Your Study Guides Map Pe....y to the Wiley CPA Review Course

Why Study with the Full CPA Review Course?

- ✓ Adaptive Review for Smarter Studying
- ✓ Unlimited Access Until You Pass
- ✓ 9 Out of 10 Students Pass

Get Your 14-Day Free Trial at **efficientlearning.com/cpatrial**

Bite-Sized Lessons Make It Easy

- ✔ Manageable lessons that can be completed in 30 to 45 minutes
- ✔ Video, text, and assessments in each lesson
- ✔ Unlimited practice exams emulate the exam day experience
- ✔ Mobile app syncs automatically with the online course and may be used offline
- ✔ Lesson progress and mastery metrics show how you're progressing

Your Plan to Pass Is Waiting

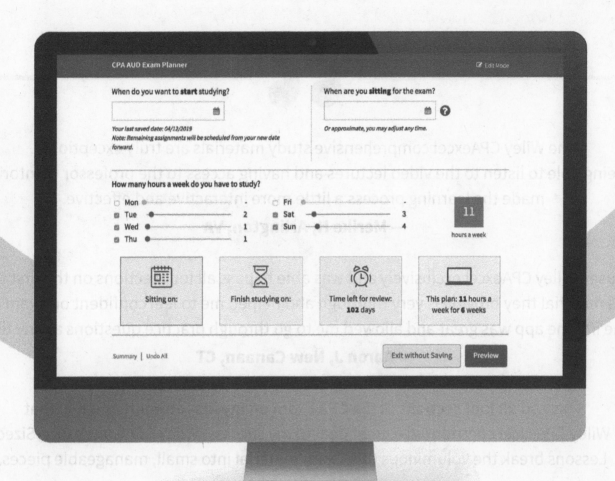

Wiley CPAexcel's Exam Planner is at the heart of why 9 out of 10 pass using our system.

- ✔ **Enter your exam date**
- ✔ **Enter your weekly study hours**
- ✔ **See 700 lessons scheduled to the day**

You Can Do This!

"

The Wiley CPAexcel comprehensive study materials are truly exceptional. Being able to listen to the video lectures and having access to the professor mentoring made the learning process a little more interactive and effective.

— Merike H, Arlington, VA

I used Wiley CPAexcel exclusively and was able to pass all four sections on the first try. The material they provide is very thorough and helped me to feel confident on exam day. The iPhone app was great and allowed me to go through practice questions at any time.

— Aaron J, New Canaan, CT

I passed all four sections of the CPA Exam on my first attempt and feel that Wiley CPAexcel contributed a great deal to my success. Wiley CPAexcel's Bite-Sized Lessons break the voluminous CPA Exam material into small, manageable pieces.

— Jason R, Emporia, KS

The video lectures, study texts, and various tools available enabled me to efficiently and effectively focus on weak areas in my review.

— Chris O, Tamuning, Guam

"

Wiley CPAexcel® Exam Review

STUDY
GUIDE

2022

AUDITING AND ATTESTATION

Wiley CPAexcel® Exam Review

STUDY GUIDE

2022

AUDITING AND ATTESTATION

Donald E. Tidrick, Ph.D., CPA, CMA, CIA
Robert A. Prentice, J.D.

Wiley Efficient Learning™

Contents

Contents

Contents

Index   459

About the Authors

Wiley CPA content is authored by a team of accounting professors and CPA Exam experts from top accounting colleges such as the University of Texas at Austin (frequently ranked the #1 accounting school in the country), Northern Illinois University (frequently ranked in the top 10 in its peer group and top 20 overall), and the University of North Alabama.

Professor Allen H. Bizzell
CPAexcel® Author and Video Lecturer
Ph.D., CPA (inactive)
Former Associate Dean and Accounting Faculty, University of Texas (Retired)
Associate Professor, Department of Accounting, Texas State University (Retired)

Professor Gregory Carnes
CPAexcel® Author, Mentor, and Video Lecturer
Ph.D., CPA
Dean, College of Business, Raburn Eminent Scholar of Accounting, University of North Alabama
Former Dean, College of Business, Lipscomb University
Former Chair, Department of Accountancy, Northern Illinois University

Professor Meghann Cefaratti
CPAexcel® Author and Video Lecturer
Ph.D.
Grant Thornton Professor of Accountancy, Department of Accountancy, Northern Illinois University

Professor Donald R. Deis Jr.
CPAexcel® Author and Video Lecturer
Ph.D., CPA, CFE
TAMUS Regents Professor and Ennis & Virginia Joslin Endowed Chair in Accounting, College of Business, Texas A&M University—Corpus Christi
Former Director, School of Accountancy, University of Missouri—Columbia
Former Professor and Director, Accounting Ph.D. Program, Louisiana State University—Baton Rouge

Instructor Elizabeth Grant
Wiley CPAexcel® Author and Video Lecturer
MAS, CPA
Instructor, Department of Accountancy, Northern Illinois University

Professor Marianne M. Jennings
CPAexcel® Author and Video Lecturer
J.D.
Professor Emeritus of Legal and Ethical Studies, W.P. Carey School of Business, Arizona State University

Instructor Tamara Phelan
Wiley CPAexcel® Author and Video Lecturer
MBA, CPA, CMA
Instructor, Department of Accountancy, Northern Illinois University

Professor Robert A. Prentice
CPAexcel® Author and Video Lecturer
J.D.
Ed and Molly Smith Centennial Professor In Business Law and Distinguished Teaching Professor, J.D. McCombs School of Business, University of Texas

Professor Pam Smith
CPAexcel® Author and Video Lecturer
Ph.D., MBA, CPA
KPMG Endowed Professor of Accountancy, Department of Accountancy, Northern Illinois University

Professor Dan N. Stone
CPAexcel® Author and Video Lecturer
Ph.D., MPA, CPA (inactive)
Rosenthal Endowed Chair, Von Allmen School of Accountancy, University of Kentucky

Professor Donald E. Tidrick
CPAexcel® Author and Video Lecturer
Ph.D., CPA, CMA, CIA
Deloitte Professor of Accountancy, Northern Illinois University
Former Associate Chair, Department of Accounting, Director of Professional Program in Accounting and
   Director of the CPA Review Course, University of Texas at Austin

About the Auditing and Attestation Professors

Professor Donald E. Tidrick is the Deloitte Professor of Accountancy at Northern Illinois University. From 1991 to 2000, Dr. Tidrick was on the faculty at the University of Texas at Austin, where he was Associate Chair of the Department of Accounting, Director of the Professional Program in Accounting and Director of UT's CPA Review Course. Among other professional distinctions, Dr. Tidrick serves on the Educators' Advisory Panel for the Comptroller General of the United States, and he is a member of the Ethics Committee of the Illinois CPA Society. In 2013, he received the AICPA's Distinguished Achievement in Accounting Education Award.

Professor Robert A. Prentice is the Ed and Molly Smith Centennial Professor of Business Law at the University of Texas, where he created a law and ethics class for accounting students. Professor Prentice has written several textbooks on law and ethics and many law review articles on business ethics, accountants' liability, and securities law. He has won more than 50 teaching awards.

Welcome to Auditing and Attestation

Welcome to Auditing and Attestation (AUD)! This lesson introduces you to the professors for the AUD lessons and provides an overview of the exam.

Passing the Auditing/Attestation Part of the CPA Exam

Candidates sometimes have a misperception about the Auditing and Attestation part of the CPA examination, believing that auditing is primarily a practice-oriented part of the exam. They may believe that having had firsthand experience doing audit work is sufficient for success on this part, or that not having had such experience is insurmountable. Sometimes candidates have a false sense of security, expressing the view that "Auditing is just common sense!" However, their view often changes when they see the specificity of the CPA exam questions that focus on the relevant concepts and the applicable professional standards. Passing the auditing part of the CPA examination is fundamentally an academic endeavor. I believe that everything you need to pass is contained in Wiley CPAexcel®—all that is required is your commitment to carefully study it.

AICPA Professional Standards

The Auditing and Attestation part of the CPA examination focuses heavily on candidates' familiarity with the applicable AICPA Professional Standards. Since the AICPA prepares the exam, it should not be surprising that they emphasize their professional literature. Indeed, a substantial majority of the points in auditing focuses on candidates' knowledge of the AICPA's Statements on Auditing Standards, the Statements on Standards for Attestation Engagements, the Statements on Standards for Accounting and Review Services, and, to a lesser extent, the Statements on Quality Control Standards. The entire set of AICPA Professional Standards tested in the Auditing and Attestation area have been addressed. Of course, the PCAOB auditing standards are "fair game" for testing and are also appropriately covered in Wiley CPAexcel®.

Wiley CPAexcel® Materials

These materials strive to achieve an optimal balance between **technical depth**, covering the topics on the AICPA Exam Blueprints, and **efficiency**, focusing on the task at hand without excess verbiage and unnecessary detail. The materials emphasize the professional standards and important concepts that are the primary object of testing in the Auditing and Attestation area.

I encourage you to review the study text in sequence, since auditing has something of a chronological order—including planning, evidence gathering, and reporting. Read the study text carefully and, very importantly, take the time to work on the knowledge checks, the multiple-choice questions, and task-based simulations that are integral to Wiley CPAexcel®'s successful approach.

Multiple-Choice Questions

Even though the number of professional standards has increased over the years, these standards often deal with only incremental changes to similar prior standards. In many cases, the underlying concepts have not changed very much. This part of the exam is not quantitative by nature, so questions cannot be updated by simply changing the "numbers." If you make a diligent effort studying these past exams' multiple-choice questions, you will very likely see some "old friends" on your examination or, at the very least, some questions that are very similar to what you have practiced.

Final Review

In addition to diligently studying the study text and practicing multiple-choice questions and exam questions, candidates invariably benefit from an intensive final review. The study text is designed to facilitate an efficient review, and I encourage you to spend a few days reviewing the study text from start to finish to refresh your memory of important concepts immediately prior to testing.

Work hard and enjoy the accomplishment of becoming a CPA for the rest of your life!

~ Prof. Donald Tidrick

In AUD, I am responsible for Area I of the CPA Exam that is devoted to Ethics, Professional Responsibilities, and General Principles. However, in your real-life career as a CPA, nothing will be more important than your ability to act ethically and professionally on a day-to-day basis.

The bulk of the material focuses on the AICPA's Code of Professional Conduct ("the Code"). However, it is also important to learn the basics of the independence and other professional requirements of the Securities Exchange Commission (SEC), the Public Company Accounting Oversight Board (PCAOB), the Government Accountability Office (GAO), and the Department of Labor (DOL). The AICPA Code is now easily accessed at the AICPA website: http://pub.aicpa.org/codeofconduct/Ethics.aspx. The Code is organized along functional lines. Most of the Code addresses the attest work done by "Members in Public Practice (MIPPs)," such as outside auditors. Some of the Code addresses the work done by "Members in Business (MIBs)," such as management accountants, internal auditors, and accountants working for government agencies and NGOs. Finally, a small portion of the Code addresses "Other Members," such as CPAs who are unemployed or retired. They still bear the title of CPA and can damage the profession's reputation by acting unprofessionally or unethically.

Please recall that the AICPA's tax-related ethics rules are located in the Regulation section. However, many Code provisions covered here—such as those related to integrity, objectivity, and advertising—generally apply to CPAs in all lines of endeavor: audit, tax, advisory services, etc.

The SEC and PCAOB material contained in this part deals primarily, though not exclusively, with additional Sarbanes-Oxley provisions aimed generally at improving the quality of financial information flowing to investors in public companies. Some of these SOX provisions are discussed inside the Code material because they override the Code's provisions where there is a conflict.

~ *Prof. Robert Prentice*

Ethics, Professional Responsibilities, and General Principles

AICPA Code of Professional Conduct

Introduction and Preface

Note: Recent questions on ethics refer to some companies as "issuers" and others as "nonissuers." It appears that this is to signal the student that some companies (issuers) are what some denominate "public companies" and others (nonissuers) are not. Issuers are subject to SEC independence rules, PCAOB rules, and Sarbanes-Oxley rules. Therefore, if there is a conflict between those rules and the Code of Professional Conduct (as there sometimes is), the federal rules override the code for issuers. However, those federal rules do not apply to nonissuers. In those questions, only the Code of Conduct applies.

After studying this lesson, you should be able to:

1. Understand the basic organizational structure of the new electronic version of the Code of Professional Conduct.

2. Explain the six key principles on which the code is based.

I. **Introduction**

   A. An electronic version of the AICPA's Code of Professional Conduct is easily accessed on the AICPA's website. This electronic version is easily updated.

   B. The code divides professional responsibilities in terms of the role that members play. Part 1 of the code sets out rules for members in public practice, such as independent auditors, tax professionals, and consultants who provide professional services to third parties. This includes, of course, independence rules but also rules regarding integrity, objectivity, and discreditable acts. Part 2 of the code sets out rules for members in business, such as internal auditors at a corporation. They need not worry about independence rules, and many of the other rules for members in business are identical (or nearly so) to the nonindependence rules that apply to members in public practice. Part 3 sets out rules for other members, such as those who are unemployed or retired, who are expected to avoid discreditable acts.

   C. The code also follows the lead of the International Federation of Accountants by putting into place a Conceptual Framework for answering questions that arise that are not answered even by the many detailed code provisions and interpretations. In virtually every subject matter area of the entire code, if there is no clear answer, the Conceptual Framework should be applied.

II. **Preface (Part 0)**

   A. **Overview**

      1. The code is divided into three main parts:

         a. Part 1 applies to members in public practice.

         b. Part 2 applies to members in business.

         c. Part 3 applies to other members.

      2. Members serving in multiple roles should choose the most restrictive applicable provisions.

   B. **Principles and rules of conduct contained in the code are supplemented by:**

      1. Interpretations

      2. Definitions

      3. Applications

      4. Where applicable, standards promulgated by other bodies such as

         a. State certified public accounting (CPA) societies

    b. Securities and Exchange Commission

    c. Public Company Accounting Oversight Board

    d. Government Accountability Office

    e. Department of Labor

    f. Various taxing authorities

C. Principles of Professional Conduct

    1. By voluntarily joining the AICPA, members assume an obligation of self-discipline above and beyond legal requirements.

    2. The six major principles call for "an unswerving commitment to honorable behavior, even at the sacrifice of personal advantage":

        a. "Responsibilities principle. In carrying out their responsibilities as professionals, members should exercise sensitive professional and moral judgments in all their activities."

            i. This principle imposes a continuing responsibility on members to "cooperate with each other to:

                1. "improve the art of accounting,

                2. "maintain the public's confidence, and

                3. "carry out the profession's special responsibilities for self-governance."

        b. "Public Interest principle. Members should accept the obligation to act in a way that will serve the public interest, honor the public trust, and demonstrate a commitment to professionalism."

        c. "Integrity principle. To maintain and broaden public confidence, members should perform all professional responsibilities with the highest sense of integrity."

            i. "Integrity is measured in terms of what is right and just"; members should always ask "Am I doing what a person of integrity would do?"

> **Note**
>
> *"A distinguishing mark of a profession is acceptance of its responsibility to the public."*

        d. "Objectivity and Independence principle. A member should maintain objectivity and be free of conflicts of interest in discharging professional responsibilities. A member in public practice should be independent in fact and appearance when providing auditing and other attestation services."

            i. "Objectivity is a state of mind" that requires:

                1. impartiality,

                2. intellectual honesty, *and*

                3. freedom from conflicts of interest.

            ii. Only members in public practice must act with independence, but all members performing all services must act with objectivity and integrity.

        e. "Due care principle. A member should observe the profession's technical and ethical standards, strive continually to improve competence and the quality of services, *and* discharge professional responsibility to the best of the member's ability."

            i. Perfection is not required.

            ii. Competence requires a commitment to continued learning—hence, continuing professional education.

            iii. Members may derive competence from research or consultation with experts.

    iv. Due care entails

        1. Adequate planning of engagements

        2. Supervision of professional activities for which members are responsible

f. "Scope and nature of services principle. A member in public practice should observe the Principles of the Code of Professional Conduct in determining the scope and nature of services to be provided."

g. At a minimum, members should:

    i. Practice in firms that have good internal quality control procedures,

    ii. Use their individual judgments to determine whether the scope and nature of services provided to an audit client would create a conflict of interest, *and*

    iii. Individually assess whether a contemplated activity is consistent with their role as professionals.

	Audit	Compilation	Tax	Consulting
Integrity	Yes	Yes	Yes	Yes
Objectivity	Yes	Yes	Yes	Yes
Independence in Fact	Yes	No	No	No
Independence in Appearance	Yes	No	No	No

D. Definitions

  1. Part 0 contains approximately 50 definitions, ranging from "Acceptable Level" to "Threats." This study guide sets out various definitions as they become relevant to the substantive provisions being discussed, but it couldn't hurt to read through the definitions.

Example

Partner Equivalent

A professional employee who is not a partner of the firm but who either (a) has the ultimate responsibility for the conduct of an attest engagement, including the authority to sign or affix the firm's name to an attest report or issue, or authorize others to issue, an attest report on behalf of the firm without partner approval; or (b) has the authority to bind the firm to conduct an attest engagement without partner approval. For example, the professional employee has the authority to sign or affix the firm's name to an attest engagement letter or contract to conduct an attest engagement without partner approval.

Members in Public Practice

MIPPs Introduction and Conceptual Framework

> Note: Recent questions on ethics refer to some companies as "issuers" and others as "nonissuers." It appears that this is to signal the student that some companies (issuers) are what some denominate "public companies" and others (nonissuers) are not. Issuers are subject to SEC independence rules, PCAOB rules, and Sarbanes-Oxley rules. Therefore, if there is a conflict between those rules and the Code of Professional Conduct (as there sometimes is), the federal rules override the code for issuers. However, those federal rules do not apply to nonissuers. In those questions, only the Code of Conduct applies.
>
> **After studying this lesson, you should be able to:**
>
> 1. Apply the Conceptual Framework to answer questions of professional responsibility that are not clearly answered in the code itself.

I. **Introduction**

   A. Part 1 of the Code of Professional Conduct applies to members in public practice (MIPPs). Public practice consists of the performance of professional services (e.g., audit, tax, consulting) for a client by a member or the member's firm.

II. **Conceptual Framework**—Where the code's rules and interpretations do not provide a clear answer to a particular situation, members should always apply the threats-and-safeguards Conceptual Framework in order to determine whether threats to a member's compliance with the rules (independence and otherwise) can be reduced to an acceptable level (defined as "a level at which a reasonable and informed third party who is aware of the relevant information would be expected to conclude that a member's compliance with the rules is not compromised") by application of safeguards.

   A. There are three main steps to applying the Conceptual Framework:

   1. Identify threats.

   2. Evaluate the significance of the threats.

   3. Identify and apply safeguards.

   B. There are seven broad categories of threats:

   1. Adverse interest threats. Examples:

      a. Client sues or threatens to sue firm.

      b. Subrogee makes claim against firm to recover payments it made to client.

   2. Advocacy threats. Examples:

      a. Member provides forensic accounting services to client in lawsuit with third party.

      b. Firm acts as investment advisor, underwriter, promoter, or registered agent for a client.

   3. Familiarity threats. Examples:

      a. Member's spouse, parent, sibling, or close friend is employed by the client.

      b. Former firm partner joins client in a key position.

   4. Management participation threats. Example:

      a. Member takes on role of client management.

5. Self-interest threats. Examples:

    a. Member has a financial interest in a client that may be affected by outcome of professional services the firm is providing.

    b. Firm relies excessively on revenue from a single client.

6. Self-review threats. Examples:

    a. Member relies on work product of own firm.

    b. Member does client's bookkeeping.

    c. Partner in firm was an officer or director of client.

7. Undue influence threats. Examples:

    a. Client threatens to fire firm or to withhold future business unless firm accedes to client's wishes.

    b. Client's major shareholder threatens to withdraw or terminate a professional service unless the member reaches desired conclusion.

C. Three kinds of safeguards exist:

1. Safeguards created by the profession, legislation, or regulation. Examples:

    a. Ethics education and training requirements, including continuing professional education (CPE)

    b. Professional standards and threat of discipline

    c. External reviews of a firm's quality controls

    d. Legislation regulating firm's professionals

    e. Licensure requirements

    f. Professional resources, such as ethics hotlines

2. Safeguards implemented by the client. The client has, for example:

    a. Knowledgeable and experienced managers

    b. Appropriate tone at the top regarding ethics and compliance

    c. Appropriate policies and procedures for compliance and fair reporting

    d. Appropriate ethics policies and procedures

    e. Appropriate governance structure, including an active audit committee

    f. Policies to prevent client from hiring a firm to provide services that would impair independence or objectivity

3. Safeguards implemented by the firm. Examples:

    a. Strong leadership emphasizing compliance and acting in the public interest

    b. Policies and procedures to implement and monitor engagement quality control

    c. Designation of qualified senior manager to oversee firm's quality control system

    d. An effective internal disciplinary system

    e. Rotation of engagement team senior personnel

    f. Policies precluding partners from being compensated for selling nonattest services to attest client

MIPPs Nonindependence Rules

Conflicts of Interest, Directorships, and Gifts

After studying this lesson, you should be able to:

Understand and be able to apply the Code of Professional Conduct's rules regarding:

1. General conflicts of interest.

2. Members serving on corporate boards.

3. Gifts and entertainment (which can pose a threat to member integrity and objectivity).

I. Conflicts of Interest

A. In evaluating possible conflicts of interest, members should ask: Would a *reasonable and informed third party* conclude that a conflict exists?

B. There are two main types of conflicts:

1. Between interests of two clients

2. Between interests of client on one hand and firm and/or its members on the other.

Examples

1. Simultaneously advising two clients trying to acquire the same company

2. Preparing valuation of assets to two clients who are simultaneously the potential seller and the potential buyer of the same assets

3. Representing both a husband and a wife in a divorce proceeding

4. Advising a client to invest in a business owned by a member or member's relatives

5. Advising a client on acquisition of assets that the firm also seeks to acquire

6. Providing forensic accounting services to one client to assist it in deciding whether to sue another client

7. Providing personal financial planning services to several members of a family or group known to have conflicting interests

8. Referring a client to a service provider that, in turn, refers clients to member under an exclusive arrangement

---

C. Identification—Before accepting an engagement, members should identify potential conflicts that threaten independence and objectivity, and should continue to monitor as engagement progresses.

1. When **network firms** are involved, members are **not** required to take specific steps to identify conflicts of interest of other network firms but should apply the conceptual framework if they **know or have reason to know** that a conflict exists or might arise.

D. Evaluation—When an actual conflict is identified by any member, the Conceptual Framework should be applied and engagements should be refused or terminated if risk of violation is unacceptably high. Safeguards that might reduce threats to an acceptable level include:

1. Implementing mechanisms to prevent unauthorized disclosure of confidential information when providing services to multiple clients with conflicting interests, including use of:

      a. Separate engagement teams

      b. Policies and procedures to limit access to client files, confidentiality agreements and physical and electronic separation of confidential information

   2. Regular review by a senior manager not involved in the engagement

   3. Consulting with third parties, such as a professional body or legal counsel

  E. Disclosure—Conflicts should be disclosed to clients and affected third parties, even if threats to compliance are at an acceptable level.

   1. General disclosure (e.g., "We audit several firms in your industry sector") may suffice.

   2. Specific disclosure (e.g., "We advise your closest competitor who would love to have access to your confidential information that we possess") may be needed, however.

  F. Documenting the threat-reducing process is wise.

  G. Members should always comply with federal (including Internal Revenue Service Circular 230), state, or local provisions that are more restrictive than the code.

II. Director Positions

  A. Objectivity is threatened when a member serves as a client entity's director.

  B. It is preferable to serve as a mere consultant to a client's board.

  C. The Conceptual Framework should be applied to determine whether the threat to objectivity is unacceptably high.

III. Gifts and Entertainment

  A. Objectivity and integrity are threatened if the client (including its officers, directors, and 10% shareholders) give gifts or entertainment to the firm or its members (or vice versa).

  B. A violation is presumed if:

   1. The member receives gifts or entertainment from a client that violate the member's or client's policies or applicable laws and regulations and

   2. The member knows or is reckless in not knowing of the violation.

  C. If no rules are violated, then there is no problem if the gifts or entertainment are "reasonable in the circumstances."

  D. Factors in determining reasonableness include:

   1. The nature of the gift or entertainment

   2. The occasion giving rise to the gift

   3. The cost or value of the gift or entertainment

   4. The nature, frequency, and value of other gifts

   5. Whether the entertainment was associated with active conduct of the business

Reporting Information and Subordination of Judgment

After studying this lesson, you should be able to:

1. Understand and be able to apply the Code of Professional Conduct's provisions regarding how to report information without violating the code.

2. Understand how to apply the rules and the process governing how to avoid a subordination of judgment.

3. Understand the rules regarding pressuring others to breach the Code's rules so that they may avoid pressuring others and not submit to such pressure themselves.

I. Preparing and Reporting Information

A. There would be a violation of the Code if a member has:

   1. Made, permitted, or directed another to make materially false and misleading entries in an entity's financial statements or records,

   2. Failed to correct misstatements when having the authority to do so,

   3. Signed, permitted, or directed another to sign misleading documents,

   4. Exercised discretion with the intent to mislead, or

   5. When relying on the work of others, either inside or outside the organizations, failed to ensure that the work was useful, honest, and accurate by taking into account such factors as the reputation, expertise, objectivity, and resources available to the third party.

B. When a member knows or has reason to know that information he or she is associated with is misleading, the member should apply appropriate safeguards to seek to resolve the matter by getting the information correct and informing users who have already been misled by it. This process may require talking to supervisors, consulting with professional bodies, and perhaps even considering resigning. These procedures are spelled out in more detail in the next section regarding subordination of judgement.

II. Subordination of Judgment

A. Assume that members have a disagreement with a superior over how to record potential earnings (or some other issue). The members are not supposed to simply do what the superior wants and subordinate their judgment.

B. The proper procedure is to:

   1. Evaluate whether the threat is at an **unacceptable level,** which occurs if the position taken would result in a material misrepresentation or legal violation. If the threat is **not significant**, then nothing further need be done.

   2. But if there is such a significant threat, the member should discuss the matter with the supervisor.

   3. If discussion with the supervisor does not resolve the difference of opinion, the member should go over the supervisor's head.

   4. If, after discussion with people up the chain, the member is still worried that the right thing is not going to be done, the member should, in no particular order, invoke the following safeguards:

      a. Determine whether the organization's policies and procedures have any additional requirements for reporting differences of opinion.

      b. Determine whether there is a duty to report to external authorities.

      c. Consult legal counsel.

d. Fully document the situation.

5. If the member ultimately concludes that the threat of misrepresentation or legal violation cannot be reduced to an acceptable level, he or she should consider quitting the firm and taking appropriate steps to eliminate his or her exposure to subordination of judgment.

6. Although the code does not **require** the member to quit, only to consider it, it goes on to say that "nothing in this interpretation precludes a member from resigning from the organization at any time."

7. Resigning from the firm would not necessarily discharge all obligations, such as to report to regulatory authorities or an external auditor.

III. Pressure to Breach the Rules

A. Members should neither pressure others to breach the Code's rules, nor submit to such pressure themselves.

B. Examples of pressure that could result in breach of the Integrity and Objectivity Rule include the following:

1. Conflict of interest: Joe is a member working for ABC Sales Co. and is charged with hiring a caterer for the company's events. Joe's supervisor's uncle is a caterer and attempts to convince Joe to accept his bid over similar bids by other caterers.

2. Presentation of information: Miko is a member working for DEF Co. and her boss strongly urges her to treat personal expenses he has incurred as business expenses so that DEF will reimburse them.

3. Due care: Member Carlos is an auditor for the GHI accounting firm and his superiors put him in charge of the audit of JKL Corporation. They give him such a small team and such a tight deadline that it will be impossible for him to do an audit that would comply with GAAS in time. When he protests, they say: "Just shut up and get it done."

4. Financial interests: CFO Mandy, a member of the AICPA, is preparing the annual revenue numbers for MNO Coporation. Her CEO, Tina, reminds Mandy that Tina will receive a huge bonus if revenue targets are met and that there are lots of accountants out there with the qualifications to replace Mandy.

5. Gifts or Entertainment: Member Lia is a tax accountant for PQR Accounting. PQR hopes to be hired by Mega Corporation to prepare its tax returns. Mega's CFO, Tad, will make the hiring decision. Lia's superior, Pat, suggests strongly that Lia buy an expensive and rare vintage milk bottle that Tad collects, and to give it to him secretly.

C. If a member finds himself or herself under inappropriate pressure to violate the Code's rules, he or she may consult with superiors or legal counsel, escalate the matter within the organization, consider resigning, etc. These procedures are very much the same for a member worried about subordination or judgement discussed in the previous section in more detail.

Advocacy, Third-Party Service Providers (TSPs), General Standards, and Accounting Principles

After studying this lesson, you should be able to:

1. Explain and apply the Code of Professional Conduct's rules regarding advocacy on behalf of clients and the outsourcing of work to third-party service providers.

2. Master the general standards that apply to members.

3. Understand members' responsibilities regarding basic accounting principles.

I. Client Advocacy

A. Members doing attest work may not advocate for their attest clients.

B. Members providing nonattest services may advocate for their clients, but should be careful and conservative so as to preserve credibility and avoid the "zealous" advocacy that lawyers often provide.

II. Use of a Third-Party Service Provider (TSP)

A. Outsourcing work to third-party service providers can threaten objectivity or integrity.

B. There is no problem if the third-party service provider provides only **administrative support** (e.g., record storage, software application hosting, authorized e-file transmittal services).

C. If substantive services are outsourced, clients should be notified, preferably in writing, before any confidential information is provided to the third-party service provider.

D. If the client objects, the member should:

1. Not outsource, *or*

2. Decline the engagement

III. General Standards

A. Members must follow rules set by appropriate bodies, meaning in part:

1. Take on jobs only if you can reasonably expect to complete them with **professional competence.**

2. You need not be perfect but should always exercise **due professional care** when providing all professional services

3. Always **adequately plan and supervise** your provision of professional services.

4. Never render conclusions or recommendations without **sufficient relevant data** to support them.

B. **Competence** means that the member or his/or her staff has appropriate technical qualifications and the member can supervise and evaluate quality of work performed.

1. Decline an engagement unless you have necessary knowledge or can acquire it through research or consultation with others.

2. If you employ a specialist to provide consulting services, you should have the ability to define the tasks and evaluate the results.

C. **Using Third-Party Service Providers**

1. Ensure any third-party service providers you use have the required professional qualifications, technical skills, and needed resources.

2. Adequately plan and supervise the third-party service providers' services and obtain the data needed to evaluate the job.

IV. Accounting Principles

A. Follow generally accepted accounting principles (GAAP) and other relevant accounting principles.

B. **Exceptions**—Departure from GAAP is appropriate if the member:

1. Demonstrates that due to unusual circumstances, following GAAP would mislead

2. Describes:

   a. The departure,

   b. Its approximate effects, and

   c. The reasons why compliance with GAAP would mislead.

C. Circumstances justifying departure include:

1. New legislation

2. Evolution of a new form of business

D. Circumstances **not** justifying departure include:

1. An unusual degree of materiality

2. Conflicting industry practice

E. Departure from GAAP is permitted when other accounting principles apply, such as:

1. Financial reporting frameworks generally accepted in foreign country

2. Frameworks prescribed by contract

3. Other special-purpose frameworks required by a law or by a domestic or foreign regulatory agency

Discreditable Acts

This lesson mostly surveys the discreditable acts, some of which are covered in more detail elsewhere (such as the confidentiality duty). But it dives into detail regarding the fairly complicated rules regarding a member's obligation to produce accounting records pursuant to a client's request.

After studying this lesson, you should be able to:

1. Understand the (nonexclusive) list of acts that the Code of Professional Conduct deems to be discreditable acts by members in public practice.

I. **Acts Discreditable**—Members shall not commit discreditable acts, including:

   A. Discrimination and harassment in employment practices

   B. Solicitation or disclosure of CPA Exam questions and answers

   C. Failure to file a tax return (including one's own personal return or his or her firm's) or failure to pay a tax liability

   D. Negligence in the preparation of financial statements or records

   E. Material departure from the audit standards of government bodies, commissions, or other regulatory agencies

   F. Failure to follow additional government standards over and above generally accepted auditing standards where applicable

   G. Improper use of indemnification and limitation of liability provisions in violation of regulatory requirements

   H. Confidential information obtained from employment or volunteer activities (more detail in the "Advertising and Confidentiality" lesson)

   I. False, misleading, or deceptive acts in promoting or marketing professional services

   J. Use of the CPA credential in violation of rules and regulations

   K. Records requests (more detail below)

   L. Removing client files or proprietary information from a firm after termination

   M. Use of confidential information obtained from a prospective client or nonclient without consent

   N. **Records Requests**

   1. **Four categories of records**

      a. **Client-provided records** are records given by the client to the member.

      b. **Member-prepared records** are those the member was not specifically engaged to prepare and are not in the client's books and records, rendering the client's financial information incomplete. Example: adjusting, closing, combining, or consolidating journal entries and supporting schedules and documents that the member proposed or prepared as part of an engagement.

      c. **Member's work products** are deliverables set forth in the engagement letter, such as a tax return.

      d. **Working papers** are all other items prepared solely for purposes of the engagement, including items prepared by both the member (e.g., audit programs, analytical review schedules, and statistical sampling and analysis) and the client (e.g., papers prepared at the member's request and reflecting testing or other work done by the member).

2. **Proper treatment of requests from client**

   a. **Client-provided records** should be delivered to the client at the client's request, even if the client has not paid its bill to the member.

   b. **Member-prepared records** related to a completed and issued work product should be delivered to the client at the client's request, **except** that they may be withheld if fees are due for that specific work product.

   c. **Work products** should be delivered to the client at the client's request, except that they may be withheld under four circumstances:

      i. Fees are due for the specific work product.

      ii. The work product is incomplete.

      iii. To comply with professional standards (e.g., withholding an audit report because of unresolved audit issues).

      iv. If threatened or outstanding litigation exists concerning the engagement or the member's work.

   d. **Working papers** are the member's property and need not be provided to the client (unless some regulation or contractual provision requires production).

3. Members may charge a reasonable fee for the time and expense incurred in producing records.

4. Members need not convert records that are not in electronic format to electronic format.

5. Sometimes state laws are more demanding of accountants, and those laws must be followed.

6. Generally, client requests should be honored within **45 days**.

7. Multiple client cases.

   a. When A engages a member to perform professional services with respect to B (example: Company A hires member to audit Company B, which Company A is considering purchasing), the member should return *client-provided records* to whoever provided them.

   b. When A engages a member to perform professional services for the benefit of B (example: Company A hires member to perform tax services for A's executive team), the member should provide a member's *work products* to the beneficiaries (the executives).

   c. When A engages a member to perform professional services with respect to B, who is not a contemplated beneficiary of the services (example: Company A hires member to value Company B's assets that Company A is considering purchasing), the member may provide its *work products* (the valuation report) only to the engaging entity (Company A).

Fees

I. Contingent Fees

A. Members shall not receive contingent fees **for any service** performed for a client for whom he or she performs any of the following attest services:

   1. A financial statement audit or review,

   2. A financial statement compilation reasonably expected to be used by a third party that does not disclose a lack of independence, or

   3. An examination of prospective financial information.

B. Nor may a member prepare an original or amended tax return or claim for a tax refund for a contingent fee for **any client**, even nonattest clients.

C. The definition of a **contingent fee** ["a fee established for the performance of any service pursuant to an arrangement in which no fee will be charged unless a specified finding or result is attained, or in which the amount of the fee is otherwise dependent upon the finding or result of such service"] excludes fees "fixed by courts or other public authorities, or, in tax matters, if determined based on the results of judicial proceedings or the finding of government agencies."

D. A member may do tax work for nonattest clients in exchange for contingent fees if Internal Revenue Service rules are not to the contrary (which they sometimes are).

E. Examples of some permitted contingent fees in the tax area include:

   1. Representing a client before a revenue agent examining the client's income tax return

   2. Filing an amended federal or state income tax return claiming a refund based on a tax issue that is the subject of a test case involving a different taxpayer

   3. Filing an amended federal or state income tax return (or refund claim) claiming a tax refund in an amount that will be examined by a tax authority, such as the Joint Committee on Taxation

   4. Helping a client obtain a private letter ruling or influencing the drafting of a regulation or statute

F. Contingent fees are not permitted if a member prepared an amended return claiming a refund because of an error in the original return.

G. The code contains additional rules regarding services performed by a member's spouse for a contingent fee and contingent fees in connection with investment advisory services that are not covered here.

II. Commissions and Referral Fees

A. Referral fees and commissions are prohibited for attest clients.

B. For nonattest clients, they are permitted, but must be disclosed in writing.

C. A member's spouse may receive a commission from the member's attest client, so long as the spouse's activities are separate from the member's practice and the member is not significantly involved in the spouse's activities.

D. Members taking title to a product and assuming risks of ownership may resell the product to a client at a profit without disclosure.

E. Similarly, members may subcontract services to third parties and mark up the cost of the services to the client without this being considered a commission.

Advertising and Confidentiality

After studying this lesson, you should be able to:

1. Explain and apply the relatively straightforward code restrictions on advertising.

2. Explain and apply the relatively more complicated rules on the confidentiality obligation that members in public practice owe to clients.

I. Advertising

A. Members are responsible not only for their own promotional efforts, but also for those of third parties if they are asked to perform professional services for the client or customer of a third party.

B. Promotional efforts are a discreditable act if they are false, misleading, or deceptive (i.e., if they contain any claim that would likely cause a reasonable person to be misled), which would be the case if they:

   1. Create false or unjustified expectations of favorable results

   2. Imply the ability to influence any court, tribunal, regulatory agency or similar body

   3. Contain a representation that the member will perform services for stated fees when it is likely at the time that the fees will be substantially increased

II. Confidential Information

A. **General Rule**—A member in public practice shall not disclose confidential client information (defined as "any proprietary information pertaining to the employer or any organization for whom the member may work in a volunteer capacity that is not known to be available to the public and is obtained as a result of such relationships") without the specific consent of the client.

   1. It is a discreditable act to inappropriately disclose confidential client information.

   2. Members should take reasonable steps to ensure that staff members do not improperly disclose confidential information.

   3. The confidentiality duty survives the employment relationship.

B. **Exceptions**—Disclosures allowed where:

   1. The client consents.

   2. Disclosure is permitted by law **and authorized by the employer**.

   3. Disclosure is **required by law**, for example, to:

      a. Comply with a validly issued and enforceable subpoena or summons

      b. Inform appropriate public authorities of violations of the law

   4. Members may have responsibility or right to disclose the information, when not prohibited by law, to:

      a. Initiate an ethics complaint with the American Institute of Certified Public Accountants (AICPA), a state board of accountancy, and so on

      b. Comply with professional standards and other ethics requirements

      c. Report potential concerns regarding questionable accounting, auditing, or other matters to the employer's confidential complaint hotline or those charged with governance

   5. Disclosure is permitted on behalf of the employer to:

      a. Obtain financing from lenders

   b. Communicate with vendors, clients, and customers

   c. Communicate with the external accountant, attorneys, regulators, and others

6. Members should be sensitive to disclosing a client's confidential information when providing services to its competitors.

7. If taking on a new client would likely lead to disclosure of confidential information from an existing, identifiable client, the member should not take on new client without informed consent from the existing client.

8. When a member withdraws from an engagement due to, say, irregularities in a client's tax return, the member should, if contacted by a potential successor firm, suggest that the potential successor firm contact the client to ask permission to discuss all matters freely with the successor.

9. When either member of a married couple hires a member to prepare a joint tax return, the two are considered to be one client, even if the member deals with only one of them. So, the member does not need consent from either spouse in order to provide information related to the joint tax return to the other spouse. When receiving conflicting directions from the spouses, the member should seek an attorney's advice.

10. When outsourcing work to a third-party service provider (TSP), a member should do one of the following **before** disclosing confidential information:

   1. Bind the third-party service provider contractually to maintain confidentiality and ensure that the third-party service provider has effective procedures in place.

   2. Obtain specific consent from the client.

11. Members involved in a peer review must keep information they receive confidential and not use it for their advantage.

12. If a third party, such as a trade association or member of academia, asks a member to disclose confidential information for purposes of publication or the like, the member should obtain the client's specific consent, preferably in writing, before disclosing.

13. Members who are directors of organizations must be cautious, because their fiduciary duty to the organization might conflict with their duty to clients who might, for example, be customers of the organization. The threats-and-safeguards conceptual framework should be utilized.

14. Disclosing clients' names is permissible, unless to do so discloses confidential information.

Example
Example: Where the member does primarily bankruptcy work and disclosing clients' identities signals that clients are in financial difficulty.

15. When A hires a member to perform a professional service to benefit B (example: Company A hires member to perform tax services for its executives), the engaging entity (Company A) and the beneficiaries (its executives) are considered *two separate clients* (so the member should not disclose the beneficiaries' confidential tax information to Company A without their consent).

16. When Company A hires a member to value the assets of Company B which it hopes to acquire, the member may assume that disclosing Company B's confidential information to Company A is permitted because A and B will typically have an agreement permitting such disclosure.

Form of Organization and Names

> **After studying this lesson, you should be able to:**
>
> 1. Explain what names they may use for denominating their firms.
>
> 2. Explain and apply the code's rules regarding what form of organization members in public practice may practice in.

I. Form of Organization

A. Basic Rules

1. Members in public practice may practice only in a form of organization permitted by law.

2. Members in public practice may not practice under misleading firm name.

3. Names of past owners may be included in the name of a successor firm.

4. A firm may not designate itself as "Members of the AICPA" unless all its CPA owners are members of the AICPA.

B. Ownership of a Separate Business

1. A member may own an interest in a separate business that performs accounting, tax, or consulting services, but if the member *controls* the separate business, then its owners and professional employees must comply with the code for issues such as commissions and referral fees. And regarding an attest client, independence rules would have to be complied with as well.

2. But if the member's interest is not a controlling one, then the code's provisions apply to him but not to the separate firm or its employees.

C. Partner Designation

1. Only members of a firm who are legally partners should use the designation "partner."

D. Responsibility for Nonmember Practitioners

1. If a member becomes an employee of a firm made up of one or more nonmembers, he or she still must comply with the code. And if the member is a partner in the firm, he or she is responsible for the firm's professional employees.

E. Attest Engagement Performed with a Former Partner

1. Two former partners may continue to jointly perform an attest engagement, but to make it clear that a partnership no longer exists, they should present their report on plain paper (with no letterhead).

F. Alternative Practice Structures

1. If a firm does attest work,

   a. CPAs must own a majority of its financial interests.

   b. CPAs must remain responsible, financially and otherwise, for a firm's attest work.

2. CPAs are responsible for compliance with laws and regulations, for enrollment in an AICPA-approved practice monitoring program, for compliance with independence rules, and for compliance with all other applicable standards within their firms.

II. Firm Name

A. If two firms merge, they may use in the newly formed firm's name the name of retired or other partners in either or both of the former firms.

B. A CPA member who is in partnership with non-CPAs may sign reports in the firm's name and also affix the designation "CPA" to his or her own signature if it is clear that the firm is not holding itself out as entirely comprised of CPAs.

C. No misleading name that causes confusion about the legal form of the firm or its owners' identities should be used.

D. Firms within a network may share a common brand or common initials as part of their firm name without misleading. To be part of a network, the firms should share one or more of the following with other network firms:

1. Common control among the firms

2. Profits or costs

3. Common business strategy

4. Significant portions of professional resources

5. Common quality control policies and procedures

6. Common brand name

MIPPs Independence Rules

Introduction to MIPPs Independence Rules

Note: Recent questions on ethics refer to some companies as "issuers" and others as "nonissuers." It appears that this is to signal the student that some companies (issuers) are what some denominate "public companies" and others (nonissuers) are not. Issuers are subject to SEC independence rules, PCAOB rules, and Sarbanes-Oxley rules. Therefore, if there is a conflict between those rules and the Code of Professional Conduct (as there sometimes is), the federal rules override the code for issuers. However, those federal rules do not apply to nonissuers. In those questions, only the Code of Conduct applies.

After studying this lesson, you should be able to:

Understand the big picture regarding the independence obligations of members in public practice and be able to answer:

1. What are the threats to independence?

2. What time period is relevant?

3. Who must comply with the rules?

I. **Introduction**

    A. Members in public practice (MIPPs) shall be independent when performing attest services.

    B. If the code and its interpretations do not resolve independence issues, **the Conceptual Framework should be applied.**

    C. **Threats and Safeguards**

        1. The *threats* to independence detailed in the code are very much the same as the threats to integrity and objectivity discussed elsewhere in these materials: adverse interest threats, advocacy threats, familiarity threats, management participation threats, self-interest threats, self-review threats, and undue influence threats.

        2. The *safeguards* that may be applied to reduce the threats to independence come from the same three sources as those relevant to integrity and objectivity:

            a. The profession, legislation, or regulation

            b. The attest client

            c. The firm

    D. The threats to independence (adverse interest, advocacy, etc.) are concentrated in four areas:

        1. **Financial relationships**—Example: An attest partner should not own stock in an audit client

        2. **Employment relationships**—Example: Attest partners should not be on an audit client's board of directors

        3. **Family relationships**—Example: An attest partner should not audit a client whose chief executive officer is the partner's spouse

        4. **Consulting relationships**—Example: An attest firm should not provide internal audit services to an attest client

    E. **Time Period**—Independence rules must be followed when relationships exist during:

        1. The period covered by the financial statements

        2. The period of the professional engagement

F. **Covered members** must comply with the independence rules for financial interests (and many others):

1. An individual on the attest engagement team (*team member*)

2. An individual in a position to influence the attest engagement (PTI)

3. A partner, partner equivalent (defined as "a person who is not a partner of the firm but either has the ultimate responsibility for the conduct of an attest engagement, or has the authority to bind the firm to conduct an attest engagement without partner approval"), or manager who provides more than 10 hours of nonattest services to the attest client within any fiscal year (*more than 10-hour person*)

4. A partner or partner equivalent in the office in which the lead attest engagement partner or partner equivalent practices in connection with the attest engagement (*other partner in office*)

5. The firm, including the firm's employee benefit plans

6. An entity whose operating, financial, or accounting policies can be controlled by any of the individuals or entities described in items (1) through (5) or two or more such individuals or entities if they act together

Network Firms and Affiliates

I. Network Firms

    A. Network firms are firms that cooperate to enhance their capabilities to provide professional services and share one or more of the following:

        1. A common brand name

        2. Common control

        3. Profits or costs

        4. A common business strategy

        5. Professional resources

        6. Common quality control policies and procedures

    B. Network firms must comply with the independence rules with respect to financial statement audit and review clients of other network firms *if* the use of the audit or review report for the client is not restricted.

    C. For all other attest clients, members should apply the Conceptual Framework to determine whether independence threats are at an unacceptable level.

II. Alternative Practice Structures

    A. The Code contains extremely complicated independence rules for firms operating in an APS environment that are not covered in these materials.

III. Use of a Nonindependent Firm

    A. If partners or professional employees of another, nonindependent firm participate on the attest engagement team, independence of the team would be impaired.

    B. Such members of another firm may work in a manner similar to internal auditors, however, without creating an independence problem so long as the firm complies with AU-C section 610 (which sets out the rules for the proper relationship between internal and external auditors).

IV. Affiliates

    A. Independence problems can obviously arise if covered members, while not having a financial, consulting, employment, etc. relationship with the attest client, have such a relationship with an "affiliate" of the client.

    B. The Code sets out numerous examples of such "affiliates," including:

        1. An entity that a client can control

        2. An entity in which a client has a direct and material financial interest

3. An entity that controls a client when the client is material to such entity

4. An entity with a direct and material financial interest in the client when that entity has significant influence over the client

5. A sister entity of a client if the client and sister entity are each material to the entity that controls both

6. A trustee that is deemed to control a trust financial statement attest client that is not an investment company

7. The sponsor of a single employer employee benefit plan financial statement attest client

C. Although there are significant exceptions (which we do not cover here), in general covered members must abide by independence rules for both their attest clients and their clients' affiliates. There are similar rules (and exceptions) when a firm audits some units, but not all, of related governmental agencies.

V. Mergers and Acquisitions

A. Independence issues can obviously arise if a member's firm acquires, is acquired by, or merges with another firm. The AICPA has recently issued detailed rules to cover such situations, focusing on (a) employment with an attest client and (b) provision of NAS.

B. Without covering those rules comprehensively, consider a situation where Maria, a partner of the ABC audit firm also works for DEF Co., which is an audit client of GHI audit firm. GHI proposes to purchase ABC. If the acquisition occurs, Maria may suddenly be an employee of her new firm's audit client. Independence should not be impaired so long as:

1. Maria terminates her relationship with DEF before the closing date of the acquisition;

2. Maria is not a team member or a PTI on the DEF audit if the engagement covers any period in which she worked for DEF;

3. Maria dissociates from DEF, including ceasing participation in its employee benefit plans if she is a covered member;

4. A responsible person within the new firm assesses Maria's prior relationship with DEF to ensure that any threats to independence are at a reasonable level. If Maria has any interaction with the attest engagement team or if the team evaluates any work done by Maria while she worked for DEF, an appropriate person within the firm should review the engagement prior to issuing the report to ensure that the team maintained integrity, objectivity, and professional skepticism; *and*

5. All safeguards should be discussed with DEF's management and the discussions should be documented.

C. Turning to NAS, the Code envisions two possibilities:

1. What if the ABC firm provides, say, internal audit services to LMN Corporation, which is audited by DEF firm? If ABC acquires DEF, ABC's independence is impaired with respect to LMN.

2. What if the ABC firm audits LMN Corporation and acquires DEF, which provides internal audit services to LMN Corporation? In this case, ABC's independence would be impaired unless all of the following conditions are met:

a. DEF must terminate the prohibited NAS prior to the closing of the acquisition;

b. Any individual who participated in the engagement to provide the NAS must not be on the LMN attest team or be a PTI; and

c. An evaluation of the threats to independence must be conducted and it must be determined that by application of safeguards they have been reduced to an acceptable level. The evaluation must attribute the NAS to ABC in making the evaluation.

Reissues, Engagement Letters, ADR, and Unpaid Fees

> **After studying this lesson, you should be able to:**
>
> 1. Explain and apply rules regarding when independent firms can no longer put their names on a report that was signed when they were independent.
>
> 2. Explain and apply rules regarding what an engagement letter may contain without impairing independence.
>
> 3. Explain and apply rules regarding when an engagement letter properly mandates alternative dispute resolution.
>
> 4. Explain and apply rules regarding under what circumstances unpaid fees endanger independence.

I. Reissued Reports

A. Covered members or their firms that were independent when they first issued an audit report may reissue that report or consent to its incorporation by reference, even if they are no longer independent, so long as they do not perform new procedures that would require updating the date (or *dual dating*) of the original report.

B. In this connection, it is acceptable if necessary to assess the effect of recent facts on the original report to:

   1. Make inquiries of successor auditors

   2. Read subsequent financial statements

   3. Undertake similar procedures

II. Engagement Contractual Terms

A. Although the Securities and Exchange Commission (SEC) and other regulators disapprove of engagement contracts that indemnify auditors for the effects of their own mistakes, it is okay for an engagement letter to require an attest client to indemnify or hold harmless a member firm for liability and costs **resulting from knowing misrepresentations by the client's management.**

B. It would impair independence for a covered member to agree to indemnify an attest client for losses resulting from the client's own acts.

III. Alternative Dispute Resolution

A. Engagement letters may require use of alternative dispute resolution (ADR) to resolve disagreements with clients.

B. However, if alternative dispute resolution is initiated, binding arbitration is sufficiently similar to litigation that it could place the member in public practice and the client in positions of material adverse interests and thereby impair independence, so the Conceptual Framework should be applied.

IV. Unpaid Fees

A. A member in public practice (MIPP) may not sign a current-year audit report if it has unpaid fees from the client for services provided more than one year prior.

B. Fees are *unpaid* even if:

   1. They are unbilled

   2. The client has issued to the firm a note receivable.

C. If the client is in bankruptcy, this rule does not apply.

Financial Interests

Overview and Unsolicited Financial Interests

> **After studying this lesson, you should be able to:**
>
> **1.** Recognize the terms that are important in understanding the financial interests that can cause independence problems for an attest firm.
>
> **2.** Know that members in public practice may not own direct or material indirect interests in an attest client.
>
> **3.** Explain and apply the rules that govern a situation where a financial interest unexpectedly comes the way of a member in public practice.

I. Overview—If a covered member has or is committed to acquire any direct (whether material or not) or any material indirect financial interest in an attest client, independence is impaired. Only if interests are both indirect and immaterial is independence not impaired.

II. Definitions

   A. Financial interest—Includes ownership (or an obligation to obtain ownership) in equity, debt, or derivatives issued by an entity.

   B. Direct financial interest—An interest:

   1. Owned directly (even if managed by others)

   2. Under one's control (even if managed by others)

   3. Beneficially owned through an investment vehicle, estate, trust, or other intermediary when the beneficiary either:

      a. Controls the intermediary, or

      b. Has the authority to supervise or participate in the intermediary's investment decisions.

   C. Indirect financial interest—An interest beneficially owned through an investment vehicle, estate, trust, or other intermediary when the beneficiary neither:

   1. Controls the intermediary, nor

   2. Has the authority to supervise or participate in its investment decisions.

   D. Beneficial ownership—Occurs when an individual or entity is not the record owner but has a right to some or all of the underlying benefits of ownership, such as to:

   1. Direct the voting

   2. Dispose of the interest

   3. Receive its economic benefits

III. Financial Interests—These rules about financial interests normally apply only to *covered members*; however, even if a partner or professional employee of a firm is not a covered member, that person (and his or her immediate family, or any group of such persons acting together) cannot own more than 5% of a client's ownership interests without impairing independence.

IV. Unsolicited Financial Interests

   A. If covered members receive or learn they will receive an unsolicited financial interest in an attest client (perhaps through gift or inheritance) that is either a direct interest or a material indirect interest, independence will not be impaired if they:

1. Dispose of the interest as soon as practicable but not later than **30 days** after having both knowledge of the interest and gaining the right to dispose of it; and

2. Do not participate on the attest engagement team after learning of the interest and before disposing of it.

B. If the covered member does not yet have the right to dispose of the interest (perhaps a relative who wrote a will is still alive), then independence will not be impaired if:

1. The member does not participate on the attest engagement team.

2. The interest is not material to the member.

Mutual Funds and Retirement Plans

After studying this lesson, you should be able to:

1. Understand the rules to avoid independence problems arising from personal investments in mutual funds and retirement plans.

2. Apply those rules in order to avoid independence problems arising from personal investments in mutual funds and retirement plans.

I. Mutual Funds

A. A covered member who owns shares in a mutual fund has a direct financial interest in the fund itself.

B. If the member owns 5% or less of the outstanding shares of a **diversified** mutual fund, the interest in the underlying investments of the fund are to be held immaterial and indirect financial interests. Immaterial and indirect interests do not impair independence.

C. However, if the covered member owns more than 5% of a diversified fund's shares or owns a financial interest in an **undiversified** fund, then the member must evaluate the fund's underlying investments to determine whether he or she holds a material indirect financial interest in any of the underlying investments.

D. **The code gives this illustration:**

> "If:
>
> a nondiversified mutual fund owns shares in attest client Company A,
>
> the mutual fund's net assets are $10,000,000,
>
> the covered member owns 1% of the outstanding shares of the mutual fund, having a value of $100,000, and
>
> the mutual fund has 10% of its assets invested in Company A,
>
> then the indirect financial interest of the covered member in Company A is $10,000 (10% × $100,000) and this amount should be measured against the covered member's net worth (including the net worth of his or her immediate family) to determine if it is material."

II. Retirement, Savings, Compensation, or Similar Plans

A. If covered members or their immediate family members (IFMs) self-direct their investments into such a plan or have the ability to supervise or participate in the plan's investment decisions, then the financial interests held by the plan are direct financial interests that impair independence even if they are immaterial.

B. Two examples:

1. A covered member is trustee of a retirement plan and supervises its investments, which include shares of an attest client.

2. A covered member participates in a retirement plan and has discretion to direct its investments, which include shares of an attest client.

C. If covered members (or their immediate family members) do not self-direct or supervise or participate in a plan's investment decisions, the underlying investments are **indirect** and therefore do not create independence issues unless they are material.

D. When a **defined benefit plan** is involved, interests held by the plan are not interests held by the covered members unless the covered members (or their immediate family members) are trustees of the plan or otherwise have the ability to supervise or participate in the plan's investment decisions.

E. Allocated shares held in an employee stock option plan are beneficially owned by the covered members but are indirect interests **until** the members have the right to dispose of them. At that point, they become direct financial interests.

Partnerships, 529s, Trust and Estates, Employee Benefit Plans

After studying this lesson, you should be able to:

1. Understand how to minimize problems in relation to investments in partnerships and limited liability corporations.

2. Understand how to minimize problems in 529 plans.

3. Understand how to minimize problems in employee benefit plans.

4. Understand how to minimize problems through trusts and estates.

I. Partnerships and Limited Liability Companies (LLCs)

A. General Partnership—A general partner (GP) has authority to influence investments, so a general partner's financial interests in both the partnership itself and its underlying investments are **direct**.

B. Limited Partnership

1. A general partner has authority to influence investments, so a general partner's financial interests in both the limited partnership itself and its underlying investments are **direct**.

2. A limited partner's interest in the limited partnership is direct, but usually he or she will not have influence over its investments so this partner's financial interest in its underlying investments will be **indirect**.

   a. If the limited partner has authority to supervise or participate in investment decisions or the ability to replace the general partner(s), then his or her interest in the underlying investments will be direct.

C. Limited Liability Companies (LLCs)

1. If a limited liability company is member-managed, then it is sufficiently like a general partnership that members' interests in both the firm and its underlying investments are direct.

2. If a limited liability company is agent-managed, then members are more like limited partners and their interests in the underlying investments are viewed as indirect unless the members have the authority to control the limited liability company or to supervise or participate in its investments.

II. Section 529 Plans

A. Prepaid Tuition Plans—Owners of a 529 account used to prepay tuition have a direct interest in the plan but only an indirect interest in its underlying investments. Owners of such plans are essentially buying tuition credits. The state has an obligation to provide the education regardless of the investments' performance.

B. Savings Plans—Owners of these accounts have a direct financial interest in both the plan and its investments because they may decide in which sponsor's 529 savings plan to invest and can determine before investing which firms the plan will invest in.

III. Trusts and Estates

A. The fact that a covered member is asked to serve as trustee of a trust or executor of an estate does not by itself create an independence problem if an attest client's shares are owned by the trust or estate. However, there is a problem if:

1. The covered member has the ability to make investment decisions for the trust or estate.

2. The trust or estate owns or is committed to acquiring more than 10% of the attest client's ownership interests, *or*

3. The value of the trust's or estate's ownership interest in the client exceeds 10% of the total assets of the trust or estate.

B. Grantor—If a covered member acts as a grantor to set up a trust, its investments are **direct** financial interests if any of the following are true:

1. The covered member has the ability to amend or revoke the trust.

2. The covered member has authority to control the trust.

3. The covered member has the ability to supervise or participate in the trust's investment decisions.

4. The underlying trust investments ultimately will revert to the covered member as the grantor.

C. Beneficiary—If a covered member is a beneficiary of a trust, then the covered member's interest in it is direct and his or her interest in the trust's underlying investments is indirect, unless the covered member controls the trust or supervises or participates in its investment decisions, in which case the interest becomes direct.

D. Blind Trust—Because the investments ultimately will revert to the grantor who typically retains the right to amend or revoke, both a blind trust **and** its underlying investments are considered to be direct financial interests of the grantor.

IV. Participation in Employee Benefit Plans (EBP)

A. Independence is impaired if a covered member participates in an employee benefit plan that is an attest client or sponsored by one. Two exceptions apply:

1. When a covered member is an employee of a government organization that sponsors an employee benefit plan and the covered member is required by law to audit the plan, then it is acceptable to do so if all of the following safeguards are in place:

a. The covered member is required to participate in the plan as a condition of employment.

b. The plan is offered to all employees in comparable positions.

c. The covered member is not a director, officer, employee, promoter, or the like of the plan.

d. The covered member has no influence or control over the investment strategy, benefits, or other management activities of the plan.

2. When the covered member formerly was associated with an attest client but is no longer, then independence is not impaired.

Depository Accounts, Brokerage Accounts, and Insurance Policies

> **After studying this lesson, you should be able to:**
>
> 1. Avoid independence problems that might arise from auditors using bank accounts and insurance policies.
>
> 2. Avoid independence problems that might arise from investing in the stock market using a stockbroker.

I. Depository Accounts

A. **Firm**—Firms may maintain depository accounts at a bank that is an attest client if they conclude that the likelihood is remote that the bank will experience financial difficulties.

B. **Individual**—Individual covered members may maintain such accounts if any of three conditions is met:

1. The balance in the depository account is fully insured, *or*

2. Any uninsured amounts were not material to the covered member's worth, *or*

3. If uninsured accounts are considered material, they are reduced to an immaterial amount within 30 days of becoming material.

II. Brokerage Accounts

A. A covered member's brokerage account at an attest client broker-dealer would not impair independence only if **both** of the following apply:

1. The attest client's services were rendered under the attest client's normal terms, procedures, and requirements.

2. Any covered member's assets subject to the risk of loss are immaterial to the covered member's net worth.

   a. In determining risk of loss, the question is not whether the assets' market value might decline but whether the client might become insolvent or commit fraud. Protection by regulators and insurance are relevant factors in determining risk of loss.

III. Insurance Policies

A. An insurance policy is not a financial interest unless it offers an investment option.

B. If there is an investment option, there would still not be an independence problem if the covered member bought the policy under normal terms and conditions, unless the covered member had either:

1. The ability to select the policy's underlying investments *or*

2. The authority to supervise or participate in the investment decision and the covered member invested in an attest client.

Loans, Leases, and Business Relationships

After studying this lesson, you should be able to:

1. Understand how to minimize the independence complications that might arise for members in public practice from:

- Borrowing money.

- Leasing (and leasing out) real estate.

- Entering into various business relationships, such as co-ownership.

I. Loans

A. If a covered member borrows from (or loans to) an attest client or any of its officers, directors, or 10% owners, there is likely an independence problem, especially if the client is not a lending institution.

B. If the attest client is a lending institution making a loan to covered members or their immediate family members, independence would not be impaired if it is (a) an immaterial unsecured loan, (b) a home mortgage, or (c) a secured loan, so long as **all** of these safeguards are met:

1. Normal lending procedures, terms, and requirements were applied.

2. The loan occurred before the lending institution become an attest client, or came from a lending institution for which independence was not required and later sold to an attest client.

3. Loans are kept current, and terms are not altered by extending maturity date, lowering interest rate, and so on.

4. The estimated fair value of the collateral equals or exceeds the outstanding balance; any deficit is not material to the covered member's net worth.

C. If a covered member keeps payments current and otherwise complies with loan or lease terms, these also do **not** impair independence:

1. Auto loans and leases collateralized by the car

2. Loans fully collateralized by cash surrender value of an insurance policy

3. Loans fully collateralized by cash deposits at the same lending institutions (e.g., passbook loans)

4. Aggregate outstanding balances from credit card and overdraft reserve accounts of $10,000 or less

II. Leases

A. Capital leases (leases to own—renamed "Finance leases" by GAAP in 2019) impair independence.

B. Operating lease arrangements do not impair independence if all of these safeguards are met:

1. The lease meets the generally accepted accounting principles criteria for an operating lease.

2. The terms and conditions are comparable with similar leases.

3. All amounts are paid in accordance with the terms of the lease.

III. Business Relationships

A. Cooperative Ventures—Cooperating with an attest client to provide services to a third party or to develop a product is problematic. A cooperative venture does not exist where all these safeguards are present:

1. Participation of the firm and client is governed by separate agreements that do not create obligations between them.

2. Neither assumes responsibilities for the other's activities or results.

3. Neither has authority to act as the other's agent.

B. Joint Closely Held Investments—Joint financial investments may create an independence problem also.

1. **Permissible:** The firm and an attest client could both own the stock of a widely held public company, like Microsoft.

2. **Impermissible:**

   a. The firm and a client both own material stakes in a small company.

   b. A covered member and an officer of an attest client jointly buy a sailboat.

Family Relationships

I. **Introduction**

    A. Two categories of family relationships create potential independence problems:

        1. **Immediate family members:** Spouses, spousal equivalents, and dependents

        2. **Close relatives**: Parents, siblings, and nondependent children.

II. **Immediate Family Members**

    A. With substantial exceptions that are about to be spelled out, immediate family members of covered members must comply with the same independence rules as covered members themselves. They may not work for attest clients or own financial interests in them (unless the interests are both indirect and immaterial).

    B. Irrespective of the exceptions below, immediate family members cumulatively may not own more than 5% of an attest client.

    C. **Immediate Family Members Employed by Attest Client**—A covered member's immediate family members may work for an attest client, just not in a "key position" such as one in which an employee has:

        1. Primary responsibility for significant accounting functions that support material components of the financial statement;

        2. Primary responsibility for the preparation of the financial statement; or

        3. The ability to exercise influence over the contents of the financial statement, including when the individual is a member of the board of directors or similar governing body, chief executive officer, president, chief financial officer, chief operating officer, general counsel, chief accountancy officer, controller, director of internal audit, director of financial reporting, treasurer, or any equivalent position.

    D. **Immediate Family Member Participation in an Employee Benefit Plan**—Immediate family members may not only work for an attest client in a nonkey position, they may also participate in an employee benefit plan that is an attest client or is sponsored by an attest client, so long as all of the following safeguards are followed:

        1. The plan is offered to all employees in comparable employment positions;

        2. The immediate family member does not serve in a position of governance for the plan; *and*

        3. The immediate family member does not have the ability to supervise or participate in the plan's investment decisions or in the selection of the investment options made available to plan participants.

    E. **Immediate Family Member Participation in an Employee Benefit Plan with Financial Interests in an Attest Client**—An immediate family member might work for a company that is not an attest client or in a non-key position in a company that is an attest client, but participate in its employee benefit plan and learn that the plan holds stock of an attest client. The general rule is that in this setting an immediate family member may hold a direct financial interest or material indirect financial interest in an attest client if all of the following safeguards are met:

1. The covered member is neither on the attest team nor in a position to influence. (So, the covered member could be a 10-hour person or other partner in the office but not a team member or in a position to influence in relationship to the attest client);

2. Such investment is an unavoidable consequence of such participation; the immediate family member had no other investment options available for selection and

3. If the plan creates an option that would allow the immediate family members to invest in a nonattest client, the immediate family members should select that option and dispose of the attest client shares as soon as practicable but within 30 days.

III. Close Relatives

A. Generally, close relatives of covered members must follow the same independence rules as the covered members themselves, but the restrictions are looser than for immediate family members and they are looser for close relatives of covered members who are not on the engagement team.

B. Independence is impaired if the close relative of an audit team member has **either** of the following:

1. A key position with the attest client, *or*

2. A financial interest in the attest client that:

   a. The team member knows or has reason to know was material to the close relative, *or*

   b. Enabled the close relative to exercise significant influence over the attest client.

C. Independence is impaired if the close relative of a person in a position to influence or other partner in the office has **either** of the following:

1. A key position with an attest client, *or*

2. A financial interest that:

   a. The person in a position to influence or other partner in office has reason to believe was material to the close relative, **and**

   b. Enabled the close relative to exercise significant influence over the attest client.

D. There are no specific restrictions on close relatives of 10-hour people (though the Conceptual Framework should always be kept in mind).

Employment Relationships

Current Employment

After studying this lesson, you should be able to:
1. Apply the rules that, to preserve independence, prevent various members of an accounting firm from working for an audit client in a wide range of positions.
2. Understand the rules that govern a situation where an attest client's employee wishes to come to work for the audit firm.

I. Current Employment

A. The employment rules focus on partners and professional employees of attest firms. They may not, without impairing independence, serve in these roles for an attest client: director, officer, employee, promoter, underwriter, voting trustee, or trustee for any pension or profit-sharing trust of the client's, or in any equivalent management position.

B. **Professors**—Partners and professional employees may serve as adjunct faculty members at a college that is an attest client so long as the following safeguards are all accurate regarding the faculty member. He or she:

1. Does not hold a key position with the client

2. Is not on the attest engagement team

3. Is not in a position to influence

4. Is on a part-time and non-tenure basis

5. Does not participate in any employee benefit plan sponsored by the school, unless participation is required

6. Does not assume any management responsibilities or set policies

C. **Honorary Director or Trustee of a Not-for-Profit Organization**—Partners and professional employees may lend the prestige of their names to a not-for-profit that is an attest client so long as all of the following safeguards are in place:

1. The position is clearly honorary.

2. The partner or professional employee cannot vote and takes no management role in the organization.

3. All externally circulated materials identify the position as honorary.

D. **Member of an Advisory Board**—If criteria similar to those mentioned in the previous section are met, partners and professional employees may serve on an attest client's advisory board without impairing independence.

E. **Member of Governmental Advisory Committee**—Independence considerations do not prevent partners or professional employees from serving on a citizen's advisory committee studying possible changes in the form of a county government that is an attest client, or on an advisory committee appointed to study the financial status of the state in which the county is located.

F. **Campaign Treasurer**—Independence considerations preclude a firm from auditing a campaign organization whose campaign manager is a partner or professional employee of the firm. Similarly, if Joe is an elected head of a governmental unit or is a candidate running for that position, an audit firm would not be independent in auditing that governmental unit if Joe's campaign manager is a partner or professional employee of the firm. However, the firm would not necessarily lack independence to audit Joe's political party. The firm should apply the threats and safeguards framework to determine whether threats to independence could be lowered to an acceptable level.

G. Member of Federated Fund-Raising Organization—If a firm's partner or professional employee serves as director or officer of a federated fund-raising organization such as United Way, which not only gives funds to a particular local charity but also exercises control over that charity, then the firm may not audit that local charity. Even if United Way does not exercise control, there are sufficient independence concerns that the Conceptual Framework should be invoked.

H. Member of Organization that Receives Funds from Fund-Raising Organization—When a partner or professional employee is a director of an organization that receives funding from a foundation that exists solely to raise funds for that organization, the firm may not audit the foundation, unless the directorship is clearly honorary.

II. Former Employment or Association with an Attest Client

A. Independence concerns arise when people who are employed by attest clients or who were associated with them as officers, directors, promoters, underwriters, voting trustees, or trustees for a pension fund or profit-sharing fund of the clients, join the firm as **covered members.**

B. Independence is impaired if one of these people participates as a **team member** or someone in a **position to influence** when the attest engagement covers any period of time when the person was employed by or associated with the audit client.

C. However, if the people become merely other partners in the office or 10-hour people, then independence is not impaired so long as they **dissociate** themselves from the client prior to becoming a covered member. Dissociation includes **all** of the following five steps:

1. Ceasing to participate in all the client's health and welfare benefit plans, unless the client is legally required to allow the covered member to participate in the plan (e.g., COBRA), and the covered member pays 100% of his or her portion of the cost

2. Ceasing to participate in all other employee benefit plans by liquidating or transferring all vested benefits in the client's defined benefit plans, defined contribution plans, and similar arrangements at the earliest permissible

3. Disposing of any direct or material indirect financial interest in the client

4. Collecting or repaying any loans to or from the client other than those specifically permitted or grandfathered by the code

5. Assessing other relationships with the client to determine if they create threats to independence that would require the application of safeguards to reduce threats to an acceptable level

Subsequent Employment

I. Considering Subsequent Employment with an Attest Client

A. When an attest team member or person in a position to influence is considering employment with the attest client, independence is impaired unless the team member:

1. Promptly reports such consideration or offer to an appropriate person in the firm, *and*

2. Removes him- or herself from the engagement until the offer is rejected or the position is no longer sought.

B. When a *covered member* learns that a team member or a person in a position to influence is considering employment with a client and has not taken the steps listed above, that member should alert the firm.

1. The firm must consider what additional procedures may be necessary to provide *reasonable assurance* that the person acted properly.

2. The policy does not explicitly cover other partners in office or 10-hour people.

II. Subsequent Employment with an Attest Client

A. A firm's independence will be considered impaired when a partner or professional employee goes to work for an attest client in a *key position,* unless all of the following conditions are met:

1. Amounts due the former employee for ownership interest in the firm and unfunded, vested retirement interests are not material to the firm, and the underlying formula used to calculate payments remains fixed.

2. The former employee is not in a position to influence the accounting firm's operations or financial policies.

3. The former employee does not participate or **appear** to participate in the firm's business and is not associated with the firm (even if unpaid). An *appearance of participation* results from such actions as:

   a. The former employee consults with the firm.

   b. The firm provides the former employee with an office and related amenities.

   c. The individual's name is included in the firm's office directory.

   d. The individual's name is included as a member of the firm in other membership lists of business, professional, or civic organizations, unless designated as retired.

4. The ongoing attest engagement team considers modifying audit procedures to adjust for the risk created by the former employee's knowledge of the audit plan that he or she has now taken to the client. Also, it should consider whether remaining team members can appropriately stand up to a former employee if they have to deal with him or/ her.

5. If the former employee joins the client in a **key position within one year of dissociating from the firm**, and has significant interaction with the attest engagement team, an appropriate professional in the firm should review the subsequent engagement to determine whether appropriate skepticism was maintained.

B. Sarbanes-Oxley (SOX) imposes stricter rules where public companies are involved. SOX imposes a one-year cooling-off period that requires the lead partner, the concurring partner, or any other member of the audit engagement team who provides more than 10 hours of audit, review, or attest services to observe a one-year cooling-off period before going to work for a client in a financial oversight position. The positions that cannot be assumed within the one-year period include (a) chief executive officer, chief financial officer, controller, chief accountancy officer, or any equivalent officers; (b) any financial oversight role; and (c) any position preparing financial statements. If a former audit firm employee violates these rules, independence is impaired. The one-year cooling-off period is that year preceding the beginning of the audit, so the cooling-off period actually can extend to nearly two years if the member has begun an audit cycle before leaving the firm.

Other Associations and Relationships

I. **Member of a Social Club**—If a covered member belongs to a social club, such as a country club, that is an attest client, there should be no independence problem if the membership is primarily a social matter.

II. **Member of a Trade Association**—If a covered member belongs to a trade association that is an attest client, independence is threatened (but not necessarily impaired if proper safeguards are applied under the conceptual framework). But if a partner or professional employee is simultaneously employed by or associated with a trade association audit client, independence would be impaired pursuant to the same rules that apply for PPE employment with any audit client.

III. **Member of a Common Interest Realty Association (CIRA)**—If a covered member buys an interest in a condominium, cooperative, or other common interest realty association, his or her firm may nonetheless audit the common interest realty association, but only if **all** of the following safeguards are met:

   A. The common interest realty association performs functions similar to local governments, such as public safety, road maintenance, and utilities;

   B. The covered member's annual assessment is not material to either the common interest realty association or the member;

   C. Liquidation of the common interest realty association or sale of common assets would not result in a distribution to the covered member; *and*

   D. The common interest realty association's creditors would not be permitted to recover out of the member's assets if the common interest realty association became insolvent.

IV. **Member of a Credit Union**—When a covered member is a member of a credit union and became eligible to join only because of the professional services he or she provided to the credit union, independence is impaired. However, if the member individually qualifies to join the credit union irrespective of professional services provided, then independence is not impaired.

V. **Gifts and Entertainment**

   A. **Gifts**—Independence is impaired if the firm, a team member, or someone in a position to influence accepts a gift from an attest client, unless the value is clearly insignificant to the recipient.

   B. **Entertainment**—Entertainment may be accepted without impairing independence so long as it is reasonable in the circumstances. The circumstances to be considered include:

      1. Nature of the gift or entertainment

      2. Occasion giving rise to the gift or entertainment

      3. Cost or value of the gift or entertainment

      4. Nature, frequency, and value of other gifts and entertainment

      5. Whether the entertainment was associated with the active conduct of business

      6. Whether other attest clients also participated in the entertainment; *and*

      7. Client and firm employees who participated in the entertainment

VI. Actual or Threatened Litigation

A. Litigation Between Client and Member—If the client (or its management) sues the audit firm (or vice versa), the key question is whether the firm and client are in threatened or actual positions of material adverse interests. A minor dispute or one not related to the engagement (such as a billing dispute) would not impair independence. However, the code gives these examples of impaired independence:

1. An **attest client's current** management sues or seriously threatens to sue firm alleging deficiencies in the audit work.

2. A **covered member** sues the client's current management alleging fraud or deceit.

B. Litigation by Client Security Holders—Client shareholders filing a suit claiming securities fraud or some other wrong by both the client and the audit firm presumptively does **not** automatically impair independence. But if there are cross-claims between the client and its managers on one hand and the attest firm of the other (or a serious risk of them), independence is impaired if there is a *significant risk* that a material settlement or judgment will result.

C. Other Third-Party Litigation—Litigation by non-shareholder third parties, such as lenders, who might also sue the auditor and/or the client is treated similarly.

D. Final resolution of litigation or other dispute eliminates the independence threat and reduces it to an acceptable level.

Nonaudit Services

Code Provisions

After studying this lesson, you should be able to:

1. Understand the differences between the code's approach and Sarbanes-Oxley's approach to the provision of nonaudit services to public company attest clients.

2. Understand and be able to apply the "big picture" code rules, such as the general requirements that always must be met for those who provide nonaudit services to attest clients.

I. Introduction

A. The code governs provision of nonaudit services to private company audit clients and indicates that communications about the following matters that would **not** normally be considered nonaudit services:

1. The client's selection and application of accounting standards or policies and financial statement disclosure requirements;

2. The appropriateness of the client's methods used in determining accounting and financial reporting;

3. Adjusting journal entries that the member has prepared or proposed for client management consideration; *and*

4. The form or content of the financial statement.

B. Covered members should monitor the total amount of their nonaudit services to ensure that their total involvement with the client does not become so extensive that it would constitute performing a separate service.

C. **Management responsibilities**—Members must not assume any management responsibilities of attest clients. "Management responsibilities involve leading and directing an entity, including making significant decisions regarding the acquisition, deployment, and control of human, financial, physical, and intangible resources." Examples of such impermissible activities include:

1. Setting policy or strategic direction for the attest client

2. Directing or accepting responsibility for actions of the attest client's employees except to the extent permitted when using internal auditors to provide assistance for services performed under auditing or attestation standards

3. Authorizing, executing, or consummating transactions or otherwise exercising authority on behalf of an attest client or having the authority to do so

4. Preparing source documents, in electronic or other form, that evidence the occurrence of a transaction

5. Having custody of an attest client's assets

6. Deciding which recommendations of the member or other third parties to implement or prioritize

7. Reporting to those charged with governance on behalf of management

8. Serving as an attest client's stock transfer or escrow agent, registrar, general counsel or equivalent

9. Accepting responsibility for the management of an attest client's project

10. Accepting responsibility for the preparation and fair presentation of the attest client's financial statements in accordance with the applicable financial reporting framework

11. Accepting responsibility for designing, implementing, or maintaining internal control

II. **General Requirements for Performing Nonaudit Services**—When covered members do provide nonaudit services for an attest client, **if other rules do not state otherwise**, independence would not be impaired if **all** of the following three safeguards are met.

A. In order to ensure that the ultimate management of the attest client stays with the client's management, the members must determine that the client and its management agree to:

1. Assume all management responsibilities;

2. Oversee the service, by designating an individual, preferably within senior management, who possesses the skill, knowledge, and/or experience to do the job. The member should assess the situation to ensure that the individual is up to the task;

3. Evaluate the adequacy and results of the services performed; *and*

4. Accept responsibility for the results of the services.

B. The members must **not** assume management responsibilities (as outlined above) and additionally must satisfy themselves that the audit client and its management will:

1. Be able to meet the criteria listed in the previous paragraph

2. Make an informed judgment on the results of the member's nonaudit services

3. Accept responsibility for making the significant judgments and decisions that are the proper responsibility of management

C. Before performing nonaudit services, members must establish (and document in writing) their understanding with the attest client regarding:

1. Objectives of the engagement

2. Services to be performed

3. The attest client's acceptance of its responsibilities

4. The member's responsibilities

5. Any limitations on the engagement

D. If all of these general requirements are met, then independence is not impaired, unless other rules (that we are about to explore) so provide.

E. If the general requirements are met, then a member may:

1. Provide advice, research materials, and recommendations to assist management in performing its functions and making decisions

2. Attend board meetings as a nonvoting advisor

3. Interpret financial statements, forecasts, or other analyses

4. Provide management with advice regarding its potential plans, strategies, or relationships

III. **Sarbanes-Oxley (SOX)**

A. SOX limits the nonattest (also known as consulting or advisory services) that attest firms may provide to attest clients that are **public companies**. SOX does not apply if the firms are not public companies, so the code governs if an accounting firm audits a private company.

B. SOX limitations on nonaudit services are based on three fundamental notions: (a) accounting firms should not audit their own work, (b) auditors should not advocate for their clients, and (c) accounting firms should not serve as their clients' managers.

C. SOX provides that an independent auditor cannot perform the following nonaudit services for a public company audit client:

1. Bookkeeping or other services related to the accounting records of financial statements

2. Financial information systems design and implementations

3. Appraisal or valuation services, fairness opinions, or contributions-in-kind reports

4. Actuarial services

5. Internal audit outsourcing services

6. Management functions or human resources

7. Broker or dealer, investment advisor, or investment banking services

8. Legal services and expert services unrelated to the audit

9. Any other service that the Public Company Accounting Oversight Board (PCAOB) determines is impermissible.

D. SOX does not prohibit attest firms from providing tax services to their attest clients, but PCAOB rules do provide that a public company's auditor's independence is impaired regarding a tax client if the firm:

1. Enters into a contingent fee arrangement with an audit client

2. Provides marketing, planning, or opinion services in favor of the tax treatment of a *confidential transaction,* or if the transaction is based on an *aggressive* interpretation of tax law

3. Provides tax services to members of management who serve in a financial reporting oversight role for a client (or to their immediate family)

E. SOX requires that rather than the audit client's management selecting the auditor, client **audit committees** should select, evaluate, and compensate the auditors. In addition, these audit committees, which are to be composed entirely of outside directors and therefore presumably independent of overt management influence, must **preapprove** any permitted nonaudit services (such as tax services) purchased by a company from its auditor.

F. Also, when a firm seeks the permission of an audit client's audit committee to provide tax services, it must: (a) describe the proposed services in writing to the committee, (b) discuss with the committee the potential effects on independence, and (c) document that discussion.

Specific Services

After studying this lesson, you should be able to:

1. Understand the types of nonaudit services that can be provided to a private company attest client.

2. Understand the types of nonaudit services that cannot be provided to a private company attest client.

Overview

Appraisal, Valuation, or Actuarial	Impaired	Not Impaired
Results would be material to the financial statement and services involve high degree of subjectivity[*]	X	
Services not requiring high degree of subjectivity[†]		X
Services performed for nonfinancial statement purposes[‡]		X

[*]Examples: valuing employee stock option plan, business combination, or appraisals of assets and liabilities.
[†]Examples: valuing a client's pension or postemployment benefit liabilities.
[‡]Examples: appraising or actuarial services for tax planning, estate and gift taxation, and divorce proceedings.

Benefit Plan Administration	Impaired	Not Impaired
Communicate summary plan data to plan trustee		X
Advise client management regarding impact of plan provisions		X
Process transactions initiated by plan participants		X
Prepare account valuations		X
Prepare and transmit participant statement to plan participants		X
Make policy decisions on client's behalf	X	
Interpret plan for participants without management's concurrence	X	
Make disbursements on plan's behalf	X	
Take custody of plan assets	X	
Serve as a plan fiduciary	X	

Bookkeeping, Payroll, and Other Disbursements	Impaired	Not Impaired
Record management-approved transactions in client's general ledger		X
Post client-coded transactions to client's general ledger		X
Prepare financial statements based on client's trial balance information		X
Post client-approved journal entry to client's trial balance		X
Propose standard, adjusting, or correcting journal entries		X
Generate unsigned checks using client's source documents		X
Process a client's payroll using client-provided records		X
Transmit client-approved payroll or other disbursement information to a financial institution chosen by client		X
Prepare reconciliation for client's evaluation		X
Determine or make changes in accounting records without client approval	X	
Approve or authorize client transactions	X	
Prepare source documents	X	
Make changes to source documents without client approval	X	
Accept responsibility to authorize payment of client funds	X	
Accept responsibility to sign or cosign checks	X	
Maintain client's bank account, take custody of client funds, or make credit or banking decisions for client	X	
Approve vendor invoices for payments	X	

Business Risk Consulting	Impaired	Not Impaired
Assist management in its assessment of client's business risk control processes		X
Recommend a plan for improving control processes and assisting in implementation		X
Make or approve business risk decisions	X	
Present business risk consideration to board on management's behalf	X	

Corporate Finance Consulting	Impaired	Not Impaired
Assist in developing corporate strategies		X
Assist in identifying sources of capital meeting client's criteria		X
Introduce management to sources of capital meeting client's criteria		X
Assist management in analyzing effects of proposed transactions		X
Advise client in transaction negotiations		X
Assist in drafting offering documents		X
Participate in transaction negotiations in advisory capacity		X
Be named as financial advisory in client's offering documents		X
Commit the client to a transaction	X	
Consummate transaction on client's behalf	X	
Act as a promoter, underwriter, broker-dealer, or guarantor of client's securities	X	
Act as a distributor of client's offering documents	X	
Maintain custody of client's securities	X	

Executive or Employee Search	Impaired	Not Impaired
Recommend position description or candidate specifications		X
Solicit, screen, and recommend candidates based on client-approved criteria		X
Recommend qualified candidates based on client-approved criteria		X
Advise employer on employee hiring or benefits		X
Hire or terminate client employees	X	
Commit client to employee compensation or benefits	X	

Forensic Accounting Services	Impaired	Not Impaired
Expert witness for a client	X	

Expert for a large group where attest clients
  a. < 20% of members, voting interest, and claims
 	
  b. are not *lead* plaintiffs, and
 	
  c. do not have sole decision-making power to select expert witness
		X

Fact witness		X
Litigation consulting: providing advice to attest client (without serving as expert witness)		X
Litigation consulting: serving as trier of fact, special master, court-appointed expert, or arbitrator	X	
Litigation consulting: mediator		X

Information Systems Services	Impaired	Not Impaired
Design, develop or implement services		
• not related to a financial information system (FIS)		X
• Related to an FIS	X	
Install a commercial off-the-shelf (COTS) FIS software solution		
• Designed by third-party vendor (3PV)		X
Configure a COTS FIS software solution		
• Using only 3PV's software		X
• Designing or developing new software code or features	X	
Customize a COTS FIS software solution to add functionality or enhancements	X	
Interface a COTS FIS software solution so it can pass data to another system (data translation services)		
• Using 3PV's application		X
• By providing interface services	X	
System and network maintenance, support, and monitoring of client's financial or nonfinancial information system (IS)		
• Operate network, such as managing client's systems or software applications	X	
• Supervise client personnel involved in operating client's IS	X	
• Have responsibility for monitoring or maintaining client's network performance	X	
• Operate or manage client's IT help desk	X	
• Have responsibility to perform ongoing network maintenance	X	
• Have responsibility for maintaining security of client's networks and systems	X	

Information Systems Services	Impaired	Not Impaired
• Analyze client's network and providing recommendations		X
• Apply virus protection solutions or updates that member did not design or develop		X
• Apply updates and patches that member did not design or develop		X
• Provide advice, training, or instruction on a software solution		X
• Assess the design or operating effectiveness of client's security over IT systems		X
• Assess client's IT securities policies or practices		X

Internal Audit	Impaired	Not Impaired
Assess whether performance complies with management policies		X
Identify opportunities for improvement		X
Recommend improvement for management consideration		X
Performing ongoing monitoring activities or control activities (e.g., reviewing customer credit info as part of sales process) that affects execution of transactions	X	
Performing separate evaluations of a significant control such that member is, in effect, performing routine operations built into client's business process	X	
Having management rely on member's work as primary basis for client's assertions on design of operating effectiveness of internal controls	X	
Determining which, if any, recommendations for improving internal control system should be implemented	X	
Reporting to board or audit committee on behalf of management regarding internal audit affairs	X	
Approving or being responsible for overall internal audit work including determining internal audit risk and scope, project priorities, and frequency of performance of audit procedures	X	
Being connected with client as employee or in any management position (e.g., being listed as an employee in client's directory)	X	

Investment—Advisory or Management	Impaired	Not Impaired
Recommend allocation of funds that client should invest in various asset classes		X
Perform bookkeeping and reporting of client's portfolio balance		X
Review management of client's portfolio by others to determine if managers are meeting client's investment objectives		X
Transmit client's investment selection to broker		X
Make investment decisions on client's behalf	X	
Execute transactions to buy or sell for client	X	
Take custody of client assets, such as a security purchased by client	X	

Tax Services *Assuming that CPA does not have custody or control over client's funds and that client employee reviews and approves tax return prior to transmission to taxing authority, and, if required for filing, signs tax return, then:*	Impaired	Not Impaired
• Preparing tax return		X
• Transmitting tax return to taxing authority		X
• Transmitting payment		X
Signing and filing tax return on behalf of client management if authorized by management and requirements are met		X
Representing client in administrative proceedings before taxing authority		X
Representing client in court to resolve a tax dispute	X	

Hosting Services *When a member provides hosting services, it is maintaining the attest client's internal control over its data or records, creating a management participation threat to independence.*	Impaired	Not Impaired
Hosting an attest client's website or other nonfinancial information system	X	
Keeping an attest client's electronic data or paper records *on client's behalf*	X	
Serving as attest client's business continuity or disaster recovery provider	X	
Keeping copies of attest client's data or records as documentation to support a service the member provided. Example: payroll data supporting payroll tax return is provided by member for client.		X
Retaining, for a *member's* records, a copy of work product prepared by the member		X
Using general ledger software to facilitate delivery of bookkeeping services to audit client. Example: Attest client maintains its software in the cloud via a third-party services provider and grants the member access to the software so that the member can perform permitted bookkeeping services for the client.		X
Retaining data collected by the member related to work product the member prepared for the attest client. Example: Member conducts employee survey for a client and retains survey data after delivering report to client.		X
Electronically exchanging data or member's work product with an attest client or on behalf of an attest client at the attest client's request. Example: Member uses a portal to deliver member's work product to a third party at attest client's request.		X
Licensing software to an attest client that it uses to input its data and receive an output that the client is responsible for maintaining, so long as the software performs no activity that, if performed directly by the member, would impair independence.		X
Possessing a depreciation schedule prepared by the member, provided the schedule and calculation are given to the attest client so that its books and records are complete		X
Retaining an attest client's original data or records to facilitate performance of an NAS. Example: Obtaining original records to prepare client's tax return, provided that the data or records are returned to the client at the end of the engagement (or at least annually if it is a multiyear engagement).		X

Members in Business

I. Introduction

A. **Members in business** are members who are "employed or engaged on a contractual or volunteer basis in an executive, staff, governance, advisory, or administrative capacity in such areas as industry, the public sector, education, the not-for-profit sector and regulatory or professional bodies." This would include staff accountants, internal auditors, and other accountants not engaged in public practice.

B. Members in business do not have to worry about independence rules. They have other responsibilities that generally mirror those of members in public practice, so it should not take long to master their part of the Code of Professional Conduct.

II. Conceptual Framework

A. The Conceptual Framework for members in business generally tracks that of members in public practice. Six of the seven threats identified for members in public practice also apply to members in business: (a) adverse interest threats, (b) advocacy threats, (c) familiarity threats, (d) self-interest threats, (e) self-review threats, and (f) undue influence threats. The examples given differ, naturally, because of the difference in work setting.

B. Examples of adverse interest threats include:

   1. A member in business's close relative is an investor in her employer's closest competitor.

   2. A member in business has sued her employer.

C. Examples of advocacy threats include:

   1. Obtaining favorable financing is dependent on the information that the member in business includes in a prospectus.

   2. The member in business gives or fails to give information that he knows will unduly influence the conclusions reached by a third party.

D. Examples of familiarity threats include:

   1. A member in business has a long relationship with a third party and therefore stops reviewing the quality of the third-party's work.

   2. A member in business hires a relative as a subordinate.

   3. A member in business regularly accepts gifts or entertainment from a firm that sells goods or services to the member's employer.

E. Self-interest threats include:

   1. A member in business's close relative owns stock in the employer.

   2. A member in business is eligible for a performance-related bonus, and its value will be directly affected by the member in business's decisions.

F. Self-review threats include:

   1. An internal auditor accepts work that she previously performed before she was promoted to her current position.

2. A member in business accepts work that she previously performed that will be the basis for providing another professional service—for example, Sally gives tax advice to her client and later, while doing attest work for the client, automatically accepts the validity of the tax advice.

G. Undue influence threats include members in business being pressured to

1. Become associated with misleading information

2. Deviate from company policy, *or*

3. Change a conclusion regarding a tax or accounting position.

H. When attempting to eliminate these threats or reduce them to an acceptable level, members in business cannot turn to safeguards generated by their accounting firm, of course, but can turn to those created by:

1. The profession, legislation, or regulation, *or*

2. Their employer.

III. Integrity and Objectivity

A. Offering or Accepting Gifts or Entertainment—Members in business should not accept any gifts or entertainment that would violate the law or the policies of other firms of their own employer. Gifts or entertainment not reasonable in the circumstances would create a violation of the integrity and objectivity rule.

B. Preparing and Reporting Information—Members in business must never:

1. Make or direct another to make a false entry;

2. Fail to correct inaccurate financial statements or entries; *or*

3. Sign or permit another to sign a document containing materially false information.

C. Subordination of Judgment—The rules against subordination of judgment for members in business are essentially identical for those of members in public practice that are contained in Part 1 of the Code of Professional Conduct.

D. Obligation of a Member to His or Her Employer's External Accountant—Members in business are to "be candid and not knowingly misrepresent facts or knowingly fail to disclose material facts to their employers" external auditor.

E. Educational Services—When teaching at a university or performing other educational services, a member in business is viewed as performing professional services and therefore must act with integrity and objectivity.

F. Pressure to Breach the Rules—MIBs should neither pressure other members to breach the rules of integrity and objectivity, nor succumb to such pressures themselves. Examples of such pressures to guard against include:

1. Pressures related to conflicts of interest (example: MIB's brother pressures MIB to select him as a vendor to the MIB's employer over competing firms).

2. Pressures to influence presentation of information (example: superiors pressure MIB to report misleading financial results to influence investors or to suppress internal audit reports containing adverse findings).

3. Pressures to act without sufficient competence or due care (example: superiors pressure MIB to finish internal audit report without having performed sufficient work or to undertake a task the MIB is not qualified for).

4. Pressures related to financial interests (example: CEO pressures MIB to manipulate financial results to indicate that performance targets qualifying the CEO for a bonus have been met).

5. Pressures related to gifts or entertainment (example: superiors pressure MIB to offer gifts to a purchasing agent to influence her to buy goods from MIB's employer rather than competitors).

IV. General Standards

A. Like members in public practice, members in business must:

1. Act with professional competence

2. Exercise due professional care

3. Adequately plan and supervise performance of professional services

4. Have sufficient relevant data to back up any conclusions or recommendations they make

B. Members in business are expected to:

1. Comply with applicable standards promulgated by bodies like the Securities and Exchange Commission and Internal Revenue Service

2. Not imply that financial statements they are preparing and submitting to third parties were prepared in accordance with independence rules when they were not

V. Accounting Principles

A. Like members in public practice, members in business may not claim that financial statements are presented in accordance with generally accepted accounting principles when they are not.

VI. Acts Discreditable—Members in business are held to essentially the same standards as members in public practice when it comes to defining discreditable acts, which include:

A. Discrimination and harassment in employment

B. Solicitation or disclosure of CPA Exam questions and answers

C. Failure to file a tax return or pay a tax liability

D. Negligence in preparing financial statement or other records

E. Failure to follow the rules for preparation of financial statements required by agencies like the Securities and Exchange Commission, Federal Communications Commission, and state commissioners

F. Entering into prohibited indemnification agreements and limited liability provisions

G. Disclosing confidential information without the employer's permission or the application of another recognized exception (such as validly issued subpoena, etc.)

H. Promoting or marketing their firm by use of false, misleading, or deceptive ads

I. Improper (misleading) use of the CPA credential

Other Members

After studying this lesson, you should be able to:

1. Recognize the two basic types of "other members"— retired and unemployed.

2. Understand that other members should not engage in discreditable acts.

I. **Definition**—*Other members* are, by definition, unemployed, retired, or otherwise not working in the profession, so most of the code that applies to members in public practice and members in business does not apply to them.

II. **Discreditable Acts**—Other members are, at a minimum, not to engage in discreditable acts, including:

A. Discrimination and harassment in employment practices

B. Solicitation or disclosure of CPA Examination questions and answers

C. Failure to file a tax return or pay a tax liability

D. Improper disclosure of confidential information obtained from former employment or previous volunteer work

E. False, misleading, or deceptive acts in promoting or marketing services

F. Improper (misleading) use of the CPA credential

Requirements of SEC and PCAOB

Securities and Exchange Commission (SEC)

After studying this lesson, you should be able to:

1. Understand the ethical requirements of the SEC.

2. Recognize situations that present threats to compliance with the ethical requirements of the SEC.

3. Apply the ethical requirements and independence rules of the SEC to situations that could present threats to compliance during an audit of an issuer.

I. Introduction

A. The SEC rules for independence are very similar to AICPA rules. Although there are some differences, the results are usually the same under both approaches. Any student who masters the AICPA Code of Professional Conduct and has knowledge of the Sarbanes-Oxley (SOX) requirements and a modicum of common sense should be able to handle questions regarding the SEC rules. Nonetheless, this lesson outlines those rules in some detail.

B. Rule 2-01 of the SEC's Regulation S-X provides specific rules regarding auditor independence in connection with public company audit clients. It also includes the SOX independence requirements. Remember that if there are any differences between the AICPA approach and the rules of the SEC or PCAOB, the latter take precedence if the audit client is a public company.

   1. Many of SOX's provisions that are relevant here are covered in more detail in the BEC lesson on corporate governance, including requirements for retention of audit records, punishment for destroying audit documents prematurely, and so on.

C. SEC independence rules are, overall, concerned with whether a relationship with or provision of a service to an audit client:

   1. Creates a conflict of interest for the auditor;

   2. Results in the accountant auditing his or her own work;

   3. Results in the accountant acting as an audit client's manager or employee; *or*

   4. Places the accountant in a position of being an advocate for the audit client.

II. Key Definitions

A. **Financial Reporting Oversight Role (FROR)**—A role in which a person is in a position to or does exercise influence over the contents of the F/S or anyone who prepares them. Examples: director, CEO, president, CFO, COO, general counsel, CAO, controller, director of internal audit, director of financial reporting, treasurer, or any equivalent position.

B. **Affiliate**—Auditors are to be independent of the firm under audit **and** its affiliates. Until 2020, "affiliate" was broadly defined, focusing on common control. Assume Company A controlled two subsidiaries—Co. B and Co. C. B's auditor would automatically have to be independent of C. Now B's auditor need be independent of C only if both B and C are "material" to A. This new "dual materiality threshold" rule makes it easier for auditors of public companies to avoid independence problems. The SEC also issued new rules making it easier to avoid independence issues when auditing "investment company complexes" (ICCs), which often include a controlling entity and scores of related funds.

C. **Audit and Professional Engagement Period**—Includes the period covered by any F/S being audited or reviewed (the "audit period") and the period of the engagement (the "professional engagement period"). The professional engagement period begins at the earlier of when the accountant signs an initial engagement letter or begins the audit and ends when the audit client or the accountant notifies the SEC that the client is no longer the accountant's audit client.

D. Close Family Member (CFM)—A CFM is defined as a person's spouse, spousal equivalent, parent, dependent, nondependent child, and sibling.

E. Covered Persons—Covered persons are defined as the following partners, principals, shareholders, and employees of an accounting firm:

1. **Audit engagement team**, which includes "all partners, principals, shareholders and professional employees participating in an audit, review, or attestation engagement of an audit client, including audit partners and all persons who consult with others on the audit engagement . . . regarding technical or industry-specific issues, transactions, or events" (comparable to AICPA "team");

2. **Chain of command**, which includes all persons who: (a) supervise or have direct management responsibility for the audit, including at all successively senior levels through the accounting firm's chief executive; (b) evaluate the performance or recommend the compensation of the audit engagement partner; *or* (c) provide quality control or other oversight of the audit (PTIs);

3. Any other partner, principal, shareholder, or managerial employee of the accounting firm who has provided 10 or more hours of nonaudit services (NAS) to the audit client for the period beginning on the date such services are provided and ending on the date the accounting firm signs the report on the F/S for the fiscal year during which those services are provided, or who expects to provide 10 or more hours of NAS to the audit client on a recurring basis (10-hour persons); *and*

4. Any other partner, principal, or shareholder from an "office" of the accounting firm in which the lead audit engagement partner primarily practices in connection with the audit other partners in the office (OPIOs).

F. Immediate Family Member (IFM)—An IFM is a person's spouse, spousal equivalent, and dependents.

III. Basic Requirements—To be qualified to audit a public company, a CPA:

A. Must be registered and in good standing under the laws of his or her state; *and*

B. Must be and appear to be independent and capable of exercising objective and impartial judgment.

IV. Financial Relationships—Investments in audit clients can imperil independence.

A. Direct Investments—The accounting firm, any of its covered persons, or any of their immediate family members (IFMs) may not have direct investments in an audit client, such as owning stocks, bonds, notes, options, and so on.

1. A "direct investment" includes one through an intermediary if:

   a. The firm, covered persons, or IFMs, alone or together, either supervise or participate in the intermediary's investment decisions, *or*

   b. The intermediary is a nondiversified mutual fund that has invested 20% or more its money in an audit client.

B. Five Percent Investments—Independence is impaired if any partner, principal, shareholder, or professional employee of the accounting firm (and any of their IFMs or CFMs) owns more than 5% or more of the client's stock.

C. Trustee of a Trust—Independence is impaired if the accounting firm or any covered persons or IFMs serve as voting trustees of a trust or executors of an estate containing an audit client's securities, *unless* they have no authority to make investment decisions for the trust or estate.

D. Material Indirect Interests—As with the AICPA Code, accounting firms, covered persons, and their IFMs may not only not have direct financial interests in an audit client (whether material or immaterial), they may not have indirect interests that are *material*. It is permitted for these persons to own 5% or less of a *diversified* investment company, even if the company owns some shares of an audit client.

E. Related Entities—Independence is destroyed if the firm, covered persons, or IFMs:

1. Have any direct or material indirect investment in an entity that is not an audit client where:

   a. An audit client has an investment in that entity that is material to the audit client and has the ability to exercise significant control over that entity, *or*

   b. The entity has an investment in an audit client that is material to that entity and has the ability to exercise significant influence over that audit client.

2. Have any material investment in an entity over which an audit client is able to exercise significant influence; *or*

3. Have the ability to exercise significant influence over an entity that has the ability to exercise significant influence over an audit client.

V. Other Financial Relationships—Independence is impaired if the firm, its covered persons, or their IMFs have:

A. Loans/Debtor Creditor Relationships—Any loan to or from an audit client, its officers or directors, or its 10% owners creates an independence problem. However, there are five exceptions where loans are obtained from a *financial institution* under its normal lending procedures, terms, and requirements:

1. Automobile loans and leases collateralized by the automobile;

2. Loans fully collateralized by the cash surrender value of an insurance policy;

3. Loans fully collateralized by cash deposits at the same financial institution;

4. Mortgage loans collateralized by the borrower's primary residence provided the loans were not obtained while the covered person was a covered person; *and*

5. Student loans provided the loans were not obtained while the covered person in the firm was a covered person.

B. Savings and Checking Accounts—Any savings, checking, or similar account at a bank, savings and loan, or similar institution that is an audit client creates an independence problem if the account has a balance that exceeds the amount insurable by the FDIC, *except* that an accounting firm may have an uninsured balance provided that the likelihood of the institution experiencing financial difficulties is remote.

C. Broker-Dealer Accounts—Brokerage or similar accounts maintained with a broker-dealer that is an audit client create an independence problem, if:

1. Any such account includes assets other than cash or securities; *or*

2. The value of assets in the accounts exceeds the amount protected by the Securities Investor Protection Corporation (SIPC), which is $500,000 for securities and $250,000 for cash.

D. Consumer Loans—Any aggregate outstanding consumer loan balance (e.g., credit card debt, retail installment loans, cell phone installment plans, and home improvement loans) greater than $10,000 owed to a lender that is an audit client creates and independence problem.

E. Insurance Products—Any individual policy issued by an insurer that is an audit client creates an independence problem, *unless*:

1. The policy was obtained when the covered person was *not* a covered person in the firm; *and*

2. The likelihood of the insurer becoming insolvent is remote.

VI. **Exceptions**—Notwithstanding the provisions in the previous two sections, independence will not be impaired in these cases:

    A. **Inheritance and Gifts**—Any person who acquires an unsolicited financial interest (as through gift or inheritance) will not lose independence if he or she disposes of the interest as soon as practicable but always less than 30 days after the person has knowledge of and the right to dispose of the interest.

    B. **New Audit Engagement**—A person has a financial interest that would normally impair independence *but* that person did not audit the client's F/S the previous year and disposes of the interest before either (a) signing an engagement letter or (b) commencing any audit procedures.

    C. **Employee Compensation and Benefit Plans**—An IFM has an impermissible financial interest in an audit client that was an unavoidable consequence of participation in his or her employer's employee compensation or benefits program, provided that the financial interest (other than unexercised employee stock options) is disposed of as soon as practicable but always no later than 30 days after the person has the right to dispose of the financial interest. This exception applies to IFMs of OPIOs and 10-hour persons.

VII. **Audit Clients' Financial Relationships**—CPAs are not independent in these cases:

    A. **Investments by the Audit Client in the Accounting Firm**—(a) An audit client has, or has agreed to acquire, any direct investment in the accounting firm, *or* (b) the audit client's officers or directors own greater than 5% of the equity securities of the accounting firm.

    B. **Underwriting**—Their firm engages an audit client to act as an underwriter, broker-dealer, market maker, promoter, or analyst for securities issued by the accounting firm.

VIII. **Employment Relationships**—An accountant is not independent if he or she has an employment relationship with the audit client such as those listed next.

    A. **Employment at Audit Client of Accountant**—A current partner, principal, shareholder, or professional employee of the accounting firm is employed by the audit client or is a member of the board of directors.

    B. **Employment at Audit Client of Certain Relatives of Accountant**—A CFM of a covered person is in an accounting role or FROR at an audit client.

    C. **Employment at Audit Client of Former Employee of Accounting Firm**

        1. A former partner, principal shareholder, or professional employee at an accounting firm is in an accounting or FROR at an audit client, *unless* the individual:

            a. Does not influence the accounting firm's operations or financial policies;

            b. Has no capital balances in the accounting firm; *and*

            c. Has no financial arrangement with the accounting firm other than one providing for regular payment of a fixed dollar amount (which is not dependent on the revenue, profits, or earnings of the accounting firm):

                i. Pursuant to a fully funded retirement plan; *or*

                ii. in the case of a former professional employee who was not a partner, principal, or shareholder of the accounting firm and who has been dissociated from the accounting firm for more than five years that is immaterial to the former employee.

        2. A former partner, principal, shareholder, or professional employee of an accounting firm is in an FROR at an audit client (except an investment company, where slightly different rules apply), *unless* the individual was not a member of the audit engagement team during the one-year period preceding the date of the initiation of the audit.

> **Example**
>
> ABC's Audit cycle runs May 15 to May 14. Sandy is on the audit team of PriceCooperHouse. She resigns on June 15, just one month into the audit cycle. She must wait until the end of that cycle and then allow a complete cycle to pass before she can go to work in an accounting or FROR capacity. Had she quit on May 14, 2017, she could have started at ABC on May 15, 2018. But since she resigned on June 15, 2017, she must wait until May 15, 2019.
>
> If the individual worked for the audit firm but did not participate in the client's audit before going to work for the client in an FROR, this is not considered a problem.
>
> Persons who provided 10 or fewer hours of attest services during the relevant period are not covered by the requirement.
>
> Nor are persons who are employed by the issuer due to a merger or because of an emergency situation.

    D. Employment at Accounting Firm of Former Employee of Audit Client—A former officer, director, or employee of an audit client becomes a partner, principal, shareholder, or professional employee of the accounting firm, *unless* the individual does not participate in, and is not in a position to influence, the audit of F/S covering any period he or she was employed by the audit client.

IX. Business Relationships

    A. An accountant is not independent if at any time during the audit and professional engagement, the accounting firm or any covered person in the firm has any direct or material indirect business relationship with an audit client or with persons associated with the audit client in a decision-making capacity, such as an audit client's officers, directors, or beneficial owners of equity securities who have significant influence over the entity under audit.

    B. Exception—An accounting firm or covered persons can provide professional services to an audit client or buy services from a client in the ordinary course of business without an impermissible business relationship arising.

X. Nonaudit Services—SOX provisions, as implemented by the SEC, indicate that independence is impaired if an auditor provides any of the following nonaudit services (NAS) to a public company audit client, *unless* it is reasonable to conclude that the results of these services will not be subject to audit procedures during the audit of the client's F/S:

    A. Bookkeeping services, including

        1. Maintaining or preparing the client's accounting records

        2. Preparing the client's F/S that are filed with the SEC

        3. Preparing or originating source data underlying the F/S

    B. Financial information systems design and implementation, including:

        1. Directly or indirectly operating, or supervising the operation of, the audit client's information system or managing the audit client's local-area network

        2. Designing or implementing a hardware or software system that aggregates source data underlying the F/S or generates information that is significant to the client's F/S

    C. Appraisal or valuation services

    D. Actuarial services

    E. Internal audit outsourcing services

    F. Management functions

    G. Human resources, such as:

        1. Searching for prospective candidates for managerial positions

2. Engaging in psychological testing, or other formal testing or evaluation programs

3. Undertaking reference checks of prospective candidates for executive or director positions

4. Acting as a negotiator on an audit client's behalf, such as determining compensation, fringe benefits, and so on

5. Recommending that the client hire a specific candidate for a specific job (although it is okay to advise a client on a candidate's competence for financial accounting, administrative, or control positions)

H. Broker-dealer, investment adviser, or investment banking services

I. Legal services

J. Expert services unrelated to the audit

> **Note**
> *Audit firms may provide these services to nonaudit clients that are public companies and to private companies (even if they are audit clients) so long as AICPA restrictions are followed. Other NAS, such as most tax services, may be performed for public company audit clients but only if (a) preapproved by the client's audit committee and (b) disclosed in the client's periodic reports filed with the SEC.*

XI. Contingent Fees—An accountant is not independent if it provides *any* service or product to a public company audit client for a contingent fee or commission.

XII. Partner Rotation—SOX mandates that:

A. There are no requirements that public companies rotate audit *firms*.

B. Lead partners and engagement quality reviewers must be rotated every five years (five on, five off).

C. Other partners providing more than 10 hours of attest services must be rotated every seven years (seven on, two off).

D. There are exemptions for firms with fewer than five public company audit clients and fewer than 10 audit partners.

XIII. Audit Committee Administration of the Engagement—SOX shifts control of the audit process from the CEO and CFO to the audit committee, and an auditor is not independent unless these new rules are followed. Both the audit engagement itself and provision of permitted NAS are to be preapproved by the audit committee.

A. Some NAS provided by the audit firm (those services providing 5% or less of total revenues from the audit client during the audit year) do not require preapproval by the audit committee. However, the audit committee must approve of these services before the current audit engagement has been completed.

XIV. Compensation—SOX provides that an accountant is not independent if any audit partner earns or receives compensation based on selling NAS to the audit client.

XV. Quality Controls—An accounting firm's independence will not be impaired solely because a covered person is not independent, *provided*:

A. The covered person did not know of the circumstances giving rise to the lack of independence;

B. The covered person's lack of independence was corrected as promptly as possible once it became known; *and*

C. The accounting firm has a quality control system in place that provides reasonable assurance that independence rules will be complied with.

D. For firms annually auditing more than 500 companies, their quality control system provides such reasonable assurance only if it has the following features:

1. Written independence policies and procedures;

2. An automated system tracking investments of partners and managerial employees that might impair independence;

3. For all professionals, a system that provides timely information about entities from which the accountant is required to maintain independence;

4. An annual or ongoing firm-wide training program on independence rules;

5. An annual internal inspection and testing program to monitor adherence to independence rules;

6. Notification to all firm employees of the name and title of the member of senior management responsible for compliance with independence rules; *and*

7. A disciplinary mechanism to ensure compliance.

XVI. Mergers and Acquisitions

A. Independence will not be impaired because an audit client engages in a merger or acquisition that gives rise to a relationship or service that would violate these independence rules, provided that:

1. The accounting firm is in compliance with applicable independence rules throughout the period to which they apply;

2. The firm has or will promptly address any conflicts that have arisen because of the merger or acquisition; *and*

3. The firm has in place a proper quality control system.

Public Company Accounting Oversight Board (PCAOB)

1. Understand the ethical requirements of the PCAOB.

2. Recognize situations that present threats to compliance with the ethical requirements of the PCAOB.

3. Apply the ethical requirements and independence rules of the PCAOB to situations that could present threats to compliance during an audit of an issuer.

4. Be able to explain the role the PCAOB plays in governing the audit profession, including in registering, inspecting, and punishing firms that audit public companies.

I. Introduction

A. In 2002, Sarbanes-Oxley (SOX) replaced decades of self-regulation by public accounting firms when it created the PCAOB to govern public company audit firms under the supervision of the SEC.

   1. The PCAOB, among other things:

      a. Registers accounting firms that audit public companies

      b. Establishes auditing, quality control, ethics, independence, and other standards

      c. Inspects firms

      d. Annual inspections are conducted for firms doing more than 100 audits per year.

      e. Inspections occur once every three years for firms auditing fewer companies.

      f. Investigates and punishes wrongdoing

B. SOX also enacted several provisions relating to auditor independence—including rules regarding which consulting services audit firms can offer to their public company audit clients, rules on audit partner rotation and cooling-off periods, and rules on auditor compensation. These rules are covered in the previous lesson on the SEC's ethics rules.

C. This lesson covers rules the PCAOB has issued on ethics and independence. An earlier lesson covered its other major responsibilities (registering public accounting firms, inspecting registered public accounting firms, issuing standards for attestation activities and quality control, enforcement).

D. All PCAOB rules must be approved by the SEC, so it is not a surprise that its ethics and independence rules are consistent with the SEC requirements explicated in a previous lesson.

E. Early on, in 2003, the PCAOB adopted the AICPA's Code of Professional Conduct provisions regarding independence as its own interim standards. Although that version of the Code has since been replaced by the current electronic version and the PCAOB has issued many of its own rules (discussed below), the substance of the rules remains the same so there remains much consistency between PCAOB rules and AICPA rules regarding independence. However, if the SEC and PCAOB issue any rules that are more restrictive than AICPA rules, they override those AICPA rules for public company audits.

II. PCAOB Independence and Ethics Rules

A. **Independence Required**—Rule 3520 provides that "a registered public accounting firm and its associated persons must be independent of the firm's audit client throughout the audit and professional engagement." No surprise there. CPAs must comply with not only PCAOB rules and SEC rules, but also "all other independence criteria applicable to the engagement."

B. **Contingency Fees and Commissions**—Rule 3521, consistent with AICPA rules, provides that if a firm or any affiliate provides "any service or product" to an audit client in exchange for a contingent fee or commission, independence is impaired. Elsewhere, the PCAOB defines contingent fee to include any arrangement in which the amount of a fee is dependent upon a specified finding or result being obtained. Consistent with AICPA rules, a fee is not considered contingent if it is fixed by courts or other public authorities and is not dependent on a particular finding or result.

C. **Tax Consulting**—Although the SEC and PCAOB considered prohibiting public company audit firms from providing any tax services to public company audit clients, they chose not to do so. However, Rule 3522 puts some limitations on those tax services by providing that firms are not independent if during their audit engagements they provide services related to marketing, planning or opining in favor of tax transactions that are:

1. **Confidential**—A "confidential transaction" is one that is offered to a taxpayer under conditions of confidentiality and for which the taxpayer has paid the advisor a fee; *or*

2. **Aggressive**—An "aggressive tax position transaction" is one initially recommended by the accounting firm and a "significant purpose" of which is tax avoidance, *unless* the proposed tax treatment is at least *more likely than not* to be allowable under applicable tax laws. Examples of such impermissible aggressive transactions are ones that are the same or similar to transactions the IRS has already determined to be tax avoidance transactions.

D. **Tax Services for FRORs**—Rule 3523 provides that public company accounting firms may also forfeit their independence by providing "any tax service" to a person in a "financial reporting oversight role" (FROR) at the audit client or to an immediate family member (IFM) (spouse, spousal equivalent, and dependents) of such a person.

1. FROR is defined as a role in which a person can or does exercise influence over the contents of financial statements or anyone who prepares them. Examples of FRORs include: directors, CEOs, presidents, CFOs, COOs, general counsel, CAOs, controllers, directors of internal audit, directors of financial reporting, treasurers, or other equivalent positions.

2. The rule contains three exceptions. Independence is not impaired if the person:

   a. Is in an FROR only because he or she is a member of the client's board of directors

   b. Is in an FROR only because of his or her relationship to an affiliate of the entity being audited where the affiliate's financial statements are not material to the consolidated financial statements of the audit client or are audited by a different audit firm.

   c. Was not in an FROR before a hiring, promotion or similar change in employment and the tax services are:

      i. Provided pursuant to an engagement in process before the change in employment; and

      ii. Completed on or before 180 days after the employment event

E. **Approving Permissible Tax Consulting**—SOX allows certain tax consulting services to be provided to public company audit clients so long as they are pre-approved by the client's audit committee. Rule 3524 sets out the procedure for seeking such approval, requiring that the accounting firm:

1. Describe in writing:

   a. The scope of the service, the fee structure for the engagement, and any other related agreement between the firm and the audit client.

   b. Any compensation arrangement or other agreement, such as a referral fee or fee-sharing arrangement between the firm and any person (other than the audit client) regarding the promoting, marketing, or recommending of a transaction covered by the service.

2. Discuss with the audit committee the potential effects of the services on the firm's independence.

3. Document the discussion.

F. Approving Permissible NAS—SOX prohibits audit firms from providing certain non-audit services (NAS) related to internal controls over financial reporting, but allows others if pre-approved by the public company client's audit committee. Regarding those that are allowed, Rule 3525 sets out the procedure for seeking such approval, providing, consistent with Rule 3524 regarding tax services, that the firm should:

1. Describe in writing to the audit committee the scope of the service;

2. Discuss with the audit committee the potential effects of the service on the firm's independence; and

3. Document the discussion.

G. Accepting New Audit Clients—Rule 3526 provides that before accepting a public company as a new audit client, a registered firm must:

1. Describe in writing to the audit committee all relationships between the firm and its affiliates on the one hand and the client and its FROR employees as of the date of the communication that "may reasonably be thought to bear on independence";

2. Discuss with the audit committee these relationships and their potential effect on independence; and

3. Document the discussion.

    a. Note: at least annually with respect to each public company audit client a firm should go through this three-step procedure regarding existing relationships and affirm to the audit committee in writing that it remains independent.

III. Other PCAOB Ethics Rules

A. Rule 3502 provides that public accountants have a responsibility to not—knowingly or recklessly, by action or omission—contribute to violations of SOX, of PCAOB rules, of federal securities laws, or of professional standards.

B. Rule 3700 establishes advisory groups to assist the PCAOB in establishing its own professional standards.

C. Relatedly, to increase transparency the PCAOB recently required firms to file a form for each issuer audit disclosing:

1. The name of the engagement partner;

2. The name, location, and extent of participation of each other accounting firm participating in the audit whose work constituted at least 5% of total audit hours; *and*

3. The number and aggregate extent of participation of all other accounting firms participating in the audit whose individual participation was less than 5% of total audit hours.

Requirements of GAO and DOL

Government Accountability Office (GAO)

After studying this lesson, you should be able to:

1. Recognize situations that present threats to compliance with the ethical requirements of the Government Accountability Office Government Auditing Standards.

I. **Government Accountability Office's Government Auditing Standards—Ethical Principles**

  A. The GAO's guidelines apply to those who conduct audits of:

    1. Government entities (e.g., federal, state and local)

    2. Entities that receive government awards (e.g., colleges, trade schools, charities, local governments) in compliance with generally accepted government auditing standards (GAGAS)

    3. **Independence and ethical principles**—Those who audit pursuant to GAGAS are expected to audit:

      a. Independently; *and*

      b. In accordance with these key ethical principles:

        i. The public interest

        ii. Integrity

        iii. Objectivity

        iv. Proper use of government information, resources, and positions—these are to be used for official purposes and not for an auditor's personal gain

        v. **Professional behavior**—Includes compliance with all relevant legal, regulatory, and professional obligations, avoidance of conflicts of interest, sensitivity to appearance of impropriety, and putting forth an honest effort to meet technical and professional standards.

II. **Independence Introduction**

  A. **Independence** comprises:

    1. **Independence of mind**—Performing an audit without being affected by influences that compromise professional judgment enables an auditor to act with integrity, objectivity, and professional skepticism.

    2. **Independence in appearance**—No reasonable and informed third party should be given reason to conclude that the integrity, objectivity, and/or professional skepticism of the auditor are compromised.

  B. **Time period**—Independence must be maintained during:

    1. Any period of time falling within the period covered by the financial statements or subject matter of the audit, *and*

    2. The period of the professional engagement, which begins at the earlier of the signing of an initial engagement letter or some other agreement to perform an audit and ends with the formal or informal notification of the termination of the professional relationship or issuance of a report, whichever is later.

C. **Four Key Independence Considerations**

1. Conceptual framework for making independence determinations

2. Requirements for and guidance on independence for audit organizations (AOs) structurally located within the entities they audit

3. Requirements for and guidance on independence for performing nonaudit services (NAS)

4. Requirements for and guidance on necessary documentation of the auditor's independence

III. **Conceptual Framework**

A. Like the AICPA and many other bodies, the GAO has adopted a conceptual framework for making independence determinations for situations where no clear rule applies. If you have mastered the AICPA conceptual framework, you should have little difficulty with the GAO conceptual framework.

B. Like the AICPA framework, the GAO's conceptual framework involves three steps:

1. **Identifying threats** to independence

2. **Evaluating the significance** of the threats identified, both individually and in the aggregate

3. **Applying safeguards** as necessary to eliminate threats or reduce them to an acceptable level

C. If threats are identified and no available safeguards can eliminate them or reduce them to an acceptable level, **independence is considered to be impaired**.

D. **Threats**—The following are broad categories of threats to independence which should be identified and evaluated:

1. **Self-interest threat**—The threat that a financial or other interest will inappropriately influence an auditor's judgment or behavior

2. **Self-review threat**—The threat that an AO will evaluate its own NAS and not appropriately evaluate the results of previous judgments made or actions taken

3. **Bias threat**—The threat that an auditor will, as a result of political, ideological, social, or other convictions, take a position that is not objective

4. **Familiarity threat**—The threat that aspects of a relationship with management or personnel of the audited entity, such as a close or long relationship or involvement of an immediate or close family member will undermine objectivity

5. **Undue influence threat**—The threat that external influences or pressures will impact an auditor's independence and objectivity

6. **Management participation threat**—The threat to objectivity resulting from an auditor's performing management functions of the audited entity

7. **Structural threat**—The threat that an AO's placement within a government entity, in combination with the structure of the entity being audited, will impact the AO's ability to perform work and report results objectively

E. **Safeguards by the Auditor**—A nonexclusive list of safeguards the AO itself might apply to eliminate the threats to independence or at least reduce them to an acceptable level include:

1. Consulting an independent third party, such as a professional organization, a regulatory body, or another auditor

2. Involving another AO to perform or re-perform part of the audit

3. Having a professional staff member who was not a member of the audit team review the work performed

4. Removing an individual from an audit team

F. Safeguards by the Audited Entity—A nonexclusive list of safeguards that might arise from the audited entity itself include:

    1. A requirement that persons other than management ratify or approve the appointment of an AO to perform the audit (as SOX requires for public companies)

    2. Internal entity procedures ensuring objective choices in commissioning NAS

    3. An entity governance structure that provides appropriate oversight and communications regarding the audit organization's services (comparable to the independent audit committee required by SOX for public companies)

G. Threats to independence should be evaluated both individually and in the aggregate.

H. Threats to independence are not acceptable if they either:

    1. Could impact the auditor's ability to perform an audit without being affected by influences that compromise professional judgment; *or*

    2. Could expose the auditor or AO to circumstances that would cause a reasonable and informed third party to conclude that integrity, objectivity, or professional skepticism of the AO, or a member of the audit team, had been compromised.

I. Mitigating Structural Threats—Independence can be threatened when auditors in government entities report either to external auditor, to senior management within the audited entity, or to both.

    1. Constitutional or statutory safeguards may mitigate the effects of structural threats to independence. For external AOs, such safeguards may include governmental organizations under which the AO is:

        a. At a level of government other than the one of which the audited entity is a part (e.g., federal auditors may be auditing a state government program, or state auditors may be auditing a county government program)

        b. Placed within a different branch of government from that of the audited entity (e.g., legislative auditors audit an executive branch program)

    2. Structural threats may be mitigated if the head of an AO meets *any* of the following criteria in accordance with constitutional or statutory requirements:

        a. Directly elected by voters of the jurisdiction being audited;

        b. Elected or appointed by a legislative body, subject to removal by a legislative body, and reports the results of audits to and is accountable to a legislative body;

        c. Appointed by someone other than a legislative body, so long as the appointment is confirmed by a legislative body and removal from the position is subject to oversight or approval by a legislative body, and reports the results of audits to and is accountable to a legislative body; *or*

        d. Appointed by, accountable to, reports to, and can only be removed by a statutorily created governing body, the majority of whose members are independently elected or appointed and are outside the organization being audited.

    3. For AOs under a different structure than those just listed, *all* of the following safeguards should be in place:

        a. Statutory protections to prevent the audited entity from abolishing the AO;

        b. Statutory protection that if the head of the AO is removed, the head of the agency reports this to the legislative body;

        c. Statutory protection preventing the audited entity from interfering with the initiation, scope, timing, and completion of any audit;

        d. Statutory protection preventing the audited entity from interfering with audit reporting, findings, conclusions or the manner, means, or timing of the AO's reports;

    e. Statutory protection requiring the AO to report regularly to a legislative body or other independent governing body;

    f. Statutory protections giving the AO sole authority over the selection, retention, advancement, and dismissal of its staff; *and*

    g. Statutory access to records and documents related to the agency, program, or function being audited and access to officials or others as needed to conduct the audit.

J. Internal Auditor Independence

  1. Internal auditors working under the direction of the audited entity's management are considered independent for purposes of reporting internally if the head of the audit organization meets *all* of the following:

    a. Accountable to head of the government entity or to those charged with governance;

    b. Reports audit results both to the head of the government entity and to those charged with governance;

    c. Located organizationally outside the staff or line management function of the areas being audited;

    d. Has access to those charged with governance; *and*

    e. Is sufficiently removed from political pressure to conduct audits and report findings objectively without fear of political reprisal.

  2. If internal auditors audit external organizations, such as contractors, and no independence impairments exist, the auditor is considered an external party to the audited entities.

IV. Provision of Nonaudit Services to Audited Entities

  A. Before providing NAS to an audited entity, the AO should determine that the audited entity has designated an individual with suitable skills, knowledge, or experience as well as a sufficient understanding to oversee the services provided by the auditor.

  1. If an AO were to assume management responsibilities for an audited entity, the management participation threat would be so great that no safeguards could reduce them to an acceptable level. Management responsibilities include leading and directing an entity, including making decisions regarding the acquisition, deployment, and control of human, financial, physical, and intangible resources. Examples of specific management actions that would impair independence include:

    a. Setting policies and strategic direction for the audited entity

    b. Directing and accepting responsibility for the actions of the audited entity's employees in the performance of their routine, recurring activities

    c. Having custody of an audited entity's assets

    d. Reporting to those charged with governance on behalf of management

    e. Deciding which of the auditor's or outside third party's recommendations to implement

    f. Accepting responsibility for the management of an audited entity's project

    g. Accepting responsibility for designing, implementing, or maintaining internal control

    h. Providing services that are intended to be used as management's primary basis for making decisions that are significant to the subject matter of the audit

    i. Developing an audited entity's performance measurement system when that system is material or significant to the subject matter of the audit

    j. Serving as a voting member of an audited entity's management committee or board of directors

B. Before performing NAS for audited entities, auditors should obtain assurances that audited entity management will do *all* the following:

1. Assume all management responsibilities

2. Oversee the NAS by designating a member within senior management who possessed suitable skill, knowledge, or experience

3. Evaluate the adequacy and results of the NAS performed

4. Accept responsibility for the results of the NAS

C. Auditors preparing to perform NAS should establish and document their understanding with the audited entity's management regarding:

1. Objectives of the NAS

2. Services to be performed

3. Audited entity's acceptance of its responsibilities

4. The auditor's responsibilities

5. Any limitations of the NAS

D. Routine Activities—Giving routine advice and responding to questions as a direct part of the audit are not considered NAS and do not impair independence. Examples of such routine activities directly related to the audit include:

1. Providing advice to the audited entity regarding an accounting matter relevant to the audit

2. Providing advice on routine business matters

3. Educating the audited entity on matters within the technical expertise of the auditors

4. Providing information to the audited entity that is readily available to the auditors, such as best practices and benchmarking studies

E. Certain NAS requirements that directly support the audited entity's operations will necessarily impair independence. Among others, these include:

1. Determining or changing journal entries, account codes or classifications for transactions, or other accounting records for the audited entity without obtaining management's approval

2. Authorizing or approving the entity's transactions

3. Preparing or making changes to source documents (e.g., purchase orders, payroll time records, general ledgers, customer orders, contracts) without management approval

F. Obviously, auditors may not accept responsibility for the preparation and fair presentation of F/S that the auditor will subsequently audit.

G. If the auditor has determined that the NAS requirements have been met and that any significant threats to independence have been eliminated or reduced to an acceptable level, then the following services, unless otherwise expressly prohibited, may be performed for an audited entity:

1. Recording transactions approved by management, or posting coded transactions to an audited entity's general ledger

2. Preparing certain line items or sections of the F/S based on information in the trial balance

3. Posting entries that an audited entity's management has approved to the entity's trial balance

4. Preparing account reconciliations that identify reconciling items for the audited entity management's evaluation

H. Internal Audit Assistance—The following will always impair independence when provided to an audit client:

1. Setting internal audit policies or the strategic direction of internal audit activities

2. Performing procedures that form part of the internal control, such as reviewing and approving changes to employee data access privileges

3. Determining the scope of the internal audit function and resulting work

Note
In 2018, the GAO eliminated from this list of services that are presumed acceptable "Preparing financial statements based on information in the trial balance."

I. Internal Control Monitoring—To perform ongoing monitoring procedures on behalf of management that are built into the routine, recurring operating activities of an organization will always constitute a management participation threat that imperils independence.

J. Information Technology Systems Service—Examples of IT NAS that would impair independence when provided to an audit client include:

1. Designing or developing a financial or other IT system that will play a significant role in the management of an area of operations that is or will be the subject matter of an audit

2. Providing services that entail making other than insignificant modifications to the source code underlying such a system

3. Supervising an audited entity's personnel in the daily operation of its information system

4. Operating an audited entity's network, financial information system, or other IT system that will play a significant role in the management of an area of operations subject to the audit

K. Valuation Services—Providing valuation services that have a material effect on the F/S will impair independence if the valuation involves a significant degree of subjectivity.

L. Miscellaneous NAS—Other NAS requirements that will always impair independence when provided to an audited entity include:

1. Advisory service

   a. Assuming any management responsibilities

2. Benefit plan administration

   a. Making policy decisions on behalf of an audited entity's management

   b. Interpreting a plan document for participants on behalf of management without first obtaining management's concurrence

   c. Making disbursements on behalf of the plan

   d. Having custody of a plan's assets

   e. Serving a plan as a fiduciary as defined by ERISA

3. Business risk consulting

   a. Making or approving business risk decisions

   b. Presenting business risk considerations to those charged with governance on behalf of management

4. Executive or employee recruiting

   a. Committing the audited entity to employee compensation or benefit arrangements

   b. Hiring or terminating audited entity employees

5. Investment—Advisory or management

   a. Making investment decisions on behalf of the audited entity's management

      b. Executing a transaction to buy or sell

      c. Having custody of an audited entity's assets, such as taking temporary possession of securities

V. Documentation—To establish independence, auditors should document:

  A. Threat to independence that requires the application of safeguards, along with the safeguards applied

  B. Safeguards required if an audit organization is structurally located within a government entity and is considered independent based on those safeguards

  C. Consideration of audited entity management's ability to effectively oversee an NAS to be provided by the auditor

  D. The auditor's understanding with an audited entity for which the auditor will perform an NAS regarding the objectives of the NAS, the NAS to be provided, the audited entity's acceptance of its responsibilities, etc.

  E. The evaluation of the significance of threats by providing any of the services

VI. Professional Judgment—This includes exercising reasonable care and professional skepticism. It represents the application of knowledge, skills, and experience.

  A. Professional judgment is used:

    1. In applying the conceptual framework to determine independence in a specific situation

    2. To assign competent staff to the audit

    3. To define the scope of the audit

    4. To determine risk in the audit

    5. To determine sufficient and appropriate audit evidence to support findings

    6. To report results

    7. To maintain appropriate quality control over the audit process

VII. Competence—The audit staff must possess professional competence adequate to address the audit objectives and perform the work in accordance with GAGAS.

  A. Competence derives from education and experience.

  B. Audit firms should have a process for recruiting, hiring, continuously developing, assigning, and evaluating staff in order to maintain a competent workforce.

  C. Competence provides the basis for sound professional judgments.

VIII. Technical Knowledge—The staff assigned to perform a GAGAS audit should collectively possess the necessary technical knowledge, skill, and experience.

IX. Continuing Professional Education (CPE)

  A. Auditors who plan, direct, perform engagement procedures for, or report on an engagement conducted in accordance with GAGAS should complete at least 80 hours of CPE in every two-year period:

    1. 24 hours of subject matter directly related to the government environment, government auditing, or the unique environment in which the audited entity operates; *and*

    2. 56 hours of subject matter that directly enhances auditors' professional expertise to conduct engagements.

  B. Examples of programs and activities that do *not* qualify as CPE, include:

    1. On-the-job training

    2. Basic or elementary courses in subjects or topics that auditors already know

3. Programs designed for personal development, such as resume writing or money management

4. Programs that demonstrate office equipment or software not used in conducting engagements

5. Programs that provide training on the audit organization's administrative operations

6. Business sessions at professional conferences that do not have a structured educational program with learning objectives

7. Conducting external quality control reviews

8. Sitting for professional certification examinations

Department of Labor (DOL)

After studying this lesson, you should be able to:

1. Understand the Department of Labor's independence rules for auditing employee benefit plans regulated by ERISA.

I. **Department of Labor**—Interpretive Bulletin Relating to Guidelines on Independence of Accountant Retained by Employee Benefit Plan.

    A. Employee Benefit Plans (plans) are broadly regulated by the Department of Labor's (DOL's) Employee Benefits Security Administration (EBSA) pursuant to the Employee Retirement Income Security Act (ERISA).

    B. Statutory law provides that an accountant retained by a plan to examine plan financial information and render an opinion on the financial statements and schedules required to be contained in a plan's annual report must be "independent."

    C. Unfortunately, despite having been strongly urged to simply adopt AICPA guidelines for independence, DOL's guidelines, contained in 29 C.F.R. 2509-75-9, date to the 1970s and are inconsistent with modern independence rules.

    D. The rules provide that an accountant will **not** be considered independent with respect to a plan, due to the following:

        1. **Financial ties**—Independence will be considered to be impaired if during the period of the engagement, at the date of the opinion, or during the period covered by the financial statements, "the accountant or his or her firm or a member thereof had, or was committed to acquire, any direct financial interest or any material indirect financial interest in such plan, or the plan sponsor . . ."

            a. Because this provision covers any member of an accountant's firm, its coverage is much broader than that of current AICPA guidelines.

            b. The term *member* means all partners or shareholder employees in the firm and all professional employees participating in the audit or located in an office of the firm participating in a significant portion of the audit.

        2. **Employment ties**—During the same period, the same entities may not be connected to a plan or plan sponsor as a:

            a. Promoter;

            b. Underwriter;

            c. Investment advisor;

            d. Voting trustee;

            e. Director;

            f. Officer; *or*

            g. Employee of the plan or plan sponsor.

        3. However, employees of a plan or plan sponsor who have left to join the accounting firm may nonetheless be deemed independent if:

            a. They have completely disassociated themselves from the plan or plan sponsor; *and*

            b. Do not participate in auditing financial statements of the plan covering any period of his or her employment by the plan or plan sponsor.

4. However, independence may be considered impaired if an accountant or a member of an accounting firm maintains financial records for the plan. An accounting firm should not audit its own work.

E. According to the rule, an engagement to provide professional services, including actuarial services, to the plan sponsor does not ruin an accountant's independence so long as the accountant does not violate the rules on financial ties and employment mentioned above.

F. However, the firm should take care not to engage in a prohibited transaction pursuant to 29 U.S.C. 1106(a)(1)(C), which prohibits certain transactions between a plan and a *party in interest* to minimize conflicts of interest and thereby prevent fiduciaries from lining their own pockets with the plan's funds.

Assessing Risk and Developing a Planned Response

Financial Statement Audits

Accounting vs. Auditing

> **After studying this lesson, you should be able to:**
>
> 1. Explain the respective responsibilities of management and the auditor in financial reporting.
> 2. Outline the role of and distinction between GAAP and GAAS.

I. **Financial Accounting**—The accounting focuses primarily on the preparation and distribution of the general-purpose, historical financial statements (balance sheet, income statement, statement of cash flows, and statement of retained earnings), which are representations of management.

   A. These financial statements are distributed to interested parties outside of the reporting entity itself, such as actual or potential shareholders and creditors, major customers and suppliers, employees, regulators, and others for their decision-making (resource allocation) needs.

   B. Users' specific decision-making circumstances will involve different issues and they may have different information priorities and concerns, but most will want to evaluate whether management has performed well.

   C. Since management's performance will be evaluated, at least in part, by financial statements prepared by management itself, users need to know whether the financial statements are reliable when evaluating the performance of management.

II. **Auditing**—The auditor's primary role is to provide an impartial (independent) report on the reliability of management's financial statements.

Purpose of an audit—"The purpose of an audit is to provide financial statement users with an opinion by the auditor on whether the financial statements are presented fairly, in all material respects, in accordance with the applicable financial reporting framework. An auditor's opinion enhances the degree of confidence that the intended users can place in the financial statements."

From the AICPA's Preface to *Codifications of Statements on Auditing Standards, Principles Underlying an Audit Conducted in Accordance with Generally Accepted Auditing Standards.*

III. **The Role of Standards**—Think of "standards" as the criteria by which quality will be evaluated. The preparation of the financial statements and the performance of the audit are subject to very different standards.

   A. Standards applicable to evaluating the presentation of the financial statements:

Applicable financial reporting framework—"The financial reporting framework adopted by management and, where appropriate, those charged with governance in the preparation of the financial statements that is acceptable in view of the nature of the entity and the objective of the financial statements, or that is required by law or regulation."

Financial reporting framework—"A set of criteria used to determine measurement, recognition, presentation, and disclosure of all material items appearing in the financial statements; for example: U.S. generally accepted accounting principles (GAAP), International Financial Reporting Standards (IFRSs), issued by the International Accounting Standards Board (IASB), or a special purpose framework."

---

   1. The financial reporting framework adopted by an entity for its financial statement presentation in the U.S. may be based on IFRSs (issued by the IASB) or U.S. GAAP.

2. **Accounting Standards Setters Associated with U.S. GAAP**—The nature of the reporting entity determines which particular accounting standards must be followed under the label of U.S. GAAP.

    a. Federal governmental entities follow pronouncements of the Federal Accounting Standards Advisory Board (FASAB).

    b. State and local governmental entities follow pronouncements of the Governmental Accounting Standards Board (GASB).

    c. Other entities (such as corporations) follow pronouncements of the Financial Accounting Standards Board (FASB).

B. Standards Applicable to Evaluating the Auditor's Performance

1. **Outside the U.S.**—"International Standards on Auditing" (ISAs) are issued by the International Auditing and Assurance Standards Board, an audit-related standard-setting body within the International Federation of Accountants, known as IFAC.

2. **Within the U.S.**—The nature of the reporting entity determines which auditing standards are applicable to an audit of the entity's financial statements.

    a. **Governmental entities**—When required by law, regulation, or agreement, Generally Accepted Government Auditing Standards (GAGAS), issued by the U.S. Government Accountability Office (GAO) are applicable.

    b. **Public companies (companies registered with the Securities and Exchange Commission, also referred to as "issuers," that is, issuers of securities to the public)** —The auditing standards of the Public Company Accounting Oversight Board (PCAOB) are Applicable.

    c. **Private companies (referred to as "nonissuers") and other entities** —The auditing standards of the AICPA's Auditing Standards Board are applicable; these pronouncements collectively are referred to by the AICPA as generally accepted auditing standards (GAAS).

ICPA's "clarity and convergence" project—The AICPA reissued substantially all of their existing Statements on Auditing Standards (SASs) in a clarified format intended to make the SASs easier to understand. In addition, the AICPA substantially converged their auditing standards to be consistent with the requirements of IFAC's International Standards on Auditing. Although some differences in those respective requirements remain (and will be covered elsewhere in CPAexcel®), those standards are now very, very similar. The recent AICPA pronouncements are referred to as "Clarified Standards."

The PCAOB adopted the then-existing AICPA auditing standards in April 2003 as "interim standards, on an initial, transitional basis." Since that time, the PCAOB has been issuing its own Auditing Standards. Much of the existing PCAOB auditing standards remain those of the AICPA existing as of April 16, 2003.

GAAS and Principles

After studying this lesson, you should be able to:

1. Identify the seven principles underlying an audit conducted in accordance with GAAS under the AICPA's "Clarified" auditing standards.

I. **Generally Accepted Auditing Standards (GAAS)**—Historically, the AICPA identified 10 standards comprising GAAS that used to serve as a framework for U.S. auditing standards. The AICPA replaced these 10 standards with seven principles in connection with its Clarified Auditing Standards. The AICPA no longer uses the term *GAAS* to refer to these 10 standards representing criteria to measure the quality of the auditor's performance. Instead the AICPA now uses the term GAAS to refer to the body of authoritative professional standards issued in the form of Statements on Auditing Standards.

II. **Clarity and Convergence Project**—In connection with its *clarity and convergence project* the AICPA has replaced its Statements on Auditing Standards to be similar to the International Standards on Auditing (ISAs) issued by the International Federation of Accountants (specifically IFAC's International Auditing & Assurance Standards Board—IAASB). As part of that effort, the AICPA has also replaced its use of 10 criteria formerly known as "Generally Accepted Auditing Standards" with seven *principles* to provide a framework for understanding and explaining an audit.

   A. The seven principles are not requirements and have no authoritative status. However, they are intended to be helpful as a framework for audit standard setting.

   B. The seven principles reflect most of the considerations that had been addressed in the previous 10 generally accepted auditing standards (the former reporting standards seem to have changed the most relative to these principles).

   C. The seven principles are organized around four primary themes—(1) purpose/premise; (2) responsibilities; (3) performance; and (4) reporting (as a memory aid, remember: PR-PR).

III. **Purpose of an Audit and Premise Upon Which an Audit Is Conducted**

   A. The purpose of an audit is to provide financial statement users with an opinion by the auditor on whether the financial statements are presented fairly, in all material respects, in accordance with the applicable financial reporting framework. An auditor's opinion enhances the degree of confidence that intended users can place in the financial statements.

   B. An audit in accordance with generally accepted auditing standards is conducted on the premise that management and, where appropriate, those charged with governance, have responsibility for

      1. The preparation and fair presentation of the financial statements in accordance with the applicable financial reporting framework; this includes the design, implementation, and maintenance of internal control relevant to the preparation and fair presentation of financial statements that are free from material misstatement, whether due to fraud or error

      2. Providing the auditor with all information, such as records, documentation, and other matters that are relevant to the preparation and fair presentation of the financial statements; any additional information that the auditor may request from management and, where appropriate, those charged with governance; and unrestricted access to those within the entity from whom the auditor determines it necessary to obtain audit evidence

   C. **Responsibilities**—Note that the term *responsibilities principle* takes the place of what previously had been called *general standards* describing characteristics the auditor brings to the engagement.

      1. Auditors are responsible for having appropriate competence and capabilities to perform the audit; complying with relevant ethical requirements; and maintaining professional skepticism and exercising professional judgment, throughout the planning and performance of the audit.

D. Performance—Note that the term *performance principle* takes the place of what previously had been called *fieldwork standards* governing the auditor's evidence-gathering activities.

1. To express an opinion, the auditor obtains reasonable assurance about whether the financial statements as a whole are free from material misstatement, whether due to fraud or error.

2. To obtain reasonable assurance, which is a high, but not absolute, level of assurance, the auditor

   a. Plans the work and properly supervises any assistants

   b. Determines and applies appropriate materiality level or levels throughout the audit

   c. Identifies and assesses risks of material misstatement, whether due to fraud or error, based on an understanding of the entity and its environment, including the entity's internal control

   d. Obtains sufficient appropriate audit evidence about whether material misstatements exist, through designing and implementing appropriate responses to the assessed risks

3. The auditor is unable to obtain absolute assurance that the financial statements are free from material misstatement because of inherent limitations, which arise from

   a. The nature of financial reporting

   b. The nature of audit procedures

   c. The need for the audit to be conducted within a reasonable period of time and so as to achieve a balance between benefit and cost

E. Reporting

1. Based on an evaluation of the audit evidence obtained, the auditor expresses, in the form of a written report, an opinion in accordance with the auditor's findings, or states that an opinion cannot be expressed. The opinion states whether the financial statements are presented fairly, in all material respects, in accordance with the applicable financial reporting framework.

Professional Standards

After studying this lesson, you should be able to:

1. Understand the role of guidance associated with Statements on Auditing Standards including interpretive publications and other auditing publications.

2. Identify the two types of professional requirements (unconditional requirements and presumptively mandatory requirements) and the wording associated with each.

I. The AICPA's Use of the Term GAAS and Guidance Associated with It

A. Statements on Auditing Standards (SASs)—The SASs constitute GAAS and must be followed by auditors when AICPA auditing standards are applicable. (Specifically, the Rule of Conduct, *Compliance With Standards,* of the AICPA Code of Professional Conduct requires that auditors adhere to the standards promulgated by the Auditing Standards Board.) Under the clarified auditing standards, any reference to GAAS now specifically means this authoritative body of professional standards (SASs) issued by the Auditing Standards Board.

    1. The auditor is expected to have sufficient knowledge of the SASs to identify those applicable to the audit.

    2. The auditor should be prepared to justify any departures from the SASs.

    3. Materiality and audit risk also underlie the application of the SASs, particularly those related to performing the audit (evidence gathering) and reporting.

B. Interpretive Publications—Consist of the appendices to the SASs, auditing interpretations of the SASs, auditing guidance included in AICPA Audit and Accounting Guides, and AICPA auditing Statements of Position.

    1. Interpretive publications are **not** considered to be auditing standards, however.

    2. These are issued under the authority of the Auditing Standards Board after all ASB members have had an opportunity to comment on the interpretive publication.

    3. Auditors should be aware of (and consider) interpretive publications applicable to their audits. When auditors do not apply such auditing guidance, they should be prepared to explain how they complied with the SAS provisions related to such interpretive publications.

C. Other Auditing Publications—Include articles in the *Journal of Accountancy* and the AICPA's *CPA Letter* (and other professional publications), continuing professional education programs, textbooks, etc.

    1. Other auditing publications have no authoritative status—they may be useful to the auditor in understanding and applying the SASs, however.

    2. To assess the appropriateness of the other auditing publications—consider the degree to which the publication is recognized as helpful in applying the SASs and the degree to which the author is recognized as an authority on auditing matters. (Other auditing publications reviewed by the AICPA Audit and Attest Standards staff are presumed to be appropriate.)

II. Categories of Professional Requirements—The various AICPA standards (i.e., Statements on Auditing Standards, Statements on Standards for Attestation Engagements, Statements on Standards for Accounting and Review Services, and Statements on Quality Control Standards) distinguish between **two types of professional requirements:**

A. Unconditional requirements—Must comply with the requirement without exception (indicated by "must" in applicable standards);

B. Presumptively mandatory requirements—In rare circumstances, the practitioner may depart from such a *requirement,* but must document the justification for the departure and how the alternate procedures performed were adequate to meet the objective of the requirement (indicated by "should" in applicable standards).

> **Note**
> *Explanatory material is descriptive guidance within the body of the standards that does not impose a requirement (indicated by may, might, or could in applicable standards).*

Quality Control Standards (SQCS)

After studying this lesson, you should be able to:

1. Describe the relationship of GAAS to the AICPA's Statements on Quality Control Standards (SQCS).

2. List the six elements that comprise a firm's quality control system.

I. **Relationship of GAAS to the SQCS**—An individual audit engagement is governed by GAAS, whereas a CPA firm's collective portfolio of accounting and auditing services (sometimes called the A&A practice, which involves entities' financial statements and, thereby, involves the public interest) is governed by the AICPA's SQCS. SQCS are issued by the AICPA's Auditing Standards Board (in particular, the section of the SQCS dealing with "A Firm's System of Quality Control" is QC10). The relevant AICPA guidance applicable to an individual audit engagement is provided by AU 220, *Quality Control for an Engagement Conducted in Accordance with [GAAS]*.

II. **Focus of the System of Quality Control**—A CPA firm is required to have a "system of quality control" for its accounting and auditing services (covering audit, attestation, compilation, and review services; note that the SQCS are not applicable to tax or consulting services) to provide reasonable assurance that engagements are performed in accordance with professional standards and applicable regulatory and legal requirements, and that the issuance of reports are appropriate in the circumstances.

    A. **Nature and Scope**—The policies and procedures will vary with the circumstances (e.g., firm size and number of offices, complexity of services offered, and the level of experience of the professional staff).

    B. **Inherent Limitations**—Similar to any internal control system, a quality control system provides "reasonable" (a high, but not absolute) assurance, reflecting implicit cost-benefit trade-offs.

III. **Six Elements of a Quality Control System**—These are interrelated (e.g., monitoring and the quality of personnel involved affect the other elements).

    A. **Leadership Responsibilities for Quality**—Policies and procedures should promote an internal culture that emphasizes a commitment to quality (sometimes called the "tone at the top"). For an individual audit engagement, the engagement partner should take responsibility for overall audit quality, although performance of certain procedures may, of course, be delegated to other members of the engagement team.

    B. **Relevant Ethical Requirements**—Policies and procedures should address the independence of personnel as necessary (should obtain written confirmation of compliance with independence requirements from all appropriate personnel at least annually).

    C. **Acceptance and Continuance of Client-Relationships and Engagements**—Policies and procedures should carefully assess the risks associated with each engagement (including issues related to management integrity) and the firm should only undertake engagements that can be completed with professional competence.

Note
The purpose of AU 220, Quality Control for an Engagement Conducted in Accordance with [GAAS], is to assist the auditor in implementing the firm's quality control procedures specifically at the engagement level. This pronouncement states that the auditor's objective is to implement quality control procedures at the engagement level that provide reasonable assurance that (a) the audit complies with professional standards and applicable legal and regulatory requirements and (b) the auditor issues an appropriate report.

Note
If the engagement team identifies a threat to independence that safeguards may not eliminate or reduce to an acceptable level, the engagement partner is required to report the matter to the relevant person(s) in the firm to determine the appropriate action (to either eliminate the threat or withdraw from the engagement when withdrawal is allowed under applicable law or regulation).

D. **Human Resources**—Policies and procedures should address important personnel issues (including initial hiring, assignments to engagements, professional development and continuing professional education, and promotion decisions).

E. **Engagement Performance**—Policies and procedures should focus on compliance with all applicable firm and professional standards and applicable regulatory requirements, and encourage personnel to consult as necessary with professional (or other) literature or other human resources within or outside of the firm for appropriate guidance.

F. **Monitoring**—Policies and procedures should provide an ongoing assessment of the adequacy of the design and the operating effectiveness of the system of quality control. Controls that are effective at one point in time, may deteriorate over time owing to neglect or changed circumstances. It is important that the controls are properly monitored so that timely adjustments can be made as necessary to keep the quality control policies and procedures working effectively over time.

IV. **Differences of Opinion**—The firm should establish policies and procedures for dealing with and resolving differences of opinion within the engagement team, with those consulted, and between the engagement partner and the engagement quality control reviewer (including that the conclusions reached are documented and implemented and that the report is not released until the matter is resolved).

V. **Documentation of the Operation of Quality Control Policies and Procedures**—The firm should establish policies and procedures requiring appropriate documentation of the operation of each element of the system of quality control.

VI. **Definitions**

A. **Engagement Partner**—The person in the firm who is responsible for the audit engagement and its performance and for the auditor's report.

B. **Engagement Quality Control Review**—A process designed to provide an objective evaluation, before the report is released, of the significant judgments the engagement team made and the conclusions it reached in formulating the auditor's report. (The engagement quality control review process is only for those audit engagements, if any, for which the firm has determined that an engagement quality control review is required, in accordance with its policies and procedures.)

C. **Engagement Quality Control Reviewer**—This is the person in the firm, a suitably qualified external person, or a team made up of such individuals, none of whom is part of the engagement team, with sufficient and appropriate experience and authority to objectively evaluate the significant judgments that the engagement team made and the conclusions it reached in formulating the auditor's report.

VII. **The Main Difference Between the Clarified SAS and the Corresponding International Standard on Auditing**—The SAS requires that the quality control review must be completed before the engagement partner releases the auditor's report, whereas the ISA requires that the quality control review be completed before the engagement partner dates the auditor's report.

Overview of Audit Process

After studying this lesson, you should be able to:

1. Identify the primary dimensions of the audit process: a) engagement planning; b) internal control considerations; c) substantive audit procedures; and d) reporting.

I. Engagement Planning

A. Decide whether to accept (or continue) the engagement—Recall the quality control standards regarding client acceptance/continuation issues.

B. Perform risk assessment procedures to address the risks of material misstatement, whether due to error or fraud.

C. Evaluate requirements for staffing and supervision.

D. Prepare the required written audit plan (sometimes called the *audit program*) that specifies the nature, timing, and extent of auditing procedures for every audit area (which is usually prepared after control risk has been assessed, so that detection risk can be appropriately set in each audit area).

II. Internal Control Considerations

A. Obtain an understanding of internal control for planning purposes as required, emphasizing the assessment of the risk of material misstatement in individual audit areas and document the understanding of internal control.

B. If contemplating *reliance* on certain identified internal control strengths as a basis for reducing substantive testing, the auditor must then perform appropriate *tests of control* to determine that those specific controls are operating effectively, that is, working as intended.

III. Substantive Audit Procedures (Evidence-Gathering Procedures Whose Purpose is to Detect Material Misstatements, if There Are Any)—Note that the word *substantive* is derived from *substantiate*, which means *to verify*. These are evidence-gathering procedures designed to verify the financial statement elements and to detect any material misstatements.

A. **Analytical Procedures**—Those evidence-gathering procedures that suggest *reasonableness* (or *unreasonableness*) based upon a comparison to appropriate expectations or benchmarks, such as prior year's financial statements, comparability to industry data (including ratios) or other interrelationships involving financial and/or nonfinancial data.

B. **Tests of Details**—Those evidence-gathering procedures consisting of either of two types:

1. **Tests of ending balances**—Where the final balance is assessed by testing the composition of the year-end balance (e.g., testing a sample of individual customers' account balances that make up the general ledger accounts receivable control account balance).

2. **Tests of transactions**—Where the final balance is assessed by examining those debits and credits that caused the balance to change from last year's audited balance to the current year's balance.

IV. Reporting—Conclusions are expressed in writing using standardized language to avoid miscommunication.

Different Types of Engagements

After studying this lesson, you should be able to:

1. Differentiate the types of engagements for which the following AICPA Professional Standards are applicable: (1) Statements on Auditing Standards (SASs); (2) Statements on Standards for Accounting and Review Services (SSARSs); and (3) Statements on Standards for Attestation Engagements (SSAEs).

2. Understand the distinction between the terms "positive assurance" and "negative assurance."

I. **AICPA's Statements on Standards for Accounting and Review Services (SSARSs)**—These are applicable when the CPA is associated with the financial statements of a private company, but that association is something less than a full-scope *audit engagement*.

    A. **Compilation**—When the CPA is engaged simply to assemble into financial statement format the financial records of a private company and issue a compilation report, without expressing any degree of assurance on the reliability of those financial statements.

    B. **Preparation engagement**—When the CPA is engaged to prepare the financial statements of a private company without issuing any report on those financial statements or expressing any form of assurance.

    C. **Review**—When the CPA is engaged to provide a lower level of assurance (relative to that of an audit) on financial statements of a private company by performing limited procedures, including performing analytical procedures, and making appropriate inquiries of client personnel. The conclusion is known as "negative assurance" that the practitioner is unaware of a need for material modification.

II. **AICPA's Statements on Standards for Attestation Engagements (SSAEs)**—These are applicable when the CPA provides assurance about written representations or subject matter other than historical financial statements (e.g., management may make representations about its superior product performance that may be made more reliable by the CPA's independent verification and report).

    A. **Examination**—When the CPA is engaged to provide an opinion (that is positive assurance) on subject matter or an assertion of a responsible party that involves something other than historical financial statements.

    B. **Review**—When the CPA is engaged to provide negative assurance on subject matter or an assertion of a responsible party that involves something other than historical financial statements.

> **Note**
> *The SSARSs and SSAEs will be explored in detail at an appropriate point later in the course materials. They are merely introduced here so that candidates will be reminded early on that the AICPA Professional Standards encompass a variety of types of standards governing different services associated with the CPA profession.*

    C. **Agreed-Upon Procedures Engagement**—When the CPA is engaged to provide assurance in the form of "procedures and findings" on subject matter or an assertion of a responsible party that involves something other than historical financial statements.

III. **Responsibilities Vary for Different Types of Engagements**

    A. **Understanding with the Client**—When associated with financial statement subject matter, AICPA Professional Standards require the CPA to establish an understanding with the entity involved as to the services to be rendered and the parties' respective responsibilities. The CPA must document that understanding in a written engagement letter between the CPA and the client entity. This should not be surprising, since the "public interest" is associated with such financial statement subject matter.

    B. **Levels of Assurance**—The level of assurance varies with the type of service involved and should be clearly addressed in the engagement letter between the CPA and the client entity.

1. **Audit** (under SASs) or Examination (under SSAEs)—An audit or examination conveys a high level of assurance (Statements on Auditing Standards apply to audits of financial statements of "nonissuers").

2. **Review** (under SSARSs or SSAEs)—A review conveys a lower (i.e., "moderate") level of assurance known as "negative assurance."

3. **Compilation** (or preparation engagement)—A compilation or preparation engagement conveys no assurance about the reliability of the financial statements (for a private company under the AICPA's SSARSs).

PCAOB Responsibilities

The Sarbanes-Oxley Act of 2002 (SOA) was enacted by Congress in response to a series of highly visible financial reporting frauds and audit failures that undermined investor confidence in the U.S. capital markets. Said to be the most significant revision of securities laws since the 1930s, SOA ended self-regulation of the accounting profession and created the Public Company Accounting Oversight Board (PCAOB), a private-sector not-for-profit corporation, to provide a new regulatory mechanism over auditors of public companies, among other things.

After studying this lesson, you should be able to:

1. Know the five primary responsibilities of the Public Company Accounting Oversight Board that were established by the Sarbanes-Oxley Act of 2002.

2. Understand the primary sections ("Titles") of the Sarbanes-Oxley Act of 2002 that directly affect auditors of public companies ("issuers").

I. **The Sarbanes-Oxley Act of 2002 and the PCAOB**

   A. **Public Company Accounting Oversight Board (PCAOB)**—Five primary responsibilities:

   1. **Registration of public accounting firms**—U.S. and non-U.S. accounting firms that prepare audit reports of any U.S. public company (*issuer* of securities) must register with the PCAOB. (This includes non-U.S. accounting firms that play a substantial role in the preparation of such audit reports.)

   2. **Inspections of registered public accounting firms**—PCAOB is directed to conduct a continuous program of inspections that assess compliance with SOA, PCAOB rules, SEC rules, and applicable professional standards. (A written report is required for each such inspection.)

      a. **Firms that provide audit reports for more than 100 issuers**—PCAOB must inspect annually.

      b. **Firms that provide audit reports for 100 or fewer issuers**—PCAOB must inspect every three years (triennially).

   3. **Standard setting**—PCAOB is directed to establish auditing and related attestation, quality control, ethics and independence standards and rules to be used by registered public accounting firms in the preparation of audit reports for issuers. (The Office of the Chief Auditor and the Standing Advisory Group (SAG) assist PCAOB in establishing such auditing and professional practice standards.)

   4. **Enforcement**—PCAOB has broad authority to investigate registered public accounting firms and persons associated with such firms.

      a. PCAOB rules require cooperation by registered public accounting firms and associated persons—must produce documents and provide testimony as directed. (PCAOB may also seek information from others, including clients of registered firms.)

      b. PCAOB sanctions may range from revocation of a firm's registration or barring a person from participating in audits of public companies to lesser sanctions such as monetary penalties or imposition of remedial measures, including additional training or new quality control procedures.

   5. **Funding**—PCAOB's budget is funded by (1) registration and annual fees from public accounting firms and (2) an annual *accounting support fee* assessed on issuers (based on their relative monthly market capitalization).

II. Overview of the Sarbanes-Oxley Act of 2002

    A. Purpose of the Legislation—To address a series of perceived corporate misconduct and alleged audit failures (including Enron, Tyco, and WorldCom, among others) and to strengthen investor confidence in the integrity of the U.S. capital markets.

    B. The Sarbanes-Oxley Act of 2002 consists of 11 *Titles* (the first four of which are directly applicable to auditors).

    C. Title I—Established the PCAOB, gave standard-setting authority to the PCAOB (regarding auditing, quality control, and independence standards), and created its role in overseeing the accounting firms required to register with the PCAOB.

    D. Title II—Established independence requirements for external auditors, which addressed perceived conflicts of interest (limiting non-audit services, establishing a five-year rotation for the audit partner and review partner, and restricting members of the audit firm from taking key management positions (including CEO, CFO, controller, or chief accounting officer) during the one-year period preceding the audit engagement).

        1. Services that the auditor is prohibited from providing: (1) bookkeeping or other services related to the accounting records; (2) financial information systems design and implementation; (3) appraisal or valuation services; (4) actuarial services; (5) internal audit outsourcing services; (6) management functions or human resources; (7) broker or dealer, investment advisor, or investment banking services; (8) legal services and expert services unrelated to the audit; and (9) any other service that the PCAOB determines is impermissible.

        2. The issuer's audit committee is required to approve any non-audit services (including tax services) that are not specifically prohibited.

    E. Title III—Established requirements related to *corporate responsibility* to make executives take responsibility for the accuracy of financial reporting (including a requirement for certification by the entity's *principal officers*) and to make it illegal for management to improperly influence the conduct of an audit.

    F. Title IV—Addressed a variety of *enhanced financial disclosures,* the most well-known of which deals with required internal control reporting (Section 404), among other matters.

PCAOB on Engagement Quality Review

After studying this lesson, you should be able to:

1. Understand the auditor's responsibilities for an "engagement quality review" (and for concurring approval of issuance) under PCAOB Auditing Standards.

2. Know the primary differences between the requirements of PCAOB Auditing Standards and the AICPA's Statements on Quality Control Standards (SQCS).

I. **Engagement Quality Review**

II. **Introduction and Overview**

  A. **Applicability of Standard**—Requires an engagement quality review (and concurring approval of issuance) for engagements conducted under PCAOB standards (1) for an audit; (2) for a review of interim financial information; and (3) for an attestation engagement regarding compliance reports of brokers and dealers (or a review engagement regarding exemption reports of brokers and dealers).

  B. **Objective of the Engagement Quality Reviewer**—To perform an evaluation of the significant judgments made by the engagement team and the related conclusions reached and in preparing any engagement report(s).

  C. **Qualifications of an Engagement Quality Reviewer** —(1) Must be an *associated person* of a registered public accounting firm; and (2) must have competence, independence, integrity, and objectivity:

> **Note**
> "An outside reviewer who is not already associated with a registered public accounting firm would become associated with the firm issuing the report if he or she ... (1) receives compensation from the firm issuing the report for performing the review or (2) performs the review as agent for the firm issuing the report."

  1. **Associated person of a registered public accounting firm**— Should be able to withstand any pressure from the engagement partner or others and may be someone from outside the firm; if the reviewer is from within the firm, he/she should be a partner or have an equivalent position. (There is no such requirement for a reviewer from outside the firm.)

  2. **Competence**—Must be qualified to serve as the engagement partner on the engagement under review.

  3. **Objectivity**—The engagement quality reviewer (and any assisting personnel) should not make engagement team decisions or assume any responsibilities of the engagement team.

  4. **"Cooling-off" restriction** —The person serving as engagement partner during either of the two audits preceding the audit subject to engagement quality review is not permitted to serve as engagement quality reviewer (unless the registered firm qualifies for a specific exemption to this requirement).

III. **Engagement Quality Review for an Audit or a Review under PCAOB Standards**

  A. **Engagement Quality Review Process**—To evaluate the significant judgments and conclusions of the engagement team, the engagement quality reviewer should (1) hold discussions with the engagement partner and other members of the engagement team; and (2) review documentation.

  B. **Evaluation of Engagement Documentation**—The engagement quality reviewer should evaluate whether the documentation that was reviewed (1) indicates that the engagement team responded appropriately to significant risks; and (2) supports the conclusions reached by the engagement team.

C. Concurring Approval of Issuance

  1. The engagement quality reviewer cannot express such approval if there is any significant engagement deficiency [when (a) the engagement team failed to obtain sufficient appropriate evidence; (b) the engagement team reached an inappropriate overall conclusion; (c) the engagement report is not appropriate; or (d) the firm is not independent of its client].

  2. The firm cannot give permission to the client to use the engagement report until the engagement quality reviewer provides concurring approval of issuance.

IV. Documentation of an Engagement Quality Review

  A. Documentation should contain sufficient information to permit an experienced auditor, having no prior association with the engagement, to understand the procedures performed and conclusions reached by the engagement quality reviewer.

  B. Documentation of an engagement quality review should be included in the engagement documentation (and be subject to other PCAOB requirements regarding retention of and changes to audit documentation).

V. PCAOB Standards Have Several Differences Relative to AICPA's Statements on Quality Control Standards (SQCS)

  A. Engagement Quality Review—SQCS do not require an engagement quality review for any type of engagement, whereas the PCAOB establishes such a requirement.

  B. Cooling-off Restriction—SQCS do not impose a "cooling-off" restriction or a requirement that the reviewer must be an associated person of a registered public accounting firm.

  C. Concurring Approval of Issuance—SQCS require any engagement quality review performed be completed before the engagement report is released without requiring a concurring approval of issuance.

  D. Documentation Retention and Changes—SQCS do not specifically require that engagement quality review documentation must be retained with other engagement documentation and be subject to specific policies regarding retention and changes.

Planning Activities

Pre-Engagement Planning Issues

> **After studying this lesson, you should be able to:**
>
> 1. Understand the auditor's requirement under the applicable Statements on Quality Control Standards as they are used to specifically consider the "acceptance and continuance of clients and engagements."
>
> 2. Understand the auditor's responsibilities in agreeing upon the terms of the audit engagement with management.
>
> 3. Understand the auditor's responsibilities to communicate with the predecessor auditor when an entity changes auditors.

I. **Statements on Quality Control Standards**—Recall the AICPA's Statements on Quality Control Standards (SQCS) that are applicable to a CPA's financial statement related services.

   A. One of the six elements of a quality control system is *acceptance and continuance of clients and engagements.* Auditors should avoid clients whose management lacks integrity or clients who are viewed as too risky owing to industry considerations or entity-specific issues.

   B. The auditor should also evaluate the compliance with applicable ethics requirements, especially regarding independence issues and competencies to properly perform the engagement, before proceeding with other significant audit-related activities.

Question
What if the successor believes that the financial statements covered by the predecessor's report require revision?

Answer:

Try to arrange a meeting with the three parties (i.e., the successor, predecessor, and client management). If the client refuses to meet to discuss issues reflecting on the appropriateness of the previously issued financial statements, the successor should consider the risks of being the entity's auditor.

Question
What if the auditor is unable to observe the beginning inventory?

Answer:

If unable to verify the beginning inventory, the auditor may be unable to reach a conclusion about the cost of goods sold and, hence, the net income. As a result, the auditor may not be able to express an opinion on the fairness of the income statement, statement of cash flows, or statement of retained earnings. However, the auditor could still express an opinion on the balance sheet itself.

II. **Terms of Engagement**—The relevant AICPA guidance is provided by AU 210, *Terms of Engagement.* This pronouncement addresses the auditor's responsibilities in agreeing upon the terms of the audit engagement with management (and those charged with governance, when appropriate).

   A. **Auditor's Objective under AU 210**—The auditor's objective is to accept an audit engagement involving a new or existing audit client only when the basis for the audit has been agreed upon by (1) establishing when the *preconditions for an audit* are present; and (2) confirming that a common understanding of the terms of the engagement exists between the auditor and management (and those charged with governance, as applicable).

Definition

Preconditions for an Audit: The use by management of an acceptable financial reporting framework in the preparation of the financial statements and the agreement of management to the premise on which an audit is conducted.

---

1. Management should acknowledge its responsibility for (a) the fair presentation of the financial statements; (b) the design and implementation of effective internal control over financial reporting; and (c) providing the auditor with all information relevant to the financial statements and any additional information requested by the auditor, and providing access to all entity personnel relevant to the audit of the financial statements. (The auditor should determine whether the financial reporting framework is appropriate and obtain an agreement that management acknowledges and understands its responsibilities.)

2. If the preconditions are not present, the auditor should not accept the engagement; instead, the auditor should discuss the matter with management.

3. If management imposes a limitation on the scope of the audit that the auditor believes would result in a disclaimer of opinion (called a *limited engagement*), the auditor normally should not accept the engagement. If such an entity is required by law or regulation to have an audit, the auditor is then allowed to accept the limited engagement, so as long as a disclaimer of opinion is acceptable under the applicable law or regulation.

4. **Agreement on audit engagement terms**—The agreement of the terms of the engagement should be documented in an audit engagement letter and address the following:

   a. The objective and scope of the audit;

   b. The auditor's responsibilities;

   c. Management's responsibilities;

   d. A statement about the inherent limitations of an audit;

   e. A statement identifying the applicable financial reporting framework;

   f. Reference to the expected content of any reports to be issued; and

   g. Other matters as warranted in the auditor's judgment.

B. **Initial audits**—*Initial audit* refers to when the prior year's financial statements have been audited by a different auditor (referred to as the *predecessor auditor*).

   1. Before accepting the engagement, the auditor should request that management authorize the predecessor auditor to respond to the auditor's inquiries relevant to the decision whether to accept the engagement.

   2. The predecessor is expected to respond fully and to indicate when the response is limited. The auditor should evaluate the predecessor's response in deciding whether to accept the engagement. If management does not authorize the predecessor to respond (or otherwise limits the predecessor's response), the auditor should consider that fact in deciding whether to accept the engagement.

   3. The auditor's communication with the predecessor auditor may be written or verbal. Typical matters expected to be addressed include the following:

      a. Information that might bear on the integrity of management

      b. Any disagreements with management about accounting or auditing issues

      c. Communications involving those charged with governance with respect to fraud and/or noncompliance with applicable laws or regulations

    d. Communications involving management and those charged with governance regarding significant deficiencies in internal control

    e. The predecessor's understanding about the reasons for the entity's change in auditors

    f. The predecessor's understanding of the nature of the entity's relationships and transactions with related parties and significant unusual transactions

---

 Question

What if the auditor believes that the financial statements covered by the predecessor's report require revision?

Answer:

Try to arrange a three-way meeting involving the auditor, predecessor, and entity management. If management refuses to meet to discuss issues related to the appropriateness of previously issued financial statements, the auditor should consider those matters in deciding whether to accept the engagement.

C. Recurring Audit Engagements—If the auditor concludes that the terms of the preceding engagement are still applicable to the current engagement, the auditor should remind management of the terms of the engagement (and document that reminder).

    1. The auditor may remind management of the terms of the engagement in writing or verbally. When the communication is oral, it is desirable to document the significant matters discussed (including with whom and when).

    2. It may be appropriate to revise the terms of the previous engagement. This is the case, for example, when there is a change in senior management or a significant change in ownership; when there is a change in the financial reporting framework adopted; when there is a change in legal or regulatory requirements; when there is any indication that management misunderstands the nature of the audit; or when there are special terms to the engagement.

D. Acceptance of a Change in the Terms of the Audit Engagement

    1. If the auditor is asked to change the audit engagement to an engagement resulting in a lower level of assurance (prior to completing the audit engagement), the auditor should determine whether reasonable justification for doing so exists; if not, the auditor should decline the request.

    2. Suppose that the auditor concludes no reasonable justification for such a change exists, but management will not permit the auditor to continue the original audit engagement. The auditor should: (a) withdraw from the audit engagement when possible; (b) communicate the circumstances to those charged with governance; and (c) determine whether there is any legal or other obligation to report the matter to any other parties.

    3. Reasonable basis for a change—Reasonable justification would exist when there is a change in circumstances affecting management's requirements, or if there was a misunderstanding about the nature of the service originally requested. The resulting report should not refer to any audit procedures performed prior to changing the engagement to a review or other service.

III. AICPA Sample Engagement Letter

CPA Firm Letterhead

Addressee: [Appropriate representative of those charged with governance of ABC Company]

[The objective and scope of the audit]

You have requested that we audit the financial statements of ABC Company, which comprise the balance sheet as of December 31, 20XX, and the related statements of income, changes in stockholders' equity, and cash flows for the year then ended, and the related notes to the financial statements. We are pleased to confirm our acceptance and our understanding of this audit engagement by means of this letter.

The objectives of our audit are to obtain reasonable assurance about whether the financial statements as a whole are free from material misstatement, whether due to fraud or error, and to issue an auditor's report that includes our opinion. Reasonable assurance is a high level of assurance but is not absolute assurance and therefore is not a guarantee that an audit conducted in accordance with auditing standards generally accepted in the United States of America (GAAS) will always detect a material misstatement when it exists. Misstatements can arise from fraud or error and are considered material if, individually or in the aggregate, they could reasonably be expected to influence the economic decisions of users made on the basis of these financial statements.

[The responsibilities of the auditor]

We will conduct our audit in accordance with GAAS. As part of an audit in accordance with GAAS, we exercise professional judgment and maintain professional skepticism throughout the audit. We also:

- Identify and assess the risks of material misstatement of the financial statements, whether due to fraud or error, design and perform audit procedures responsive to those risks, and obtain audit evidence that is sufficient and appropriate to provide a basis for our opinion. The risk of not detecting a material misstatement resulting from fraud is higher than for one resulting from error, as fraud may involve collusion, forgery, intentional omissions, misrepresentations, or the override of internal control.

- Obtain an understanding of internal control relevant to the audit in order to design audit procedures that are appropriate in the circumstances, but not for the purpose of expressing an opinion on the effectiveness of the entity's internal control. However, we will communicate to you in writing concerning any significant deficiencies or material weaknesses in internal control relevant to the audit of the financial statements that we have identified during the audit.

- Evaluate the appropriateness of accounting policies used and the reasonableness of significant accounting estimates made by management, as well as evaluate the overall presentation of the financial statements, including the disclosures, and whether the financial statements represent the underlying transactions and events in a manner that achieves fair presentation.

- Conclude, based on the audit evidence obtained, whether there are conditions or events, considered in the aggregate, that raise substantial doubt about ABC Company's ability to continue as a going concern for a reasonable period of time.

Because of the inherent limitations of an audit, together with the inherent limitations of internal control, an unavoidable risk that some material misstatements may not be detected exists, even though the audit is properly planned and performed in accordance with GAAS.

[The responsibilities of management and identification of the applicable financial reporting framework]

Our audit will be conducted on the basis that *[management and, when appropriate, those charged with governance]* acknowledge and understand that they have responsibility

a. for the preparation and fair presentation of the financial statements in accordance with accounting principles generally accepted in the United States of America;

b. for the design, implementation, and maintenance of internal control relevant to the preparation and fair presentation of financial statements that are free from material misstatement, whether due to fraud or error; and

c. to provide us with

    i. access to all information of which management is aware that is relevant to the preparation and fair presentation of the financial statements, such as records, documentation, and other matters;

    ii. additional information that we may request from management for the purpose of the audit; and

    iii. unrestricted access to persons within ABC Company from whom we determine it necessary to obtain audit evidence.

As part of our audit process, we will request from *[management and, when appropriate, those charged with governance]* written confirmation concerning representations made to us in connection with the audit.

[Other relevant information]

[Insert other information, such as fee arrangements, billings, and other specific terms, as appropriate.]

[Reporting]

[Insert appropriate reference to the expected form and content of the auditor's report; an example follows:]

We will issue a written report upon completion of our audit of ABC Company's financial statements. Our report will be addressed to the board of directors of ABC Company. Circumstances may arise in which our report may differ from its expected form and content based on the results of our audit. Depending on the nature of these circumstances, it may be necessary for us to modify our opinion, add an emphasis-of-matter paragraph or other-matter paragraph to our auditor's report, or, if necessary, withdraw from the engagement.

We also will issue a written report on *[insert appropriate reference to other auditor's reports expected to be issued]* upon completion of our audit.

Please sign and return the attached copy of this letter to indicate your acknowledgment of, and agreement with, the arrangements for our audit of the financial statements including our respective responsibilities.

XYZ & Co.

Acknowledged and agree on behalf of ABC Company

[Signed]

[Name and Title]

[Date]

Planning and Supervision

1. Understand the auditor's responsibility to adequately plan an audit engagement based on applicable AICPA Professional Standards.

Recall the AICPA's specific Performance Principle dealing with "planning, materiality, risk assessment, and evidence," which states: "To obtain reasonable assurance, which is a high, but not absolute, level ofassurance, the auditor: plans the work and properly supervises any assistants."

I. **AICPA Guidance**—The relevant AICPA guidance is provided by AU 300, *Planning An Audit*. This pronouncement states that the auditor's objective is to plan the audit so that it will be performed in an effective manner.

   A. **Involvement of Key Engagement Team Members** —The engagement partner and other key members of the audit team should be involved in planning activities.

      1. The nature and extent of planning varies with the size and complexity of the entity, the audit team's experience with the entity, and changes in circumstances occurring during the engagement. Likewise, the extent of supervision and review can vary depending upon the size and complexity of the entity, the nature of the audit area involved, the assessed risks of material misstatement, and the competence of the audit personnel involved.

      2. Planning is an ongoing iterative process, not a one-time activity. Planning encompasses risk assessment procedures, understanding the applicable legal and regulatory framework, the determination of materiality, the involvement of specialists, and so forth.

      3. The engagement partner may delegate portions of planning and supervision to other personnel, but a discussion about the risk of material misstatement (including fraud risks) among key members of the audit team, including the engagement partner, is required.

   B. **Preliminary Engagement Activities** —The auditor should address the following matters at the beginning of the engagement:

      1. Perform appropriate procedures to address quality control issues related to the continuance of the client relationship and the specific audit engagement (including consideration of issues regarding management integrity).

      2. Evaluate compliance with relevant ethical requirements related to quality control considerations (particularly regarding independence issues).

      3. Establish an understanding of the terms of the engagement.

   C. **Planning Activities**

      1. The auditor should establish an *overall audit strategy* dealing with the scope and timing of the audit work, which affects the development of the required *audit plan*. (An audit plan is more detailed than the overall strategy and deals with the nature, timing, and extent of audit procedures to be performed.) In establishing the overall audit strategy, the auditor should:

         a. Identify relevant characteristics of the engagement affecting its scope.

         b. Identify the reporting objectives of the engagement and required communications.

         c. Consider the factors that are significant in utilizing the audit team.

         d. Consider the results of preliminary engagement activities.

         e. Determine the nature, timing, and extent of necessary resources for the engagement.

    f. The overall strategy affects the auditor's decisions regarding the allocation of audit resources to specific audit areas and how those resources are managed and supervised.

    g. Communication with those charged with governance—The auditor is required to communicate with those charged with governance about an overview of the planned scope and timing of the engagement. The auditor may discuss planning issues with management, but should be careful to avoid divulging details that might reduce the effectiveness of the audit by making the auditor's procedures and scope too predictable.

  2. The auditor should also develop an *audit plan*. (In practice, the term *audit program* is often used in place of what the AICPA calls the *audit plan*.) The audit plan encompasses (a) the nature and extent of planned risk assessment procedures; (b) the nature, timing, and extent of planned *further audit procedures* at the relevant assertion level; and (c) other planned audit procedures necessary to comply with GAAS. Note: Because planning is an iterative process, the auditor should make appropriate changes to the overall strategy and to the audit plan as necessary during the course of the audit if unexpected circumstances are encountered.

D. Specialized Skills—The auditor should determine whether there is a need for specialized skills on the engagement. In the past, the AICPA used the term specialist to describe what they now call "a professional possessing specialized skills."

  1. A professional having specialized skills may be someone within or outside of the audit firm. Examples include valuation experts, appraisers, actuaries, tax specialists, IT professionals, etcetera.

  2. The auditor should be sufficiently knowledgeable about the matters involved to communicate the objectives of the work, to evaluate whether the planned procedures will meet the auditor's needs, and to evaluate the results of the procedures performed.

E. Documentation—The auditor should address the following matters in the audit documentation: (1) the overall audit strategy; (2) the audit plan; and (3) any significant changes made to the audit strategy or the audit plan during the audit engagement, along with the reasons for any such changes.

II. PCAOB Standards—The relevant PCAOB guidance is provided by their auditing standards on *Audit Planning*. The auditor's planning-related responsibilities are virtually the same under the PCAOB standards as they are under the AICPA standards.

Materiality

I. **AICPA Guidance**—The relevant AICPA guidance is provided by AU 320, *Materiality in Planning and Performing An Audit*. This pronouncement states that the auditor's objective is to apply the concept of materiality appropriately in planning and performing the audit.

II. **Materiality**—The concept of materiality can be described as "an understanding of what is important" in financial reporting based on the auditor's perception of the users' needs.

   A. A definition of *materiality* from the FASB's Conceptual Framework project (specifically, Statement on Financial Accounting Concepts No. 2) follows:

   "The magnitude of an omission or misstatement of accounting information that, in the light of surrounding circumstances, makes it probable that the judgment of a reasonable person relying on the information would have been changed or influenced by the omission or misstatement." (Note that this definition emphasizes that materiality judgments involve both quantitative and qualitative considerations.)

   The AICPA issued SAS No. 138, "Amendments to the Description of the Concept of Materiality," to better align AICPA Professional Standards with the treatment of materiality by the U.S. courts, the PCAOB, the SEC, and the FASB.

   SAS No. 138 describes materiality as follows: "Misstatements, including omissions, are considered to be material if there is a substantial likelihood that, individually or in the aggregate, they would influence the judgment made by a reasonable user based on the financial statements."

   B. The determination of materiality is a matter of professional judgment, and involves both **quantitative** (the relative magnitude of the items in question) and **qualitative** (the surrounding circumstances) considerations.

   C. The auditor considers the concept of materiality throughout the audit process, including (a) in planning and performing the audit; (b) in evaluating the effect of uncorrected misstatements on the entity's financial statements; and (c) in forming the auditor's opinion.

      1. **In planning the audit** —The auditor should determine the materiality for the financial statements as a whole in connection with establishing the overall audit strategy. The auditor should determine **performance materiality** in connection with assessing the risks of material misstatement and determining the nature, timing, and extent of further audit procedures at the relevant assertion level.

Definitions

Performance Materiality: The amount(s) set by the auditor at less than materiality for the financial statements as a whole to reduce to an appropriately low level the probability that the aggregate of uncorrected and undetected misstatements exceeds materiality for the financial statements as a whole; if applicable, it is also the amount(s) set by the auditor at less than the materiality level(s) for particular classes of transactions, account balances, or disclosures.

Tolerable Misstatement: The application of performance materiality to a particular sampling procedure.

> **Note**
> *Previous AICPA auditing standards distinguished between* planning-stage materiality *and* evaluation-stage materiality. *Current standards no longer make that distinction, but, instead, introduce the term* performance materiality, *which seems similar to what was meant by the term* planning-stage materiality *in the past.*

2. **Revision during the audit** —The auditor should revise materiality for the financial statements as a whole and, if applicable, the materiality level(s) for specific classes of transactions or account balances when the auditor becomes aware of information affecting the auditor's initial judgments. The auditor should also determine whether "performance materiality" should be revised and whether the nature, timing, and extent of further audit procedures are appropriate.

D. **Documentation**—The auditor should document the following matters:

1. Materiality for the financial statements as a whole

2. Materiality level(s) for particular classes of transactions, account balances, or disclosures, as applicable

3. Performance materiality

4. Any revision of those considerations during the audit engagement

E. **Considerations that May Affect the Auditor's Materiality Judgment**

1. **Quantitative guidelines**—In practice, auditors frequently apply a variety of "benchmarks" as a starting point in determining the appropriate materiality levels. A few examples of frequently used general guidelines follow (these are not specifically identified in the AICPA auditing standards, however):

   a. 5% to 10% of net income or earnings before taxes

   b. 0.50% to 2% of the larger of net sales or total assets

   c. 5% of owners' equity for private companies

2. **Qualitative matters**—The surrounding circumstances and perceived risks might affect the auditor's judgment of what is material to the users. There are too many such factors to list here, but two examples follow:

   a. **Public versus private companies**— A lower materiality threshold may apply to public companies owing to more exposure to litigation and because the owners of private companies may be closer to the day-to-day operations and, therefore, have different information needs.

   b. **Unstable versus stable industry**— A lower materiality threshold may apply to a company in an unstable industry, which is by nature more susceptible to business failure.

3. **Tolerable misstatement** (which, in practice, is sometimes referred to as "tolerable error")— This term refers to the maximum error in a population that the auditor is willing to accept. This should be established in such a way that tolerable misstatement, combined for the entire audit plan, does not exceed materiality for the financial statements taken as a whole.

III. **PCAOB Standards**—The relevant PCAOB guidance is provided by *Consideration of Materiality in Planning and Performing an Audit*. The auditor's responsibilities regarding materiality under the PCAOB standards are very similar to those under AICPA standards, although the PCAOB standard does not use the term "performance materiality."

Audit Risk

After studying this lesson, you should be able to:

1. Understand the concept (and definition) of *audit risk* that underlies a risk-based audit approach relevant to planning, fieldwork, and audit reporting.

2. Understand the components of the "audit risk model" that are applicable to individual audit areas or major classes of transactions to be audited.

I. Audit Risk

   A. Definition of Audit Risk— "The risk that the auditor expresses an inappropriate audit opinion when the financial statements are materially misstated. Audit risk is a function of the risks of material misstatement and detection risk." (Source—AU 200, *Overall Objectives of the Independent Auditor and the Conduct of an Audit in Accordance with [GAAS].*) Note that the concept of audit risk is really a probability and that audit risk and materiality are interrelated by the definition of audit risk.

   B. The presence of audit risk is indicated in the auditor's report by reference to *reasonable assurance,* meaning that audit risk cannot be reduced to a zero probability (which would imply "absolute assurance") owing to the inherent limitations of an audit. *Reasonable assurance* is defined as follows: "In the context of an audit of financial statements, a high, but not absolute, level of assurance." Note that *reasonable assurance* means a "high level of assurance" and a "low level of audit risk."

II. Basic Auditor Responsibility—
The auditor should properly plan and perform the audit to obtain reasonable assurance that material misstatements, whether caused by errors or fraud, are detected.

III. Considerations at the Financial Statement Level—
The one overriding audit planning objective is to limit audit risk to an appropriately low level (as determined by the auditor's judgment), which involves the following:

   A. Determining the extent and nature of the auditor's risk assessment procedures

   B. Identifying and assessing the risk of material misstatement

   C. Determining the nature, timing, and extent of further audit procedures

   D. Evaluating whether the financial statements taken as a whole are presented fairly in conformity with GAAP

IV. Risk of Material Misstatement—
The *risk of material misstatement* (RMM) is defined as: "The risk that the financial statements are materially misstated prior to the audit." RMM exists at two levels: (1) the overall financial statement level; and (2) the assertion level for classes of transactions, account balances, and disclosures.

   A. RMM at the Overall Financial Statement Level— This refers to risks that are "pervasive" to the financial statements and that potentially affect many assertions.

   B. RMM at the Assertion Level— The auditor assesses RMM at the assertion level for the purpose of determining the nature, timing, and extent of further audit procedures to obtain sufficient appropriate audit evidence. RMM at the assertion level consists of two components: (1) inherent risk; and (2) control risk (see below).

   C. At the assertion level, audit risk consists of three component risks: (1) inherent risk (IR); (2) control risk (CR); and detection risk (DR). RMM consists of inherent risk and control risk.

$$AR = IR \times CR \times DR$$

Definitions

Inherent Risk (IR): The probability that a material misstatement would occur in the particular audit area in the absence of any internal control policies and procedures.

Control Risk (CR): The probability that a material misstatement that occurred in the first place would not be detected and corrected by internal controls that are applicable.

Detection Risk (DR): The probability that a material misstatement that was not prevented or detected and corrected by internal control was not detected by the auditor's substantive audit procedures (i.e., an undetected material misstatement exists in a relevant assertion).

V. Variations on the above Audit Risk Model

A. $AR = RMM \times DR$, where:

    1. "Risk of material misstatement" (RMM)—the auditor's combined assessment of inherent risk and control risk (if IR and CR are not separately assessed).

> Note that $RMM = IR \times CR$

B. $AR = RMM \times TD \times AP$, where:

    1. DR can be broken into two components involving the likelihood that the auditor's two basic categories of substantive procedures fail to detect a material misstatement that exists (1) "tests of details risk" (TD) and (2) "substantive analytical procedures risk (AP)."

> Note that $DR = TD \times AP$

C. $AR = IR \times CR \times TD \times AP$

VI. Quantification of the Risk Components

A. The component risks do not necessarily have to be quantified; for example, they could be assessed qualitatively as high, medium, or low.

B. Each component is considered from left to right in order: audit risk is set, then inherent risk is assessed, then control risk is assessed, and finally the implications for the appropriate level of detection risk are considered.

C. "Detection risk" is the only component risk that is specifically the auditor's responsibility —"inherent risk" arises because of the particular audit area under investigation and "control risk" reflects management's responsibility to design and implement internal controls. Note that the auditor must "assess" inherent risk and control risk, but the auditor actually makes the decisions that, in effect, result in some level of detection risk, which should take into consideration the auditor's assessment of the risk of material misstatement.

    1. If IR and CR are seen by the auditor as too high, the auditor must compensate by decreasing DR.

    2. If IR and CR are perceived as low, the auditor may consider accepting a higher DR.

D. Increasing or decreasing DR is accomplished by adjusting the nature, timing, and/or extent of the auditor's substantive audit procedures. These might be viewed as the auditor's three strategic variables that, in effect, "set" DR based on the auditor's professional judgment about the following:

1. **Nature**—What specific audit procedures to perform (perhaps shifting the relative emphasis placed on the "soft evidence" analytical procedures versus the "hard evidence" tests of details)?

2. **Timing**—When will the procedures be performed? At an "interim" date (prior to year-end) or at "final" (after year-end when the books have been closed) and the auditor is actually auditing the numbers that the entity intends to report in its financial statements)?

3. **Extent**—Are large samples required for the auditor's test work or can somewhat smaller sample sizes be justified? How extensively should substantive procedures be performed?

Analytical Procedures

I. AICPA Guidance

The relevant AICPA guidance is provided by AU 520, *Analytical Procedures*. This pronouncement states that the auditor's objectives are to: (1) obtain relevant and reliable audit evidence when using substantive analytical procedures; and (2) design and perform analytical procedures near the end of the audit that assist the auditor when forming an overall conclusion about whether the financial statements are consistent with the auditor's understanding of the entity.

Definition

Analytical Procedures: Evaluations of financial information through analysis of plausible relationships among both financial and nonfinancial data

---

II. Purposes Associated with Analytical Procedures

A. Used in planning for risk assessment purposes—Required, must be performed

B. Used for substantive purposes as a partial basis for conclusions—Not technically required for this purpose, but still widely used on a voluntary basis; referred to as "substantive analytical procedures" in this context

C. Used as a final review to determine that sufficient appropriate evidence has been gathered to support audit conclusions—Required, must be performed

III. Substantive Analytical Procedures

A. Steps comprising the auditor's performance of substantive analytical procedures:

1. Determine the suitability of the analytical procedures for the identified assertions involved.

2. Evaluate the reliability of the data used to develop the auditor's expectation.

3. Develop the auditor's expectation of the recorded amounts (or ratios), and evaluate whether the expectation is sufficiently precise.

4. Compare the recorded amounts (or ratios) to the auditor's expectation.

5. Determine whether any difference relative to the auditor's expectation requires further investigation (such as inquiry of management or other actions).

B. Key factors that determine the effectiveness and efficiency of using analytical procedures for substantive purposes—This topic will be considered further later in connection with the "Overview of Substantive Procedures" lesson.

1. **Nature of the assertion**—Analytical procedures may be particularly effective (compared to tests of details) in detecting omissions of transactions (regarding the "completeness" assertion); tests of details may not be effective in detecting omissions when there are no underlying source documents associated with unrecorded transactions

2. **Plausibility and predictability of the relationship**—The auditor's expectation improves with the increased predictability of an account balance or ratio; predictability is affected by several considerations:

   a. Relationships in a stable environment are usually more predictable than those in a dynamic environment.

   b. Relationships involving income statement accounts tend to be more predictable than those involving balance sheet accounts (since the income statement deals with a period of time rather than a single moment in time).

   c. As management discretion increases, the predictability of an account balance or ratio tends to decrease.

3. **Availability and reliability of data**—Analytical procedures are improved as the reliability of the data used increases; the following considerations tend to enhance the reliability of the data used:

   a. When data have been subject to audit testing (either currently or in the past), the reliability of the data is enhanced.

   b. When data have been obtained from independent external sources (rather than from the client entity), the reliability of the data is enhanced.

   c. When data obtained from the client entity are developed under conditions of effective internal control (rather than ineffective internal control), the reliability of the data is enhanced.

4. **Precision of the expectation**—The likelihood of detecting a misstatement increases as the level of aggregation of the data decreases.

   a. Relationships of interest to the auditor may be obscured by the noise in the data at high levels of aggregation of the data.

   b. For example, simply comparing the current year's sales in total to the prior year's total sales is a high level of aggregation; a more precise analysis (at a lower level of aggregation) would be analyzing the sales by month broken down by product line.

IV. Analytical Procedures in Forming Overall Conclusions

A. Purpose—To assist the auditor in forming an overall conclusion as to whether the financial statements are consistent with the auditor's understanding of the entity

B. Similarity to risk assessment procedures—The auditor should read the financial statements and consider any unusual or unexpected relationships that were not previously identified.

C. Revise risk assessment as necessary—The auditor may revise the assessment of the risk of material misstatement and modify the planned further audit procedures as necessary.

V. Documentation Requirements

A. The auditor's expectation and the factors considered in developing it

B. The results of comparing the recorded amounts (or ratios) with the auditor's expectation

C. The results of any additional auditing procedures performed to investigate significant differences identified by that comparison

Audit Data Analytics

After studying this lesson, you should be able to:

1. State (or paraphrase) the definition and purposes of an "audit data analytic" (ADA).

2. Understand the five-step process associated with using an ADA in the various phases of an audit.

3. State (or paraphrase) the definition and purpose of "visualization" associated with the application of an ADA.

I. Introduction

A. Definition of audit data analytics (ADAs)

The AICPA's *Guide to Audit Data Analytics* defines ADAs as follows: "the science and art of discovering and analyzing patterns, identifying anomalies, and extracting other useful information in data underlying or related to the subject matter of an audit through analysis, modeling, and visualization for the purpose of planning or performing the audit"

B. Purposes of ADAs—ADAs may be used for multiple purposes, including to perform (1) risk assessment, (2) tests of control, (3) substantive procedures, or (4) evaluating conclusions.

C. The Guide identifies a five-step approach applicable to using ADAs: (1) plan the ADA, (2) access and prepare the data for purposes of the ADA, (3) consider the relevance and reliability of the data used, (4) perform the ADA, and (5) evaluate the results and decide whether the purpose and specific objectives have been achieved. These will be discussed further below.

> **Note**
> *The AICPA's Guide does not address using ADAs as tests of control. The Guide does not establish any auditor requirements beyond those associated with the AICPA's Statements on Auditing Standards.*

II. The Five-Step Approach to Using ADAs

A. Step #1—Plan the audit data analytic.

1. Procedures

   a. Describe the objective of an ADA—Recall that ADAs may be used for risk assessment or substantive purposes.

   i. Risk assessment procedures involve obtaining an understanding of the entity and its environment, including the entity's internal control, to identify and assess risks of material misstatement.

   ii. Substantive procedures are designed to detect material misstatements at the relevant assertion level—These can be classified as either tests of details or substantive analytical procedures.

   b. Brainstorm potential ADAs—Involves the audit team's discussion of where the potential ADAs and related objectives can be applied

2. Understand the relationship between specific audit assertions and ADAs.

B. Step #2—Access and prepare the data for use in an ADA.

1. Accessing the data—Request and access the data from a client or third party considering the objectives of the ADA; determine the relevant characteristics of the data and the related technology.

a. Types of data

    i. Structured—The data conform to a specified organization; for example, data in a relational database or a spreadsheet that is organized in the format of rows and columns.

    ii. Semi-structured—The data are tagged, for example, as in HTML, XML, or XBRL.

    iii. Unstructured—Data such as text, audio, or video

b. File types—Auditors should understand and document the types of files they are requesting and using. Common file types include the following:

    i. Comma-separated values files (.csv)

    ii. Database files (.db or .dbf)

    iii. Microsoft Access database files (.mdb)

    iv. Structured Query Language (SQL) database files (.sql)

    v. Extensible Markup Language (XML) files (.xml)

    vi. Image files (for example, .jpg, .png, .bmp, .tif)

    vii. Video files (for example, .mp4, .avi)

c. Data storage—Auditors should understand and document where the data are stored prior to extraction.

d. Extraction methodologies—Auditors should understand and document how the data were extracted and by whom.

e. Metadata—Characteristics that provide context and additional information about the data (such as file name, file type, file size, creation date/time, last modification date/time, and identification of who can access and/or update the data)

f. Understand and document the accounting system(s) and the flow of transactions with an emphasis on the entity's business processes.

g. Understand and document how the IT general controls and application controls impact the integrity of the data.

2. Preparing the data for use in the ADA—The process used is known as "ETL" (which stands for extract, transform, and load)

a. Extract—The process of extracting the appropriate data from the data set

b. Transform—The process of cleaning the extracted data so that it can be appropriately analyzed. Note that errors in the data may indicate that controls over the data are not operating effectively.

    i. Field format inconsistency—Should identify and correct inconsistencies in data fields (for example, some data may be presented as Month-Day-Year, whereas other data in the same field could be presented as Day-Month-Year)

    ii. Blank fields—Should verify that blank fields are appropriate and not a result of missing data

    iii. Field-type mistakes—Should identify and correct instances where fields contain the wrong type of data; for example, an intended numerical field might consist of letters (text) instead of numbers

c. Load—The process of uploading the cleaned data in the software that will be used to perform the ADA

C. Step #3—Consider the relevance and reliability of the data used.

    1. Data should have the following attributes:

        a. Accuracy—Data are free from significant errors.

        b. Completeness—Data contain all the requisite data (that is, there are no omissions of data that should be present).

        c. Consistency—Data fields are well defined and managed.

        d. Freshness—Data contain the most up-to-date changes/additions.

        e. Timeliness—Data are available when needed.

        f. Clarity and relatedness—Data fields are clearly defined and related to the objective(s) being tested.

    2. Consider the integrity of the data (with emphasis on accuracy and completeness over the data's life cycle) —Determine whether data have been protected whenever acquired and/or delivered.

        a. Determine whether files are encrypted to protect access to data.

        b. Critically examine a data set and the procedures used to obtain the data to understand where it originated (regarding freshness, timeliness, and clarity and relatedness).

    3. Actions primarily directed at ensuring the accuracy and completeness of the data set

        a. Reconciliations—Prepare or review reconciliations of underlying data.

        b. Sequence checks—Verify the appropriateness of the sequence; gaps may indicate possible omissions.

        c. Record counts—Verify that the appropriate number of records are accounted for.

    4. Consider the impact of changes to the environment that may increase the risks of errors in the data—For example, changes in management or changes in the accounting system (such as an ERP system)

D. Step #4—Perform the ADA.

    1. Simple ADAs might be used to test journal entry posting, cash accounts, accounts receivable, accounts payable, and inventory.

    2. The auditor should identify and address any "notable items."

> **Definition**
>
> *Notable Item:* "An item identified from the population being analyzed that has one or more characteristics that, for the relevant assertions, may do the following: (a) Be indicative of a risk of material misstatement that (i) was not previously identified (a new risk) or (ii) is higher than originally assessed by the auditor; (b) Provide information that is useful in designing or tailoring procedures to address risks of material misstatement."

        a. When a large number of notable items is identified—The auditor may use a grouping and filtering process to identify characteristics of interest common to the groups; should perform appropriate procedures to address the risks of each group

        b. When a small number of notable items is identified—The auditor may perform manual risk assessment procedures; further audit procedures should be responsive to the assessed risks of material misstatement

3. When using ADAs in forming an overall conclusion—The auditor may decide it appropriate to revise previous risk assessments and perform further audit procedures in response.

4. ADAs may be used to test management's analytics, including those in footnote disclosures and even in Management's Discussion and Analysis (MD&A) presentation for consistency with other information known by the auditor.

E. **Step #5**—Evaluate the results and decide whether the purpose and specific objectives have been achieved.

1. The auditor should develop preliminary conclusions or recommendations for an ADA.

2. The auditor should evaluate whether the ADA has been appropriately planned and performed—If not, the auditor should refine and reperform the ADA.

3. Documentation—The auditor should document the performance and results of the ADAs; any screenshots of graphics necessary to support the auditor's work should also be retained.

III. Visualization

Definition

Visualization: "… the use of various types of graphics (for example, charts, scatter diagrams, trend lines), tables, or combinations thereof in formats such as dashboards."

A. The purpose of such visualization techniques is to make relationships of interest in very large data sets more easily identifiable.

B. The form and content of such graphics and/or tables when performing ADAs requires the auditor's professional judgment.

C. A variety of software (including Excel) may recommend using a trend line, bar chart, histogram, pie chart, or scatterplot, for example, which can be a useful starting point.

Detecting Fraud

After studying this lesson, you should be able to:

1. Understand (and be able to state) the auditor's fundamental responsibility to detect and communicate matters related to fraud in a financial statement audit.

2. Identify and distinguish between the two types of "fraud" that might be relevant to a financial statement audit, as discussed in the AICPA Professional Standards.

3. Identify the three categories of "risk factors" that the auditor is required to consider when assessing the risk of material misstatement due to fraud, based on AICPA Professional Standards.

I. AICPA Guidance—The relevant AICPA guidance is provided by AU 240, *Consideration of Fraud in a Financial Statement Audit*. This pronouncement states that the auditor's objectives are to: (1) identify and assess the risks of material misstatement due to fraud; (2) obtain sufficient appropriate audit evidence regarding the assessed risks of material misstatement due to fraud, through designing and implementing appropriate responses; and (3) respond appropriately to fraud or suspected fraud identified during the audit.

Definitions

Fraud: An intentional act by one or more individuals among management, those charged with governance, employees, or third parties, involving the use of deception that results in a misstatement in the financial statements.

Fraud Risk Factors: Events or conditions that indicate (a) an incentive or pressure to perpetrate fraud; (b) provide an opportunity to commit fraud; or (c) indicate attitudes or rationalizations to justify a fraudulent action.

Significant Unusual Transactions: Significant transactions that are outside the normal course of business for the entity or that otherwise appear to be unusual due to their timing, size, or nature.

A. There are two different types of misstatements that are relevant to the auditor's consideration of fraud:

1. **Fraudulent financial reporting**—This type of fraud involves misstatements that are intended to deceive financial statement users (e.g., the intent is to inflate the entity's stock price). Fraudulent financial reporting often involves management override of controls, recording fictitious journal entries, concealing facts, and altering underlying records to achieve the deception. This scenario is typically associated with a conspiracy involving multiple members of senior management to deceive the auditors, as well as financial statement users.

2. **Misappropriation of assets**—This type of fraud involves theft of assets causing the financial statements to be misstated owing to false entries intended to conceal the theft. Misappropriation of assets often involves embezzlement of receipts, stealing physical assets or intellectual property, and diverting the entity's assets for personal use. This scenario is typically associated with an individual bad actor operating individually to perpetrate and conceal the theft.

II. The Auditor's Basic Responsibility Relates to Planning

A. In general, the auditor is required to design (plan) the audit to provide "reasonable assurance" of detecting misstatements that are material to the financial statements. In particular, the auditor should

> **Note**
> *AICPA Professional Standards focus on the auditor's responsibility for providing reasonable assurance of detecting material misstatements, whether due to error or fraud. The distinction depends upon whether the misstatement is intentional (which is the essence of fraud) or not. Intent may be difficult to determine, for example, when addressing accounting estimates, which are subjective by nature.*

specifically assess the risk of material misstatement due to fraud (in addition to error), and design the audit procedures to be responsive to that risk assessment. That risk assessment should be performed at both the financial statement level and the assertion level.

B. Specifically, key audit team members must have a "brainstorming" discussion to consider how and where the financial statements might be susceptible to material misstatement owing to fraud and to emphasize the importance of maintaining professional skepticism. That discussion involving key members of the engagement team should consider such matters as the following:

1. Known internal and external fraud risk factors relevant to the entity

2. The risk of management override of controls

3. Indications of "earnings management"

4. The importance of maintaining professional skepticism throughout the engagement

5. How the auditor might respond to the risk of material fraud

---

Question

Does failure to detect a material misstatement imply a substandard audit?

Answer:

No! An auditor may be unable to detect a material misstatement owing to forgery, collusion, or upper management involvement, etc.

III. **Inquiry and Analytical Procedures**—To obtain information needed to identify the risks of material fraud the auditor emphasizes "inquiry" and "analytical procedures." (The auditor's important inquiries should be documented in the Management Representations Letter at the end of fieldwork!)

A. **Inquiry**—The auditor should question management personnel about their knowledge of fraud, suspected fraud, allegations of fraud, and any significant unusual transactions (including related-party involvement); inquire about specific controls that management has implemented to mitigate fraud risks; and inquire about management's communications with those charged with governance about fraud-related issues. The auditor may also choose to question others (e.g., audit committee, internal auditors, operating personnel, in-house legal counsel, etc.) about fraud-related issues.

B. **Analytical Procedures**—The auditor should perform analytical procedures involving revenue accounts, in particular. In general, the auditor should consider whether any unexpected results associated with analytical procedures might have been intentional.

C. There is a presumption that improper revenue recognition is a fraud risk. The auditor should ordinarily presume that there is a risk of material misstatement owing to fraud related to revenue recognition, and perform appropriate audit procedures (such as analytical procedures).

IV. **Fraud Risk Factors**—The auditing standards identify three characteristics generally associated with fraud: (1) incentive/pressure; (2) opportunity; and (3) attitude/rationalization. These three categories of risk factors are sometimes referred to as the *fraud triangle*.

A. **Fraudulent Financial Reporting**—Example risk factors the auditor should consider:

1. **Incentive/pressure**—Reasons that management might be motivated to commit fraudulent financial reporting.

a. **Financial stability/profitability**—When the entity is threatened by deteriorating economic conditions, for example: operating losses threaten bankruptcy; there are recurring negative cash flows from operations; there is vulnerability to rapid changes due to technology or other factors; there are increasing business failures in the industry; or the entity reports unusual profitability relative to others in the industry.

b. **Excessive pressure to meet the expectations of outsiders**—Senior management may face significant pressure to meet external expectations, for example: there are overly optimistic press releases; the entity is only barely able to meet the stock exchange's listing requirements; the entity is having difficulty meeting debt covenants; or the entity must obtain additional outside financing to retool production to be competitive.

2. **Opportunities**—Circumstances that might give management a way to commit fraudulent financial reporting.

    a. **Nature of the industry or the entity's operations**—For example: significant unusual transactions with related parties; ability to dominate suppliers or customers in a certain industry sector; unnecessarily complex transactions close to year-end raise "substance over form" issues; significant bank accounts or business operations in "tax-haven" jurisdictions with no clear business justification; major financial statement elements that involve significant estimates by management that are difficult to corroborate.

    b. **Ineffective monitoring of management**—For example, domination of management by a single person or small group without compensating controls or; ineffective oversight by those charged with governance.

    c. **Complex or unstable organizational structure**—For example, organization consists of unusual legal entities; high turnover of senior management, counsel, or board members.

    d. **Internal controls are deficient**—For example, inadequate monitoring of controls; high turnover rates in accounting, internal auditing, and information technology staff; ineffective accounting and information systems (There are significant deficiencies that rise to the level of material weaknesses.)

3. **Attitudes/rationalizations**—Attitudes, behaviors, or justifications of management that might be associated with fraudulent financial reporting:

    a. Lack of commitment to establishing and enforcing ethical standards

    b. Previous violations of securities laws (or other regulations)

    c. Excessive focus by management on the entity's stock price

    d. Management's failure to correct reportable conditions

    e. Pattern of justifying inappropriate accounting as immaterial

    f. Management has a strained relationship with the predecessor or current auditor

B. **Misappropriation of Assets**—Example risk factors the auditor should consider:

1. **Incentive/pressure**—An employee or member of management might be motivated to commit the misappropriation for a variety of reasons, such as the following: employees who have access to cash (or other assets susceptible to theft), may have personal financial problems, or they may have adverse relationships with the entity under audit, (perhaps in response to anticipated future layoffs or recent decreases to their benefits or compensation levels).

2. **Opportunities**—Circumstances that might give someone a way to commit the misappropriation include the following:

    a. **When assets are inherently vulnerable to theft**— For example, there are large amounts of liquid assets on hand, or inventory items are small, but valuable.

    b. **Inadequate internal control over assets**— For example, there is inadequate segregation separation of duties, inadequate documentation or reconciliation for assets, or inadequate management understanding related to information technology.

3. **Attitudes/rationalizations**—The individual perpetrating the misappropriation might possess attitudes or justifications that might be associated with that rationalize the improper behaviors and avoid any feelings of remorse for this misconduct. Generally, the auditor cannot normally observe these attitudes, but should consider the implications of such matters when they are discovered. The following might be of interest to the auditor:

    a. The employee's behavior indicates dissatisfaction with the entity under audit.

    b. There are changes in the employee's behavior or lifestyle that are suspicious.

    c. The employee exhibits a disregard for internal control related to assets by overriding existing controls or failing to correct known deficiencies.

C. Consideration of the Effects of the Risk Factors

    1. The auditor should use judgment in considering the individual or collective effects of the risk factors and recognize that the effects of these risk factors vary widely.

    2. Specific controls may mitigate the associated risks, and specific control deficiencies may add to the risks.

D. Conditions may be discovered during fieldwork that cause the assessment of these risks in the planning stage to be modified. Factors that might cause the auditor's concerns to increase include the following examples:

    1. There are discrepancies in the accounting records including inaccuracies or unsupported balances.

    2. There is conflicting or missing evidence including missing documents or the absence of original documents that should be available (perhaps only photocopies are available).

    3. There is a problematic relationship between the auditor and the entity including restricted access of the auditor to records or personnel and undue time pressures imposed by management.

E. Responses to Risk Assessment—In response to this risk assessment related to fraud, the auditor may conclude that the planned procedures should be modified or that control risk should be reconsidered. The auditor might make some "overall responses" (at the financial statement level, such as assigning more experienced staff to the engagement) and make other responses "at the assertion level" (by designing audit procedures for which the nature, timing, and extent of those procedures are responsive to the assessed risks of fraud).

    1. Overall responses—The auditor may decide to assign more experienced personnel or information technology specialists to the engagement. The auditor should incorporate a degree of "unpredictability" in audit testing, whether at the financial statement level or the assertion level (e.g., visiting some locations for inventory counts on an unannounced basis) or selecting some items for testing that are below materiality levels.

    2. Responses at the assertion level—The auditor may decide to increase the emphasis on audit procedures that provide a stronger basis for conclusions or to confirm the terms of sales transactions, in addition to receivable balances; the auditor may move important audit testing to year-end, instead of performing those tests at an interim date; and/or the auditor may increase sample sizes for audit testing.

    3. Addressing management override of controls—The auditor should obtain an understanding of the entity's controls over journal entries and inquire about unusual activity. Selected journal entries at the end of the period should be examined. The auditor should also review accounting estimates for bias, and might perform a "retrospective review" of significant accounting estimates in the prior year. The auditor should specifically evaluate any significant unusual transactions outside the entity's normal course of business.

F. Management Override—Auditors should plan procedures specifically to address management override of internal control. Management override means that upper management may not be affected by controls that are imposed on subordinates throughout the organization. (Therefore, management may be able to sidestep those controls without leaving an audit trail for discovery.)

    1. Examine adjusting journal entries—The auditor should be especially attentive to nonstandard journal entries (involving unusual accounts or amounts and those involving complex issues or significant uncertainty). Likewise, the auditor should also be especially attentive to journal entries near the end of the reporting period (both for the fiscal year and any applicable interim reporting periods, such as quarterly reports).

2. **Evaluate accounting estimates for bias**—The auditor should consider performing a "retrospective review," which means evaluating prior years' estimates for reasonableness in light of facts occurring after those estimates were made. In other words, did later events support or refute the appropriateness of management's estimates in prior periods? That may affect the auditor's perception of the reliability of management's estimates in the current period.

3. **Evaluate the business rationale for any unusual transactions**—The auditor should look for appropriate authorization of any unusual transactions by those charged with governance.

Fraud: Evaluation and Communication

1. Understand the auditor's responsibility to evaluate fraud issues in light of the overall results of the audit procedures performed.

2. Identify the specific fraud issues that the auditor should document.

3. Understand the auditor's responsibility to communicate the identified fraud issues to management, those charged with governance, or others.

I. **Evaluation of Audit Test Results**—Near the end of the audit, the auditor should evaluate whether the results of the auditing procedures affect the auditor's initial assessment of material fraud risk. (The analytical procedures related to revenue should be performed through the end of the period.)

    A. When evaluating identified misstatements of the financial statements, the auditor should consider whether such misstatements might be indicative of fraud. For example, the auditor might consider the organizational level involved. If a misstatement may be the result of fraud involving management, the auditor should reevaluate the assessment of material fraud risk and the auditor's response to the assessed risks.

    B. If the misstatement is (or may be) the result of fraud and the effect could be material to the financial statements (or if the auditor has been unable to evaluate the materiality involved):

        1. Attempt to obtain additional evidence to determine the facts as to the cause and whether the financial statements are misstated. Discuss the issues and any further investigation required with an appropriate level of management (at least one level above those believed to be involved) and with those charged with governance (especially if senior management appears to be involved).

        2. If the auditor encounters circumstances related to fraud that call into question whether it is appropriate to continue the audit, the auditor should determine the applicable professional and legal responsibilities, and consider whether it is appropriate to withdraw from the engagement. If the auditor withdraws, then the matter should be discussed with management and those charged with governance. (Circumstances that may call into question the auditor's ability to continue the audit include the following: (a) the entity does not take appropriate action regarding fraud; (b) audit evidence suggests that there is a significant risk of pervasive fraud; and (c) the auditor has significant concerns about the competence or integrity of management or those charged with governance.)

II. **Required Documentation**—The auditor should document the following matters related to the consideration of fraud in the financial statement audit:

    A. The discussion among engagement personnel about fraud in planning the audit, including how and when the discussion occurred, the team members who participated, and the subject matter discussed;

    B. The procedures performed to obtain information necessary to assess the risks of material fraud:

    C. Specific risks of material fraud that were identified at the financial statement level and at the assertion level, including a description of how the auditor responded to those identified risks (including the linkage of audit procedures to the risk assessment);

    D. Reasons supporting the auditor's conclusion if revenue recognition was not identified as a fraud risk contrary to the presumption that revenue recognition is a fraud risk;

    E. The results of procedures performed to further address the risk of management override of controls;

    F. Other conditions and analytical relationships that caused the auditor to perform additional auditing procedures; *and*

G. The nature of any communication about fraud made to management, those charged with governance, regulators, and others.

III. Required Communications When Fraud Is Detected or Suspected—The auditor's communication of fraud issues with management (or those charged with governance) may be written or oral, but should be timely. As indicated above, such communication should be documented in the audit documentation.

A. If the fraud is not material to the financial statements and senior management is not involved in the fraud, the appropriate level of management (which is usually considered to be at least one level above where the fraud is believed to have occurred) should be notified. Determining the appropriate level of management for such communication is a matter of judgment, and includes consideration of the likelihood of collusion within management.

B. If the fraud is material to the financial statements or if senior management is involved in the fraud, those charged with governance should be notified.

C. Other Matters Related to Fraud—The auditor may choose to discuss a variety of other matters with those charged with governance, including the following:

1. Concerns about the adequacy of management's assessment of the entity's controls to prevent and detect fraud

2. Failure by management to respond appropriately to identified fraud or to address identified significant deficiencies in internal control

3. Concerns about the entity's control environment, including the competence or integrity of management

4. Concerns about management's efforts to "manage earnings"

5. Concerns about the authorization of transactions that do not appear to be within the normal course of the entity's business

D. The auditor should consider whether any identified fraud risk factors may constitute a "significant deficiency" (or material weakness) regarding internal control that should be reported to senior management and those charged with governance.

E. Whistleblowing—Informing others (outside) the entity such as regulatory and enforcement authorities, is ordinarily prohibited by the auditor's confidentiality requirements, although the duty of confidentiality may be overridden by law or regulation (or the requirements of audits for governmental entities). Accordingly, it would be appropriate for the auditor to seek legal guidance when facing such circumstances. The auditing (and ethical) standards historically have identified four basic exceptions to the auditor's confidentiality requirements:

1. The auditor must respond truthfully to a valid legal subpoena.

2. The auditor must comply with applicable legal and regulatory requirements (including complying with the SEC's 8-K requirements about important matters, such as the entity's decision to change auditors).

3. A predecessor auditor must respond appropriately to the successor auditor's inquiries when the former client has given permission for the predecessor auditor to respond to the auditor's questions.

4. The auditor must report fraud to the applicable funding agency under the requirements of government auditing standards.

Detecting Illegal Acts

After studying this lesson, you should be able to:

1. State the auditor's fundamental responsibility to detect and communicate illegal acts in a financial statement audit.

I. **AICPA Guidance**—The relevant AICPA guidance is provided by AU 250, *Consideration of Laws and Regulations in an Audit of Financial Statements*. This pronouncement states that the auditor's objectives are to: (1) obtain sufficient appropriate audit evidence regarding material amounts and disclosures about laws and regulations generally recognized to have a direct effect on the financial statements; (2) perform specified audit procedures that may identify instances of noncompliance with other laws and regulations that may have a material effect on the financial statements; and (3) respond appropriately to noncompliance (or suspected noncompliance) with laws and regulations identified during the audit.

> **Definition**
>
> *Legal and Regulatory Framework*: Those laws and regulations to which an entity is subject; noncompliance may result in fines, litigation, or other consequences that may have a material effect on the financial statements.

A. **Fundamental Auditor Responsibility**—The essence of the auditor's responsibility is to obtain reasonable assurance that the financial statements are free from material misstatement, whether caused by fraud or error, considering the applicable legal and regulatory framework.

1. **Inherent limitations**—The auditor cannot be expected to detect all noncompliance with all laws and regulations, since that is a legal determination and because many laws focus on an entity's operations instead of on the financial statements. (Note that the personal misconduct of management, those charged with governance, or others is outside the meaning of the term *noncompliance*.)

2. The SAS distinguishes between two categories of considerations:

    a. Laws and regulations **having a direct effect** on the amounts and/or disclosures in the financial statements—The auditor should obtain sufficient appropriate audit evidence regarding material amounts and disclosures.

    b. Other laws and regulations **not having a direct effect** on the financial statements—The auditor should perform specified audit procedures that may identify noncompliance that may have a material effect on the financial statements. The specified audit procedures include inquiry of management and those charged with governance about compliance issues, inspection of any correspondence with regulatory authorities, reading minutes, and so forth.

B. **Auditor's Consideration of Compliance with Laws and Regulations**—In obtaining an understanding of the entity and its environment, the auditor should obtain an understanding of

1. The entity's applicable legal and regulatory framework; *and*
2. How the entity is complying with that framework.

C. **Audit Procedures when Noncompliance is Identified or Suspected**

1. **If information suggests possible noncompliance**—The auditor should obtain an understanding of the circumstances of the act involved and gather further information to evaluate the financial statement effect. The auditor should also evaluate the implications of noncompliance to other aspects of the audit engagement, including risk assessment and the reliability of written representations.

   2. If the auditor suspects noncompliance—The auditor should discuss the matter with management (at least one level above those suspected to be involved) and with those charged with governance, as appropriate.

   3. If unable to obtain sufficient information as to compliance—The auditor should evaluate the effect of the lack of sufficient appropriate audit evidence on the auditor's report (and consider the need for obtaining legal advice).

D. Reporting of Identified or Suspected Noncompliance

   1. Reporting noncompliance to those charged with governance—The auditor should communicate with those charged with governance any noncompliance with laws and regulations (unless it is clearly inconsequential). When management or those charged with governance is involved, the auditor should communicate to the next higher level of authority. If no higher level of authority within the entity exists, the auditor should consider obtaining legal advice.

   2. Reporting noncompliance in the auditor's report—If a material effect on the financial statements has not been appropriately reported, the auditor should modify the opinion (expressing either a qualified or adverse opinion). If the auditor has been prevented from obtaining sufficient appropriate audit evidence to evaluate the financial statement impact of the matter, the auditor should modify the opinion (expressing either a qualified opinion or disclaimer of opinion) for a scope limitation.

   3. Reporting noncompliance to regulatory/enforcement authorities—The auditor should determine whether there is a responsibility to report the matter to parties outside the entity, which may take priority over confidentiality responsibilities. The auditor should consider obtaining legal advice about this issue.

   4. Withdrawal—If the entity refuses to accept a modified opinion and if withdrawal is possible under applicable law or regulation, the auditor may withdraw from the engagement and inform those charged with governance of the reasons in writing. Likewise, if the entity does not take the appropriate corrective action regarding noncompliance issues, the auditor may withdraw if such action is permitted by applicable law or regulation.

E. Documentation—The auditor should document the identified or suspected noncompliance and the results of the discussion with management, those charged with governance, and others, as applicable. Such documentation might include:

   1. Copies of records or documents

   2. Minutes of the discussion with management, those charged with governance, and others

Using the Work of a "Specialist"

I. **AICPA Guidance**—The relevant AICPA guidance is provided by AU 620, *Using the Work of an Auditor's Specialist*. This pronouncement states that the auditor's objectives are to determine: (1) whether to use the work of an auditor's specialist; and (2) whether the work of the auditor's specialist is adequate for the auditor's purposes.

> **Definitions**
>
> *Auditor's Specialist*: An individual or organization possessing expertise in a field other than accounting or auditing, whose work in that field is used by the auditor to assist the auditor in obtaining sufficient appropriate audit evidence.
>
> *Management's Specialist*: An individual or organization possessing expertise in a field other than accounting or auditing, whose work in that field is used by the entity to assist the entity in preparing the financial statements.

    A. Note that the auditor is still responsible for the expressed opinion, so the auditor's responsibility is not reduced by using the work of an auditor's specialist.

    B. Examples of a "field of expertise other than accounting or auditing" include the following: the valuation of complex financial instruments; actuarial calculations of liabilities for employee benefits; the valuation of environmental liabilities and cleanup costs; estimation of oil and other mineral reserves; and the interpretation of contracts, laws, and regulations; and so forth.

II. **Basic Requirements of the Auditor with Respect to Using an Auditor's Specialist**—Some considerations may differ for an *internal* auditor's specialist (who is affiliated with the auditor's firm or a firm that is part of an affiliated network) or an *external* auditor's specialist (who is not affiliated with the auditor's firm).

    A. **Determining the Need**—The auditor should determine whether an auditor's specialist is needed to obtain sufficient appropriate audit evidence, taking into consideration the following:

        1. The nature of the matter involved;

        2. The risks of material misstatement involved;

        3. The significance of the matter to the audit;

        4. The auditor's experience with any previous work of the auditor's specialist; *and*

        5. Whether the auditor's specialist is subject to the audit firm's quality controls (which would apply to an internal specialist, but not to an external one).

    B. **Competence, Capabilities, and Objectivity of the Specialist**—The auditor should evaluate the competence, capabilities, and objectivity of the auditor's specialist for the auditor's purposes.

1. The auditor should consider information about the competence, capabilities, and objectivity of an auditor's specialist, which might be obtained from the following:

   a. Personal experience with the specialist's previous work

   b. Discussions with the specialist or with other auditors familiar with the specialist

   c. Knowledge of the specialist's credentials or professional/industry affiliations, including whether the work is subject to any particular technical performance standards or industry requirements

   d. Any journal articles or books written by the specialist

2. For an external auditor's specialist, the auditor should inquire about any relationships that might threaten the specialist's objectivity. The auditor should consider any threats to the specialist's objectivity, along with any safeguards that might reduce such threats to an acceptable level.

C. Obtaining an Understanding of the Field of Expertise—The auditor should obtain a sufficient understanding of the field of expertise of the auditor's specialist so that the auditor can

1. Determine the nature, scope, and objectives of the work; *and*

2. Evaluate the adequacy of that work for the auditor's purposes. This understanding may be obtained from having experience with other entities requiring that same field of expertise, through specific education in that field, or through discussion with the auditor's specialist.

D. Agreement with the Auditor's Specialist—The auditor and the auditor's specialist should agree (in writing when appropriate) about the following:

1. The nature, scope, and objectives of the work involved;

2. Their respective roles and responsibilities;

3. The nature, timing, and extent of communications between the auditor and the auditor's specialist, including any reports to be delivered; *and*

4. The requirements for the auditor's specialist to adhere to confidentiality considerations applicable to an audit engagement. The agreement between the auditor and the external specialist is usually in the form of an engagement letter.

E. Evaluating the Adequacy of the Work

1. The auditor should evaluate the adequacy of the work performed by the auditor's specialist, including the following matters:

   a. The relevance and reasonableness of the conclusions;

   b. The relevance and reasonableness of any underlying assumptions and the methods used; *and*

   c. The relevance, completeness, and accuracy of any source data used by the auditor's specialist.

2. The auditor may perform specific procedures to evaluate such work, including:

   a. Making inquiries of the specialist;

   b. Reviewing the specialist's working papers; *and*

   c. Performing certain corroborative procedures, such as performing analytical procedures, examining published data, or confirming some matters with third parties, among other possibilities.

F. If the Work is not Adequate—The auditor and the auditor's specialist should agree on any further work to be performed, or the auditor should perform additional audit procedures that are appropriate to the circumstances (which could include engaging another auditor's specialist). If the auditor is unable to resolve the matter, it could constitute a scope limitation that would result in a modified opinion.

G. Reference to the Auditor's Specialist in the Auditor's Report

1. If the auditor's report contains an *unmodified* opinion, the auditor should not refer to the work of an auditor's specialist.

2. If the auditor's report contains a *modified* opinion and the auditor believes that it would help readers understand the reason for the modification, the auditor may reference the work of an external auditor's specialist. Normally, such a reference would first require the permission of the auditor's specialist. The auditor should also point out, in the auditor's report, that such a reference does not reduce the auditor's responsibility for the expressed opinion.

III. PCAOB Guidance—The PCAOB issued its Auditing Standard No. 44 involving the use of specialists (approved by the SEC in July 2019), which is effective for audits for fiscal years ending on or after December 15, 2020. The effect was to modify or replace three specific sections of the PCAOB's codified auditing standards related to three different categories of specialists.

Definitions

Specialist: Similar to the AICPA, the PCAOB defines a specialist as follows: "... a person (or firm) possessing special skill or knowledge in a particular field other than accounting or auditing."

The PCAOB classifies "specialists" into the following three categories:

1. **Company's specialist**—A specialist employed or engaged by the company

2. **Auditor-employed specialist**—A specialist employed by the auditor's firm

3. **Auditor-engaged specialist**—A specialist engaged by the auditor's firm

---

A. Amendments to PCAOB AS § 1105 ("Audit Evidence")

1. Added an appendix to supplement the requirements when using the work of a company's specialist

   a. The auditor should obtain an understanding of the work and report/communication of the company's specialist and related company controls.

   b. The auditor should obtain an understanding of and assess the knowledge and skills of a company's specialist, including any relationship with the entity engaging the specialist – Should consider applicable certification/licensure along with the specialist's reputation, experience, and areas of specialization.

   c. The auditor should perform procedures to evaluate the work of a company's specialist, including evaluating: (a) the data, significant assumptions, and methods used; and (b) the relevance and reliability of the specialist's work to the relevant assertion(s).

2. Aligned the requirements for using the work of a company's specialist with the PCAOB's risk assessment standards—The auditor should consider (1) the significance of the specialist's work to the auditor's conclusion(s), and (2) the risk of material misstatement of the relevant assertion(s).

3. Identified factors to be considered in determining the evidence needed to support the auditor's conclusion at the relevant assertion level when using the work of a company's specialist

B. Amendments to PCAOB AS § 1201 ("Supervision of the Audit Engagement")

1. Added an appendix to supplement the requirements for supervision when using the work of an auditor-employed specialist

   a. The auditor should inform the auditor-employed specialist of the work to be done and should document that understanding.

   b. The auditor should coordinate the work of the auditor-employed specialist with other audit team members.

    c. The auditor should review the work of the auditor-employed specialist to determine whether it provides sufficient appropriate audit evidence – Should consider whether the work is consistent with the established understanding and whether the findings are consistent with the work of the specialist and other audit evidence obtained.

  2. Identified factors to be considered in determining the extent of supervision needed when using the work of an auditor-employed specialist—The extent of the supervision needed depends on (1) the significance of the specialist's work to the auditor's conclusion(s); (2) the risk of material misstatement of the relevant assertion; and (3) the specialist's expertise.

C. **Replaced PCAOB AS § 1210 (now entitled "Using the Work of an Auditor-Engaged Specialist")**

  1. Provides requirements for using the work of an auditor-engaged specialist to assist in obtaining/evaluating audit evidence

  2. Provides requirements for obtaining an understanding with the auditor-engaged specialist on the work to be done and documenting that understanding

  3. Provides requirements for assessing the knowledge, skills, and objectivity of the auditor-engaged specialist – Should consider applicable certification/licensure along with the specialist's reputation, experience, and areas of specialization

  4. Identifies factors for determining the extent of review needed when using the work of an auditor-engaged specialist

    a. The auditor should consider whether the specialist's work is consistent with the established understanding and whether the findings are consistent with the work of the specialist and other audit evidence obtained.

    b. The extent of the supervision needed depends on (1) the significance of the specialist's work to the auditor's conclusion(s); (2) the risk of material misstatement of the relevant assertion; and (3) the specialist's expertise.

Required Communications with Those Charged with Governance

After studying this lesson, you should be able to:

1. State the specific matters that the auditor is required to communicate "with those charged with governance" (and be able to define that term).

2. Understand the importance of effective two-way communication with those charged with governance on the audit engagement.

I. **AICPA Guidance**—The relevant AICPA guidance is provided by AU 260, *The Auditor's Communication with Those Charged with Governance*. This pronouncement states that the auditor's objectives are to: (1) communicate clearly the auditor's responsibilities related to the audit and an overview of the planned scope and timing of the audit and (2) obtain from those charged with governance information relevant to the audit.

Definitions

Those Charged with Governance: The person(s) or organization(s) with responsibility for overseeing the strategic direction of the entity and the obligations related to the accountability of the entity (encompasses the term "board of directors" or "audit committee" used elsewhere in the auditing standards).

Management: The person(s) with executive responsibility for the conduct of the entity's operations.

A. **Basic Auditor Responsibility**—The auditor should communicate those matters that are significant and relevant to the responsibilities of those charged with governance in overseeing the financial reporting process.

Note
The auditor is not required to perform any specific procedures to identify such matters to communicate with those charged with governance.

B. **Benefits**—Effective two-way communication with those charged with governance is important to having a constructive relationship, obtaining information relevant to the audit, and assisting those charged with governance in their role of overseeing financial reporting.

II. **Communication with Management**—The auditor may choose to discuss some matters with management before communicating them with those charged with governance, unless that is inappropriate. For example, the auditor would not normally discuss issues involving management's competence or integrity. Likewise, the auditor may choose to discuss some matters with the internal auditor(s) before communicating the matters with those charged with governance.

III. **Matters Required to Be Communicated with Those Charged with Governance**—(Note that the auditor may choose to communicate additional matters.)

A. **The Auditor's Responsibilities under GAAS**—The auditor should communicate the auditor's responsibility for expressing an opinion on the fairness of the financial statements, and point out that management is responsible for presenting the financial statements in conformity with the applicable financial reporting framework. These responsibilities could be communicated by an engagement letter.

B. **The Planned Scope and Timing of the Audit**—The auditor should communicate an overview of the planned scope and timing of the audit engagement, including any specialized skills needed and the planned use of an auditor's specialist.

C. **Significant Findings from the Audit**—The auditor should communicate:

1. The auditor's views about the qualitative aspects of the entity's significant accounting policies including the quality (not just the acceptability) of significant accounting practices, accounting estimates (including fair value estimates), and disclosures;

2. Significant difficulties encountered during the audit including significant delays caused by management, unreasonable time pressure, unavailability of expected information, etc.;

3. Significant risks identified (and why they require special audit consideration), including any significant unusual transactions;

4. Circumstances that affect the form and content of the auditor's report;

5. Disagreements with management over accounting and auditing matters whether or not those disagreements were satisfactorily resolved; *and*

6. Any other matters that the auditor believes would be important to those charged with governance in their oversight of financial reporting.

D. **Uncorrected misstatements**—The auditor should request that uncorrected misstatements be corrected and communicate any uncorrected misstatements accumulated by the auditor, including the financial statement effect (currently or in the future).

E. **Other matters**—The auditor should communicate the following matters:

1. Material misstatements communicated to management that were corrected;

2. Any significant findings or issues discussed with management;

3. Any known instances where management consulted with other accountants about accounting or auditing matters; *and*

4. The written representations that the auditor requested from management.

IV. **The Communication Process**—Clear communication by the auditor facilitates effective two-way communication with those charged with governance. Generally, the communication may be oral or in writing (effective communication may include formal presentations, written reports, or informal discussions, as determined by the auditor's judgment).

A. The auditor should communicate the significant findings from the audit in writing when oral communication is inadequate in the auditor's judgment.

B. When a significant matter is discussed with an individual member or subset of those charged with governance (such as the chair of the audit committee or others), the auditor should evaluate whether the matter should be summarized in a subsequent communication to all those charged with governance.

C. **Timing of Communications**—The auditor should communicate on a timely basis so that those charged with governance can take appropriate action. However, that timing may vary depending upon the circumstances.

D. **Adequacy of the Communication Process**—The auditor should evaluate whether the two-way communication has been adequate for purposes of the audit.

1. An inadequate two-way communication may suggest an unsatisfactory control environment, which the auditor should consider.

2. If the two-way communication is inadequate, the auditor should consider whether a scope limitation may exist and consider the possible effect on the assessment of the risks of material misstatement. This might warrant modification of the opinion, or even withdrawal.

V. **Documentation of the Communication**—The auditor should document matters communicated orally, and (when communicated in writing, the auditor should keep a copy of that communication).

VI. **Other Statements on Auditing Standards**—Other statements require that certain specific matters should be communicated to those charged with governance regarding:

A. **Illegal Acts**—The auditor should communicate any illegal acts that come to the auditor's attention.

B. When substantial doubt about the entity's ability to continue as a going concern remains after considering management's strategy, the auditor should communicate (1) the nature of the conditions identified; (2) the possible effect on the financial statements and disclosures; and (3) the effects on the auditor's report:

C. Fraud—The auditor should:

1. Inquire of the audit committee about the risks of fraud and the audit committee's knowledge of any fraud or suspected fraud;

2. Communicate any fraud discovered involving senior management and any fraud that causes a material misstatement (whether or not management is involved); *and*

3. Obtain an understanding with those charged with governance regarding communications about misappropriations committed by lower-level employees.

D. Communicating Internal Control Matters Identified in an Audit—The auditor should communicate to management and those charged with governance any identified significant deficiencies in internal control (including material weaknesses).

E. When Engaged to Communicate Key Audit Matters—In addition to adding a "Key Audit Matters" section to the auditor's report, the auditor should communicate with those charged with governance about (1) those matters determined to be key audit matters or (2) the determination that there are no key audit matters to communicate in the report.

PCAOB on Communications with Audit Committees

After studying this lesson, you should be able to:

1. Recognize the matters about which the auditor is obligated to communicate with the company's audit committee under PCAOB auditing standards.

2. Know the meaning of the terms "critical accounting estimate" and "critical accounting policies and practices" as used by the PCAOB.

3. Know the PCAOB's requirements regarding the form and timing of the auditor's communications with a company's audit committee.

I. Introduction

The PCAOB encourages effective *two-way communication* between the auditor and the audit committee. Specifically, it requires the auditor to communicate with a company's audit committee regarding the conduct of an audit and to obtain information from the audit committee relevant to the audit. It also requires the auditor to establish an understanding of the terms of the engagement with the audit committee and to obtain an engagement letter. Communications are required only to the extent that the matters are relevant to the integrated audit, so there may be fewer matters to communicate when auditing a smaller, less complex company.

Definitions

Audit Committee: A committee (or equivalent body) established by and among the board of directors of a company for the purpose of overseeing the accounting and financial reporting processes of the company and audits of the financial statements of the company; if no such committee exists with respect to the company, the entire board of directors of the company.

Critical Accounting Estimate: An accounting estimate where (a) the nature of the estimate is material due to the levels of subjectivity and judgment necessary to account for highly uncertain matters or the susceptibility of such matters to change and (b) the impact of the estimate on financial condition or operating performance is material.

Critical Accounting Policies and Practices: A company's accounting policies and practices that are both most important to the portrayal of the company's financial condition and results, and require management's most difficult, subjective, or complex judgments, often as a result of the need to make estimates about the effects of matters that are inherently uncertain.

II. Objectives

The auditor's objectives are to: (1) communicate to the audit committee the auditor's responsibilities regarding the audit and establish an understanding of the terms of the audit engagement with the audit committee; (2) obtain information from the audit committee relevant to the audit; (3) communicate to the audit committee information about the strategy and timing of the audit; and (4) provide the audit committee with timely observations about the audit that are significant.

III. Appointment and Retention

A. Significant Issues Discussed with Management in Connection with the Auditor's Appointment or Retention—The auditor should discuss with the audit committee any significant issues that the auditor discussed with management in connection with the auditor's appointment/retention.

B. Establishing an Understanding of the Terms of the Audit

1. The auditor should establish an understanding of the terms of the engagement with the audit committee, including the following matters: (a) the objective of the audit; (b) the auditor's responsibilities; and (c) management's responsibilities.

2. The auditor should provide an engagement letter to the audit committee annually.

IV. Obtaining Information and Communicating the Audit Strategy

A. Obtaining Information Relevant to the Audit —The auditor should inquire of the audit committee about matters relevant to the audit, including their knowledge of (possible) violations of laws or regulations.

B. Overall Audit Strategy, Timing of the Audit, and Significant Risks —The auditor should communicate an overview of the audit strategy (including timing of the audit) and discuss any significant risks identified during the auditor's risk assessment. The auditor should communicate the need for specialized skills or knowledge and plans to use the work of the entity's internal auditors or others (including other CPA firms) in the integrated audit.

V. Results of the Audit

A. Accounting Policies and Practices, Estimates, and Significant Unusual Transactions—The auditor should communicate the following matters: (1) *significant* accounting policies and practices; (2) *critical accounting policies and practices* (and the reasons they are considered critical); (3) *critical accounting estimates* (including a description of management's processes, significant assumptions, and significant changes to those processes or assumptions); and (4) significant unusual transactions (matters that are outside the normal course of business). If management communicates any of those matters, the auditor is not required to communicate them again at the same level of detail.

B. Auditor's Evaluation of the Quality of Financial Reporting—The auditor should communicate the following matters:

1. Qualitative aspects of significant accounting policies and practices (including any indications of management bias);

2. Assessment of critical accounting policies and practices;

3. Conclusions regarding critical accounting estimates;

4. Significant unusual transactions (and their business rationale);

5. The conformity of the financial statement presentation with applicable financial reporting framework;

6. Any new accounting pronouncements affecting financial reporting; *and*

7. Alternative accounting treatments discussed with management.

C. Other Information in Documents Containing Audited Financial Statements —The auditor should communicate the auditor's responsibilities for *other information* presented in documents containing the audited financial statements.

D. Difficult or Contentious Matters—The auditor should communicate any difficult or contentious matters for which the auditor consulted outside the engagement team.

E. Management Consultation with Other Accountants—The auditor should communicate views about any known instances where management consulted with other accountants about significant accounting or auditing matters.

F. Going-Concern Issues —The auditor should communicate about the following going-concern matters: (1) The conditions or events causing the auditor to have *substantial doubt about the company's ability to continue for a going concern for a reasonable period of time* ; (2) the basis for the auditor's conclusion, if the auditor concludes that such substantial doubt is alleviated by management's plans; and (3) if the auditor concludes that substantial doubt remains after considering management's plans, the effect on the financial statements and the auditor's report.

G. Uncorrected and Corrected Misstatements

1. **Uncorrected misstatements**—The auditor should provide the audit committee with a schedule of uncorrected misstatements that the auditor presented to management, and discuss with the audit committee the basis for the determination that the uncorrected misstatements were immaterial.

2. **Corrected misstatements**—The auditor should communicate those corrected misstatements (other than those that are clearly *trivial*) that were detected by the auditor, and discuss the implications of those matters relative to internal control over financial reporting.

H. Material Written Communications—The auditor should communicate other *material written communications* between the auditor and management.

I. Departure from the Auditor's Standard Report —When the auditor expects to modify the opinion or include explanatory language to the audit report (or an explanatory paragraph), the auditor should communicate the reasons for that.

J. Disagreements with Management—The auditor should communicate any disagreements with management over significant matters, whether or not satisfactorily resolved.

K. Difficulties Encountered in Performing the Audit —The auditor should communicate any significant difficulties encountered, such as: (1) significant delays or the unavailability of personnel; (2) unreasonable time pressures to complete the audit; (3) unreasonable management restrictions; and (4) unexpected difficulties in obtaining sufficient appropriate audit evidence.

L. Other Matters—The auditor should communicate any other matters arising out of the audit that are significant to overseeing the company's financial reporting.

VI. Form and Documentation of Communications—The auditor's communications may be oral or in writing, unless otherwise specified.

VII. Timing—The auditor should communicate all of these required matters to the audit committee on a timely basis and prior to the issuance of the auditor's report.

Internal Control—Concepts and Standards

Obtaining an Understanding of Internal Control

> **After studying this lesson, you should be able to:**
>
> 1. Understand the auditor's responsibility to obtain an understanding of an entity's internal control (in connection with the second Standard of Fieldwork under GAAS, which is now associated with one of the AICPA's "Performance Principles" underlying an audit under GAAS).
>
> 2. Explain three different ways that an auditor might document the understanding of internal control.

I. **Review Phase**—The auditor should obtain an initial understanding of internal controls and document that understanding.

    A. The auditor obtains an **understanding of internal control** and the flow of documents related to the entity's transactions primarily through:

        1. Inquiry of appropriate personnel

        2. Observation of client activities

        3. Review of documentation—The auditor reviews relevant documentation, including the client's accounting manuals, prior-year's audit documentation (working papers), etc.

    B. The auditor's internal control analysis tends to focus on the entity's major transaction cycles.

    C. **Transaction Cycle**—Defined to be a group of essentially homogeneous transactions, that is, transactions of the same type.

    D. **Implication**—A specific transaction cycle is the highest level of aggregation about which meaningful generalizations of control risk can be made, since control risk is constant within that transaction cycle. Each transaction within a specific transaction cycle is captured, processed, and recorded subject to the same set of internal control policies and procedures.

    E. **Examples of Typical Transaction Cycles**—Typical examples, include the following:

        1. Revenue/receipts

        2. Expenditures/disbursements

        3. Payroll

        4. Financing/investing activities

        5. Inventory, especially if inventory is manufactured, rather than purchased

    F. **Document the Auditor's Understanding**—The auditor should document that understanding of internal control. The extensiveness of the review and documentation varies with the circumstances (e.g., the emphasis on understanding internal controls increases if reliance on internal control is planned):

        1. **Flow charts of transaction cycles**—A graphical depiction of the client's accounting systems for major categories of transactions with emphasis on the origination, processing, and distribution of important underlying accounting documents.

            a. **Advantages**—A fairly systematic approach that is unlikely to overlook important considerations; tailored to client-specific circumstances; fairly easy for others to review and understand; and fairly easy to update from year to year.

b. **Disadvantages**—Can be rather tedious and time consuming to prepare initially although available commercial software today may eliminate much of that difficulty; the auditor might fail to recognize relevant internal control deficiencies by getting too absorbed in the details of documenting the client's system.

Computer operation/process

Document

Manual operation (off-line)

Decision point

Off-line storage (e.g., filing)

2. **Internal control questionnaires (ICQs)**—Questionnaires consisting of a listing of questions about client's control procedures and activities; a "no" answer is usually designed to indicate a control weakness.

a. **Advantages**—Generic questionnaires can be prepared in advance for clients in various industry categories with every conceivable question, so that no important question related to controls is likely to be omitted; deficiencies are easily identified by a client's "no" response to any question.

b. **Disadvantages**—Generic questionnaires are not tailored to client-specific circumstances and irrelevant questions are annoying to client personnel; the client personnel responding to the checklist of questions may conceal deficiencies by inaccurate answers without the auditor's knowledge.

3. **Narrative write-ups**—A written memo describing the important control-related activities in the transaction cycles under consideration.

a. **Advantages**—Memos can be tailored to a client's unique circumstances, can be as detailed or general as desired, and are relatively easy to prepare (and easy for reviewers to read it).

b. **Disadvantages**—It is relatively easy to overlook relevant internal control issues (strengths or weaknesses) because the analysis is fairly unstructured.

G. **Perform a Walkthrough**—The auditor may select a few transactions to trace them through the client's accounting system. The purpose is merely to get some feedback as to whether the auditor has accurately understood (and documented) the way the client entity is processing transactions. The walkthrough is not considered evidence or a form of documentation and should not be confused with tests of control.

Evaluating Internal Control

I. **Preliminary Evaluation of Internal Control**—The auditor may initially consider whether reliance on certain specific internal control strengths is appropriate. The auditor may consider assessing control risk at less than the maximum level.

   A. Consider the apparent **adequacy of controls (regarding design effectiveness)**—If internal control is perceived to be "ineffective," the auditor would assess control risk at the maximum level.

   1. Consider the possible types of errors or problems that could occur.

   2. Consider the kinds of procedures that would prevent and/or detect such errors or problems.

   3. Determine whether such controls are in place.

   4. Evaluate the implications of any identified weaknesses.

   B. Consider **cost-benefit trade-offs**—Reliance on internal controls "buys" a reduction of substantive audit work to some degree, but it "costs" additional effort to perform tests of control (and this may or may not be cost beneficial, even if the design of internal control is perceived to be effective).

   C. The auditor should document the basis for conclusions about internal control either way, whether internal control is perceived to be effective or ineffective.

II. **Perform Tests of Controls**—If reliance is planned (regarding operating effectiveness)—*Reliance* means the same thing as *to assess control risk at less than the maximum level* for purposes of accepting a somewhat higher level of detection risk.

   A. Perform tests of controls—but only for those specific control policies and procedures (strengths that justify accepting a somewhat higher level of detection risk) on which reliance is planned.

   B. The purpose of performing tests of control is to verify that the controls that looked good on paper (design effectiveness) were actually working as intended throughout the period (**operating effectiveness**).

   C. Circumstances that warrant performing tests of control (associated with a reliance strategy): (1) when the auditor's risk assessment includes an expectation regarding the operating effectiveness of controls; or (2) when the performance of substantive procedures alone do not limit audit risk to an acceptably low level.

   D. **When Performing Tests of Controls**—Select a sample of transactions and verify that the control procedures of interest were, in fact, performed on the transactions in the sample which usually requires that the control procedure be documented as it is performed. Undocumented controls may be tested by the auditor's observation of the entity's performance of such controls.

III. **Reevaluate Planned Reliance Based on the Results of These Tests of Controls**—Determine whether the results of the tests of controls are consistent with the planned reliance on internal controls. (What looked good on paper may not be working satisfactorily in reality.)

IV. **Develop a Detailed Audit Plan**—(Also referred to as an *audit program*) The auditor should prepare a written audit plan that specifies the nature, timing, and extent of further audit procedures to be performed, and the auditor should document the conclusions about control risk in planning the audit:

    A. A wholly substantive audit approach means *no reliance* on internal control (which means the same thing as *assessing control risk at the maximum level*). In other words, the auditor plans to meet the audit risk objectives by performing only substantive audit procedures without any expectation about the operating effectiveness of internal control. Tests of control would not be performed.

    B. Auditors may base their audit conclusions on both tests of controls and substantive audit procedures, although the auditor must always perform substantive procedures to some extent (i.e., the auditor cannot rely entirely on the operating effectiveness of internal control as a sole basis for conclusions), related to detection risk in the audit risk model.

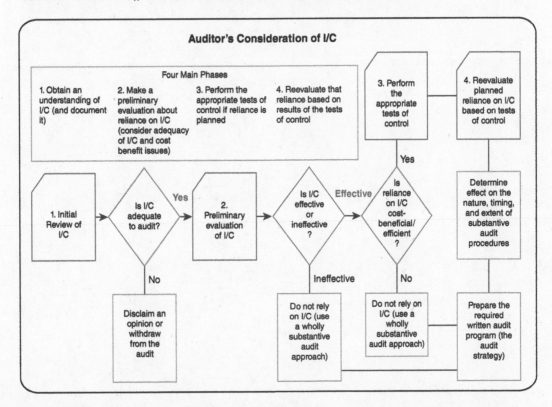

V. **Inherent Limitations**—The design and implementation of internal control is a management function (not the auditor's responsibility!) and management must evaluate the applicable costs and benefits in the design and implementation of their internal control policies and procedures.

    A. The costs of internal controls should not outweigh the benefits attributable to those controls. As a result, controls provide reasonable (not absolute) assurance.

    B. Mistakes may occur as a result of employees' misunderstandings, misjudgments, carelessness, fatigue, etc.

    C. Segregation of duties may break down due to collusion (a conspiracy among employees or management to circumvent internal controls) or management's "override" of controls—override refers to management imposing controls downward on subordinates without intending to be affected by those controls themselves.

Question
Why must auditors consider an entity's internal control in planning the audit engagement?

Answer: In order to plan an effective and efficient audit, auditors must assess control risk as a basis for setting the appropriate level of detection risk related to their substantive auditing procedures (specifically, to determine the nature, timing, and extent of those substantive procedures).

Assessing Control Risk Under AICPA Standards

After studying this lesson, you should be able to:

1. Understand the auditor's responsibility to perform risk assessment procedures.

2. Understand the entity and its environment, including internal control (with emphasis on the five interrelated components of internal control), in accordance with AICPA Professional Standards.

I. Responsibilities under AICPA Professional Standards

A. The relevant AICPA guidance is provided by AU 315, *Understanding the Entity and Its Environment and Assessing the Risks of Material Misstatement*. This pronouncement states that the auditor's objective is to "identify and assess the risks of material misstatement, whether due to fraud or error, at the financial statement and relevant assertion levels through understanding the entity and its environment, including its internal control, thereby providing a basis for designing and implementing responses to the assessed risks of material misstatement."

> This SAS provides guidance related to one of the Performance Principles. "To obtain reasonable assurance, which is a high, but not absolute, level of assurance, the auditor . . . identifies and assesses risks of material misstatement, whether due to fraud or error, based on an understanding of the entity and its environment, including the entity's internal control."

B. The AU section focuses on the auditor's requirements related to

1. Risk assessment procedures
2. Understanding the entity and its environment, including its internal control
3. Assessing the risks of material misstatement
4. Documentation

II. Risk Assessment Procedures

—The auditor should perform risk assessment procedures to obtain an understanding of the entity and its environment, including its internal control (the nature, timing, and extent of the risk assessment procedures vary with the engagement's circumstances, such as the entity's size and complexity and the auditor's experience with it).

A. **Inquiries of Management and Others**—The auditor should obtain information from inquiries made of management and others, including internal auditors, production and marketing personnel, those charged with governance, and outsiders (such as external legal counsel or valuation experts used by the entity).

B. **Observation and Inspection**—The auditor's risk assessment procedures should include observation of entity operations, inspection of documents (e.g., internal control manuals), reading reports prepared by management and those charged with governance (e.g., minutes of meetings), and visits to the entity's facilities.

C. **Analytical Procedures**—The auditor's analytical procedures performed in planning may assist the auditor in understanding the entity and its environment and identify specific risks relevant to the audit.

D. **Review Information**—The auditor should review information about the entity and its environment obtained in prior periods. The auditor should consider whether changes may have affected the relevance of that information (perhaps by making inquiries or performing a walkthrough of transactions through the entity's systems).

E. **Discussion among Audit Team Members**—The audit team should discuss the susceptibility of the entity's financial statements to material misstatements.

1. **Key members should be involved in the discussion**—But professional judgment is required to determine who should be included in that discussion. (For a multilocation audit, there may be multiple discussions for key members at each major location.)

2. **Objective of this discussion**—The purpose of the discussion is for members of the audit team to understand the potential for material misstatements of the financial statements (due to error or fraud) in specific areas assigned to them and how their work may affect other parts of the audit.

3. **The discussion should include critical issues**—Such matters include the areas of significant audit risk, the potential for management override of controls; important controls; materiality at the financial statement level and the relevant assertion level; etc.

III. **Understanding the Entity and Its Environment**—Including its internal control.

    A. The auditor's understanding of the entity and its environment consists of understanding the following: (1) industry, regulatory, and other external factors; (2) nature of the entity; (3) objectives and strategies and related business risks that may cause material misstatement of the financial statements; (4) measurement and review of the entity's financial performance; and (5) internal control.

1. **Industry, regulatory, and other external factors**—There may be specific risks of material misstatement due to the nature of the business, the degree of regulation, or other economic, technical, and competitive issues.

2. **Nature of the entity**—This refers to the entity's operations, ownership, governance, financing, etc. (Understanding these considerations may help the auditor understand the classes of transactions, account balances, and disclosures that are relevant to the financial statements.)

3. **Objectives and strategies**—The auditor should obtain an understanding of the entity's objectives and strategies, including any related business risks that may cause material misstatement of the financial statements. Strategies are operational approaches by which management intends to achieve its objectives. Business risks result from circumstances that could adversely affect the entity's ability to achieve its objectives. (Note that the auditor does not have a responsibility to identify all business risks.)

4. **Measurement and review of the entity's financial performance**—The auditor should obtain an understanding of the entity's performance measures (and their review) and indicate aspects of the entity's performance that management considers important, which may help the auditor to understand whether such pressures increase the risks of material misstatement.

5. **Obtain a sufficient understanding of internal control**—The auditor should perform risk assessment procedures to evaluate the design of controls relevant to the audit to identify types of potential misstatements. Note that inquiry alone is not sufficient to evaluate the design and implementation of a control. Consider factors that affect the risks of material misstatement; and design the tests of controls, if applicable, and the substantive procedures that are appropriate in the circumstances.

> **Note**
> *The auditor must perform substantive tests to some degree for all significant audit areas—cannot assess control risk so low that substantive testing is omitted entirely!*

    B. **The Auditor's Consideration of Internal Control**—Internal control may also be referred to as *internal control structure*. The auditor should obtain a sufficient understanding of internal control to evaluate the design of controls relevant to the audit.

> **Definition**
> *Internal Control*: A process—effected by those charged with governance, management, and other personnel—that is designed to provide reasonable assurance about the achievement of the entity's objectives with regard to reliability of financial reporting, effectiveness and efficiency of operations, and compliance with applicable laws and regulations.

C. **The Auditor's Primary Consideration**—The auditor should consider whether (and how) a specific control prevents, or detects and corrects, material misstatements in relevant assertions related to classes of transactions, account balances, or disclosures.

D. Internal control consists of five interrelated components:

1. **Control environment**—The policies and procedures that determine the overall control consciousness of the entity, sometimes called "the tone at the top."

> The auditor should evaluate the following elements that comprise the entity's control environment:
>
> Communication and enforcement of integrity and ethical values
>
> Commitment to competence
>
> Participation of those charged with governance (including their interaction with internal and external auditors)
>
> Management's philosophy and operating style
>
> The entity's organizational structure
>
> The entity's assignment of authority and responsibility (including internal reporting relationships)
>
> Human resource policies and practices

2. **Risk assessment**—The policies and procedures involving the identification, prioritization, and analysis of relevant risks as a basis for managing those risks.

> The auditor's responsibilities include:
>
> Inquiring about business risks that management has identified relevant to financial reporting and considering their implications to the financial statements
>
> Considering how management identified (and decided how to manage) business risks relevant to financial reporting
>
> Considering the implications to the risk assessment process when the auditor identifies business risks that management failed to identify

3. **Information and communication systems**—The policies and procedures related to the identification, capture, and exchange of information in a form and time frame that enable people to carry out their responsibilities.

> The auditor's responsibilities include obtaining the following:
>
> Sufficient knowledge to understand the classes of transactions that are significant to the financial statements and the procedures and relevant documents related to financial reporting
>
> An understanding of how incorrect processing of transactions is resolved
>
> An understanding of the automated (IT) and manual procedures used to prepare the financial statements and how misstatements may occur
>
> An understanding of how transactions originate with the entity's business processes
>
> Sufficient knowledge to understand how the entity communicates financial reporting roles and responsibilities

4. Control activities—The policies and procedures that help ensure that management directives are carried out, especially those related to

    a. Authorization,

    b. Segregation of duties,

    c. Performance reviews,

    d. Information processing, *and*

    e. Physical controls.

> The auditor's responsibilities include:
>
> Obtaining an understanding of how IT affects control activities relevant to planning the audit (especially with respect to application controls and general controls); and
>
> Considering whether the entity has established effective controls related to IT (especially with respect to maintaining the integrity of information and the security of data).

5. Monitoring—The policies and procedures involving the ongoing assessment of the quality of internal control effectiveness over time.

> The auditor should obtain an understanding of the sources of the information related to the entity's monitoring activities and the basis upon which management considers the information to be reliable.

E. Inherent Limitations of Internal Control—Internal control provides reasonable, not absolute, assurance about achieving the entity's objectives. Internal control may be ineffective owing to human failures (mistakes and misunderstandings) and controls may be circumvented by collusion or management override of controls. The cost of an internal control procedure should not exceed the benefit expected to be derived from it.

Performing Procedures in Response to Assessed Risks

After studying this lesson, you should be able to:

1. Assess the risk of material misstatement.

2. Document various internal control matters.

3. Link audit responses to the risks of material misstatement at the financial-statement level and the relevant-assertion level, in accordance with AICPA Professional Standards.

I. Responsibilities under AICPA Professional Standards

A. The primary relevant AICPA guidance is provided by AU 315, *Understanding the Entity and Its Environment and Assessing the Risks of Material Misstatement*. This pronouncement states that the auditor's objective is to "identify and assess the risks of material misstatement, whether due to fraud or error, at the financial statement and relevant assertion levels through understanding the entity and its environment, including its internal control, thereby providing a basis for designing and implementing responses to the assessed risks of material misstatement."

B. Additional relevant guidance is provided by AU 330, *Performing Audit Procedures in Response to Assessed Risks and Evaluating the Audit Evidence Obtained*. The auditor's objective is "to obtain sufficient appropriate audit evidence regarding the assessed risks of material misstatement through designing and implementing appropriate responses to those risks."

II. Assessing the Risk of Material Misstatement

A. Auditor's Responsibility—The auditor should identify and assess the risks of material misstatement

1. At the financial statement level; *and*

2. At the relevant assertion level related to classes of transactions, account balances, and disclosures.

B. Internal Control Considerations—A weak control environment (such as management's lack of competence) may have pervasive financial statement effects and require an overall response by the auditor. The auditor's understanding of internal control may also raise questions about the auditability of the entity's financial statements (e.g., sufficient appropriate evidence may not be available).

C. Significant Risks—These are risks that the auditor believes require special audit consideration. The auditor should consider the nature of the risks identified (e.g., whether the risk may relate to fraud, significant economic developments, the complexity of transactions, related-party transactions, subjective measurement, or nonroutine transactions that are unusual for the entity).

D. Risks for which Substantive Procedures Alone do not Provide Sufficient Appropriate Audit Evidence—The auditor should evaluate the design and implementation of controls over such risks, since it is not possible to reduce detection risk to an acceptably low level with substantive procedures by themselves: for example, when IT is a significant part of the entity's information system and transactions are initiated, authorized, recorded, processed, and reported electronically without an audit trail.

E. Revision of Risk Assessment—Risk assessment is an iterative process and the assessment of risks may change as additional evidence is obtained. (For example, when performing tests of controls, evidence may be obtained that controls are ineffective, or when performing substantive procedures, misstatements may be detected that suggest that controls are ineffective.)

III. **Documentation**—The form of the documentation requires professional judgment and varies with the circumstances, including the complexity of the entity and the extent to which IT is used. The documentation may include narrative descriptions, questionnaires, flowcharts, and checklists.

    A. The auditor should document the following matters:

        1. The discussion with members of the audit team about the potential for misstatements due to error or fraud including how and when that discussion occurred, the subject matter discussed, the team members involved, and significant decisions reached about the planned responses to those risks;

        2. Major elements of the understanding of each of the five components of internal control to assess the risk of material misstatement, the sources of information used for that understanding, and the risk assessment procedures performed;

        3. The assessment of the risks of material misstatement (both at the financial statement level and at the relevant assertion level) and the basis for that assessment; *and*

        4. The risks identified and the related controls the auditor evaluated.

    B. Another standard (AU 330) focuses on the auditor's requirements related to:

        1. Overall responses to the risks of material misstatement at the financial statement level;

        2. Responses to the risks of material misstatement at the relevant assertion level (in determining the nature, timing, and extent of further audit procedures, including tests of the operating effectiveness of controls and substantive procedures);

        3. Evaluating the sufficiency and appropriateness of the audit evidence obtained; *and*

        4. Documentation.

IV. **Overall Responses to the Risks of Material Misstatement at the Financial Statement Level**

    A. As the risk of material misstatement increases, the auditor may assign more experienced staff to the engagement; provide closer supervision; use specialists; use more unpredictable audit procedures; and/or make appropriate changes in the nature, timing, or extent of further audit procedures.

    B. The assessment of the risk of material misstatement may influence the auditor's strategy in using a *substantive approach* or a *combined approach* that uses both tests of controls (regarding the operating effectiveness of controls) and substantive procedures.

V. **Responses to the Risks of Material Misstatement at the Relevant Assertion Level**—The assessment of the risk of material misstatement may affect the auditor's decisions regarding the nature, timing, and extent of further audit procedures, including the tests of the operating effectiveness of controls and the substantive procedures.

    A. Substantive procedures must be performed to some degree for all relevant assertions related to each material class of transactions, account balance, or disclosure (i.e., the auditor cannot rely totally on the effectiveness of the entity's internal controls).

    B. **Nature**—This refers to the purpose of further audit procedures (tests of controls or substantive procedures) and their type (inspection, observation, inquiry, confirmation, recalculation, reperformance, or analytical procedures).

    C. **Timing**—This refers to when the further audit procedures are performed (at year-end or before year-end, called "interim"); performing substantive procedures at year-end is usually more effective with a higher risk of material misstatement.

    D. **Extent**—This refers to the quantity of an audit procedure to be performed (such as sample size) based on the auditor's judgment; computer-assisted audit techniques (CAATs) may be used to extensively test electronic transactions/files.

    E. **Tests of Controls**—To determine the operating effectiveness of controls

1. The auditor should perform tests of controls when the auditor's risk assessment includes an expectation of the operating effectiveness of controls. (Note that this is frequently referred to as "relying" on internal control as a partial basis for the auditor's conclusions, or "assessing control risk at less than the maximum level.")

2. The auditor should also perform tests of control when substantive procedures alone do not provide sufficient appropriate evidence at the relevant assertion level. For example, when the entity uses IT extensively and no audit trail exists.

3. **Nature of tests of controls**—Tests of control might include making inquiries of entity personnel; inspection of documents, reports, or files, indicating performance of the control; observation of the application of the control; and auditor reperformance of the control. Note that inquiry alone is not sufficient to test controls. When controls are not documented, the auditor may be able to obtain evidence about their operating effectiveness by observation or the use of CAATs.

> **Note**
> When the auditor identifies a significant risk of material misstatement, but plans to rely on the effectiveness of controls that mitigate that risk, the auditor should test those controls in the current period.

4. **Timing of tests of controls**—When obtaining evidence about the effectiveness of controls for an interim period, the auditor should determine what evidence is required for the remaining period. If planning to rely on controls that have changed since last tested, the auditor should test those controls currently. If planning to rely on controls that have not changed since last tested, the auditor should test the operating effectiveness of those controls at least every third year (i.e., no more than two years should pass before retesting such controls).

5. **Extent of tests of controls**—When a control is applied on a transaction basis (e.g., matching approved purchase orders to suppliers' invoices) and if the control operates frequently, the auditor should use audit sampling techniques to test operating effectiveness; when a control is applied on a periodic basis (e.g., monthly reconciliation of the accounts receivable subsidiary ledger to the general ledger), the auditor should perform procedures appropriate for testing smaller populations.

F. **Substantive Procedures**—The issues related to the auditor's search for material misstatements will be discussed later in connection with lessons on audit evidence.

VI. **Evaluating the Sufficiency and Appropriateness of the Audit Evidence Obtained**

A. An audit is an iterative process, so the planned audit procedures may need to be modified; for example, identified misstatements from substantive procedures may alter the auditor's judgment about the effectiveness of controls.

B. Consider all relevant audit evidence—The auditor should consider all relevant audit evidence, whether it appears to corroborate or contradict the relevant assertions.

VII. **Documentation**—The auditor should document the following:

A. The overall responses to address the assessed risk of misstatement at the financial statement level;

B. The nature, timing, and extent of the further audit procedures;

C. The linkage of those procedures with the assessed risks at the relevant assertion level;

D. The results of the audit procedures; *and*

E. The conclusions reached in the current audit about the operating effectiveness of controls tested in a prior audit.

Required Communications

After studying this lesson, you should be able to:

1. Know the meaning of the terms *significant deficiency* and *material weakness*.

2. Understand the auditor's responsibility to communicate identified internal control deficiencies to management and those charged with governance, in accordance with AICPA Professional Standards.

I. Required Communications Related to Internal Control Deficiencies (Weaknesses)

Definitions

Control Deficiency: When the design or operation of a control does not allow management or employees, in the normal course of performing their assigned functions, to prevent or detect misstatements on a timely basis.

Deficiency in Design: When a control necessary to meet the control objective is missing, or when the control objective is not always met, even if the control operates as designed.

Deficiency in Operation: When a properly designed control does not operate as designed, or when the person performing the control does not have the authority or competence to effectively perform the control.

Significant Deficiency: A deficiency (or combination of deficiencies) in internal control that is less severe than a material weakness, yet important enough to merit attention by those charged with governance.

Material Weakness: A deficiency (or combination of deficiencies) in internal control such that there is a reasonable possibility that a material misstatement of the entity's financial statements will not be prevented or detected and corrected on a timely basis.

A. **Evaluating Control Deficiencies**—The auditor must determine whether identified deficiencies are significant deficiencies or material weaknesses.

1. The auditor should consider both the likelihood and potential magnitude of misstatement in making that evaluation—multiple control deficiencies affecting the same financial statement item increases the likelihood of misstatement.

2. The auditor may wish to consider the possible mitigating effects of compensating controls that can reduce the severity of the effects of a deficiency.

3. Risk factors that affect whether there is a reasonable possibility that a deficiency will result in a misstatement include the following:

    a. The nature of the accounts, classes of transactions, disclosures, and assertions involved;

    b. The susceptibility of the related asset or liability to loss or fraud;

    c. The subjectivity, complexity, or extent of judgment involved;

    d. The interaction or relationship of the control with other controls;

    e. The interaction among the deficiencies; *and*

    f. The possible future consequences of the deficiency.

4. Specific indicators of material weaknesses include the following:

    a. Identification of any fraud involving senior management (whether or not material);

    b. Restatement of previously issued financial statements to correct a material misstatement due to error or fraud;

    c. Identification of a material misstatement in the financial statements by the auditor that would not have been identified by the entity's internal control; *and*

    d. Ineffective oversight of the entity's financial reporting and internal control by those charged with governance.

II. Communicating Identified Control Deficiencies—The auditor must communicate the significant deficiencies and material weaknesses identified in the audit.

  A. Form of Communication—Identified significant deficiencies and material weaknesses must be communicated in writing to management and those charged with governance. Certain matters may not be communicated to management when communication would be inappropriate (e.g., matters that raise questions about management integrity or competence). Lesser matters (not significant deficiencies) may be communicated to the appropriate level of operational management with the authority to take remedial action. Such lesser matters may be communicated either orally or in writing.

  B. Timing—The required communication is best made by the "report release date" and should be made no later than 60 days following the report release date. The "report release date" is the date that the auditor grants the entity permission to use the auditor's report in connection with the audited financial statements.

  C. Early Communication is Permitted—The auditor may choose to verbally communicate certain significant deficiencies and material weaknesses during the audit (e.g., to permit timely correction). However, all identified significant deficiencies and material weaknesses must still be communicated in writing no later than 60 days following the report release date, including those matters communicated orally during the audit.

> **Note**
> There is a slight difference as to timing between AICPA requirements and those of the PCAOB. The AICPA requires "timely" communication of these internal control matters (no later than the "documentation completion date," that is, 60 days after the report release date). The PCAOB requires such matters be communicated prior to the release of the auditor's report.

  D. Other Matters—The auditor may choose to communicate other matters believed to be beneficial to the entity (including deficiencies that are not "significant deficiencies") either in writing or verbally. If communicated verbally, the auditor must document such communication.

  E. The written communication about significant deficiencies and material weaknesses should:

    1. State that the purpose of the audit was to express an opinion on the financial statements, not to express an opinion on the effectiveness of internal control

    2. State that the auditor is not expressing an opinion on the effectiveness of internal control

    3. State that the auditor's consideration of internal control was not designed to identify all significant deficiencies or material weaknesses.

    4. Include the definition of the terms *material weakness* and *significant deficiency*, as applicable.

    5. Identify the matters that are considered to be material weaknesses and significant deficiencies, as applicable.

    6. State that the communication is intended solely for the use of management, those charged with governance, and others within the organization (it should not be used by anyone other than those specified parties)—if such a communication is required to be given to a governmental authority, that specific reference may be added.

> **Note**
> The auditor may include additional statements regarding the general inherent limitations of internal control, including the possibility of management override, but such comments are not required.

Sample Written Communication about Internal Control Deficiencies

In planning and performing our audit of the financial statements of ABC Company (the "Company") as of and for the year ended December 31, 20XX, in accordance with auditing standards generally accepted in the United States of America, we considered the Company's internal control over financial reporting (internal control) as a basis for designing our auditing procedures for the purpose of expressing our opinion on the financial statements, but not for the purpose of expressing an opinion on the effectiveness of the Company's internal control. Accordingly, we do not express an opinion on the effectiveness of the Company's internal control.

Our consideration of internal control was for the limited purpose described in the preceding paragraph and was not designed to identify all deficiencies in internal control that might be significant deficiencies or material weaknesses and therefore, there can be no assurance that all deficiencies, significant deficiencies, or material weaknesses have been identified. However, as discussed below, we identified certain deficiencies in internal control that we consider to be material weaknesses (and other deficiencies that we consider to be significant deficiencies—*add this phrase only if applicable*).

A deficiency in internal control exists when the design or operation of a control does not allow management or employees, in the normal course of performing their assigned functions, to prevent, or detect and correct misstatements on a timely basis. A material weakness is a deficiency, or a combination of deficiencies, in internal control, such that there is a reasonable possibility that a material misstatement of the entity's financial statements will not be prevented, or detected and corrected on a timely basis. (We consider the following deficiencies in the Company's internal control to be material weaknesses:)

(*Describe the material weaknesses that were identified.*)

(A significant deficiency is a deficiency, or a combination of deficiencies, in internal control that is less severe than a material weakness, yet important enough to merit attention by those charged with governance. We consider the following deficiencies to be significant deficiencies in internal control:)

(*Describe the significant deficiencies that were identified.*)

This communication is intended solely for the information and use of management, (*identify the body or individuals charged with governance*), others within the organization, and (*identify any specified governmental authorities*) and is not intended to be and should not be used by anyone other than these specified parties.

F. The auditor should not issue a written communication stating that no significant deficiencies were identified—However, the auditor is permitted to add a comment that no material weaknesses were identified, perhaps as requested to submit to a governmental authority.

G. Management may issue a written response to the auditor's communication to indicate corrective action taken or planned or stating management's belief that the costs of correction exceed the benefits—If such a written response is included with the auditor's communication, the auditor should add a paragraph to disclaim an opinion on management's written response.

Using the Work of an Internal Audit Function

After studying this lesson, you should be able to:

1. Understand the independent auditor's responsibilities to evaluate the internal auditors' competence and objectivity when considering the role of an entity's internal audit function for purposes of assessing control risk and/or providing assistance with substantive procedures.

I. **AICPA Guidance**—The relevant AICPA guidance is provided by AU 610 (SAS No. 128), *Using the Work of Internal Auditors,* which has been clarified to be consistent with International Standards on Auditing.

Note

The requirements of this standard do not apply if (1) the activities of the internal audit function are not relevant to the audit, or (2) the external auditor does not expect to use the work of the internal audit function in obtaining audit evidence. There is no requirement that external auditors use the work of an internal audit function.

The AICPA defines an **internal audit function** as "a function of an entity that performs assurance and consulting activities designed to evaluate and improve the effectiveness of the entity's governance, risk management, and internal control processes."

II. **Two Ways to Use the Work of an Internal Audit Function**—The external auditor may use the internal audit function to (1) obtain audit evidence that modifies the nature, timing, or extent of audit procedures to be performed by the external auditor; and/or (2) provide direct assistance to the external auditor under the external auditor's direction, supervision, and review.

A. Using the internal audit function **to obtain audit evidence** means, in effect, substituting the internal auditors' work (related to tests of controls and/or substantive procedures) in place of work that would otherwise be performed by the external auditor.

1. There are three necessary conditions before the external auditor may use the internal audit function to obtain audit evidence

a. **Objectivity**—The internal audit function's organizational status (dealing with the level to whom the function reports, such as those charged with governance, rather than middle management) and relevant policies and procedures must support the objectivity of the internal auditors.

b. **Competence**—The internal auditors must be competent (related to their education, experience, certification, etc.) to perform reliable work.

c. **Systematic and disciplined approach**—The internal audit function must apply a "systematic and disciplined approach, including quality control." The external auditor should not rely on "internal audit–like" work that is conducted in an informal, unstructured, or ad hoc way. However, the degree of formality and structure may vary with the nature, size, and complexity of the entity involved.

2. **Significant judgments**—The external auditor should make all significant audit judgments.

3. The external auditor should perform more of the work directly when (a) the degree of judgment involved increases, (b) the assessed risk of material misstatement increases, (c) the organizational status and objectivity of the internal auditors decreases, or (d) the competence of the internal auditors decreases.

4. Procedures to be performed by the external auditor when using the work of the internal audit function to obtain audit evidence include the following:

    a. The external auditor should read the internal audit function's reports related to the work the external auditor plans to use;

    b. The external auditor should perform procedures to determine whether the internal audit function's work was adequately planned, performed, reviewed, and documented, and whether the conclusions reached were appropriate; *and*

    c. The external auditor should reperform some of the internal audit function's work that the external auditor plans to use.

5. **Communication with those charged with governance**—The external auditor should communicate plans to use the work of the internal audit function to obtain audit evidence.

B. Using the internal audit function **to provide direct assistance** means using internal auditors to perform audit procedures subject to the external auditor's direction, supervision, and review.

1. There are two necessary conditions before the external auditor may use the internal audit function to obtain audit evidence.

    a. **Objectivity**—The internal audit function's organizational status and relevant policies and procedures must support the objectivity of the internal auditors.

    b. **Competence**—The internal auditors must be competent to perform reliable work.

2. **Determining the nature and extent of the internal auditors' direct assistance**—The external auditor should consider the internal audit function's objectivity and competence, the assessed risk of material misstatement, and the amount of judgment involved.

> **Note**
> *A systematic and disciplined approach is not a requirement for using the internal audit function to provide direct assistance, since the internal auditors' work is subject to the direction, supervision, and review of the external auditor.*

3. Procedures to be performed by the external auditor when using the internal audit function to provide direct assistance

    a. The external auditor should obtain written acknowledgment from management or those charged with governance (either as part of the engagement letter or as a separate document) that the internal auditors will be allowed to follow the external auditor's directives without interference.

    b. The external auditor should appropriately direct, supervise, and review the work performed by the internal auditors.

    c. The external auditor should test some of the work performed by the internal auditors.

4. Communication with those charged with governance—The external auditor should communicate how the auditor plans to use the internal auditors to provide direct assistance.

III. Documentation Requirements

A. When using the internal audit function to obtain audit evidence, the external auditor should document the following:

1. The evaluation of the internal audit function's organizational status and objectivity of the internal auditors, the function's competence, and the application of a systematic and disciplined approach;

2. The nature and extent of the work used and the basis for that decision; *and*

3. The external auditor's procedures performed to evaluate the work of the internal audit function.

B. When using the internal audit function to provide direct assistance— the external auditor should document the following:

1. The evaluation of the internal audit function's organizational status and objectivity of the internal auditors and the function's competence;

2. The basis for the external auditor's decision about the nature and extent of the work performed by the internal auditors; and

3. Identification of the working papers prepared by the internal auditors, and the nature and extent of the external auditor's review and testing of the internal auditors' work.

Note

There is no division of responsibility regarding the work of the internal auditors. The external auditor's report should not refer to the internal auditors' work in the audit report! The external auditor remains fully responsible for all the conclusions expressed.

Performing Further Procedures and Obtaining Evidence

Internal Control: Transaction Cycles

Specific Transaction Cycles

> **After studying this lesson, you should be able to:**
>
> 1. Understand what is meant by the term *transaction cycle* and why auditors tend to focus on transaction cycles when assessing control risk.
>
> 2. Identify several examples of transaction cycles that an auditor might consider.

I. **Transaction Cycle**—A transaction cycle is a group of essentially homogeneous transactions, that is, transactions of a particular type. The bulk of a company's economic activities can be grouped into a relative few categories called transaction cycles.

II. **Implication**—Within a given category of transactions, control risk is essentially constant, since all transactions within that category are processed subject to the same configuration of internal control policies and procedures. A transaction cycle is, therefore, the highest level of aggregation for which control risk may be viewed as a constant.

III. **Transaction Cycles Covered in This Lesson**

  A. Revenue/receipts

  B. Expenditures/disbursements

  C. Payroll

  D. Inventory, especially manufactured inventory (since purchased inventory would be similar to expenditures/disbursements as presented here)

  E. Fixed assets

  F. Investing/financing

Exam Hint

As a tool to analyze the audit considerations of internal control policies and procedures in each transaction cycle, remember that internal controls (specifically, "control activities") should "SCARE"! Note that this is intended to be a helpful memory aid simply to recall some basic points of emphasis that are useful to auditors in looking at the relative strength or weakness of controls in a particular transaction cycle. In this context, "SCARE" represents:

Segregation of duties,

Controls (as in physical controls),

Authorization,

Reviews (as in performance reviews), *and*

EDP/IT (information processing).

IV. **The Framework "SCARE"**—This acronym is easy to remember and it is helpful in identifying relevant internal control considerations that are associated with "control activities" in the AICPA Professional Standards:

  A. **Segregation of Duties**—This is also referred to as separation of duties and involves separating incompatible functions to the extent possible. The same employee should not normally (1) authorize transactions (execution function), (2) have access to the related assets (custody function), and (3) perform accounting activities (record keeping function) in the ordinary course of duties. In essence, these three activities are like points on a triangle and each point of the triangle should ideally be vested in different employees, subject to cost-benefit considerations.

Note
The applicable SAS describes control activities in terms of five specific considerations: (1) authorization; (2) segregation of duties; (3) physical controls; (4) information processing; and (5) performance reviews.

B. Controls (Physical Controls)—Access to assets (and to important accounting documents and computer systems) should be limited to authorized personnel. In addition, assets should be periodically counted, as appropriate, and compared to the corresponding accounting records for agreement. This is important in safeguarding assets and in establishing accountability for assets.

C. Authorization—Transactions should be executed in accordance with management's authorization.

D. Reviews (Performance Reviews)—Actual performance should be compared to appropriate budgets and forecasts. Internal data should be compared to external sources of information as appropriate. Analyses of relationships should be performed and investigative and corrective action should be taken as needed.

E. EDP/IT (Information Processing)—Information technology (IT) controls consist of two basic categories:

1. General controls, which are policies and procedures that have widespread effect on many specific applications

2. Application controls, which refer specifically to the processing of particular computer applications

Note
EDP *as used here is an outdated reference to* electronic data processing *that has been replaced by the more contemporary term* IT *for information technology.*

Revenue/Receipts—Sales

I. Flow Chart of Typical Internal Controls for Sales

II. Internal Control Objectives—The objectives of internal controls in this area are to provide reasonable assurance that:

A. Goods and services are provided in accordance with management's authorization (and based on approved orders).

B. Terms of sale (including prices and any discounts) are in accordance with management's authorization.

C. Credit terms and limits are properly established (as authorized).

D. Deliveries of goods and services result in accurate and timely billings.

E. Any sales-related discounts and adjustments (including returns) are in accordance with management's authorization.

III. Audit Considerations (Framed by "SCARE")—The entity's control activities should address the following matters:

A. **Segregation of duties**—Separate the execution (authorization), record-keeping (accounting), and custody (access) functions.

1. Credit to customers should be granted by an independent department (separate from sales staff which may be paid on commission and which may have an incentive to view everyone as creditworthy).

2. An independent employee should review the statements to customers.

3. Returns should be accounted for by an independent clerk in the shipping/receiving area.

B. Controls (Physical Controls)

   1. Computer passwords should be used to limit unauthorized access to the accounting systems.

   2. Any inventory involved should be secured with access limited to authorized personnel.

C. Authorization—The entity's transactions should be executed as authorized by management.

   1. Management should review the terms of sales transactions and indicate that approval on the sales invoice (billing).

   2. Management should usually establish general approvals of transactions within specified limits and specifically approve transactions outside of those prescribed limits.

   3. Management should approve the entity's adjusting journal entries.

D. Reviews (Performance Reviews)

   1. The entity's recorded sales should be compared to appropriate budgets and forecasts.

   2. Related accounting documents should be compared on a timely basis—for example, sales invoices and shipping documents should be compared to verify that the sales transactions were recorded in the proper period, which is referred to as proper cutoff.

E. EDP/IT (Information Processing)—The auditor should agree the financial statement amount(s) to the applicable general ledger account(s).

   1. Important accounting documents (e.g., shipping documents and sales invoices) should be prenumbered and the numerical sequence should be accounted for.

   2. An aged trial balance for accounts receivable should be agreed (or reconciled) to the general ledger control account; the aging provides important information about the quality of the receivables and the need for follow-up audit procedures.

Revenue/Receipts—Cash

After studying this lesson, you should be able to:

1. Identify the primary accounting documents and internal control objectives associated with an entity's revenue-receipts cycle (with emphasis on cash collection).

2. Understand the primary control activities normally associated with an entity's revenue-receipts cycle (with emphasis on cash collection).

I. Flow Chart of Typical Processing of Cash Receipts

II. Internal Control Objectives—The objectives of internal controls in this area are to provide reasonable assurance that:

A. Access to cash receipts records and accounts receivable records is limited to authorized personnel.

B. Detailed cash and account balance records are reconciled with control accounts and bank statements at least monthly.

C. All cash receipts are correctly recorded in the period received.

III. Audit Considerations (Framed by "SCARE")—The entity's control activities should address the following matters:

A. Segregation of Duties

1. A listing of cash receipts (sometimes referred to as a *remittance listing* or *log of cash receipts*) is prepared upon opening the mail in the mail room; checks are restrictively endorsed immediately ("for deposit only . . . ")

2. Cash-related activities, which are handled by separate personnel as appropriate are as follows:

a. Opening the mail—handling the checks received, and verifying the accuracy of the payment indicated on the enclosed "remittance advice" (the stub returned with the customer's payment on account)

b. Making the deposit—deposits should be made daily

c. Applying payments received to the appropriate customers' accounts receivable

d. Preparing the bank reconciliation on a timely basis

B. Controls (Physical Controls)

1. Employees with access to cash receipts should be "bonded," which is a type of insurance for which the employer pays an insurance premium and which involves background checks on the applicable employees.

2. Receipts should be deposited daily, not accumulated in someone's desk drawer for an occasional deposit.

3. Access to cash receipts (including access to documents) should be limited to those authorized—that includes the appropriate use of passwords.

4. The company might use a *lockbox* whereby payments from customers are directly received by the bank, thereby avoiding the company's mail room.

C. Authorization—The entity's transactions should be executed as authorized by management.

1. Adjusting journal entries should be approved by management.

2. Bank reconciliations should be appropriately reviewed with the reviewer's approval indicated.

D. Reviews (Performance Reviews)

1. The initial cash receipts listing from the mail room should be compared to the total according to the cash receipts journal, and traced to that day's bank deposit to show that what was received was, in fact, deposited.

2. The cash accounts should be reconciled with the bank statements on a timely basis by someone not involved in handling cash receipts or updating the accounting records.

E. EDP/IT (Information Processing)

1. In general, there should be adequate documentation supporting transactions and account balances (important documents should be prenumbered and the numerical sequence properly accounted for).

2. For cash transactions received *on site,* there should be adequate *point of sale* cash registers and use of prenumbered receipts.

Expenditures/Disbursements

After studying this lesson, you should be able to:

1. Identify the primary accounting documents and internal control objectives associated with an entity's expenditure/disbursements cycle.

2. Understand the primary control activities normally associated with an entity's expenditure/disbursements cycle.

I. Flow Chart of Typical Processing for Expenditures/Disbursements

II. Objectives of Internal Controls over Purchases and Accounts Payable—The objectives are to provide reasonable assurance that:

A. Goods and services are obtained in accordance with management's authorization and based on approved orders—considering quantity, quality, vendors, etc. This is usually handled by a separate "Purchasing Department" to centralize these activities.

B. The terms of acquisitions (including prices and quantities) are in accordance with management's authorization.

C. All goods and services received are accurately accounted for on a timely basis.

D. Adjustments to vendor accounts are made according to management's authorization.

E. Only authorized goods and services are accepted and paid for (and payments are timely to take advantage of any cash discounts available for prompt payment).

F. Amounts payable for goods and services received are accurately recorded and properly classified.

G. Access to purchasing, receiving, and accounts payable records is limited to authorized personnel.

III. Objectives of Internal Controls over Cash Disbursements—The objectives are to provide reasonable assurance that:

A. Disbursements are for authorized expenditures as approved by management.

B. Disbursements are recorded at the proper amounts and with the appropriate classifications.

C. Periodic comparisons are made between the supporting detailed accounting records (including bank reconciliations) and the general ledger control accounts.

D. Any adjusting journal entries for cash accounts are in accordance with management's authorization.

E. Access to cash and disbursement records is limited to authorized personnel.

IV. Audit Considerations (Framed by "SCARE")—The entity's control activities should address the following matters related to the expenditures/disbursement transactions cycle:

A. Segregation of Duties

1. A separate purchasing department handles the purchasing activities (after a duly approved request for goods or services has been received from the department making the request).

2. The purchasing personnel (execution function) are independent of those in receiving (custody function) and in accounting (record-keeping function), including the accounts payable personnel. The accounts payable personnel should also be independent of those involved in processing the related cash disbursements.

3. Bank reconciliations are prepared by someone not having other involvement in handling cash receipts, cash disbursements, or record keeping.

B. Controls (Physical Controls)

1. There should be appropriate physical control over unused checks to limit access to authorized personnel.

2. Employees with the ability to initiate cash disbursements should be "bonded."

3. Access to cash disbursements or to related documents should be limited to authorized personnel.

C. Authorization—The entity's transactions should be executed as authorized by management.

1. All adjusting journal entries should be approved by management.

2. Only authorized personnel should be able to order goods and services on the company's behalf.

3. The department requesting the purchase of goods or services should indicate their acceptance of the goods or services received and approval, before payment is made.

D. Reviews (Performance Reviews)

1. An appropriate employee should compare the suppliers' monthly statements with recorded payables.

2. An appropriate employee should compare the purchase order, "receiver," and vendor's invoice for agreement to establish that the invoice is for goods and services received and as authorized. (The invoice should be approved before payment is made and available cash discounts for prompt payment should be taken.)

E. EDP/IT (Information Processing)

1. Detailed records should be maintained to support the general ledger payable account.

2. Prenumbered purchase orders should be used (and the numerical sequence accounted for).

3. Prenumbered checks should be used (and the numerical sequence accounted for).

4. The supporting documents (including vendors' invoices) should be canceled as "paid" immediately upon payment to prevent double payments.

5. Two signatures should be required on checks. (Any signature plates should be kept in a secure place to prevent unauthorized use.)

F. Note the difference between a "vouchers payable" system and an "accounts payable" system:

1. An **accounts payable** system keeps track of payables by the name of the vendor. (Hence, payables are identified by the total amount owed to the various individual suppliers.)

2. A **vouchers payable** system keeps track of individual transactions without summarizing amounts owed in total to individual vendors. (There can be numerous vouchers payable to an individual vendor, but the payables are identified by voucher number, not by vendor name. An entity that uses a vouchers payable system can confirm individual transactions, but cannot confirm the total amount owed to a given vendor, which has implications to the vendor's auditor and how confirmation requests should be designed.)

Payroll Cycle

After studying this lesson, you should be able to:

1. Identify the primary accounting documents and internal control objectives associated with an entity's payroll cycle.

2. Understand the primary control activities normally associated with an entity's payroll cycle.

I. Flow Chart of Typical Internal Controls for Payroll

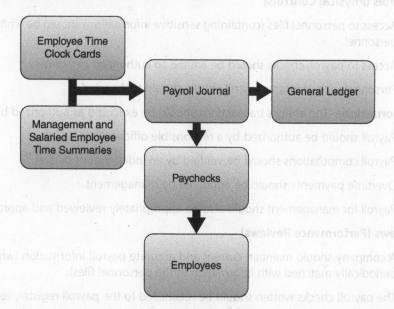

II. Objectives of Internal Controls over Payroll—The objectives are to provide reasonable assurance that:

A. Payroll withholdings and deductions are based on appropriate supporting authorizations.

B. Compensation is made only to valid employees at authorized rates and for services actually rendered.

C. Gross pay, withholdings, deductions, and net pay are correctly computed.

D. Payroll costs and liabilities are appropriately classified and summarized in the proper periods.

E. Appropriate comparisons are made of personnel, payroll, and work records at reasonable intervals.

F. Net pay and related withholdings are remitted to the appropriate employees and agencies.

G. Access to sensitive personnel files and payroll records is limited to authorized personnel.

III. Audit Considerations (Framed by "SCARE")—The entity's control activities should address the following matters:

A. Segregation of Duties

1. The following activities should be performed by different personnel when circumstances permit:

   a. Establishing and maintaining employee files in the personnel department

   b. Timekeeping

      c. Payroll preparation and updating the accounting records

      d. Check distribution

      e. Reconciling the payroll bank account with the general ledger account

  2. The treasurer should typically sign the payroll checks.

  3. An appropriate departmental supervisor should distribute the payroll checks to employees in that department.

  4. Unclaimed checks should be controlled. That is, they should be returned to treasury, secured, and eventually destroyed, if not claimed within an appropriate time.

B. Controls (Physical Controls)

  1. Access to personnel files (containing sensitive information) should be limited to authorized personnel.

  2. Access to payroll checks should be limited to authorized personnel.

  3. Personnel with access to payroll checks should be bonded.

C. Authorization—The entity's transactions should be executed as authorized by management.

  1. Payroll should be authorized by a responsible official.

  2. Payroll computations should be verified by an independent person.

  3. Overtime payments should be approved by management.

  4. Payroll for management should also be appropriately reviewed and approved.

D. Reviews (Performance Reviews)

  1. A company should maintain current and accurate payroll information (which should be periodically matched with information in the personnel files).

  2. The payroll checks written should be reconciled to the payroll register, serving as the supporting accounting record for each payroll period.

  3. Other appropriate reconciliations should be made on a timely basis: for example, in a manufacturing environment, someone should reconcile the job cost time sheets to time clock cards. (For strict internal control purposes, a company should use time clocks where possible.)

E. EDP/IT (Information Processing)

  1. Payroll checks should be prenumbered (and the numerical sequence accounted for).

  2. A company should maintain a separate checking account specifically for payroll transactions to establish more accountability and control over these important transactions.

Miscellaneous Cycles

After studying this lesson, you should be able to:

1. Identify the internal-control objectives associated with miscellaneous transaction cycles (manufactured inventory, fixed assets, and investing/financing).

2. Understand the primary control activities normally associated with miscellaneous transaction cycles.

I. Production/Manufacturing Inventory

A. **The Major Objectives of Internal Controls**—In this area, the primary objectives are to provide reasonable assurance that:

1. The resources obtained and used in production (including raw materials, work-in-process, and finished goods) are accurately recorded on a timely basis.

2. Transfers of finished products to customers or others are accurately recorded.

3. Related expenditures are appropriately classified.

4. Access to all categories of inventory (and inventory-related documents) is limited to authorized personnel.

5. Comparisons of actual inventory on hand are made to recorded amounts at least annually.

B. **Audit Considerations (Framed by "SCARE")**—The entity's control activities should address the following matters:

1. **Segregation of duties**

   a. To the extent possible, the company should separate the authorization of inventory-related transactions, the custody of (or access to) inventory, and the accounting record keeping activities.

   b. Sales returns (inventory) should be immediately counted by the receiving clerk and a *receiver* (i.e., a receiving document) prepared to verify the quantity and condition of the goods received.

2. **Controls (physical controls)**

   a. Access to the inventory should be limited to authorized personnel (the inventory should be physically secured with access restricted to personnel having authorized keys or passcodes).

   b. Access to the important accounting documents, including applicable shipping documents, should be limited to authorized personnel.

3. **Authorization**—The entity's transactions should be executed as authorized by management.

   a. The acquisition and distribution of inventory should be consistent with management's authorization.

   b. Management should establish general approvals of transactions within specified limits, and specifically approve transactions above those limits.

   c. Any adjusting journal entries (including sales returns and allowances, or adjustments to inventory, such as write-downs) should be approved by management.

4. **Reviews (performance reviews)**

   a. Actual inventory should be compared periodically to recorded inventory (and any unusual differences should be investigated).

b. In a manufacturing context, appropriate reconciliations should be made of underlying accounting records (including applicable job order cost sheets or process cost worksheets) to the applicable inventory-related general ledger accounts.

5. **EDP/IT (information processing)**

a. The company should use prenumbered purchase orders for raw materials and components of production, along with prenumbered receivers, the receiving document. (The numerical sequence of these documents should be properly accounted for.)

b. The company should consider using a perpetual inventory system for items with high cost per unit.

c. The company should maintain adequate support for related general ledger control accounts.

II. **Fixed Assets Cycle**—The major objectives of internal controls in this area are to provide reasonable assurance that:

A. Transactions involving property, plant, and equipment are accurately recorded and classified; and are in accordance with management's authorization.

B. Estimates used in the determination of depreciation, depletion, and amortization of the assets' cost basis are reasonable and consistent over time; any changes should be properly approved.

C. Fixed assets are reasonably secure from loss with appropriate property insurance in force.

D. Supporting detailed records are maintained and periodically compared to the assets on hand.

E. Any adjusting journal entries related to fixed assets are approved by the management.

III. **Investing/Financing Cycle**—The major objectives of internal controls in this area are to provide reasonable assurance that:

A. Transactions involving investments and financing are accurately recorded and classified on a timely basis; and as authorized by management.

1. **Investing**—As used here, this refers to decisions related to the composition of the company's portfolio of investment assets, both current and noncurrent.

2. **Financing**—This refers to decisions related to the structure of the company's noncurrent liabilities and stockholders' equity sections of the balance sheet.

B. Investment assets should be reasonably secure from loss with procedures established to monitor the associated risks. Access should be limited to authorized personnel with appropriate segregation of duties.

C. Supporting detailed records should be maintained and compared periodically to actual investment-related assets of the company.

D. Any adjusting journal entries related to investment-related assets, liabilities, or stockholders' equity are approved by management.

Audit Evidence: Concepts and Standards

Overview of Substantive Procedures

This lesson contains supplemental documents:

After studying this lesson, you should be able to:

1. Know the two categories of "substantive" audit procedures (and the two categories of "tests of details").

2. Know the meaning of the term *analytical procedures*, the three general purposes served by analytical procedures, and the four considerations that determine the efficiency and effectiveness of analytical procedures that are used for substantive purposes.

3. Familiarize yourself with the fundamental ratios that are most often associated with the auditor's substantive analytical procedures.

I. **The Audit Risk Model**—Recall the *audit risk model* that applies to the assertion level for classes of transactions, account balances, and disclosures (note that this audit risk model does not apply at the overall financial statement level): $AR = IR \times CR \times DR$; where detection risk is the only component within the auditor's direct influence and which is essentially set by specifying the nature, timing, and extent of the auditor's substantive audit procedures.

  A. **Nature**—The auditor has to decide what specific substantive procedures to perform. This includes determining how much emphasis should be placed on *tests of details* (which tend to be labor intensive and expensive, but which provide a relatively stronger basis for conclusions for most financial statement assertions) versus substantive *analytical procedures* (which tend to be less labor intensive and less expensive, but which provide a relatively weaker basis for conclusions for most financial statement assertions).

  B. **Timing**—The auditor has to decide whether to perform the important substantive procedures, at an "interim" date (meaning any date prior to year-end and before the books are closed) or at "final" (at year-end and after the books are closed).

  C. **Extent**—The auditor has to decide how large the samples sizes should be. Since the audit work is performed on a test basis, should the sample sizes be relatively large or can smaller sample sizes be justified?

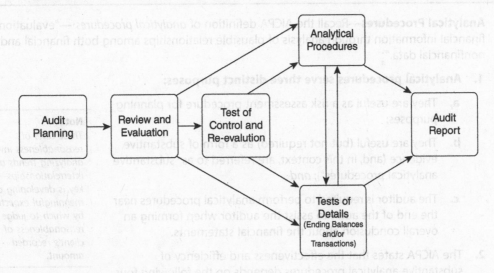

D. **AU 330,** *Performing Audit Procedures in Response to Assessed Risks and Evaluating the Audit Evidence Obtained,* **states:**

> "In some cases, the auditor may find it impossible to design effective substantive procedures that, by themselves, provide sufficient appropriate audit evidence at the relevant assertion level. This may occur when an entity conducts its business using IT and no documentation of transactions is produced or maintained, other than through the IT system."

In such cases, the auditor would be required to perform tests of the relevant controls, in addition to the planned substantive procedures.

Question
Under these circumstances, what would be the consequences if the required tests of controls indicate that internal control is ineffective and cannot be relied on?

Answer:

If the auditor's substantive procedures by themselves are insufficient and if internal control is ineffective, the auditor would not have obtained sufficient appropriate evidence to afford a reasonable basis for the opinion. In other words, these circumstances would constitute a scope limitation!

II. **Substantive Audit Procedures**—These are audit procedures that are directly related to the financial statement elements and disclosures. Recall that the word substantive is derived from substantiate, which means "to verify that substantive procedures are those audit procedures designed to verify the entity's financial statement elements and disclosures" or, in other words, "to search for material misstatements if there are any."

A. **Tests of Details**—These are the relatively precise (but usually rather expensive, labor-intensive) procedures (that suggest whether the client's recorded amounts are right or not).

Definitions
Tests of Ending Balances: Verifying the client's recorded amounts by directly testing the composition making up the ending account balance.

Tests of Transactions: Verifying the client's recorded amounts by testing those relative few debits and credits (the transactions) that caused the account balance to change from last year's audited balance to this year's recorded balance.

B. **Analytical Procedures**—Recall the AICPA definition of *analytical procedures* —"evaluations of financial information through analysis of plausible relationships among both financial and nonfinancial data."

    1. **Analytical procedures serve three distinct purposes:**

        a. They are useful as a risk assessment procedure for planning purposes;

        b. They are useful (but not required) as a form of substantive evidence (and, in this context, are referred to as "substantive analytical procedures"); *and*

        c. The auditor is required to perform analytical procedures near the end of the audit to assist the auditor when forming an overall conclusion about the financial statements.

    2. The AICPA states that the effectiveness and efficiency of substantive analytical procedures depends on the following four factors or considerations:

Note
These tests of reasonableness involve analyzing trends and interrelationships—the key is developing a meaningful expectation by which to judge the reasonableness of the client's recorded amount.

164

a. **Nature of the assertion**—Substantive analytical procedures may be particularly effective in testing for omissions of transactions that would be hard to detect with procedures that focus on recorded amounts. In other words, the skillful use of analytical procedures may be more effective than tests of details in addressing the completeness assertion, since there may be no supporting documents to examine for transactions that were not recorded in the first place!

b. **Plausibility and predictability of the relationship**—Developing a meaningful expectation to compare to the client's recorded balance is critical to the skillful use of analytical procedures, so the predictability of the relationship is very important.

   i. Relationships in a stable environment are usually more predictable than those in a dynamic environment.

   ii. Relationships involving income statement accounts tend to be more predictable than those involving balance sheet accounts (since the income statement deals with a period of time rather than a single moment in time).

   iii. Relationships involving transactions subject to management discretion tend to be less predictable.

c. **Availability and reliability of data used**—The reliability of the expectation increases when the data used is (1) obtained from independent outside sources; (2) when it is subject to audit testing (either currently or in the past); or (3) is developed under conditions of effective internal control.

d. **Precision of the expectation**—The likelihood of detecting a misstatement decreases as the level of aggregation of the data increases. (That is, procedures would be less effective for "high altitude" global comparisons than for more focused, specific comparisons. In other words, relationships of interest to the auditor might be obscured by the noise in the data at a high level of aggregation, whereas those relationships might be more identifiable at a lower level of aggregation. For example, the auditor could focus on sales by month broken down by product line instead of simply comparing current annual sales currently to the prior year.)

3. **Selected ratios**—Such ratios may be tested in Auditing and Attestation as *analytical procedures* or in Financial Accounting and Reporting as *financial statement analysis*.

Definition
Liquidity Ratios (also known as solvency ratios): Measures of an entity's short-term ability to meet its obligations.

---

a. *Working Capital* = Current assets – Current liabilities. This is a definition, not a ratio.

b. *Current ratio* = Current assets/Current liabilities

c. *Quick ratio(acid-test ratio)* = (Cash + Marketable securities + A/R)/Current liabilities

d. *Current cash to debt ratio* = Net cash from operations/Average current liabilities

---

Definition
Activity Ratios (also known as turnover or efficiency ratios): Measures of an entity's effectiveness putting its assets to use.

---

e. *Asset turnover* = Net sales/Average total assets

f. *Receivable turnover* = Net (credit) sales/Average trade receivable (net)

g. *Number of days sales in receivables* = 365 days/Receivable turnover

h. *Inventory turnover* = Cost of goods sold/Average inventory

i. *Number of days sales in inventory* = 365 days/Inventory turnover

> **Definition**
>
> *Profitability Ratios:* Measures of an entity's operating success (failure) for a period of time.

    j. *Profit margin on sales* = Net income/Net sales

    k. *Gross profit percentage* = (Sales – Cost of goods sold)/Sales

    l. *Rate of return on assets* = Net income/Average total assets

    m. *Rate of return on common stockholders' equity* = (Net income – Dividends attributable to preferred stockholders)/Average common stockholders' equity

    n. *Earnings per share* = (Net income – Preferred dividends)/Average number of common shares outstanding

    o. *Price earnings ratio(P-E ratio)* = Market price of stock/earnings per share

> **Definition**
>
> *Coverage Ratios (also known as leverage ratios):* Measures of the entity's ability to meet its obligations over time (i.e., measures of long-term risk to creditors and the extent to which the entity has borrowed up to its available capacity).

    p. *Debt to total assets ratio* = Total liabilities/Total assets

    q. *Debt to equity ratio* = Total liabilities/Total stockholders' equity

    r. *Times interest earned* = Income before interest expense and income taxes/Interest expense

    s. *Cash to debt coverage ratio* = Net cash from operations/Average total liabilities

The Nature of Audit Evidence

After studying this lesson, you should be able to:

1. Understand the meaning of the terms "sufficient" and "appropriate."

2. Know what constitutes "audit evidence."

3. Identify the financial statement assertions specified in AICPA auditing standards (separately by category of assertion: account balances and related disclosures at period-end and transactions and events and related disclosures during the period; and those specified in PCAOB auditing standards, which can be used as broad audit objectives for which evidence must be obtained.

I. Responsibilities under AICPA Professional Standards

The relevant AICPA guidance is provided by AU 500, *Audit Evidence*. This pronouncement states that the auditor's objective is to "obtain sufficient appropriate audit evidence to be able to draw reasonable conclusions on which to base the auditor's opinion."

One of the "Performance Principles" addresses the importance of obtaining sufficient appropriate audit evidence: "To obtain reasonable assurance, which is a high but not absolute level of assurance, the auditor obtains sufficient appropriate audit evidence about whether material misstatements exist, through designing and implementing appropriate responses to the assess risks."

II. Audit Evidence

Definitions

Audit Evidence: Information used by the auditor in arriving at the conclusions on which the auditor's opinion is based. Audit evidence includes both information contained in the accounting records underlying the financial statements and other information.

Accounting Records: The records of initial accounting entries and supporting records, such as checks and records of electronic fund transfers, invoices, contracts, the general and subsidiary ledgers, journal entries and other adjustments to the financial statements that are not reflected in journal entries, and records, such as work sheets and spreadsheets, supporting cost allocations, computations, reconciliations and disclosures.

Other Information Constituting Audit Evidence: Includes minutes of meetings, confirmations, industry analysts' reports, internal control manuals, and any other information obtained by inquiry, observation, and inspection.

III. Sufficient Appropriate Audit Evidence

"Sufficient" refers to the quantity of evidence, whereas "appropriate" refers to the quality of evidence in terms of its relevance and reliability.

A. The quantity of evidence required (related to "sufficient") is directly related to the risk of misstatement (the greater the risk, the more evidence is needed) and inversely related to the quality of evidence (the higher the quality, the less evidence is needed).

B. "Reliability" is affected by the source and nature of evidence and depends upon individual circumstances however, the SAS offers the following guidelines:

Note

The auditor should obtain audit evidence by testing the accounting records, by analysis, review, and reconciling related information; however, the accounting records by themselves do not provide sufficient appropriate audit evidence.

1. Evidence obtained directly by the auditor is more reliable than evidence obtained indirectly or by inference (e.g., observation of the application of a control is more reliable than inquiry of entity personnel about the application of a control).

2. Evidence is more reliable when obtained from independent (knowledgeable) sources outside the entity;

3. Evidence generated internally is more reliable when the related controls are effective;

4. Evidence is more reliable when it exists in documentary form (whether paper or electronic); and

5. Evidence provided by original documents is more reliable than evidence based on photocopies/facsimiles (faxes).

C. The auditor should consider the reliability of information used, but the auditor is not normally responsible for authenticating the entity's documents. The auditor should obtain evidence about the accuracy and completeness of information used to perform further audit procedures (either in connection with the actual audit procedure or by testing controls related to the information).

D. More assurance is obtained from consistent audit evidence obtained from different sources or of a different nature ("corroborating" information) than from evidence considered individually. When evidence from different sources is inconsistent, the auditor should determine what audit procedures are needed to resolve the inconsistency.

E. Professional judgment is required for "reasonable assurance," and the auditor does not examine all available evidence. The auditor may appropriately consider the cost of information relative to its usefulness, although cost alone is not a valid basis for omitting an audit procedure. Audit evidence is usually "persuasive" (or suggestive) and is rarely "conclusive" (or compelling). The auditor should not be satisfied with evidence that is less than persuasive.

IV. **Using "Assertions" to Obtain Audit Evidence**—In stating that the financial statements are consistent with GAAP, management makes several "assertions" (which are implicit or explicit statements of fact).

A. Historically, the auditing standards discussed five traditional financial statement assertions (and the PCAOB standards still focus on these 5 assertions):

1. Existence/occurrence;

2. Completeness;

3. Rights and obligations;

4. Valuation and allocation; *and*

5. Presentation and disclosure.

B. AICPA Professional Standards, as amended by SAS No. 134, classify assertions in two separate categories for the auditor's consideration, related to:

1. Account balances (and related disclosures) at period-end; and

2. Classes of transactions and events (and related disclosures) for the period under audit.

C. There are six assertions specific to account balances (and related disclosures) at period-end:

1. **Existence**—That the assets, liabilities, and equity interests exist.

2. **Completeness**—That all assets, liabilities, and equity interests that should have been recorded have been recorded. There are no omissions, and all appropriate disclosures have been included.

3. **Rights and obligations**—That the entity holds or controls the rights to its assets, and the liabilities are the obligations of the entity. Any restrictions on the rights to the assets or obligations for the liabilities must be disclosed.

4. **Accuracy, valuation and allocation**—That assets, liabilities, and equity interests are included in the financial statements at appropriate amounts (relative to the requirements of GAAP) and any resulting valuation or allocation adjustments are appropriately recorded. Related disclosures have been appropriately measured and described.

5. **Classification**—Assets, liabilities, and equity interests have been recorded in the proper accounts.

6. **Presentation**—Assets, liabilities, and equity interests are appropriately aggregated or disaggregated and clearly described. Related disclosures are relevant and understandable.

D. **There are six assertions about classes of transactions and events during the period (and related disclosures).**

1. **Occurrence**—That transactions and events that have been recorded have occurred. In other words, they are properly recorded and valid.

2. **Completeness**—That all transactions and events that should have been recorded have been recorded. There are no omissions.

3. **Cutoff**—That transactions and events have been recorded in the correct accounting period. Note that there are only two ways to record a transaction in the wrong period. One is by recording a transaction prematurely, which violates the "occurrence" assertion; and the other is to record a transaction belatedly, which violates the "completeness" assertion.

4. **Accuracy**—That amounts and other data have been recorded appropriately, and that all related disclosures have been appropriately measured and described.

Note

"Cutoff" is actually redundant in this context, since establishing "occurrence" (that the recorded transactions are properly recorded) and "completeness" (that there are no omissions of transactions that should have been recorded) together establish that the transactions, in fact, have been recorded in the correct accounting period ("cutoff"). However, "cutoff" is an important issue that auditors must address, so this redundancy emphasizes an important auditing concept.

---

5. **Classification**—That transactions and events have been recorded in the proper accounts.

6. **Presentation**—That transactions and events are appropriately aggregated or disaggregated and clearly described. Related disclosures are relevant and understandable.

	Categories of Assertions	
	Account Balances (and Disclosures) at Period-End	**Transactions or Events (and Disclosures) During the Period**
Existence/Occurrence	Applicable (existence)	Applicable (occurrence)
Completeness	Applicable	Applicable
Rights and Obligations	Applicable	**Not applicable**
Cutoff	**Not applicable**	Applicable
Accuracy, valuation, and allocation	Applicable	Applicable (accuracy)
Classification	Applicable	Applicable
Presentation	Applicable	Applicable

E. The auditor may use the assertions as presented above or express them differently as long as the relevant issues have been addressed. For example, the auditor may combine the assertions about transactions and events with those about account balances; and the auditor may decline to identify a separate assertion about "cutoff" if occurrence and completeness have been established.

F. The auditor should use relevant assertions (those that have a meaningful bearing on whether the account is fairly stated) to assess the risk of material misstatement. The auditor should evaluate the nature of the assertion, the volume of transactions or data involved, and the complexity of the systems (including IT) by which the entity processes and controls the information related to the assertion.

Assertions and Types of Audit Procedures

After studying this lesson, you should be able to:

1. Understand the auditor's responsibility to plan and perform substantive procedures in order to be responsive to the assessed risks of material misstatement, according to AICPA Professional Standards.

2. Know the three categories of audit procedures.

I. **Audit Procedures for Obtaining Evidence**—The auditor's basis for conclusion is comprised of three categories of procedures:

   A. Risk assessment procedures

   B. Tests of controls

   C. Substantive procedures

Definitions

Risk Assessment Procedures: The audit procedures performed to obtain an understanding of the entity and its environment, including the entity's internal control, to identify and assess the risks of material misstatement, whether due to fraud or error, at the financial statement and relevant assertion levels.

Tests of Control: An audit procedure designed to evaluate the operating effectiveness of controls in preventing, or detecting and correcting, material misstatements at the assertion level. (Note that the auditor must perform tests of controls when the risk assessment includes an expectation of the operating effectiveness of controls or when the substantive procedures alone do not provide sufficient appropriate audit evidence.)

Substantive Procedures: An audit procedure designed to detect material misstatements at the assertion level. Substantive procedures comprise (a) tests of details (classes of transactions, account balances, and disclosures) and (b) substantive analytical procedures.

II. **Menu of Specific Substantive Audit Procedures**—The auditor may use computer-assisted audit techniques (CAATs) to assist the auditor when information is in electronic form:

   A. **Inspection of Records/Documents**—Examining records or documents, whether internal or external, whether paper or electronic, or other media;

   B. **Inspection of Tangible Assets**—Physical examination of the assets;

   C. **Observation**—Looking at a process or procedure being performed by others;

   D. **Inquiry**—Seeking information of knowledgeable persons inside or outside the entity and evaluating their responses. Note that inquiry alone does not provide sufficient appropriate audit evidence either for substantive purposes or for tests of controls.

   E. **Confirmation**—Obtaining a representation directly from a knowledgeable third party;

   F. **Recalculation**—Checking the mathematical accuracy of documents;

   G. **Reperformance**—The auditor's execution of procedures or controls originally performed as part of the entity's internal controls;

   H. **Analytical Procedures**—Includes "scanning" to review accounting data to identify unusual items to be tested further. CAATs may be especially useful in identifying significant or unusual items.

> **Note**
> *Analytical procedures are defined as "evaluations of financial information through analysis of plausible relationships among both financial and nonfinancial data."*

III. **The Auditor Should Plan and Perform Substantive Procedures**—The auditor should design the substantive procedures to be responsive to the assessed risks of material misstatements. The purpose of substantive procedures is to detect material misstatements at the relevant assertion level.

A. The auditor should perform some substantive procedures for all relevant assertions related to each material class of transactions, account balance, and disclosure (regardless of the assessed risk of material misstatement), since there are inherent limitations to internal control and the assessment of risk is judgmental.

B. The auditor's substantive procedures should include the following related to the financial reporting process:

1. Agree the financial statement information to the underlying accounting records.

2. Examine material journal entries and other adjustments made during the preparation of the financial statements.

C. **Nature of Substantive Procedures**—These should be responsive to the planned level of detection risk; they consist of:

1. Tests of details

2. Substantive analytical procedures (should consider testing the controls over the preparation of information used in connection with analytical procedures)

D. **Timing of Substantive Procedures**—May be performed at an interim date (before year-end) or at final (at or after year-end)

1. Performing substantive procedures at an interim date increases detection risk. The auditor should perform additional substantive procedures (or substantive procedures combined with tests of control) to mitigate the increased risk and provide a reasonable basis for extending the audit conclusions from the interim date to year-end.

2. It is not necessary to rely on internal controls (i.e., test the operating effectiveness of controls) to extend the audit conclusions from the interim date to year-end. However, the auditor should consider whether only performing additional substantive procedures is sufficient.

3. When planning to perform substantive analytical procedures for the period following the interim date, the auditor should consider whether the period-end balances are reasonably predictable as to amount, relative significance, and composition.

E. **Extent of Substantive Procedures**—Determine the implications to sample sizes (considering the planned level of detection risk, materiality, tolerable misstatement, expected misstatement, and the nature of the population).

F. **Evaluating the Sufficiency and Appropriateness of the Audit Evidence Obtained**

1. **Consider all relevant audit evidence**—The auditor should consider whether the audit evidence appears to corroborate or to contradict the relevant assertions in the financial statements.

2. The sufficiency and appropriateness of audit evidence as a basis for the auditor's conclusions are matters of professional judgment. The auditor's judgment may be influenced by factors such as the following:

   a. The significance of the potential misstatement and the likelihood that it may have a material effect

   b. The understanding of the entity and its environment, including internal control

   c. The effectiveness of management's responses and controls to address the risks

   d. The results of the audit procedures performed (including whether the procedures identified instances of fraud or error)

   e. The persuasiveness of the audit evidence obtained

    f.   The source and reliability of available information

    g.   The experience gained in previous audits with such misstatements

3. **Documentation**—As covered in the course materials on internal controls, the auditor should document the following matters:

    a.   The overall responses to address the assessed risk of misstatement at the financial statement level

    b.   The nature, timing, and extent of the further audit procedures

    c.   The linkage of those procedures with the assessed risks at the relevant assertion level;

    d.   The results of the audit procedures

    e.   The conclusions reached in the current audit about the operating effectiveness of controls tested in a prior audit

PCAOB Risk Assessment Audit Standards

After studying this lesson, you should be able to:

1. Recognize the set of pronouncements that comprise the PCAOB's "risk assessment" project.

2. Understand the auditor's fundamental responsibilities associated with the various risk assessment Auditing Standards issued by the PCAOB.

3. Know the primary differences between the risk-assessment-related standards of the PCAOB and those of the AICPA.

I. PCAOB Risk Assessment Standards

The PCAOB issued a suite of eight Auditing Standards comprising its "risk assessment" project in 2010. In general, these PCAOB risk assessment standards are remarkably similar to the risk assessment standards previously issued (and now clarified) by the AICPA (Statements on Auditing Standards) and by the International Federation of Accountants (International Standards on Auditing), although a few (mostly minor) differences are identified below.

A. PCAOB Auditing Standard No. 8, *Audit Risk* [AS 1101]

B. PCAOB Auditing Standard No. 9, *Audit Planning* [AS 2101]

C. PCAOB Auditing Standard No. 10, *Supervision of the Audit Engagement* [AS 1201]

D. PCAOB Auditing Standard No. 11, *Consideration of Materiality in Planning and Performing an Audit* [AS 2105]

E. PCAOB Auditing Standard No. 12, *Identifying and Assessing Risks of Material Misstatement* [AS 2110]

F. PCAOB Auditing Standard No. 13, *The Auditor's Responses to the Risks of Material Misstatement* [AS 2301]

G. PCAOB Auditing Standard No. 14, *Evaluating Audit Results* [AS 2810]

H. PCAOB Auditing Standard No. 15, *Audit Evidence* [AS 1105]

II. PCAOB vs. AICPA—Structural Differences

These PCAOB Auditing Standards are applicable to integrated audits of an issuer's financial statements and the internal controls over financial reporting. In contrast, the AICPA's Statements on Auditing Standards focus solely on audits of nonissuers' financial statements.

III. Summaries—Summaries of the essence of these PCAOB risk assessment standards.

A. PCAOB on Audit Risk

1. **Auditor's objective** —To conduct the audit of financial statements in a manner that reduces audit risk to an appropriately low level.

2. **"Reasonable assurance" means reducing audit risk to an appropriately low level**— The auditor must plan and perform the audit to obtain reasonable assurance about whether the financial statements are free of material misstatements due to error or fraud.

3. The auditor should assess the risks of material misstatement at two levels: (1) at the financial statement level (where the risk of material misstatement is pervasive and potentially involves many assertions); and (2) at the assertion level (where the risk of material misstatement involves inherent risk and control risk).

B. PCAOB on Audit Planning

1. **Auditor's objective** —To plan the audit so that the audit is conducted effectively.

2. "Planning the audit includes establishing the overall audit strategy for the engagement and developing an audit plan, which includes, in particular, planned risk assessment procedures and planned responses to the risks of material misstatement. Planning is not a discrete phase of an audit but, rather, a continual and iterative process that might begin shortly after (or in connection with) the completion of the previous audit and continues until the completion of the current audit."

   a. **Overall strategy**—Involves rather high-level audit resource allocation issues involving the scope, timing, and direction of the audit (guides the development of the more specific audit plan).

   b. **Audit plan**—Deals with the planned nature, timing, and extent of the risk assessment procedures, the tests of controls, the substantive procedures, and any other procedures required to comply with PCAOB standards.

3. **Engagement partner responsibilities**—"The engagement partner is responsible for the engagement and its performance. Accordingly, the engagement partner is responsible for planning the audit and may seek assistance from appropriate engagement team members in fulfilling this responsibility."

C. PCAOB on Supervision of the Audit Engagement

1. **Auditor's objective**—To supervise the audit engagement so that the work is performed as directed and supports the conclusions reached.

2. The extent of supervision required varies with the engagement's circumstances, including the size and complexity of the company, the nature of the work assigned to engagement personnel, the capabilities of each engagement team member, and the risks of material misstatement. (The extent of supervision should be commensurate with those risks.)

3. **Engagement partner responsibilities**—"The engagement partner is responsible for the engagement and its performance. Accordingly, the engagement partner is responsible for proper supervision of the work of engagement team members and for compliance with PCAOB standards, including standards regarding using the work of specialists, other auditors, internal auditors, and others who are involved in testing controls."

D. PCAOB on Consideration of Materiality in Planning and Performing an Audit

1. **Auditor's objective**—To apply the concept of materiality appropriately in planning and performing audit procedures.

2. The auditor should plan and perform the audit to detect misstatement that, individually or in the aggregate, would result in material misstatement of the financial statements.

3. The auditor should use the same materiality considerations for planning the audit of internal control over financial reporting as for the audit of the financial statements.

4. The materiality level for the financial statements should be expressed as a specified amount to determine the nature, timing, and extent of audit procedures.

5. The auditor should determine tolerable misstatement for purposes of assessing risks of material misstatement at the account or disclosure levels.

E. PCAOB on "Identifying and Assessing Risks of Material Misstatement"

1. **Auditor's objective**—To identify and appropriately assess the risks of material misstatement, thereby providing a basis for designing and implementing responses to the risks of material misstatement.

2. The auditor should perform risk assessment procedures sufficient to provide a reasonable basis for identifying and assessing the risks of material misstatement and designing further audit procedures.

3. These risk assessment procedures should include (a) obtaining an understanding of the company and its environment; (b) obtaining an understanding of internal control over financial reporting; (c) considering information from the client acceptance/retention

evaluation, planning activities, prior audits, and other engagements for the company; (d) performing analytical procedures; and (e) inquiring of the audit committee, management, and others within the company about the risks of material misstatement.

4. The auditor should begin by identifying and assessing the risks of material misstatement at the financial statement level and then work down to the significant accounts and disclosures and their relevant assertions.

F. PCAOB on "The Auditor's Responses to the Risks of Material Misstatement"

1. **Auditor's objective**—To address the risks of material misstatement through appropriate overall audit responses and audit procedures.

2. **Overall responses** —The auditor should consider (a) making appropriate assignments of responsibilities based on capabilities of team members; (b) providing appropriate supervision; (c) incorporating a degree of unpredictability in planned procedures; (d) evaluating the company's selection and application of significant accounting principles (especially in subjective areas); and (e) determining whether it is necessary to make pervasive changes to the nature, timing, and extent of audit procedures.

3. **Responses involving the nature, timing, and extent of audit procedures** —The auditor should address the assessed risks of material misstatement for each relevant assertion of each significant account and disclosure.

   a. There are two categories of audit procedures performed in response to the assessed risks of material misstatement: (1) tests of controls; and (2) substantive procedures.

   b. The auditor should perform substantive procedures that are responsive to any identified significant risks (including fraud risks).

   c. In responding to fraud risks, the auditor should address the risk of management override of controls by examining journal entries, reviewing accounting estimates for biases, and evaluating the business rationale for significant unusual transactions.

G. PCAOB on "Evaluating Audit Results"

1. **Auditor's objective** —To evaluate the results of the audit to determine whether the audit evidence obtained is sufficient and appropriate to support the opinion.

2. The auditor must reach a conclusion as to whether sufficient appropriate audit evidence has been obtained to support the opinion.

3. The auditor should consider all relevant audit evidence (whether it corroborates or contradicts the financial statements) and evaluate the following:

   a. The results of analytical procedures performed as the overall review

   b. Misstatements (other than "trivial" ones) accumulated during the audit (with emphasis on uncorrected misstatements)

   c. The qualitative aspects of the company's accounting practices, including potential for management bias

   d. Conditions identified related to fraud risk

   e. The presentation of the financial statements (including disclosures) relative to the applicable financial reporting framework

   f. The sufficiency and appropriateness of the evidence obtained

H. PCAOB on "Audit Evidence"

1. **Auditor's objective** —To plan and perform the audit to obtain appropriate audit evidence that is sufficient to support the opinion.

2. **Sufficient appropriate audit evidence**

   a. Sufficiency relates to the *quantity* of evidence required—the amount of evidence needed increases as the risk of material misstatement increases; The amount of evidence needed decreases as the quality of the underlying evidence increases.

   b. Appropriateness relates to the *quality* of evidence, which involves (1) relevance and (2) reliability.

3. Financial statement assertions are factual representations that are implicitly or explicitly made by management—The PCAOB identified the five traditional financial statement assertions previously presented in a now-superseded Statement on Auditing Standards:

   a. **Existence or occurrence**—That the assets or liabilities exist at a given date or that the recorded transactions have occurred during a given period

   b. **Completeness**—That there are no omissions of transaction or accounts that should have been recorded

   c. **Rights and obligations**—That the company has the rights to the assets and the obligations for the liabilities at a given date

   d. **Valuation or allocation**—That the financial statement elements are presented at appropriate amounts relative to the applicable accounting framework

   e. **Presentation and disclosure**—That the elements of the financial statements are properly classified, described, and disclosed relative to the applicable accounting framework

---

Note

The PCAOB's discussion about these five traditional financial statement assertions is a relatively major difference compared to the AICPA's Statement on Auditing Standards dealing with assertions. The AICPA presents the discussion of assertions in two categories: (1) account balances (and related disclosures) at the period end (six assertions); and (2) transactions and events (and related disclosures) during the period (six assertions).

The PCAOB commented on the alternative treatments of assertions: "The auditor may base his or her work on financial statement assertions that differ from those in this standard if the assertions are sufficient for the auditor to identify the potential misstatements..."

IV. **Summary of Differences**—Summary of fundamental differences between the PCAOB risk assessment standards and the AICPA Auditing Standards Board risk assessment standards.

   A. The PCAOB risk assessment standards apply to integrated audits of issuers (encompassing both the company's financial statements and internal control over financial reporting), whereas the AICPA risk assessment standard apply solely to audits of non-issuers' financial statements.

   B. The PCAOB standards tended to provide a bit more specific guidance in certain areas (such as the engagement partner's responsibilities) that were originally addressed in somewhat more general terms in the AICPA standards; however, the AICPA's clarified auditing standards are now very similar to PCAOB auditing standards in these areas.

   C. A more significant difference involves the treatment of "assertions" in their respective standards dealing with the topic of audit evidence—the PCAOB focuses on the five traditional financial statement assertions (as presented in an earlier SAS that has since been superseded in an attempt to align U.S. auditing standards more closely with international standards); the current AICPA standard classifies 12 assertions into two broad categories: (1) account balances (and related disclosures) at the period end (for which there are six assertions); and (2) transactions and events (and related disclosures) for the period (for which there are six assertions).

Evaluation of Misstatements Identified During the Audit

After studying this lesson, you should be able to:

1. Understand the auditor's responsibility to accumulate and evaluate the effect of identified misstatements on the audit and to evaluate the effects of uncorrected misstatements on the financial statements

2. Understand the auditor's responsibility to communicate identified misstatements to management, and the auditor's responsibility when management refuses to correct some (or all) of the identified misstatements.

3. Identify the specific matters related to misstatements that the auditor is required to document.

I. **Responsibilities under AICPA Professional Standards**—The relevant AICPA guidance is provided by AU 450, *Evaluation of Misstatements Identified During the Audit*. This pronouncement states that the auditor's objectives are to evaluate the effect of (1) identified misstatements on the audit; and (2) uncorrected misstatements, if any, on the financial statements.

Definitions

Misstatement: A difference between the amount, classification, presentation, or disclosure of a reported financial statement item and the amount, classification, presentation, or disclosure that is required for the item to be in accordance with the applicable reporting framework. (Misstatements also involve matters deemed necessary for the financial statements to be presented fairly, in all material respects.)

Uncorrected Misstatements: Misstatements that the auditor has accumulated during the audit and that have not been corrected.

II. **Expectations Regarding Identified Misstatements and Uncorrected Misstatements**

A. **Accumulation of Identified Misstatements**—The auditor should accumulate all misstatements identified during the audit (except for those that are *clearly trivial*, which means *inconsequential*). The auditor may wish to distinguish among the following three types of misstatements:

1. **Factual misstatements**—Misstatements for which there is no doubt.

2. **Judgmental misstatements**—Differences due to the judgments of management that the auditor considers unreasonable or to the selection of accounting policies that the auditor views as inappropriate.

3. **Projected misstatements**—The auditor's best estimate of misstatements in populations as suggested by audit sampling.

B. **Consideration of Identified Misstatements as the Audit Progresses**—The auditor should determine whether the overall audit strategy and audit plan need to be revised as a result of the identified misstatements. That would be necessary if the aggregate of accumulated misstatements (and other misstatements that may exist) approaches what is considered to be material.

C. **Communication and the Correction of Misstatements**—The auditor should communicate all misstatements accumulated during the audit on a timely basis with the *appropriate level* of management and request they correct the misstatements. The appropriate level is the one that has the authority to evaluate the misstatements and take necessary action.

1. If management has examined a class of transactions or account balance at the auditor's request (e.g., as a result of an audit sample that indicates a misstatement) and has made a correction—The auditor should perform additional procedures to determine whether any misstatements remain.

2. If management refuses to correct some (or all) of the misstatements—The auditor should obtain an understanding of management's reasons and take that into consideration when evaluating whether the financial statements are materially misstated.

D. Evaluating the Effect of Uncorrected Misstatements

1. **Reassess materiality**—The auditor should reassess materiality to verify that it is appropriate in view of the entity's actual financial results.

2. **Determine whether uncorrected misstatements are material**—The auditor should consider (a) the size and nature of the misstatements; and (b) the effect of uncorrected misstatements related to prior periods.

3. Other (undetected) misstatements may exist when a misstatement results from a break down in internal control, or when inappropriate assumptions or valuation methods have been widely used. The auditor should consider whether the detected and undetected misstatements might exceed materiality.

4. Circumstances affecting the evaluation of materiality include the following: (a) compliance and regulatory requirements; (b) debt covenants; (c) the effect on future periods' financial statements; (d) the effects on changes in earnings (such as changing income to a loss or vice versa) or other trends; (e) the impact on ratios; (f) the effects on segment information; (g) an effect that increases management compensation; (h) the omission of information important to users' understanding; and (i) the misclassification between operatingnon-operating items or recurringnon-recurring items.

E. Documentation of misstatements—The auditor should document the following three matters in the audit documentation: (1) the amount below which misstatements would be viewed as *clearly trivial* ; (2) all misstatements accumulated during the audit and whether they have been corrected; and (3) the auditor's conclusion (and the basis for that conclusion) about whether the uncorrected misstatements are material, individually or in the aggregate.

Audit Documentation

I. **Responsibilities under AICPA Professional Standards**—The relevant AICPA guidance is provided by AU 230, *Audit Documentation*. This pronouncement states that the auditor's objective is "to prepare documentation that provides:

   A. A sufficient and appropriate record of the basis for the auditor's report; *and*

   B. Evidence that the audit was planned and performed in accordance with (GAAS) and applicable legal and regulatory requirements."

Definition

Audit Documentation: This is the record of audit procedures performed, relevant audit evidence obtained, and conclusions reached (terms such as *working papers* or *work papers* are also sometimes used).

II. **Purposes of Audit Documentation**

   A. Provides the principal support for the auditor's report (regarding the procedures performed and the conclusions reached).

   B. Documents the auditor's compliance with GAAS and any applicable legal and regulatory requirements;

   1. That the work was adequately planned and supervised;

   2. That an understanding of the entity and its environment, including internal control, was obtained and evaluated as necessary to assess the risks of material misstatement and to design the audit to be responsive to those risks; *and*

   3. That the procedures applied and the evidence obtained provide a reasonable basis for the opinion expressed.

   C. The audit documentation assists in controlling the audit work—that is, breaking the overall audit project into manageable tasks that can be delegated to the various members of the audit team (while documenting the work performed and the conclusions reached, and identifying the work yet to be completed).

III. **Ownership and Custody Issues**

   A. **Ownership**—Audit documentation is the auditor's property (the auditor should safeguard it and establish a formal retention policy).

   B. **Confidentiality**—The audit documentation is subject to the restrictions imposed by AICPA ethics rules on confidentiality. (The auditor should prevent unauthorized access to the audit documentation, since it contains entity-specific confidential information.)

   C. Auditors should apply appropriate controls over the audit documentation to protect the integrity of the information at all stages of the audit, to prevent unauthorized changes, and to limit access to authorized personnel.

IV. AICPA Requirements

    A. Audit documentation should permit an experienced auditor without prior connection to the audit to understand the following:

        1. The nature, timing, and extent of procedures performed;

        2. The results of those procedures;

        3. The conclusions reached on significant matters; *and*

        4. Whether the accounting records agree or reconcile with the audited financial statements.

    B. Audit documentation should include abstracts or copies of significant contracts or agreements examined—if needed by an experienced auditor to understand the basis for conclusions.

    C. Audit documentation should identify the specific items tested by the auditor (or the *identifying characteristics* of items tested in connection with the substantive procedures and any tests of control so that the items tested can be determined as necessary).

    D. The auditor should also document audit findings or issues that are *significant* (including actions taken to address them and the basis for conclusions reached), and should also document discussions of significant findings or issues with management (including issues discussed, and when and with whom). Such findings and issues include:

        1. Significant matters regarding the selection, application, and consistency of accounting principles

        2. Circumstances causing difficulty in applying necessary audit procedures

        3. Results of audit procedures indicating a possible material misstatement

        4. Findings that could result in modification of the audit report

        5. Audit adjustments (whether or not recorded by management) that could have a material effect individually or when aggregated

    E. If information is identified that contradicts or is inconsistent with the auditor's final conclusions—the auditor should document how the auditor addressed the contradiction or inconsistency in forming the conclusions.

    F. Identification of preparer and reviewer—the auditor should document who performed the audit work and who reviewed the specific audit documentation.

    G. Should document the *report release date*—That is defined as the date the auditor grants the entity permission to use the auditor's report on the audited financial statements.

V. Revisions—Any revisions to audit documentation after the date of the auditor's report should comply with the following requirements:

    A. Documentation Completion Date—The auditor should complete the assembly of the final audit file no later than 60 days after the report release date. The PCAOB specifies a limit of 45 days for audits of public companies.

    B. Before the Documentation Completion Date—The auditor may add information received after the report date or delete unnecessary documentation up to the documentation completion date.

    C. After the Documentation Completion Date—The auditor must not delete any audit documentation before the end of the retention period; the auditor may add to the documentation, but must document any materials added, by whom, when, reasons for the change, and the effect, if any, on the auditor's conclusions.

    D. Retention Requirements—The AICPA requires that the audit documentation be retained for at least five years from the report release date. (The PCAOB requires retention for at least seven years for audits of public companies.)

VI. Additional Documentation—Other Statements on Auditing Standards require additional specific documentation, including, for example, the following:

  A. Aggregated Misstatements—The auditor must document:

  1. The nature and effect of misstatements that the auditor aggregates

  2. The auditor's conclusions as to whether the aggregated misstatements are material to the financial statements

  B. Analytical Procedures—The auditor must document:

  1. The expectation and factors (sources) considered in developing it, when not otherwise apparent

  2. The results of the comparison of that expectation to the recorded amounts (or to ratios based on recorded amounts)

  3. Any additional procedures performed (and the results of those procedures) to investigate unexpected differences from that comparison

  C. Going-Concern Issues—The auditor must document:

  1. The conditions giving rise to the going concern issue

  2. The elements of management's plan considered important to overcoming the situation

  3. Evidence obtained to evaluate the significant elements of management's plans

  4. The auditor's conclusion as to whether *substantial doubt* remains

  5. The auditor's conclusion as to whether a "Going Concern" section should be added to the auditor's report

VII. Quantity of Content—The quantity, type, and content of the audit documentation depends on the auditor's professional judgment and may include consideration of the following matters:

  A. The risk of material misstatement in the area involved

  B. The amount of judgment involved in performing the work and interpreting the results (including the nature of the audit procedures involved)

  C. The nature and extent of any exceptions identified

  D. The significance of the evidence to the assertion involved

  E. The need to document a conclusion not readily determinable from the documentation of the work performed

VIII. Types of Files Related to Audit Working Papers

  A. Permanent File—Involves matters having ongoing audit significance and may include:

  1. Description of the client's industry, a brief history of client, and a description of the client's facilities

  2. Abstracts or copies of important legal documents and important long-term contracts—documents such as the company's articles of incorporation and bylaws and contracts such as debt agreements, leases, and labor contracts (including pension plans and profit-sharing agreements)

  3. Documentation of the auditor's understanding of internal control for the major transaction cycles

  4. **Historical financial information**—Such as ratio analysis of the client's operations or other data having ongoing usefulness

  B. Current Year's Audit Files—The current year's audit files include the auditor's documentation of important administrative matters (such as the audit team's time budget) along with the supporting working papers related to the financial statement items.

1. Audit plan (sometimes called the audit program).

2. Memoranda (documenting planning activities, consideration of fraud, assessment of internal control, etc.).

3. Abstracts or copies of relevant client documents (including minutes of board of directors' meetings or meetings of those charged with governance).

4. Letters (confirmations, attorney letters, management representation letter, engagement letter, etc.).

5. Analyses and schedules (either prepared by client personnel or by the audit team).

C. **Bulk File**—Where documentation that is too voluminous can be stored (e.g., magnetic tapes, extensive computer printouts, etc.).

D. **Correspondence File**—Where letters and e-mail messages to and from clients are organized so that the audit team can conveniently review communications related to each client organization.

E. **Report File**—Where prior years' audit reports and management letters are organized (by client) so that the audit team can conveniently review formal reports previously issued for each client.

PCAOB on Audit Documentation

After studying this lesson, you should be able to:

1. Know the documentation requirements under PCAOB Auditing Standards.

2. Know the primary differences between PCAOB documentation requirements for issuers relative to AICPA documentation requirements for nonissuers (regarding documentation retention and the documentation completion date).

I. Audit Documentation

Definition
Audit Documentation: The written record of the basis for the auditor's conclusions that provides the support for the auditor's representations. Also serves as a **basis for the review** of the quality of the audit work—the documentation should be prepared in sufficient detail to permit an experienced auditor without prior connection to the engagement to understand the procedures performed and the conclusions reached (and to determine who performed the work and on what date).

II. Basic Documentation Requirement

—(1) Demonstrate that the engagement complied with PCAOB standards; (2) support the basis for the auditor's conclusions regarding every relevant financial statement assertion; and (3) demonstrate that the underlying accounting records agree to or reconcile with the financial statement elements.

III. Documentation of Specific Matters

A. Document audit procedures involving inspection of documents (including walkthroughs, tests of controls, and substantive tests of details)—Identify the specific items tested (or the source and specific selection criteria); include abstracts or copies of significant contracts or agreements examined.

B. For matters documented in a **central repository** or in a particular office of the public accounting firm (including issues such as auditor independence, staff training, client acceptance/retention, etc.)—The audit documentation should appropriately reference the central repository.

C. Must document all **significant findings or issues** (also document the actions taken to address them and the basis for the conclusions reached)—Including the application of accounting principles, circumstances causing modification of planned audit procedures, matters that could result in modification of the auditor's report, material misstatements, significant deficiencies or material weaknesses in internal control over financial reporting, difficulties in applying audit procedures, and disagreements among members of the engagement team about final conclusions on significant matters, among other things.

D. All significant findings or issues must be identified in an **engagement completion document** in sufficient detail so that a reviewer can obtain a thorough understanding of the matters.

IV. Retention of and Subsequent Changes to Audit Documentation

A. **Must retain audit documentation for seven years from the report release date**—The report release date is when the auditor grants permission to use the auditor's report in connection with the issuance of the company's financial statements. (Recall that the AICPA requires a retention period of five years for audits of *nonissuers.*)

B. **A complete and final set of audit documentation should be assembled no later than 45 days after the report release date**—That is called the **documentation completion date.** (Recall that the AICPA allows auditors of nonissuers to have a maximum of 60 days for this purpose.)

C. **After the documentation completion date**—No documentation can be deleted, but documentation can be added (must indicate the date the information was added, the name of the person preparing the additional documentation, and the reason for adding it).

D. **The office of the firm issuing the auditor's report is responsible for ensuring that all documentation complies with PCAOB requirements**—Documentation of other auditors associated with the engagement (in other offices of the firm or in different firms) must be retained or accessible to the office issuing the report.

Confirmation

I. **Responsibilities under AICPA Professional Standards**—The relevant AICPA guidance is provided by AU 505, *External Confirmations*. This pronouncement states that the auditor's objective is "to design and perform external confirmations to obtain relevant and reliable audit evidence."

Definitions

External Confirmation: Audit evidence obtained as a direct written response to the auditor from a third party ("the confirming party"), either in paper form or by electronic or other medium (e.g., through the auditor's direct access to information held by a third party).

Positive Confirmation Request: A request that the confirming party respond directly to the auditor by providing the requested information or indicating whether the confirming party agrees or disagrees with the information in the request.

Negative Confirmation Request: A request that the confirming party respond directly to the auditor only if the confirming party disagrees with the information provided in the request.

II. **Tailor Objectives/Assertions**—The auditor should tailor the confirmations to the specific audit objectives/assertions. Confirmations are most useful in addressing the existence/occurrence assertion. There are two basic types of confirmation requests:

   A. **Positive Confirmation Request**—Where a response is requested whether or not the other party agrees with the client's recorded amount. A nonresponse is viewed as a "loose end" that must be addressed.

      1. When individual accounts are large

      2. Requires second (or possibly third) requests as a follow-up procedure for nonresponses

      3. If no response is obtained, the auditor must perform *alternative procedures*.

   B. **Negative Confirmation Request**—Where a response is only requested in the event of **disagreement**. A nonresponse is viewed as evidence of agreement by the recipient:

      1. Could easily misinterpret a nonresponse as suggesting agreement when, instead, the other party did not even open the envelope!

      2. Therefore, negative confirmations usually require a larger sample size than would positive confirmations.

      3. The auditor may justify using negative confirmations when:

         a. The population consists of a large number of small, rather homogeneous items;

         b. The assessed risk of material misstatement is low, and the relevant controls are operating effectively; *and*

         c. Recipients are expected to pay attention to the request, and a low rate of exceptions is expected.

C. **Alternative Procedures**—Alternative (sometimes called "alternate") audit procedures are usually required when no response is received for a positive confirmation request:

1. **Receivables**—The auditor would first look to see whether cash was received subsequent to the date of the confirmation request. Second best, the auditor would examine the documents underlying the apparent validity of the recorded transaction.

2. **Payables**—The auditor would usually verify subsequent cash disbursements as evidence of payment of the account.

III. **Control of Requests and Responses**—The auditor should "maintain control over the confirmation requests and responses." If the response is by fax, the auditor should consider a direct call to the respondent; and if the response is verbal, encourage a written reply.

IV. **Responding to Risks of Material Misstatement**—AU 330, *Performing Audit Procedures in Response to Assessed Risks and Evaluating the Audit Evidence Obtained,* states, "The auditor should use external confirmation procedures for accounts receivable, except when one or more of the following is applicable:

A. The overall account balance is immaterial.

B. External confirmation procedures for accounts receivable would be ineffective.

C. The auditor's assessed level of risk of material misstatement at the relevant assertion level is low, and the other planned substantive procedures address the assessed risk. In many situations, the use of external confirmation procedures for accounts receivable and the performance of other substantive procedures are necessary to reduce the assessed risk of material misstatement to an acceptably low level."

AU 330 also states, "If the auditor has determined that an assessed risk of material misstatement at the relevant assertion level is a significant risk, the auditor should perform substantive procedures that are specifically responsive to that risk."

Example
If the auditor identified that management is under pressure to meet earnings expectations, there may be a risk that management is inflating sales by improperly recognizing revenue related to sales agreements with terms that preclude revenue recognition or by invoicing sales before shipment. In these circumstances, the auditor may, for example, design external written confirmation requests not only to confirm outstanding amounts, but also to confirm the details of the sales agreements, including date, any rights of return, and delivery terms. In addition, the auditor may find it effective to supplement such external written confirmations with inquiries of nonfinancial personnel in the entity regarding any changes in sales agreements and delivery terms.

Accounting Estimates

After studying this lesson, you should be able to:

1. Understand the auditor's responsibilities to apply a risk-based audit approach to evaluate the reasonableness of accounting estimates in accordance with AICPA Professional Standards and in accordance with PCAOB auditing standards.

2. Know the definition of "estimation uncertainty" and how that concept may result in a "significant risk."

3. Know the auditor's responsibilities when an accounting estimate results in a "significant risk."

I. **Responsibilities under AICPA Professional Standards**—The relevant AICPA guidance is provided by AU 540, *Auditing Accounting Estima tes, Including Fair Value Accounting Estimates and Related Disclosures*. This pronouncement states that the auditor's objective is to obtain sufficient appropriate audit evidence about whether the accounting estimates (including fair value accounting estimates) are reasonable and whether the related disclosures are adequate in view of the applicable financial reporting framework.

Definitions

Accounting Estimate: An approximation of a monetary amount in the absence of a precise means of measurement.

Auditor's Point Estimate (or Auditor's Range): The amount (or range of amounts) derived from audit evidence for use in evaluating the recorded or disclosed amount(s).

Estimation Uncertainty: The susceptibility of an accounting estimate and related disclosures to an inherent lack of precision in its measurement.

Management's Point Estimate: The amount selected by management for recognition or disclosure as an accounting estimate.

Outcome of an Accounting Estimate: The actual monetary amount that results from resolution of the underlying matter addressed by the accounting estimate.

II. **The Risk-Based Audit Approach**

A. **Basis for Risk Assessment**—The auditor should obtain an understanding of the following:
1. The requirements of the applicable financial reporting framework
2. How management makes the accounting estimates and the data used, including how management has assessed the effect of estimation uncertainty

B. **Identifying and Assessing Risks of Material Misstatement**—The auditor should evaluate the degree of estimation uncertainty involved, and determine whether any of those accounting estimates result in significant risks. (Recall that significant risks require the auditor to obtain an understanding of whether relevant controls mitigate such risks.)

C. **Responding to the Assessed Risks of Material Misstatement**
1. The auditor should determine whether management has complied with the requirements of the applicable financial reporting framework, and whether the methods used to make the estimate are appropriate and consistently applied.
2. In responding to the assessed risks, the auditor should do one (or more) of the following:
   a. Determine whether events occurring up to the date of the auditor's report provide evidence about the accounting estimate;
   b. Test how management made the estimate, along with the data used;

      c. Test the operating effectiveness of applicable controls, along with performing appropriate substantive procedures; *and/or*

      d. Develop a point estimate (or range) to evaluate management's point estimate.

  3. The auditor should consider the need for specialized skills or knowledge.

D. Further Substantive Procedures to Respond to Significant Risks—The auditor should evaluate the following:

  1. How management addressed estimation uncertainty in making the accounting estimate;

  2. Whether management's significant assumptions are reasonable; *and*

  3. When relevant, whether management has the intent and ability to carry out specific actions.

E. Evaluating the Reasonableness of the Accounting Estimates—The auditor should evaluate whether the accounting estimates are reasonable (or are misstated) relative to the applicable financial reporting framework. The auditor is not responsible for predicting future conditions, transactions, or events, however.

F. Disclosures—The auditor should obtain sufficient appropriate audit evidence as to whether the disclosures meet the requirements of the applicable financial reporting framework. For accounting estimates resulting in significant risks, the auditor should evaluate the adequacy of the disclosure of estimation uncertainty.

G. Indicators of Possible Management Bias—The auditor should consider whether the accounting estimates might indicate possible management bias.

H. Documentation—The auditor should include documentation regarding (1) the basis for the auditor's conclusions about the reasonableness of accounting estimates resulting in significant risks and their disclosure; and (2) any indications of possible management bias. The auditor usually obtains written representations as to whether management believes assumptions used in making accounting estimates are reasonable.

III. Additional Guidance Regarding Estimation Uncertainty

A. Nature of Estimation Uncertainty—The nature of estimation uncertainty varies with the nature of the accounting estimate, the extent to which there is an accepted method (or model) to be used, and the subjectivity of any assumptions or the degree of judgment involved. The risks of material misstatement increase when there is high estimation uncertainty.

B. Understanding Management's Assessment—In obtaining an understanding of whether and how management has assessed estimation uncertainty, the auditor might consider whether management has performed a *sensitivity analysis* and monitors outcomes of prior accounting estimates.

C. When the Estimation Uncertainty is High—The auditor may consider a combination of responses to the assessed risks, including reviewing outcomes, testing how management made its estimate, testing applicable controls, and developing a point estimate (or range) to evaluate management's point estimate.

D. Narrowing a Range—The auditor's range should encompass all reasonable outcomes, not all possible outcomes. A high estimation uncertainty (significant risk) may be indicated if it is not possible to narrow the range to less than or equal to performance materiality.

E. Reporting—When there is significant uncertainty, the auditor may add an emphasis-of-matter paragraph to the auditor's report.

IV. PCAOB Guidance

PCAOB Auditing Standard No. 43 addresses accounting estimates, including fair value measurements. PCAOB AS § 2501 (*Auditing Accounting Estimates, Including Fair Value Measurements*) replaces three previous PCAOB standards separately dealing with (1) accounting estimates, (2) fair value measurements, and (3) derivative instruments. It was approved by the SEC in July 2019 and is effective for audits for fiscal years ending on or after December 15, 2020.

A. Overview of PCAOB's Standard on Auditing Accounting Estimates

1. Requires auditors to give greater attention to potential management bias involving accounting estimates

   a. Requires a discussion among audit team members about the potential for management bias

   b. Emphasizes the importance of exercising professional skepticism

   c. Requires auditors to consider contradictory evidence as well as corroborating evidence regarding assertions related to such estimates

   d. Requires auditors to identify significant assumptions (and evaluate their reasonableness) related to estimates, including those that are susceptible to bias

   e. Requires auditors to obtain an understanding of management's analysis of "critical accounting estimates"

   f. Requires auditors to evaluate whether data was appropriately used and whether any change in the source of data is appropriate

2. Extends key requirements in the fair value standard to other significant accounting estimates to achieve a more uniform approach to substantive testing

   a. Describes the auditor's responsibilities for testing the methods, data, and significant assumptions used by the company in developing the estimate

   b. Describes the auditor's responsibilities for evaluating the company's methods for developing the estimate, including whether the methods conform with the requirements of the applicable financial reporting framework and are appropriate in the circumstances

3. Integrates requirements with the PCAOB's risk assessment standards to emphasize estimates having greater risk of material misstatement

   a. Addresses risk factors to identify significant accounts and disclosures associated with accounting estimates

   b. Acknowledges that it might be impossible to design effective substantive procedures alone that would provide sufficient appropriate audit evidence when dealing with accounting estimates that involve complex models or processes

4. Updates other requirements related to auditing accounting estimates

   a. Broadens the general description of accounting estimates to include fair value measurements

   b. Establishes more specific requirements for developing an independent expectation depending on the source of the data, assumptions, or methods used by the auditor

5. Provides more specific requirements when auditing the fair value of financial instruments

   a. Requires a determination of whether pricing information obtained from third parties (e.g., pricing services and brokers or dealers) provides sufficient appropriate audit evidence

   b. Requires the auditor to obtain an understanding of how any unobservable inputs were determined and to evaluate their reasonableness

B. Additional Specific Considerations under PCAOB Auditing Standards

1. To test accounting estimates—Should perform one or more of the following:

   a. Test the company's process for developing the accounting estimate.

   b. Develop an independent expectation for comparison.

   c. Evaluate evidence from events occurring after the measurement date.

2. When the company changed the method used to determine the accounting estimate—The auditor should evaluate the appropriateness of the change.

3. Identification of significant assumptions

    a. Significant assumptions—Those that are important to the recognition or measurement of the accounting estimate.

    b. Examples that usually would be considered significant assumptions—Assumptions that are (1) sensitive to variation, (2) susceptible to manipulation or bias, (3) involve unobservable data, or (4) depend on the company's intent and ability to carry out specific actions.

4. Evaluating the reasonableness of significant assumptions—The auditor should determine whether the company has a reasonable basis for significant assumptions used and whether the significant assumptions are consistent with the following, when applicable:

    a. Relevant industry and other external factors, including economic factors

    b. The company's objectives, strategies, and business risks

    c. External market information

    d. Relevant historical or recent experience

    e. Other significant assumptions used by the company in other estimates tested by the auditor

5. Critical accounting estimates

    a. Definition: "An accounting estimate where (a) the nature of the estimate is material due to the levels of subjectivity and judgment necessary to account for highly uncertain matters or the susceptibility of such matters to change and (b) the impact of the estimate on financial condition or operating performance is material."

    b. The auditor should obtain an understanding of management's analysis of the sensitivity of its significant assumptions to change when evaluating the reasonableness of the significant assumptions and potential for bias.

Fair Value Estimates

After studying this lesson, you should be able to:

1. Understand the auditor's responsibilities to apply a risk-based audit approach to evaluate the reasonableness of fair value accounting estimates in accordance with AICPA Professional Standards and in accordance with PCAOB auditing standards.

2. Recognize the role of "observable inputs" and "unobservable inputs" in evaluating estimation uncertainty for fair value accounting estimates.

I. **Responsibilities under AICPA Professional Standards**—The relevant AICPA guidance is provided by AU 540, *Auditing Accounting Estimates, Including Fair Value Accounting Estimates and Related Disclosures*. This pronouncement states that the auditor's objective is to obtain sufficient appropriate audit evidence about whether the accounting estimates (including fair value accounting estimates) are reasonable and whether the related disclosures are adequate in view of the applicable financial reporting framework.

II. **The Risk-Based Audit Approach**

Note
The prior discussion related to auditing accounting estimates is also applicable to the discussion here related to auditing fair value accounting estimates, which is based on the same Statement on Auditing Standards. The focus here is on audit considerations that are specific to fair value measurements and disclosures.

A. **Basis for Risk Assessment**—The auditor should obtain an understanding of the applicable financial reporting requirements, and how management makes the fair value accounting estimate (and data used), including how management assessed the effect of estimation uncertainty.

B. **Identifying and Assessing Risks of Material Misstatement**—The auditor should evaluate the degree of estimation uncertainty involved and determine whether any of those fair value accounting estimates result in significant risks.

C. **Responding to the Assessed Risks of Material Misstatement**—The auditor should determine whether management complied with the applicable financial reporting requirements, and whether the methods used to make the fair value accounting estimate are appropriate and are consistently applied. The auditor should consider the need for specialized skills or knowledge.

D. **Further Substantive Procedures to Respond to Significant Risks**—The auditor should evaluate how management addressed estimation uncertainty; whether management's significant assumptions are reasonable; and, when relevant, whether management has the intent and ability to carry out specific actions.

E. **Evaluating the Reasonableness of the Estimates**—The auditor should evaluate whether the fair value accounting estimates are reasonable relative to the requirements of the applicable financial reporting framework.

F. **Disclosures**—The auditor should obtain sufficient appropriate audit evidence as to whether the disclosures meet the requirements of the applicable financial reporting framework. The auditor should also evaluate the adequacy of disclosure of the estimation uncertainty for any identified significant risks.

G. **Indicators of Possible Management Bias**—The auditor should consider whether the fair value accounting estimates might indicate possible management bias.

H. **Documentation**—The auditor should document the following:

   1. The basis for the auditor's conclusions about the reasonableness of fair value accounting estimates resulting in significant risks and their disclosure, *and*

   2. Any indications of possible management bias.

III. Additional Guidance Regarding Estimation Uncertainty Particularly for Fair Value Accounting Estimates

A. Nature of Estimation Uncertainty—High estimation uncertainty results in an increased risk of material misstatement when, for example:

1. Fair value accounting estimates for derivative instruments are not publicly traded.

2. Fair value accounting estimates are based on a highly specialized entity-developed model or when the assumptions (inputs) cannot be observed in the marketplace.

> " ... the existence of published price quotations ordinarily is the best audit evidence of fair value."

B. Examples of Fair Value Accounting Estimates—Complex financial instruments (not traded in an open market); share-based payments; property held for disposal; certain assets or liabilities acquired in a business combination, including intangibles; and nonmonetary exchange of assets.

C. For fair value accounting estimates, assumptions (inputs) affect estimation uncertainty and vary as follows:

1. **Observable inputs**—Assumptions that market participants would use in pricing an asset or liability based on market data from sources independent of the reporting entity or

2. **Unobservable inputs**—An entity's own judgments about what assumptions market participants would use. Estimation uncertainty increases when the fair value estimates are based on unobservable inputs.

D. Testing how Management Makes the Estimate—The auditor may decide to test how management made their estimate (and the data used) when the accounting estimate is a fair value accounting estimate using observable and unobservable inputs.

E. Evaluating the Method of Measurement—Determining whether the method or model used by management is appropriate requires professional judgment.

F. Evaluating the Use of Models for Fair Value Accounting Estimates—Matters the auditor may consider in testing the model include the following:

1. Whether the model is validated for suitability prior to usage

2. Whether appropriate controls exist over changes

3. Whether the model is periodically tested for validity (when inputs are subjective)

4. Whether adjustments are made to the model's outputs

5. Whether the model is adequately documented, including key parameters and limitations

G. Considering Specialized Skills or Knowledge—In considering the need for specialized skills or knowledge, the auditor may consider whether any complex calculations or models are involved in making fair value accounting estimates when no observable market exists.

H. Indicators of Possible Management Bias—An example of an indicator of possible management bias would be the use of an entity's own assumptions for fair value accounting estimates that are inconsistent with observable market conditions.

I. Communication with Those Charged with Governance—Another SAS requires the auditor to communicate the auditor's views about the qualitative aspects of the entity's significant accounting practices, including accounting estimates. The auditor should determine that they are informed about the process used by management in developing sensitive accounting estimates, as well as the auditor's basis for conclusions about those matters.

IV. PCAOB Guidance

PCAOB Auditing Standard No. 43 addresses accounting estimates, including fair value measurements. PCAOB AS § 2501 (*Auditing Accounting Estimates, Including Fair Value Measurements*) replaces three previous PCAOB standards separately dealing with (1) accounting estimates, (2) fair value measurements, and (3) derivative instruments. It was approved by the SEC in July 2019 and is effective for audits for fiscal years ending on or after December 15, 2020.

A. "In general, fair values of financial instruments based on trades of identical financial instruments in an active market have a lower risk of material misstatement than fair values derived from observable trades of similar financial instruments or unobservable inputs."

B. **Using Pricing Information from a Pricing Service**

1. The reliability of pricing information provided is affected by (a) the pricing service's experience and expertise and (b) whether the pricing service has a relationship with the company

2. The relevance of pricing information used as audit evidence is affected by the following:

   a. Whether the values are based on quoted prices in active markets for identical financial instruments

   b. When the values are based on transactions of similar financial instruments—The auditor should consider how those transactions were determined to be comparable.

   c. When no recent transactions have occurred for the financial instrument being valued (or for similar financial instruments)—The auditor should consider whether the inputs used are representative of the assumptions that market participants would use for valuation purposes; the auditor should perform additional procedures to evaluate the appropriateness of the method used by the pricing service.

C. **Using Pricing Information from Multiple Pricing Services**—Less information is required when the following conditions are met:

1. There are recent trades of identical or similar financial instruments.

2. The type of financial instrument is routinely priced by several pricing services.

3. Prices are reasonably consistent across the various pricing services.

4. The pricing information is based on inputs that are observable.

D. **Using Pricing Information from a Broker or Dealer**

1. The relevance and reliability of the evidence provided depends on whether

   a. The broker or dealer has a relationship with the company.

   b. The broker or dealer is a "market maker" that deals in the same type of financial instrument.

   c. The quote reflects market conditions as of the financial statement date.

   d. The quote is binding on the broker or dealer.

   e. There are any restrictions, limitations, or disclaimers in the quote.

2. "Broker quotes generally provide more relevant and reliable evidence when they are timely, binding quotes, without any restrictions, limitations, or disclaimers, from unaffiliated market makers transacting in the same type of financial instrument."

E. **When Unobservable Inputs Are Significant to the Valuation**—The auditor should evaluate the reasonableness of the unobservable inputs.

F. **When Changes Are Made to Observable Information**—The auditor should consider whether the assumptions used are consistent with what market participants would use for pricing purposes.

Lawyer's Letters

After studying this lesson, you should be able to:

1. Understand procedures the auditor would perform related to legal liability issues.

2. Understand the agreement between the AICPA and American Bar Association regarding matters that can be communicated to the auditor in the "lawyer's letter" in response to a "letter of inquiry" (with emphasis on "asserted" and "unasserted claims").

3. Be familiar with the language used in a typical "letter of inquiry to legal counsel."

I. **Responsibilities under AICPA Professional Standards**—The relevant AICPA guidance is provided by AU 501, *Audit Evidence—Specific Considerations for Selected Items*. This pronouncement states that the auditor's objective is "to obtain sufficient appropriate audit evidence regarding the completeness of litigation, claims, and assessments involving the entity" (among other matters specifically addressed by the SAS).

II. **Audit Procedures Related to Legal Contingencies**

A. Management is the primary source of information about these legal contingencies. The auditor should make appropriate inquiries of management.

B. The auditor should read the minutes of all meetings of those charged with governance where significant issues, including matters related to legal liability, affecting the financial statements likely would be discussed.

C. To corroborate management's responses to the auditor's inquiries about the identity of lawyers who have rendered significant legal services to the client (and to whom a letter of inquiry should be sent)—the auditor should examine the charges to the related expense account and then examine (vouch to) the appropriate underlying invoices.

D. The auditor should draft a *letter of inquiry* for management to send to those lawyers who have rendered litigation-related services to the entity. The lawyer's response to the letter of inquiry is simply called the *lawyer's letter* (or *attorney's letter*). The primary purpose of the lawyer's letter is to corroborate management's responses to the auditor's inquiries about legal-related contingencies. When the entity's in-house counsel has responsibility for such litigation-related matters, the auditor should send a similar letter of inquiry to the in-house counsel and obtain a written response.

E. One or more lawyer's letters are expected to be included in the audit documentation. However, the SAS allows for the possibility that the entity may not have any relevant "litigation, claims, or assessments" having financial reporting significance. In that case, the auditor would include a specific statement of fact in the management representations letter stating that the entity had no legal counsel to address current or potential litigation issues.

III. **Inquiries of the Client's Lawyer(s)**—The letter of inquiry normally includes the entity's listing of various legal matters that the lawyer is handling (classified separately as Asserted Claims and Unasserted Claims) to facilitate the lawyer's response.

IV. **Asserted Claims**—With respect to asserted claims and active litigation "asserted" means that someone has already filed a claim or has at least announced the intention to make such a claim, which is synonymous with the AICPA's term "pending or threatened litigation." According to the American Bar Association, the lawyer should inform the auditor directly about any omissions of asserted claims in the lawyer's letter responding to the letter of inquiry.

V. Unasserted Claims—With respect to unasserted claims and potential litigation, "unasserted" means that the entity has exposure to litigation, but no one has yet announced an intention to sue.

   A. The lawyer cannot (according to the American Bar Association's *Statement of Policy Regarding Lawyers' Responses to Auditors' Requests for Information*) inform the auditor directly about any omission of unasserted claims as identified in the letter of inquiry.

   B. However, lawyers must tell their client about any such omissions and request that client management then inform the auditors.

   C. Note that this issue (whether the entity's lawyer has informed management of any omission of an unasserted claim that management should discuss with their auditors) is implicitly addressed in the management representations letter.

   D. An unasserted claim must be disclosed according to GAAP if the following two conditions exist:

   1. It is probable that a claim will be asserted, *and*

   2. It is at least reasonably possible that a material unfavorable outcome will occur.

VI. Scope Limitation—A limitation in the lawyer's response is a scope limitation sufficient to preclude an unmodified opinion (a nonresponse would likely result in a disclaimer of opinion owing to a major scope limitation).

VII. Sample Letter of Inquiry to Legal Counsel

Illustrative Letter of Inquiry to Legal Counsel

(Prepared on Client's Letterhead)

(*Date*[1])

(*Name of Lawyer*)

(*Address of Lawyer*)

Dear _____ :

In connection with an audit of our financial statements at (*balance-sheet date*) and for the (*period*) then ended, management of the Company has prepared, and furnished to our auditors (*state name and address of auditors*), a description and evaluation of certain contingencies, including those set forth below involving matters with respect to which you have been engaged and to which you have devoted substantive attention on behalf of the Company in the form of legal consultation or representation. These contingencies are regarded by management of the Company as material for this purpose.[2]

Pending or Threatened Litigation (excluding unasserted claims)

(Ordinarily, the information would include the following: (1) the nature of the litigation; (2) the progress of the case to date; (3) how management is responding or intends to respond to the litigation (e.g., to contest the case vigorously or to seek an out-of-court settlement); and (4) an evaluation of the likelihood of an unfavorable outcome and an estimate, if one can be made, of the amount or range of potential loss.)

Please furnish to our auditors such explanation, if any, that you consider necessary to supplement the foregoing information, including an explanation of those matters as to which your views may differ from those stated and an identification of the omission of any pending or threatened litigation, claims, and assessments or a statement that the list of such matters is complete.

Unasserted Claims and Assessments (considered by management to be probable of assertion, and that, if asserted, would have at least a reasonable possibility of an unfavorable outcome)

(Ordinarily, the information would include the following: (1) the nature of the litigation; (2) how management intends to respond if the claim is asserted; and (3) an evaluation of the likelihood of an unfavorable outcome and an estimate, if one can be made, of the amount or range of potential loss.)

Please furnish to our auditors such explanation, if any, that you consider necessary to supplement the foregoing information, including an explanation of those matters as to which your views may differ from those stated.

We understand that whenever, in the course of performing legal services for us with respect to a matter recognized to involve an unasserted possible claim or assessment that may call for financial statement disclosure, if you have formed a professional conclusion that we should disclose or consider disclosure concerning such possible claim or assessment, as a matter of professional responsibility to us, you will so advise us and will consult with us concerning the question of such disclosure and the applicable requirements of Statement of Financial Accounting Standards No. 5. Please specifically confirm to our auditors that our understanding is correct.

Please specifically identify the nature of and reasons for any limitation on your response.

(The auditor may request the client to inquire about additional matters, for example, unpaid or unbilled charges or specified information on certain contractually assumed obligations of the company, such as guarantees of indebtedness of others.)

Very truly yours,

(*Authorized Signature for Client*)[3]

---

[1]The sending of this letter should be timed so that the lawyer's response is dated as close as practicable to the date of the auditor's report. However, the auditor and client should consider early mailing of a draft inquiry as a convenience for the lawyer in preparing a timely response to the formal letter of inquiry.

[2]Management may indicate a specific materiality limit if an understanding has been reached with the auditor. Your response should include matters that existed at (*balance-sheet date*) and during the period from that date to the date of your response.

[3]If a client has not needed to retain legal counsel, the auditors may express an unmodified opinion on the financial statements even though they have not obtained a letter from legal counsel of the Company. In these circumstances, the auditors should obtain written representation from the Company that legal counsel has not been retained for matters concerning business operations that may involve current or prospective litigation.

Management Representations Letters

I. **Responsibilities under AICPA Professional Standards**—The relevant AICPA guidance is provided by AU 580, *Written Representations*. This pronouncement states that the auditor's objectives are

   A. "To obtain written representations from management that they believe they have fulfilled their responsibility for the preparation and fair presentation of the financial statements and for the completeness of information provided to the auditor;

   B. Support other audit evidence relevant to the financial statements by means of written representations determined necessary by the auditor; *and*

   C. Respond appropriately to written representations provided by management … or if management … (does) not provide the written representations requested by the auditor."

II. **Document Verbal Responses to Auditor's Inquiries**

   A. An auditor is required to obtain written representations from management to corroborate management's verbal responses to important inquiries by the auditor.

   B. This letter from management is addressed directly to the auditors.

   C. The letter should be signed by those members of management with overall responsibility for financial and operating matters—ordinarily the chief executive officer (CEO) and the chief financial officer (CFO).

      1. Their unwillingness to sign the management representations letter would be a scope limitation probably resulting in a disclaimer of opinion or withdrawal from the engagement.

      2. If any such representations are contradicted by other evidence—the auditor should investigate the circumstances and evaluate the implications to reliance on other management representations.

   D. The representations letter should cover all periods encompassed by the auditor's report. If current management was not present for all periods covered, tailor the representations to the circumstances.

   E. Date of the management representations letter—the representations letter should be dated the same as the date of the auditor's report.

III. **The Specific Content of the Representations Depend on the Circumstances**—Usually include the following provisions as applicable.

   A. **Regarding the Financial Statements:**

      1. That management is responsible for the fairness of the financial statements

      2. That management is responsible for internal control over financial reporting

      3. That management is responsible for internal control to prevent and detect fraud

      4. That significant assumptions used for any accounting estimates are reasonable

      5. That related party transactions have been properly accounted for and disclosed

      6. That subsequent events have been properly accounted for and disclosed

7. That any uncorrected misstatements are immaterial

8. That the effects of litigation and claims have been properly accounted for and disclosed

B. Regarding the Information Provided:

1. That all relevant financial records and unrestricted access to personnel were made available to the auditor

2. That all transactions have been recorded

3. That management has made available the results of their assessment of fraud risks

4. That regarding fraud, there is no fraud involving management or employees having significant internal control responsibilities, or others where the financial statement effect could be material

5. That management has no knowledge of suspected fraud communicated by employees, former employees, or others

6. That management has disclosed all instances of noncompliance with laws and regulations relevant to financial reporting

7. That there are no (undisclosed) litigations, claims, and assessments relevant to the financial statements

8. That management has disclosed all known related party relationships and transactions

C. Sample Management Representations Letter

Illustrative Management Representation Letter

(Prepared on the Entity's Letterhead)

(To Auditor)

(Date)

This representation letter is provided in connection with your audit of the financial statements of ABC Company, which comprise the balance sheet as of December 31, 20XX, and the related statements of income, changes in stockholders' equity, and cash flows for the year then ended, and the related notes to the financial statements, for the purpose of expressing an opinion on whether the financial statements are presented fairly, in all material respects, in accordance with accounting principles generally accepted in the United States (U.S. GAAP).

Certain representations in this letter are described as being limited to matters that are material. Items are considered material, regardless of size, if they involve an omission or misstatement of accounting information that, in the light of surrounding circumstances, makes it probable that the judgment of a reasonable person relying on the information would be changed or influenced by the omission or misstatement.

Except where otherwise stated below, immaterial matters less than $[insert amount] collectively are not considered to be exceptions that require disclosure for the purpose of the following representations. This amount is not necessarily indicative of amounts that would require adjustment to or disclosure in the financial statements.

We confirm that (*to the best of our knowledge and belief, having made such inquiries as we considered necessary for the purpose of appropriately informing ourselves*) [*as of (date of auditor's report),*]:

Financial Statements

– We have fulfilled our responsibilities, as set out in the terms of the audit engagement dated (insert date), for the preparation and fair presentation of the financial statements in accordance with U.S. GAAP.

– We acknowledge our responsibility for the design, implementation, and maintenance of internal control relevant to the preparation and fair presentation of financial statements that are free from material misstatement, whether due to fraud or error.

– We acknowledge our responsibility for the design, implementation, and maintenance of internal control to prevent and detect fraud.

– Significant assumptions used by us in making accounting estimates, including those measured at fair value, are reasonable.

– Related party relationships and transactions have been appropriately accounted for and disclosed in accordance with the requirements of U.S. GAAP.

– All events subsequent to the date of the financial statements and for which U.S. GAAP requires adjustment or disclosure have been adjusted or disclosed.

– The effects of uncorrected misstatements are immaterial, both individually and in the aggregate, to the financial statements as a whole. A list of the uncorrected misstatements is attached to the representation letter.

– The effects of all known actual or possible litigation and claims have been accounted for and disclosed in accordance with U.S. GAAP.

(Any other matters that the auditor may consider appropriate.)

Information Provided

– We have provided you with:

• Access to all information, of which we are aware that is relevant to the preparation and fair presentation of the financial statements such as records, documentation, and other matters;

• Additional information that you have requested from us for the purpose of the audit; and

• Unrestricted access to persons within the entity from whom you determined it necessary to obtain audit evidence.

– All transactions have been recorded in the accounting records and are reflected in the financial statements.

– We have disclosed to you the results of our assessment of the risk that the financial statements may be materially misstated as a result of fraud.

– We have *(no knowledge of any)* *(disclosed to you all information that we are aware of regarding)* fraud or suspected fraud that affects the entity and involves:

• Management;

• Employees who have significant roles in internal control; or

• Others when the fraud could have a material effect on the financial statements

– We have *(no knowledge of any)* *(disclosed to you all information that we are aware of regarding)* allegations of fraud, or suspected fraud, affecting the entity's financial statements communicated by employees, former employees, analysts, regulators or others.

– We have disclosed to you all known instances of noncompliance or suspected noncompliance with laws and regulations whose effects should be considered when preparing financial statements.

– We *(have disclosed to you all known actual or possible)* *(are not aware of any pending or threatened)* litigation, claims, and assessments whose effects should be considered when preparing the financial statements [and we have not consulted legal counsel concerning litigation, claims, or assessments].

– We have disclosed to you the identity of the entity's related parties and all the related party relationships and transactions of which we are aware.

(Any other matters that the auditor may consider necessary.)

(Name and Signature of Chief Executive Officer with Title)

(Name and Signature of Chief Financial Officer with Title)

Related-Party Issues

After studying this lesson, you should be able to:

1. Know the definition of the term *related parties*.

2. Understand the auditor's responsibility to address related-party issues, in accordance with AICPA Professional Standards.

I. **Responsibilities under AICPA Professional Standards**—The relevant AICPA guidance is provided by the clarified SAS, AU-C 550, *Related Parties*. This pronouncement states that the auditor's objectives are:

    A. To obtain an understanding of related-party relationships and transactions to address fraud risk factors and evaluate whether the financial statements achieve fair presentation and

    B. To obtain sufficient appropriate audit evidence about whether related-party relationships and transactions are properly accounted for and adequately disclosed in the financial statements.

II. **Definitions**

    A. FASB definition of *related parties*: The essence of this definition is that one party has the ability to influence the conduct of the other party.

> "Affiliates of the enterprise; entities for which investments are accounted for by the equity method by the enterprise; trusts for the benefit of employees, such as pension and profit-sharing trusts that are managed by or under the trusteeship of management; principal owners of the enterprise; its management; members of the immediate families of principal owners of the enterprise and its management; and other parties with which the enterprise may deal if one party controls or can significantly influence the management or operating policies of the other to an extent that one of the transacting parties might be prevented from fully pursuing its own separate interests."

    B. AICPA definition of *arm's-length transaction*:

> "A transaction conducted on such terms and conditions between a willing buyer and a willing seller who are unrelated and are acting independently of each other and pursuing their own best interests. "

III. **The Historical Cost Principle**—The historical cost principle in accounting is based on the notion of an exchange price negotiated in an arms-length transaction, which results in an accurate measure of the value exchanged. However, related parties could potentially set the transaction price at whatever value they wish, without regard to the "real" economic value. Auditors are generally not in a position to provide reliable, independent appraisals of transaction prices between related parties. As a result, auditors are particularly concerned with the adequacy of disclosure about transactions between related parties.

IV. **The Auditor's Responsibilities Under the SAS**

    A. **Risk Assessment**—The auditor should assess the risk of material misstatement that could result from the entity's related-party relationships and transactions. The auditor should view any significant related-party transactions outside the entity's normal course of business as significant risks.

        1. The auditor should inquire of management and others within the entity about

            a. The identity of the entity's related parties

            b. The nature of the relationships involved

    c. The business purpose of entering into a transaction with a related party (instead of an unrelated party)

    d. Whether the entity entered into, modified, or terminated any transactions with related parties; if so, the type and business purpose of the transactions

2. The auditor should also inquire about (and perform other risk assessment procedures) to obtain an understanding of the applicable controls established to (a) identify and account for such related-party relationships and transactions; (b) authorize and approve significant transactions with related parties, as well as those that may be significant unusual transactions. (The risk of management override of controls is higher when management has significant influence with parties with whom the entity does business.)

    a. Should inquire about any related-party transactions that were not subject to established controls for authorization and approval; inquire about the reasons for any such exceptions.

    b. Examples of arrangements that may indicate undisclosed related-party relationships

        i. Participation in partnerships with other parties

        ii. Agreements with other parties having conditions outside the normal course of business

        iii. Guarantees involving other parties

    c. Examples of transactions that may be significant unusual transactions (i.e., outside the normal course of business)

        i. Complex equity transactions (restructurings or acquisitions)

        ii. Transactions with offshore entities

        iii. Sales transactions with unusually large discounts

        iv. Transactions with circular arrangements (such as repurchase agreements)

    d. The auditor should stay alert for any indications of related-party relationships or transactions that management has failed to disclose to the auditor. The auditor should be attentive to such matters when

        i. Reviewing bank confirmations and other records or documents

        ii. Reading the minutes of meetings of those charged with governance

    e. Relevant information about the related parties should be shared with the members of the engagement team.

3. Response to Risk Assessment—The auditor should obtain sufficient appropriate audit evidence about the assessed risks of material misstatement due to related-party relationships and transactions.

    a. When there is a significant risk about related-party transactions—The auditor may perform substantive procedures such as the following:

        i. Confirm specific terms of the transactions with the related parties

        ii. Inspect evidence in the possession of the entity or the related party

        iii. Confirm (or discuss) information with intermediaries, such as banks or others

        iv. Review audited financial statements, income tax returns, or reports issued by regulatory agencies to assess the financial condition of the other party

    b. Procedures to obtain an understanding of the business relationships involving a related party (and to determine the need for further substantive procedures) include the following:

     i. Inquiries of management and those charged with governance

     ii. Inquiries of the related parties

     iii. Inspection of contracts with the related party

     iv. Review of employee whistleblowing reports, if available

     v. Background research, perhaps using the Internet

4. Evaluation—The auditor should evaluate whether the identified related-party relationships and transactions have been appropriately accounted for and properly disclosed and whether the financial statements achieve *fair presentation* regarding those related-party relationships and transactions. The substance of the transactions is normally more important than their legal form.

  a. If the auditor identifies related-party transactions not previously disclosed by management—The auditor should:

     i. Communicate relevant information to members of the engagement team

     ii. Ask management to identify all transactions with the newly identified related party

     iii. Inquire about why the entity's controls did not identify the related-party relationship

     iv. Perform appropriate substantive audit procedures

     v. Reconsider the risk that there may be other undisclosed related-party relationships

     vi. Evaluate whether management's failure to disclose the matter might have been intentional

  b. If the auditor identifies related-party transactions that are required to be disclosed or are considered to be a significant risk—The auditor should determine whether those transactions have been appropriately authorized. The auditor should also inspect any underlying agreements to evaluate the business purpose and whether the terms are consistent with management's explanations or whether the business rationale might suggest fraud.

5. Communication—The auditor should communicate with those charged with governance any significant matters involving the entity's related parties and inquire about any concerns those charged with governance may have about relationships or related-party transactions.

6. Documentation—The auditor should include in the audit documentation the names of the identified related parties and the nature of the related-party relationships and transactions.

B. Procedures to Identify the Existence of Related Parties

1. Inquire of management as to the existence of any related-party relationships; for any identified significant unusual transactions, inquire whether related parties could be involved.

2. Review prior year's audit documentation for continuing engagements.

3. Might inquire of the predecessor auditors for a first-year engagement (if applicable).

4. Review any applicable SEC filings (for public companies) that list related parties.

5. Review stockholder listings of closely held companies to identify major stockholders.

C. Procedures to Identify Transactions with the Related Parties

1. Inquire of management about any such transactions. Review any conflict-of-interest statements furnished to the company by management.

2. Review minutes of board of directors' meetings for mention of significant activities with related parties.

3. Review the accounting records for any large, unusual, or nonrecurring transactions, especially near the end of the reporting period.

4. Examine underlying documents for unusual or large transactions (such as investment transactions) and transactions that have terms or conditions that are inconsistent with prevailing market conditions (such as loans with abnormal interest rates or without stated maturity dates):

   a. Guarantees of loans (either payable or receivable) might be identified on confirmations of such loans

   b. Transactions with major customers, suppliers, borrowers, or lenders might indicate undisclosed relationships

   c. Invoices from law firms might indicate work performed for related parties or related-party transactions

PCAOB on Related Parties

After studying this lesson, you should be able to:

1. Understand how to identify and assess the risks of material misstatement involving related party relationships and transactions under PCAOB auditing standards.

2. Understand how to respond to the assessed risks of material misstatement involving related party relationships and transactions and to evaluate their financial statement effects under PCAOB auditing standards.

3. Know the auditor's responsibilities for communicating with an entity's audit committee about related party relationships and transactions under PCAOB auditing standards.

I. **Related Parties**

II. **Introduction and Overview**

A. Until 2014, the PCAOB guidance with respect to related-party issues was a now-superseded AICPA Statement on Auditing Standards adopted by the PCAOB on a temporary basis in 2003. The PCAOB updated its guidance on related-party relationships and transactions by incorporating the PCAOB's risk assessment standards issued in 2010.

B. **Objective**—The auditor's objective is "to obtain sufficient appropriate audit evidence to determine whether related parties and relationships and transactions with related parties have been properly identified, accounted for, and disclosed in the financial statements."

C. **Risk Assessment**—The auditor should identify and assess the risks of material misstatement at the financial statement and assertion levels, including the risks of material misstatement associated with related parties and transactions with related parties.

D. **Response to Risk Assessment**—The auditor should design and implement audit responses addressing the assessed risks of material misstatement, including the risks of material misstatement associated with related parties and transactions with related parties.

> **Note**
> *If management makes an assertion that transactions with related parties were conducted on terms equivalent to those prevailing in arm's-length transactions, the auditor should determine whether evidence obtained supports or refutes such assertions. Such an assertion may result in a qualified or adverse opinion, since it may be impossible for management to determine what the terms would have been had the parties not been related.*

III. **Perform Risk Assessment Procedures**—The auditor should perform procedures to obtain an understanding of the nature of the relationships between the company and its related parties, including the terms and business purposes of transactions with related parties.

A. The auditor should obtain an understanding of the company's process for

1. Identifying related parties and transactions with related parties;

2. Authorizing and approving transactions with related parties; *and*

3. Accounting for and disclosing relationships and transactions with related parties in the financial statements.

B. The auditor should make appropriate inquiries of management, others who may be knowledgeable about related-party issues, and the audit committee (or chair).

1. Inquire of management about the following:

a. The names of the company's related parties, the nature of the relationships, and any changes from the prior period;

b. Background information about the related parties, including location, industry, size, etc.;

  c. The transactions involving related parties during the period, including the terms and business purposes of those transactions; *and*

  d. Any related-party transactions that were not authorized according to the company's established policies (including any exceptions that were granted and the reasons).

 2. Inquire of others who may have knowledge of the matters identified above. These may include internal auditors, in-house legal counsel, the chief compliance/ethics officer, and the human resources director.

 3. Inquire of the audit committee (or its chair) about the audit committee's understanding of the company's relationships, significant related-party transactions, and whether any member of the audit committee has any concerns about related-party issues.

C. Communication—The auditor should communicate relevant information about related-party issues to engagement team members (and, when using the work of other auditors, the auditor should communicate relevant information about related-party issues to those other auditors).

IV. Response to Risk Assessment —The auditor should respond appropriately to the assessed risks of material misstatement associated with related parties and transactions with related parties.

A. For any related-party transactions that are required to be disclosed or that are determined to be a significant risk, the auditor should do the following:

 1. Read the underlying documents for consistency with explanations from inquiries and other audit evidence about the business purpose;

 2. Determine whether the transaction has been authorized and approved in accordance with the company's established policies and whether any exceptions to the company's established policies were granted;

 3. Evaluate the financial capability of the related parties with respect to significant responsibilities (relevant information might include the audited financial statements of the related parties, reports of regulatory agencies, financial publications, and income tax returns if available); *and*

 4. Perform other procedures as necessary regarding the assessed risks of material misstatement.

B. Intercompany Accounts —The auditor should address the risks of material misstatement regarding the company's intercompany accounts.

V. Evaluation of Financial Statement Treatment —The auditor should evaluate whether the company has properly identified its related parties and transactions with related parties.

A. The auditor should read the minutes of board meetings and evaluate any significant unusual transactions, including transactions with executives.

B. If the auditor believes that previously undisclosed related-party relationships or transactions may exist, the auditor should perform procedures (beyond inquiry of management) to determine whether those relationships or transactions do exist.

C. If the auditor determines that previously undisclosed related-party relationships or transactions exist, the auditor should do the following:

 1. Inquire of management about the possible existence of other transactions with the related party previously undisclosed;

 2. Evaluate why the matter was previously undisclosed to the auditor;

 3. Communicate relevant information to other members of the audit team;

 4. Consider the need to perform additional procedures to identify other relationships or transactions previously undisclosed;

 5. Perform the procedures identified above for transactions with related parties required to be disclosed or determined to be a significant risk; *and*

6. Reconsider the auditor's risk assessment: (1) Evaluate the implications to the auditor's assessment of internal control; (2) reassess the risk of material misstatement and perform additional procedures as necessary; and (3) evaluate the implications for the audit if the auditor believes the undisclosed matter indicates that fraud or an illegal act may be involved.

D. Communications with the Audit Committee

A. In general, the auditor should communicate the auditor's evaluation of the company's identification and financial reporting of related-party relationships and transactions.

B. The auditor should also communicate other significant matters associated with related-party relationships and transactions, such as the following:

1. Related-party relationships or transactions with parties that were previously undisclosed to the auditor

2. Significant related-party transactions that have not been authorized in accordance with the company's established policies or for which exceptions to the company's established policies were made

3. Related-party transactions identified by the auditor that appear to lack an appropriate business purpose

4. Management's assertion included in the financial statements that the terms of a related-party transaction were equivalent to that of an arm's-length transaction (and the evidence obtained by the auditor that is consistent or inconsistent with that assertion)

E. Indicators of Related Parties and Transactions Undisclosed to the Auditor

The PCAOB provides examples of information (and sources of information) that may indicate to the auditor that related parties or related-party transactions previously undisclosed to the auditor might exist.

A. Examples of **information** that may indicate that related parties or transactions with related parties previously undisclosed to the auditor might exist

1. Purchasing or selling at significantly different than market prices

2. Sales transactions that have unusual terms (e.g., "bill and hold" transactions) or engaging in transactions that lack economic substance

3. Borrowing or lending at significantly different than normal terms

4. Advancing funds that are used to pay for an otherwise uncollectible receivable

5. Guarantees outside the normal course of business

B. Examples of **sources of information** that may indicate that related parties or transactions with related parties previously undisclosed to the auditor might exist:

1. Filings with the SEC and other regulatory agencies

2. Confirmation responses and lawyer letters

3. Internal reports (e.g., reports prepared by the entity's internal auditors and records from the company's whistleblower program)

4. Shareholder registers identifying major shareholders

5. Contracts and other agreements with management or others involving significant unusual transactions

Subsequent Events and Related Issues

After studying this lesson, you should be able to:

1. Know what is meant by the term *subsequent events*, and distinguish between those that require adjustments to the financial statement and those that require disclosure without adjustment.

2. Understand the auditing procedures associated with identifying subsequent events issues.

3. Recognize the effect that subsequent events issues may have on dating the auditor's report.

4. Understand the auditor's responsibilities when subsequently discovered facts become known to the auditor before (and after) the report release date.

5. Understand the predecessor auditor's responsibility when considering the reissuance of the auditor's report on prior period financial statements.

I. **Responsibilities under AICPA Professional Standards**—The relevant AICPA guidance is provided by AU 560, *Subsequent Events and Subsequently Discovered Facts*. This pronouncement states that the auditor's objectives are

   A. To obtain sufficient appropriate audit evidence about whether subsequent events are properly reflected in the financial statements;

   B. To respond appropriately to subsequently discovered facts; and

   C. For a predecessor auditor who is requested to reissue a previously issued report, to perform specified procedures to determine whether the previously issued report is still appropriate.

Definitions

Subsequent Events: Events occurring between the date of the financial statements and the date of the auditor's report.

Subsequently Discovered Facts: Facts that become known to the auditor after the date of the auditor's report that, had they been known to the auditor at that date, may have caused the auditor to revise the auditor's report.

II. **Subsequent Events Requiring Adjustment**—Where such an event provides new or better information about circumstances in existence as of the balance sheet date.

Example
A lawsuit that could only be estimated at the balance sheet date was settled for a fixed amount prior to the issuance of the audit report; with the benefit of this new information, there is no need to estimate the financial statement consequences, since the actual consequence is now known and can be used to adjust the income statement and balance sheet.

III. **Subsequent Events Requiring Disclosure Only**—Where disclosure of a material event or transaction is necessary so that the financial statements will not be misleading, even though the subsequent events issue is unrelated to circumstances existing at the balance sheet date.

Example
After the balance sheet date, a tornado wiped out the company's facilities and the company had no casualty insurance; disclosure would be required to prevent financial statement readers from being misled about the entity's circumstances, but adjustment would not be required since the financial statement presentation was appropriate at year-end.

IV. **Audit Procedures Regarding Subsequent Events**

    A. **Inquire of Management**—Include an appropriate reference to such subsequent events in the management representations letter. The auditor should also obtain an understanding of management's procedures to identify subsequent events, as appropriate.

    B. Review the minutes of meetings of those charged with governance. (Include all meetings up to the date of the audit report.)

    C. The lawyer's letter may be relevant to this issue (regarding legal contingencies).

    D. Scan journals and ledgers subsequent to year-end (through fieldwork) for any unusual items.

V. **Subsequently Discovered Facts Known Before the Report Release Date**—Subsequently discovered facts that became known to the auditor before the report release date

    A. The auditor should discuss the matter with management (and possibly those charged with governance) and determine whether the financial statements require revision. If so, the auditor should inquire as to how management will address the matter.

    B. **If Management Revises the Financial Statements**—The auditor should perform appropriate audit procedures on the revision.

    C. **If Management Does Not Revise the Financial Statements**—If the auditor believes that revision is necessary, the auditor should appropriately modify the opinion.

VI. **Subsequently Discovered Facts Known After the Report Release Date**

    A. The auditor should discuss the matter with management (and possibly those charged with governance) and determine whether the financial statements require revision. If so, the auditor should inquire as to how management will address the matter.

    B. **If Management Revises the Financial Statements**—The auditor should

        1. Perform appropriate audit procedures on the revision;

        2. Assess whether management's actions are timely and appropriate to ensure that users are informed; *and*

        3. If the opinion on the revised financial statements differs from that previously expressed; add an emphasis-of-matter or other matter paragraph (that identifies the date of the previous report, the opinion previously expressed, and the reason for the different opinion now expressed).

    C. **If Management Does Not Revise the Financial Statements**—If the auditor believes that revision is necessary, the auditor should determine whether those financial statements have already been made available to third parties.

        1. If the financial statements have not been made available to third parties, the auditor should notify management and those charged with governance that the financial statements should not be made available to third parties before making necessary revisions and a new audit report has been provided.

        2. If the financial statements have been made available, the auditor should determine whether management has taken timely and appropriate steps to ensure that users have been informed not to rely on those financial statements.

        3. If management does not take the necessary steps to inform the users, the auditor should notify management and those charged with governance that the auditor will try to prevent users' reliance on the auditor's report.

VII. If a Predecessor Auditor Reissues the Auditor's Report

A. The predecessor should perform the following procedures to determine whether the previously issued auditor's report is still appropriate:

1. Read the financial statements of the subsequent period (and compare those financial statements with the ones previously audited and reported on to identify any significant changes);

2. Inquire of and request written representations from management about any issues, including subsequent events, that might affect the previous representations from management; *and*

3. Obtain a representation letter from the successor auditor about any known matters affecting the financial statements audited by the predecessor.

B. If a Subsequently Discovered Fact Becomes Known to the Predecessor

1. The predecessor auditor should discuss the matter with management (and possibly those charged with governance) and determine whether the financial statements require revision. If so, the auditor should inquire as to how management will address the matter.

2. If management revises the financial statements and the predecessor auditor plans to issue a new auditor's report—the predecessor should:

   a. Perform the procedures necessary to evaluate the revision (and date the audit report appropriately or dual-date the report for the revision);

   b. Assess steps taken by management to ensure that users do not rely on the erroneous financial statements; *and*

   c. If the opinion on the revised financial statements differs from that previously expressed, add an emphasis-of-matter or other matter paragraph (that identifies the date of the previous report, the opinion previously expressed, and the reason for the different opinion now expressed).

VIII. Dating the Auditor's Report—Applicable to subsequent events, as well as to subsequently discovered facts involving the auditor or the predecessor auditor.

A. Dating the Auditor's Report—The auditor's report should not be dated earlier than the date on which the auditor has obtained "sufficient appropriate audit evidence to support the opinion."

1. Earlier auditing standards used to emphasize the *completion of fieldwork* as the relevant date for the audit report.

2. Current standards emphasize that the audit report should not be dated before the completion of fieldwork, and may be dated later than that. For example, management must take responsibility for the financial statement presentation, including footnotes; and the auditor must review and evaluate the audit documentation before having *sufficient appropriate evidence* both of which may follow the so-called completion of fieldwork.

3. When reissuing an audit report on financial statements that require disclosure, but not adjustment, for a material subsequent event, the reissued audit report may use the original report date if the entity under audit includes a separate footnote to the financial statements labeled something like "Event (Unaudited) Subsequent to the Date of the Independent Auditor's Report."

B. Subsequent Events—Dating the auditor's report when a subsequent event occurs after the completion of fieldwork but prior to the issuance of the auditor's report

1. If the financial statements are adjusted without any accompanying disclosure, the report should be dated whenever the auditor has obtained *sufficient appropriate audit evidence* (which may be the completion of fieldwork or later). In this case, there is no need to consider *dual dating*.

2. If the financial statements are (a) adjusted along with additional footnote disclosure; or (b) disclosure is added without adjustment—the audit report may be either "dual dated" (using one date for the overall audit report and a later date to address a specific subsequent event) or the entire audit report may be dated as of the later date (which makes the auditor responsible, in general, for all subsequent events up to that later date).

Example
Dual-Dating the Audit Report
"February 16, 20X1, except for Note XY, as to which the date is March 1, 20X1"

C. Subsequently Discovered Facts—If management revised the financial statements

1. Before the report release date—The auditor should either date the auditor's report as of a later date (and extend the audit procedures to the new date and obtain an updated management representations letter as of the new date) or dual-date the auditor's report for the revision.

2. After the report release date (also applicable to a predecessor auditor)—The auditor should date the audit report appropriately or dual-date the report for the revision.

Going Concern Issues

This lesson addresses the auditor's responsibilities under AICPA *Professional Standards* when there is substantial doubt about an entity's ability to continue as a going concern. The focus includes the additional audit procedures that may be required and the implications to the auditor's report when substantial doubt about an entity's ability to continue as a going concern exists.

After studying this lesson, you should be able to:

1. Identify the types of indicators that would cause the auditor to have "substantial doubt about an entity's ability to continue as a going concern" (and the routine audit procedures that would likely detect such issues).

2. Describe the additional evidence-gathering responsibilities (and documentation requirements) the auditor has when substantial doubt about the entity's ability to continue as a going concern exists.

3. Understand the audit reporting implications of going concern issues.

I. **Responsibilities Under AICPA *Professional Standards*—**The relevant AICPA guidance is provided by AU-C 570, *The Auditor's Consideration of an Entity's Ability to Continue as a Going Concern*. This pronouncement identifies the following audit objectives:

    A. To obtain sufficient appropriate audit evidence whether management's use of the going concern basis of accounting is appropriate when used in the preparation of the financial statements;

    B. To conclude whether substantial doubt about an entity's ability to continue as a going concern for a reasonable period of time exists;

    C. To evaluate the possible financial statement effects (including disclosure) regarding the entity's ability to continue as a going concern for a reasonable period of time; *and*

    D. To report appropriately in accordance with this SAS.

Definition

Reasonable Period of Time: "The period of time required by the applicable financial reporting framework or, if no such requirement exists, within one year after the date that the financial statements are issued (or within one year after the date that the financial statements are available to be issued, when applicable)."

II. **Management's Responsibility for the Evaluation of Going Concern Issues**

    A. FASB requires management to evaluate whether substantial doubt exists within one year of the issuance of the financial statements; GASB has a similar requirement for governmental entities.

    B. Financial statements are prepared using the "going concern basis of accounting" unless the "liquidation basis of accounting" is appropriate.

III. **Auditor Requirements**

    A. **Perform Risk Assessment Procedures—**Should consider whether conditions or events exist that raise substantial doubt; should determine whether management has performed an evaluation of any such conditions or events.

        1. **If management has made an evaluation—**Should discuss the evaluation with management and obtain an understanding of management's plans to mitigate the effects of conditions or events causing substantial doubt.

        2. **If management has not made an evaluation—**Should discuss management's intended use of the going concern basis of accounting and inquire whether management may have substantial doubt about the entity's ability to continue as a going concern for a reasonable time.

B. Auditor's Evaluation of Management's Evaluation and Supporting Analysis

1. Should consider all relevant information known to the auditor; and should consider the same period that management used in its evaluation.

2. **Period beyond management's evaluation**—Should inquire of management about any conditions or events after the period of management's evaluation that may be relevant to the entity's ability to continue as a going concern.

3. **When conditions or events are identified that raise substantial doubt**—Should perform additional audit procedures, including consideration of any mitigating factors

   a. Request that management make an evaluation if they have not already done so.

   b. Evaluate whether management's plan as to whether it is probable that the plans can be implemented and would effectively mitigate the conditions or events that raise the going concern issue.

   c. **When financial support by "supporting parties" (either third parties or the entity's owner-manager) are important to management's plans**—Should obtain sufficient appropriate audit evidence (specifically, in writing) about the supporting parties' **intent** and **ability** of those parties to provide the necessary support.

   d. **When the analysis of the entity's cash flow forecast is significant to management's plans**—Should evaluate the reliability of the underlying data and the adequacy of the support for the underlying assumptions.

> **Note**
> The intent of the supporting parties may be established by obtaining from management the "support letter" from the supporting party or by confirming the commitment directly with the supporting parties. The auditor should consider the legality and enforceability of the commitments. Ability may be established by evidence of past support given, along with evidence of the solvency of the supporting party (e.g., reviewing bank statements or the valuation of assets held by the supporting party).

4. **Procedures to identify conditions or events that raise going concern issues**

   a. **Audit procedures routinely performed in any audit engagement are normally sufficient to identify relevant conditions or events**—Need not design specific procedures to identify the conditions or events that would raise substantial doubt.

   b. These procedures include performing substantive analytical procedures, reviewing for subsequent events, reviewing the entity's compliance with requirements of its debt agreements (regarding breach of contract matters that could accelerate the due date of the debt), reading the minutes of meetings of those charged with governance, and sending a letter of inquiry to the entity's attorney(s) to request a lawyer's letter regarding litigation issues.

   c. **When conditions or events raise substantial doubt**—There may be a need for additional audit procedures (e.g., analyzing and discussing the entity's latest interim financial statements or relevant forecasts, determining the adequacy of support for planned disposals of assets, etc.).

5. **Going concern issues might be indicated by the following circumstances:**

   a. **Negative financial trends**—Recurring operating losses, negative cash flow from operations, adverse financial ratios, etc.

   b. **Other indications**—Already in default, entity is denied usual trade credit, cash dividends are in arrears, the entity is selling pieces its business, etc.

  c. Internal matters—Facing work stoppages, dependence on a particular project or customer, etc.

  d. External matters—Uninsured casualty losses, significant litigation, changing technology, etc.

C. Written Representations—Should request written representations from management (1) about management's plans intended to mitigate the relevant conditions or events, and (2) whether disclosure of all relevant matters is appropriate (including the conditions or events involved and management's plans).

D. Auditor Conclusions—The auditor should reach a conclusion about the following:

1. **Use of the going concern basis of accounting**—Should conclude on the appropriateness of management's use of the going concern basis of accounting in the preparation of the financial statements.

2. **Substantial doubt**—Should conclude on whether there are conditions or events that raise substantial doubt about the entity's ability to continue as a going concern for a reasonable period of time.

3. **Adequacy of disclosure**—Should conclude whether disclosure is adequate (whether or not substantial doubt has been alleviated by management's plans).

E. Communication with Those Charged with Governance—Should include the following in such communication:

1. Whether there are conditions or events that constitute substantial doubt for a reasonable period of time;

2. Auditor's consideration of management's plans;

3. Whether management's use of the going concern basis of accounting in its financial statements is appropriate;

4. The adequacy of disclosures in the financial statements; *and*

5. The implications of these going concern issues for the auditor's report.

F. Audit Documentation—Should document the following:

1. The conditions or events causing the auditor to have substantial doubt for a reasonable period of time;

2. Elements of management's plans considered to be significant in mitigating those conditions or events;

3. Audit procedures performed (and results obtained) to evaluate the significant elements of management's plans;

4. Auditor's conclusion as to whether the substantial doubt remains or is alleviated and the evaluation of the adequacy of related disclosures; *and*

5. Auditor's conclusion with respect to the effects on the auditor's report.

G. Implications of Going Concern Issues for the Auditor's Report

1. **When the use of the going concern basis of accounting is inappropriate**—Should express an adverse opinion when liquidation is imminent and management's use of the going concern basis of accounting in inappropriate.

2. **If disclosure is inadequate**—Should either express a qualified or adverse opinion, as appropriate.

3. **If the auditor is unable to obtain sufficient appropriate audit evidence**—Should either express a qualified opinion or disclaimer of opinion, as appropriate.

4. **When there is substantial doubt about the entity's ability to continue as a going concern (but the use of the going concern basis of accounting is appropriate) and disclosure is adequate** — Should include a "Going Concern" section to the auditor's report (after the "Opinion" and "Basis for Opinion" sections).

5. **Prohibited the inappropriate use of conditional language** — The SAS prohibits using "conditional language" in expressing a conclusion about the existence of substantial doubt; for example, the SAS offered the following as inappropriate: "The Company has been unable to renegotiate its expiring credit agreements. Unless the Company is able to obtain financial support, there is substantial doubt about its ability to continue as a going concern."

Note

The following "Going Concern" section should be added to the auditor's report when (1) the auditor concludes that substantial doubt exists; (2) management's plans do not alleviate that substantial doubt; and (3) the entity is required by applicable (FASB) reporting standards to include a note to the financial statements that substantial doubt exists:

Substantial Doubt About the Company's Ability to Continue as a Going Concern

The accompanying financial statements have been prepared assuming that the Company will continue as a going concern. As discussed in Note X to the financial statements, the Company has suffered recurring losses from operations, has a net capital deficiency, and has stated that substantial doubt exists about the Company's ability to continue as a going concern. Management's evaluation of the events and conditions and management's plans regarding these matters are also described in Note X. The financial statements do not include any adjustments that might result from the outcome of this uncertainty. Our opinion is not modified with respect to this matter.

Audit Evidence: Specific Audit Areas

Introduction to Auditing Individual Areas

After studying this lesson, you should be able to:

1. Identify the six assertions for account balances at the end of the period as broad audit objectives applicable to balance-sheet line items for which the auditor must gather evidence as a basis for evaluation.

2. Identify certain audit procedures that are generally applicable to these assertions and other audit procedures that are generally applicable to every individual audit area.

I. **Audit Procedures Generally Applicable to the Six Assertions for Account Balances**—Note that these assertions represent broad audit objectives for which the auditor must gather evidence to determine whether the financial statement elements are fairly presented in accordance with the applicable accounting framework (e.g., GAAP).

   A. **Existence**—Related to the validity of recorded items.

      1. **Confirmation**—(Especially when concerned about overstatements.) For example, cash, accounts receivable, inventory held by others, and investments held by others.

      2. **Observation**—Especially for inventory or investment securities held by the entity.

      3. **Agree (vouch) to underlying documents**—Agree items from the accounting records to the supporting source documents to evaluate the appropriateness of recorded items: for example, as an alternate procedure for accounts receivable; to verify additions to property, plant, and equipment accounts; and for various liabilities, such as notes payable.

   B. **Completeness**—Related to omissions of amounts that should have been recorded.

      1. **Cutoff tests**—Trace from supporting source documents back to the accounting records looking for omissions. For example, trace from shipping documents to cost of goods sold or to the sales journal, or perform a "search for unrecorded liabilities."

      2. **Analytical procedures**—These are applicable to every audit area, but be specific: calculate a particular ratio or compare something specific to another specific thing!

   C. **Rights and Obligations**—Related to any restrictions to the entity's rights to their assets or to the obligations for their liabilities.

      1. **Inquire of applicable client personnel**—Inquire about compensating balances with banks, the use of specific assets as collateral for debts, review debt agreements for collateral, etc.; the management representation letter should document these inquiries regarding important matters.

      2. **Examine authorization of transactions**—to ascertain whether any unusual conditions apply.

   D. **Accuracy, Valuation, and Allocation**—Related to the appropriateness of dollar measurements.

      1. **Recalculate account balances**—(Verify the client's calculations), for example, for depreciation expense and prepaid insurance.

      2. **Trace to subsequent cash receipts or disbursements**—Includes tracing to cash receipts or cash disbursements journal and to the applicable bank statement.

      3. **Analytical procedures**—review the aged trial balance for accounts receivable to evaluate the apparent reasonableness of the allowance for uncollectibles. (In connection with such

analytical procedures, the auditor may also inspect underlying sales invoices or shipping documents to test the accuracy of the entity's data underlying the analytical procedures.)

4. **Examine published price quotations for fair value measurements, when applicable**—Verify mathematical accuracy. Verify that the supporting ledgers or other accounting records agree to the reported balance per the general ledger before performing other audit procedures on those supporting accounting records for purposes of reaching a conclusion about the fairness of the general ledger account balance involved. *Foot* and *cross-foot* the underlying records to verify that they, in fact, add up.

E. **Classification**—Related to the use of appropriate accounts for the financial statement elements.

1. **Inquire of applicable client personnel**—For example, inquire about receivables due from management/employees that should be separated from normal trade receivables.

2. **Review lending agreements**—to distinguish amounts that should be reported as current (versus noncurrent) liabilities.

F. **Presentation**—Related to the appropriate level of aggregation of financial statement elements and the appropriate disclosures associated with them.

1. Review footnote disclosures relative to the auditor's disclosure checklist.

2. Inquire of management about related-party issues and management's going-concern assessment.

II. Audit Procedures Generally Applicable to Every Individual Audit Area

A. **Consider the Implications of Internal Control**—Remember the acronym **"SCARE"** [for "segregation of duties, controls (as in physical controls), authorization, reviews (as in performance reviews), and EDP (for information processing)]" discussed in the "Internal Control Concepts and Standards" section") to identify control activities of interest to the auditor relevant to planning the **nature, timing, and extent of substantive procedures** that underlie detection risk, based on the assessed level of control risk.

B. **Substantive Procedures usually Performed in Every Individual Audit Area**

1. Agree the financial statement elements (or the trial balance from which the financial statement elements are derived) to the underlying accounting records (i.e., to the general ledger).

2. Scan the entity's journals and ledgers for any unusual items.

3. Make appropriate inquiries of management and other personnel (and document those important inquiries and management's responses in the management representations letter).

4. Perform specific analytical procedures—consider historical trends and events within the industry.

Cash

After studying this lesson, you should be able to:

1. Be familiar with the content of the standard bank confirmation form.

2. Verify the appropriateness of each of the items on an entity's bank reconciliation that supports the entity's reported cash balance.

3. Understand what is meant by the term kiting and how the auditor might address this issue.

I. Review the Client's Bank Reconciliation for Each Cash Account

A. Request a **cutoff bank statement** approximately 10 days after year-end, to test the reconciling items on the year-end bank reconciliation. (This request must come from management to the entity's financial institution to provide information directly to the entity's auditors.)

1. **Deposits in-transit**—Verify that items listed as deposits in transit on the bank reconciliation have been processed as deposits on the cutoff bank statement (testing for existence/occurrence regarding the validity of those reconciling items); these should appear in chronological order on the cutoff bank statement.

2. **Outstanding checks**—Look for checks processed with the cutoff bank statement and having a date prior to year-end; trace those items to the client's list of outstanding checks for completeness. (Note that checks outstanding at year-end will not necessarily clear the bank in order or within the period encompassed by the cutoff bank statement.)

B. **Confirm** directly with the bank the balance according to the bank statement (usually confirm two separate bank-related matters: (1) cash balances with emphasis on the existence assertion; and (2) liabilities to the bank with emphasis on the completeness assertion)—Note that such evidence obtained from independent sources outside the client organization is viewed as very reliable evidence.

Sample Bank Reconciliation As of 12/31/X1:

Balance per bank @ 12/31/X1	$X[1]
Add: Deposits in transit	X[2]
Less: Outstanding checks	(X)[3]
Adjusted balance as of 12/31/X1	$X
Balance per books @ 12/31/X1	X[4]
Add: Credits directly by bank (e.g., interest)	X[5]
Less: Charges by bank (service charges, etc.)	(X)
Adjusted balance as of 12/31/X1	$X

[1] Confirmed as of 12/31/X1... (A-3).

[2] Agreed to bank cutoff statement (A-4).

[3] Reviewed canceled checks (dated December or earlier and processed in January) returned with bank cutoff statement (A-4); no omissions from the outstanding check listing were noted.

[4] Agreed to General Ledger as of 12/31/X1.

[5] Agreed to client's December bank statement.

"Tick Mark Legend" (with reference to supporting working papers)

a - Confirmed with the bank as of 12/31/X1... (see W/P A-3)

b - Agreed to bank cut-off statement received directly from the bank for the first 10 days of January (see W/P A-4)

c - Reviewed canceled checks returned with bank cut-off statement for the first 10 days of January (see W/P A-4); agreed the canceled checks (> $X) dated in December (or earlier) to the client's outstanding check list. No omissions were detected

d - Agreed to the General Ledger as of 12/31/X1

e - Agreed to client's December bank statement

Standard Form to Confirm Account
Balance Information with Financial Institutions

_____
Customer Name

Financial Institution's Name and Address

[ ]

[ ]

We have provided to our accountants the following information as of the close of business on_____, 20___, regarding our deposit and loan balances. Please confirm the accuracy of the information, noting any exceptions to the information provided. If the balances have been left blank, please complete this from by furnishing the balance in the appropriate space below.* Although we do not request nor expect you to conduct a comprehensive, detailed search of your records, if during the process of completing this confirmation additional information about other deposit and loan accounts we may have with you comes to your attention, please include such information below. Please use the enclosed envelope to return the form directly to our accountants.

1. At the close of business on the date listed above, our records indicated the following deposit balance(s):

Account Name	Account No.	Interest Rate	Balance

2. We were directly liable to the financial institution for loans at the close of business on the date listed above as follows:

Account No./Description	Balance	Due Date	Interest Rate	Date through which interest is paid	Description of Collateral

_____
Customer's Authorized Signature

_____
Date

The information presented above by the customer is in agreement with our records. Although we have not conducted a comprehensive, detailed search of our records, no other deposit or loan accounts have come to our attention except as noted below.

_____
Financial Institution Authorized Signature / Title

_____
Date

Exceptions and/or comments

Please return this form directly to our accountants: [ ]

*Ordinarily, balances are intentionally left blank if they are not available at the time the form is prepared.

[ ] D 451 5951

Approved 1990 by American Bankers Association, American Institute of Certified Public Accountants, and Bank Administration Institute.

Additional forms available from: AICPA - Order Department, P.O. Box 1003, NY, NY 10108-1003

II. Multiple Checking Accounts with Transfers Among Them

    A. Prepare a schedule of interbank (or intercompany) transfers to verify that both sides of the transfer are properly accounted for (i.e., verify that the cash receipts journal and the cash disbursements journal both reflect the transfer in the same proper period) and to detect any **kiting.**

    B. Kiting is an overstatement of the true cash balance at year-end caused by recording the receipt, while failing to record the disbursement, associated with a transfer between cash accounts. (Note that recording the disbursement, while failing to record the receipt part of a transfer between cash accounts would result in a misstatement—however, it would be an understatement of the cash balance and, therefore, would be inconsistent with kiting, which results specifically in an overstatement.)

III. If Fraud (Misappropriation) Is Suspected—The auditor may prepare a **proof of cash**. This compares the beginning balance per the bank plus deposits minus checks clearing the bank versus the beginning balance per the books plus receipts minus disbursements according to the books.

IV. Petty Cash—May count cash on hand at the client's request. (If the auditor chooses to perform any specific audit procedures for an immaterial account, such as petty cash, analytical procedures are usually sufficient, such as simply comparing the current year's general ledger balance to the prior year's general ledger balance.)

V. Inquire of Management—About any **restrictions on cash balances**. If there is a minimum balance requirement for cash, then that restriction should be disclosed.

> **Note**
> *The* management representations letter *usually addresses any* compensating balances *(minimum balance requirements) that constitute a restriction on spendable cash. (The usual management representations comment that addresses all general restrictions on the entity's rights to its assets is: "The company has satisfactory title to all owned assets, and there are no liens or encumbrances on such assets nor has any asset been pledged as collateral.")*

Accounts Receivable

I. **Recall the assertions** that AICPA Professional Standards identify for account balances (and related disclosures) at the end of the period: (1) existence; (2) completeness; (3) rights and obligations; (4) accuracy, valuation, and allocation; (5) classification; and (6) presentation.

   A. **Related to the Existence Assertion**—Confirm selected individual customers' accounts.

   B. Verify that the subsidiary A/R ledger agrees or reconciles with the A/R general ledger balance:

   1. Recall that the *accounting records* constitute one category of evidence. The second category is *other information* according to AICPA Professional Standards and is covered in the review module on Audit Evidence.

   2. It is important to establish the logical connection between the detailed accounting records being used for the audit procedure (in this case, the subsidiary ledger of individual customer accounts) and that which is the object of the auditor's intended conclusions (specifically, the general ledger balance for A/R).

   C. **Confirm all accounts** that are determined to be individually material and confirm selected other accounts on a test basis.

   1. **Positive confirmations**—Request a response whether the individual customer agrees or disagrees with the stated balance. A nonresponse indicates a situation that should be followed up by the auditor.

   2. **Negative confirmations**—Request a response only if the individual customer disagrees with the stated balance.

      a. A nonresponse is taken as evidence supporting the client's representation.

      b. The risk is that the recipient of the request might have thrown it away without even verifying the balance owed.

      c. Accordingly, negative confirmations are usually used only for rather small balances under conditions of effective internal control (i.e., low control risk).

   D. **Investigate All Exceptions (Disagreements) Received**—Determine whether the client's records are accurate and, if not, whether the financial statements are materially misstated.

   E. If no response is received to a positive confirmation request, the auditor should send a second confirmation request, and perform **alternate procedures** if still no response is received.

   1. **Subsequent cash receipts (the preferred alternate procedure)**—Trace collections on the account subsequent to the date of the confirmation to the cash receipts journal and to the bank statement (suggests the balance was valid if it was subsequently collected).

   2. **Vouch to (inspect) the underlying documents (the last resort if the account has not been collected)**—Examine the documents (customer's purchase order, client's sales invoice, and shipping documents) supporting the validity (*occurrence*) of the transactions comprising the account balance.

II. Related to the Accuracy, Valuation, and Allocation Assertion—Evaluate the reasonableness of management's estimates of the *allowance for uncollectibles* and the *allowance for sales returns*.

A. Note that confirmations may contribute, in part, to the auditor's conclusions about the **fairness of the dollar valuation**; however, that contribution relates to establishing the reasonableness of the gross A/R and additional procedures are required to assess the net realizable value of the A/R.

B. Review the Client's Aged Trial Balance of Accounts Receivable

    1. Inquire about any large, delinquent items.

    2. Estimate the percentage of uncollectible accounts within each category of age (based on prior year's working papers tempered by current economic conditions).

C. Review **receivers (documents used by the entity's receiving department to capture deliveries) after year-end** for sales returns; consider prior years' returns in view of current economic conditions.

D. Review **adjusting journal entries** (e.g. write-offs) for appropriate authorization.

III. Related to the Completeness Assertion

A. Perform a **cutoff test** of sales. Examine the shipping documents for the last few shipments before year-end and the first few shipments after year-end; compare these shipping documents with the related sales invoices to assess whether the sales were recorded in the appropriate period.

B. Compare these shipping documents around the end of the period with the related sales invoices (related to the sales journal) to assess whether the sales were recorded in the appropriate period.

C. Proper cutoff involves two assertions (existence/occurrence and completeness). Usually the auditor performs certain specific audit procedures directed at testing the validity of recorded transactions (i.e., existence/occurrence) but completeness is primarily addressed by these cutoff procedures (along with applicable analytical procedures).

IV. Related to the Rights and Obligations Assertion—Inquire of management:

A. About receivables pledged as collateral for debts (and review loan agreements to identify such collateral)

B. About shipments on consignment that are not actual sales

C. Document such inquiries (and management's response) in the management representations letter.

V. Related to the Classification and Presentation Assertions

A. Inquire of management about any receivables due from employees or management that should be presented separately from ordinary trade accounts receivable.

B. Inquire of management about any sales/receivables involving related parties for which specific disclosure is required.

C. Document such inquiries (and management's response) in the management representations letter.

Note

Lapping is an attempt to cover up a theft of receipts, where a clerk might try to apply a later receipt to the prior customer's account (and so on) until the scam ends by writing off someone's account as uncollectible. Lapping is a type of fraud (specifically, misappropriation of assets) that is associated with an improper segregation of duties whereby someone with access to the customer's payment also has the authority to make entries in the accounting records to cover up the theft.

Inventory

After studying this lesson, you should be able to:

1. Recognize that the assertions for account balances (and related disclosures) at the end of the period represent a framework for preparing an audit plan to evaluate the fairness of inventory.

2. Identify appropriate substantive audit procedures to address those assertions when auditing inventory.

Recall the assertions that that AICPA Professional Standards identify for account balances at the end of the period: (1) existence; (2) completeness; (3) rights and obligations; (4) accuracy, valuation, and allocation; (5) classification; and (6) presentation.

I. **Relevant AICPA Guidance**—The relevant AICPA guidance is provided by AU 501, *Audit Evidence—Specific Considerations for Selected Items*. Part of this standard focuses specifically on inventory, which is summarized here. The standard states that the auditor's objective is to obtain sufficient appropriate audit evidence about the **existence and condition** of inventory.

II. **Related to the Existence Assertion**—The auditor participates in the client's physical count of inventory (the observation of inventory):

A. **Note**—The **client counts** the entire inventory and the **auditor observes** the client's taking of the inventory (while taking independent *test counts*). The auditor participates in this process for two primary reasons, referred to as *dual purpose* tests.

1. **Internal control objectives**—The auditor should study the client's written procedures and instructions given to the employees or others counting the inventory to assess the adequacy of the design of these procedures in achieving an accurate physical count; the auditor's focus here is assessing control risk related to inventory reporting.

2. **Substantive audit objectives**—The auditor should take a sample of inventory items and verify the physical existence of quantities reflected in the client's detailed records supporting the ending inventory; the auditor's focus here is assessing the fairness of the reported inventory.

Recall that the *direction* of the test is critical to the inference associated with an audit procedure:

To test existence for inventory—The auditor should select items from the client's (final) inventory listing, which is essentially the subsidiary ledger for the adjusted general ledger balance. The auditor should agree those selected items to the underlying inventory count tags (and the auditor's own count sheets) that serve as source documents.

To test completeness for inventory—The direction of the test is just the opposite. The auditor should select items from the underlying inventory count tags (including the auditor's own count sheets) and agree those to the client's inventory listing to establish that there were no omissions from the client's inventory listing.

B. **Related to Audit Procedures**—Emphasizing quantities:

1. **Auditor's attendance at physical inventory counting**—Involves (a) inspecting the inventory to ascertain its existence and evaluate its condition (and performing test counts); (b) observing compliance with management's instructions and the performance of procedures for recording and controlling the results of the physical count; and (c) obtaining audit evidence about the reliability of management's count procedures

2. Review the client's written inventory-taking procedures to determine that the physical count will be complete and accurate (regarding dates, locations, personnel involved, and instructions about accounting for the prenumbered inventory tags, cutoff procedures, and error resolution procedures)

3. Assessing the accuracy of the client's reported inventory **quantities**. The auditor should perform test counts for a sample of the prenumbered inventory tags, trace these counts into the client's count sheets (to verify the accuracy of the client's counts on a test basis) and to the client's final inventory listing that supports the general ledger balance. Note that the entity's final inventory listing (reflecting both quantities and dollar amounts) serves as the "subsidiary ledger" for inventory and represents the dollar amount for inventory to which the general ledger account will be adjusted.

4. Focus on the client's prenumbered inventory tags. Determine that all tags have been properly accounted for (i.e., all tags are used, unused and returned, or have been voided and returned to a responsible official).

5. The auditor should be alert for and inquire about obsolete or damaged items (e.g., dusty or damaged cartons) related to the valuation assertion; the auditor should also be alert for empty containers or hollow spaces.

C. If the physical count of inventory occurs on a date other than the date of the financial statements, the auditor should perform audit procedures to determine whether changes in inventory between those dates are properly recorded.

D. If the auditor is unable to attend physical inventory counting due to unforeseen circumstances, the auditor should make some physical counts on an alternative date and perform audit procedures on intervening transactions.

E. If attendance at physical inventory counting is impracticable, the auditor should perform alternative audit procedures to obtain sufficient appropriate audit evidence regarding the existence and condition of inventory. If that is not possible, then the auditor should appropriately modify the auditor's opinion.

F. If there is a material amount of inventory stored in a **public warehouse**, the auditor can confirm such inventory with the custodian (or could consider physical observation).

III. **Related to the Accuracy, Valuation, and Allocation Assertion**

A. **Price Tests**—Regarding the **unit costs** (not selling prices!) attributed to inventory items:

1. Affected by the client's inventory methods (perpetual versus periodic inventory system) and cost flow assumptions (LIFO, FIFO, average)

2. For merchandising (nonmanufacturing) inventory—Examine the appropriate underlying invoices

3. For manufactured inventory—Review the supporting job order cost records (or the process cost worksheets) and test to underlying documents.

B. **Test Extensions**—Recalculate the product of quantity times cost/unit for selected items:

1. Add up these extensions to verify that the items tested are reflected in the total of the detailed inventory listing supporting the client's general ledger balance. This can be described as "verifying the mathematical accuracy" to establish the connection between the general ledger balance and the supporting detailed listing;

2. Scan the detailed inventory listing for any unusual items;

3. Review the client's reconciliation (or the adjusting journal entry) of the general ledger balance to the detailed inventory listing.

C. **Lower of Cost or Market Considerations (and Lower of Cost or Net Realizable Value)**—Inquire of management as to the existence of any damaged, obsolete, or excess inventory items that might require a write-down from historical cost to net realizable value; be attentive to these issues when participating in the observation of inventory.

IV. Related to the Completeness Assertion—Procedures that might identify material omissions of inventory:

   A. Test **inventory cutoff** (recall "FOB-shipping point" versus "FOB-destination" as a technical issue determining when ownership of goods is transferred):

      1. Related to increases in inventory—Review "receivers" (receiving documents used by the entity's receiving department to capture deliveries) for a few days before and after year-end (part of "purchases" cutoff test);

      2. Related to decreases to inventory—Review shipping documents for a few days before and after year-end (related to "sales" and, hence, "cost of goods sold" cutoff test).

   B. Analytical Procedures (Perhaps by Location or by Product-Line)—Compare the current year to the prior year and inquire about any significant differences in:

      1. Gross profit rates

      2. Inventory turnover (primarily applicable to the valuation assertion regarding slow-moving inventory)

      3. Shrinkage rates

      4. Total inventory

V. Related to the Rights and Obligations Assertion

   A. Inquire of management about any inventory that might be pledged as collateral for borrowings (and review loan agreements to identify such collateral).

   B. Document such inquiries (and management's response) in the management representations letter.

VI. Related to the Classification and Presentation Assertions

   A. Inquire about any inventory that is held on consignment for which the entity under audit retains the risk of ownership; such goods should be included in reported inventory.

   B. For manufacturing entities, examine the appropriateness of the reported raw materials, work in process, and finished goods categories of inventory.

VII. Other Issues Related to Auditing Inventory

   A. Use of Specialists—An auditor may need to engage an outside expert if the determination of **quantities** and/or **quality** is too complex (e.g., electronics, precious jewels).

   B. If an auditor is unable to verify the **beginning** inventory for a first-year audit, but is able to verify the **ending** inventory:

      1. The auditor may render an opinion on the balance sheet and disclaim an opinion on the income statement, statement of retained earnings, and the statement of cash flows (due to the inability to verify cost of goods sold and, hence, net income).

      2. It may be possible to establish the reasonableness of a new client's beginning inventory from alternate procedures—through the use of analytical procedures or by reviewing a predecessor auditor's working papers.

Investments in Securities and Derivative Instruments

> **After studying this lesson, you should be able to:**
>
> **1.** Understand the auditor's responsibilities, under AICPA Professional Standards, when auditing investments (including derivative instruments and hedging activities).
>
> **2.** Recognize that the assertions for account balances (and related disclosures) at the end of the period represent a framework for preparing an audit plan to evaluate the fairness of investments.
>
> **3.** Identify appropriate substantive audit procedures to address those assertions when auditing investments.

I. Relevant AICPA Guidance—The relevant AICPA guidance is provided by AU 501, *Audit Evidence—Specific Considerations for Selected Items* (part of this Standard with investments in securities and derivative instruments as summarized here), with additional guidance provided by a related AICPA Audit Guide.

   A. The objective of AU 501 (as it relates to investments)—To obtain sufficient appropriate audit evidence regarding the valuation of investments in securities and derivative instruments.

   B. Definition of "estimation uncertainty" (from AU 540 regarding accounting estimates)—"The susceptibility of an accounting estimate and related disclosures to an inherent lack of precision in its measurement."

      1. Estimation uncertainty increases with the increasing complexity of the financial instrument and with the increasing variability of the cash flows involved.

      2. The risk of material misstatement (RMM) increases with estimation uncertainty.

   C. The Audit Guide introduced several additional concepts of risk.

      1. Credit (or counterparty) risk—"[The] risk that one party to a financial instrument will cause a financial loss to another party by failing to discharge an obligation, and it is often associated with default."

      2. Market risk—"[The] risk that the fair value or future cash flows of a financial instrument will fluctuate because of changes in market prices"; examples include currency risk, interest rate risk, and commodity and equity price risk.

      3. Liquidity risk—"[The] risk of not being able to buy or sell a financial instrument at an appropriate price in a timely manner due to a lack of marketability for that financial instrument."

      4. Operational risk—"Operational risk relates to the specific processing required for financial instruments. Operational risk may increase as the complexity of a financial instrument increases, and poor management of operational risk may increase other types of risk."

   D. Purposes Served by Financial Instruments—(1) Hedging purposes to mitigate risk exposures and (2) speculative purposes (either trading purposes related to short-term market changes or investment purposes related to long-term returns).

   E. Distinction between the term "derivative" and the term "hedge":

      1. Derivative—A derivative is a financial instrument or other contract whose value is derived (hence the name "derivative") from its relationship to something else, known as the underlying. The underlying can be another financial instrument, a physical commodity, currency, etc.

      2. Hedge—A hedge is a derivative used specifically as a defensive strategy designed to protect against the risk of adverse price or interest rate movements to achieve a state of balance.

F. The Audit Guide referenced FASB's "fair value hierarchy" that classifies inputs into three different levels; estimation uncertainty and RMM increases as the financial instrument moves from level 1 to level 2 to level 3 (in other words, moving away from observable inputs toward unobservable inputs increases estimation uncertainty).

    1. Level 1 inputs—Quoted prices in active markets for identical financial assets or liabilities; usually viewed as sufficient appropriate evidence of fair value.

    2. Level 2 inputs—Inputs other than quoted market prices (level 1) that are observable either directly (as prices) or indirectly (derived from prices); may involve similar assets or liabilities or markets that are not very active.

    3. Level 3 inputs—Unobservable inputs for the asset or liability with little or no market activity at the measurement date.

G. Models may be used to establish valuation when the market price is not observable.

    1. Models range from simple (e.g., using a bond pricing formula) to complex (e.g., using software tools involving level 3 inputs)—A frequently used model for option-pricing purposes is known as Black-Scholes.

    2. Models consist of three primary components: (a) a methodology; (b) underlying assumptions; and (c) data used—These should be adequately documented.

H. **Third-Party Pricing Sources**

    1. Smaller entities or those that have a relatively low volume of transactions for financial instruments may base the valuation on third-party pricing sources.

    2. Third-party pricing sources usually fall into two categories: (a) pricing services (including consensus pricing services) or (b) brokers providing broker quotes.

        a. Pricing services—Valuations are based on market data and prices collected from a wide variety of sources to derive estimated fair values (often using level 2 inputs).

        b. Consensus pricing services—Such services obtain pricing information about an instrument from participating subscribers who submit prices; the service returns to each subscriber the consensus price (usually an average after eliminating outliers); consensus pricing may be the best available data for some financial instruments, such as exotic derivatives.

        c. Brokers providing broker quotes (often used for instruments with level 3 inputs)— Broker quotes may be "executable" or "indicative": (a) Executable quotes are strong evidence of fair value and represent a price at which the broker is willing to transact; (b) indicative quotes are a weaker evidence of fair value, since there is a lack of transparency of methods used.

I. **Use of Valuation Specialists by Management**—The methodology and data used are usually readily available to management; management is still responsible for the valuation used, whether obtained from a specialist or not.

J. **General Auditing Considerations for Financial Instruments**

    1. Planning considerations—Auditors normally focus on:

        a. Understanding the accounting and disclosure requirements.

        b. Understanding the purpose and risks associated with the financial instruments.

        c. Determining whether specialized skills and knowledge are required, including possibly engaging an auditor's specialist to assist.

        d. Understanding and evaluating the relevant internal controls.

        e. Understanding management's processes for valuing the financial instruments.

        f. Assessing and responding to the RMM for the financial instruments.

2. **Internal control considerations**—The auditor should obtain an understanding of the relevant internal controls associated with financial instruments to properly assess the RMM to determine the nature, timing, and extent of further audit procedures.

   a. The Audit Guide framed the discussion of internal control issues around the five components: (1) control environment, (2) risk assessment, (3) information and communication system, (4) control activities, and (5) monitoring.

   b. The discussion of control activities emphasized the importance of segregation of duties in this context—Financial instrument activities may be segregated into these functions: (1) executing the transaction (dealing); (2) initiating payments or handling receipts (settlements); (3) sending out trade confirmations and reconciling any differences; (4) recording transactions in the accounting records; (5) monitoring risk limits; and (6) monitoring positions and valuing financial instruments.

   c. Testing the operating effectiveness of controls—When an entity has a trading function for financial instruments, substantive tests alone may be insufficient as a basis for the auditor's conclusions; however, tests of control will not be sufficient by themselves.

3. **Assessing and responding to the RMM**

   a. Overall considerations—RMM increases with the complexity (e.g., having a high degree of uncertainty and variability of future cash flows); RMM is also affected by the volume, terms, and nature of the financial instruments.

   b. At the relevant assertion level—RMM consists of inherent risk and control risk.

   c. The Audit Guide identified characteristics that might affect inherent risk (and RMM), along with the assertions involved—These are summarized below.

Characteristics That Might Affect Inherent Risk (and RMM)

1. **Management's objective**

   a. Indication of higher risk—Financial instruments used as hedges

   b. Indications of lower risk—Financial instruments held as investments

   c. Related assertion(s)—Rights and obligations, accuracy/valuation, classification, and presentation

2. **Management's intent and ability**

   a. Indication of higher risk—Accounting treatment based on intent and ability

   b. Indications of lower risk—Accounting treatment based on objective criteria

   c. Related assertion(s) —Accuracy/valuation, classification, and presentation

3. **Complexity of the financial instrument**

   a. Indication of higher risk—More complex (e.g., futures contracts, swaps, etc.)

   b. Indications of lower risk—Less complex (common stock, U.S. Treasury securities, etc.)

   c. Related assertion(s)—Rights and obligations, accuracy/valuation, classification, and presentation

4. Whether there is an exchange of cash at inception of the financial instrument

   a. Indication of higher risk—No exchange of cash at inception

   b. Indications of lower risk—Cash exchanged at inception

   c. Related assertion(s)—Completeness, classification, and presentation

---

5. Whether the derivative is "freestanding" versus "embedded"

   a. Indication of higher risk—Embedded derivative

   b. Indications of lower risk—Freestanding derivative

   c. Related assertion(s)—Completeness, classification, and presentation

6. Credit risk

   a. Indication of higher risk—High counterparty credit risk

   b. Indications of lower risk—Low counterparty credit risk

   c. Related assertion(s)—Accuracy/valuation

7. Market risk

   a. Indication of higher risk—Volatile values or interest rates

   b. Indications of lower risk—Relatively stable values or interest rates

   c. Related assertion(s)—All

8. Nature of security and related accounting principles

   a. Indication of higher risk—Rapidly evolving

   b. Indications of lower risk—Relatively stable

   c. Related assertion(s)—All

9. Assumptions about future conditions

   a. Indication of higher risk—Significant subjective assumptions

   b. Indications of lower risk—Relatively objective and verifiable assumptions

   c. Related assertion(s)—All

K. **Addressing the Accuracy/Valuation Assertion in Connection with Financial Instruments**

1. Basic responsibility—The auditor is required to obtain an understanding of how management makes its valuation, including the methodology used, and to evaluate the reasonableness of that valuation relative to the requirements of the applicable financial reporting framework.

2. When management uses a model to estimate fair value—

   a. Audit testing normally consists of either of two approaches: (1) evaluating the appropriateness of the model used by management, the reasonableness of the assumptions and data used, and the mathematical accuracy; or (2) developing the auditor's own estimate and then comparing that with the entity's valuation (i.e., an analytical procedures approach).

   b. Evaluating the reasonableness of management's assumptions—The auditor focuses on significant assumptions that might materially affect the valuation and those that are susceptible to bias.

3. When management uses a specialist to estimate fair value—The auditor might evaluate the competence and objectivity of the specialist and obtain an understanding of the specialist's work, including the techniques used and assumptions involved.

4. Investments reported based on an investee's financial results (i.e., using the equity method)

   a. Group versus component—The auditor of the investor's financial statements (the group financial statements) should obtain an understanding of the investee's financial statements (audited by the component auditor) and decide whether to reference the component auditor's work in the auditor's report.

    b. Obtaining and reading the audited financial statements of the equity investee may constitute sufficient appropriate audit evidence as to the equity investment.

5. Impairment losses

    a. Applicable financial reporting frameworks may require recognition of an impairment loss when a decline in fair value is other than temporary—The auditor should evaluate management's conclusions about the need to recognize an impairment loss and obtain sufficient appropriate audit evidence regarding the recorded impairment loss.

    b. Examples of indicators of impairment include the following: (1) Fair value is significantly below cost and the decline has existed for an extended period of time; (2) The security has been downgraded by a rating agency; (3) The financial conditions of the issuer or counterparty have deteriorated; and (4) Dividends have been reduced or eliminated, or scheduled interest payments have not been made.

L. Other audit procedures may provide evidence related to the existence, completeness, and rights and obligations assertions as follows:

    1. External confirmation of bank accounts, trades, and custodian statements.

Note

Traded financial instruments are usually maintained in electronic form and street name, and therefore cannot be inspected. Their existence may be supported by examining supporting documentation, such as:

- Transaction confirmations
- Agreements or contracts
- Minutes of investment committees
- Instructions to portfolio managers or custodians

---

    2. Reviewing reconciliations of statements or data feeds from custodians with the entity's own records.

    3. Reviewing journal entries and the controls over recording such entries.

    4. Reading individual contracts and reviewing supporting documentation, including accounting records, related to financial instruments.

    5. Performing tests of control for relevant internal controls.

    6. Reviewing the entity's complaint-management systems.

M. **Other Audit Considerations Related to Financial Instruments**

    1. Procedures dealing with presentation and disclosure—Auditors focus on disclosures related to risks and sensitivity analysis: (a) entity's objectives and strategies for using financial instruments, including stated accounting policies; (b) entity's internal control framework for managing the risks; and (c) the risks and uncertainties associated with the financial instruments.

    2. Written representations—Depending on the volume and complexity of financial instrument activities, additional specific written representations may be needed to support other audit evidence obtained.

    3. Departures from the applicable financial reporting framework—Could arise from disagreements about the appropriateness of the valuation method or the reasonableness of significant valuation assumptions.

4. Communication with those charged with governance—General matters to be communicated include: (a) nature and consequences of significant assumptions used; (b) degree of subjectivity involved in developing the assumptions; and (c) relative materiality of the items measured at fair value to the financial statements as a whole.

II. Summary of Audit Procedures for Traditional Investments (i.e., Stocks and Bonds)

A. Related to the Existence Assertion—Auditors primarily use inspection and confirmation.

1. Physically inspect securities in the possession of the client entity.

2. Confirm stocks and bonds held by an independent custodian.

B. Related to the Completeness Assertion—Auditors primarily use analytical procedures to address the risk of omissions.

1. Evaluate investment income or loss accounts:

   a. Verify revenue through confirmation when investments are held by an independent custodian.

   b. May trace recorded cash receipts to a bank statement.

   c. May recalculate the interest income on debt instruments or dividends received on stock investments.

2. Compare dividends, interest, or other investment income (loss) to prior year's workpapers for reasonableness; dividends can be verified by consulting dividend record books produced by commercial investment advisory services.

3. Review the minutes of the meetings of those charged with governance for approval of any large investment-related transactions.

C. Related to the Accuracy, Valuation, and Allocation Assertion—The appropriate audit procedures will vary with the nature of the securities involved.

1. For bonds to be held to maturity:

   a. Verify the interest earned by calculations (based on the face value, interest yield, and period held).

   b. Review the amortization of any premium or discount.

   c. Inquire about management's intent and ability to hold the security to maturity (and document that inquiry in the management representations letter).

2. For investments (in stocks or bonds) that are marked to market as required by the applicable financial reporting framework:

   a. Compare the carrying value at the beginning of the period to the prior year's workpapers; agree to underlying documents, examine canceled checks for any current-year additions to investments, and trace the proceeds of any sales to a bank statement.

   b. Verify the year-end fair value (trace to an independent outside source, such as the *Wall Street Journal* or other appropriate quotation)—Evaluate the adequacy of disclosure as required by the applicable financial reporting framework.

   c. Inquire of management about any impairments that may be other than temporary.

D. Related to the Rights and Obligations Assertion—Auditors primarily use inquiry and review.

1. Inquire of management about any restrictions applicable to investments (including any securities pledged as collateral for debt).

2. Review cash receipts and cash disbursements subsequent to year-end for any material transactions affecting investments, perhaps requiring disclosure.

E. Related to the Classification and Presentation Assertions—Verify the appropriateness of the classification of investments in certain equity and debt securities.

1. **Investment in Equity Securities**

   a. Fair value—Equity investments when there is no significant influence and fair value is readily determinable; report at fair value with unrealized gains and losses included in earnings.

   b. Cost—Equity investments when there is no significant influence and fair value is *not* readily determinable; report at cost and test for impairment.

   c. Equity method accounting—Equity investments when there is significant influence; report using the equity method of accounting (can elect the fair value option if the entity chooses to do so).

2. **Investment in Debt Securities**

   a. Held-to-maturity—For debt securities when the entity has the intent and ability to hold the investment to maturity

   b. Trading—For debt securities intended for sale in the near term

Fixed Assets

Since the composition of the fixed assets' balances is usually substantially carried over from one period to the next, the auditor usually emphasizes substantive tests of transactions (that is, the continuing auditor usually verifies the ending balance by examining the debits and credits that caused the balance to change from the prior year).

After studying this lesson, you should be able to:

1. Recognize that the assertions for account balances (and related disclosures) at the end of the period represent a framework for preparing an audit plan to evaluate the fairness of fixed assets.

2. Identify the appropriate substantive audit procedures to address those assertions when auditing fixed assets.

Recall the assertions that AICPA Professional Standards identify for account balances (and related disclosures) at the end of the period: (1) existence; (2) completeness; (3) rights and obligations; (4) accuracy, valuation, and allocation; (5) classification; and (6) presentation.

I. Related to the Existence Assertion

A. Consider the adequacy of the accounting records. Verify that the client's detailed fixed asset listing supports the related general ledger account balance.

B. **For Additions**—Vouch to (inspect) the underlying documents (examine the purchase order, vendor's invoice, and the entity's canceled check if payment has been made); look for approval in the minutes of meetings of those charged with governance if the addition is a "major" one.

C. **For Disposals**—Trace any proceeds received to the cash receipts journal and bank statement; review for appropriate approval.

Note

Instead of performing tests of ending balances, the continuing auditor will normally verify the appropriateness of the year-end balance of fixed assets by performing substantive tests of transactions. In other words, if there are relatively few transactions that have caused the fixed asset balance to change from last year to this year, the auditor will, in effect, back into the ending balance by taking the beginning balance (audited last year), add any additions, and subtract any disposals. Since there are likely only a few additions and/or disposals, it is more efficient to examine those few transactions, rather than verify a sample of the individual items that comprise the year-end fixed asset balance.

II. Related to the Accuracy, Valuation, and Allocation Assertion

A. Review the calculations for depreciation expense—compare the useful lives and methods used to prior years for consistency, and recalculate on a test basis.

B. Consider whether there have been any *impairments* of long-lived assets requiring a write-down from the historical cost-based carrying value—make appropriate inquiries of management (and document such inquiries and management's response in the management representations letter).

III. Related to the Completeness Assertion

A. Review the client's *repairs and maintenance expense* account and examine underlying documents for material items to determine whether any of those recorded expenses should instead be capitalized.

B. Review any lease agreements to determine if lease capitalization might be required.

IV. Related to the Rights and Obligations Assertion

    A. Inquire of management about any fixed assets pledged as security for borrowings (and review loan agreements to identify such collateral).

    B. Document such inquiries (and management's response) in the management representations letter.

V. Related to the Classification and Presentation Assertions

    A. Inquire of management about any fixed assets that have been taken out of operation and retained for possible future purposes and that should be reclassified

    B. Document such inquiries (and management's response) in the management representations letter.

Current Liabilities

I. Accounts Payable (or Vouchers Payable)—Primarily use substantive tests of ending balances.

    A. Recall the difference between **accounts payable and vouchers payable** systems described in the lessons in the "Internal Control" subsection.

        1. Accounts payable—In an accounts payable system, the payables are tracked by the name of the vendor. The total payable to another party, which constitutes a receivable to them, is susceptible to confirmation if desired.

        2. Vouchers payable—In a vouchers payable system, the payables are tracked by individual transaction without summarizing the amounts owed by vendor name. The total payable to another party is not susceptible to confirmation, only individual transactions could be confirmed.

    B. Recall the assertions that AICPA Professional Standards identify for account balances (and related disclosures) at the end of the period: (1) existence; (2) completeness; (3) rights and obligations; (4) accuracy, valuation, and allocation; (5) classification; and (6) presentation.

    C. Related to the Completeness Assertion (for liabilities, the auditor's primary concern involves completeness not existence!)—Perform a **search for unrecorded liabilities.** This is done toward the end of fieldwork to provide the best chance of detecting any significant unrecorded liabilities.

        1. Review cash disbursements **subsequent to year-end** and, for all disbursements over some specified dollar amount (>$X), examine the related vendors' invoices and the entity's related receiving documents to identify transactions that should have been reported as liabilities as of year-end; compare those apparent liabilities to the details comprising the recorded payables to identify apparent liabilities that are unrecorded.

        2. Examine any unpaid invoices on hand at the date of the "search" along with the entity's related receiving documents to identify any transactions that should have been reported as a liability as of year-end.

        3. Inquire of management about their knowledge of any unrecorded liabilities and whether all invoices have been made available to the auditor. Document such inquiries and management's response in the management representations letter.

    D. Related to the Existence and Accuracy/Valuation Assertions

        1. Verify the mathematical accuracy of payables by comparing the general ledger balance to the supporting detailed listing of payables.

        2. Vouch selected items to the underlying vendor's invoices.

        3. Could confirm selected payables, but usually do not—Confirmation primarily establishes the validity (existence) of the recorded items, but there is a relatively low risk that the company would overstate its true liabilities; the far bigger risk is that material liabilities may have been omitted (i.e., completeness).

        4. Usually valuation is not a significant audit issue, since there is a presumption that the client will pay 100% of what is owed; the auditor should look to see that the client takes advantage of any available cash discounts for prompt payment.

    E. Related to the Rights and Obligations Assertion—Inspect the specific terms of the payables and inquire about any related party transactions.

    F. Related to the Classification and Presentation Assertions—Verify that notes payable or other liabilities are reported separately from accounts payable for ordinary operating activities.

II. Other Current Liabilities—The auditor uses analytical procedures extensively to evaluate other miscellaneous payables:

    A. Wages and Salaries Payable—The auditor can compute the estimated accrual, in view of the number of days to be accrued relative to a whole pay period.

    B. Dividends Payable—The auditor can compute, in view of the declared dividends/share (per the minutes of meetings of those charged with governance) times the number of shares outstanding.

    C. Interest Payable (and the Related Interest Expense)—The auditor can compute an estimate of accrued interest for the time period involved, based on the interest rate (and payment dates) specified in the underlying debt agreements.

Long-Term Liabilities

After studying this lesson, you should be able to:

1. Recognize that the assertions for account balances (and related disclosures) at the end of the period represent a framework for preparing an audit plan to evaluate the fairness of long-term liabilities.

2. Identify appropriate substantive audit procedures to address those assertions when auditing long-term liabilities.

Recall the assertions that AICPA Professional Standards identify for account balances (and related disclosures) at the end of the period: (1) existence; (2) completeness; (3) rights and obligations; (4) accuracy, valuation, and allocation; (5) classification; and (6) presentation.

I. **Related to the Completeness Assertion**—Use substantive tests of transactions (to address decreases in debt):

   A. Verify due dates for payments in the loan agreements.

   B. Trace cash disbursements from the accounting records to the bank statement.

   C. Examine canceled notes if paid in full.

   D. Could confirm year-end balances, but confirmations are most applicable to establishing the validity of recorded items (i.e., existence).

II. **Related to the Existence Assertion**—Use substantive tests of transactions (to address increases in debt):

   A. Obtain copies of new loan agreements for the auditor's review and documentation.

   B. Verify authorization of new debt in minutes of meetings of those charged with governance.

   C. Trace receipts from the accounting records to the bank statement.

III. **Related to the Accuracy, Valuation, and Allocation Assertion**—There are few measurement issues associated with most liabilities, but long-term liabilities should be based on present values:

   A. Trace related cash receipts and disbursements from the accounting records to the bank statements.

   B. Examine the underlying loan contracts related to the stated dollar amounts.

   C. Recalculate the amortization of any premium or discount using the effective interest method.

   D. Apply analytical procedures to the related expense accounts (e.g., interest)—Note that the balance sheet item and the related income statement item are usually addressed on the same audit documentation (working paper).

IV. **Related to the Rights and Obligations Assertion**—The auditor should make appropriate inquiries of management and review the loan documents:

   A. **Debt Covenants**—Important restrictions should be disclosed. (Note that violations of such covenants can cause the entire balance to become immediately payable.)

   B. **Collateral**—Any assets pledged as security for the debt should be disclosed.

V. **Related to the Classification and Presentation Assertions**—The current portion of long-term debt should be reclassified to current liabilities and presented separately.

   A. Read the loan documents to identify the principal to be paid within the next year.

   B. Examine the cash payments for the current-year installment paid if the debt is scheduled to be paid in equal installments.

Stockholders' Equity

> **After studying this lesson, you should be able to:**
>
> 1. Recognize that the assertions for account balances (and related disclosures) at the end of the period represent a framework for preparing an audit plan to evaluate the fairness of stockholders' equity.
>
> 2. Identify appropriate substantive audit procedures to address those assertions when auditing stockholders' equity.

> Recall the assertions that AICPA Professional Standards identify for account balances at the end of the period: (1) existence; (2) completeness; (3) rights and obligations; (4) accuracy, valuation, and allocation; (5) classification; and (6) presentation.

I. **Related to the Existence Assertion**—Confirm the outstanding shares of stock if there is an external registrar. (Verify that the stock was issued in accordance with the company's articles of incorporation and with the approval of those charged with governance.)

II. **Related to the Completeness Assertion**

    A. Review the minutes of meetings of those charged with governance to identify authorized transactions.

    B. Account for all certificate numbers to establish that no unauthorized shares were issued.

III. **Related to the Rights and Obligations Assertion**

    A. Review the minutes of board meetings to verify that any stock and dividend transactions were duly authorized by those charged with governance.

    B. Review contracts with employee stock option plans to verify compliance with such agreements.

    C. Inquire of management about any restrictions that might exist on the availability of retained earnings for purposes of dividend distribution—the financial statements should disclose any restrictions on retained earnings available for dividend distribution.

IV. **Related to the Accuracy, Valuation, and Allocation Assertion**

    A. Review cash receipts and disbursements (and minutes of meetings of those charged with governance) for increases or decreases in stock accounts.

    B. Compare the subsidiary ledger to the general ledger stock accounts. (Examine stock certificates or read the applicable minutes of meetings of those charged with governance to verify the par or stated value per share.)

V. **Related to the Classification and Presentation Assertions**

    A. Review the appropriateness of the various classifications of paid-in capital accounts.

    B. Review the adequacy of disclosures relative to the audit firm's disclosure checklists.

Payroll

When the auditor chooses to examine the payroll function handled in-house by the company (as opposed to an outside payroll service), recall the internal control considerations associated with the payroll transaction cycle covered in the lesson "Specific Transaction Cycles."

After studying this lesson, you should be able to:

1. Recognize that the assertions for transactions and events (and related disclosures) during the period represent a framework for preparing an audit plan to evaluate the fairness of income statement items, such as payroll expense.

2. Identify appropriate substantive audit procedures to address payroll expense.

Recall the assertions that AICPA Professional Standards identify for "classes of transactions and events (and related disclosures) for the period under audit": (1) existence; (2) completeness; (3) rights and obligations; (4) accuracy, valuation, and allocation; (5) classification; and (6) presentation.

I. Related to the Accuracy, Valuation, and Allocation and Occurrence Assertions

    A. Examine personnel records on a test basis, to determine that the levels of compensation and support for all deductions exist for all employees. (Officers' compensation should be documented in the minutes of meetings of those charged with governance.)

    B. Trace selected transactions from the payroll register to the general ledger and to the payroll bank account.

    C. Recalculate selected entries on the payroll register.

II. Related to the Completeness Assertion

    A. Review time reports and time cards to verify support for production records.

    B. Apply analytical procedures (and recalculation) to verify that the payroll-related accruals at year-end are reasonable.

III. Related to the Cutoff Assertion—Cutoff is effectively addressed when occurrence and completeness have been addressed; in other words, when the auditor has established that recorded transactions are properly recorded and that there are no omissions of transactions that should have been recorded, the auditor has established that the transactions have been recorded in the correct accounting period.

AICPA Professional Standards also state, "… there may not be a separate assertion related to cutoff of transactions and events when the occurrence and completeness assertions include appropriate consideration of recording transactions in the correct accounting period." (AU-C 315.A132)

IV. Related to the Classification and Presentation Assertions

    A. The comments related to accuracy and occurrence apply to recording the transactions in the proper accounts, as well.

    B. Review outside reports related to pension, other post-retirement benefits (e.g., insurance), and profit-sharing plans.

    C. Verify payroll deductions and taxes, trace cash disbursements for withholdings to appropriate agencies.

D. Note that ordinarily, income statement elements (including revenue and expense items) are primarily audited by analytical procedures. Typically, tests of details will be performed only when the analytical procedures suggest that a risk of material misstatement exists and that a more detailed investigation is warranted. Payroll-related expenses would normally be subject to such analytical procedures, too. The discussion above is presented to provide insights about how such transactions could be tested in detail if the auditor deemed that appropriate.

Audit Sampling

Introduction to Sampling

After studying this lesson, you should be able to:

1. Understand the distinction between statistical and nonstatistical audit sampling.

2. Understand the distinction between sampling risk and nonsampling risk.

3. Understand the distinction between false rejection (a Type 1 Error) and false acceptance (a Type 2 Error) comprising sampling risks that are applicable to control and substantive procedures tests.

Definition

Sampling: "The selection and evaluation of less than 100% of the population of audit relevance such that the auditor expects the items selected to be representative of the population ..."

I. **Responsibilities under AICPA Professional Standards**—The relevant AICPA guidance is provided by AU 530, *Audit Sampling*. This pronouncement states that the auditor's objective is to provide a reasonable basis for the auditor to draw conclusions about the population from which the sample is selected.

II. **There Are Two General Approaches to Sampling**—May depend on the auditor's perceptions of cost/benefit trade-offs.

   A. **Nonstatistical Sampling**—Also called judgmental sampling

   B. **Statistical**—The benefits relate to objectivity:

   1. Relates to the **sufficiency** of the evidence—The determination of the sample size in a statistical sampling application establishes how much evidence is required.

   2. The results may seem more defensible to others (such as the courts).

   3. A common misconception is that statistical sampling eliminates the need for judgment. Actually, numerous judgments must be made; however, these judgments are made more explicit.

   4. Sampling applications occur in either of two contexts:

Definitions

Attributes Sampling: Sampling for purposes of deciding whether internal controls are working as designed (tests of controls).

Variables Sampling: Sampling for purposes of deciding whether account balances (such as inventory or receivables) are fairly stated (substantive tests of details).

III. **Uncertainty and Audit Sampling—Risk Considerations** (Recall the definition of *audit risk*)—The probability that the auditor fails to modify the opinion on financial statements containing a material misstatement. Auditors may use the following model to evaluate the risk components explicitly:

AR = RMM * AP * TD, where

AR = audit risk;

RMM = risk of material misstatement, consisting of the combined assessments of inherent risk and control risk;

AP = risk that analytical procedures performed for substantive purposes will not detect a material misstatement that occurred; and

TD = risk that tests of details will fail to detect a material misstatement that was not otherwise detected.

IV. **Whether Nonstatistical Sampling or Statistical Sampling Is Used**—The auditor is fundamentally seeking a sample that is truly representative of the population, so that the auditor gets an accurate signal about the population's characteristics in a highly efficient way.

V. **Sampling Risk**—Is the risk that the sample may not be truly representative of the population; in other words, the chance of an erroneous conclusion that the auditor takes by examining a subset of the population, rather than the entire population.

    A. **Type 1 Errors (False Rejection)**

       1. Tests of controls => the risk of **underreliance** on internal controls (also known as risk of assessing control risk too high).

       2. Substantive testing => the risk of incorrect rejection.

       3. Type 1 errors relate to efficiency—the auditor will probably achieve the appropriate conclusions, although not in the most efficient manner (perhaps taking more than one sample, maybe at the urging of the client who has faith in the effectiveness of the internal control or the fairness of the financial statement element).

    B. **Type 2 Errors (False Acceptance)**

       1. Tests of controls => the risk of **overreliance** on internal controls (also known as the risk of assessing control risk too low).

       2. Substantive testing => the risk of incorrect acceptance.

       3. Type 2 errors relate to effectiveness—now the auditor may have failed to meet the overall objective, which is to limit audit risk to an acceptably low level. (The client will have no incentive to argue about this conclusion, so the auditors will not have any reason to take a second look.)

VI. **Nonsampling Risk**—Refers to any other mistakes by the auditor (i.e., other than sampling risk), not a direct consequence of using a sampling approach:

    A. Inappropriate auditing procedures.

    B. Failure to correctly identify "errors" or amounts sampled, misinterpreting the results, etc.

> **Note**
> *If there were no variation within a population (i.e., if all items were homogeneous), the auditor would only need a sample of one item to assess the whole population! The variability of the population causes the sample size to increase and is responsible for the sampling risk.*

Attributes Sampling

After studying this lesson, you should be able to:

1. Understand the meaning of the term "attributes sampling."

2. Know the eight steps that comprise an attributes-sampling application.

3. Know how to determine the sample size for an attributes sampling application using AICPA tables.

I. **Attributes Sampling**—Statistical sampling for the purpose of identifying the percentage frequency of a characteristic in a population of interest to the auditor; this term is usually used to refer to audit sampling to ascertain the operating effectiveness of internal control (where, for each transaction in the sample, the control procedure of interest was either performed or not performed—there are only two outcomes, similar to '"hit or miss" or "heads or tails")

II. **Eight Steps Comprise an Attributes Sampling**

A. **Identify the Sampling Objective**—That is, the purpose of the test.

B. **Define What Constitutes an Occurrence**—Sometimes called a deviation or error when a control procedure of interest was not properly performed.

C. **Identify the Relevant Population**

1. Specify the relevant time period.

2. Specify the sampling unit—what it is that the auditor is selecting (e.g., sales transactions).

D. **Determine the Sampling Method**—How the specific items (or transactions) are to be selected for the sample.

1. **Statistical sampling approaches**

a. **Random number**—Each transaction has the same probability of being selected (the best approach).

b. **Systematic**—For example, selecting every 100th item

2. **Judgmental sampling approaches**—not appropriate for attributes sampling!

a. **Block**—A group of contiguous items (e.g., the sales transactions for the entire month of June)

b. **Haphazard**—Arbitrary selection, with no conscious biases. Subconscious biases may exist without the auditor's awareness, however.

E. **Determine the Sample Size**—Based on AICPA tables.

Factor (holding all others constant)	Relationship
Expected error rate (related to the variation in population)	Direct
Tolerable (deviation) rate (related to precision)	Inverse
Risk of overreliance	Inverse
Risk of underreliance (implicit)	Inverse
Population size (implicit)	Direct

F. **Select the Sample**—Identify the occurrences associated with all the items in the sample.

G. **Evaluate the Sample Results**—This means make a decision as to whether the auditor can rely on the effectiveness of the internal control procedure under consideration.

1. Calculate the **observed deviation rate** = (# errors)/n.

2. Determine the point estimate, the best single indicator of the percentage of times that the control procedure was performed as designed in the population (ignoring, for the moment, the uncertainty surrounding whether the sample is truly representative of the population).

3. Calculate a confidence interval for the **achieved upper precision limit** (in view of the actual errors observed). There are AICPA tables to determine the achieved upper precision limit. *(The topic determination of confidence intervals is not likely to be tested on the CPA Exam!)*

4. Compare the achieved upper precision limit to the stated **tolerable rate**; the auditor can only rely on the internal control procedure if the error rate, based on the upper bound of the confidence interval (the achieved upper precision limit from the tables) is less than or equal to the stated tolerable rate.

5. Consider the **qualitative characteristics** of the internal control deviations for any implication to the rest of the audit.

6. Make the appropriate decision—Should the auditor rely on the specific control procedure (i.e., **assess control risk at less than the maximum**) or not?

H. Document the Auditor's Sampling Procedures

III. Attributes Sampling Example

Statistical Sample Sizes for Tests of Controls

5% Risk of Overreliance						
Expected Population	Tolerable Rate					
Deviation Rate	2%	3%	4%	5%	6%	7%
.25	236	157	117	93	78	66
.50	*	157	117	93	78	66
.75	*	208	117	93	78	66
1.00	*	*	156	**93**	78	66
1.25	*	*	156	124	78	66
1.50	*	*	192	124	103	66
1.75	*	*	227	153	103	88
2.00	*	*	*	181	127	88
*Sample size is too large to be cost-effective for most audit applications.						

Note: This table has been adapted from material copyrighted by the American Institute of Certified Public Accountants, Inc.

IV. Attributes Sampling—Numerical Example

A. Suppose that an auditor specified the following parameters for a statistical sampling application related to internal controls in the revenue/receipts transaction cycle:

Acceptable risk of overreliance on	
Internal control (a Type II error)	**5%**
(The auditor is willing to rely on the control procedure if the statistical test indicates that the control is working as prescribed at least 95% of the time.)	
Estimated population deviation rate	**1%**
Tolerable deviation rate	**5%**

B. Requirement—Identify the required sample size using the AICPA tables for attributes sampling.

C. Solution—The 5% **risk of overreliance** (Type II Error) determines the applicable page of the AICPA tables; the 5% **tolerable rate** determines the applicable column of the AICPA table; and the 1% **estimated population deviation rate** determines the applicable row of the AICPA table.

1. The resulting sample size is **93**.

Variables Sampling

After studying this lesson, you should be able to:

1. Understand the meaning of the term "variables sampling" and the various specific approaches (difference estimation, ratio estimation, mean-per-unit estimation, and probability-proportionate-to-size sampling).

2. Know the eight steps that comprise a variables-sampling application.

3. Know the factors that affect the sample size for a variables-sampling application.

4. Understand the role of "stratification" in audit sampling.

I. **Relies Heavily on the Classic Normal Distribution**—(With the bell-shaped curve.)

   A. This distribution is determined by two parameters:

      1. The **mean**, related to central tendency; and

      2. **Variance** (or its square root, standard deviation), related to dispersion or variability.

II. **Basic Steps**—The **eight basic steps in a variables sampling plan** are practically the same as in the attributes sampling case:

   A. **Identify the Sampling Objective**—The purpose of "variables sampling" is to determine the inferred audit value of a population of interest (e.g., for accounts receivable or inventory).

   B. Identify the Relevant Population:

      1. Specify what constitutes the sampling unit.

      2. Be careful to assure that conclusions are properly extended to the appropriate population (i.e., completeness of the population).

   C. **Select the Specific Sampling Technique**—The choices are difference estimation, ratio estimation, mean-per-unit estimation, or probability-proportionate-to-size sampling.

   D. **Calculate the Sample Size**—Since tables do not exist for this in variables sampling. Recall the **five factors and relationships** to sample size identified for attributes sampling applications—these factors are still applicable to variables sampling.

> **Note**
> If 68% of the area is under the bell-shaped curve, it is within one standard deviation of the mean; if 95.5% of the area is under the bell-shaped curve, it is within two standard deviations of the mean.

> **Note**
> Auditors should examine all the items that are individually material (i.e., we are not sampling these).

Factor	(holding all others constant) Relationship
Estimated population standard deviation (related to the variation in population)	Direct
Allowance for sampling risk (also called "tolerable misstatement") [related to precision]	Inverse
Risk of incorrect acceptance (Type II)	Inverse
Population size (explicitly considered for variables sampling)	Direct
Risk of incorrect rejection (Type I error, only implicitly considered)	Inverse

The **basic formula**, based on classical statistics:

$n = (S * \text{Z-coefficient} * N / A)^2$

where:

n represents the sample size to be determined

S represents the estimated population standard deviation (related to the variability of the population).

Z-coefficient represents a measure of reliability for some level of specified "confidence" (typically about 2)

N represents the size of the population (number of accounts or items of inventory, etc.)

A represents the specified allowance for sampling risk, related to the statistical concept of "precision."

Note

It is very unlikely that the AICPA will require calculations of sample size! However, they frequently test these concepts. In particular, they might ask questions related to the factors that influence the sample size and whether that influence is directly or inversely related. The formula identified above is a useful way to keep these relationships straight.

    E. **Determine the Method of Selection**—Random (the preferred approach) or systematic.

    F. **Conduct the Sample**

    G. **Evaluate the Sample** and project to population:

        1. Calculate a point estimate (the implied audit value) for the population based on the sample's audited values.

        2. Construct a confidence interval to determine whether to accept or reject the client's recorded balance as consistent with the audit evidence.

Note

The AICPA has rarely tested calculations in this area. On a few occasions, they have required calculations of a "point estimate" for a population; however, calculations of the confidence interval surrounding a point estimate are beyond the scope of the CPA Exam!

    H. **Document the Auditor's Sampling Procedures and Judgments.**

Definition

Stratification: The auditor may reduce the overall variability within a population by classifying similar items into sub-populations (within each group, the variability may be much smaller); the resulting aggregate sample size may be smaller as a result of reducing the combined effects of variability.

III. **Variables Sampling—Specific Sampling Techniques**—Note that the CPA Exam has rarely emphasized calculations related to statistical sampling; however, the exam has historically tested the concepts related to sampling.

    A. **Difference Estimation**—This approach involves identifying the dollar differences between the sample's audit values and applicable book values.

        1. **Sample size**—As previously described. Note that we usually need at least 30 differences between audit and book values in our sample when using "difference estimation."

        2. Estimate the population's implied audit value.

    B. Calculate the average difference between the audit value (av) and book value (bv) for items in the sample:

$$d = (av - bv)/n$$

   C. Extend that average difference to the population by multiplying it by the number of items in the population:

$$D = d * N$$

   D. Calculate the implied population audit value (the "point estimate") by adding the calculated difference for the population to the population's book value:

$$AV = BV + D, \text{ where } D \text{ can be either positive or negative}$$

     1. Construct a confidence (precision) interval around the population's audit value to compare to the client's recorded balance—This is beyond the scope of the CPA Examination.

   E. **Ratio Estimation**—This approach involves identifying the ratio of the audit values and book values for the sampled items.

     1. Note that this approach is useful when the dollar amount of the differences between the audit and the book values is expected to be proportional to the book values.

     2. Sample size—as previously described.

     3. Estimate the population's implied audit value:

   F. Calculate the ratio for the sample, where the ratio has the sample's audit value in the numerator and the sample's book value in the denominator:

$$R = av/bv$$

   G. Estimate the population's audit value (a point estimate) by multiplying the population's book value by that "ratio:"

$$AV = R * BV$$

     1. Construct a confidence (precision) interval around the population's audit value to compare to the client's recorded balance—this is beyond the scope of the CPA Examination.

   H. **Mean-per-Unit Estimation (MPU)**

     1. Useful when difference or ratio estimation cannot be used—for example, for inventory when perpetual records do not exist (i.e., there is no "book" value for each individual sample item).

     2. Sample size—as previously described.

     3. Estimate the population's implied audit value.

       a. Calculate the average audit value for items in the sample:

$$MPU = av/n$$

       b. Multiply that average (MPU) times the number of items in the population:

$$AV = MPU * N$$

4. Construct a confidence (precision) interval around the population's audit value to compare to the client's recorded balance—this is beyond the scope of CPA Exam!

I. **Probability-Proportional-to-Size (PPS) Sampling**—An introduction:

1. The *sampling unit* is an individual dollar (when a given dollar is selected for the sample, it attaches to the related account or item which is then examined in its entirety); note that individually material items are automatically selected.

2. PPS is useful if there are relatively few differences between audit and book values; otherwise, the sample size can become very large and the PPS application then becomes inefficient.

3. The main advantage is efficiency—it can achieve the maximum possible stratification (which then minimizes the effects of variability on sample size).

4. The main disadvantage is that PPS does not work very well in auditing negative balances (understatements) or zero (unrecorded) balances. Applies best to audit concerns involving overstatements (e.g., accounts receivable or inventory when few misstatements are expected).

PPS sampling will be addressed in more depth in the next lesson.

Probability-Proportional-to-Size (PPS) Sampling

After studying this lesson, you should be able to:

1. Understand the relevant sampling unit for probability-proportionate-to-size sampling.

2. Determine the sample size and the sampling interval for a probability-proportionate-to-size sampling application.

3. Determine the projected misstatement for a probability-proportionate-to-size sampling application.

I. **PPS "Sampling Unit"**—PPS sampling defines the "sampling unit" to be an individual dollar associated with the financial statement element involved. (Variations of this approach are referred to as dollar-unit sampling or monetary-unit sampling.) For example, suppose accounts receivable consists of 7500 customer accounts having a total balance of $3,000,000. The population is viewed as consisting of 3,000,000 individual items (dollars) rather than 7500 accounts. However, when an individual dollar is selected as part of the sample, it attaches to the related account or logical record, which is then examined in its entirety. Accordingly, the probability that an individual account will be selected is "proportional" to that individual account's balance relative to the total for all accounts.

II. **Primary Advantage of PPS Sampling**—The main advantage of PPS sampling is efficiency. If there are few differences between audit and book values, PPS sampling may result in smaller sample sizes than the other sampling methods. If there are many differences, however, PPS sample sizes can become too large to be practical.

III. **Primary Disadvantage of PPS Sampling**—The main disadvantage of PPS sampling is that it does not work very well in auditing negative balances (understatements) or zero (unrecorded) balances. It applies best to audit circumstances involving concerns about overstatements, such as for accounts receivable or inventory; and, then, only when few misstatements are expected.

IV. **Basic Steps in a PPS Sampling Application**

   A. **Determine the Sample Size**—based on three considerations:

   1. The "reliability factor" (from an AICPA table based on the risk of incorrect acceptance and the number of overstatements permitted—see the table below);

   2. The population book value; *and*

   3. The tolerable misstatement (net of any expected misstatements).

$$n = \frac{\text{Reliability factor (from tables)} \times \text{Book value}}{\text{Tolerable misstatement, net of expected misstatements}}$$

Alternatively, **n = Book value/Sampling interval**, where:

Sampling interval = Tolerable misstatement (net of expected misstatements)/Reliability factor

Reliability Factors

Number of Overstatements	Risk of Incorrect Acceptance				
	1%	5%	10%	15%	20%
0	4.61	3.00	2.31	1.90	1.61
1	6.64	4.75	3.89	3.38	3.00
2	8.41	6.30	5.33	4.72	4.28
3	10.05	7.76	6.69	6.02	5.52
4	11.61	9.16	8.00	7.27	6.73
5	13.11	10.52	9.28	8.50	7.91

B. Select the Sample—PPS samples are usually selected using "systematic selection" with a random starting point and a specified "sample interval."

$$\text{Sample interval} = \frac{\text{Population book value}}{\text{Sample size}}$$

C. Evaluate the Recorded Book Value—To "evaluate" the entity's recorded balance relative to the implied audit value for the population, the auditor should calculate the "upper limit on misstatement," which corresponds to the upper limit of a confidence interval. Such computations are beyond the scope of CPA Exam, but a few concepts (especially "projected misstatement") may be worth remembering.

Upper limit on misstatement

= [Basic precision + Projected misstatement + Incremental allowance]

where:

Basic precision:

$$\text{Basic precision} = \text{Reliability factor} \times \text{Sample interval (for 0 misstatements)}$$

Projected misstatement:

For accounts having a book value greater than or equal to the sample interval, the actual misstatement should be used to determine the "projected misstatement."

For accounts having book values less than the sample interval, the auditor would have to apply the "tainting percentage" to the sample interval from which that account was selected. Suppose that the sample interval is $2,000 and that an account having a book value of $250 has an audit value of $200. The "tainting" is $50/$250 = .20; and, since the account's book value is less than the sample interval, the projected misstatement for this account would be .20 × $2,000 = $400.

When there are no misstatements in the sample, the projected misstatement is zero.

Incremental allowance:

The incremental allowance is zero if there are no misstatements of accounts having book values less than the sample interval. The concept is only relevant when there are misstatements of accounts having book values less than the sample interval, but the calculation itself is a technical issue that is beyond the scope of the CPA Exam.

IT (Computer) Auditing

IT General & Application Controls

After studying this lesson, you should be able to:

1. Understand the meaning of the term "general controls" relevant to an IT (computerized) environment.

2. Know the five categories of general controls identified by AICPA Professional Standards.

3. Understand the meaning of the term "application controls" relevant to an IT (computerized) environment.

4. Know the three categories of application controls (input, processing, and output) and specific examples of controls associated with each.

I. Introduction

AICPA Professional Standards comment on the implications of an entity's use of information technology (IT) on the auditor's consideration of internal control issues. Specifically, AU 315, Understanding the Entity and Its Environment and Assessing the Risks of Material Misstatement, is applicable. AU 315 distinguishes "general controls" and "application controls" in the auditor's consideration of IT-related controls. In auditing standards years ago, the AICPA used the term "electronic data processing" (EDP), which has been replaced by modern references to IT.

A. The use of IT affects the way that specific control activities are implemented, but the control objectives are the same as those for a manual accounting system.

B. Advantages Associated with IT—Data processing is uniform (consistent) and efficiency may be enhanced, especially for routine and recurring transactions.

C. Disadvantages Associated with IT—The intended segregation of duties may be undercut if someone gets unauthorized access to the computer system; also, a traditional "audit trail" (i.e., paper trail) may not exist in an electronic environment.

D. AICPA Professional Standards point out that, if IT is a significant aspect of an entity's accounting system, then the auditor may find it necessary to adopt a reliance audit approach; in other words, substantive procedures alone may not provide sufficient appropriate audit evidence.

"When such routine business transactions are subject to highly automated processing with little or no manual intervention, it may not be possible to perform only substantive procedures regarding the risk. For example, the auditor may consider this to be the case when a significant amount of an entity's information is initiated, authorized, recorded, processed, or reported only in electronic form, such as in an integrated system." (AU 315.A157)

II. IT General Controls

A. These controls have pervasive effects on the various specific data processing applications.

"General IT controls are policies and procedures that relate to many applications and support the effective functioning of application controls. They apply to mainframe, miniframe, and end-user environments." (AU 315.A111)

B. IT general controls associated with maintaining the integrity of data and protecting the security of data can be classified into five categories, as follows (AU 315.A107):

1. Data center and network operations

2. System software acquisition, change, and maintenance

3. Program change

4. Access security

5. Application system acquisition, development, and maintenance

III. Discussion of the Five Categories of IT General Controls

A. Data Center and Network Operations

1. Data-related controls emphasize the importance of selecting the proper files, typically associated with the IT librarian's responsibility for keeping track of the programs and data files and verifying that access is limited to authorized personnel.

2. Operations-related controls emphasize the importance of maintaining an appropriate segregation of duties within the IT function as well as between the IT function and the various user departments.

3. To the extent possible, the following IT-related functions should be separated:

   a. Systems analyst—Responsible for designing the IT system

   b. Operator—Responsible for running the IT system

   c. Programmer—Responsible for writing the code that makes up the specific programs

   d. Librarian—Responsible for keeping track of the programs and files and verifying that access is limited to authorized personnel

   e. Security—Responsible for protecting the programs and data files and implementing procedures to safeguard the system

B. System Software Acquisition, Change, and Maintenance

1. "System software" refers to programs that run the computer system, including the operating system and database management systems.

2. The entity should have appropriate controls to approve the acquisition of new system software and any changes to the existing system software.

3. System software typically includes certain "built-in" controls:

   a. Parity check—This term is associated with transmissions of information between system hardware components; a "bit" is added to each character so that the loss of any portion of transmitted data can be detected.

   b. Echo check—This term is associated with transmissions of information over the phone lines; a signal establishes that what was sent was, in fact, received.

   c. Diagnostic routines—This term is associated with the internal operation of hardware components, particularly when booting up the system.

C. Program Change—The entity should have appropriate controls to prevent unauthorized changes to any system or application programs; authorized changes should be properly tested and documented.

D. Access Security

1. The entity should have appropriate controls to prevent unauthorized access to (a) the computer equipment, (b) the software, and (c) the data files.

2. Examples of such controls include locked doors to secure the computer operation with access allowed by keys or swipe cards, passcodes, or biometrics (e.g., fingerprints or retina scans).

3. An entity's IT "librarian" should have physical control over the application programs and data files to prevent unauthorized access.

4. Access to the computer system via remote terminals should be limited to authorized personnel. The entity should appropriately implement firewalls, establish access controls requiring appropriate identification and passwords, and use encrypted data to reduce the risk of unauthorized access.

5. Disaster recovery procedures—The entity should have appropriate procedures to back up important data files, including off-site storage, to protect against losses due to fire, flood, earthquake, tornado, and other disasters.

E. Application System Acquisition, Development, and Maintenance

1. The acquisition of hardware and software should be properly authorized.

2. Changes in the entity's hardware and software should be properly tested and documented.

IV. IT Application Controls

A. IT application controls relate to specific computer processing activities, referred to as "applications."

B. Application controls are usually classified into three categories of controls: (1) input, (2) processing, and (3) output.

"*Application controls* are manual or automated procedures that typically operate at a business process level and apply to the processing of transactions by individual applications. Application controls can be preventive or detective and are designed to ensure the integrity of the accounting records." (AU315.A113)

V. Discussion of the Three Categories of IT Application Controls

A. **Input Controls**—The objective of input controls is that the input of data is accurate and as authorized.

1. Data validation controls—Input controls focus particularly on establishing the validity of data prior to (or at the time of) data input.

2. Logic checks—Common controls used for data validation purposes that involve computer edit routines to identify errors in data include the following:

   a. Limit test—To establish that numeric data do not exceed a predetermined amount

   b. Field test—To establish that a field properly consists of all alphabetical or all numeric characters

   c. Validity check—To establish that a field properly contains an item from a predetermined menu of appropriate possibilities

   d. Missing data check—To establish that there are no omissions from fields in which data should be present

   e. Sequence check—To establish that data are in the appropriate order (either numerically or alphabetically)

      f. Check digit—A "check digit" refers to an arithmetic manipulation of a numerical field that captures the information content of the field; the check digit typically gets tacked onto the end of the numeric field to establish that the original value was properly input.

  3. Control totals may be used as an input control—Comparisons are made to verify that all the appropriate data were input.

      a. Record count—Comparing the number of records that were actually input to the number of records that were supposed to be input

      b. Batch totals—Totals that are subject to meaningful interpretation (e.g., the day's cash withdrawals at a specific ATM location)

      c. Hash totals—Totals that have no meaningful interpretation as such, even though a total can be arithmetically determined (e.g., adding up employees' Social Security numbers to verify that no employees were omitted from a payroll application)

  4. Error resolution procedures—Whenever the control procedures flag a data input error, there should be specific procedures to fix the error and resubmit the data for input.

B. **Processing Controls**—The objective is that the processing of data is accurate and as authorized.

  1. Logic checks—The various logic checks identified above as input controls may also be used as processing controls (e.g., limit tests, etc.).

  2. Control totals, especially batch totals and hash totals, may also be used as processing controls, as described above with respect to input control.

  3. Limit on processing time—A predetermined limit for computer processing time can be specified; if that limit is exceeded, the program will terminate.

  4. Checkpoint/restart—For particularly long processing runs, there can be built-in checkpoint/restart locations; if the program crashes, it can be resumed without having to go back to the beginning.

  5. Error resolution procedures—Whenever the control procedures flag a data processing error, there should be specific procedures to fix the problem and resume processing.

C. **Output Controls**—The objective is that the output, specifically the distribution of any related reports, is accurate and as authorized.

  1. Control totals, especially batch totals and hash totals, may also be used as output controls, as described above with respect to input control.

  2. Output limits—A predetermined page or time limit might be specified; if such a limit is exceeded, the output activity will be stopped.

  3. Report distribution log—The entity should maintain a log that identifies when reports are to be generated, who is supposed to receive the reports, and the date of such distribution.

  4. Error resolution procedures—Whenever the control procedures flag an output error, there should be specific procedures to fix the problem and proceed with the proper generation and distribution of reports.

Other IT Considerations

1. Recognize the term "computer-assisted audit techniques" (CAATs) and the distinction between generalized audit software and customizing audit software.

2. Understand specific procedures that the auditor may perform in an IT environment to test relevant application controls.

3. Understand the basic terminology associated with an IT environment and common networks.

I. Computer-Assisted Audit Techniques (CAATs)

> **Note**
> CAATS can be used to test an entity's IT application controls and/or to gather substantive audit evidence related to an entity's computer files.

A. Generalized Audit Software—Commercially available software that can be used to access data and perform routine functions using clients' electronic files and databases

    1. Software commonly used in audit practice includes (a) ACL (formerly known in full as "Audit Command Language") and (b) IDEA (formerly known in full as "Interactive Data Extraction and "Analysis"); ACL and IDEA are sometimes referred to as data mining software.

    2. Routine functions include (a) extracting electronic data for analysis; (b) performing numerical tasks, such as adding up columns and rows of data; (c) stratifying data meeting specified criteria; (d) selecting audit samples; and (e) generating a variety of requested reports.

    3. Advantages—Generalized audit software tends to be applicable to a wide variety of client systems, so it does not require specific programming expertise and is rather user friendly; very large populations can be examined completely.

    4. Disadvantages—Generalized audit software is applicable only to data extracted from files/databases after being processed, not while the data are being processed; the software can be pricey, but that cost can be spread across many clients.

B. Customized Audit Software—Programs written specifically to access and manipulate the files/databases of a particular client

    1. Advantages—Customized audit software is tailored to specific circumstances and auditor needs.

    2. Disadvantages—Customized audit software may require a long planning horizon to develop, and the cost (on a per-client basis) may be high; any changes in the client's systems may also require changes to the customized software.

II. Audit Procedures Specific to Testing IT Application Controls

A. Test Data—Involves processing "dummy" transactions under the auditor's control

    1. The data includes known errors of interest to the auditor to test the entity's controls by checking whether the client's system detects those errors.

    2. The auditor need not include every possible type of error; only those specific errors that are of interest to the auditor must be included.

3. It is important that the auditor run such test data using the actual programs used for processing by the client entity while being careful not to contaminate the client entity's actual data with the test data.

B. Integrated Test Facility (ITF)—A fictitious division or department created by the auditor within the client entity where dummy data is processed along with the client's actual "live" data. It is important to avoid contaminating the client's actual data.

C. Parallel Simulation—Processing the client's actual data using the auditor's system and software; the auditor then compares the auditor's output to the entity's output for agreement.

D. Embedded Audit Modules and Audit Hooks—These involve auditing during an entity's processing, which is useful for systems that lack an audit trail.

1. Embedded audit modules—Routines that are built into application programs to perform ongoing audit functions

2. Audit hooks—Exit points that are built into application programs where an audit module can be added at a later time.

> **Note**
> The procedures identified in this section apply when testing IT application controls that are internal to an entity's systems and that are unobservable. Inquiry, observation, and inspection can be appropriately used to gather audit evidence about external, observable IT-related controls even if they are undocumented.

III. Miscellaneous IT-Related Terminology

A. Hardware and Software

1. Hardware—The central processing unit (CPU) and all the other related equipment

2. Software—The various systems and application programs

    a. Operating system—The instructions that run the CPU and related peripheral equipment

    b. Compiler—The software that translates the "source program" (written in a specific programming language, such as COBOL) into the "object program" (the instructions in machine-readable form)

B. Modes of Operation—The timing of when transactions are processed

1. Batch processing—Transactions are grouped for periodic processing (e.g., daily updates for an ATM machine).

2. Online, real-time processing—"Online" refers to being in direct communication with the CPU; "real-time" refers to immediately updating the underlying data files.

C. Database systems—Sets of interconnected files that eliminate the redundancy associated with maintaining separate files for different subsets of the organization; a major concern is limiting users' access to the parts of the database they have authorization to access.

1. Hierarchical database structures—Data elements at one level encompass the data elements immediately below them (constructed similar to a company's organizational chart); these structures are now uncommon.

2. Relational database structures—Integrated databases having the structure of a spreadsheet (each row consists of fields related to a particular customer or item, and each column consists of a specific information field that is applicable to each customer or item)

3. Distributed system—Single database that is distributed across multiple computers connected to the host server; each location can have its own input, processing, and output capabilities.

D. Network Jargon

1. Local area network (LAN)—A network interconnected throughout a building or campus, usually limited to a few miles in area.

2. Wide area network (WAN)—A larger version of a LAN that might span a whole city or country.

3. Intranet—A local area network that uses internet technology to facilitate communications throughout an organization.

4. Extranet—A local area network, similar to an intranet, that also connects important external constituents, such as major customers or suppliers.

5. Electronic data interchange (EDI)—An electronic transaction between a buyer and seller. EDIs exist in a variety of forms; in creating an EDI system, the elements of an entity's system should be mapped into the elements of the standardized format established for EDI activities.

   a. Direct EDI (also called "point-to-point EDI")—Involves a specific connection between the buyer and seller; Walmart is known for having these connections

   b. Value-added network (VAN)—A facilitating network maintained by an independent company that provides support services; VAN-based EDI is less common since the development of the internet, but it still exists.

   c. Web-based EDI—Involves using online forms via a standard internet browser; tends to be associated with small and medium-size entities that only have occasional EDI transactions

   d. EDI outsourcing (also called "B2B managed/outsourced services") —Involves engaging an external service provider to manage an entity's EDI activities

Forming Conclusions and Reporting

Audit Reports

Introduction to Audit Reports

Note: Changes to the AICPA's audit reporting model associated with SAS #134 (and several subsequent SASs) have been postponed by the AICPA and will **not** be eligible for testing until **January 2022**.

After studying this lesson, you should be able to:

1. State the Reporting Principle under the AICPA's clarified auditing standards.
2. Know the structure and content of the **unmodified** auditor's report.
3. Recognize the various alternative audit reports in addition to the unmodified auditor's report.

I. Reporting Principle

Recall that the seven principles identified as a framework for audit standard setting in the clarified auditing standards include one principle specifically directed at reporting:

"Based on an evaluation of the audit evidence obtained, the auditor expresses, in the form of a written report, an opinion in accordance with the auditor's findings, or states that an opinion cannot be expressed. The opinion states whether the financial statements are presented fairly, in all material respects, in accordance with the applicable financial reporting framework."

II. Relevant AICPA Guidance

The relevant AICPA clarified auditing standard is AU 700, *Forming an Opinion on Financial Statements*, which states that the auditor's objectives are to form an opinion on the financial statements based on an evaluation of the audit evidence obtained and to clearly express that opinion through a written report.

III. Overview of an Unmodified Audit Report

Under the AICPA's Clarified Standards (as amended by SAS No. 134, issued in 2019), the auditor's usual unmodified report has been reformatted and expanded to consist of the following four primary sections (in order) along with a signature block:

A. **Opinion**—The first sentence identifies the specific financial statements audited; the second sentence expresses the auditor's opinion on those financial statements.

B. **Basis for Opinion**—The second section consists of 4 sentences, including a comment on the applicable auditing standards, the auditor's independence, and the evidence providing a basis for the opinion.

C. **Responsibilities of Management for the Financial Statements**—The third section identifies management's responsibility for the preparation and fair presentation of the entity's financial statements as well as management's responsibility for the design, implementation, and maintenance of internal control over financial reporting; in addition, this section includes a comment about management's responsibility to evaluate the entity's ability to continue as a going concern.

D. **Auditor's Responsibilities for the Audit of the Financial Statements**—The fourth section consists of rather detailed comments about the auditor's responsibilities under GAAS, including comments regarding reasonable assurance, fraud, materiality, and going-concern issues, among other matters; the concluding sentence comments on the auditor's responsibility for communication with those charged with governance.

E. **Signature block**—The auditor's report also includes a signature block consisting of the manual or typed signature of the auditor's firm name, identification of the city and state of the office primarily responsible for conducting the audit, and the date of the auditor's report (when sufficient appropriate audit evidence has been obtained as a basis for the opinion).

IV. Alternative Audit Reports (to be discussed in detail in subsequent lessons)

A. Unmodified audit report that includes an "emphasis-of-matter" paragraph

B. Unmodified audit report that includes an "other-matter" paragraph

C. Modified audit reports—There are three types of modified audit reports:

1. **Qualified opinion**—The auditor expresses one or more reservations about (a) the financial statement presentation (due to a departure from the requirements of the applicable financial reporting framework that is material but not pervasive) or (b) the audit engagement (due to a scope limitation about a matter for which the auditor was unable to obtain desired audit evidence, the possible effect of which is material but not pervasive).

2. **Adverse opinion**—The auditor states that the financial statements are not fairly stated due to one or more departures from the requirements of the applicable financial reporting framework that is/are material and pervasive.

3. **Disclaimer of opinion**—The auditor does not express any conclusion about the fairness of the entity's financial statements due to a scope limitation that is material and pervasive.

V. Comparative Financial Statements

The continuing auditor's report should comment appropriately on the financial statements of each period presented that the auditor has audited. The type of opinion need not be the same for each period. (Sample reports are provided in subsequent lessons in connection with specific lessons on the various modified audit reports.)

A. Prior period's financial statements audited by a predecessor auditor whose report is reissued— The predecessor should obtain a representation letter from the (successor) auditor regarding matters that might affect the predecessor's prior-period audit report; the predecessor should not refer to the successor auditor in the predecessor auditor's reissued audit report.

B. Prior period's financial statements audited by a predecessor auditor whose report is not reissued— The auditor should add an other-matter paragraph to the auditor's report pointing out (1) that the financial statements of the prior period were audited by a predecessor auditor; (2) the type of opinion expressed by the predecessor (and the reason for any modification); (3) the nature of any emphasis-of-matter or other-matter paragraph(s); and (4) the date of the predecessor's report.

C. If the prior period's financial statements were not audited

1. If those financial statements were compiled or reviewed (and the report on the prior period's financial statements is not reissued)— The auditor should include an other-matter paragraph that identifies (a) the nature of the service performed in the prior period; (b) a description of any modifications reported; (c) a statement that the service does not provide a basis for an opinion; and (d) the date of the report.

2. If those financial statements were not audited, reviewed, or compiled—The auditor's report should include an other-matter paragraph pointing out that fact.

VI. Sample Auditor's Reports Presented Below

A. Unmodified auditor's report on the current-year (and prior-year) comparative financial statements without reference to legal and regulatory requirements

B. Unmodified auditor's report presented on a sentence-by-sentence basis (to facilitate the review of the contents of such an auditor's report)

C. Unmodified auditor's report on the current-year (and prior-year) comparative financial statements including a reference to legal and regulatory requirements

Sample Audit Report: Unmodified Report on GAAP-Based Financial Statements (without a "Report on Other Legal and Regulatory Requirements")

Independent Auditor's Report

[*Appropriate Addressee*]

Opinion

We have audited the financial statements of ABC Company, which comprise the balance sheets as of December 31, 20X1 and 20X0, and the related statements of income, changes in stockholders' equity, and cash flows for the years then ended, and the related notes to the financial statements.

In our opinion, the accompanying financial statements present fairly, in all material respects, the financial position of ABC Company as of December 31, 20X1 and 20X0, and the results of its operations and its cash flows for the years then ended in accordance with accounting principles generally accepted in the United States of America.

Basis for Opinion

We conducted our audits in accordance with auditing standards generally accepted in the United States of America (GAAS). Our responsibilities under those standards are further described in the Auditor's Responsibilities for the Audit of the Financial Statements section of our report. We are required to be independent of ABC Company and to meet our other ethical responsibilities, in accordance with the relevant ethical requirements relating to our audits. We believe that the audit evidence we have obtained is sufficient and appropriate to provide a basis for our audit opinion.

Responsibilities of Management for the Financial Statements

Management is responsible for the preparation and fair presentation of the financial statements in accordance with accounting principles generally accepted in the United States of America, and for the design, implementation, and maintenance of internal control relevant to the preparation and fair presentation of financial statements that are free from material misstatement, whether due to fraud or error.

In preparing the financial statements, management is required to evaluate whether there are conditions or events, considered in the aggregate, that raise substantial doubt about ABC Company's ability to continue as a going concern for [*insert the time period set by the applicable financial reporting framework*].

Auditor's Responsibilities for the Audit of the Financial Statements

Our objectives are to obtain reasonable assurance about whether the financial statements as a whole are free from material misstatement, whether due to fraud or error, and to issue an auditor's report that includes our opinion. Reasonable assurance is a high level of assurance but is not absolute assurance and therefore is not a guarantee that an audit conducted in accordance with GAAS will always detect a material misstatement when it exists. The risk of not detecting a material misstatement resulting from fraud is higher than for one resulting from error, as fraud may involve collusion, forgery, intentional omissions, misrepresentations, or the override of internal control. Misstatements are considered material if, individually or in the aggregate, they could reasonably be expected to influence the economic decisions of users made on the basis of these financial statements.

In performing an audit in accordance with GAAS, we:

o Exercise professional judgment and maintain professional skepticism throughout the audit.

o Identify and assess the risks of material misstatement of the financial statements, whether due to fraud or error, and design and perform audit procedures responsive to those risks. Such procedures include examining, on a test basis, evidence regarding the amounts and disclosures in the financial statements.

o Obtain an understanding of internal control relevant to the audit in order to design audit procedures that are appropriate in the circumstances, but not for the purpose of expressing an opinion on the effectiveness of ABC Company's internal control. Accordingly, no such opinion is expressed.[1]

○ Evaluate the appropriateness of accounting policies used and the reasonableness of significant accounting estimates made by management, as well as evaluate the overall presentation of the financial statements.

○ Conclude whether, in our judgment, there are conditions or events, considered in the aggregate, that raise substantial doubt about ABC Company's ability to continue as a going concern for a reasonable period of time.

We are required to communicate with those charged with governance regarding, among other matters, the planned scope and timing of the audit, significant audit findings, and certain internal control-related matters that we identified during the audit.

[*Signature of the auditor's firm*]

[*City and state where the auditor's report is issued*]

[*Date of the auditor's report*]

---

[1]When the auditor also has a responsibility to express an opinion on the effectiveness of internal control in connection with the audit of a nonissuer's financial statements, omit the following: "but not for the purpose of expressing an opinion on the effectiveness of ABC Company's internal control. Accordingly, no such opinion is expressed."

Sample Audit Report: Unmodified Report on GAAP-Based Financial Statements (without a "Report on Other Legal and Regulatory Requirements") Sentence-by-Sentence

Independent Auditor's Report

[*Appropriate Addressee*]

Opinion (2 paragraphs)

[First Paragraph]

1. We have audited the financial statements of ABC Company, which comprise the balance sheets as of December 31, 20X1 and 20X0, and the related statements of income, changes in stockholders' equity, and cash flows for the years then ended, and the related notes to the financial statements.

[Second Paragraph]

2. In our opinion, the accompanying financial statements present fairly, in all material respects, the financial position of ABC Company as of December 31, 20X1 and 20X0, and the results of its operations and its cash flows for the years then ended in accordance with accounting principles generally accepted in the United States of America.

Basis for Opinion (1 paragraph)

1. We conducted our audits in accordance with auditing standards generally accepted in the United States of America (GAAS).

2. Our responsibilities under those standards are further described in the Auditor's Responsibilities for the Audit of the Financial Statements section of our report.

3. We are required to be independent of ABC Company and to meet our other ethical responsibilities, in accordance with the relevant ethical requirements relating to our audits.

4. We believe that the audit evidence we have obtained is sufficient and appropriate to provide a basis for our audit opinion.

Responsibilities of Management for the Financial Statements (2 paragraphs)

[First Paragraph]

1. Management is responsible for the preparation and fair presentation of the financial statements in accordance with accounting principles generally accepted in the United States of America, and for the design, implementation, and maintenance of internal control relevant to the preparation and fair presentation of financial statements that are free from material misstatement, whether due to fraud or error.

[Second Paragraph]

2. In preparing the financial statements, management is required to evaluate whether there are conditions or events, considered in the aggregate, that raise substantial doubt about ABC Company's ability to continue as a going concern for [*insert the time period set by the applicable financial reporting framework*].

Auditor's Responsibilities for the Audit of the Financial Statements (3 paragraphs, 5 bullets)

[First Paragraph]

1. Our objectives are to obtain reasonable assurance about whether the financial statements as a whole are free from material misstatement, whether due to fraud or error, and to issue an auditor's report that includes our opinion.

2. Reasonable assurance is a high level of assurance but is not absolute assurance and therefore is not a guarantee that an audit conducted in accordance with GAAS will always detect a material misstatement when it exists.

3. The risk of not detecting a material misstatement resulting from fraud is higher than for one resulting from error, as fraud may involve collusion, forgery, intentional omissions, misrepresentations, or the override of internal control.

4. Misstatements are considered material if, individually or in the aggregate, they could reasonably be expected to influence the economic decisions of users made on the basis of these financial statements.

[Second Paragraph with 5 bullets]

5. In performing an audit in accordance with GAAS, we:

○ Exercise professional judgment and maintain professional skepticism throughout the audit.

○ Identify and assess the risks of material misstatement of the financial statements, whether due to fraud or error, and design and perform audit procedures responsive to those risks. Such procedures include examining, on a test basis, evidence regarding the amounts and disclosures in the financial statements.

○ Obtain an understanding of internal control relevant to the audit in order to design audit procedures that are appropriate in the circumstances, but not for the purpose of expressing an opinion on the effectiveness of ABC Company's internal control. Accordingly, no such opinion is expressed.[2]

○ Evaluate the appropriateness of accounting policies used and the reasonableness of significant accounting estimates made by management, as well as evaluate the overall presentation of the financial statements.

○ Conclude whether, in our judgment, there are conditions or events, considered in the aggregate, that raise substantial doubt about ABC Company's ability to continue as a going concern for a reasonable period of time.

[Third Paragraph]

6. We are required to communicate with those charged with governance regarding, among other matters, the planned scope and timing of the audit, significant audit findings, and certain internal control-related matters that we identified during the audit.

[*Signature of the auditor's firm*]

[*City and state where the auditor's report is issued*]

[*Date of the auditor's report*]

---

[2]When the auditor also has a responsibility to express an opinion on the effectiveness of internal control in connection with the audit of a nonissuer's financial statements, omit the following: "but not for the purpose of expressing an opinion on the effectiveness of ABC Company's internal control. Accordingly, no such opinion is expressed."

Sample Audit Report: Unmodified Report on GAAP-Based Financial Statements (when including a "Report on Other Legal and Regulatory Requirements")

Independent Auditor's Report

[*Appropriate Addressee*]

Report on the Audit of the Financial Statements[3]

Opinion

We have audited the financial statements of ABC Company, which comprise the balance sheets as of December 31, 20X1 and 20X0, and the related statements of income, changes in stockholders' equity, and cash flows for the years then ended, and the related notes to the financial statements.

In our opinion, the accompanying financial statements present fairly, in all material respects, the financial position of ABC Company as of December 31, 20X1 and 20X0, and the results of its operations and its cash flows for the years then ended in accordance with accounting principles generally accepted in the United States of America.

Basis for Opinion

We conducted our audits in accordance with auditing standards generally accepted in the United States of America (GAAS). Our responsibilities under those standards are further described in the Auditor's Responsibilities for the Audit of the Financial Statements section of our report. We are required to be independent of ABC Company and to meet our other ethical responsibilities, in accordance with the relevant ethical requirements relating to our audits. We believe that the audit evidence we have obtained is sufficient and appropriate to provide a basis for our audit opinion.

Responsibilities of Management for the Financial Statements

Management is responsible for the preparation and fair presentation of the financial statements in accordance with accounting principles generally accepted in the United States of America, and for the design, implementation, and maintenance of internal control relevant to the preparation and fair presentation of financial statements that are free from material misstatement, whether due to fraud or error.

In preparing the financial statements, management is required to evaluate whether there are conditions or events, considered in the aggregate, that raise substantial doubt about ABC Company's ability to continue as a going concern for [*insert the time period set by the applicable financial reporting framework*].

Auditor's Responsibilities for the Audit of the Financial Statements

Our objectives are to obtain reasonable assurance about whether the financial statements as a whole are free from material misstatement, whether due to fraud or error, and to issue an auditor's report that includes our opinion. Reasonable assurance is a high level of assurance but is not absolute assurance and therefore is not a guarantee that an audit conducted in accordance with GAAS will always detect a material misstatement when it exists. The risk of not detecting a material misstatement resulting from fraud is higher than for one resulting from error, as fraud may involve collusion, forgery, intentional omissions, misrepresentations, or the override of internal control. Misstatements are considered material if, individually or in the aggregate, they could reasonably be expected to influence the economic decisions of users made on the basis of these financial statements.

In performing an audit in accordance with GAAS, we:

○ Exercise professional judgment and maintain professional skepticism throughout the audit.

○ Identify and assess the risks of material misstatement of the financial statements, whether due to fraud or error, and design and perform audit procedures responsive to those risks. Such procedures include examining, on a test basis, evidence regarding the amounts and disclosures in the financial statements.

○ Obtain an understanding of internal control relevant to the audit in order to design audit procedures that are appropriate in the circumstances, but not for the purpose of expressing an opinion on the effectiveness of ABC Company's internal control. Accordingly, no such opinion is expressed.[4]

○ Evaluate the appropriateness of accounting policies used and the reasonableness of significant accounting estimates made by management, as well as evaluate the overall presentation of the financial statements.

○ Conclude whether, in our judgment, there are conditions or events, considered in the aggregate, that raise substantial doubt about ABC Company's ability to continue as a going concern for a reasonable period of time.

We are required to communicate with those charged with governance regarding, among other matters, the planned scope and timing of the audit, significant audit findings, and certain internal control-related matters that we identified during the audit.

Report on Other Legal and Regulatory Requirements

[*The form and content of this section of the auditor's report would vary depending on the nature of the auditor's other reporting responsibilities.*]

[*Signature of the auditor's firm*]

[*City and state where the auditor's report is issued*]

[*Date of the auditor's report*]

---

[3]This subtitle is not needed when the second subtitle ("Report on Other Legal and Regulatory Requirements") is not applicable.

[4]When the auditor also has a responsibility to express an opinion on the effectiveness of internal control in connection with the audit of a nonissuer's financial statements, omit the following: "but not for the purpose of expressing an opinion on the effectiveness of ABC Company's internal control. Accordingly, no such opinion is expressed."

Reporting Key Audit Matters

Overview for Reporting Key Audit Matters

After studying this lesson, you should be able to:

1. Define the term "key audit matters."

2. Know how to determine what constitutes a key audit matter.

3. Know how identified key audit matters should be addressed in the auditor's report when the auditor has been engaged to report key audit matters in connection with an audit of an entity's financial statements as a whole.

Reporting Key Audit Matters

I. Relevant AICPA Guidance

The relevant AICPA guidance in the clarified auditing standards is provided by AU 701, *Communicating Key Audit Matters in the Independent Auditor's Report*.

A. Scope of AU 701—This standard applies only when the auditor has been engaged to communicate key audit matters; if not specifically engaged to do so, the auditor is not required to identify and report key audit matters.

B. Objectives of AU 701—To identify key audit matters and to communicate those matters in the auditor's report

II. Definition

Definition

Key audit matters—"Those matters that, in the auditor's professional judgment, were of most significance in the audit of the financial statements of the current period. Key audit matters are selected from matters communicated with those charged with governance."

III. Determining Key Audit Matters

A. Involving Significant Auditor Attention—The auditor should determine those matters requiring significant auditor attention from those matters communicated with those charged with governance.

B. The auditor considers matters requiring significant auditor attention:

1. Significant risks identified, including areas of higher risk of material misstatement; matters that challenge the auditor in obtaining sufficient appropriate audit evidence

2. Areas of the financial statements involving significant management judgment, such as accounting estimates that have high estimation uncertainty requiring significant auditor attention; matters that involve complex auditor judgments

3. Significant unusual transactions or events identified as significant risks that require significant auditor attention

4. Significant changes to an IT system may be an area of significant auditor attention, especially if it has a significant effect on the auditor's overall strategy or relates to an identified significant risk.

5. Revisions to the auditor's risk assessment that result in higher assessed risk of material misstatement and the reevaluation of planned audit procedures that require significant auditor attention

C. **Matters of Most Significance**—Key audit matters are those matters that required significant auditor attention and that the auditor determines were of most significance in the audit; this reflects the auditor's judgment as to the relative importance of the identified significant risks.

1. Communications with those charged with governance may serve as an indication of which matters are considered most significant to the audit.

2. Long lists of key audit matters may be inconsistent with the concept of "most significance"; determining which (and how many) matters that required significant auditor attention were of most significance is a matter of professional judgment.

IV. Communicating Key Audit Matters

A. **Add a "Key Audit Matters" Section to the Auditor's Report**—Placing that section close to the "Opinion" and "Basis for Opinion" sections gives emphasis to such information; AU 701 does not specify exactly where this section should be located.

1. The introductory comments in that section should define "key audit matters" and state that those matters were identified in connection with forming an opinion on the financial statements as a whole.

2. Describe each key audit matter; reference any related disclosures; and explain why the matter was identified as a key audit matter and how the matter was addressed in the audit

   a. The order of the presentation of the individual key audit matters is a matter of professional judgment.

   b. The description of the information associated with identified key audit matters should be concise and understandable; the auditor should avoid standardized language.

   c. The auditor should not normally provide original information about the entity; if it is necessary to provide original information in the description of a key audit matter, management may wish to expand or supplement the entity's disclosures about such a matter.

3. A key audit matter should not be communicated in the following circumstances:

   a. When such disclosure is prohibited by law or regulation—For example, when a matter relates to a government contractor and involves security clearances

   b. When such disclosure has adverse consequences that outweigh the public interest benefits of that communication—For example, management may claim that the entity's commercial negotiations or competitive position may be adversely affected; however, this rationale is expected to be extremely rare

4. The "Key Audit Matters" section of the auditor's report should not include (a) matters that caused a qualified opinion or (b) matters that caused substantial doubt about an entity's ability to continue as a going concern; those issues are appropriately reported in accordance with other auditing standards.

5. If there are no key audit matters to be communicated—The auditor should include a specific statement as to that fact in the "Key Audit Matters" section of the auditor's report.

6. If the auditor expresses either an adverse opinion or disclaims an opinion—The auditor is prohibited from communicating key audit matters.

B. **Communication with Those Charged with Governance**—The auditor should communicate (1) those matters determined to be key audit matters or (2) the determination that there are no key audit matters to communicate in the report.

C. Documentation—The auditor should document the following:

1. Matters that required significant auditor attention and the rationale as to whether each such matter is a key audit matter

2. The rationale for determining that there are no key audit matters to communicate

3. The rationale to not communicate in the auditor's report any matter identified as a key audit matter

PCAOB on Audit Reports

After studying this lesson, you should be able to:

1. Know the structure and content of the audit report for an audit of an issuer under PCAOB Auditing Standards.

2. State the required disclosures associated with the PCAOB's Form AP.

3. Define the term "critical audit matters" and understand how such critical audit matters impact the auditor's report under PCAOB auditing standards.

I. Evolution of the PCAOB's Audit Reporting Model

A. The PCAOB adopted the AICPA's auditing standards in existence on April 16, 2003, as "interim standards, on an initial, transitional basis." An early PCAOB auditing standard made several minor changes to the AICPA's audit reporting language at that time.

B. Accordingly, the audit report under PCAOB auditing standards essentially consisted of three paragraphs known as the introductory, scope, and opinion paragraphs, in that order. The paragraphs were not individually labeled.

C. **Form AP**—The PCAOB subsequently required each registered public accounting firm to file a Form AP, *Auditor Reporting of Certain Audit Participants,* for every audit of an issuer. These Form APs are accessible on the PCAOB's website. The Form AP requires disclosure of the following:

1. The engagement partner's name;

2. The name, location, and extent of participation of any other accounting firm whose participation in the audit accounts for 5% or more of the total audit hours; *and*

3. The number and extent in total of all other accounting firms whose participation in the audit accounts for less than 5% of the total audit hours.

D. In 2017, the PCAOB issued (and the SEC approved) a new PCAOB auditing standard that changed the PCAOB's audit reporting model fairly significantly.

II. Relevant PCAOB Guidance

A. Basic guidance as to the PCAOB's audit reporting model is provided in the reorganized auditing standards: AS 3101, *The Auditor's Report on an Audit of Financial Statements When the Auditor Expresses an Unqualified Opinion.*

B. Other PCAOB standards apply when an unqualified opinion cannot be expressed: AS 3105, *Departures from Unqualified Opinions and Other Reporting Circumstances.*

III. Overview of the Revised PCAOB Audit Reporting Model

A. Most of the changes might be seen as relatively minor.

1. The opinion section was moved to the first part of the report;

2. Labels were added to clearly identify the sections of the report: (a) Opinion on the Financial Statements; (b) Basis for Opinion; and (c) Critical Audit Matters;

3. Commentary regarding the auditor's responsibilities was changed somewhat to be more descriptive and included an explicit statement about the auditor's independence requirements; *and*

4. The report must state the year when the auditor first began serving consecutively as the company's auditor (regarding "auditor tenure"). (The location of this statement is not prescribed by the PCAOB, but the sample report includes this disclosure within the signature block.)

B. The most significant (and controversial) change in the PCAOB's audit reporting model involves reporting **critical audit matters** (CAMs).

1. **Definition**—"Any matter arising from the audit of the financial statements that was communicated or required to be communicated to the audit committee and that relates to accounts or disclosures that are material to the financial statements and involved especially challenging, subjective, or complex auditor judgment."

2. Note that this definition encompasses matters (a) that were required to be communicated to the audit committee and (b) other matters that were actually communicated, although not required.

3. Among other things, the PCAOB requires the following matters to be communicated to a company's audit committee:

   a. Significant risks the auditor identified;

   b. Relevant matters regarding the company's accounting policies and estimates;

   c. Significant unusual transactions;

   d. Matters regarding the auditor's evaluation of any related parties and transactions with those related parties; *and*

   e. Other matters identified that are significant to the oversight of the company's financial reporting process.

4. For each current-year CAM, the auditor's report should communicate the following:

   a. The identification of the specific CAM;

   b. A description of the considerations that caused the auditor to identify the matter as a CAM;

   c. A description of how the CAM was addressed in the audit; *and*

   d. Reference to the related financial statement accounts or disclosures.

5. Communication of CAMs in reports not containing unqualified opinions:

   a. **Qualified opinion**—Such a report should also include communication of CAMs, if applicable.

   b. **Adverse opinion**—Such a report should not include any communication of CAMs, since the reason for the adverse opinion is most important.

   c. **Disclaimer of opinion**—Such a report should not include any communication of CAMs, since the reason for the disclaimer is most important.

Excerpt

Sample PCAOB Unqualified Audit Report with Critical Audit Matters

Report of Independent Registered Public Accounting Firm

To the shareholders and the board of directors of X Company

Opinion on the Financial Statements

We have audited the accompanying balance sheets of X Company (the "Company") as of December 31, 20X2 and 20X1, the related statements of [titles of the financial statements, e.g., income, comprehensive income, stockholders' equity, and cash flows] for each of the three years in the period ended December 31, 20X2, and the related notes [and schedules] (collectively referred to as the "financial statements"). In our opinion, the financial statements present fairly, in all material respects, the financial position of the Company as of [at] December 31, 20X2 and 20X1, and the results of its operations and its cash flows for each of the three years in the period ended December 31, 20X2, in conformity with [the applicable financial reporting framework].

Basis for Opinion

These financial statements are the responsibility of the Company's management. Our responsibility is to express an opinion on the Company's financial statements based on our audits. We are a public accounting firm registered with the Public Company Accounting Oversight Board (United States) ("PCAOB") and are required to be independent with respect to the Company in accordance with the U.S. federal securities laws and the applicable rules and regulations of the Securities and Exchange Commission and the PCAOB.

We conducted our audits in accordance with the standards of the PCAOB. Those standards require that we plan and perform the audit to obtain reasonable assurance about whether the financial statements are free of material misstatement, whether due to error or fraud. Our audits included performing procedures to assess the risks of material misstatement of the financial statements, whether due to error or fraud, and performing procedures that respond to those risks. Such procedures included examining, on a test basis, evidence regarding the amounts and disclosures in the financial statements. Our audits also included evaluating the accounting principles used and significant estimates made by management as well as evaluating the overall presentation of the financial statements. We believe that our audits provide a reasonable basis for our opinion.

Critical Audit Matters [if applicable]

The critical audit matters communicated below are matters arising from the current-period audit of the financial statements that were communicated or required to be communicated to the audit committee and that: (1) related to accounts or disclosures that are material to the financial statements and (2) involved our especially challenging, subjective, or complex judgments. The communication of critical audit matters does not alter in any way our opinion on the financial statements, taken as a whole, and we are not, by communicating the critical audit matters below, providing separate opinions on the critical audit matters or on the accounts or disclosures to which they relate.

[Include discussion of critical audit matters]

[Signature]

We have served as the Company's auditor since [year].

[City and State or Country]

[Date]

Note

If the auditor determines that there are no critical audit matters for the current period's audit (which seems unlikely), the auditor should include the following passage in the auditor's report:

Critical Audit Matters

Critical audit matters are matters arising from the current-period audit of the financial statements that were communicated or required to be communicated to the audit committee and that: (1) relate to accounts or disclosures that are material to the financial statements and (2) involved our especially challenging, subjective, or complex judgments. We determined that there are no critical audit matters.

Sample "Old" PCAOB Unqualified Audit Report (Now Superseded)

Report of Independent Registered Public Accounting Firm

We have audited the accompanying balance sheets of ABC Company at December 31, 20X3 and 20X2, and the related statements of operations, stockholders' equity, and cash flows for each of the three years in the period ended December 31, 20X3. These financial statements are the responsibility of the Company's management. Our responsibility is to express an opinion on these financial statements based on our audits.

We conducted our audits in accordance with the standards of the Public Company Accounting Oversight Board (United States). Those standards require that we plan and perform the audit to obtain reasonable assurance about whether the financial statements are free of material misstatement. An audit includes examining, on a test basis, evidence supporting the amounts and disclosures in the financial statements. An audit also includes assessing the accounting principles used and significant estimates made by management, as well as evaluating the overall financial statement presentation. We believe that our audits provide a reasonable basis for our opinion.

In our opinion, the financial statements referred to above present fairly, in all material respects, the financial position of ABC Company at December 31, 20X3 and 20X2, and the results of its operations and its cash flows for each of the three years in the period ended December 31, 20X3, in conformity with U.S. generally accepted accounting principles.

(Signature)

(City and State or Country)

(Date)

Audits of Group Financial Statements

> **After studying this lesson, you should be able to:**
>
> 1. Know how a reference to a component auditor affects the auditor's report.
> 2. Understand the difference between a component and a group, and distinguish between the group's auditor and a component auditor.

I. Relevant AICPA Guidance

The relevant AICPA guidance is provided by AU 600, *Special Considerations—Audits of Group Financial Statements (Including the Work of Component Auditors)*. The standard states that the auditor's objectives are to determine whether to act as the auditor of the group financial statements, and, if so, (1) to determine whether to make reference to the audit of the component auditor; (2) to communicate clearly with component auditors; and (3) to obtain sufficient appropriate audit evidence regarding the financial information of the components and the consolidation process to express an opinion on the group financial statements.

II. Selected Definitions

> **Definitions**
>
> *Component*: An entity for which group or component management prepares financial information that is required by the applicable financial reporting framework to be included in the group financial statements.
>
> *Component Auditor*: An auditor who performs work on the financial information of a component that will be used as audit evidence for the group audit. (**A component auditor may be part of the group engagement partner's firm, a network-affiliated firm, or another unrelated firm.**)
>
> *Group*: All the components whose financial information is included in the group financial statements. A group always has more than one component.
>
> *Group Financial Statements*: Financial statements that include the financial information of more than one component. This term also refers to combined financial statements aggregating the financial information prepared by components that are under common control.
>
> *Group-Wide Controls*: Controls designed, implemented, and maintained by group management over group financial reporting.
>
> *Significant Component*: A component identified by the group engagement team that (a) is of individual financial significance to the group; or (b) due to its specific nature, is likely to include significant risks of material misstatement of the group financial statements.

III. Responsibilities of the Group Engagement Partner and the Group Engagement Team

A. **Group Engagement Partner**—The group engagement partner is responsible for (1) the supervision and performance of the group audit engagement in compliance with professional standards and applicable regulatory requirements; and (2) determining whether the auditor's report is appropriate in the circumstances.

B. **Acceptance and Continuance**—The group engagement team should obtain an understanding of the group, its components, and their environments sufficient to identify the significant components.

   1. The group engagement partner should evaluate whether sufficient appropriate audit evidence will be obtained, including the use of the component auditors' work, to act as the auditor of the group financial statements.

2. If sufficient appropriate audit evidence would not be obtained, the auditor should not accept a new engagement or should withdraw from a continuing engagement. (If withdrawal is not permitted, the auditor should disclaim an opinion.)

C. Assess the Risks of Material Misstatement of the Group Financial Statements—The auditor should obtain an understanding of the group, its components, and their environments (including group-wide controls) and obtain an understanding of the consolidation process and the instructions issued by group management to components.

D. Obtain an Understanding of the Component Auditor(s)

1. Recall that the term component auditor applies to auditors of other offices of the group engagement partner's firm (for an engagement involving multiple offices of the same firm), to a network-affiliated firm, or to another unrelated firm (that is not subject to the quality controls of the group engagement partner's firm).

2. The group engagement team should obtain an understanding of (a) the component auditor's independence and professional competence; (b) the extent to which the group engagement team will be involved in the work of the component auditor; (c) whether the group engagement team will be able to obtain information affecting the consolidation process from the component auditor.

E. The group engagement team should determine materiality (1) for the group financial statements as a whole, (2) for the components to be audited by the group engagement team or by component auditors, and (3) the threshold for determining clearly trivial to the group financial statements.

F. Responding to Assessed Risks—If work to be performed on the consolidation process or the financial information of the components is based on an expectation that group-wide controls are operating effectively, the group engagement team (or the component auditor) should test the operating effectiveness of those controls.

G. Consolidation Process—The group engagement team should perform further audit procedures on the consolidation process to respond to the assessed risks of material misstatement associated with the consolidation process, including evaluating whether all components have been included and whether there are any indicators of possible management bias or fraud.

H. Communications with a Component Auditor—The group engagement team should communicate its requirements of the component on a timely basis, and request that the component auditor communicate matters relevant to the group engagement team's conclusions.

I. Involvement in the Work of the Component Auditors—For a significant component for which the auditor of the group financial statements is assuming responsibility for the component auditor's work, the auditor should (a) discuss with the component auditor the significance of the component to the group and the susceptibility of the component to material misstatement; and (b) review the component auditor's documentation of identified significant risks of material misstatement to the group financial statements.

J. Documentation—The group engagement team's audit documentation should include the following:

1. An analysis of components indicating those that are significant (and the type of work performed);

2. Written communications between the group engagement team and the component auditors about the group engagement team's requirements;

3. Those components for which reference to the component auditors' reports were made in the auditor's report; *and*

4. The financial statements of the component and the report of the component auditor for components referenced in the auditor's report on the group financial statements.

K. Determining Whether to Reference a Component Auditor in the Auditor's Report

1. Reference to the component auditor should not be made unless: (a) the component's financial statements are prepared using the same financial reporting framework used by the group; (b) the component auditor has performed an audit on the component's financial statements in accordance with GAAS (or PCAOB standards, if applicable); and **(c) the component auditor has issued an audit report on the component's financial statements that is not restricted as to use.**

2. **If the group engagement partner decides to assume responsibility for the component auditor's work**—No reference should be made to the component auditor in the auditor's report.

3. **If the group engagement partner decides to name the component auditor in the auditor's report**—The component auditor's permission should be obtained and the component auditor's report should be presented along with the auditor's report on the group financial statements.

L. Effect of Reference to a Component Auditor on the Auditor's Report

1. The "Opinion" section should refer to "In our opinion, **based on our audit(s) and the report of the other auditors, ...**" The opinion section should include an additional paragraph that identifies the component(s) audited by other auditors and the relative magnitude of the financial statements involved.

2. The "Basis for Opinion," "Management Responsibilities," and "Auditor's Responsibilities" sections are unchanged by the reference to component auditors.

M. Sample Report that Refers to a Component Auditor

Independent Auditor's Report

[Appropriate Addressee]

Opinion

We have audited the consolidated financial statements of ABC Company and its subsidiaries, which comprise the consolidated balance sheets as of December 31, 20X1 and 20X0, and the related consolidated statements of income, changes in stockholders' equity, and cash flows for the years then ended, and the related notes to the financial statements.

In our opinion, based on our audits and the report of the other auditors, the accompanying consolidated financial statements present fairly, in all material respects, the financial position of ABC Company and its subsidiaries as of December 31, 20X1 and 20X0, and the results of their operations and their cash flows for the years then ended in accordance with accounting principles generally accepted in the United States of America.

We did not audit the financial statements of B Company, a wholly owned subsidiary, which statements reflect total assets constituting 20 percent and 22 percent, respectively, of consolidated total assets at December 31, 20X1 and 20X0, and total revenues constituting 18 percent and 20 percent, respectively, of consolidated total revenues for the years then ended. Those statements were audited by other auditors, whose report has been furnished to us, and our opinion, insofar as it relates to the amounts included for B Company, is based solely on the report of the other auditors.

Basis for Opinion

We conducted our audits in accordance with auditing standards generally accepted in the United States of America (GAAS). Our responsibilities under those standards are further described in the Auditor's Responsibilities for the Audit of the Financial Statements section of our report. We are required to be independent of ABC Company and to meet our other ethical responsibilities, in accordance with the relevant ethical requirements relating to our audits. We believe that the audit evidence we have obtained is sufficient and appropriate to provide a basis for our audit opinion.

Responsibilities of Management for the Financial Statements

Management is responsible for the preparation and fair presentation of the consolidated financial statements in accordance with accounting principles generally accepted in the United States of America, and for the design, implementation, and maintenance of internal control relevant to the preparation and fair presentation of consolidated financial statements that are free from material misstatement, whether due to fraud or error.

In preparing the consolidated financial statements, management is required to evaluate whether there are conditions or events, considered in the aggregate, that raise substantial doubt about ABC Company's ability to continue as a going concern for [insert the time period set by the applicable financial reporting framework].

Auditor's Responsibilities for the Audit of the Financial Statements

Our objectives are to obtain reasonable assurance about whether the consolidated financial statements as a whole are free from material misstatement, whether due to fraud or error, and to issue an auditor's report that includes our opinion. Reasonable assurance is a high level of assurance but is not absolute assurance and therefore is not a guarantee that an audit conducted in accordance with GAAS will always detect a material misstatement when it exists. The risk of not detecting a material misstatement resulting from fraud is higher than for one resulting from error, as fraud may involve collusion, forgery, intentional omissions, misrepresentations, or the override of internal control. Misstatements are considered material if there is a substantial likelihood that, individually or in the aggregate, they would influence the judgment made by a reasonable user based on the consolidated financial statements.

In performing an audit in accordance with GAAS, we:

- Exercise professional judgment and maintain professional skepticism throughout the audit.

- Identify and assess the risks of material misstatement of the consolidated financial statements, whether due to fraud or error, and design and perform audit procedures responsive to those risk. Such procedures include examining, on a test basis, evidence regarding the amounts and disclosures in the financial statements.

- Obtain an understanding of internal control relevant to the audit in order to design audit procedures that are appropriate in the circumstances, but not for the purpose of expressing an opinion on the effectiveness of ABC Company's internal control. Accordingly, no such opinion is expressed.

- Evaluate the appropriateness of accounting policies used and the reasonableness of significant accounting estimates made by management, as well as evaluate the overall presentation of the consolidated financial statements.

- Conclude whether, in our judgment, there are conditions or events, considered in the aggregate, that raise substantial doubt about ABC Company's ability to continue as a going concern for a reasonable period of time.

We are required to communicate with those charged with governance regarding, among other matters, the planned scope and timing of the audit, significant audit findings, and certain internal control–related matters that we identified during the audit.

Other Information [or another title, if appropriate, such as "Information Other Than the Financial Statements and Auditor's Report Thereon"]

[Reporting in accordance with the reporting requirements in section 720, The Auditor's Responsibilities Relating to Other Information Included in Annual Reports, if applicable.]

[Signature of auditor's firm]

[City and state where the auditor's report is issued]

[Date of the auditor's report]

Emphasis-of-Matter Paragraphs and Other-Matter Paragraphs

> **After studying this lesson, you should be able to:**
>
> 1. Know the definition of (and distinction between) emphasis-of-matter and other-matter paragraphs in the auditor's report.
>
> 2. Know the matters for which an emphasis-of-matter paragraph is required.
>
> 3. Know how an emphasis-of-matter and/or other-matter paragraph would be presented in the auditor's report.

I. Relevant AICPA Guidance

The relevant AICPA clarified auditing standard is AU 706, Emphasis-of-Matter Paragraphs and Other-Matter Paragraphs in the Independent Auditor's Report, which states that the auditor's objective is to draw the users' attention, as necessary, to (1) a matter, already appropriately presented/disclosed in the financial statements, that is important to the users' understanding of the financial statements (emphasis-of-matter paragraph); or (2) any other matter that is relevant to the users' understanding of the audit, the auditor's responsibilities, or the auditor's report (other-matter paragraph).

II. Definitions

A. **Emphasis-of-matter paragraph**: "A paragraph included in the auditor's report that is required by GAAS, or is included at the auditor's discretion, and that refers to a matter appropriately presented or disclosed in the financial statements that, in the auditor's professional judgment, is of such importance that it is fundamental to users' understanding of the financial statements."

B. **Other-matter paragraph**: "A paragraph included in the auditor's report that is required by GAAS, or is included at the auditor's discretion, and that refers to a matter other than those presented or disclosed in the financial statements that, in the auditor's professional judgment, is relevant to users' understanding of the audit, the auditor's responsibilities, or the auditor's report."

III. Emphasis-of-Matter Paragraph

A. Circumstances for which an emphasis-of-matter paragraph is required:

1. When there is a change in accounting measurement principles (i.e., an inconsistency) the effect of which is properly accounted for and disclosed

2. When the financial statements are prepared properly in accordance with a special-purpose framework; this topic will be discussed in another lesson

B. Examples of circumstances for which an auditor may choose to add an emphasis-of-matter paragraph: (1) an uncertainty regarding the outcome of important litigation or regulatory action; (2) a significant subsequent event; (3) a major event or catastrophe having significant effects on the entity; or (4) significant transactions with related parties

C. Effect of the emphasis-of-matter paragraph on the auditor's report

1. Should have an appropriate label, such as "Emphasis of Matter; presented after the "Opinion" and "Basis for Opinion" sections of the audit report

2. Should reference the specific matter being emphasized and identify where relevant disclosures can be found in the financial statements

3. Include a statement that the opinion is not modified with respect to the matter being emphasized

D. Example of an emphasis-of-matter paragraph:

> **Emphasis of Matter**
>
> As discussed in Note X to the financial statements, subsequent to the date of the financial statements, there was a fire in ABC Company's production facilities. Our opinion is not modified with respect to this matter.

IV. Other-Matter Paragraph

A. Circumstances for which an other-matter paragraph is required:

1. When the opinion expressed on the prior year's financial statements is different from the opinion previously expressed (due to management's correction of a material departure from the applicable financial reporting framework)

   a. Identify the date of the auditor's previous report.

   b. Identify the type of opinion previously expressed and point out that the auditor's opinion on the revised financial statements differs from the opinion previously expressed.

   c. State the reason(s) for expressing a different opinion.

2. When the prior period's financial statements were audited by a predecessor auditor whose report on those financial statements is not reissued

   a. State that the prior period's financial statements were audited by a predecessor auditor.

   b. Identify the type of opinion expressed by the predecessor and the reasons for any modification of the opinion; identify the nature of any emphasis-of-matter or other-matter paragraphs included.

   c. Identify the date of the predecessor's audit report.

3. When the current period's financial statements have been audited and the prior period's financial statements were compiled or reviewed (discussed in later lessons related to Statements on Standards for Accounting and Review Services) and the report on the prior period's financial statement is not reissued

   a. Identify the nature of the service performed in the prior period and identify the date of the compilation or review report involved.

   b. Describe any material modifications associated with that report.

   c. For a review report—Include a statement that the service was substantially less in scope than an audit and disclaim an opinion.

   d. For a compilation report—Include a statement that disclaims an opinion or any other form of assurance on the prior period's financial statements.

4. When the prior period's financial statements were not audited, reviewed, or compiled—The status of those financial statements should be so marked; the other-matter paragraph should state that those financial statements have not been audited, reviewed, or compiled.

5. When financial statements have been presented using certain special-purpose frameworks (discussed further in a separate lesson titled "Financial Statements with Special-Purpose Frameworks")— An other-matter paragraph should be added to restrict the distribution of the auditor's report to specified parties when the financial statements are based on:

   a. A contractual basis of accounting

   b. A regulatory basis of accounting (not intended for general distribution)

   c. A so-called "other basis of accounting"

   d. Note: No such restriction is required when the special-purpose financial statements are presented using (1) cash basis, (2) tax basis, or (3) a regulatory basis that is intended for general use

6. When the entity presents "supplementary information" (derived from the underlying accounting records) with the financial statements and the auditor does not issue a separate report on that supplementary information—The auditor should add an other-matter paragraph to address the supplementary information; the content of such an other-matter paragraph is addressed in a separate lesson titled "Supplementary Information Related to Financial Statements."

7. When a designated accounting standard-setting body requires certain supplementary information to be reported in the financial statements—The auditor should add an other-matter paragraph to address the supplementary information; the content of such an other-matter paragraph is addressed in a separate lesson titled "Required Supplementary Information."

8. When a report on compliance with contractual or regulatory requirements is combined with the auditor's report on financial statements—The auditor should add an other-matter paragraph to address those compliance issues and to restrict the distribution of the report to specified parties; the content of such an other-matter paragraph is addressed in a separate lesson titled "Reporting on Compliance with Requirements in an F/S Audit."

9. When auditing the financial statements of an employee benefit plan subject to ERISA (discussed in a separate lesson titled "Auditing Employee Benefit Plans")— The auditor should add an other-matter paragraph to address the supplemental schedules required by ERISA.

B. In general, the auditor may choose to add an other-matter paragraph to the auditor's report to address issues relevant to users' understanding of the audit, the auditor's responsibilities, or the auditor's report

C. Effect of the other-matter paragraph on the auditor's report—Should have an appropriate label, such as "Other Matter"; presented after the "Opinion" and "Basis for Opinion" sections (and after any emphasis-of-matter paragraphs).

D. Departure from promulgated accounting principles in unusual circumstances—There is a strong presumption that compliance with promulgated accounting principles by designated standard-setting bodies will result in proper financial statements.

1. However, if compliance with such a promulgated accounting principle would itself cause the financial statements to be misleading, departure from such a principle is permitted for purposes of achieving fairness in financial reporting; this situation is addressed by the "Accounting Principles Rule" (ET sec. 1.320.001) of the AICPA Code of Professional Conduct.

2. In such a case, the auditor may issue an unmodified audit report with an appropriate other-matter paragraph (or possibly an emphasis-of-matter paragraph, depending on the financial statement treatment of the departure), to describe the departure, its approximate effects, and the reason(s) why compliance with the promulgated principle would cause the financial statements to become misleading.

E. Example of an other-matter paragraph:

Other Matter

In our report dated March 1, 20X1, we expressed an opinion that the 20X0 financial statements did not fairly present the financial position, results of operations, and cash flows of ABC Company in accordance with accounting principles generally accepted in the United States of America because of two departures from such principles: (1) ABC Company carried its property, plant, and equipment at appraisal values and provided for depreciation on the basis of such values, and (2) ABC Company did not provide for deferred income taxes with respect to differences between income for financial reporting purposes and taxable income. As described in Note X, the Company has changed its method of accounting for these items and restated its 20X0 financial statements to conform with accounting principles generally accepted in the United States of America. Accordingly, our present opinion on the restated 20X0 financial statements, as presented herein, is different from that expressed in our previous report.

V. Communication with Those Charged with Governance

The auditor should communicate with those charged with governance about the proposed wording of any expected emphasis-of-matter or other-matter paragraph(s).

VI. "Going Concern" Section of the Auditor's Report

A. In the past, the auditor was required to add an emphasis-of-matter paragraph to the auditor's report when the auditor had substantial doubt about the entity's ability to continue as a going concern for a reasonable period of time (assuming those uncertainties were adequately disclosed in accordance with the applicable financial reporting framework)

B. SAS No. 134, *Auditor Reporting and Amendments, Including Amendments Addressing Disclosures in the Audit of Financial Statements*, was issued in 2019—Among other things, SAS No. 134 changed the auditor's reporting requirements with respect to going concern issues

    1. When the auditor has substantial doubt about the entity's ability to continue as a going concern for a reasonable period of time (and those uncertainties are properly disclosed)—The auditor should add a "Going Concern" section to the auditor's report that

        a. Is labeled "Substantial Doubt About the Entity's Ability to Continue as a Going Concern."

        b. References the financial statement note that discloses the conditions/events identified by management's plan to address those issues causing substantial doubt the entity's ability to continue as a going concern for a reasonable period of time.

        c. Includes a statement that the auditor's report is not modified with respect to this matter.

    2. Example of a "Going Concern" section of the auditor's report:

Substantial Doubt About the Company's Ability to Continue as a Going Concern

The accompanying financial statements have been prepared assuming the Company will continue as a going concern. As discussed in Note X to the financial statements, the Company has suffered recurring losses from operations, has a net capital deficiency, and has stated that substantial doubt exists about the Company's ability to continue as a going concern. Management's evaluation of the events and conditions and management's plans regarding these matters are also described in Note X. The financial statements do not include any adjustments that might result from the outcome of this uncertainty. Our opinion is not modified with respect to this matter.

C. When the auditor concludes that substantial doubt about the entity's ability to continue as a going concern has been alleviated by management's plans (and that disclosure of those issues is adequate)—The auditor may add an emphasis-of-matter paragraph to draw the users' attention to those circumstances.

D. The topic of going concern issues is addressed in more detail in the lesson titled "Going Concern Issues."

Qualified for Scope Limitation

After studying this lesson, you should be able to:

1. Understand when and how to express a qualified audit opinion for a scope limitation affecting the auditor's basis for conclusions.

I. Relevant AICPA Guidance

The relevant AICPA guidance is provided by AU 705, *Modifications to the Opinion in the Independent Auditor's Report*. The standard states that the auditor's objective is to express clearly an appropriately modified opinion when (1) the auditor concludes that the financial statements as a whole are misstated; or (2) **the auditor is unable to obtain sufficient appropriate audit evidence to conclude that the financial statements as a whole are free from material misstatement.** This lesson focuses on the second matter, which is known as a scope limitation.

> **Definitions**
>
> *Modified opinion*: A qualified opinion, an adverse opinion, or a disclaimer of opinion.
>
> *Pervasive*: (a) Effects that are not confined to specific elements, accounts or items of the financial statements; (b) effects that, if so confined, represent or could represent a substantial proportion of the financial statements; or (c) regarding disclosures, are fundamental to users' understanding of the financial statements.

II. Opinion Scope Limitation Involves Judgment

A. Qualified Opinion—The auditor should express a qualified opinion when the auditor is unable to obtain sufficient appropriate audit evidence, and the auditor concludes that the possible effect on the financial statements, if any, could be **material, but not pervasive**. (This lesson focuses on the qualified opinion in connection with a scope limitation.)

B. Disclaimer of Opinion—The auditor should express a disclaimer of opinion when the auditor is unable to obtain sufficient appropriate audit evidence, and the auditor concludes that the possible effect on the financial statements, if any, could be **material and pervasive**. (A separate lesson focuses on the disclaimer of opinion.)

III. Circumstances Resulting in a Scope Limitation

A. Circumstances beyond the Control of the Entity—For example, the entity's accounting records have been destroyed.

B. Circumstances Related to the Nature or Timing of the Auditor's Work—For example, the auditor determines that substantive procedures alone are not sufficient and the entity's controls are ineffective; the auditor is unable to obtain audited financial statements of an investee (accounted for using the equity method); or the timing of the auditor's appointment does not permit the auditor to observe the physical counting of inventories.

C. Limitations Imposed by Management—For example, management prevents the auditor from requesting external confirmation of certain account balances. The auditor should request that management remove any such limitation.

1. If management refuses—the auditor should communicate the matter to those charged with governance and determine whether it is possible to perform alternative procedures to obtain sufficient appropriate audit evidence.

2. If unable to obtain sufficient appropriate audit evidence (and if the effects could be both material and pervasive)—the auditor should withdraw from the audit (when practicable) or issue a disclaimer of opinion.

IV. Effect of a Qualification for a Scope Limitation on the Auditor's Report

A. Opinion—Qualify the opinion using appropriate language such as: "In our opinion, **except for the possible effects of the matter described in the "Basis for Qualified Opinion" section**, the financial statements referred to above present fairly . . .; label the "Opinion" section "Qualified Opinion."

B. "Basis for Qualified Opinion" section—(1) Add a paragraph at the beginning of that section to explain the reason for the qualified opinion; (2) modify the last sentence of the second paragraph to state: "We believe that the audit evidence we have obtained is sufficient and appropriate to provide a basis for our qualified audit opinion."

C. "Management's Responsibilities" section—No changes

D. "Auditor's Responsibilities" section—No changes

V. Sample Audit Report Qualified Due to Scope Limitation

Independent Auditor's Report

[*Appropriate Addressee*]

Qualified Opinion

We have audited the consolidated financial statements of ABC Company and its subsidiaries, which comprise the consolidated balance sheets as of December 31, 20X1 and 20X0, and the related consolidated statements of income, changes in stockholders' equity, and cash flows for the years then ended, and the related notes to the financial statements.

In our opinion, except for the possible effects of the matter described in the Basis for Qualified Opinion section of our report, the accompanying consolidated financial statements present fairly, in all material respects, the financial position of ABC Company and its subsidiaries as of December 31, 20X1 and 20X0, and the results of their operations and their cash flows for the years then ended in accordance with accounting principles generally accepted in the United States of America.

Basis for Qualified Opinion

We were unable to obtain audited financial statements supporting the Company's investment in a foreign affiliate stated at $XXXX and $XXXX at December 31, 20X1 and 20X0, respectively, or its equity in earnings of that affiliate of $XXXX and $XXXX, which is included in net income for the years then ended as described in Note X to the consolidated financial statements; nor were we able to satisfy ourselves as to the carrying value of the investment in the foreign affiliate or the equity in its earnings by other auditing procedures.

We conducted our audits in accordance with auditing standards generally accepted in the United States of America (GAAS). Our responsibilities under those standards are further described in the Auditor's Responsibilities for the Audit of the Financial Statements section of our report. We are required to be independent of ABC Company and to meet our other ethical responsibilities, in accordance with the relevant ethical requirements relating to our audit. We believe that the audit evidence we have obtained is sufficient and appropriate to provide a basis for our qualified audit opinion.

Responsibilities of Management for the Financial Statements

Management is responsible for the preparation and fair presentation of the consolidated financial statements in accordance with accounting principles generally accepted in the United States of America, and for the design, implementation, and maintenance of internal control relevant to the preparation and fair presentation of consolidated financial statements that are free from material misstatement, whether due to fraud or error.

In preparing the consolidated financial statements, management is required to evaluate whether there are conditions or events, considered in the aggregate, that raise substantial doubt about ABC Company's ability to continue as a going concern for [*insert the time period set by the applicable financial reporting framework*].

Auditor's Responsibilities for the Audit of the Financial Statements

Our objectives are to obtain reasonable assurance about whether the consolidated financial statements as a whole are free from material misstatement, whether due to fraud or error, and to issue an auditor's report that includes our opinion. Reasonable assurance is a high level of assurance but is not absolute assurance and therefore is not a guarantee that an audit conducted in accordance with GAAS will always detect a material misstatement when it exists. The risk of not detecting a material misstatement resulting from fraud is higher than for one resulting from error, as fraud may involve collusion, forgery, intentional omissions, misrepresentations, or the override of internal control. Misstatements are considered material if, individually or in the aggregate, they could reasonably be expected to influence the economic decisions of users made on the basis of these consolidated financial statements.

In performing an audit in accordance with GAAS, we:

- Exercise professional judgment and maintain professional skepticism throughout the audit.

- Identify and assess the risks of material misstatement of the consolidated financial statements, whether due to fraud or error, and design and perform audit procedures responsive to those risks. Such procedures include examining, on a test basis, evidence regarding the amounts and disclosures in the financial statements.

- Obtain an understanding of internal control relevant to the audit in order to design audit procedures that are appropriate in the circumstances, but not for the purpose of expressing an opinion on the effectiveness of ABC Company's internal control. Accordingly, no such opinion is expressed.

- Evaluate the appropriateness of accounting policies used and the reasonableness of significant accounting estimates made by management, as well as evaluate the overall presentation of the consolidated financial statements.

- Conclude whether, in our judgment, there are conditions or events, considered in the aggregate, that raise substantial doubt about ABC Company's ability to continue as a going concern for a reasonable period of time.

We are required to communicate with those charged with governance regarding, among other matters, the planned scope and timing of the audit, significant audit findings, and certain internal control-related matters that we identified during the audit.

[*Signature of the auditor's firm*]

[*City and state where the auditor's report is issued*]

[*Date of the auditor's report*]

Qualified for Misstatement

After studying this lesson, you should be able to:

1. Understand when and how to express a qualified audit opinion for a misstatement (including inadequate disclosure) affecting the fair presentation of an entity's financial statements.

I. Relevant AICPA Guidance

The relevant AICPA guidance is provided by AU 705, *Modifications to the Opinion in the Independent Auditor's Report*. The standard states that the auditor's objective is to express clearly an appropriately modified opinion when (1) **the auditor concludes that the financial statements as a whole are misstated**; or (2) the auditor is unable to obtain sufficient appropriate audit evidence to conclude that the financial statements as a whole are free from material misstatement. (This lesson focuses on the first matter, since the scope limitation is discussed in a separate lesson.)

Definitions

Modified Opinion: A qualified opinion, an adverse opinion, or a disclaimer of opinion.

Pervasive: (a) Effects that are not confined to specific elements, accounts, or items of the financial statements; (b) effects that, if so confined, represent or could represent a substantial proportion of the financial statements; or (c) regarding disclosures, are fundamental to users' understanding of the financial statements.

II. Opinion Choice for a Misstatement (Including Inadequate Disclosure) Involves Judgment

   A. Qualified Opinion—The auditor should express a qualified opinion when the auditor concludes that misstatements are **material, but not pervasive** to the financial statements.

   B. Adverse Opinion—The auditor should express an adverse opinion when the auditor concludes that misstatements are **material and pervasive** to the financial statements. (A separate lesson focuses on the adverse opinion.)

III. Effect of a Qualification for a Misstatement on the Auditor's Report

   A. Opinion—Qualify the opinion using appropriate language such as: "In our opinion, **except for the effects of the matter described in the Basis for Qualified Opinion paragraph**, the financial statements referred to above present fairly . . ."; label the Opinion section "Qualified Opinion."

   B. Basis for Qualified Opinion—(1) Add a paragraph at the beginning of that section to explain the reason(s) for the qualified opinion and the effects on the financial statements; should quantify the financial effects or provide the omitted information when "practicable" (e.g., would not be required to include a missing statement of cash flows); (2) modify the last sentence of the second paragraph to state "We believe that the audit evidence we have obtained is sufficient and appropriate to provide a basis for our qualified audit opinion."

   **C. "Management's Responsibilities" section—No changes

   **D. "Auditor's Responsibilities" section—No changes

IV. Sample Audit Report Qualified Due to GAAP Departure/Misstatement

---

Independent Auditor's Report

[Appropriate Addressee]

Qualified Opinion

We have audited the financial statements of ABC Company, which comprise the balance sheets as of December 31, 20X1 and 20X0, and the related statements of income, changes in stockholders' equity, and cash flows for the years then ended, and the related notes to the financial statements.

In our opinion, except for the effects of the matter described in the Basis for Qualified Opinion section of our report, the accompanying financial statements present fairly, in all material respects, the financial position of ABC Company as of December 31, 20X1 and 20X0, and the results of its operations and its cash flows for the years then ended in accordance with accounting principles generally accepted in the United States of America.

Basis for Qualified Opinion

ABC Company has stated inventories at cost in the accompanying balance sheets. Accounting principles generally accepted in the United States of America require inventories to be stated at the lower of cost or market. If the Company stated inventories at the lower of cost or market, a write down of $XXX and $XXX would have been required as of December 31, 20X1 and 20X0, respectively. Accordingly, cost of sales would have been increased by $XXX and $XXX, and net income, income taxes, and stockholders' equity would have been reduced by $XXX, $XXX, and $XXX, and $XXX, $XXX, and $XXX, as of and for the years ended December 31, 20X1 and 20X0, respectively.

We conducted our audits in accordance with auditing standards generally accepted in the United States of America (GAAS). Our responsibilities under those standards are further described in the Auditor's Responsibilities for the Audit of the Financial Statements section of our report. We are required to be independent of ABC Company and to meet our other ethical responsibilities, in accordance with the relevant ethical requirements relating to our audits. We believe that the audit evidence we have obtained is sufficient and appropriate to provide a basis for our qualified audit opinion.

Responsibilities of Management for the Financial Statements

Management is responsible for the preparation and fair presentation of the financial statements in accordance with accounting principles generally accepted in the United States of America, and for the design, implementation, and maintenance of internal control relevant to the preparation and fair presentation of financial statements that are free from material misstatement, whether due to fraud or error.

In preparing the financial statements, management is required to evaluate whether there are conditions or events, considered in the aggregate, that raise substantial doubt about ABC Company's ability to continue as a going concern for *[insert the time period set by the applicable financial reporting framework]*.

Auditor's Responsibilities for the Audit of the Financial Statements

Our objectives are to obtain reasonable assurance about whether the financial statements as a whole are free from material misstatement, whether due to fraud or error, and to issue an auditor's report that includes our opinion. Reasonable assurance is a high level of assurance but is not absolute assurance and therefore is not a guarantee that an audit conducted in accordance with GAAS will always detect a material misstatement when it exists. The risk of not detecting a material misstatement resulting from fraud is higher than for one resulting from error, as fraud may involve collusion, forgery, intentional omissions, misrepresentations, or the override of internal control. Misstatements are considered material if, individually or in the aggregate, they could reasonably be expected to influence the economic decisions of users made on the basis of these financial statements.

In performing an audit in accordance with GAAS, we:

- Exercise professional judgment and maintain professional skepticism throughout the audit.

- Identify and assess the risks of material misstatement of the financial statements, whether due to fraud or error, and design and perform audit procedures responsive to those risks. Such procedures include examining, on a test basis, evidence regarding the amounts and disclosures in the financial statements.

- Obtain an understanding of internal control relevant to the audit in order to design audit procedures that are appropriate in the circumstances, but not for the purpose of expressing an opinion on the effectiveness of ABC Company's internal control. Accordingly, no such opinion is expressed.

- Evaluate the appropriateness of accounting policies used and the reasonableness of significant accounting estimates made by management, as well as evaluate the overall presentation of the financial statements.

- Conclude whether, in our judgment, there are conditions or events, considered in the aggregate, that raise substantial doubt about ABC Company's ability to continue as a going concern for a reasonable period of time.

We are required to communicate with those charged with governance regarding, among other matters, the planned scope and timing of the audit, significant audit findings, and certain internal control-related matters that we identified during the audit.

[*Signature of the auditor's firm*]

[*City and state where the auditor's report is issued*]

[*Date of the auditor's report*]

Adverse Opinion

After studying this lesson, you should be able to:

1. Understand how to express an adverse audit opinion when a material and pervasive misstatement causes an entity's financial statement presentation to be misleading.

I. Relevant AICPA Guidance

The relevant AICPA guidance is provided by AU 705, *Modifications to the Opinion in the Independent Auditor's Report*. The standard states that the auditor's objective is to express clearly an appropriately modified opinion when (1) **the auditor concludes that the financial statements as a whole are misstated**; or (2) the auditor is unable to obtain sufficient appropriate audit evidence to conclude that the financial statements as a whole are free from material misstatement. (This lesson focuses on the first matter, since the scope limitation is discussed elsewhere.)

Definitions

Modified Opinion: A qualified opinion, an adverse opinion, or a disclaimer of opinion.

Pervasive: (a) Effects that are not confined to specific elements, accounts, or items of the financial statements; (b) effects that, if so confined, represent or could represent a substantial proportion of the financial statements; or (c) regarding disclosures, are fundamental to users' understanding of the financial statements.

II. Opinion Choice for a Misstatement (Including Inadequate Disclosure) Involves Judgment

A. **Qualified Opinion**—The auditor should express a qualified opinion when the auditor concludes that misstatements are *material, but not pervasive* to the financial statements. (A separate lesson focuses on the qualified opinion.)

B. **Adverse Opinion**—The auditor should express an adverse opinion when the auditor concludes that misstatements are *material, and pervasive* to the financial statements.

III. Effect of an Adverse Opinion on the Auditor's Report

A. Opinion—Express the adverse opinion using appropriate language such as: "In our opinion, **because of the significance of the matter discussed in the Basis for Adverse Opinion section of our audit report, the financial statements referred to above do not present fairly . . .**; label the "Opinion" section "Adverse Opinion."

B. Basis for Adverse Opinion—(1) Add a paragraph to describe the reason(s) for the adverse opinion (and, when practicable, to quantify the financial statement effects or to include the omitted information); (2) modify the last sentence of that section to state "We believe that the audit evidence we have obtained is sufficient and appropriate to provide a basis for our adverse audit opinion."

C. "Management's Responsibilities" section—No changes

D. "Auditor's Responsibilities" section—No changes

IV. Sample Audit Report with an Adverse Opinion for Misstatement Due to GAAP Departure/ Misstatement

Independent Auditor's Report

[*Appropriate Addressee*]

Adverse Opinion

We have audited the consolidated financial statements of ABC Company and its subsidiaries, which comprise the consolidated balance sheet as of December 31, 20X1, and the related consolidated statements of income, changes in stockholders' equity, and cash flows for the year then ended, and the related notes to the financial statements.

In our opinion, because of the significance of the matter discussed in the Basis for Adverse Opinion section of our report, the accompanying consolidated financial statements do not present fairly the financial position of ABC Company and its subsidiaries as of December 31, 20X1, or the results of their operations or their cash flows for the year then ended in accordance with accounting principles generally accepted in the United States of America.

Basis for Adverse Opinion

As described in Note X, ABC Company has not consolidated the financial statements of subsidiary XYZ Company that it acquired during 20X1 because it has not yet been able to ascertain the fair values of certain of the subsidiary's material assets and liabilities at the acquisition date. This investment is therefore accounted for on a cost basis by the Company. Under accounting principles generally accepted in the United States of America, the subsidiary should have been consolidated because it is controlled by the Company. Had XYZ Company been consolidated, many elements in the accompanying consolidated financial statements would have been materially affected. The effects on the consolidated financial statements of the failure to consolidate have not been determined.

We conducted our audit in accordance with auditing standards generally accepted in the United States of America (GAAS). Our responsibilities under those standards are further described in the Auditor's Responsibilities for the Audit of the Financial Statements section of our report. We are required to be independent of ABC Company and to meet our other ethical responsibilities, in accordance with the relevant ethical requirements relating to our audits. We believe that the audit evidence we have obtained is sufficient and appropriate to provide a basis for our adverse audit opinion.

Responsibilities of Management for the Financial Statements

Management is responsible for the preparation and fair presentation of the consolidated financial statements in accordance with accounting principles generally accepted in the United States of America, and for the design, implementation, and maintenance of internal control relevant to the preparation and fair presentation of consolidated financial statements that are free from material misstatement, whether due to fraud or error.

In preparing the consolidated financial statements, management is required to evaluate whether there are conditions or events, considered in the aggregate, that raise substantial doubt about ABC Company's ability to continue as a going concern for [*insert the time period set by the applicable financial reporting framework*].

Auditor's Responsibilities for the Audit of the Financial Statements

Our objectives are to obtain reasonable assurance about whether the consolidated financial statements as a whole are free from material misstatement, whether due to fraud or error, and to issue an auditor's report that includes our opinion. Reasonable assurance is a high level of assurance but is not absolute assurance and therefore is not a guarantee that an audit conducted in accordance with GAAS will always detect a material misstatement when it exists. The risk of not detecting a material misstatement resulting from fraud is higher than for one resulting from error, as fraud may involve collusion, forgery, intentional omissions, misrepresentations, or the override of internal control. Misstatements are considered material if, individually or in the aggregate, they could reasonably be expected to influence the economic decisions of users made on the basis of these consolidated financial statements.

In performing an audit in accordance with GAAS, we:

- Exercise professional judgment and maintain professional skepticism throughout the audit.

- Identify and assess the risks of material misstatement of the consolidated financial statements, whether due to fraud or error, and design and perform audit procedures responsive to those risks. Such procedures include examining, on a test basis, evidence regarding the amounts and disclosures in the financial statements.

- Obtain an understanding of internal control relevant to the audit in order to design audit procedures that are appropriate in the circumstances, but not for the purpose of expressing an opinion on the effectiveness of ABC Company's internal control. Accordingly, no such opinion is expressed.

- Evaluate the appropriateness of accounting policies used and the reasonableness of significant accounting estimates made by management, as well as evaluate the overall presentation of the consolidated financial statements.

- Conclude whether, in our judgment, there are conditions or events, considered in the aggregate, that raise substantial doubt about ABC Company's ability to continue as a going concern for a reasonable period of time.

We are required to communicate with those charged with governance regarding, among other matters, the planned scope and timing of the audit, significant audit findings, and certain internal control-related matters that we identified during the audit.

[Signature of the auditor's firm]

[City and state where the auditor's report is issued]

[Date of the auditor's report]

Disclaimer of Opinion

After studying this lesson, you should be able to:

1. Understand how to express a disclaimer of opinion for a scope limitation when the possible effects are viewed as *material and pervasive*.

I. Relevant AICPA Guidance

The relevant AICPA guidance is provided by AU 705, *Modifications to the Opinion in the Independent Auditor's Report*. The standard states that the auditor's objective is to express clearly an appropriately modified opinion when (1) the auditor concludes that the financial statements as a whole are misstated; or (2) the auditor is unable to obtain sufficient appropriate audit evidence to conclude that the financial statements as a whole are free from material misstatement. This lesson focuses on the second matter, which is known as a *scope limitation*.

> **Definitions**
>
> *Modified Opinion*: A qualified opinion, an adverse opinion, or a disclaimer of opinion.
>
> *Pervasive*: (a) Effects that are not confined to specific elements, accounts, or items of the financial statements; (b) effects that, if so confined, represent or could represent a substantial proportion of the financial statements; or (c) regarding disclosures, are fundamental to users' understanding of the financial statements.

II. Opinion Choice for a Scope Limitation Involves Judgment

A. **Qualified Opinion**—The auditor should express a qualified opinion when the auditor is unable to obtain sufficient appropriate audit evidence, and the auditor concludes that the possible effect on the financial statements, if any, could be *material, but not pervasive* . (Another lesson focuses on the qualification for a scope limitation.)

B. **Disclaimer of Opinion**—The auditor should express a disclaimer of opinion when the auditor is unable to obtain sufficient appropriate audit evidence, and the auditor concludes that the possible effect on the financial statements, if any, could be *material and pervasive*.

III. Circumstances Resulting in a Scope Limitation

A. **Circumstances beyond the Control of the Entity**—For example, the entity's accounting records have been destroyed.

B. **Circumstances Related to the Nature or Timing of the Auditor's Work**—For example, the auditor determines that substantive procedures alone are not sufficient and the entity's controls are ineffective; the auditor is unable to obtain audited financial statements of an investee (accounted for using the equity method); or the timing of the auditor's appointment does not permit the auditor to observe the physical counting of inventories.

C. **Limitations Imposed by Management**—For example, management prevents the auditor from requesting external confirmation of certain account balances. The auditor should request that management remove any such limitation.

1. If management refuses—The auditor should communicate the matter to those charged with governance and determine whether it is possible to perform alternative procedures to obtain sufficient appropriate audit evidence.

2. If unable to obtain sufficient appropriate audit evidence (and if the effects could be both material and pervasive)—The auditor should withdraw from the audit (when practicable) or issue a disclaimer of opinion.

IV. **Effect of a Disclaimer of Opinion on the Auditor's Report**

    A. Disclaimer of Opinion—Disclaim an opinion using appropriate language such as: **"Because of the significance of the matter described in the Basis for Disclaimer of Opinion section of our report, we have not been able to obtain sufficient appropriate audit evidence to provide a basis for an audit opinion on these financial statements."**

    B. Basis for Disclaimer of Opinion—Describe the circumstances resulting in the disclaimer; identify the dollar amounts involved as applicable.

    C. "Responsibilities of Management" section—No changes

    D. "Auditor's Responsibilities" section—Provide a limited description consisting of 3 sentences (without any bullet points), including a reference to the "Basis for Disclaimer of Opinion" section.

    E. When disclaiming an opinion on the entity's financial statements—The auditor is prohibited from including an "Other Information" section in the auditor's report; likewise, the auditor cannot communicate key audit matters when disclaiming an opinion.

V. **Sample Audit Report with a Disclaimer of Opinion Due to Scope Limitation**

Independent Auditor's Report
[Appropriate Addressee]

Disclaimer of Opinion

We were engaged to audit the financial statements of ABC Company, which comprise the balance sheet as of December31,20X1, and the related statements of income, changes in stockholders' equity, and cash flows for the year then ended, and the related notes to the financial statements. We do not express an opinion on the accompanying financial statements of ABC Company. Because of the significance of the matters described in the Basis for Disclaimer of Opinion section of our report, we have not been able to obtain sufficient appropriate audit evidence to provide a basis for an audit opinion on these financial statements.

Basis for Disclaimer of Opinion

We were not engaged as auditors of ABC Company until after December 31, 20X1, and, therefore, did not observe the counting of physical inventories at the beginning or end of the year. We were unable to satisfy ourselves by other auditing procedures concerning the inventory held at December 31, 20X1, which is stated in the balance sheet at $XXX. In addition, the introduction of a new computerized accounts receivable system in September 20X1 resulted in numerous misstatements in accounts receivable. As of the date of our audit report, management was still in the process of rectifying the system deficiencies and correcting the misstatements. We were unable to confirm or verify by alternative means accounts receivable included in the balance sheet at a total amount of $XXX at December 31, 20X1. As a result of these matters, we were unable to determine whether any adjustments might have been found necessary in respect of recorded or unrecorded inventories and accounts receivable, and the elements making up the statements of income, changes in stockholders' equity, and cash flows.

Responsibilities of Management for the Financial Statements

Management is responsible for the preparation and fair presentation of the financial statements in accordance with accounting principles generally accepted in the United States of America, and for the design, implementation, and maintenance of internal control relevant to the preparation and fair presentation of financial statements that are free from material misstatement, whether due to fraud or error.

In preparing the financial statements, management is required to evaluate whether there are conditions or events, considered in the aggregate, that raise substantial doubt about ABC Company's ability to continue as a going concern for [insert the time period set by the applicable financial reporting framework].

Auditor's Responsibilities for the Audit of the Financial Statements

Our responsibility is to conduct an audit of ABC Company's financial statements in accordance with auditing standards generally accepted in the United States of America and to issue an auditor's report. However, because of the matters described in the Basis for Disclaimer of Opinion section of our report, we were not able to obtain sufficient appropriate audit evidence to provide a basis for an audit opinion on these financial statements.

We are required to be independent of ABC Company and to meet our other ethical responsibilities, in accordance with the relevant ethical requirements relating to our audit.

[Signature of the auditor's firm]

[City and state where the auditor's report is issued]

[Date of the auditor's report]

Consistency of Financial Statements

After studying this lesson, you should be able to:

1. Identify how the auditor's report should address a material inconsistency in the financial statements caused by a change in accounting principle or a correction of previously issued financial statements.

I. **Relevant AICPA Guidance**—The relevant AICPA guidance is provided by AU 708, *Consistency of Financial Statements*. The standard states that the auditor's objectives are to (1) evaluate the consistency of the financial statements for the periods presented; and (2) communicate appropriately in the auditor's report when comparability has been materially affected (a) by a change in accounting principle or (b) by adjustments to correct a material misstatement in previously issued financial statements.

II. **Evaluating Consistency**

   A. The auditor should evaluate whether the comparability between periods has been affected by either a material change in accounting principle or a material restatement of financial statements.

   B. **When the Auditor's Opinion Covers Two (or More) Periods**—The auditor should evaluate the consistency between such periods, as well as the consistency of the earliest period covered by the auditor's opinion with the prior period.

   C. **Change in Accounting Principle**

   D. The auditor should evaluate a change in accounting principles about four matters:

   1. Whether the adopted principle is in accordance with the applicable financial reporting framework;

   2. Whether the method of accounting for the effect of the change is in accordance with the applicable financial reporting framework;

   3. Whether the disclosures about the change are adequate; *and*

   4. Whether the entity has justified that the alternative adopted is **preferable**. (The issuance of an accounting pronouncement that requires or expresses a preference for an accounting principle is considered sufficient justification for a change in principle.)

   E. **When Those Four Criteria are Met (and the Change has a Material Effect on the Financial Statements)**—The auditor should include an *emphasis-of-matter* paragraph in the auditor's report to describe the change and reference the footnote disclosure applicable to the change. The auditor should state that the auditor's opinion is not modified regarding the matter.

   1. Include the emphasis-of-matter paragraph in subsequent periods until the new principle is applied in all periods presented.

   2. If the change is accounted for by retrospective application to the financial statements, the emphasis-of-matter paragraph is only needed in the period of the change.

   F. **When Those Four Criteria Have not all been Met (and the Change has a Material Effect on the Financial Statements)**—The auditor should evaluate whether the change results in a material misstatement and consider whether the auditor's report should be modified.

   G. **When a Change in the Reporting Entity Results in Financial Statements that are Essentially Those of a Different Reporting Entity**—The auditor should include an emphasis-of-matter paragraph in the auditor's report describing the change in the entity and referencing the entity's disclosure. However, that is unnecessary when the change in entity results from a transaction or event, such as the purchase or disposition of a subsidiary.

H. Correction of a Material Misstatement in Previously Issued Financial Statements

1. **When the financial statements are restated to correct a prior material misstatement—** The auditor should include an emphasis-of-matter paragraph in the auditor's report. (That paragraph need not be included in subsequent periods.) The auditor should state that the auditor's opinion is not modified regarding the matter.

2. **If the financial statement disclosures relating to the restatement are not adequate—** The auditor should evaluate the inadequacy of disclosure and consider whether the auditor's report should be modified.

3. A change from an accounting principle that is not in accordance with the applicable financial reporting framework to one that is in accordance is a correction of a misstatement.

III. Effect on the Auditor's Report

A. The auditor need not refer to consistency, unless there is an inconsistency due to a material change in accounting principle or restatement.

B. Sample emphasis-of-matter paragraph for a voluntary change in principle:

Emphasis-of-Matter

As discussed in Note X to the financial statements, the entity has elected to change its method of accounting for (*describe accounting method change*) in (*insert year(s) of financial statements that reflect the accounting method change*). Our opinion is not modified with respect to this matter.

C. Sample emphasis-of-matter paragraph for a restatement:

Emphasis-of-Matter

As discussed in Note X to the financial statements, the 20X2 financial statements have been restated to correct a misstatement. Our opinion is not modified with respect to this matter.

PCAOB on Evaluating Consistency of Financial Statements

> **After studying this lesson, you should be able to:**
>
> **1.** Understand the auditor's responsibilities under PCAOB Auditing Standards to identify "consistency" issues involving either a change in accounting principle or a restatement to correct previously issued financial statements.

I. Evaluating Consistency of Financial Statements

II. Purpose of These PCAOB Auditing Standards

To establish requirements and provide direction for the auditor's evaluation of the consistency of financial statements and the effect of that evaluation on the auditor's report.

A. Identifies two types of issues related to consistency that might affect the auditor's report: (1) a change in accounting principle; and (2) an adjustment to correct a misstatement in previously issued financial statements (i.e., *restatements*).

B. **When Reporting on Two or More Periods** —The auditor should evaluate the consistency between those periods and with the prior period, if that prior period is presented along with the financial statements reported on.

III. Changes in Accounting Principle

Involving a change from one generally accepted accounting principle to another, including the situation where the accounting principle formerly used is no longer generally accepted.

A. GAAP is specified by FASB guidance entitled *Accounting Changes and Error Corrections*. The PCAOB auditing standards point out that, when a company uses retrospective application to account for a change in accounting principle, the financial statements generally will be viewed as consistent. (However, the previous years' financial statements will appear different from those that the auditor previously reported on.)

B. **When There is a Change in Accounting Principle** —The auditor should evaluate whether **(1) the newly adopted principle is GAAP; (2) the method of accounting for the effect of the change conforms to GAAP; (3) the disclosures related to the change are adequate; and (4) the company has justified that the alternative accounting principle is preferable.**

    1. **When the four criteria have been met** —The auditor should add an explanatory paragraph to the auditor's report to identify the inconsistency.

    2. **When the four criteria have not been met** —The auditor should treat the matter as a GAAP departure and modify the audit report appropriately.

    3. **When an investor uses the "equity method" and the investee has a change in accounting principle that is material to the investor's financial statements** —The auditor should add an explanatory paragraph to emphasize the matter.

C. **When There is a Change in Accounting Estimate Effected by a Change in Accounting Principle** —The auditor should evaluate and report on the matter like other changes in accounting principle.

D. **When There is a Change in the Reporting Entity Resulting from a Transaction or Event, Such as the Purchase or Disposition of a Subsidiary**—It does not require recognition in the auditor's report. (However, if there is a change in the reporting entity that does not result from such a transaction or event, then an explanatory paragraph would be required.)

IV. Correction of a Material Misstatement in Previously Issued Financial Statements

    A. The correction of a material misstatement in previously issued financial statements should be recognized in the auditor's report by the addition of an explanatory paragraph.

    B. Restatements of previously issued financial statements require related disclosures to be made— The auditor should evaluate the adequacy of the company's disclosures.

V. Change in Classification

    A. Changes in classification in previously issued financial statements normally do not require recognition in the auditor's report (unless the change represents a change in accounting principle or the correction of a material misstatement).

    B. Accordingly, the auditor should evaluate a material change in financial statement classification (and the related disclosure) to determine whether such a change is also a change in accounting principle or a correction of a material misstatement.

The auditing requirements under PCAOB auditing standards are substantially the same as those of the AICPA's Clarified Auditing Standards (specifically, AU 708, *Consistency of Financial Statements.* The now-superseded SAS No. 1 (specifically, AU 420, *Consistency of Application of [GAAP]*) previously stated that "error correction not involving principle" (e.g., mathematical mistakes, oversight, or misuse of facts) did not have to be identified in the auditor's report. However, the guidance in the Clarified Auditing Standard now treats restatements as an inconsistency that warrants mention in the auditor's report, similar to PCAOB requirements.

Opening Balances—Initial Audits

After studying this lesson, you should be able to:

1. Describe the auditor's responsibility for verifying *opening balances* (and consistency) in an initial audit engagement.

2. Know that the auditor cannot refer to the predecessor as providing a partial basis for the auditor's report.

3. Know how the inability to verify beginning inventory would impact the auditor's report when the effect is material and pervasive.

I. Relevant AICPA Guidance

The relevant AICPA guidance is provided by AU 510, *Opening Balances—Initial Audit Engagements, Including Reaudit Engagements*. The standard states that the auditor's objective is to obtain sufficient audit evidence about whether (a) opening balances contain misstatements that materially affect the current period's financial statements; and (b) appropriate accounting policies reflected in the opening balances have been consistently applied in the current period (or changes are appropriately accounted for and adequately presented and disclosed).

II. Selected Definitions

Definitions

Initial Audit Engagement: An engagement in which (a) the financial statements for the prior period were not audited; or (b) the financial statements for the prior period were audited by a predecessor auditor.

Opening Balances: Those account balances that exist at the beginning of the period. (also include matters requiring disclosure that existed at the beginning of the period, such as contingencies and commitments).

Predecessor Auditor: The auditor from a different audit firm who has reported on the most recent audited financial statements (or was engaged to perform, but did not complete, an audit of the financial statements).

Reaudit: An initial audit engagement to audit financial statements that have been previously audited by a predecessor auditor.

III. Audit Procedures

A. The auditor should read the most recent financial statements and any predecessor's audit report for information relevant to opening balances.

B. The auditor should request management to authorize the predecessor to respond fully to inquiries by the auditor and to allow the auditor to review the predecessor auditor's audit documentation.

   1. The predecessor may request a *consent and acknowledgment letter* from the entity to document the authorization regarding the communication with the auditor. Such a letter is not required, but the SAS provides an example.

   2. The predecessor may also request a *successor auditor acknowledgment letter* to document the auditor's agreement regarding the use of the predecessor auditor's audit documentation before permitting access to it. Such a letter is not required, but the SAS provides an example.

3. The extent to which the predecessor permits access to the audit documentation is a matter of professional judgment.

4. The auditor's use of the predecessor's information is influenced by the auditor's assessment of the predecessor's competence and independence.

C. Evaluate the Entity's Opening Balances

1. Obtain sufficient appropriate audit evidence as to whether opening balances contain misstatements affecting the current period financial statements by (a) determining whether the prior closing balances have been properly brought forward; (b) determining whether the opening balances reflect the application of appropriate accounting policies; and (c) evaluating whether current period audit procedures provide evidence relevant to the opening balances (such as reviewing the predecessor's audit documentation).

2. If the opening balances contain material misstatements affecting the current period, the auditor should determine the effect on the current period's financial statements and communicate the misstatements to the appropriate level of management and those charged with governance.

D. Evaluate the Consistency of Accounting Policies—The auditor should obtain sufficient appropriate audit evidence as to whether the accounting policies reflected in the opening balances have been consistently applied in the current period (and whether any changes have been properly reported).

E. Discovery of possible material misstatements in financial statements reported on by a predecessor auditor.

1. The auditor should request management to inform the predecessor of the situation and arrange a three-way meeting to resolve the matter.

2. If management does not cooperate (or if the auditor is not satisfied with the resolution of the matter), the auditor should evaluate the implications to the current engagement and whether to withdraw. The auditor may also wish to consult with legal counsel for guidance.

IV. Audit Reporting Considerations

A. Reference to Predecessor—The auditor should not refer to the predecessor's work or report as a partial basis for the auditor's opinion.

B. Opening Balances

1. If unable to obtain sufficient appropriate audit evidence regarding the opening balances, the auditor should either express a qualified opinion or disclaim an opinion, as appropriate.

2. If there is a material misstatement in the opening balances, the auditor should either express a qualified or adverse opinion, as appropriate.

C. Consistency of Accounting Policies—The auditor should either express a qualified or adverse opinion (as appropriate) if the current period's accounting policies are not consistently applied in relation to the opening balances (or if any material changes are not properly reported).

V. Sample Report—A sample report follows with a disclaimer of opinion on results of operations and cash flows and an unmodified opinion on financial position (due to the inability to verify opening inventory such that the effect is deemed to be material and pervasive).

A. Add a heading for "Opinions"—Include a single sentence: "We have audited the balance sheet … and were engaged to audit the related statements of income, changes in stockholders' equity, and cash flows …"

B. Add a heading for "Disclaimer of Opinion on the Results of Operations and Cash Flows"—Provide a disclaimer of opinion and reference the Basis for Opinions section of the report.

C. Add a separate heading for "Opinion on the Financial Position"—Provide an opinion on the entity's financial position.

D. Basis for Opinions—Explain the reason(s) for the disclaimer of opinion on the results of operations and cash flows; comment on the basis for the opinion on financial position.

E. Responsibility of Management for the Financial Statements—No changes

F. Auditor's Responsibilities for the Audit of the Financial Statements—Change the first paragraph to reference the "Basis for Opinions" section of the report regarding the scope limitation resulting in a disclaimer of opinion on the results of operations and cash flows.

G. See the sample report below having a disclaimer of opinion on results of operations and cash flows and an unmodified opinion on financial position (due to the inability to verify the beginning inventory for the period under audit).

Independent Auditor's Report

[*Appropriate Addressee*]

Opinions

We have audited the balance sheet of ABC Company as of December 31, 20X1, and were engaged to audit the related statements of income, changes in stockholders' equity, and cash flows for the year then ended, and the related notes to the financial statements.

Disclaimer of Opinion on the Results of Operations and Cash Flows

We do not express an opinion on the results of operations and cash flows of ABC Company for the year ended December 31, 20X1. Because of the significance of the matter described in the Basis for Disclaimer of Opinion on the Results of Operations and Cash Flows section of our report, we have not been able to obtain sufficient appropriate audit evidence to provide a basis for an audit opinion on the results of operations and cash flows for the year ended December 31, 20X1.

Opinion on the Financial Position

In our opinion, the balance sheet presents fairly, in all material respects, the financial position of ABC Company as of December 31, 20X1, in accordance with accounting principles generally accepted in the United States of America.

Basis for Opinions

We were not engaged as auditors of the Company until after December 31, 20X0, and, therefore, did not observe the counting of physical inventories at the beginning of the year. We were unable to satisfy ourselves by performing other auditing procedures concerning the inventory held at December 31, 20X0. Since opening inventories enter into the determination of net income and cash flows, we were unable to determine whether any adjustments might have been necessary in respect of the profit for the year reported in the income statement and the net cash flows from operating activities reported in the cash flow statement.

We conducted our audit of the balance sheet in accordance with auditing standards generally accepted in the United States of America. Our responsibilities under those standards are further described in the Auditor's Responsibilities for the Audit of the Financial Statements section of our report. We are required to be independent of the Company and to meet our other ethical responsibilities, in accordance with the relevant ethical requirements relating to our audit.

We believe that the audit evidence we have obtained is sufficient and appropriate to provide a basis for our unmodified opinion on the financial position.

Responsibility of Management for the Financial Statements

Management is responsible for the preparation and fair presentation of these financial statements in accordance with accounting principles generally accepted in the United States of America, and for the design, implementation, and maintenance of internal control relevant to the preparation and fair presentation of financial statements that are free from material misstatement, whether due to fraud or error.

In preparing the financial statements, management is required to evaluate whether there are conditions or events, considered in the aggregate, that raise substantial doubt about ABC

Company's ability to continue as a going concern for [*insert the time period set by the applicable financial reporting framework*].

Auditor's Responsibilities for the Audit of the Financial Statements

Our responsibility is to conduct an audit of the Company's financial statements in accordance with auditing standards generally accepted in the United States of America. However, because of the matters described in the Basis for Opinions section of our report, we were not able to obtain sufficient appropriate audit evidence to provide a basis for an audit opinion on the results of operations and cash flows.

Our objectives are to obtain reasonable assurance about whether the financial statements as a whole are free from material misstatement, whether due to fraud or error, and to issue an auditor's report that includes our opinion. Reasonable assurance is a high level of assurance but is not absolute assurance and therefore is not a guarantee that an audit conducted in accordance with generally accepted auditing standards (GAAS) will always detect a material misstatement when it exists. The risk of not detecting a material misstatement resulting from fraud is higher than for one resulting from error, as fraud may involve collusion, forgery, intentional omissions, misrepresentations, or the override of internal control. Misstatements are considered material if there is a substantial likelihood that, individually or in the aggregate, they would influence the judgment made by a reasonable user based on the financial statements.

In performing an audit in accordance with GAAS, we:

- Exercise professional judgment and maintain professional skepticism throughout the audit.

- Identify and assess the risks of material misstatement of the financial statements, whether due to fraud or error, and design and perform audit procedures responsive to those risks. Such procedures include examining, on a test basis, evidence regarding the amounts and disclosures in the financial statements.

- Obtain an understanding of internal control relevant to the audit in order to design audit procedures that are appropriate in the circumstances, but not for the purpose of expressing an opinion on the effectiveness of ABC Company's internal control. Accordingly, no such opinion is expressed.

- Evaluate the appropriateness of accounting policies used and the reasonableness of significant accounting estimates made by management, as well as evaluate the overall presentation of the financial statements.

- Conclude whether, in our judgment, there are conditions or events, considered in the aggregate, that raise substantial doubt about ABC Company's ability to continue as a going concern for a reasonable period of time.

We are required to communicate with those charged with governance regarding, among other matters, the planned scope and timing of the audit, significant audit findings, and certain internal control–related matters that we identified during the audit.

[*Signature of the auditor's firm*]

[*City and state where the auditor's report is issued*]

[*Date of the auditor's report*]

Responsibilities for Other Information in Annual Reports

After studying this lesson, you should be able to:

1. Identify the auditor's responsibility for *other information* included in an entity's annual report along with audited financial statements.

2. Understand how the "Other Information" section should be presented in the auditor's report.

I. Relevant AICPA Guidance

The relevant clarified AICPA guidance is provided by AU 720, *The Auditor's Responsibilities Relating to Other Information Included in Annual Reports* (SAS No. 137 issued in 2019).

II. Definitions

A. Annual Report—A document, or combination of documents, typically prepared on an annual basis by management or those charged with governance in accordance with law, regulation, or custom, the purpose of which is to provide owners (or similar stakeholders) with information on the entity's operations and the entity's financial results and financial position as set out in the financial statements. An annual report contains, accompanies, or incorporates by reference the financial statements and the auditor's report thereon and usually includes information about the entity's developments, its future outlook and risks and uncertainties, a statement by the entity's governing body, and reports covering governance matters.

B. Other Information—Financial or nonfinancial information (other than financial statements and the auditor's report thereon) included in an entity's annual report.

Some examples of "other information" include the following: (1) chair's statement; (2) management report, management commentary, or operating and financial review; (3) corporate governance statement; (4) management's internal control and risk assessment reports; (5) financial summaries or highlights, including financial ratios; (6) employment data; (7) names of officers and directors; and (8) selected quarterly data.

C. Misstatement of the Other Information—A misstatement of the other information exists when the other information is incorrectly stated or is otherwise misleading.

III. Auditor's Responsibilities for the Other Information

A. Obtaining the Other Information

1. Obtain management's written acknowledgment as to which documents comprise the annual report.

2. Make arrangements with management for the timely receipt of the final version of those documents.

3. If any of those documents will not be available until after the date of the auditor's report on the financial statements—Request a written representation from management that the final version of such documents will be provided to the auditor prior to the documents' issuance.

B. Communication with Those Charged with Governance—Communicate (1) the auditor's responsibility regarding the other information, (2) the procedures performed regarding the other information, and (3) the results of those procedures

C. Reading the Other Information

1. The auditor should read the other information and consider whether there is a material inconsistency relative to the audited financial statements or a material misstatement of fact regarding the other information

   a. Material inconsistency—Involves differences between the other information and the auditor's knowledge obtained in the audit

   b. Material misstatement of fact—Involves other information that is otherwise misleading

2. Omitted other information—Auditors are not responsible for searching for omitted information or for the completeness of the other information.

D. When a Material Inconsistency Appears to Exist—The auditor should discuss the matter with management and determine whether a material misstatement of the other information (or a material misstatement of the financial statements) exists.

E. Responding When the Auditor Concludes that a Material Misstatement of the Other Information Exists

1. Request that management correct the other information—If management agrees, then verify that the correction has been made; if management refuses, communicate the matter to those charged with governance with a request to make the correction.

2. If the other information has not been corrected after communicating with those charged with governance (prior to the date of the auditor's report)— The auditor should take appropriate action (e.g., withhold the audit report).

3. If the material misstatement in the other information is determined after the date of the auditor's report—(a) If the other information is corrected, perform the procedures necessary in the circumstances; (b) if the other information is not corrected (after communicating with those charged with governance), consider the legal rights and obligations of communicating with anyone in receipt of the auditor's report on the financial statements.

F. Reporting Issues

1. The auditor should add a separate section in the auditor's report (after the "Auditor's Responsibilities" section) with an appropriate heading, such as "Other Information."

2. The "Other Information" section should include the following:

   a. A statement that management is responsible for the other information

   b. An identification of the other information

   c. Disclaimer—A statement that the auditor's opinion on the financial statements does not cover the other information and that the auditor does not express an opinion or any form of assurance on it.

   d. A statement that the auditor is responsible to read the other information and consider whether a material inconsistency exists between the other information and the financial statements (or the other information otherwise appears to be materially misleading)

   e. A statement that, if the auditor concludes that an uncorrected material misstatement of the other information exists, the auditor is required to describe it in the auditor's report

   f. If the auditor has concluded that an uncorrected material misstatement of the other information exists—The auditor should add a statement that an uncorrected material misstatement of the other information exists along with a description of it in the auditor's report.

3. Reporting considerations when the auditor's opinion is modified

   a. For a qualified or adverse opinion—May need to modify the "Other Information" section of the auditor's report if the reason for the qualified or adverse opinion is relevant to the description of an uncorrected material misstatement of the other information.

   b. For a disclaimer of opinion—In this case, the auditor's report should omit the "Other Information" section (providing such a section could overshadow the disclaimer of opinion).

G. Documentation—The auditor's documentation should include (1) procedures performed under SAS #137 and (2) the final version of the other information addressed by the auditor's procedures.

IV. Sample "Other Information" Section When the Auditor Has Not Identified Any Uncorrected Material Misstatements of the Other Information

---

Other Information [*Included in the Annual Report*]

Management is responsible for the other information [*included in the annual report*]. The other information comprises the [*information included in the annual report*] but does not include the financial statements and our auditor's report thereon. Our opinion on the financial statements does not cover the other information, and we do not express an opinion or any form of assurance thereon.

In connection with our audit of the financial statements, our responsibility is to read the other information and consider whether a material inconsistency exists between the other information and the financial statements, or the other information otherwise appears to be materially misstated. If, based on the work performed, we conclude that an uncorrected material misstatement of the other information exists, we are required to describe it in our report.

Supplementary Information Related to Financial Statements

> **After studying this lesson, you should be able to:**
>
> 1. Identify the auditor's responsibilities when engaged to report on *supplementary information in relation to the audited financial statements*.
>
> 2. Prepare an appropriate "Supplementary Information" section to the auditor's report when expressing an opinion on the supplementary information in relation to the audited financial statements in a combined report on the audited financial statements.

I. Relevant AICPA Guidance

The relevant AICPA guidance is provided by AU 725, *Supplementary Information in Relation to the Financial Statements as a Whole*. The standard states that the auditor's objective is to evaluate the presentation of the supplementary information and report on whether it is fairly stated, in all material respects, in relation to the financial statements as a whole.

II. Definition

Supplementary Information—"Information presented outside the basic financial statements, excluding required supplementary information that is not considered necessary for the financial statements to be fairly presented in accordance with the applicable financial reporting framework. Such information may be presented in a document containing the audited financial statements or separate from the financial statements."

III. Fairly Stated

Fairly Stated—When engaged to determine whether supplementary information is fairly stated in relation to the financial statements.

A. The auditor should determine whether:

1. The supplementary information was derived from (or directly related to) the underlying records used to prepare the financial statements.

2. The supplementary information relates to the same period as the financial statements.

3. The auditor served as the auditor of the financial statements.

4. Either an unmodified or qualified opinion was expressed on the financial statements (must not have issued an adverse opinion or disclaimer of opinion).

5. The supplementary information will either accompany the entity's audited financial statements or the audited financial statements will be made *readily available* by the entity. (Note: *Readily available* means without further action by the entity. Being available upon the user's request is not considered *readily available*).

B. The auditor should obtain management's agreement that management has responsibility for:

1. Preparing the supplementary information in accordance with applicable criteria

2. Providing the auditor with written representations

3. Including the auditor's report on the supplementary information in any document containing the supplementary information that references the auditor's association with it

4. Presenting the supplementary information with the audited financial statements (or making the audited financial statements *readily available* to the intended users of the supplementary information)

C. The auditor should perform the following procedures:

1. Inquire of management about the purpose of the supplementary information and the criteria used to prepare it.

2. Obtain an understanding about the methods used and whether those methods have changed (and if changed, the reasons for any changes).

3. Compare and reconcile the supplementary information to the financial statements or to the underlying records used for the financial statements.

4. Inquire of management about any significant assumptions used.

5. Evaluate the appropriateness and completeness of the supplementary information in relationship to the audited financial statements.

6. Obtain appropriate written representations from management.

IV. Reporting on Supplementary Information in Relation to Audited Financial Statements

A. Form of Report—The auditor may issue a separate report on the supplementary information (in addition to the report on the audited financial statements) or combine the report on the supplementary information with the report on the financial statements. (If the latter, then add a separate section labeled "Supplementary Information" regarding the supplementary information.)

B. If the auditor expressed an adverse opinion or a disclaimer of opinion on the financial statements, the auditor is prohibited from reporting on the supplementary information.

C. If the supplementary information is materially misstated in relation to the financial statements, the auditor should discuss the matter with management and propose appropriate revision. If management does not revise the supplementary information, the auditor should either appropriately modify the opinion on the supplementary information or withhold the separate report on it.

D. Sample "Supplementary Information" section when the auditor expresses an unmodified opinion on the financial statements and on the supplementary information in a combined report:

Supplementary Information
Our audit was conducted for the purpose of forming an opinion on the financial statements as a whole. The (*identify accompanying supplementary information*) is presented for purposes of additional analysis and is not a required part of the financial statements. Such information is the responsibility of management and was derived from and relates directly to the underlying accounting and other records used to prepare the financial statements. The information has been subjected to the auditing procedures applied in the audit of the financial statements and certain additional procedures, including comparing and reconciling such information directly to the underlying accounting and other records used to prepare the financial statements or to the financial statements themselves, and other additional procedures in accordance with auditing standards generally accepted in the United States of America. In our opinion, the information is fairly stated in all material respects in relation to the financial statements as a whole.

Required Supplementary Information

I. Relevant AICPA Guidance

The relevant AICPA guidance is provided by AU 730, *Required Supplementary Information*. The standard states that the auditor's objectives are to (1) describe in the auditor's report whether required supplementary information is presented, and (2) communicate when the supplementary information has not been presented in accordance with the established guidelines (or when material modification is necessary).

Definitions

Required supplementary information: Information that a designated accounting standards setter requires to accompany an entity's basic financial statements. Required supplementary information is not part of the basic financial statements; however, a designated accounting standards setter considers the information to be an essential part of financial reporting for placing the basic financial statements in an appropriate operational, economic, or historical context. In addition, authoritative guidelines for the methods of measurement and presentation of the information have been established.

Designated accounting standard setter: A body designated by the Council of the AICPA to promulgate GAAP pursuant to the "Compliance with Standards Rule" (ET sec. 1.310.001) and the "Accounting Principles Rule" (ET sec. 1.320.001) of the AICPA Code of Professional Conduct.

II. Procedures to Be Performed by the Auditor

A. Inquire of management about the methods used to prepare the information, including (1) whether it is measured and presented in accordance with prescribed guidelines; (2) whether the methods of measurement or presentation have been changed relative to prior period; and (3) whether any significant assumptions affect the measurement or presentation of it.

B. Compare the information for consistency with (1) management's responses to the auditor's inquiries; (2) the basic financial statements; and (3) other knowledge obtained during the audit of the basic financial statements.

III. Reporting Implications

A. The auditor should include a separate section in the auditor's report labeled something like "Required Supplementary Information" commenting appropriately on the required supplementary information. The supplementary information cannot affect the auditor's opinion on the financial statements, since it is outside of those financial statements.

B. The specific language to be used depends upon the particular circumstances.

1. Whether the required supplementary information is included and the auditor has applied the procedures described above (no material departures);

2. Whether the required supplementary information is omitted;

3. Whether some required supplementary information is missing and some is presented in accordance with prescribed guidelines;

4. Whether the auditor has identified any material departures from prescribed guidelines;

5. Whether the auditor is unable to complete required procedures; or

6. Whether the auditor has unresolved doubts as to whether the required supplementary information is presented in accordance with prescribed guidelines.

IV. Required Supplementary Information

Example language when the required supplementary information is included and the auditor has performed the applicable procedures without identifying any material departures:
[*Identify the applicable financial reporting framework (e.g., accounting principles generally accepted in the United States of America)*] require that the (*identify the required supplementary information*) on page XX be presented to supplement the basic financial statements. Such information is the responsibility of management and, although not a part of the basic financial statements, is required by (*identify designated accounting standard setter*) who considers it to be an essential part of financial reporting for placing the basic financial statements in an appropriate operational, economic, or historical context. We have applied certain limited procedures to the required supplementary information in accordance with auditing standards generally accepted in the United States of America, which consisted of inquiries of management about the methods of preparing the information and comparing the information for consistency with management's responses to our inquiries, the basic financial statements, and other knowledge we obtained during our audit of the basic financial statements. We do not express an opinion or provide any assurance on the information because the limited procedures do not provide us with sufficient evidence to express an opinion or provide any assurance.

PCAOB on Auditing Supplemental Information

After studying this lesson, you should be able to:

1. Know the meaning of the term "supplemental information" as used by the PCAOB.

2. Know the auditor's responsibility for performing audit procedures on supplemental information under PCAOB auditing standards.

3. Know the auditor's responsibilities for reporting on supplemental information under PCAOB auditing standards.

I. Auditing Supplemental Information Accompanying Audited Financial Statements

II. Introduction and Overview

A. The PCAOB issued this guidance primarily because of recent changes in the regulatory environment. For example, the 2010 Dodd-Frank Act gave the PCAOB oversight responsibility for audits of brokers and dealers registered with the SEC. These brokers and dealers are required to file certain schedules of information with the SEC. The previous PCAOB standards on supplemental information (adopted from the AICPA standards in 2003) addressed supplemental information only in *auditor-submitted documents* and did not specify audit procedures to be applied to supplemental information that is filed with a regulatory authority, such as the SEC. The current PCAOB standards apply to supplemental information, whether it is required by regulatory authorities or provided voluntarily, when audited in connection with financial statements audited under PCAOB auditing standards.

B. **Objective**—The auditor's objective is "to obtain sufficient appropriate audit evidence to express an opinion on whether the supplemental information is fairly stated, in all material respects, in relation to the financial statements as a whole."

Definition

Supplemental Information: "Refers to the following information when it accompanies audited financial statements:

a. Supporting schedules that brokers and dealers are required to file pursuant to Rule 17a-5 under the Securities Exchange Act of 1934;

b. Supplemental information (i) required to be presented pursuant to the rules and regulations of a regulatory authority and (ii) covered by an independent public accountant's report on that information in relation to financial statements that are audited in accordance with PCAOB standards; or

c. Information that is (i) ancillary to the audited financial statements, (ii) derived from the company's accounting books and records, and (iii) covered by an independent public accountant's report on that information in relation to the financial statements that are audited in accordance with PCAOB standards."

C. **Overview of the Performance and Reporting Requirements**

1. The auditor is required to perform audit procedures specifically to test the supplemental information.

2. The auditor is required to evaluate (a) whether the supplemental information is fairly presented in relation to the audited financial statements; and (b) whether the supplemental information complies with the relevant regulatory requirements (or other criteria, if applicable).

3. The auditor is required to coordinate audit work on the supplemental information with audit work on the related financial statements.

4. The auditor is required to clearly report the auditor's responsibilities and conclusions when reporting on supplemental information.

III. Performing Audit Procedures on the Supplemental Information

A. The nature, timing, and extent of the procedures to be applied to the supplemental information may vary with the circumstances, including the following: (1) the risk of material misstatement; (2) the applicable materiality levels relevant to the information; (3) the audit evidence obtained with respect to the financial statements; and (4) the type of opinion expressed on the financial statements.

B. In performing procedures on the supplemental information, the auditor should:

1. Obtain an understanding of the purpose of the information and the criteria used by management for its presentation;

2. Obtain an understanding of the methods used to prepare the information, evaluate the appropriateness of those methods, and determine whether those methods are consistent with those used in the prior period;

3. Inquire of management about any significant assumptions underlying the presentation of the information;

4. Determine that the information reconciles to the financial statements or other applicable records;

5. Perform procedures to test the completeness and accuracy of the information (if not already tested in connection with the audit of the financial statements);

6. Evaluate whether the information complies with relevant regulatory requirements (or other applicable criteria); *and*

7. Obtain appropriate management representations: (a) that management acknowledges responsibility for the fair presentation of the information; (b) that management believes the information is fairly stated; (c) that the methods used have not changed from the prior period (if changed, state that the reasons for the changes are appropriate); (d) that the information complies with regulatory requirements or other applicable criteria; and (e) that management believes any underlying assumptions are appropriate.

IV. Evaluation of Audit Results

A. Overall Evaluation—The auditor should evaluate whether the information is fairly stated in relation to the financial statements, including whether the information is presented in conformity with regulatory requirements or other applicable criteria.

B. Accumulated Misstatements—The auditor should communicate accumulated misstatements to management to give management a chance to make corrections.

C. Uncorrected Misstatements—The auditor should evaluate whether uncorrected misstatements are material (based on relevant quantitative and qualitative factors).

V. Reporting on Supplemental Information

A. Combined or Separate Reports Permitted—Unless prohibited by regulatory requirements, the auditor may either issue a separate report on the supplemental information and the financial statements or issue a combined report on both.

B. Effects of Modifications to the Report on Financial Statements—The auditor should evaluate whether any modification of the report on the financial statements is relevant to the opinion to be expressed on the supplemental information.

1. **Qualified opinion on the financial statements**—The auditor should express a qualified opinion on the supplemental information if the basis for the qualification also applies to the supplemental information.

2. **Adverse opinion (or disclaimer) on the financial statements**—The auditor should likewise express an adverse opinion (or disclaimer) on the supplemental information.

PCAOB's Sample (Separate) Report on Supplemental Information:
The (identify supplemental information) has been subjected to audit procedures performed in conjunction with the audit of (Company's) financial statements. The (supplemental information) is the responsibility of the Company's management. Our audit procedures included determining whether the (supplemental information) reconciles to the financial statements or the underlying accounting and other records, as applicable, and performing procedures to test the completeness and accuracy of the information presented in the (supplemental information). In forming our opinion on the (supplemental information), we evaluated whether the (supplemental information), including its form and content, is presented in conformity with (specify the relevant regulatory requirement or other criteria, if any). In our opinion, the (identify supplemental information) is fairly stated, in all material respects, in relation to the financial statements as a whole.

Alert to Restrict Report

I. Relevant AICPA Guidance—The relevant AICPA guidance is provided by AU 905, *Alert That Restricts the Use of the Auditor's Written Communication*. The standard states that the auditor's objective is to restrict the use of the auditor's written communication by including an alert when the potential exists for that communication to be misunderstood if taken out of the context of its intended use.

II. Using an Alert to Restrict the Use of the Auditor's Report—Such an alert should be included as a separate paragraph of the report when:

    A. The subject matter is based on criteria that are only suitable for (or available to) a limited number of users; *or*

    B. The matters are presented in a *by-product report* that is not the primary objective of the engagement.

    C. Including an Alert—The auditor is not prohibited from including such an alert in any other auditor's report or written communication.

    D. Purpose of the Alert—The purpose of the alert is to restrict the use of the auditor's written communication because of the potential for misunderstanding if taken out of the context for which the written communication is intended.

    E. Content of the Alert—The auditor should state that the written communication is intended solely for the use of the specified parties (and either identify or refer to those parties).

    F. Adding Other Specified Parties—The auditor should obtain acknowledgment in writing from such other parties as to their understanding of the nature of the engagement, the criteria used, and the auditor's written communication. They can be added after the release of the auditor's written communication (by amending the written communication to add them, but without changing the original date of the auditor's written communication).

    G. Distribution of the Auditor's Written Communication—The auditor is not responsible for enforcing the distribution of the auditor's written communication after its release. The purpose of the alert is to appropriately communicate such restricted distribution.

III. Sample Reporting Language for an Alert to Restrict the Use of the Auditor's Report

    A. A typical alert consists of one sentence at the end of the auditor's report:

> This (report, letter, presentation, or communication) is intended solely for the information and use of (list or refer to the specified parties) and is not intended to be and should not be used by anyone other than these specified parties.

    B. Alert for engagements performed in accordance with Government Auditing Standards:

> The purpose of this (*report, letter, presentation, or communication*) is solely to (*describe the purpose of the auditor's written communication, such as to describe the scope of our testing of internal control over financial reporting and compliance, and the results of that testing, and not to provide an opinion on the effectiveness of the entity's internal control over financial reporting or on compliance*). This (*report, letter, presentation, or communication*) is an integral part of an audit performed in accordance with

Government Auditing Standards in considering (*describe the results that are being assessed, such as the entity's internal control over financial reporting and compliance*). Accordingly, this (*report, letter, presentation, or communication*) is not suitable for any other purpose.

Financial Statements Using Another Country's Framework

After studying this lesson, you should be able to:

1. Identify the auditor's responsibilities when engaged to report on financial statements prepared in accordance with a financial reporting framework generally accepted in another country.

2. Identify the reporting language that would be appropriate when issuing an audit report on financial statements prepared in accordance with a financial reporting framework generally accepted in another country.

I. Relevant AICPA Guidance

The relevant AICPA guidance is provided by AU 910, *Financial Statements Prepared in Accordance With a Financial Reporting Framework Generally Accepted in Another Country*. The standard states that the auditor's objective, when engaged to report on financial statements prepared in accordance with a financial reporting framework generally accepted in another country, is to address appropriately the special considerations that are relevant to: (1) the acceptance of the engagement; (2) the planning and performance of the engagement; and (3) the formation of an opinion and reporting on the financial statements.

II. Acceptance of the Engagement

A. Considerations—The auditor should obtain an understanding of (1) the purpose for which the financial statements are prepared; (2) the intended users of the financial statements; and (3) steps taken by management to determine that the framework is acceptable in the circumstances.

B. Users—The auditor should consider whether the intended users are likely to be familiar with the applicable financial reporting framework.

III. Performance of the Engagement

A. Use Solely Outside the U.S.—When auditing financial statements intended for use solely outside the U.S., the auditor should comply with GAAS, except for requirements related to the form and content of the auditor's report. The auditor should obtain an understanding of the entity's selection and application of accounting policies.

B. Consultation with Others—The auditor may wish to consult with others having expertise in applying that country's reporting framework.

IV. Reporting

A. For Use Only Outside the U.S.—The auditor should report either using (1) a U.S. form of report (including a statement that refers to the note to the financial statements that describes the basis of presentation, including the country involved); or (2) the report form and content of the other country (identify the other country in the report).

B. For Use Both Outside and Inside the U.S.—If the financial statements are also intended for use in the U.S., the auditor should report using the U.S. form of report, including an emphasis-of-matter paragraph that (1) identifies the financial reporting framework used; (2) refers to the note to the financial statements describing that framework; and (3) indicates that such a framework differs from U.S. GAAP.

C. Summary of the Differences in the Audit Reporting Language Relative to U.S. Form.

1. Opinion—The opinion would be changed as follows: "In our opinion, the accompanying financial statements present fairly, in all material respects, ... in accordance with (*specify the financial reporting framework generally accepted*) in (*name of country*)."

2. **Basis of Opinion**—State: "We conducted our audit in accordance with auditing standards generally accepted in the United States of America and in [*name of country*]" if the audit also followed the other country's auditing standards.

3. **"Responsibilities of Management" section**—State: "Management is responsible for the preparation and fair presentation of the financial statements in accordance with [*specify the financial reporting framework generally accepted*] in [*name of country*] ..."

4. **"Auditor's Responsibilities" section**—No changes

V. Sample Audit Report: Financial Statements Prepared in Accordance With a Another Country's Financial Reporting Framework (for Use Outside of U.S.)

Independent Auditor's Report
[Appropriate Addressee]

Opinion

We have audited the financial statements of ABC Company, which comprise the balance sheet as of December 31, 20X1, and the related statements of income, changes in stockholders' equity, and cash flows for the year then ended, and the related notes to the financial statements, which, as described in note X to the financial statements, have been prepared on the basis of [*specify the financial reporting framework generally accepted*] in [*name of country*].

In our opinion, the accompanying financial statements present fairly, in all material respects, the financial position of ABC Company as of December 31, 20X1, and the results of its operations and its cash flows for the year then ended in accordance with [specify the financial reporting framework generally accepted] in [*name of country*].

Basis for Opinion

We conducted our audit in accordance with auditing standards generally accepted in the United States of America (*and [in name of country]*). Our responsibilities under those standards are further described in the Auditor's Responsibilities for the Audit of the Financial Statements section of our report. We are required to be independent of ABC Company and to meet our other ethical responsibilities, in accordance with the relevant ethical requirements relating to our audit.

Responsibilities of Management for the Financial Statements

Management is responsible for the preparation and fair presentation of the these financial statements in accordance with [*specify the financial reporting framework generally accepted*] in [*name of country*], and for the design, implementation, and maintenance of internal control relevant to the preparation and fair presentation of financial statements that are free from material misstatement, whether due to fraud or error.

[*Describe management's responsibilities for evaluating whether there are conditions or events, considered in the aggregate, that raise substantial doubt about the entity's ability to continue as a going concern, when the applicable financial reporting framework includes such a requirement.*]

Auditor's Responsibilities for the Audit of the Financial Statements

Our objectives are to obtain reasonable assurance about whether the financial statements as a whole are free from material misstatement, whether due to fraud or error, and to issue an auditor's report that includes our opinion. Reasonable assurance is a high level of assurance but is not absolute assurance and therefore is not a guarantee that an audit conducted in accordance with generally accepted auditing standards will always detect a material misstatement when it exists. The risk of not detecting a material misstatement resulting from fraud is higher than for one resulting from error, as fraud may involve collusion, forgery, intentional omissions, misrepresentations, or the override of internal control. Misstatements are considered material if, individually or in the aggregate, they could reasonably be expected to influence the economic decisions of users made on the basis of these financial statements.

In performing an audit in accordance with GAAS, we:

○ Exercise professional judgment and maintain professional skepticism throughout the audit.

○ Identify and assess the risks of material misstatement of the financial statements, whether due to fraud or error, and design and perform audit procedures responsive to those risks. Such procedures include examining, on a test basis, evidence regarding the amounts and disclosures in the financial statements.

○ Obtain an understanding of internal control relevant to the audit in order to design audit procedures that are appropriate in the circumstances, but not for the purpose of expressing an opinion on the effectiveness of the entity's internal control. Accordingly, no such opinion is expressed.

○ Evaluate the appropriateness of accounting policies used and the reasonableness of significant accounting estimates made by management, as well as evaluate the overall presentation of the financial statements.

○ Conclude whether, in our judgment, there are conditions or events, considered in the aggregate, that raise substantial doubt about the entity's ability to continue as a going concern for a reasonable period of time.

We are required to communicate with those charged with governance regarding, among other matters, the planned scope and timing of the audit, significant audit findings, and certain internal control–related matters that we identified during the audit.

[Signature of the auditor's firm]

[City and state where the auditor's report is issued]

[Date of the auditor's report]

Reporting on Summary Financial Statements

After studying this lesson, you should be able to:

1. Identify the auditor's responsibilities when engaged to report on an entity's *summary financial statements*.

2. Identify the reporting language that would be appropriate when issuing an audit report on summary financial statements.

I. Relevant AICPA Guidance

The relevant AICPA guidance is provided by AU 810, *Engagements to Report on Summary Financial Statements*. The standard states that the auditor's objectives are (1) to determine whether it is appropriate to accept the engagement to report on summary financial statements; and (2) if engaged, to perform the necessary procedures, to form an opinion on whether the summary financial statements are consistent with the audited financial statements from which they have been derived, and to clearly express that opinion (and the basis for it) through a written report.

Definitions

Applied Criteria: The criteria applied by management in the preparation of the summary financial statements.

Summary Financial Statements: Historical financial information that is derived from financial statements but that contains less detail than the financial statements, while still providing a structured representation consistent with that provided by the financial statements of the entity's economic resources or obligations at a point in time or the changes therein for a period of time. Summary financial statements are separately presented and are not presented as comparative information.

II. Engagement Acceptance

A. The auditor must have been engaged to audit the financial statements as a whole in order to accept an engagement to report on summary financial statements.

B. Before accepting an engagement to report on summary financial statements—The auditor should (1) determine whether the applied criteria are acceptable; and (2) obtain a written agreement from management acknowledging their responsibilities and accepting the expected form and content of the auditor's report.

III. Procedures to Be Performed by the Auditor

A. Evaluate whether the summary financial statements adequately disclose their summarized nature and identify the audited financial statements.

B. When unaccompanied by the audited financial statements, evaluate whether the audited financial statements are **readily available** to users.

C. Evaluate whether the summary financial statements adequately disclose the applied criteria.

D. Compare the summary financial statements with the related audited financial statements.

E. Evaluate whether the summary financial statements are prepared in accordance with the applied criteria.

> **Note**
> *Audited financial statements are viewed as readily available if users can obtain them without any further action by the entity. Management's statement that they are available upon request, would **not** be considered readily available.*

F. Evaluate whether the summary financial statements contain necessary information at an appropriate level of aggregation so they are not misleading.

G. Obtain a written representations letter that addresses the following matters:

1. Management has prepared the summary financial statements in accordance with the applied criteria (and that the applied criteria are acceptable).

2. Management has made the audited financial statements readily available to the intended users.

3. If the date of the report on the summary financial information is later than the date of the report on the audited financial statements, include a statement as to whether management believes any of its previous representations need to be modified and whether any subsequent events require adjustment to or disclosure in the audited financial statements.

4. The representation letter should be dated the same as the auditor's report.

IV. Form of the Auditor's Opinion

A. Only an Unmodified or Adverse Opinion is Permitted—The summary financial statements are either consistent or not consistent with the audited financial statements; accordingly, a qualified opinion is not permitted.

1. Unmodified opinion—When issuing an unmodified opinion on the summary financial statements, the opinion should state that they are consistent, in all material respects, with the audited financial statements from which they have been derived, in accordance with the applied criteria.

2. Adverse opinion—When issuing an adverse opinion on the summary financial statements, the opinion should state that the financial statements are not consistent, in all material respects, with the audited financial statements in accordance with the applied criteria.

B. Adverse Opinion or Disclaimer of Opinion—When the auditor's report on the audited financial statements contains an adverse opinion or a disclaimer of opinion, the auditor should either withdraw from the engagement to report on the summary financial statements (when withdrawal is possible) or disclaim an opinion on the summary financial statements.

V. Auditor's Report on Summary Financial Statements—Include the following elements:

A. A title that includes the word *independent*

B. Addressee

C. "Opinion" section—That (1) identifies the audited financial statements (along with the type of opinion expressed and (2) expresses an opinion on whether the summary financial statements are consistent with the audited financial statements (from which the summary financial statements are derived).

D. "Summary Financial Statement" section—State that (1) the summary financial statements do not contain all the disclosures associated with the audited financial statements; (2) reading the summary financial statements (with the auditor's report) is not a substitute for reading the audited financial statements; and (3) the summary financial statements do not reflect subsequent events that occurred after the date of the report on the audited financial statements

E. "Responsibility of Management" section—State that management is responsible for the preparation of the summary financial statements.

F. "Auditor's Responsibility" section—That (1) identifies the responsibility to express an opinion whether the summary financial statements are consistent with the audited financial statements; (2) describe the procedures performed; and (3) point out that no procedures were performed on the audited financial statements after the date of the auditor's report on those financial statements.

G. Signature block—Sign the report and identify the city/state and date of the report.

VI. Sample Audit Report on Summary Financial Statements

Independent Auditor's Report on Summary Financial Information

[Appropriate Addressee]

Opinion

The summary financial statements, which comprise the summary balance sheet as of December 31, 20X1, the summary income statement, summary statement of changes in stockholders' equity, and summary cash flow statement for the year then ended, and the related notes, are derived from the audited financial statements of ABC Company as of and for the year ended December 31, 20X1. We expressed an unmodified audit opinion on those audited financial statements in our report dated February 15, 20X2.

In our opinion, the accompanying summary financial statements of ABC Company as of and for the year ended December 31, 20X1 referred to above are consistent, in all material respects, with the audited financial statements from which they have been derived, on the basis described in Note X.

Summary Financial Statements

The summary financial statements do not contain all the disclosures required by [*describe financial reporting framework applied in the preparation of the financial statements of ABC Company*]. Reading the summary financial statements and the auditor's report hereon, therefore, is not a substitute for reading the audited financial statements and the auditor's report thereon. The summary financial statements and the audited financial statements do not reflect the effects of events that occurred subsequent to the date of our report on the audited financial statements.

Responsibility of Management for the Summary Financial Statements

Management is responsible for the preparation of the financial statements in accordance with the criteria described in Note X.

Auditor's Responsibility

Our responsibility is to express an opinion on whether the summary financial statements are consistent, in all material respects, with the audited financial statements based on our procedures, which were conducted in accordance with auditing standards generally accepted in the United States of America. The procedures consisted principally of comparing the summary financial statements with the related information in the audited financial statements from which the summary financial statements have been derived and evaluating whether the summary financial statements are prepared in accordance with the basis described in Note X. We did not perform any audit procedures regarding the audited financial statements after the date of our report on those financial statements.

[Signature of the auditor's firm]

[City and state where the auditor's report is issued]

[Date of the auditor's report]

Interim Financial Information

After studying this lesson, you should be able to:

1. Identify the auditor's responsibilities when engaged to report on an entity's *interim financial information*.

2. Identify the reporting language that would be appropriate when issuing a review report on an audit entity's interim financial information.

I. Relevant AICPA Guidance

The relevant AICPA guidance is provided by AU 930: *Interim Financial Information*. The standard states that the auditor's objective is to obtain a basis for reporting whether the auditor is aware of any material modifications that should be made to the interim financial information for it to be in accordance with the applicable financial reporting framework through performing limited procedures.

Definition

Interim Financial Information: Financial information prepared and presented in accordance with an applicable financial reporting framework that comprises either a complete or condensed set of financial statements covering a period(s) less than one full year or covering a 12-month period ending on a date other than the entity's fiscal year-end.

II. Engagement Acceptance

A. Before accepting an engagement to review the interim financial information, the auditor should (1) determine whether the financial reporting framework to be applied is acceptable; and (2) obtain the agreement of management regarding the engagement terms.

B. Agreement on Engagement Terms—The auditor should agree upon the terms of the engagement with management (or those charged with governance) and record those terms in an engagement letter that includes: (1) the objectives and scope of the engagement; (2) the responsibilities of management; (3) the responsibilities of the auditor; (4) the limitations of a review engagement; and (5) identification of the applicable financial reporting framework.

III. Engagement Performance

A. Obtain an understanding of the entity and its environment, including internal control related to the preparation of annual and interim financial information. This should be sufficient to (1) identify the types of potential misstatements (and likelihood of occurrence) and (2) select the inquiries and analytical procedures for the auditor's basis for conclusions.

B. Analytical Procedures, Inquiries, and Other Review Procedures

1. **Analytical procedures**—The auditor should apply analytical procedures to the interim information to identify unusual items that may indicate a material misstatement, including the following:

   a. Comparing the interim financial information with comparable information for the immediately preceding period and with the corresponding period(s) in the previous year;

   b. Comparing recorded amounts or ratios developed from recorded amounts to expectations; and

   c. Comparing disaggregated revenue data.

2. Inquiries and other review procedures—The auditor should make the following inquiries and perform the following other procedures in a review of interim financial information.

    a. Read the available minutes of meetings of stockholders, directors, and appropriate committees;

    b. Obtain reports from any component auditors related to reviews of significant components or inquire of those auditors if reports have not been issued;

    c. Inquire of management about the matters normally associated with a management representations letter;

    d. Obtain evidence that the interim financial information agrees to (or reconciles with) the accounting records;

    e. Read the interim financial information; *and*

    f. Read other information in documents containing the interim financial information to see if any of it is materially inconsistent.

3. Inquiry concerning litigation, claims, and assessments—The auditor should inquire of legal counsel if information about litigation, claims, and assessments does not appear to be presented in accordance with the applicable financial reporting framework.

4. Going-concern issues—If information indicates that there may be substantial doubt about an entity's ability to continue as a going concern, the auditor should inquire of management about plans for dealing with adverse effects and consider the adequacy of disclosure about such matters.

5. The auditor should consider the reasonableness and consistency of management's responses, but the auditor is not required to corroborate management's responses with other evidence.

C. Evaluating the Results of Interim Review Procedures—The auditor should evaluate, individually and in the aggregate, misstatements to determine whether material modification should be made to the interim financial information.

D. Written Representations from Management—The auditor should obtain written representations from management for all interim financial information presented as of the date of the auditor's review report. If management does not provide the written representation requested, the auditor should withdraw from the engagement to review the interim financial information.

IV. Reporting on a Review of Interim Financial Information

A. Form of the Review Report—The report should be in writing and include the following:

    1. Title

    2. Addressee

    3. A section called "Results of Review"

    4. A section called "Basis for Review Results"

    5. A section called "Responsibilities of Management"

    6. The signature, city and state, and date of the review report

B. Each page of the interim financial information should be clearly marked *unaudited*.

C. If Comparative Information Is Presented that Has Not Been Reviewed—The report should indicate that the auditor assumes no responsibility for it.

D. Modification of the Auditor's Review Report—When the interim financial information has not been prepared in accordance with the applicable financial reporting framework in all material respects, the auditor should consider whether modification of the review report is sufficient to address the matter.

1. **If modification is sufficient**—The auditor should modify the review report by describing the nature of the departure, and stating the effects on the interim financial information (or providing the appropriate information when disclosure is inadequate), if practicable.

2. **If modification is not sufficient**—The auditor should withdraw from the review engagement.

3. See Sample Review Report—Modified for Inadequate Disclosure below—Affects only the first section dealing with the "Results of the Review" (the second and third paragraphs)

E. **Interim Financial Information Accompanying Audited Financial Statements**—The auditor should include an *other-matter paragraph* in the report on audited financial statements when the following conditions exist:

1. The interim financial information that has been reviewed is included in a document containing the audited financial statements.

2. The interim information accompanying the audited financial statements does not appear to be presented in accordance with the applicable financial reporting framework.

3. The auditor's separate review report, which refers to the departure, is not presented with the interim financial information.

F. Add a separate section "Substantial Doubt About an Entity's Ability to Continue as a Going Concern" if either of the following:

1. Such a section was included in the prior year's auditor's report and the conditions continue to exist and raise substantial doubt; or

2. Such a section was not included in the prior year's auditor's report but the applicable reporting framework requires management to include a note that substantial doubt exists and management has included a note to the interim financial information stating that substantial doubt exists.

V. Sample Review Report of the Entity's Auditor

Independent Auditor's Review Report
[Appropriate Addressee]

Results of Review of Interim Financial Information

We have reviewed the accompanying [*describe the interim financial information or statements reviewed*] of ABC Company and its subsidiaries as of September 30, 20X1, and for the three-month and nine-month periods then ended, and the related notes (collectively referred to as the interim financial information).

Based on our review, we are not aware of any material modifications that should be made to the accompanying interim financial information for it to be in accordance with [*identify the applicable financial reporting framework; for example, accounting principles generally accepted in the United States of America*].

Basis for Review Results

We conducted our review in accordance with auditing standards generally accepted in the United States of America (GAAS) applicable to reviews of interim financial information. A review of interim financial information consists principally of applying analytical procedures and making inquiries of persons responsible for financial and accounting matters. A review of interim financial information is substantially less in scope than an audit conducted in accordance with GAAS, the objective of which is an expression of an opinion regarding the financial information as a whole, and accordingly, we do not express such an opinion. We are required to be independent of ABC Company and to meet our other ethical responsibilities in accordance with the relevant ethical requirements relating to our review. We believe that the results of the review procedures provide a reasonable basis for our conclusion.

Responsibilities of Management for the Interim Financial Information

Management is responsible for the preparation and fair presentation of the interim financial information in accordance with [*identify the applicable financial reporting framework; for example, accounting principles generally accepted in the United States of America*] and for the design, implementation, and maintenance of internal control relevant to the preparation and fair presentation of interim financial information that is free from material misstatement, whether due to fraud or error.

[Signature of the auditor's firm]

[City and state where the auditor's report is issued]

[Date of the auditor's report]

VI. Sample Review Report—Modified for Inadequate Disclosure

Independent Auditor's Review Report

[Appropriate Addressee]

Results of Review of Interim Financial Information

We have reviewed the accompanying [*describe the interim financial information or statements reviewed*] of ABC Company and its subsidiaries as of September 30, 20X1, and for the three-month and nine-month periods then ended, and the related notes (collectively referred to as the interim financial information).

Based on our review, with the exception of the matters described in the following paragraph, we are not aware of any material modifications that should be made to the accompanying interim financial information for it to be in accordance with [*identify the applicable financial reporting framework; for example, accounting principles generally accepted in the United States of America*].

Management has informed us that the Company is presently defending a claim regarding [*describe the nature of the loss contingency*] and that the extent of the Company's liability, if any, and the effect on the accompanying interim financial information is not determinable at this time. The interim financial information fails to disclose these matters, which we believe are required to be disclosed in accordance with [*identify the applicable financial reporting framework; for example, accounting principles generally accepted in the United States of America*].

VII. Filings with the SEC Under Federal Securities Statutes

A. Relevant AICPA Guidance

The relevant AICPA guidance is provided by AU 925, *Filings with the U.S. SEC Under the Securities Act of 1933*. The standard states that the auditor's objective is to perform specified procedures at or shortly before the effective date of the registration statement to sustain the burden of proof that the auditor has performed a reasonable investigation [under Section 11(b)(3)(B)].

Definitions

Auditor's Consent: A statement signed and dated by the auditor giving consent to use the auditor's report in a registration statement.

Awareness Letter: A letter signed and dated by the auditor to acknowledge the auditor's awareness that the review report on interim financial information is being used in a registration statement (also known as an *acknowledgment letter*).

Effective Date of the Registration: The date on which the registration statement becomes effective for purposes of evaluating the auditor's liability under Section 11 of the Securities Act of 1933.

B. Responsibilities under Federal Securities Statutes—The Securities Act of 1933 promotes fair disclosure and prohibits fraud in initial public offerings of securities.

1. **Management's** responsibilities are the same as with the financial statements used for other purposes—that is, the financial statements are the representations of management.

2. The **independent accountant's** responsibilities are similar to other types of reporting—Section 11 of the 1933 Act prohibits false or misleading statements (or material omissions) in registration statements.

   a. Section 11 defense—After a reasonable investigation, the independent accountant had reasonable grounds to believe that the financial statements were fairly stated (but the CPA has the burden of proof).

   b. Statutory responsibility is determined in light of the circumstances on the effective date of the registration statement.

   c. The CPA should read the relevant parts of any prospectus filed under the 1933 Act to verify that the independent accountant's name is not being used inappropriately. (Note that a *prospectus* is an informational document required to be filed with the SEC in connection with a registration statement to offer securities for sale; the prospectus cannot be used to finalize sales of such securities until the registration statement is declared effective by the SEC.)

   d. When the registration statement references the interim financial information reviewed by the accountant—the prospectus should clearly indicate that the review report is not part of the registration statement within the meaning of the 1933 Act. The auditor's review report is only required if the registration statement indicates that the unaudited interim information has been reviewed. (If unaudited financial statements are presented along with audited financial statements in a filing with the SEC, the unaudited financial statements should be labeled "unaudited" and should not be referenced in the auditor's report.)

C. Subsequent Events Procedures in Connection with Filings under the Securities Act of 1933

1. Extend the procedures regarding subsequent events from the audit report date up to (or as near as practicable) to the effective date of the registration statement.

2. Following fieldwork, the auditor may usually rely on inquiries of appropriate client personnel—obtain written representations from management regarding those financial and accounting matters.

3. An auditor who has reported on the financial statements from prior periods, but not the most recent audited financial statements included in the registration statement, is responsible for events subsequent to the date of the prior-period's audited financial statements. The auditor should:

   a. Read the applicable portions of the prospectus and registration statement.

   b. Obtain a letter of representations from the successor auditor as to whether the successor's audit identified any matters that might have a material effect on the prior period's financial statements.

Note

In 2017, the AICPA amended AU-C 925, referenced above, by issuing AU-C 945 (SAS 133), "Auditor Involvement With Exempt Offering Documents." Prior to that, guidance on so-called exempt offering documents was provided in certain specific AICPA Audit and Accounting Guides.

I. Introduction

A. Definition of "exempt offering document"—"The disclosure document that provides financial and nonfinancial information related to the entity issuing the exempt offering (or in the case of a franchise offering, the franchisor) and the offering itself."

B. Examples—(1) Securities transactions that are exempt from the registration requirements of the Securities Act of 1933 (for example, private placement offerings, exempt public offerings, and municipal securities offerings) and (2) franchise offerings regulated by the Federal Trade Commission or under state franchise laws

C. Applicability—When the auditor is "involved with the exempt offering document," that occurs when (1) the auditor's report is included or referenced in an exempt offering, and (2) the auditor performs one or more activities enumerated in the SAS (for example, preparing information included in the document, reading a draft of the document, providing comments on the document, etc.)

II. Requirements

A. Other information included in the exempt offering document—Perform the procedures associated with other information in documents containing audited financial statements to identify inconsistencies

B. Subsequent events and subsequent discovered facts—Perform the appropriate procedures to identify such relevant events (including inquiry of management and reading applicable minutes); obtain updated written representations from management

Other Types of Reports

Reports on Application of Requirements of Framework

After studying this lesson, you should be able to:

1. Identify the reporting accountant's responsibilities when engaged to provide a second opinion on the requirements of the applicable financial reporting framework.

2. Identify the reporting language that would be appropriate when issuing a written report on the requirements of the applicable financial reporting framework.

I. **Relevant AICPA Guidance** —The relevant AICPA guidance is provided by AU 915, *Reports on Application of Requirements of an Applicable Financial Reporting Framework*. The standard states that the auditor's objective, when engaged to issue a written report or provide oral advice on the application of the requirements of an applicable financial reporting framework to a specific transaction or on the type of report that may be issued on a specific entity's financial statements, is to appropriately address: (1) the acceptance of the engagement; (2) the planning and performance of the engagement; and (3) reporting on the specific transaction or type of report.

Definitions

Hypothetical Transaction: A transaction or financial reporting issue that does not involve facts or circumstances of a specific entity.

Reporting Accountant: An accountant, other than a continuing accountant, who prepares a written report or provides oral advice on the application of the requirements of an applicable financial reporting framework to a specific transaction or on the type of report that may be issued on a specific entity's financial statements. (A reporting accountant who is also engaged to provide accounting advice to a specific entity on a recurring basis is commonly referred to as an *advisory accountant*.)

Specific Transaction: A completed or proposed transaction or group of related transactions or a financial reporting issue involving facts and circumstances of a specific entity.

II. **Engagement Acceptance**

   A. The reporting accountant should consider the following: (1) the circumstances under which the written report or oral advice is requested; (2) the purpose of the request; and (3) the intended use of the written report or oral advice.

   B. The reporting accountant should not accept any engagement involving a *hypothetical transaction*.

   C. If it is appropriate to accept an engagement under this SAS, the reporting accountant should establish an understanding with the requesting party that: (1) management is responsible for the proper accounting treatment and should consult with the continuing accountant; (2) management acknowledges that the reporting accountant may need to consult with the continuing accountant and, if requested, that management will authorize the continuing accountant to respond to the reporting accountant's inquiries; and (3) management will notify those charged with governance and the continuing accountant about the engagement.

III. Engagement Planning and Performance

A. The reporting accountant should:

1. Obtain an understanding of the specific transaction(s) or the conditions relevant to the type of report that may be issued;

2. Review the requirements of the applicable financial reporting framework;

3. Consult with other professionals or others, if appropriate;

4. Consider existing relevant precedents or analogies;

5. Request permission from management to consult with the continuing accountant and request that management authorize the continuing accountant to respond fully to the reporting accountant's inquiries; *and*

6. Consult with the continuing accountant regarding the facts.

B. Consulting with the Continuing Accountant—The reporting accountant (who is engaged to issue a written report or provide oral advice on the application of the requirements of an applicable financial reporting framework to a specific transaction) should consult with the continuing accountant **unless**:

1. The reporting accountant is engaged to provide recurring accounting and reporting advice and (a) **does not believe that a second opinion is being requested**; (b) has full access to management; and (c) believes that the relevant information has been obtained.

2. The reporting accountant deems it unnecessary to consult with the continuing accountant, the reporting accountant should **document** the justification for not consulting.

C. Continuing Accountant's Responses—The continuing accountant's responsibilities for responding to inquiries of the reporting accountant are the same as those of a predecessor auditor responding to an auditor's inquiries. The continuing accountant may indicate whether the method of accounting recommended by the continuing accountant is disputed by management and convey the continuing accountant's conclusion on the application of the requirements of an applicable financial reporting framework.

IV. Written Report

A. The report should be addressed to the requesting party and include the following:

1. A description of the engagement and reference to this SAS;

2. Identification of the specific entity, a description of any specific transaction(s), and a statement about the source of information;

3. A statement describing the application of the requirements of an applicable financial reporting framework (and country involved);

4. A statement that management is responsible for the proper accounting treatment and they should consult with their continuing accountants;

5. A statement that any differences in the facts or circumstances may change the report; *and*

6. A restriction that the report is intended solely for the specified parties. (The restricted distribution of the report does not prevent distribution of the report to the continuing accountant.)

B. The requirements associated with the written report may be useful when providing oral advice, too.

V. Sample Written Report to the Requesting Party

> ### Introduction
>
> We have been engaged to report on the appropriate application of the requirements of accounting principles generally accepted in the United States of America to the specific transaction described below. This report is being issued to ABC Company for assistance in evaluating accounting policies for the described specific transaction. Our engagement has been conducted in accordance with Statement on Auditing Standards Reports on Application of Requirements of an Applicable Financial Reporting Framework.
>
> ### Description of Transactions
>
> The facts, circumstances, and assumptions relevant to the specific transaction as provided to us by the management of ABC Company are as follows:
>
> (*Include text discussing the facts, circumstances, and assumptions relevant to the specific transaction.*)
>
> ### Appropriate Accounting Principles
>
> (*Include text discussing accounting principles generally accepted in the United States of America and how they apply to the described transaction.*)
>
> ### Concluding Comments
>
> The ultimate responsibility for the decision on the appropriate application of the requirements of accounting principles generally accepted in the United States of America for an actual transaction rests with the preparers of financial statements, who should consult with their continuing accountant. Our conclusion on the appropriate application of the requirements of accounting principles generally accepted in the United States of America for the described specific transaction is based solely on the facts provided to us as previously described; should these facts and circumstances differ, our conclusion may change.
>
> ### Restricted Use
>
> This report is intended solely for the information and use of those charged with governance and management of ABC Company and is not intended to be and should not be used by anyone other than these specified parties.

F/S with Special Purpose Frameworks

After studying this lesson, you should be able to:

1. Identify the different bases of accounting associated with the term *special purpose framework*.

2. Identify the reporting language that would be appropriate when issuing an audit report on financial statements prepared using a special purpose framework, and the differences in such reporting language depending upon the particular basis of accounting involved.

I. **Relevant AICPA Guidance**—The relevant AICPA guidance is provided by AU 800, *Special Considerations—Audits of Financial Statements Prepared in Accordance With Special Purpose Frameworks*. The standard states that the auditor's objectives are to (1) the acceptance of the engagement; (2) the planning and performance of that engagement; and (3) forming an opinion and reporting on the financial statements.

> **Definition**
> *Special Purpose Framework*: A financial reporting framework other than GAAP that is one of the following bases of accounting: (1) cash basis, (2) tax basis, (3) regulatory basis, or (4) contractual basis, or (5) other basis (that "uses a definite set of logical, reasonable criteria that is applied to all material items appearing in financial statements").

II. **Engagement Acceptance**

    A. **Acceptability of the Financial Reporting Framework**—The auditor should obtain an understanding of (a) the purpose for which the financial statements are prepared; (b) the intended users; and (c) the steps taken by management to determine that the applicable financial reporting framework is acceptable in the circumstances.

    B. **Preconditions for an Audit**—The auditor should obtain the agreement of management that it understands its responsibility to include all informative disclosures that are appropriate for the special purpose framework used, including (a) a description of the special purpose framework; (b) informative disclosures similar to those required by GAAP; (c) a description of any significant interpretations of the contract on which the special purpose financial statements are based, when applicable; and (d) additional disclosures beyond those specifically required that may be necessary to achieve fair presentation.

III. **Engagement Planning and Performance**

    A. **When the Engagement Is Based on an Underlying Contract**—The auditor should obtain an understanding of any *significant interpretations* of the contract that management made.

    B. An interpretation is significant when adoption of another reasonable interpretation would have produced a material difference.

IV. **Forming an Opinion and Reporting Considerations**

    A. **Description of the Applicable Financial Reporting Framework**—The auditor should consider whether the financial statements are appropriately titled (should not use financial statement names that imply GAAP), include a summary of significant accounting policies, and adequately describe how the special purpose framework differs from GAAP. These differences do not have to be quantified, however.

    B. **Fair Presentation**—The auditor should determine whether informative disclosures are included similar to those required by GAAP, and whether additional disclosures are needed to achieve fair presentation.

    C. **Auditor's Report**—The report should describe the *purpose for which the financial statements are prepared* (**if regulatory basis or contractual basis**) or reference a note containing that information about the special purpose framework used.

D. Alerting Readers in an Emphasis-of-Matter Paragraph —The auditor's report on special purpose financial statements should include an *emphasis-of-matter* ("Basis of Accounting") paragraph that (1) indicates that the financial statements are prepared in accordance with the applicable special purpose framework; (2) refers to the note that describes that framework; and (3) states that the special purpose framework is a basis of accounting other than GAAP. (The only exception to such an alert involves *regulatory basis financial statements intended for general use* for which no such alert is needed.)

E. Restricting the Use of the Auditor's Report to the Intended Users—The auditor's report should also include an *other-matter* paragraph that restricts the use of the auditor's report to those within the entity, the parties to the contract agreement, or the regulatory agencies to whom the entity is subject **when the financial statements are prepared in accordance with either** (1) a contractual basis of accounting; or (2) a regulatory basis of accounting. (The only exception to such a restriction involves *regulatory basis financial statements intended for general use* for which no such restriction is needed. And no such restriction applies to cash basis or tax basis.)

F. Regulatory Basis Financial Statements Intended for General Use—If the financial statements are prepared in accordance with a regulatory basis of accounting and are intended for general use, the auditor should not include the *emphasis-of-matter* or *other-matter* paragraphs. Instead, the auditor should express (1) an opinion as to whether the financial statements are prepared in accordance with GAAP (which they are not); and (2) an opinion in a separate paragraph as to whether the financial statements are prepared in accordance with the special purpose framework.

G. Auditors Report Prescribed by Law or Regulation—If the prescribed specific layout, form, or wording of the auditor's report is not acceptable (or would cause the auditor to make an inappropriate statement), the auditor should either reword the prescribed form or attach separately an appropriately worded audit report.

Question
Which special purpose frameworks require a *description of purpose for which such financial statements are prepared*?

Answer:

Only regulatory basis (whether intended for general use or not) and contractual basis. (Cash basis and tax basis do not!)

Question
Which special purpose frameworks require an *emphasis-of-matter* paragraph alerting readers to the special purpose framework?

Answer:

Cash basis, tax basis, regulatory basis (if restricted), and contractual basis do. (Only regulatory basis intended for general use does not require such an alert!)

Question
Which special purpose frameworks require an *other-matter* paragraph to restrict the distribution of the auditor's report to specified users?

Answer:

Only regulatory basis (if restricted) and contractual basis do. (Cash basis, tax basis, and regulatory basis intended for general use do not require such a restriction!)

V. Sample Audit Report for Financial Statements Prepared on a Cash Basis

Independent Auditor's Report

[Appropriate Addressee]

Opinion

We have audited the financial statements of ABC Partnership, which comprise the statement of assets and liabilities arising from cash transactions as of December 31, 20X1, and the related statement of revenue collected and expenses paid for the year then ended, and the related notes to the financial statements.

In our opinion, the accompanying financial statements present fairly, in all material respects, the assets and liabilities arising from cash transactions of ABC Partnership as of December 31, 20X1, and its revenue collected and expenses paid during the year then ended in accordance with the cash basis of accounting described in Note X.

Basis for Opinion

We conducted our audit in accordance with auditing standards generally accepted in the United States of America (GAAS). Our responsibilities under those standards are further described in the Auditor's Responsibilities for the Audit of the Financial Statements section of our report. We are required to be independent of ABC Partnership, and to meet our other ethical responsibilities, in accordance with the relevant ethical requirements relating to our audit. We believe that the audit evidence we have obtained is sufficient and appropriate to provide a basis for our audit opinion.

Emphasis of Matter — Basis of Accounting

We draw attention to Note X of the financial statements, which describes the basis of accounting. The financial statements are prepared on the cash basis of accounting, which is a basis of accounting other than accounting principles generally accepted in the United States of America. Our opinion is not modified with respect to this matter.

Responsibilities of Management for the Financial Statements

Management is responsible for the preparation and fair presentation of the financial statements in accordance with the cash basis of accounting described in Note X, and for determining that the cash basis of accounting is an acceptable basis for the preparation of the financial statements in the circumstances. Management is also responsible for the design, implementation, and maintenance of internal control relevant to the preparation and fair presentation of financial statements that are free from material misstatement, whether due to fraud or error.

Auditor's Responsibilities for the Audit of the Financial Statements

Our objectives are to obtain reasonable assurance about whether the financial statements as a whole are free from material misstatement, whether due to fraud or error, and to issue an auditor's report that includes our opinion. Reasonable assurance is a high level of assurance but is not absolute assurance and therefore is not a guarantee that an audit conducted in accordance with GAAS will always detect a material misstatement when it exists. The risk of not detecting a material misstatement resulting from fraud is higher than for one resulting from error, as fraud may involve collusion, forgery, intentional omissions, misrepresentations, or the override of internal control. Misstatements are considered material if there is a substantial likelihood that, individually or in the aggregate, they would influence the judgment made by a reasonable user based on the financial statements.

In performing an audit in accordance with GAAS, we:

o   Exercise professional judgment and maintain professional skepticism throughout the audit.

o   Identify and assess the risks of material misstatement of the financial statements, whether due to fraud or error, and design and perform audit procedures responsive to those risks. Such procedures include examining, on a test basis, evidence regarding the amounts and disclosures in the financial statements.

○ Obtain an understanding of internal control relevant to the audit in order to design audit procedures that are appropriate in the circumstances, but not for the purpose of expressing an opinion on the effectiveness of ABC Partnership's internal control. Accordingly, no such opinion is expressed.

○ Evaluate the appropriateness of accounting policies used and the reasonableness of significant accounting estimates made by management, as well as evaluate the overall presentation of the financial statements.

○ Conclude whether, in our judgment, there are conditions or events, considered in the aggregate, that raise substantial doubt about ABC Partnership's ability to continue as a going concern for a reasonable period of time.

We are required to communicate with those charged with governance regarding, among other matters, the planned scope and timing of the audit, significant audit findings, and certain internal control-related matters that we identified during the audit.

[Signature of the auditor's firm]

[City and state where the auditor's report is issued]

[Date of the auditor's report]

Audits of Single F/S and Specific Elements, Accounts, or Items

After studying this lesson, you should be able to:

1. Identify the auditor's responsibilities when engaged to report on a single financial statement or specific element of a financial statement.

2. Identify the reporting language that would be appropriate when issuing an audit report on a single financial statement or specific element of a financial statement.

I. Relevant AICPA Guidance—The relevant AICPA guidance is provided by AU 805, *Special Considerations—Audits of Single Financial Statements and Specific Elements, Accounts, or Items of a Financial Statement*. The standard states that the auditor's objective is to appropriately address the special considerations that are relevant to (1) the acceptance of the engagement; (2) the planning and performance of the engagement; and (3) reporting on the single financial statement or the specific element.

II. Engagement Acceptance

A. Application of GAAS—If not engaged to audit the complete set of financial statements, the auditor should determine whether the audit of a single financial statement or a specific element of those financial statements in accordance with GAAS is practicable.

B. Acceptability of the Financial Reporting Framework—The auditor should obtain an understanding of (a) the purpose for which the single financial statement or specific element of a financial statement is prepared; (b) the intended users; and (c) the steps taken by management to determine that the application of the financial reporting framework is acceptable and that disclosure is adequate.

III. Engagement Planning and Performance

A. If the Specific Element is Based on Stockholders' Equity—The auditor should obtain sufficient appropriate evidence to enable the auditor to express an opinion about financial position. (This effectively means that the auditor should have audited the whole balance sheet in order to report on an element based on stockholders' equity.)

B. If the Specific Element is Based upon the Entity's Net Income or the Equivalent—The auditor should obtain sufficient appropriate evidence to enable the auditor to express an opinion about both financial position and results of operations. (This effectively means that the auditor should have audited the complete set of financial statements in order to report on an element based on net income.)

C. Considerations when Planning and Performing the Audit—Written representations from management about the complete set of financial statements would be replaced by representations about the single financial statement or the specific element in accordance with the applicable financial reporting framework.

IV. Forming an Opinion and Reporting Considerations

A. Reporting on the Entity's Complete Set of Financial Statements and a Single Financial Statement or a Specific Element of Those Financial Statements:

1. If the auditor is engaged to audit a single financial statement or a specific element of a financial statement in connection with an audit of the complete set of financial statements—The auditor should (1) issue a separate report and express a separate opinion for each engagement, and (2) indicate in the report on a specific element of a financial statement the date of the auditor's report on the complete set of financial statements and the nature of that opinion under an appropriate heading.

2. An audited single financial statement or an audited specific element of a financial statement may normally be published along with the entity's audited complete set of financial statements if the single financial statement or specific element is sufficiently differentiated from the complete set of financial statements.

3. If the presentation does not sufficiently differentiate the single financial statement or specific element from the audited financial statements—The auditor should ask management to address the situation; and the auditor should not release the auditor's report until satisfied with the resolution.

B. **Modified Opinion, Emphasis-of-Matter Paragraph, or Other-Matter Paragraph in the Auditor's Report on the Entity's Financial Statements:**

1. **If the modified opinion on the set of financial statements is relevant to the audit of the specific element (i.e., the modification is material and pervasive with respect to the specific element)**—The auditor should (a) express an adverse opinion on the specific element when the modification applicable to the set of financial statements is a result of a material misstatement in the financial statements; or (b) disclaim an opinion on the specific element when the modification applicable to the set of financial statements is a result of a scope limitation. (Note: Otherwise that would be equivalent to expressing a *piecemeal opinion*, which is prohibited.)

2. **If the modified opinion on the set of financial statements is relevant to the audit of the specific element and the auditor still considers it appropriate to express an unmodified opinion on that specific element**—The auditor should only do that if (a) that opinion is expressed in a report that does not accompany the report containing the adverse opinion or disclaimer of opinion, and (b) the specific element does not constitute a major portion of the entity's complete set of financial statements or the specific element is not based on stockholders' equity or net income or equivalent.

3. A single statement constitutes a major portion of a complete set of financial statements, so the auditor should not express an unmodified opinion on the single financial statements when an adverse opinion or disclaimer of opinion is expressed on the complete set of financials.

4. **If the report on the complete set of financial statements includes an emphasis-of-matter or other-matter paragraph relevant to the single financial statement or the specific element**—The auditor should include a similar emphasis-of-matter or other-matter paragraph in the report on the single financial statement or specific element.

C. **Reporting on an Incomplete Presentation (that is otherwise in Accordance with GAAP)**— The auditor should include an emphasis-of-matter paragraph in the auditor's report that (1) states the purpose for which the presentation is prepared and refers to a note in the financial statements that describes the basis of presentation; and (2) indicates that the presentation is not intended to be a complete presentation.

V. Sample Report on a Single Financial Statement (Balance Sheet only)

Independent Auditor's Report

[Appropriate Addressee]

Opinion

We have audited the balance sheet of ABC Company as of December 31, 20X1, and the related notes (the financial statement).

In our opinion, the accompanying financial statement presents fairly, in all material respects, the financial position of ABC Company as of December 31, 20X1, in accordance with accounting principles generally accepted in the United States of America.

Basis for Opinion

We conducted our audit in accordance with auditing standards generally accepted in the United States of America (GAAS). Our responsibilities under those standards are further described in the Auditor's Responsibilities for the Audit of the Financial Statement section of our report. We are required to be independent of ABC Company and to meet our other ethical responsibilities, in accordance with the relevant ethical requirements relating to our audit. We believe that the audit evidence we have obtained is sufficient and appropriate to provide a basis for our audit opinion.

Responsibilities of Management for the Financial Statement

Management is responsible for the preparation and fair presentation of the financial statement in accordance with accounting principles generally accepted in the United States of America, and for the design, implementation, and maintenance of internal control relevant to the preparation and fair presentation of the financial statement that is free from material misstatement, whether due to fraud or error.

Auditor's Responsibilities for the Audit of the Financial Statement

Our objectives are to obtain reasonable assurance about whether the financial statement as a whole is free from material misstatement, whether due to fraud or error, and to issue an auditor's report that includes our opinion. Reasonable assurance is a high level of assurance but is not absolute assurance and therefore is not a guarantee that an audit conducted in accordance with GAAS will always detect a material misstatement when it exists. The risk of not detecting a material misstatement resulting from fraud is higher than for one resulting from error, as fraud may involve collusion, forgery, intentional omissions, misrepresentations, or the override of internal control. Misstatements are considered material if there is a substantial likelihood that, individually or in the aggregate, they would influence the judgment made by a reasonable user based on the financial statement.

In performing an audit in accordance with GAAS, we:

○ Exercise professional judgment and maintain professional skepticism throughout the audit.

○ Identify and assess the risks of material misstatement of the financial statement, whether due to fraud or error, and design and perform audit procedures responsive to those risks. Such procedures include examining, on a test basis, evidence regarding the amounts and disclosures in the financial statement.

○ Obtain an understanding of internal control relevant to the audit in order to design audit procedures that are appropriate in the circumstances, but not for the purpose of expressing an opinion on the effectiveness of ABC Company's internal control. Accordingly, no such opinion is expressed.

○ Evaluate the appropriateness of accounting policies used and the reasonableness of significant accounting estimates made by management, as well as evaluate the overall presentation of the financial statement.

○   Conclude whether, in our judgment, there are conditions or events, considered in the aggregate, that raise substantial doubt about ABC Company's ability to continue as a going concern for a reasonable period of time.

We are required to communicate with those charged with governance regarding, among other matters, the planned scope and timing of the audit, significant audit findings, and certain internal control-related matters that we identified during the audit.

[Signature of the auditor's firm]

[City and state where the auditor's report is issued]

[Date of the auditor's report]

Reporting on Compliance with Requirements in an F/S Audit

After studying this lesson, you should be able to:

1. Identify the auditor's responsibilities when engaged to report on an entity's compliance with contractual or regulatory requirements in connection with an audit of the entity's financial statements.

2. Identify the reporting language that would be appropriate when issuing a report on compliance with contractual or regulatory requirements in a combined report on the audited financial statement and on compliance issues.

I. **Relevant AICPA Guidance**—The relevant AICPA guidance is provided by AU 806, *Reporting on Compliance with Aspects of Contractual Agreements or Regulatory Requirements in Connection with Audited Financial Statements*. The standard states that the auditor's objective, when requested to report on an entity's compliance with aspects of contractual agreements or regulatory requirements in connection with the audit of financial statements, is to report appropriately on such matters.

II. **Reports on Compliance with Aspects of Contractual Agreements or Regulatory Requirements**

   A. The auditor should include a statement that nothing came to the auditor's attention to cause the auditor to believe that the entity failed to comply with the specified aspects of the contractual agreements or regulatory requirements only if: (1) the auditor did not identify any such noncompliance; (2) the auditor expressed an unmodified or qualified opinion on the financial statements involved; and (3) the covenants or regulatory requirements related to accounting matters that have been subjected to procedures applied in the audit.

   B. **When Instances of Noncompliance have been Identified**—The auditor's report on compliance should describe that noncompliance. Note: If the entity has obtained a waiver for such noncompliance, the auditor may include a statement that a waiver has been obtained; but, all instances of noncompliance must be described in the report, including those for which a waiver has been obtained.

   C. **When the Auditor has Issued an Adverse Opinion or Disclaimed an Opinion**—The auditor should issue a report on compliance only when instances of noncompliance were identified.

   D. The report on compliance should be in writing and should be presented either as a separate report or may be combined with the auditor's report on the financial statements.

   E. Include a paragraph conveying an *appropriate alert* that restricts the distribution of the report on compliance issues to the specified users.

III. **A Separate Report on Compliance with Aspects of Contractual Agreements When No Instances of Noncompliance Are Identified**

Independent Auditor's Report

(Appropriate Addressee)

We have audited, in accordance with auditing standards generally accepted in the United States of America, the financial statements of XYZ Company, which comprise the balance sheet as of December 31, 20X2, and the related statements of income, changes in stockholders' equity, and cash flows for the year then ended, and the related notes to the financial statements, and have issued our report thereon dated February 16, 20X3.

In connection with our audit, nothing came to our attention that caused us to believe that XYZ Company failed to comply with the terms, covenants, provisions, or conditions of sections XX to YY, inclusive, of the Indenture dated July 21, 20X0, with ABC Bank, insofar as they relate to accounting matters. However, our audit was not directed primarily toward obtaining knowledge of such noncompliance. Accordingly, had we performed additional procedures, other matters may have come to our attention regarding the Company's noncompliance with the above-referenced terms, covenants, provisions, or conditions of the Indenture, insofar as they relate to accounting matters.

This report is intended solely for the information and use of the board of directors and management of XYZ Company and ABC Bank and is not intended to be and should not be used by anyone other than these specified parties.

(Auditor's signature)

(Auditor's city and state)

(Date of the auditor's report)

IV. A Separate Report on Compliance with Aspects of Contractual Agreements When Instances of Noncompliance Are Identified

Independent Auditor's Report

(Appropriate Addressee)

We have audited, in accordance with auditing standards generally accepted in the United States of America, the financial statements of XYZ Company, which comprise the balance sheet as of December 31, 20X2, and the related statements of income, changes in stockholders' equity, and cash flows for the year then ended, and the related notes to the financial statements, and have issued our report thereon dated March 5, 20X3.

In connection with our audit, we noted that XYZ Company failed to comply with the Working Capital provision of section XX of the Loan Agreement dated March 1, 20X2, with ABC Bank. Our audit was not directed primarily toward obtaining knowledge as to whether XYZ Company failed to comply with the terms, covenants, provisions, or conditions of sections XX to YY, inclusive, of the Loan Agreement, insofar as they relate to accounting matters. Accordingly, had we performed additional procedures, other matters may have come to our attention regarding noncompliance with the above-referenced terms, covenants, provisions, or conditions of the Loan Agreement, insofar as they relate to accounting matters.

This report is intended solely for the information and use of the board of directors and management of XYZ Company and ABC Bank and is not intended to be and should not be used by anyone other than these specified parties.

(Auditor's signature)

(Auditor's city and state)

(Date of the auditor's report)

V. A Combined Report on Audited Financial Statements and Compliance with Aspects of Contractual Agreements When No Instances of Noncompliance Are Identified

Independent Auditor's Report

[Appropriate Addressee]

Opinion

We have audited the financial statements of ABC Company, which comprise the balance sheet as of December 31, 20X1, and the related statements of income, changes in stockholders' equity, and cash flows for the year then ended, and the related notes to the financial statements.

In our opinion, the accompanying financial statements present fairly, in all material respects, the financial position of ABC Company as of December 31, 20X1, and the results of its operations and its cash flows for the year then ended in accordance with accounting principles generally accepted in the United States of America.

Basis for Opinion

We conducted our audit in accordance with auditing standards generally accepted in the United States of America (GAAS). Our responsibilities under those standards are further described in the Auditor's Responsibilities for the Audit of the Financial Statements section of our report. We are required to be independent of ABC Company and to meet our other ethical responsibilities, in accordance with the relevant ethical requirements relating to our audit. We believe that the audit evidence we have obtained is sufficient and appropriate to provide a basis for our audit opinion.

Responsibilities of Management for the Financial Statements

Management is responsible for the preparation and fair presentation of the financial statements in accordance with accounting principles generally accepted in the United States of America, and for the design, implementation, and maintenance of internal control relevant to the preparation and fair presentation of financial statements that are free from material misstatement, whether due to fraud or error.

In preparing the financial statements, management is required to evaluate whether there are conditions or events, considered in the aggregate, that raise substantial doubt about ABC Company's ability to continue as a going concern for [*insert the time period set by the applicable financial reporting framework*].

Auditor's Responsibilities for the Audit of the Financial Statements

Our objectives are to obtain reasonable assurance about whether the financial statements as a whole are free from material misstatement, whether due to fraud or error, and to issue an auditor's report that includes our opinion. Reasonable assurance is a high level of assurance but is not absolute assurance and therefore is not a guarantee that an audit conducted in accordance with GAAS will always detect a material misstatement when it exists. The risk of not detecting a material misstatement resulting from fraud is higher than for one resulting from error, as fraud may involve collusion, forgery, intentional omissions, misrepresentations, or the override of internal control. Misstatements are considered material if there is a substantial likelihood that, individually or in the aggregate, they would influence the judgment made by a reasonable user based on the financial statements.

In performing an audit in accordance with GAAS, we:

o   Exercise professional judgment and maintain professional skepticism throughout the audit.

o   Identify and assess the risks of material misstatement of the financial statements, whether due to fraud or error, and design and perform audit procedures responsive to those risks. Such procedures include examining, on a test basis, evidence regarding the amounts and disclosures in the financial statements.

o   Obtain an understanding of internal control relevant to the audit in order to design audit procedures that are appropriate in the circumstances, but not for the purpose of expressing an opinion on the effectiveness of ABC Company's internal control. Accordingly, no such opinion is expressed.

o   Evaluate appropriateness of accounting policies used and the reasonableness of significant accounting estimates made by management, as well as evaluate the overall presentation of the financial statements.

o   Conclude whether, in our judgment, there are conditions or events, considered in the aggregate, that raise substantial doubt about ABC Company's ability to continue as a going concern for a reasonable period of time.

We are required to communicate with those charged with governance regarding, among other matters, the planned scope and timing of the audit, significant audit findings, and certain internal control-related matters that we identified during the audit.

Other Matter

In connection with our audit, nothing came to our attention that caused us to believe that ABC Company failed to comply with the terms, covenants, provisions, or conditions of sections XX to YY, inclusive, of the Indenture dated July 21, 20X0 with XYZ Bank, insofar as they relate to accounting matters. However, our audit was not directed primarily toward obtaining knowledge of such noncompliance. Accordingly, had we performed additional procedures, other matters may have come to our attention regarding the Company's noncompliance with the above-referenced terms, covenants, provisions, or conditions of the Indenture, insofar as they relate to accounting matters.

Restricted Use Relating to the Other Matter

The communication related to compliance with the aforementioned Indenture described in the Other Matter paragraph is intended solely for the information and use of the boards of directors and management of ABC Company and XYZ Bank and is not intended to be and should not be used by anyone other than these specified parties.

[*Signature of the auditor's firm*]

[*City and state where the auditor's report is issued*]

[*Date of the auditor's report*]

Service Organizations—User Auditors

After studying this lesson, you should be able to:

1. Identify the user auditor's responsibilities when auditing a *user entity* that has outsourced some degree of transaction processing to a *service organization*.

2. Understand the implications that a service auditor's report may have to the user auditor's report on the user entity's financial statement.

I. **Relevant AICPA Guidance**—The relevant AICPA guidance is provided by AU-C 402, *Audit Considerations Relating to an Entity Using a Service Organization*. The standard states that the user auditor's objectives, when the user entity uses the services of a service organization, are to: (1) obtain an understanding of the nature and significance of the services provided and their effect on the user entity's internal control relevant to the audit sufficient to assess the risks of material misstatement, and (2) design and perform audit procedures that are responsive to those risks.

Definitions

Complementary User Entity Controls: Controls that management of the service organization assumes, in the design of its service, will be implemented by user entities, and which, if necessary to achieve the control objectives stated in management's description of the service organization's system, are identified as such in that description.

Service Auditor: A practitioner who reports on controls at a service organization

Service Organization: An organization or segment of an organization that provides services to user entities that are relevant to those user entities' internal control over financial reporting.

Subservice Organization: A service organization used by another service organization to perform some of the services provided to user entities that are relevant to those user entities' internal control over financial reporting. (This SAS also applies to subservice organizations.)

Type 1 Report: Report on management's description of a service organization's system and the **suitability of the design** of controls.

Type 2 Report: Report on management's description of a service organization's system and the **suitability of the design and operating effectiveness of controls**.

User Auditor: An auditor who audits and reports on the financial statements of a user entity.

User Entity: An entity that uses a service organization and whose financial statements are being audited.

II. **User Auditor Responsibilities**

A. **Obtain an Understanding of the Services Provided by a Service Organization, Including Internal Controls**

1. The services of a service organization are relevant to the audit of a user entity when those services (and the controls over those services) affect the user entity's information system related to financial reporting and safeguarding assets.

2. The user auditor should evaluate the design and implementation of relevant controls at the user entity related to the service organization's services.

3. The user auditor should determine whether a sufficient understanding of the nature and significance of the service organization's services and their effect on the user entity's internal control relevant to the audit have been obtained to assess the risks of material misstatement.

4. **If the user auditor is unable to obtain a sufficient understanding from the user entity**—the user auditor should obtain that understanding by:

    a. Obtaining and reading the service auditor's Type 1 or Type 2 report;

    b. Contacting the service organization (through the user entity) to obtain specific information, or visiting the service organization and performing necessary procedures about relevant controls; *or*

    c. Using another auditor to perform procedures to provide the necessary information about controls at the service organization.

5. **Using a Type 1 or Type 2 Report to Support the User Auditor's Understanding**

    a. The user auditor should be satisfied about (1) the service auditor's professional competence and independence and (2) the standards that the service auditor followed in issuing the report.

    b. The user auditor should (1) evaluate whether the report provides sufficient appropriate evidence for understanding the user entity's relevant internal controls and (2) determine whether any *complementary user entity controls* identified by the service organization are relevant in assessing the risks of material misstatement.

B. **Responding to the Assessed Risks of Material Misstatement**

1. **Evidence at the user entity**—The user auditor should determine whether sufficient appropriate audit evidence is available at the user entity; and, if not, perform further audit procedures at the service organization.

2. **Tests of controls**—When the user auditor's risk assessment includes an expectation that controls at the service organization are operating effectively, the user auditor should obtain evidence about such operating effectiveness by either obtaining a Type 2 report or performing appropriate tests of controls at the service organization (or using another auditor to perform those tests of controls).

3. **A user entity may outsource some or all of its finance function to a service organization**—In that case, a significant portion of the audit evidence resides at the service organization. Necessary substantive procedures may be performed at the service organization by the user auditor or by the service auditor on the user auditor's behalf. The user auditor is still responsible for obtaining sufficient appropriate audit evidence.

C. **Inquiry about Fraud, Noncompliance, and Uncorrected Misstatements**—The user auditor should inquire of the user entity's management as to whether they are aware of any fraud, noncompliance with laws and regulations, or uncorrected misstatements at the service organization affecting the financial statements of the user entity.

III. **Reporting Issues to the User Auditor**

A. **Modified Opinion**

1. **Scope limitation**—If the user auditor is unable to obtain sufficient appropriate audit evidence about the services provided by the service organization relevant to the user entity's financial statements, the user auditor should modify the opinion for a scope limitation.

2. **Reference to service auditor**—The user auditor may refer to the service auditor in the user auditor's report containing a modified opinion if that reference would be relevant to understanding the user auditor's modification. The user auditor should indicate that such reference does not change the user auditor's responsibility for that opinion.

B. **Unmodified Opinion**—The user auditor should not refer to the service auditor in the user auditor's report containing an unmodified opinion. The user auditor is responsible for the opinion expressed, and *no division of responsibility* is permitted.

Service Organizations—Service Auditors

After studying this lesson, you should be able to:

1. Understand the service auditor's requirements under AICPA Attestation Standards when engaged to report on internal control over financial reporting at a service organization.

2. Identify the nature of the two different types of reports on internal control that a service auditor may be engaged to issue.

I. Relevant AICPA Guidance

The relevant AICPA guidance applicable to the service auditor is provided by AT-C 320, *Reporting on an Examination of Controls at a Service Organization*.

II. Distinction Between the Service Auditor and the User Auditor

Definitions

Service Auditor: Practitioner who reports on controls at a service organization.

User Auditor: An auditor who audits and reports on the financial statements of a user entity. (In other words, the auditor of an entity that has outsourced the processing of its transactions to the service organization for whom such processing may be more efficient; the user auditor must consider relevant internal controls of the service organization in auditing the financial statements of such a user entity.)

III. Applicability

A. **The Attestation Standards Apply to Internal Control Reporting by the Service Auditor**— The service auditor may be engaged to issue either of two types of reports on internal control applicable to a service organization.

1. **On the adequacy of the design of internal control** (Called a "Type 1 engagement" by AICPA Professional Standards)—Whether the control policies and procedures are suitably designed and placed in operation.

2. **On the operating effectiveness of internal control (based on tests of controls)** (called a "Type 2 engagement" by AICPA Professional Standards)—Whether the policies and procedures are suitably designed and working effectively to provide reasonable assurance of achieving the stated control objectives.

B. **Examples of Such Services** —Bank trust departments, mortgage banks that service mortgages for others, IT centers (e.g., processing checks for financial institutions or handling the details of subscriptions for magazine publishers).

C. Management of the service organization is required to provide the service auditor with a written assertion (1) about the fairness of the presentation of the description of the system and (2) about the suitability of the design; and, in a *Type 2 engagement* , management is also required to provide a written assertion (3) about the operating effectiveness of the controls. Those assertions should either accompany the service auditor's report or be included in the service organization's description of the system of internal control.

IV. Responsibilities of Service Auditors (Governed by SSAEs) —Must be independent of service organization, but not necessarily independent of all **user** entities.

A. **Procedures**

1. **Inquiry**—of service organization management and other personnel.

2. **Inspection**—of documentation (flowcharts, narrative memoranda, or questionnaires).

3. **Observation**—of internal control activities.

4. Obtainment of management's written representations as deemed appropriate.

5. **Performance of test of control**—If reporting on the operating effectiveness of internal control, the service auditor must perform appropriate **tests of controls**.

B. **Reporting on the Adequacy of the Design of Internal Control** (i.e., reporting on the internal control policies and procedures placed in operation, which are also known as a "Type 1" engagement)—the service auditor's report ordinarily consists of the following sections:

1. **Scope**—Identify the nature of the engagement and the **specific date** involved.

2. **Service organization's responsibilities**

3. **Service auditor's responsibilities**—Reference the attestation standards established by the AICPA and describe an examination; also, **disclaim an opinion on operating effectiveness**

4. **Inherent limitations of internal control**

5. **Opinion**—(1) that the description fairly presents the system that was designed and implemented as of the specific date; and (2) that the controls related to the stated control objectives were suitably designed to provide reasonable assurance that the control objectives would be achieved if the controls operated effectively as of the specific date.

6. **Restricted use** —Distribution should be restricted to the service organization, user entities, and the user entities' independent auditors.

C. **Reporting on the operating effectiveness of internal control** (i.e., reporting on the policies and procedures placed in operation **and** on their operating effectiveness, which are also known as a "Type 2" engagement)—the service auditor's report ordinarily consists of the following sections:

1. **Scope**—Identify the nature of the engagement and the period involved.

2. **Service organization's responsibilities**

3. **Service auditor's responsibilities**—Reference the attestation standards established by the AICPA and describe an examination.

4. **Inherent limitations of internal control**

5. **Opinion**—(1) that the description fairly presents the system that was designed and implemented throughout the period; (2) that the controls related to the stated control objectives were suitably designed to provide reasonable assurance that the control objectives would be achieved if the controls operated effectively throughout the period; and (3) that the controls tested operated effectively throughout the period.

6. **Description of tests of controls**—Reference the pages of the service auditor's report identifying the specific controls tested and the nature, timing, and results of those tests.

7. **Restricted use** —Distribution should be restricted to the service organization, user entities, and the user entities' independent auditors.

> **Note**
> *Management specifies the control objectives to be tested—Should cover a reporting period of **at least six months.***

V. **System and Organization Control Reports**—The AICPA has developed a "menu" of assurance-related service opportunities for CPAs under the heading of **System and Organization Control Reports** (called **SOC** Reports):

A variety of resources, including the "SOC for Service Organizations Toolkit" is available on the AICPA's website at: http://www.aicpa.org/interestareas/frc/assuranceadvisoryservices/pages/soctoolkit_firms.aspx

SOC 1 Report:

"To give the auditor of a user entity's financial statements information about controls at a service organization that may be relevant to a user entity's internal control over financial reporting. A Type 2 SOC 1 report includes a detailed description of tests of controls performed by the CPA and results of the tests." [Such a report must be restricted to specified users.]

Note

The service auditor's report under AT-C 320 is an SOC 1 report.

SOC 2 Report:

"To give management of a service organization, user entities and others a report about controls at a service organization relevant to the security, availability or processing integrity of the service organization's system, or the confidentiality and privacy of the data processed by that system. A Type 2 SOC 2 report includes a detailed description of tests of controls performed by the CPA and results of the tests." [Such a report must be restricted to specified users.]

SOC 3 Report:

"To give users and interested parties a report about controls at the service organization related to security, availability, processing integrity, confidentiality or privacy. SOC 3 reports are a short-form report (i.e., no description of tests of controls and results) and may be used in a service organization's marketing efforts." [This is the only SOC report that is appropriate for "general use; the others must be restricted to specified users.]

Comfort Letters

After studying this lesson, you should be able to:

1. Understand the purpose of *comfort letters* provided by accountants to underwriters and other financial intermediaries in connection with an entity's stock issuance.

2. Understand the basic structure of comfort letters and the nature of the assurance specifically provided by the entity's accountants/auditors.

I. **Relevant AICPA Guidance**—The relevant AICPA guidance is provided by AU 920: *Letters for Underwriters and Certain Other Requesting Parties*. The standard states that the auditor's objectives, when engaged to issue a letter to a requesting party in connection with a nonissuer entity's financial statements included in a securities offering, are to appropriately address: (1) the acceptance of the engagement and the scope of services, and (2) issue a letter with the appropriate form and content.

II. **Purpose**—Section 11 of the Securities Act of 1933 (the Act) provides for liability to underwriters and certain others (such as a broker-dealer or a financial intermediary) when there is a material omission or misstatement to a registration statement.

   A. A c*omfort letter* from the entity's auditor may help underwriters or others having a statutory due diligence defense under Section 11 of the Act to establish a *reasonable investigation* (i.e., *due diligence*).

   B. Comfort letters are not required and are not filed with the SEC.

   C. The scope is specified in the underwriting agreement (between the entity and the underwriters or others); a copy of the agreement should be given to the auditor. The auditor should obtain from the requesting party either (1) a written opinion from legal counsel that the requesting party has a statutory due diligence defense under Section 11 of the 1933 Act, or (2) an appropriate representation letter that meets certain technical requirements. (Without that, the auditor should not provide negative assurance on the financial statements or on any of the requested matters.)

   D. The auditor should meet with the underwriters (or other requesting parties) to establish their specific needs and give them a *draft* of the expected comfort letter in advance to avoid misunderstandings.

   E. The auditor should avoid implying that the procedures performed were sufficient for the underwriter's (or other parties') purposes, since that is a legal determination.

III. **A Typical Comfort Letter**—Usually consists of the following:

   A. An introductory paragraph that identifies the particular registration statement and the audited financial statements and schedules with which the auditor is associated

   B. A statement as to the auditor's independences

   C. **Positive Expression of Opinion**—Whether the **audited** financial statements and schedules **comply as to form** with the accounting requirements of the Act and the SEC (if a review under GAAS has been performed); if a review of the interim information has not been performed, the auditor is limited to reporting the procedures performed along with the findings

   D. **Negative Assurance**—Whether the **unaudited** condensed interim financial information complies as to form with the requirements of the Act and the SEC

   E. **Negative Assurance**—Whether any material modifications should be made to the unaudited condensed consolidated financial statements

   F. **Negative Assurance**—Whether there has been any change during a specified period in capital stock, increase in long-term debt, or any decrease in other specified financial statement items

G. A concluding paragraph that limits the distribution of the comfort letter to specified parties for the purposes stated

IV. Other Reporting Considerations

A. Dating of the Letter—A comfort letter is usually dated on or shortly before the effective date of the registration; the letter should state that the procedures identified in the letter did not cover the period after the cut-off date (to which the procedures apply) to the date of the letter.

B. Addressee—A comfort letter should be addressed only to the entity, named underwriters, broker-dealer, or the financial intermediary related to the securities.

C. Comment on the Previously Audited Financial Statements Referred to in the Registration Statement

1. Give **positive assurance** (opinion) as to whether the audited financial statements comply with the **form** and content required by the SEC.

2. Use the following language: "In our opinion (include the phrase 'except as disclosed in the registration statement,' if applicable) the consolidated financial statements and financial statement schedules audited by us and included in the registration statement comply as to form in all material respects with the applicable accounting requirements of the 1933 Act and the related rules and regulations adopted by the SEC."

D. Commenting on the Unaudited Financial Statements, Condensed Interim Financial Information, or Capsule Financial Information—The auditor should obtain an understanding of internal control over financial reporting.

1. **Unaudited financial statements and schedules and unaudited condensed interim financial information** —The auditor may express negative assurance that interim information complies as to form with SEC requirements, if the auditor has performed a review of the interim financial information. (If a review of the interim financial information has not been performed, the auditor is limited to reporting the procedures performed and the findings.)

2. **Capsule financial information** —This term refers to unaudited summarized interim information in narrative or tabular form. The auditor is permitted to express negative assurance on capsule financial information if (a) the auditor has appropriate knowledge of the entity's financial reporting practices; and (b) the auditor conducted an audit of the annual financial statements involved (or conducted a review of the interim financial information involved). Otherwise, the auditor is limited to reporting the procedures performed along with the findings.

E. Commenting on Financial Forecasts; Subsequent Changes; or Tables, Statistics, and Other Financial Information

1. **Forecasts**—The comfort letter should not provide negative assurance on the results of any procedures performed with respect to financial forecasts.

2. **Subsequent changes** —Comments usually relate to any changes in capital stock, increase in long-term debt, or decreases in other specified financial statement items (subsequent to the latest financial statements included in the registration statement).

3. The comfort letter may express negative assurance regarding "subsequent changes" within 135 days of the most recent period for which an audit or review was performed. The procedures usually are limited to reading the minutes and making inquiries of management (and obtaining the appropriate written representations). (After 135 days from the most recent period for which the auditor has performed an audit or review, the auditor is limited to reporting the procedures performed along with the findings.)

4. **Tables, statistics, and other financial information**—For the auditor to comment on tables, statistics, and other financial information in the comfort letter, there are several requirements: (a) the auditor must have conducted an audit of the entity's financial statements for a period including (or immediately preceding) the unaudited period (or have

completed an audit for a later period); (b) the auditor must have obtained an understanding of the entity's internal control over financial reporting; (c) the information must be expressed in dollars (or percentages based on dollars); and (d) the information must be derived from the accounting records subject to the entity's internal control over financial reporting. The auditor's comments should clearly identify the specific information involved, and report the procedures performed and the findings.

F.   A comfort letter should state that the auditor make no representation involving legal interpretations.

Typical Comfort Letter for a 1933 Act Offering
June 28, 20X6

[Addressee]

Dear Ladies and Gentlemen:

We have audited the consolidated financial statements of the Nonissuer Company, Inc. (the company) and subsidiaries, which comprise the consolidated balance sheets as of December 31, 20X5 and 20X4, and the related consolidated statements of income, changes in stockholders' equity, and cash flows for each of the years in the three-year period ended December 31, 20X5, and the related notes to the consolidated financial statements, all included in The Issuer Company's (the registrant) registration statement (no. 33-00000) on Form S-1 filed by the registrant under the Securities Act of 1933 (the Act); our report with respect thereto is also included in that registration statement. The registration statement, as amended on June 28, 20X6, is herein referred to as the registration statement.

In connection with the registration statement—

1.   We are independent certified public accountants with respect to the company within the meaning of the 1933 Act and the applicable rules and regulations thereunder adopted by the SEC.

2.   In our opinion [include the phrase "except as disclosed in the registration statement" if applicable], the consolidated financial statements audited by us and included in the registration statement comply as to form in all material respects with the applicable accounting requirements of the Act and the related rules and regulations adopted by the SEC.

3.   We have not audited any financial statements of the company as of any date or for any period subsequent to December 31, 20X5; although, we have conducted an audit for the year ended December 31, 20X5, the purpose (and, therefore, the scope) of the audit was to enable us to express our opinion on the consolidated financial statements as of December 31, 20X5, and for the year then ended, but not on the financial statements for any interim period within that year. Therefore, we are unable to and do not express any opinion on the unaudited condensed consolidated balance sheet as of March 31, 20X6, and the unaudited condensed consolidated statements of income, stockholders' equity, and cash flows for the three-month periods ended March 31, 20X6 and 20X5, included in the registration statement, or on the financial position, results of operations, or cash flows as of any date or for any period subsequent to December 31, 20X5.

4.   For purposes of this letter we have read the 20X6 minutes of meetings of the stockholders, the board of directors, and [include other appropriate committees, if any] of the company and its subsidiaries as set forth in the minute books at June 23, 20X6, officials of the company having advised us that the minutes of all such meetings through that date were set forth therein and having discussed with us the unapproved minutes of meetings held on [dates]; we have carried out other procedures to June 23, 20X6, as follows (our work did not extend to the period from June 24, 20X6 to June 28, 20X6, inclusive):

   a.   With respect to the three-month periods ended March 31, 20X6 and 20X5, we have—

      i.   Performed the procedures specified for a review in accordance with auditing standards generally accepted in the United States of America applicable to reviews of interim financial information, on the unaudited condensed consolidated balance sheet as of March 31, 20X6, and the unaudited condensed consolidated statements of income, stockholders' equity, and cash flows for the three-month periods ended March 31, 20X6 and 20X5, included in the registration statement.

ii. Inquired of certain officials of the company who have responsibility for financial and accounting matters whether the unaudited condensed consolidated financial statements referred to in a(i) comply as to form in all material respects with the applicable accounting requirements of the Act and the related rules and regulations adopted by the SEC.

b. With respect to the period from April 1, 20X6 to May 31, 20X6, we have—

i. Read the unaudited consolidated financial information of the company and subsidiaries for April and May of both 20X5 and 20X6 furnished to us by the company, officials of the company having advised us that no financial statements as of any date or for any period subsequent to May 31, 20X6, were available. (If applicable: The financial information for April and May of both 20X5 and 20X6 is incomplete in that it omits the statements of cash flows and other disclosures.)

ii. Inquired of certain officials of the company who have responsibility for financial and accounting matters whether the unaudited consolidated financial information referred to in b(i) is stated on a basis substantially consistent with that of the audited consolidated financial statements included in the registration statement.

The foregoing procedures do not constitute an audit conducted in accordance with generally accepted auditing standards. Also, they would not necessarily reveal matters of significance with respect to the comments in the following paragraph. Accordingly, we make no representations regarding the sufficiency of the foregoing procedures for your purposes.

5. Nothing came to our attention as a result of the foregoing procedures, however, that caused us to believe that—

a.

i. Any material modifications should be made to the unaudited condensed consolidated financial statements described in 4a(i), included in the registration statement, for them to be in conformity with generally accepted accounting principles.

ii. The unaudited condensed consolidated financial statements described in 4a(i) do not comply as to form in all material respects with the applicable accounting requirements of the Act and the related rules and regulations adopted by the SEC.

b.

i. At May 31, 20X6, there was any change in the capital stock, increase in long-term debt, or decrease in consolidated net current assets or stockholders' equity of the consolidated companies as compared with amounts shown in the March 31, 20X6 unaudited condensed consolidated balance sheet included in the registration statement, or

ii. for the period from April 1, 20X6 to May 31, 20X6, there were any decreases, as compared to the corresponding period in the preceding year, in consolidated net sales or in income from continuing operations or of net income, except in all instances for changes, increases, or decreases that the registration statement discloses have occurred or may occur.

6. As mentioned in 4b, company officials have advised us that no consolidated financial statements as of any date or for any period subsequent to May 31, 20X6, are available; accordingly, the procedures carried out by us with respect to changes in financial statements items after May 31, 20X6, have, of necessity, been even more limited than those with respect to the periods referred to in 4. We have inquired of certain officials of the company who have responsibility for financial

and accounting matters whether (a) at June 23, 20X6, there was any change in the capital stock, increase in long-term debt, or any decreases in consolidated net current assets or stockholders' equity of the consolidated companies as compared with amounts shown in the March 31, 20X6, unaudited condensed consolidated balance sheet included in the registration statement, or (b) for the period from April 1, 20X6 to June 23, 20X6, there were any decreases as compared with the corresponding period in the preceding year, in consolidated net sales or in income from continuing operations or of net income. On the basis of these inquiries and our reading of the minutes as described in 4, nothing came to our attention that caused us to believe that there was any such change, increase, or decrease, except in all instances for changes, increases, or decreases that the registration statement discloses have occurred or may occur.

7. This letter is solely for the information of the addressees and to assist the underwriters in conducting and documenting their investigation of the affairs of the company in connection with the offering of the securities covered by the registration statement, and it is not to be used, circulated, quoted, or otherwise referred to within or without the underwriting group for any other purpose, including but not limited to the registration, purchase, or sale of securities, nor is it to be filed with or referred to in whole or in part in the registration statement or any other document, except that reference may be made to it in the underwriting agreement or in any list of closing documents pertaining to the offering of the securities covered by the registration statement.

Government Auditing Standards

> **After studying this lesson, you should be able to:**
>
> 1. Understand the distinction between "GAAS" and "GAGAS" (issued by the U.S. Government Accountability Office) and the additional responsibilities resulting from the Government Auditing Standards.
>
> 2. Understand the circumstances in which the Single Audit Act is applicable.

I. **Government Auditing Standards**—Government Auditing Standards (also known as Generally Accepted Government Auditing Standards or GAGAS) are issued by the U.S. Government Accountability Office (in GAO's Yellow Book) under the authority of the Comptroller General of the United States.

A. GAGAS must be followed when required by applicable law, regulation, or agreement. These standards may apply to a variety of different governmental engagements, including financial audits, performance audits, and attestation engagements.

B. GAO's 2018 edition of the Yellow Book made a number of noteworthy changes relative to the 2011 edition.

1. Adopted a new format that distinguishes professional requirements (consisting of unconditional requirements and presumptively mandatory requirements) from the related application guidance.

2. Updated the independence guidance, which includes adding a threats and safeguards framework for evaluating independence issues.

3. Updated the internal control guidance (and clarified connections to GAO's "Green Book" dealing with Standards for Internal Control in the Federal Government), particularly regarding performance audits.

4. Revised applicable peer review requirements for audit organizations performing audit engagements under GAGAS.

C. **Summary of the Primary Reporting Differences Associated with GAGAS (Relative to Engagements under GAAS):**

1. **Additional reporting requirements regarding internal control**—Government Auditing Standards require a written report on internal control in every financial audit under GAGAS. This includes commentary about the auditor's understanding of internal control for planning purposes and the assessment of control risk, as well as the scope of the auditor's testing of internal control. When the auditor communicates *significant deficiencies*, the auditor should also obtain a response from officials of the entity and include a copy of management's written response (or a summary of management's oral response) in the auditor's report.

2. **Additional reporting requirements regarding compliance with applicable laws and regulations**—Government Auditing Standards require a written report on compliance with applicable laws and regulations. This report should distinguish between (a) *general requirements* that apply to all federal financial programs; and (b) *specific requirements* that apply to a particular program by a specific statutory (legislative) requirement.

a. The auditor should design the audit to provide reasonable assurance of detecting instances of noncompliance that have a "material and direct effect" on the entity's financial statements. (Similarly, the auditor should design the audit to provide reasonable assurance of detecting fraud that is material to the entity's financial statements.)

b. Management is responsible for identifying laws and regulations that have a direct and material effect on the entity's financial statements, and it is common for auditors to obtain written representations from management that all such laws and regulations have been appropriately identified.

c. The auditor's report on compliance should comment on the scope of the auditor's testing of the entity's compliance with applicable laws and regulations.

d. The auditor's report on compliance should also include (1) any known instances of fraud that are viewed as more than inconsequential; (2) any known instances of illegal acts that are viewed as more than inconsequential; (3) other identified violations of contracts or grants that are material; and (4) any known instances of "abuse" that are material.

e. Auditors may have a duty to report instances of fraud, illegal acts, or abuse to authorities outside the entity (such as a federal inspector general, etc.) when (1) management fails to meet its legal requirements to report such matters; or (2) when management fails to appropriately respond to identified instances of fraud, illegal acts, or abuse.

3. Additional reporting requirements regarding illegal acts—Government Auditing Standards also require the auditor to report any known instances of illegal acts that could result in **criminal prosecution**.

II. Single Audit Act of 1984, as Amended—The Single Audit Act is applicable to state and local governmental entities that have expenditures of federal assistance (grants) aggregating at least $750,000 in a given year. It imposes certain requirements on such entities and their auditors that go beyond GAAS and even GAGAS.

A. Management's Responsibilities under the Single Audit Act Include the Following:

1. Prepare the financial statements along with a schedule of expenditures of federal assistance.

2. Prepare a *corrective action plan* to respond to any current-year audit findings.

3. Submit certain necessary forms, including the audit report to the designated Federal Audit Clearinghouse on a timely basis.

B. The Auditor's Responsibilities under the Single Audit Act Include the Following:

1. The audit should be conducted in accordance with GAGAS.

2. The auditor should identify each *major program* to be audited based on appropriate risk assessment considerations (and materiality should be determined separately for each major program).

3. The auditor should evaluate whether the financial statements and schedule of expenditures of federal assistance are fairly presented using appropriate criteria.

4. The auditor should obtain an appropriate understanding of internal control over the federal assistance programs and perform testing of internal control over designated major programs.

5. The auditor should evaluate the entity's compliance with applicable laws, regulations, or other requirements having a direct and material effect on designated major programs.

6. The auditor should report any identified audit findings, including material instances of noncompliance with applicable laws, regulations, or other requirements involving designated major programs; identified instances of fraud; and significant deficiencies in internal controls over designated major programs.

C. Summary Comments Regarding the Single Audit Act

1. Efficiency—A single coordinated audit of the aggregate federal financial assistance provided to a state or local governmental entity (with emphasis on the entity's major programs) is intended to result in greater efficiency compared to the alternative, which would be having multiple audits of the entity conducted on a grant-by-grant basis.

2. **Added requirements**—A single coordinated audit of the aggregate federal financial assistance involves more than just a financial statement audit. Additional testing of internal control is required for major programs, and additional testing is also required for major programs regarding the entity's compliance with applicable laws, regulations, or other requirements applicable to major programs.

3. **Multiple reports**—The auditor should issue reports on (a) the fairness of the entity's financial statements (and schedule of expenditures of federal assistance); (b) internal control over financial reporting (with emphasis on major programs); and (c) compliance with applicable laws, regulations, and other requirements. If audit findings were identified, the auditor should also prepare a "Schedule of Findings and Questioned Costs."

Compliance Audits

After studying this lesson, you should be able to:

1. Understand the circumstances to which AICPA auditing standards, entitled *Compliance Audits,* apply, along with the auditor's responsibilities.

2. Know the structure and content of an auditor's combined report on an entity's compliance and its internal control over compliance.

I. **Relevant AICPA Guidance**—The relevant AICPA clarified guidance is provided by AU 935, *Compliance Audits*. The standard states that the auditor's objectives are to (1) obtain sufficient appropriate audit evidence to form an opinion and report whether the entity complied in all material respects with applicable compliance requirements (at the level specified in the governmental audit requirement), and (2) identify audit and reporting requirements specified in the governmental audit requirements that are supplementary to GAAS and Government Auditing Standards and perform procedures to address those requirements.

II. **Applicability**—When an auditor is engaged to perform a compliance audit in accordance with (1) generally accepted auditing standards (GAAS), (2) Government Auditing Standards (also called Generally Accepted Government Auditing Standards (GAGAS) from GAO's Yellow Book issued under the authority of the Comptroller General of the United States), and (3) a governmental audit requirement or program-specific audit guide.

   A. This SAS applies to the compliance audit, but not to the financial statement audit part of such an engagement.

   B. **Definition of Governmental Audit Requirement**— "A governmental requirement established by law, regulation, rule, or provision of contracts or grant agreements requiring that an entity undergo an audit of its compliance with applicable compliance requirements related to one or more government programs that the entity administers."

III. **Compliance Auditing—Requirements and Guidance**

   A. **This SAS Incorporated the AICPA's Risk Assessment Standards**

      1. The auditor should perform risk assessment procedures to obtain an understanding of the applicable compliance requirements and internal controls over compliance—the nature and extent of the risk assessment procedures may vary with the circumstances (such as the complexity of the compliance requirements and the depth of the auditor's knowledge of internal control over compliance).

      2. The auditor should assess the risks of material noncompliance (whether due to fraud or error) for each applicable compliance requirement and consider whether any of those are *pervasive* to compliance.

      3. The auditor should perform further audit procedures in response to the assessed risks, such as develop an overall response to any risks that are pervasive to the entity's compliance; perform appropriate tests of details; and perform tests of controls when there is an expectation of operating effectiveness or when required to do so. (Note that an example of a *pervasive* risk of noncompliance would be financial difficulty that increases the risk that grant funds will be used for unauthorized purposes.)

   B. **Supplementary Audit Requirements**—The auditor should identify *supplementary audit requirements* (beyond GAAS and GAGAS) specified in the governmental audit requirement.

      1. Some governmental audit requirements specifically identify the applicable compliance requirements, whereas others provide a framework for the auditor to determine the applicable compliance requirements.

2. Historically, the Office of Management and Budget (OMB) Circular A-133, *Audits of States, Local Governments and Non-Profit Organizations*, provided a framework (Compliance Supplement) to determine the compliance requirements. [Note: That OMB Circular A-133 was combined along with several other OMB circulars into a "super circular" now associated with Title 2 U.S. Code of Federal Regulations (CFR) Part 200, Uniform Administrative Requirements, Cost Principles, and Audit Requirements for Federal Awards (known as the Uniform Guidance)].

3. Examples of supplementary audit requirements in the Uniform Guidance include requirements for the auditor to (a) perform specified procedures to identify major programs and (b) follow up prior audit findings.

C. Written Representations—The auditor should obtain written representations from management tailored to the entity and the governmental audit requirement.

D. Subsequent Events—The auditor should perform procedures up to the date of the auditor's report to identify subsequent events related to the entity's compliance (e.g., reports from grantors regarding noncompliance or information about noncompliance obtained through other professional engagements for the entity); an example of a subsequent event warranting disclosure is the discovery of noncompliance causing the grantor to stop the funding.

E. Evaluating the Evidence and Forming an Opinion—Most governmental audit requirements specify that the auditor's opinion on compliance is at the *program* level (and materiality is usually determined based on the program taken as a whole).

1. The auditor should consider *likely questioned costs* (not just *known questioned costs*) and other noncompliance that may not result in questioned costs.

2. The auditor may include a variety of factors in assessing the risk of noncompliance, including: (a) the complexity of the compliance requirements; (b) how long the entity has been subject to those compliance requirements; (c) the degree of judgment involved in compliance; and (d) the entity's compliance in prior years.

F. Reporting—The auditor may issue (1) a separate report on compliance only; (2) a combined report on compliance and on internal control over compliance; or (3) a separate report on internal control over compliance. [*See the sample combined report below.*]

G. Documentation—The auditor should document the risk assessment procedures performed, responses to the assessed risks of material noncompliance, the basis for materiality levels, and the auditor's compliance with applicable *supplementary audit requirements*.

H. Communication—The auditor should communicate the following matters with those charged with governance: the auditor's responsibilities under GAAS, GAGAS, and the governmental audit requirements; an overview of the planned scope and timing of the compliance audit; and any significant findings.

I. Reissuance of the Compliance Report—When reissuing a compliance report, the auditor should add an other-matter paragraph describing why the report is being reissued and noting any changes from the previously issued report; if additional audit procedures are performed, the auditor's report date should be updated.

IV. Sample (Unmodified) Combined Report on Compliance with Applicable Requirements and Internal Control Over Compliance

Independent Auditor's Report

[*Appropriate Addressee*]

Report on Compliance

Opinion on [*indicate the reporting level pursuant to governmental audit requirements*]

We have audited Example Entity's compliance with the [*identify the applicable compliance requirements or refer to the document that describes the applicable compliance requirements*] applicable to Example Entity's [*identify the government program(s) audited or refer to a separate schedule that identifies the program(s)*] for the year ended June 30, 20X1.

In our opinion, Example Entity complied, in all material respects, with the compliance requirements referred to above that are applicable to [*indicate the reporting level pursuant to governmental audit requirement*] for the year ended June 30, 20X1.

Basis for Opinion

We conducted our audit of compliance in accordance with auditing standards generally accepted in the United States of America (GAAS); the standards applicable to financial audits contained in Government Auditing Standards (Government Auditing Standards) issued by the Comptroller General of the Comptroller General of the United States; and [*insert the name of the governmental audit requirement or program-specific audit guide*]. Our responsibilities under those standards and [*insert the name of the governmental audit requirement or program-specific audit guide*] are further described in the Auditor's Responsibilities for the Audit of Compliance section of our report.

We are required to be independent of Example Entity and to meet our other ethical responsibilities, in accordance with relevant ethical requirements relating to our audit. We believe the audit evidence we have obtained is sufficient and appropriate to provide a basis for our opinion. Our audit does not provide a legal determination of Example Entity's compliance with the compliance requirements referred to above.

Responsibilities of Management for Compliance

Management is responsible for compliance with the requirements referred to above and for the design, implementation, and maintenance of effective internal control over compliance with the requirements of laws, statutes, regulations, rules, and provisions of contracts or grant agreements applicable to the Example Entity's government programs.

Auditor's Responsibilities for the Audit of Compliance

Our objectives are to obtain reasonable assurance about whether material noncompliance with the compliance requirements referred to above occurred, whether due to fraud or error, and express an opinion on Example Entity's compliance based on our audit. Reasonable assurance is a high level of assurance but is not absolute assurance and therefore is not a guarantee that an audit conducted in accordance with GAAS, Government Auditing Standards, and [*insert the name of the governmental audit requirement or program-specific audit guide*] will always detect material noncompliance when it exists. The risk of not detecting material noncompliance resulting from fraud is higher than for that resulting from error, as fraud may involve collusion, forgery, intentional omissions, misrepresentations, or the override of internal control. Noncompliance with the compliance requirements referred to above is considered material if there is a substantial likelihood that, individually or in the aggregate, it would influence the judgment made by a reasonable user of the report on compliance about Example Entity's compliance with the requirements of the government program as a whole.

In performing an audit in accordance with GAAS, Government Auditing Standards, and [*insert the name of the governmental audit requirement or program-specific audit guide*], we:

- Exercise professional judgment and maintain professional skepticism throughout the audit.

- Identify and assess the risks of material noncompliance, whether due to fraud or error, and design and perform audit procedures responsive to those risks. Such procedures include examining, on a test basis, evidence regarding Example Entity's compliance with the compliance requirements referred to above and performing such other procedures as we considered necessary in the circumstances.

- Obtain an understanding of Example Entity's internal control over compliance relevant to the audit in order to design audit procedures that are appropriate in the circumstances and to test and report on internal control over compliance in accordance with [*insert the name of the governmental audit requirement or program-specific audit guide*], but not for the purpose of expressing an opinion on the effectiveness of Example Entity's internal control over compliance. Accordingly, no such opinion is expressed.

We are required to communicate with those charged with governance regarding, among other matters, the planned scope and timing of the audit and any significant deficiencies and material weaknesses in internal control over compliance that we identified during the audit.

Report on Internal Control Over Compliance

A deficiency in internal control over compliance exists when the design or operation of a control over compliance does not allow management or employees, in the normal course of performing their assigned functions, to prevent, or detect and correct, noncompliance on a timely basis. A material weakness in internal control over compliance is a deficiency, or combination of deficiencies, in internal control over compliance, such that there is a reasonable possibility that material noncompliance with a compliance requirement will not be prevented, or detected and corrected, on a timely basis. A significant deficiency in internal control over compliance is a deficiency, or a combination of deficiencies, in internal control over compliance that is less severe than a material weakness in internal control over compliance, yet important enough to merit attention by those charged with governance.

Our consideration of internal control over compliance was for the limited purpose described in the Auditor's Responsibilities for the Audit of Compliance section above and was not designed to identify all deficiencies in internal control over compliance that might be material weaknesses or significant deficiencies in internal control over compliance. Given these limitations, during our audit we did not identify any deficiencies in internal control over compliance that we consider to be material weaknesses, as defined above. However, material weaknesses or significant deficiencies in internal control over compliance may exist that have not been identified.

Our audit was not designed for the purpose of expressing an opinion on the effectiveness of internal control over compliance. Accordingly, no such opinion is expressed.

The purpose of this report on internal control over compliance is solely to describe the scope of our testing of internal control over compliance and the results of that testing based on the [*insert the name of the governmental audit requirement or program-specific audit guide*]. Accordingly, this report is not suitable for any other purpose.

[Signature of the auditor's firm]

[City and state where the auditor's report is issued]

[Date of the auditor's report]

SSARSs—General Principles

The Clarified SSARSs and General Principles

The Statements on Standards for Accounting and Review Services (SSARS) are issued by the AICPA's Accounting and Review Services Committee (ARSC) and are applicable to certain financial statement-related services that a CPA may provide to nonissuers. In October, 2014, the ARSC replaced substantially all of the then-existing SSARSs with *clarified* SSARSs, similar to what the Auditing Standards Board previously did with the Statements on Auditing Standards. The purpose of this project was to make the clarified SSARSs easier to read and understand and, therefore, to improve the application of these standards in practice.

Accordingly, the ARSC adopted clarity drafting conventions, such as the following: (1) specified objectives for each of the clarified sections of the AR-C (i.e., the clarified SSARS sections); (2) included a section on definitions, as applicable, in each AR-C; (3) separated the professional *requirements* from the *application and other explanatory material* parts of each AR-C; and (4) adopted formatting techniques (e.g., using bullet lists) to improve the flow and readability of each AR-C.

The clarified SSARSs were issued as SSARS No. 21, *Statements on Standards for Accounting and Review Services: Clarification and Recodification* . It is comprised of four primary sections:

- Section 60, General Principles for Engagements Performed in Accordance with [SSARS]

- Section 70, Preparation of Financial Statements

- Section 80, Compilation Engagements

- Section 90, Review of Financial Statements

Historically, the SSARSs involved two types of engagements: (1) reviews; and (2) compilations. The clarified SSARSs added a third type of engagement: engagements to prepare financial statements for a client without issuing an accompanying report.

Compliance with the SSARSs is enforceable under the AICPA Code of Professional Conduct, including the Rule of Conduct dealing with *Compliance with Standards*.

I. **Requirements**—The General Principles retained the two categories of requirements for SSARSs: (1) *unconditional* and *presumptively mandatory*.

    A. **Unconditional Requirements**—Indicated by the word **must**, the accountant is required to comply with such a requirement without exception whenever the requirement is relevant.

    B. **Presumptively Mandatory Requirements**—Indicated by the word **should**, the accountant is expected to comply with such a requirement, except in rare circumstances.

        1. Noncompliance is allowed if a required procedure would be ineffective in achieving the intent of the requirement for a specific engagement.

2. When not complying with such a requirement, the accountant should perform alternative procedures to achieve the intent of the presumptively mandatory requirement.

C. **Application and Other Explanatory Material (Including Appendices of the SSARSs)**—These are not requirements and are presented separately within the SSARSs. Indicated by the words **may, might**, or **could**, they may explain what a requirement means or provide examples of appropriate procedures.

II. The Role of Interpretive and Other Publications

A. **Interpretive Publications**—The accountant should consider the guidance of applicable interpretive publications in performing the engagement. These are recommendations on the application of the SSARSs in particular circumstances as issued by ARSC after ARSC members have had the opportunity to comment on the proposed interpretations.

> **Definition**
> *Interpretive Publications*: "Interpretations of SSARSs; exhibits to SSARSs; AICPA Guide, *Compilation and Review Engagements*; guidance on preparation, compilation, and review engagements included in AICPA Audit and Accounting Guides; and AICPA Statements of Position, to the extent that those statements are applicable to such engagements."

B. **Other Preparation, Compilation and Review Publications**—The accountant should evaluate the relevance and appropriateness of such guidance to the engagement.

> **Definition**
> *Other Preparation, Compilation, and Review Publications*: "Publications other than interpretive publications."

1. These other publications may be useful in understanding the SSARSs, but they have no authoritative status and the accountant is not required to be aware of all such other publications.

2. Other publications issued by the AICPA that have been approved by the AICPA's Audit and Attest Standards team are presumed to be appropriate. Those that have not been reviewed by the AICPA's Audit and Attest Standards team may be considered by the accountant, but their influence may be affected by the publication's stature and whether the author is a known expert.

III. Preconditions

Circumstances affecting acceptance and continuance of engagements in accordance with the SSARSs

A. The accountant should not accept an engagement to be performed in accordance with the SSARSs if any of the following circumstances exist:

1. There is reason to believe that relevant ethical requirements (e.g., independence requirements) will not be satisfied;

2. Information that is needed to perform the engagement is unlikely to be either available or reliable; *or*

3. There is reason to doubt management's integrity.

B. Prior to accepting an engagement to be performed in accordance with the SSARSs, the accountant should perform the following actions:

1. Determine whether the financial reporting framework adopted by management is acceptable; *and*

2. Obtain an agreement that management acknowledges and understands its responsibilities for the following:

a. The selection of the financial reporting framework;

b. The design, implementation, and maintenance of internal control relevant to the financial statements;

c. The prevention and detection of fraud;

d. Compliance with applicable laws and regulations;

e. The accuracy and completeness of the records, documents, and explanations, including significant judgments made by management for the financial statements; *and*

f. Providing the accountant with access to all relevant information related to the fair presentation of the financial statements, additional information requested by the accountant, and unrestricted access to personnel.

SSARSs—Preparation of Financial Statements

After studying this lesson, you should be able to:

1. Distinguish between preparation engagements for which AR-C 70, "*Preparation of Financial Statements*" is applicable and other engagements for which AR-C 70 is not applicable.

2. Understand the accountant's obligation to obtain written agreement of the terms of the preparation engagement.

3. Know the requirements associated with a preparation engagement, including the accountant's documentation requirements.

Note

In the past, the SSARSs dealt with only two types of engagements: (1) reviews; and (2) compilations. The clarified SSARSs added a third type of engagement: engagements to prepare financial statements for a client without issuing an accompanying report, which is the focus of AR-C 70, *Preparation of Financial Statements*. When engaged to prepare financial statements, the accountant is also required to comply with the requirements of AR-C 60, *General Principles*, including meeting the preconditions for accepting the engagement. The accountant is not required to be independent for a preparation engagement.

I. Obtain an Agreement on the Terms of the Engagement

A. The accountant and management (or those charged with governance, as applicable) should agree on the terms of the engagement, which should be documented in writing (typically in an engagement letter, but a contract would also be acceptable). The following should be documented:

   1. The engagement's objective;

   2. Management's responsibilities;

   3. The accountant's responsibilities;

   4. That each page of the financial statements will include a statement that no assurance is provided (if such a statement is not included on each page, then the accountant will issue a disclaimer to make that point clear);

   5. The limitations of the engagement;

   6. Identification of the applicable financial reporting framework; *and*

   7. Whether the financial statements are to contain known departures from the applicable financial reporting framework (including misstatements or omission of some or all of the required footnote disclosures).

B. The agreement should be signed by the accountant (or firm) and management (or those charged with governance). If signed by those charged with governance, the accountant still should obtain management's agreement and understanding of its responsibilities (associated with preconditions for accepting the engagement).

II. Prepare the Financial Statements

A. Each page of the financial statements should include a statement that "no assurance is provided" (or other words to that effect). The accountant's name (or firm) need not be identified. If that statement cannot be added to each page, the accountant should issue a disclaimer as to any assurance or perform a compilation engagement in accordance with AR-C 80 or withdraw from the engagement.

B. The accountant is required to obtain an appropriate understanding of the financial reporting framework to be used and the significant accounting policies applicable to the financial statements.

C. If the financial statements use a special purpose framework, the accountant should include a description of the financial reporting framework on the face of the financial statements or in a footnote.

D. When assisting management with significant judgments, the accountant should discuss those judgments with management so that management understands those judgments and can take responsibility for them.

E. When records, documents, or other information used in preparing the financial statements are viewed as incomplete or inaccurate, the accountant should request additional or corrected information.

F. When financial statements contain known departures from the applicable financial reporting framework (including omission of some or all required disclosures), the accountant should discuss the matter with management and disclose those departures in the financial statements. If management fails to provide the necessary information, the accountant should disclose the corrected information or withdraw from the engagement.

III. Documenting a Preparation Engagement

A. The accountant should document the preparation engagement in enough detail to clearly show the work performed and should include (1) the engagement letter (or other written documentation); and (2) a copy of the financial statements prepared.

B. Noncompliance with a *presumptively mandatory requirement* —In rare circumstances, the accountant may depart from a relevant presumptively mandatory requirement; however, the accountant must document the reason(s) for the departure and how alternative procedures satisfied the intent of that presumptively mandatory requirement.

IV. Applicability of AR-C 70

A. In addition to preparing traditional financial statements, this section also applies to preparation of the following:

1. Specified elements, accounts, or financial statement items;

2. Supplementary information and required supplementary information;

3. Pro forma financial information; *and*

4. Prospective financial information (forecasts or projections).

B. An appendix identified the following examples to which AR-C 70 applies:

1. Preparing financial statements prior to audit or review by another accountant;

2. Preparing financial statements to be presented **alongside** the tax return;

3. Preparing personal financial statements for presentation **alongside** a financial plan;

4. Preparing single financial statements (e.g., just a balance sheet) with substantially all disclosures omitted; *and*

5. Preparing financial statements using general ledger information outside of an accounting software system.

C. AR-C 70 identified certain engagements to which AR-C 70 does not apply:

1. Engagements to perform audit, review, or compilation services;

2. Preparing financial statements for submission to taxing authorities;

3. Preparing financial statements as part of personal financial planning;

4. Preparing financial statements in connection with litigation services or business valuation services; *or*

5. Performing bookkeeping services (i.e., merely assisting with preparing financial statements, rather than preparing).

SSARSs—Compilation Engagements

> **After studying this lesson, you should be able to:**
>
> 1. Know what is meant by the term "compilation."
>
> 2. Understand the accountant's responsibilities when performing a compilation engagement.
>
> 3. Know the structure and content of the accountant's report for a compilation engagement.

Note

A "compilation" engagement involves assisting management in presenting the financial statements (or other historical, pro forma, or prospective financial information) along with the accountant's accompanying report, which provides no assurance about those financial statements (or other financial information). The accountant is also required to comply with the requirements of AR-C 60, *General Principles*, including meeting the "preconditions" for accepting the compilation engagement. The accountant is not required to be independent for a compilation engagement, since no assurance is provided. Guidance is provided in the Clarified SSARSs, specifically by AR-C 80, *Compilation Engagements*.

I. **Obtain an Agreement on the Terms of the Engagement**

   A. The accountant and management (or those charged with governance, as applicable) should agree on the terms of the engagement, which should be documented in writing (typically in an engagement letter, but a contract would also be acceptable). The following should be documented:

   1. The engagement's objective;

   2. Management's responsibilities;

   3. The accountant's responsibilities;

   4. The limitations of the engagement (see the note below);

   5. Identification of the applicable financial reporting framework; *and*

   6. The expected form and content of the compilation report (and a statement that, depending on circumstances, the actual report issued may differ from the expected report in form and content).

Note

An exhibit to AR-C 80 provides a sample engagement letter for a compilation engagement, which includes the following example of a limitation of the engagement (regarding the accountant's liability):

"You agree to hold us harmless and to release, indemnify, and defend us from any liability or costs, including attorney's fees, resulting from management's knowing misrepresentations to us."

   B. The agreement should be signed by the accountant (or firm) and management (or those charged with governance). If signed by those charged with governance, the accountant should still obtain management's agreement and understanding of its responsibilities (associated with the "preconditions" for accepting an engagement).

II. Performance Responsibilities for a Compilation Engagement

A. Understanding the Applicable Reporting Framework—The accountant should obtain an appropriate understanding of the financial reporting framework and the significant accounting policies applicable to the entity's financial statements.

B. Read the Financials—The accountant should read the financial statements to evaluate whether they are free of obvious material misstatements.

C. Incomplete/Unsatisfactory Records—If the accountant believes that the records or other information is incomplete or inaccurate, the accountant should request further or corrected information.

D. Revisions Required—If the accountant discovers a need for revision to the financial statements, the accountant should propose appropriate revisions to management.

E. Withdrawal—If management has failed to provide records or information as requested or if management does not make appropriate adjustments as proposed by the accountant, the accountant should withdraw (and inform management of the reasons for withdrawing).

III. Reporting Responsibilities for a Compilation Engagement

A. The accountant's compilation report normally consists of the following:

1. A statement that management (owners) of the identified entity is (are) responsible for the financial statements and that identifies the financial statements (and date/period) involved;

2. A statement that the compilation was performed in accordance with SSARSs promulgated by the AICPA's Accounting and Review Services Committee;

3. A statement that the accountant did not audit or review the financial statements, etc., and the accountant does not provide any assurance on them;

4. A statement that disclaims an opinion or any form of assurance; *and*

5. The signature of the accountant (or the accountant's firm), along with the city and state of the office, and the date of the report. (Presenting the report on the accountant's letterhead is an acceptable way to identify the accountant's city and state.)

Note

The accountant may request that management add a reference to each page of the financial statements, such as "See Accountant's Compilation Report" (or something similar), but that is not required.

Sample Compilation Report (Under Clarified SSARSs)
Accountant's Compilation Report

Management is responsible for the accompanying financial statements of XYZ Company, which comprise the balance sheets as of December 31, 20X1 and 20X2, the related statements of income, changes in stockholders' equity, and cash flows for the years then ended, and the related notes to the financial statements in accordance with accounting principles generally accepted in the United States of America. I (We) have performed compilation engagements in accordance with Statements on Standards for Accounting and Review Services promulgated by the Accounting and Review Services Committee of the AICPA. I (We) did not audit or review the financial statements nor was (were) I (we) required to perform any procedures to verify the accuracy or completeness of the information provided by management. Accordingly, I (we) do not express an opinion, a conclusion, or provide any form of assurance on these financial statements.

[Signature of accounting firm or accountant, as appropriate]

[Accountant's city and state]

[Date of the accountant's report]

B. In summary, the compilation report normally consists of four sentences:

    1. Management is responsible for the accompanying financial statements of XYZ Company, which comprise the balance sheets as of December 31, 20X1 and 20X2, the related statements of income, changes in stockholders' equity, and cash flows for the years then ended, and the related notes to the financial statements in accordance with accounting principles generally accepted in the United States of America.

    2. I (We) have performed compilation engagements in accordance with Statements on Standards for Accounting and Review Services promulgated by the Accounting and Review Services Committee of the AICPA.

    3. I (We) did not audit or review the financial statements nor was (were) I (we) required to perform any procedures to verify the accuracy or completeness of the information provided by management.

    4. Accordingly, I (we) do not express an opinion, a conclusion, or provide any form of assurance on these financial statements.

IV. Compilation Report when Financial Statements Use a Special-Purpose Framework

A. When using a special-purpose framework, the report should include a separate paragraph stating that the financial statements are prepared in accordance with the particular special-purpose framework and that refers to the note to the financial statement describing the framework.

B. When the financial statements are prepared using a regulatory basis or a contractual basis of accounting, the report should identify the purpose for which the financial statements were prepared (or refer to a note that provides that information).

C. Unless the financial statements omit substantially all disclosures, the accountant should modify the report when the financial statements omit (a) a description of the special-purpose framework; (b) a summary of significant accounting policies; (c) a description of how the special-purpose framework differs from GAAP (although the differences need not be quantified); or (d) appropriate informative disclosures.

V. Reporting when the Accountant Is Not Independent

A. The last paragraph of the report should state that the accountant was not independent [either a single sentence without indicating the reason or with additional commentary indicating the reason(s) for the impairment].

B. If stating any reason(s) for the impairment, the accountant should identify all applicable reasons for the lack of independence.

VI. Reporting when Substantially All Disclosures Are Omitted

A. If the omission of disclosures appears to be intended to mislead financial statement readers, the accountant should not issue a compilation report.

B. When the financial statements omit substantially all disclosures, the compilation report should include a paragraph pointing out that fact, including a statement that the financial statements are not designed for those who are uninformed about such matters. (The accountant should not issue a report on "comparative" financial statements of one year that omit substantially all disclosures along with financial statements of another year that include applicable disclosures. Such financial statements would not be viewed as comparable.)

C. If most disclosures are presented but selected disclosures are omitted, the report should identify the nature of the departure and any known effects.

VII. Reporting Known Departures from the Applicable Financial Reporting Framework

    A. Material departures that are not disclosed in the notes should be reported in a modified compilation report in a separate paragraph. (If the accountant believes that modification of the report is not an adequate way to communicate the deficiencies, the accountant should withdraw.)

    B. The effects of the departure should be disclosed if known. The accountant is not required to determine the effects, however, and can state in the report that management has not made such a determination.

    C. The accountant should not add a statement to the report stating that the "financial statements are not in conformity with [the applicable financial reporting framework]," which is equivalent to expressing a conclusion.

VIII. Documentation Requirements for a Compilation Engagement—The documentation should provide a clear understanding of the accountant's work and, at a minimum, include the following:

    A. The engagement letter (or other appropriate written documentation);

    B. A copy of the financial statements; *and*

    C. A copy of the compilation report.

SSARSs—Review Engagements

Note

A "review" engagement involves obtaining "limited assurance" (primarily by analytical procedures and inquiry of management) as to whether material modifications should be made to an entity's financial statements to be presented in accordance with the applicable financial reporting framework. The accountant is also required to comply with the requirements of AR-C 60 (*General Principles*), including meeting the "preconditions" for accepting the review engagement. The accountant is required to be independent for a review engagement, since "negative assurance" is provided. Guidance is provided in the Clarified SSARSs, specifically by AR-C 90, *Review Engagements*.

Definitions

Limited Assurance: "A level of assurance that is less than the reasonable assurance obtained in an audit engagement but is at an acceptable level as the basis for the conclusion expressed in the accountant's review report."

Modified Conclusion: "A qualified conclusion or an adverse conclusion."

I. **Obtain an Agreement on the Terms of the Engagement**

A. The accountant and management (or those charged with governance, as applicable) should agree on the terms of the engagement, which should be documented in writing (typically in an engagement letter). The following should be documented:

1. The engagement's objective;

2. Management's responsibilities;

3. The accountant's responsibilities;

4. The limitations of the engagement, including that the accountant will not express an opinion;

5. Identification of the applicable financial reporting framework; *and*

6. The expected form and content of the review report (and a statement that, depending on circumstances, the actual report issued may differ from the expected report in form and content).

B. The agreement should be signed by the accountant (or firm) and management (or those charged with governance). If signed by those charged with governance, the accountant should still obtain management's agreement and understanding of its responsibilities (associated with the "preconditions" for accepting an engagement).

C. **Understanding of the Industry and Knowledge of the Entity**—The accountant should obtain an understanding of the entity's industry, its business (including its organization and operations) and the accounting principles and practices used (including the nature of its financial statement elements).

II. **Designing and Performing Review Procedures**—The accountant should design and perform analytical procedures and make inquiries (and perform any other procedures as needed) to obtain "sufficient appropriate review evidence" as a basis for the review report; if unable to obtain sufficient appropriate review evidence, the accountant should withdraw from the engagement.

A. **Risk Assessment**—The accountant should focus the review procedures in the areas believed to be at higher risk of material misstatements. However, the accountant does not obtain an understanding of internal control for purposes of assessing control risk.

B. **Analytical Procedures**—The accountant should use analytical procedures as a basis for inquiry about relationships that appear unusual and should investigate significant differences relative to expectations by inquiring of management and performing other review procedures as needed.

C. **Inquiries of Management**—The accountant should inquire about (but is not required to corroborate) the following:

1. Whether the financial statements have been prepared and fairly presented in accordance with the applicable financial reporting framework, including how management determined that significant accounting estimates are reasonable

2. Identification of related parties and related-party transactions (including the purpose of such transactions)

3. Whether there are significant, unusual, or complex transactions or events (including significant changes in operations, significant adjustments, etc.)

4. The existence of any actual, suspected, or alleged (a) fraud or (b) noncompliance with laws and regulations (including tax and pension laws)

5. Whether there are subsequent events that require adjustment or disclosure

6. The basis for management's assessment about the entity's ability to continue as a going concern along with any conditions causing doubt

7. Material commitments, obligations, or contingencies affecting the financial statements

8. Material nonmonetary transactions

9. Communications from applicable regulatory agencies

10. Any litigation, claims, and assessments affecting the financial statements

11. Actions taken at meetings of stockholders, board of directors, or others that may affect the financial statements

12. Any other matters that the accountant considers necessary

D. **Reading the Financial Statements**—The accountant should read the financial statements for any indications of departures from the applicable framework.

E. **Reconciling to Underlying Records**—The accountant should verify that the financial statements agree to (or reconcile to) the accounting records.

F. **Incomplete/Unsatisfactory Records**—If the accountant believes that the records or other information is incomplete or inaccurate, the accountant should request further or corrected information.

G. **Written Representations**—The accountant should obtain written representations from the appropriate members of management (usually the chief executive officer and chief financial officer); the representations letter should have the same date as the review report. (If management does not provide the required representations, the accountant should withdraw.)

III. Reporting Responsibilities for a Review Engagement

A. The accountant's review report having an unmodified conclusion consists of the following:

1. A title, such as "Independent Accountant's Review Report"

2. An appropriate addressee

3. An introductory paragraph (without a label) that identifies the financial statements that were reviewed (and dates/periods involved), that states that a review consists primarily of analytical procedures and inquiries, and that states that a review is substantially less in scope than an audit (with a disclaimer of opinion)

4. A section entitled "Management's Responsibility for the Financial Statements" that identifies management's responsibilities for the financial statements and internal control

5. A section entitled "Accountant's Responsibility" that references the SSARSs promulgated by the ARSC of the AICPA and refers to "limited assurance" as a basis for reporting

6. A section entitled "Accountant's Conclusion" that provides negative assurance on the financial statements *and*

7. The signature of the accountant or the accountant's firm, the city and state where the accountant practices, and the date of the report.

Sample Unmodified Review Report on Comparative Financial Statements

Independent Accountant's Review Report

[Appropriate Addressee]

I (We) have reviewed the accompanying financial statements of XYZ Company, which comprise the balance sheets as of December 31, 20X2 and 20X1, and the related statements of income, changes in stockholders' equity, and cash flows for the years then ended, and the related notes to the financial statements. A review includes primarily applying analytical procedures to management's (owners') financial data and making inquiries of company management (owners). A review is substantially less in scope than an audit, the objective of which is the expression of an opinion regarding the financial statements as a whole. Accordingly, I (we) do not express such an opinion.

Management's Responsibility for the Financial Statements

Management (Owners) is (are) responsible for the preparation and fair presentation of these financial statements in accordance with accounting principles generally accepted in the United States of America; this includes the design, implementation, and maintenance of internal control relevant to the preparation and fair presentation of financial statements that are free from material misstatement whether due to fraud or error.

Accountant's Responsibility

My (Our) responsibility is to conduct the review engagements in accordance with Statements on Standards for Accounting and Review Services promulgated by the Accounting and Review Services Committee of the AICPA. Those standards require me (us) to perform procedures to obtain limited assurance as a basis for reporting whether I am (we are) aware of any material modifications that should be made to the financial statements for them to be in accordance with accounting principles generally accepted in the United States of America. I (We) believe that the results of my (our) procedures provide a reasonable basis for my (our) conclusion.

We are required to be independent of XYZ Company and to meet our other ethical responsibilities, in accordance with the relevant ethical requirements related to our reviews.

Accountant's Conclusion

Based on my (our) reviews, I am (we are) not aware of any material modifications that should be made to the accompanying financial statements in order for them to be in accordance with accounting principles generally accepted in the United States of America.

[Signature of accounting firm or accountant, as appropriate]

[Accountant's city and state]

[Date of the accountant's report]

B. Review report when financial statements use a special-purpose framework.

1. When using a special-purpose framework, the report should include an "emphasis-of-matter" paragraph stating that the financial statements are prepared in accordance with the special purpose framework and referencing the note to the financial statement describing the framework.

2. When the financial statements are prepared using a contractual basis of accounting, the report should identify the purpose for which the financial statements were prepared (or refer to a note that provides that information) and restrict the distribution of the report.

3. The accountant should modify the report when the financial statements omit (a) a description of the special-purpose framework, (b) a summary of significant accounting policies, (c) a description of how the special-purpose framework differs from GAAP (although the differences need not be quantified), or (d) appropriate informative disclosures.

C. Going Concern Section and Emphasis-of-Matter and Other-Matter Paragraphs

1. "Going Concern" section—When there is substantial doubt about the entity's ability to continue as a going concern for a reasonable period of time (and disclosure of those uncertainties are adequate), add a "Going Concern" section to the review report labeled "Substantial Doubt About the Entity's Ability to Continue as a Going Concern"; if disclosure is not adequate, the matter would be addressed in the "Basis for Qualified (Adverse) Conclusion" section of the review report.

2. Emphasis-of-matter paragraphs—The accountant may add an emphasis-of-matter paragraph to the review report to draw readers' attention to a matter that is appropriately reported or disclosed in the financial statements; the accountant should add an emphasis-of-matter paragraph when the financial statements have been restated to correct a misstatement in previously issued financial statements.

3. Other-matter paragraphs—The accountant may add an "other-matter" paragraph to the review report to draw readers' attention to a matter that is relevant to their understanding of the review, the review report, or the accountant's responsibilities.

D. Modified conclusion—When the accountant determines that the financial statements are materially misstated

1. **Qualified conclusion**—The accountant should express a qualified conclusion using the phrase "… except for the effect of the matter described in the Basis for Qualified Conclusion paragraph …" when the misstatement is material but not pervasive to the financial statements; see the sample review report with a qualified conclusion below.

2. **Adverse conclusion**—The accountant should express an adverse conclusion using the phrase "… due to the significance of the matter described in the Basis for Adverse Conclusion paragraph, the financial statements are not in accordance with …" when the misstatement is material and also pervasive to the financial statements; see the sample review report with an adverse conclusion below.

Sample Review Report with Qualified Conclusion

Independent Accountant's Review Report

[Appropriate Addressee]

I (We) have reviewed the accompanying financial statements of XYZ Company, which comprise the balance sheets as of December 31, 20X2 and 20X1, and the related statements of income, changes in stockholders' equity, and cash flows for the years then ended, and the related notes to the financial statements. A review includes primarily applying analytical procedures to management's (owners') financial data and making inquiries of company management (owners). A review is substantially less in scope than an audit, the objective of which is the expression of an opinion regarding the financial statements as a whole. Accordingly, I (we) do not express such an opinion.

Management's Responsibility for the Financial Statements

Management (Owners) is (are) responsible for the preparation and fair presentation of these financial statements in accordance with accounting principles generally accepted in the United States of America; this includes the design, implementation, and maintenance of internal control relevant to the preparation and fair presentation of financial statements that are free from material misstatement whether due to fraud or error.

Accountant's Responsibility

My (Our) responsibility is to conduct the review engagements in accordance with Statements on Standards for Accounting and Review Services promulgated by the Accounting and Review Services Committee of the AICPA. Those standards require me (us) to perform procedures to obtain limited assurance as a basis for reporting whether I am (we are) aware of any material modifications that should be made to the financial statements for them to be in accordance with accounting principles generally accepted in the United States of America. I (We) believe that the results of my (our) procedures provide a reasonable basis for our conclusion.

We are required to be independent of XYZ Company and to meet our other ethical responsibilities, in accordance with the relevant ethical requirements related to our reviews.

Basis for Qualified Conclusion

As disclosed in Note X to these financial statements, the company has adopted [*description of newly adopted method*], whereas it previously used [*description of previous method*]. Although the [*description of newly adopted method*] is in accordance with accounting principles generally accepted in the United States of America, the company does not appear to have reasonable justification for making a change as required by FASB Accounting Standards Codification 250, *Accounting Changes and Error Corrections*.

Qualified Conclusion

Based on my (our) reviews, except for the effect of the matter described in the Basis for Qualified Conclusion paragraph, I am (we are) not aware of any material modifications that should be made to the accompanying financial statements in order for them to be in accordance with accounting principles generally accepted in the United States of America.

[Signature of accounting firm or accountant, as appropriate]

[Accountant's city and state]

[Date of the accountant's report]

Sample Review Report with Adverse Conclusion

Independent Accountant's Review Report

[Appropriate Addressee]

I (We) have reviewed the accompanying financial statements of XYZ Company, which comprise the balance sheet as of December 31, 20X1, and the related statements of income, changes in stockholders' equity, and cash flows for the year then ended, and the related notes to the financial statements. A review includes primarily applying analytical procedures to management's (owners') financial data and making inquiries of company management (owners). A review is substantially less in scope than an audit, the objective of which is the expression of an opinion regarding the financial statements as a whole. Accordingly, I (we) do not express such an opinion.

Management's Responsibility for the Financial Statements

Management (Owners) is (are) responsible for the preparation and fair presentation of these financial statements in accordance with accounting principles generally accepted in the United States of America; this includes the design, implementation, and maintenance of internal control relevant to the preparation and fair presentation of financial statements that are free from material misstatement whether due to fraud or error.

Accountant's Responsibility

My (Our) responsibility is to conduct the review engagement in accordance with Statements on Standards for Accounting and Review Services promulgated by the Accounting and Review Services Committee of the AICPA. Those standards require me (us) to perform procedures to obtain limited assurance as a basis for reporting whether I am (we are) aware of any material modifications that should be made to the financial statements for them to be in accordance with accounting principles generally accepted in the United States of America. I (We) believe that the results of my (our) procedures provide a reasonable basis for our conclusion.

We are required to be independent of XYZ Company and to meet our other ethical responsibilities, in accordance with the relevant ethical requirements related to our reviews.

Basis for Adverse Conclusion

As disclosed in Note X to these financial statements, the Company has not consolidated the financial statements of subsidiary ABC Company it acquired during 20X1 because it has not yet been able to ascertain the fair values of certain of the subsidiary's material assets and liabilities at the acquisition date. This investment is therefore accounted for on a cost basis by the Company. Under accounting principles generally accepted in the United States of America, the subsidiary should have been consolidated because it is controlled by the Company. Had XYZ Company been consolidated, many elements in the accompanying consolidated financial statements would have been materially affected. The effects on the consolidated financial statements of the failure to consolidate have not been determined.

Adverse Conclusion

Based on my (our) review, due to the significance of the matter described in the Basis for Adverse Conclusion paragraph, the financial statements are not in accordance with accounting principles generally accepted in the United States of America.

[Signature of accounting firm or accountant, as appropriate]

[Accountant's city and state]

[Date of the accountant's report]

E. **Review Documentation**

   1. In general, the documentation should permit an experienced accountant with no prior connection to the engagement to understand the following:

      a. The nature, timing, and extent of review procedures performed in compliance with the SSARSs

      b. The evidence obtained from the procedures performed *and*

      c. Significant findings, conclusions reached, and significant professional judgments involved

   2. Specifically, the documentation should include the following

      a. The engagement letter (or other written documentation)

    b. Communications with management about emphasis-of-matter or other-matter paragraph(s) in the accountant's review report

    c. Communications with management and those charged with governance about significant matters during the engagement

    d. Communications with other accountants associated with the financial statements of significant components

    e. Any identified information that is inconsistent with the findings regarding significant matters (and how the inconsistency was addressed)

    f. The representation letter obtained from management *and*

    g. A copy of the financial statements and the review report

SSARSs—Other Topics

SSARS No. 22 provides guidance on *Compilation of Pro Forma Financial Information* in clarified format (designated AR-C section 120). That topic will be addressed here.

In addition, certain other technical topics applicable to preparation engagements, compilations, and reviews in accordance with the SSARSs will also be addressed below.

After studying this lesson, you should be able to:

1. Know how the accountant's report (for a compilation and for a review engagement) is affected when "required supplementary information" is relevant to the entity's financial statements.

2. Understand the accountant's responsibilities under SSARSs when "subsequently discovered facts" are identified before the report release date, as well as after the report release date.

3. Understand the accountant's responsibilities under SSARSs when engaged to compile "pro forma" financial information.

4. Know how the accountant's report (for a compilation and for a review engagement) is affected when the entity's financial statements are accompanied by "supplemental information."

5. Know the distinction between a "forecast" and a "projection" and the different types of professional services that are permitted for such prospective financial information.

I. Compilation of Pro Forma Financial Information

> **Note**
>
> The purpose of "pro forma" financial information is to show the significant effects on historical financial information that might have resulted had an actual or proposed transaction occurred at an earlier date. The Statements on Standards for Attestation Engagements provide guidance to practitioners when performing an "examination" or "review" engagement involving pro forma information. Compilation of pro forma financial information is addressed in the SSARSs.

A. **A Requirement to Perform a Compilation of Pro Forma Financial Information**—The historical financial statements on which the pro forma information is based must have been compiled, reviewed, or audited.

B. **Engagement Letter**—The accountant and the entity (management) should establish an understanding in writing as to the nature and limitations of the services to be performed and the nature of the report to be issued.

1. That understanding should specifically state that the engagement cannot be relied on to disclose errors, fraud, or illegal acts.

2. That understanding also should state that the accountant will inform the appropriate level of management of any material errors and of any information coming to the accountant's attention that fraud or illegal acts may have occurred (excluding matters that are "clearly inconsequential").

C. **Performance Requirements**—The accountant should read the compiled pro forma financial information (including the summary of significant assumptions) and consider whether that information appears to be free of obvious material errors.

D. **Reporting Requirements**

1. The pro forma financial information should be clearly labeled in a manner that distinguishes it from historical financial statements.

2. Each page of the compiled pro forma financial information should include a reference such as "See Accountant's Compilation Report."

3. The accountant is not required to be independent since no assurance is provided. If the accountant is not independent, the compilation report should indicate that fact.

4. The accountant may "assist" with the preparation of pro forma financial information without issuing a compilation report (when the accountant has not been engaged to "compile" such information).

5. The compilation report should not describe any other procedures performed by the accountant either prior to or during the compilation engagement.

II. Supplemental Information

> **Note**
> When the financial statements are accompanied by "supplemental information" associated with either a compilation or review engagement, the accountant should indicate the responsibility taken, if any, for such supplemental information either (1) in an other-matter paragraph in the compilation or review report or (2) in a separate report on that supplemental information.

A. When the Accountant Has Reviewed the Supplementary Information along with the Financial Statements—The report should state that (1) the supplementary information is presented for additional analysis and is not required as part of the financial statements; (2) the supplementary information is the responsibility of management; (3) the supplementary information was subjected to the review procedures applied to the review of the financial statements (and indicate whether the accountant is aware of any material modifications that should be made to it); and (4) the accountant has not audited the supplementary information and does not express an opinion on it.

B. When the Accountant Has Not Reviewed the Supplementary Information along with the Financial Statements—The report should state that (1) the supplementary information is presented for additional analysis and is not required as part of the financial statements; (2) the supplementary information is the responsibility of management; and (3) the accountant has not audited or reviewed the supplementary information, and does not express an opinion, a conclusion, or any assurance on it.

III. Required Supplementary Information

> **Note**
> When "required supplementary information" is relevant to financial statements associated with either a compilation or review engagement, the accountant's compilation or review report should include an "other-matter" paragraph that comments on the applicable circumstances:

A. That the required supplementary information is included and the accountant performed a compilation or review engagement on it;

B. That the required supplementary information is included and the accountant did not perform a compilation, review, or audit on it;

C. That the required supplementary information is omitted;

D. That some required supplementary information is included and some is omitted

E. That the accountant identified departures from the prescribed guidelines (established by the designated accounting standard-setting body); *or*

F. That the accountant has doubts as to whether the information is presented in accordance with the prescribed guidelines.

IV. Preparation or Compilation of Prospective Financial Information

Definitions

Prospective financial information: "Any financial information about the future. The information may be presented as complete financial statements or limited to one or more elements, items, or accounts."

Financial forecast: "Prospective financial statements that present, to the best of the responsible party's knowledge and belief, an entity's expected financial position, results of operations, and cash flows. A financial forecast is based on the responsible party's assumptions reflecting conditions it expects to exist and the course of action it expects to take."

Financial projection: Prospective financial statements that present, to the best of the responsible party's knowledge and belief, given one or more hypothetical assumptions, an entity's expected financial position, results of operations, and cash flows. A financial projection is sometimes prepared to present one or more hypothetical courses of action for evaluation, as in response to a question that begins for instance, "What would happen if ...?'"

A. Under the Clarified SSARSs

1. The accountant may perform either a preparation engagement or a compilation of prospective financial information (a review of such prospective financial information is not permitted).

2. When engaged to prepare prospective financial information or issue a compilation report on prospective financial information:

   a. Significant assumptions—The accountant should not prepare (or issue a compilation report on) prospective financial information that omits disclosure of the summary of significant assumptions; the entity's financial statements should also include a summary of significant accounting policies.

   b. Financial projections—The accountant should not prepare or issue a compilation report on a financial projection that (a) fails to identify the hypothetical assumptions or that (b) omits a description of the limitations of the usefulness of the projection; any report on a projection should be restricted to specified users, consisting of third parties in direct negotiation with the responsible party (which allows them to ask questions about the presentation).

3. When issuing a compilation report on prospective financial information—The report should include statements that (a) the forecasted/projected results may not be achieved; and (b) the accountant assumes no responsibility to update the report for matters occurring after the date of the report. (Any report on a "projection" must have restricted distribution; only a report on a "forecast" is permitted to have general distribution.)

B. Under the Clarified Statements on Standards for Attestation Engagements (SSAEs) —The accountant may be engaged to perform an "examination" or an "agreed-upon procedures engagement" on prospective financial information (again, a review of prospective financial information is not permitted under the SSAEs). Examinations and agreed-upon procedures engagements under the SSAEs are addressed in other lessons of Wiley CPAexcel˚.

1. **Examination engagements**—An examination results in a positive expression of opinion (similar to an audit report) focusing on the preparation of the prospective information and management's underlying assumptions; an examination report on a forecast is allowed to be issued for general distribution (but any report on a projection should have restricted distribution).

2. **Agreed-upon procedures engagements**—Any agreed-upon procedures report must be restricted to the specified users who take responsibility for the sufficiency of the procedures for their purposes; assurance is provided in the form of "procedures" and "findings".

V. Review Engagements—Other Miscellaneous Topics

A. Subsequent Events and Subsequently Discovered Facts

1. **Subsequent events**—The accountant should request that management consider the appropriateness of the financial statement treatment when subsequent events are identified.

2. **Subsequently discovered facts *before* the report release date:**

   a. The accountant should discuss the matter with management (and those charged with governance, as applicable) and determine how management intends to deal with the matter when the financial statements require revision.

   b. If management revises the financial statements, the accountant should perform review procedures on the revision and either change the date on the review report or "dual-date" the report.

   c. If management does not revise the financial statements, the accountant should modify the review report appropriately.

3. **Subsequently discovered facts *after* the report release date:**

   a. The accountant should discuss the matter with management (and those charged with governance, as applicable) and determine how management intends to deal with the matter when the financial statements require revision.

   b. If management revises the financial statements, the accountant should perform review procedures on the revision, and either change the date on the review report or "dual-date" the report. The accountant also should determine whether third parties possess those released financial statements and evaluate whether management is taking appropriate steps to inform them that the financial statements should not be used.

   c. If management is not taking the appropriate steps, including revision, the accountant should notify management and take action to prevent the use of the accountant's review report. The accountant may wish to seek legal guidance in that event.

B. Comparative Financial Statements

1. The report should refer to each applicable period for which financial statements are presented. (The type of engagement need not be the same for each period presented. For example, one period might be a compilation and another period might be a review; or one period might be a review and another period might be an audit.)

2. A continuing accountant should update the report on any prior periods' financial statements that are presented along with the current period.

3. **Reporting when the prior period was audited**—If the audit report on the prior period's financial statements is not presented, the review report should include an "other-matter" paragraph to indicate that the prior period's financials were audited; to identify the date of that audit report and the type of opinion expressed (and the reasons for any modifications); and to state that no audit procedures were performed after the date of the audit report.

4. **When changing reference to a previously reported departure**—The review report should include an "other-matter" paragraph to explain the removal of the previously reported departure.

C. Changing the Engagement from an Audit to a Review

1. The accountant should decide whether such a change is appropriate and consider (1) the reason(s) expressed for the change and (2) the incremental effort and cost to complete the audit.

2. A change in circumstances or a misunderstanding about the nature of an audit or review engagement usually would be considered a satisfactory reason for requesting a change in the engagement.

3. If an accountant was engaged to perform an audit but management refused to allow correspondence with the entity's attorney, the accountant normally would be prohibited from changing the engagement to review the entity's financial statements.

Other Professional Services

AICPA on Reporting on Internal Control in an Integrated Audit

> **After studying this lesson, you should be able to:**
>
> 1. Understand the auditor's responsibilities when reporting on internal control over financial reporting in an integrated audit of a non-issuer's financial statements in accordance with AICPA Professional Standards.
>
> 2. Know the structure of the report on internal control over financial reporting for an engagement, whether the report is issued separately or combined with the audit report on the entity's financial statements.

I. **Applicability and Objectives**

A. **Applicability**—This guidance applies when an auditor is engaged to audit internal control over financial reporting (ICFR) along with an audit of a nonissuer's financial statements, known as an integrated audit. The AICPA issued a Statement on Auditing Standards to replace the guidance that was previously included among the Statements on Standards for Attestation Engagements. The AICPA guidance is closely aligned with the corresponding PCAOB Auditing Standards applicable to an integrated audit of an issuer.

> **Note**
> AICPA guidance is provided by Statement on Auditing Standards (SAS) No. 130, *An Audit of Internal Control Over Financial Reporting That Is Integrated with an Audit of Financial Statements*, as amended (AU-C 940).

B. **Objectives**—There are two objectives: (1) To obtain reasonable assurance whether material weaknesses exist at the "as of" date in management's assessment of ICFR; and (2) to express an opinion on the effectiveness of ICFR and communicate appropriately with management and those charged with governance.

II. **Underlying Concepts**

A. If any (one or more) "material weaknesses" exist, then the entity's internal control cannot be considered effective. The auditor should plan and perform the audit of ICFR to obtain sufficient appropriate evidence to provide reasonable assurance whether material weaknesses exist as of the date specified by management's report.

B. The auditor is not required to search for deficiencies that are less severe than a material weakness (such as significant deficiencies or other lesser matters).

C. The auditor should use the same suitable and available control criteria to perform the audit of ICFR that management uses for its assessment of the effectiveness of ICFR.

D. **Preconditions for the Audit of ICFR:**

1. Management must accept responsibility for the effectiveness of ICFR.

2. Management must provide the auditor with an assessment of ICFR using suitable and available criteria (e.g., COSO's Internal Control-Integrated Framework).

3. Management must support its assessment of ICFR with sufficient documentation.

4. Management must provide its written assessment about the effectiveness of ICFR in a report that accompanies the auditor's report. (If management refuses to furnish a written assessment, the auditor should withdraw from the audit of ICFR.)

E. **The Auditor's Basic Responsibilities**—The auditor should plan and perform the integrated audit to achieve the objectives of both engagements simultaneously; that is, design the tests of control to (1) obtain sufficient appropriate evidence to support the auditor's opinion on ICFR at the "as of" date in management's report; and (2) obtain sufficient appropriate evidence to support the auditor's control risk assessments for purposes of the audit of the financial statements.

III. Planning the Audit of ICFR

A. Risk Assessment, in General—The auditor should use the same risk assessment process to focus attention on the areas of highest risk in the audit of ICFR and the audit of the entity's financial statements.

B. Fraud Risk Assessment—The auditor should evaluate whether the entity's controls adequately address the risks of material misstatement due to fraud as well as the risk of management override of controls.

C. Entities with Multiple Locations—The auditor should assess the risk of material misstatement associated with the various locations/business units and correlate the amount of work with the degree of risk.

D. Materiality—The auditor should use the same materiality for the audit of ICFR and for the audit of the entity's financial statements.

E. Using the Work of Internal Auditors or Others—The auditor should assess the competence and objectivity of persons when planning to use them either (1) to obtain audit evidence or (2) to provide direct assistance in the audit of ICFR. (The need for the auditor to perform the work increases as the risk associated with a control increases.)

F. Scaling the Audit—The size and complexity of the entity, its business processes, and the business units may affect the way in which the entity achieves its control objectives. (Less control testing may be needed for smaller, less complex entities.)

G. Use a "Top-Down Approach"—The auditor should (1) begin at the financial statement level; (2) use the auditor's understanding of the overall risks to internal control; (3) focus on "entity-level controls" (e.g., the control environment, the entity's risk assessment process, monitoring controls, etc.); (4) focus on significant classes of transactions, accounts, disclosures, and relevant assertions that have a reasonable possibility of material misstatement to the financial statements; (5) verify the auditor's understanding of the risks in the entity's processes (includes performing walkthroughs); and (6) select controls for testing based on the assessed risk of material misstatement to each relevant assertion.

IV. Testing Controls and Evaluating Identified Deficiencies—The evidence that should be obtained increases with the risk of the control being tested. (The objective is to express an opinion on ICFR overall, not on the effectiveness of individual controls.)

A. Evaluating "Design Effectiveness"—Procedures include a mix of inquiry, observation of the entity's operations, and inspection of relevant documentation. (A walkthrough is usually sufficient to evaluate design effectiveness.)

B. Testing "Operating Effectiveness"—Procedures include a mix of inquiry, observation of the entity's operations, inspection of relevant documentation, recalculation, and reperformance of the control. (Note that these procedures are presented in order of increasing persuasiveness of the resulting evidence.) Inquiry alone is insufficient for evaluating the operating effectiveness of controls.

C. The Severity of a Deficiency—Depends on the magnitude of the potential misstatement and the degree of likelihood (whether there is a "reasonable possibility") of a failure; it does not require that an actual misstatement occur.

D. Risk Factors Affecting whether a Misstatement may Occur—(1) The size and composition of the account; (2) susceptibility to misstatement; (3) volume of activity and complexity; (4) nature of the account, transactions, or disclosure; (5) accounting and reporting complexities associated with the account, transactions, or disclosures; (6) exposure to losses in the account; (7) possibility of significant contingent liabilities resulting; (8) existence of related party transactions; *and* (9) changes from the prior period.

E. Multiple Deficiencies—May cause a material weakness even though the deficiencies individually may be less severe.

F. Compensating Controls—May mitigate the severity of a deficiency, although they do not eliminate the deficiency entirely.

G. Indicators of Material Weaknesses—(1) Discovery of any fraud involving senior management, whether material or not; (2) restatement of previously issued financial statements to correct a material misstatement; (3) identification of any material misstatement during the audit that was not detected by internal control; and (4) ineffective oversight of reporting and controls by those charged with governance.

V. Concluding Procedures

A. Review Reports of Other Parties—The auditor should review the reports of others (such as internal auditors) during the period that address internal control issues.

B. Obtain written representations from management specific to the audit of ICFR; management's failure to provide these representations is a scope limitation.

C. Communicate Certain Internal Control Matters Identified during the Integrated Audit.

1. **Communicating material weaknesses and significant deficiencies**—Should be communicated in writing to those charged with governance and management by the report release date. (For governmental entities only, the written communication must occur within 60 days of the report release date.)

2. **Communicating other lesser deficiencies**—Should be communicated in writing to management within 60 days of the report release date; should also inform those charged with governance of that communication.

3. **Communicating an absence of deficiencies**— The auditor should **not** issue any report stating that "no material weaknesses" (or no deficiencies less severe than a material weakness) were identified in an audit of ICFR.

VI. Reporting on ICFR

A. The Auditor's Separate Written Report on ICFR Should Include the Following Elements:

1. A title that includes the word "independent"

2. An appropriate addressee

3. "Opinion on [ICFR]" section that (a) identifies the entity involved; (b) states that ICFR has been audited; (c) identifies the applicable measurement criteria (e.g., COSO); (d) expresses an opinion on ICFR; and (e) includes a paragraph that cross-references the auditor's report on the entity's financial statements

4. "Basis for Opinion" section that (a) references GAAS; (b) refers to the requirement to be independent and meet other ethical responsibilities; and (c) expresses the belief that sufficient appropriate audit evidence was obtained

5. "Responsibilities of Management for [ICFR]" section that identifies management's responsibilities for ICFR and references the title of the accompanying management report

6. "Auditor's Responsibilities for the Audit of [ICFR]" section that identifies the objectives of the audit and defines reasonable assurance; and comments on the role of professional judgment, professional skepticism, and risk assessment, among other matters

7. "Definition and Inherent Limitations of [ICFR]" section that (a) defines ICFR and (b) includes a paragraph commenting on the inherent limitations of internal control

8. The manual or printed signature of the auditor's firm;

9. The city and state where the auditor's report is issued

10. The date of the auditor's report

B. Report Date—The auditor's report on ICFR should not be dated before the auditor has obtained sufficient appropriate audit evidence to support the auditor's opinion, including evidence that the audit documentation has been reviewed; the audit reports on ICFR and on the financial statements should have the same date.

C. Five Reasons to Depart from the Usual Unmodified Wording in the Auditor's Report on ICFR

1. **Adverse opinion issued**—When there is at least one material weakness, the report should include the definition of "material weakness" and reference the description in management's report or point out that management's report did not identify the matter; the report also should determine the effect on the audit of the entity's financial statements (state whether the opinion on the financial statements was affected by adding an other-matter paragraph or commenting in the paragraph that identifies the material weakness).

2. **Elements of management's report are incomplete or improperly presented**—If management does not revise its report, the auditor should add an other-matter paragraph to describe the reasons for the determination that elements of the report are incomplete or improperly presented.

3. **Scope limitations**—The auditor should either withdraw from the engagement or disclaim an opinion on ICFR (stating the reasons for the disclaimer) and consider the effect on the audit of financial statements.

4. **Making reference to a component auditor**—The auditor should not make such a reference unless the component auditor has followed appropriate professional standards and has issued a report on a component's ICFR that is not restricted.

5. **Management's report includes additional information**—The auditor should add an other-matter paragraph to disclaim an opinion on the other information in management's report; if such other information is included in a document containing management's report, the auditor should read the additional information to evaluate whether there are material inconsistencies with management's report. (If there are, the auditor should try to persuade management to make appropriate changes to resolve any inconsistency.)

VII. Sample Reports That Follow

A. Example of a management report (with no material weaknesses reported)

B. Auditor's unmodified opinions on an entity's financial statements and ICFR (presented as a combined report on both parts of the integrated audit)

C. Auditor's unmodified opinion on ICFR (presented as a separate report on ICFR)

D. Auditor's adverse opinion on ICFR (presented as a separate report on ICFR)

Example Management Report (with No Material Weaknesses Reported)
Management's Report on Internal Control Over Financial Reporting

ABC Company's internal control over financial reporting is a process effected by those charged with governance, management, and other personnel, designed to provide reasonable assurance regarding the preparation of reliable financial statements in accordance with [*applicable financial reporting framework, such as accounting principles generally accepted in the United States of America*]. An entity's internal control over financial reporting includes those policies and procedures that: (1) pertain to the maintenance of records that, in reasonable detail, accurately and fairly reflect the transactions and dispositions of the assets of the entity; (2) provide reasonable assurance that transactions are recorded as necessary to permit preparation of financial statements in accordance with [*applicable financial reporting framework, such as accounting principles generally accepted in the United States of America*] and that receipts and expenditures of the entity are being made only in accordance with authorizations of management and those charged with governance; and (3) provide reasonable assurance regarding prevention, or timely detection and correction, of unauthorized acquisition, use, or disposition of the entity's assets that could have a material effect on the financial statements.

Management of ABC Company is responsible for designing, implementing, and maintaining effective internal control over financial reporting. Management assessed the effectiveness of ABC Company's internal control over financial reporting as of December 31, 20XX, based on [identify criteria]. Based on that assessment, management concluded that, as of December 31, 20XX, ABC Company's internal control over financial reporting is effective, based on [identify criteria].

Internal control over financial reporting has inherent limitations. Internal control over financial reporting is a process that involves human diligence and compliance and is subject to lapses in judgment and breakdowns resulting from human failures. Internal control over financial reporting also can be circumvented by collusion or improper management override. Because of its inherent limitations, internal control over financial reporting may not prevent, or detect and correct, misstatements. Also, projections of any assessment of effectiveness to future periods are subject to the risk that controls may become inadequate because of changes in conditions or that the degree of compliance with the policies or procedures may deteriorate.

ABC Company

[Report signers, if applicable]

[Date]

Unmodified Opinions on Financial Statements and ICFR (Combined Report)
Independent Auditor's Report

[Appropriate Addressee]

Opinions on the Financial Statements and Internal Control Over Financial Reporting

We have audited the financial statements of ABC Company, which comprise the balance sheet as of December 31, 20XX, and the related statements of income, changes in stockholders' equity, and cash flows for the year then ended, and the related notes to the financial statements. In our opinion, the accompanying financial statements present fairly, in all material respects, the financial position of ABC Company as of December 31, 20XX, and the results of its operations and its cash flows for the year then ended in accordance with accounting principles generally accepted in the United States of America.

We also have audited ABC Company's internal control over financial reporting as of December 31, 20XX, based on [identify criteria; for example, "criteria established in the Internal Control – Integrated Framework (2013), issued by the Committee of Sponsoring Organizations of the Treadway Commission (COSO)."] In our opinion, ABC Company maintained, in all material respects, effective internal control over financial reporting as of December 31, 20XX, based on [identify criteria].

Basis for Opinions

We conducted our audits in accordance with auditing standards generally accepted in the United States of America (GAAS). Our responsibilities under those standards are further described in the Auditor's Responsibilities for the Audits of the Financial Statements and Internal Control Over Financial Reporting section of our report. We are required to be independent of ABC Company and to meet our other ethical responsibilities, in accordance with the relevant ethical requirements relating to our audits. We believe that the audit evidence we have obtained is sufficient and appropriate to provide a basis for our audit opinions.

Responsibilities of Management for the Financial Statements and Internal Control Over Financial Reporting

Management is responsible for the preparation and fair presentation of the financial statements in accordance with accounting principles generally accepted in the United States of America, and for the design, implementation, and maintenance of effective internal control over financial reporting relevant to the preparation and fair presentation of financial statements that are free from material misstatement, whether due to fraud or error. Management is also responsible for its assessment about the effectiveness of internal control over financial reporting, included in the accompanying [*title of management's report*].

In preparing the financial statements, management is required to evaluate whether there are conditions or events, considered in the aggregate, that raise substantial doubt about ABC Company's ability to continue as a going concern [*insert the time period set by the applicable financial reporting framework*].

Auditor's Responsibilities for the Audits of the Financial Statements and Internal Control Over Financial Reporting

Our objectives are to obtain reasonable assurance about whether the financial statements as a whole are free from material misstatement, whether due to fraud or error, and about whether effective internal control over financial reporting was maintained in all material respects, and to issue an auditor's report that includes our opinions.

Reasonable assurance is a high level of assurance but is not absolute assurance and therefore is not a guarantee that an audit of financial statements or an audit of internal control over financial reporting conducted in accordance with GAAS will always detect a material misstatement or a material weakness when it exists. The risk of not detecting a material misstatement resulting from fraud is higher than for one resulting from error, as fraud may involve collusion, forgery, intentional omissions, misrepresentations, or the override of internal control. Misstatements are considered to be material if there is a substantial likelihood that, individually or in the aggregate, they would influence the judgment made by a reasonable user based on the financial statements.

In performing an audit of financial statements and an audit of internal control over financial reporting in accordance with GAAS, we:

- Exercise professional judgment and maintain professional skepticism throughout the audits.

- Identify and assess the risks of material misstatement of the financial statements, whether due to fraud or error, and design and perform audit procedures responsive to those risks. Such procedures include examining, on a test basis, evidence regarding amounts and disclosures in the financial statements.

- Obtain an understanding of internal control relevant to the financial statement audit in order to design audit procedures that are appropriate in the circumstances.

- Obtain an understanding of internal control over financial reporting relevant to the audit of internal control over financial reporting, assess the risks that a material weakness exists, and test and evaluate the design and operating effectiveness of internal control over financial reporting based on the assessed risk.

- Evaluate the appropriateness of accounting policies used and the reasonableness of significant accounting estimates made by management, as well as evaluate the overall presentation of the financial statements.

- Conclude whether, in our judgment, there are conditions or events, considered in the aggregate, that raise substantial doubt about ABC Company's ability to continue as a going concern for a reasonable period of time.

We are required to communicate with those charged with governance regarding, among other matters, the planned scope and timing of the audit, significant audit findings, and certain internal control-related matters that we identified during the financial statement audit.

Definition and Inherent Limitations of Internal Control Over Financial Reporting

An entity's internal control over financial reporting is a process effected by those charged with governance, management, and other personnel, designed to provide reasonable assurance regarding the preparation of reliable financial statements in accordance with accounting principles generally accepted in the United States of America. An entity's internal control over financial reporting includes those policies and procedures that (1) pertain to the maintenance of records that, in reasonable detail, accurately and fairly reflect the transactions and dispositions of the assets of the entity; (2) provide reasonable assurance that the transactions are recorded as necessary to permit preparation of financial statements in accordance with accounting principles generally accepted in the United States of America, and that receipts and expenditures of the entity are being made only in accordance with authorizations of management and those charged with governance; and (3) provide reasonable assurance regarding prevention, or timely detection and correction of unauthorized acquisition, use, or disposition of the entity's assets that could have a material effect on the financial statements.

Because of its inherent limitations, internal control over financial reporting may not prevent, or detect and correct, misstatements. Also, projections of any assessment of effectiveness to future periods are subject to the risk that controls may become inadequate because of changes in conditions, or that the degree of compliance with the policies or procedures may deteriorate.

[Signature of the auditor's firm]

[City and state where the auditor's report is issued]

[Date of the auditor's report]

Unmodified Opinion on ICFR (Separate Report on ICFR)
Independent Auditor's Report

[Appropriate Addressee]

Opinion on Internal Control Over Financial Reporting

We have audited ABC Company's internal control over financial reporting as of December 31, 20XX, based on [identify criteria; for example, "criteria established in the Internal Control – Integrated Framework (2013), issued by the Committee of Sponsoring Organizations of the Treadway Commission (COSO)."] In our opinion, ABC Company has maintained, in all material respects, effective internal control over financial reporting as of December 31, 20XX, based on [identify criteria].

We also have audited, in accordance with auditing standards generally accepted in the United States of America (GAAS), the [identify financial statements] of ABC Company, and our report dated [date of report, which should be the same as the date of the report on the audit of ICFR] expressed [include nature of opinion].

Basis for Opinion

We conducted our audit in accordance with auditing standards generally accepted in the United States of America (GAAS). Our responsibilities under those standards are further described in the Auditor's Responsibilities for the Audit of Internal Control Over Financial Reporting section of our report. We are required to be independent of ABC Company and to meet our other ethical responsibilities, in accordance with the relevant ethical requirements relating to our audits. We believe that the audit evidence we have obtained is sufficient and appropriate to provide a basis for our audit opinion.

Responsibilities of Management for Internal Control Over Financial Reporting

Management is responsible for designing, implementing, and maintaining effective internal control over financial reporting, and for its assessment about the effectiveness of internal control over financial reporting, included in the accompanying [title of management's report].

Auditor's Responsibilities for the Audit of Internal Control Over Financial Reporting

Our objectives are to obtain reasonable assurance about whether effective internal control over financial reporting was maintained in all material respects, and to issue an auditor's report that includes our opinion on internal control over financial reporting. Reasonable assurance is a high level of assurance but is not absolute assurance and therefore is not a guarantee that an audit of internal control over financial reporting conducted in accordance with GAAS will always detect a material weakness when it exists.

In performing an audit of internal control over financial reporting in accordance with GAAS, we:

- Exercise professional judgment and maintain professional skepticism throughout the audit.

- Obtain an understanding of internal control over financial reporting, assess the risks that a material weakness exists, and test and evaluate the design and operating effectiveness of internal control over financial reporting based on the assessed risk.

Definition and Inherent Limitations of Internal Control Over Financial Reporting

An entity's internal control over financial reporting is a process effected by those charged with governance, management, and other personnel, designed to provide reasonable assurance regarding the preparation of reliable financial statements in accordance with accounting principles generally accepted in the United States of America. An entity's internal control over financial reporting includes those policies and procedures that (1) pertain to the maintenance of records that, in reasonable detail, accurately and fairly reflect the transactions and dispositions of the assets of the entity; (2) provide reasonable assurance that the transactions are recorded as necessary to permit preparation of financial statements in accordance with accounting principles generally accepted in the United States of America, and that receipts and expenditures of the entity are being made only in accordance with authorizations of management and those charged with governance; and (3) provide reasonable assurance regarding prevention, or timely detection and correction of unauthorized acquisition, use, or disposition of the entity's assets that could have a material effect on the financial statements.

Because of its inherent limitations, internal control over financial reporting may not prevent, or detect and correct, misstatements. Also, projections of any assessment of effectiveness to future periods are subject to the risk that controls may become inadequate because of changes in conditions, or that the degree of compliance with the policies or procedures may deteriorate.

[Signature of the auditor's firm]

[City and state where the auditor's report is issued]

[Date of the auditor's report]

Adverse Opinion on ICFR (Separate Report on ICFR)
Independent Auditor's Report

[Appropriate Addressee]

Adverse Opinion on Internal Control Over Financial Reporting

We have audited ABC Company's internal control over financial reporting as of December 31, 20XX, based on [identify criteria; for example, "criteria established in the Internal Control – Integrated Framework (2013), issued by the Committee of Sponsoring Organizations of the Treadway Commission (COSO)."] In our opinion, because of the effect of the material weakness described in the Basis for Adverse Opinion section on the achievement of the objectives of [identify criteria], ABC Company has not maintained effective internal control over financial reporting as of December 31, 20XX, based on [identify criteria].

We also have audited, in accordance with auditing standards generally accepted in the United States of America (GAAS), the [identify financial statements] of ABC Company, and our report dated [date of report, which should be the same as the date of the report on the audit of ICFR] expressed [include nature of opinion].

We considered the material weakness described in the Basis for Adverse Opinion on Internal Control Over Financial Reporting section in determining the nature, timing, and extent of audit procedures applied in our audit of the 20XX financial statements, and this report does not affect such report on the financial statements.

Basis for Adverse Opinion on Internal Control Over Financial Reporting

A material weakness is a deficiency, or a combination of deficiencies, in internal control over financial reporting, such that there is a reasonable possibility that a material misstatement of the entity's financial statements will not be prevented, or detected and corrected, on a timely basis. The following material weakness has been identified and included in the accompanying [*title of management's report*].

[*Identify the material weakness described in management's report.*]

We conducted our audit in accordance with auditing standards generally accepted in the United States of America (GAAS). Our responsibilities under those standards are further described in the Auditor's Responsibilities for the Audit of Internal Control Over Financial Reporting section of our report. We are required to be independent of ABC Company and to meet our other ethical responsibilities, in accordance with the relevant ethical requirements relating to our audits. We believe that the audit evidence we have obtained is sufficient and appropriate to provide a basis for our audit opinion.

Responsibilities of Management for Internal Control Over Financial Reporting

Management is responsible for designing, implementing, and maintaining effective internal control over financial reporting, and for its assessment about the effectiveness of internal control over financial reporting, included in the accompanying [*title of management's report*].

Auditor's Responsibilities for the Audit of Internal Control Over Financial Reporting

Our objectives are to obtain reasonable assurance about whether effective internal control over financial reporting was maintained in all material respects, and to issue an auditor's report that includes our opinion on internal control over financial reporting. Reasonable assurance is a high level of assurance but is not absolute assurance and therefore is not a guarantee that an audit of internal control over financial reporting conducted in accordance with GAAS will always detect a material weakness when it exists.

In performing an audit of internal control over financial reporting in accordance with GAAS, we:

- Exercise professional judgment and maintain professional skepticism throughout the audit.

- Obtain an understanding of internal control over financial reporting, assess the risks that a material weakness exists, and test and evaluate the design and operating effectiveness of internal control over financial reporting based on the assessed risk.

Definition and Inherent Limitations of Internal Control Over Financial Reporting

An entity's internal control over financial reporting is a process effected by those charged with governance, management, and other personnel, designed to provide reasonable assurance regarding the preparation of reliable financial statements in accordance with accounting principles generally accepted in the United States of America. An entity's internal control over financial reporting includes those policies and procedures that (1) pertain to the maintenance of records that, in reasonable detail, accurately and fairly reflect the transactions and dispositions of the assets of the entity; (2) provide reasonable assurance that the transactions are recorded as necessary to permit preparation of financial statements in accordance with accounting principles generally accepted in the United States of America, and that receipts and expenditures of the entity are being made only in accordance with authorizations of management and those charged with governance; and (3) provide reasonable assurance regarding prevention, or timely detection and correction of unauthorized acquisition, use, or disposition of the entity's assets that could have a material effect on the financial statements.

Because of its inherent limitations, internal control over financial reporting may not prevent, or detect and correct, misstatements. Also, projections of any assessment of effectiveness to future periods are subject to the risk that controls may become inadequate because of changes in conditions, or that the degree of compliance with the policies or procedures may deteriorate.

[Signature of the auditor's firm]

[City and state where the auditor's report is issued]

[Date of the auditor's report]

PCAOB on Reporting on Internal Control in an Integrated Audit

The AICPA issued Statement on Auditing Standards (SAS) No. 130, *An Audit of Internal Control Over Financial Reporting that is integrated with an Audit of Financial Statements*. This SAS is applicable to integrated audits nonissuers (private companies), and it makes the professional requirements under the AICPA standards substantially the same as the requirements for integrated audits of issuers under PCAOB standards.

After studying this lesson, you should be able to:

1. Understand the auditor's responsibilities when reporting on internal control over financial reporting in an integrated audit of an issuer's financial statements in accordance with PCAOB Auditing Standards.

2. Familiarize yourself with the structure of the report on internal control over financial reporting for such an engagement, whether the report is issued separately or combined with the audit report on the entity's financial statements.

I. **"An Audit of Internal Control Over Financial Reporting That Is Integrated with an Audit of Financial Statements"**

II. **Applicability of Standard**—When engaged to "perform an audit of management's assessment of the effectiveness of internal control over financial reporting" (ICFR), the objective of such an engagement is to express an opinion on the effectiveness of ICFR.

III. **Some Important Definitions**

   A. **Control Deficiency**—When the design or operation of a control does not allow management or employees, in the normal course of performing their assigned functions, to prevent or detect misstatements on a timely basis.

   1. **Deficiency in design**—When a control necessary to meet the control objective is missing or when an existing control is not properly designed so that, even if the control operates as designed, the control objective is not always met.

   2. **Deficiency in operation**—When a properly designed control does not operate as designed or when the person performing the control does not possess the necessary authority or qualifications to perform the control effectively.

   B. **Material Weakness**—A deficiency, or a combination of deficiencies, in ICFR such that there is a reasonable possibility that a material misstatement of the company's annual or interim financial statements will not be prevented or detected on a timely basis. (If one or more material weaknesses exist, the company's ICFR is not considered to be effective.)

   C. **Significant Deficiency**—A deficiency, or a combination of deficiencies, in ICFR that is less severe than a material weakness, yet important enough to merit attention by those responsible for oversight of the company's financial reporting.

IV. **Planning the Audit**—The audit of ICFR should be integrated with the audit of the financial statements (i.e., the tests of controls should be designed to address both the objectives of the audit of ICFR and the audit of the financial statements).

   A. **Role of Risk Assessment**—"Risk assessment underlies the entire audit process described by this standard, including the determination of significant accounts and disclosures and relevant assertions, the selection of controls to test, and the determination of the evidence necessary for a given control."

   1. There is a direct relationship between the risk of material weakness and the amount of audit attention that is needed.

2. **Materiality**—Should use the same materiality considerations in planning the audit of ICFR as for the audit of the company's annual financial statements.

B. **Using the Work of Others**—The auditor may use the work of others to reduce the work the auditor might otherwise have to perform.

1. Includes internal auditors, other company personnel, service auditors (when a service organization is involved), and third parties working under the direction of management or the audit committee; the auditor should assess the competence and objectivity of those whose work the auditor plans to use.

2. As the risk associated with a control increases, the auditor should take increasing responsibility for performing the work instead of using the work of others.

V. **Using a Top-Down Approach**—Begins at the financial statement level and with the auditor's understanding of the overall risks to ICFR; the auditor then focuses on *entity-level* controls and works down to significant accounts and disclosures and their relevant assertions.

A. **Identifying Entity-Level Controls**—The auditor must test those entity-level controls that are important to the conclusion about the effectiveness of ICFR.

1. **Entity-level controls**—Include controls related to the control environment, controls over management override, the company's risk assessment process, controls to monitor results of operations or other controls, controls over the period-end financial reporting process; and policies that address significant business control and risk management practices.

2. **Control environment**—Because of its importance to ICFR, the auditor must evaluate the control environment at the company.

3. **Period-end financial reporting process**—Because of its importance to ICFR, the auditor must evaluate the period-end financial reporting process.

B. **Identifying Significant Accounts and Disclosures and their Relevant Assertions**

1. **Relevant assertions**—Those financial statement assertions that have a reasonable possibility of containing a material misstatement. (PCAOB auditing standards specifically refer to the following asertions (1) existence or occurrence; (2) completeness; (3) valuation or allocation; (4) rights and obligations; and (5) presentation and disclosure.)

2. **Risk factors**—The auditor should consider risk factors relevant to the identification of significant accounts and disclosures and their relevant assertions, including the nature of the account or disclosure; size and composition of the account; susceptibility to misstatement, volume of activity and complexity of transactions; and changes from the prior period, among others.

C. **Understanding Likely Sources of Misstatement**

1. **The auditor should achieve these control objectives**—(a) Understand the flow of transactions related to the relevant assertions; (b) verify that the auditor has identified the points within the company's processes at which a material misstatement could arise; (c) identify the controls that management has implemented to address these potential misstatements; and (d) identify the controls that management has implemented over the company's assets that could materially misstate the financial statements.

2. **Performing walkthroughs**—Following a transaction from origination through the company's processes until reflected in the financial records is frequently the most effective way to achieve the objectives above. (Procedures usually include inquiry, observation, inspection of relevant documentation, and re-performance of controls.)

D. **Selecting Controls to Test**—The auditor should test those controls that are important to the conclusion about whether the company's controls sufficiently address the assessed risk of misstatement to each relevant assertion.

VI. Testing Controls

A. Nature of Tests of Controls (From least to most persuasive)—Inquiry, observation, inspection of relevant documentation, and re-performance of a control:

1. **Testing design effectiveness**—Procedures include inquiry of appropriate personnel, observation of the company's operations, and inspection of relevant documentation (may be addressed by appropriate walkthroughs).

2. **Testing operating effectiveness**—Procedures include inquiry of appropriate personnel, observation of the company's operations, inspection of relevant documentation, and re-performance of the control.

B. Timing of Tests of Controls—Testing controls over a greater period of time provides more evidence than testing over a shorter period of time; testing closer to the date of management's assessment provides more evidence than testing performed earlier in the year.

C. Extent of Tests of Controls—The more extensively a control is tested, the greater the evidence to evaluate the effectiveness of the control.

D. Roll-Forward Procedures—When operating effectiveness has been tested at an interim date, the auditor should consider what additional testing for the remaining period may be necessary.

VII. Evaluating Identified Deficiencies

A. Basic Responsibility—The auditor must evaluate identified control deficiencies to determine whether, individually or in combination, they constitute material weaknesses as of the date of management's assessment (based on whether there is a "reasonable possibility" that the controls will fail to prevent or detect a material misstatement, not whether a misstatement has actually occurred).

B. Indicators of Material Weaknesses—Examples include (1) identification of fraud involving senior management (whether or not material); (2) restatement of previously issued financial statements; (3) identification by the auditor of a material misstatement of the financial statements in the current period; and (4) ineffective oversight of the company's external financial reporting and internal control by the company's audit committee.

C. Communicating Identified Deficiencies

1. The auditor must communicate (in writing) all **material weaknesses** identified to **management and the audit committee**.

2. The auditor must also communicate (in writing) other **significant deficiencies** identified to the **audit committee**.

3. The auditor should communicate (in writing) all other identified deficiencies in ICFR to **management** and inform the audit committee that such a communication has been made.

4. If the auditor concludes that the audit committee's oversight of financial reporting and ICFR is ineffective, he or she must communicate that conclusion in writing to the board of directors.

VIII. Reporting on Internal Control over Financial Reporting

A. Separate or Combined Reports—The auditor may choose to issue a combined report on the financial statements and on ICFR or separate reports.

B. Title of report should include the word "independent" (e.g., "Report of Independent Registered Public Accounting Firm").

C. Combined Report—An unqualified report on the financial statements and on ICFR consists of five paragraphs: (1) introduction; (2) scope; (3) definition; (4) inherent limitations; and (5) opinion.

D. Separate Reports—The auditor should add an additional paragraph to the audit report on the financial statements that references the report on ICFR; and the auditor should add an

additional paragraph to the report on ICFR that references the audit report on the financial statements.

E. Report Date—If separate reports are issued, they should be dated the same (the date as of which the auditor has obtained sufficient competent evidence).

F. If One (or More) Material Weakness Exists—The auditor must express an adverse opinion (unless there is a scope limitation).

1. **When expressing an adverse opinion**—The auditor's report must include the definition of a material weakness and refer to management's assessment of the material weakness. (If not included in management's assessment, the auditor's report should state that fact.)

2. Should determine the effect the adverse opinion on ICFR has on the opinion on the entity's financial statements.

G. If There is a Scope Limitation—The auditor should disclaim an opinion or withdraw from the engagement.

Sample Report on the Effectiveness of Internal Control Over Financial Reporting
Report of Independent Registered Public Accounting Firm

Separate Audit Report on ICFR

(Introductory paragraph)

We have audited ABC Company's internal control over financial reporting as of December 31, 20X2, based on (*Identify control criteria, e.g., "criteria established in Internal Control—Integrated Framework issued by the Committee of Sponsoring Organizations of the Treadway Commission (COSO)"*). ABC Company's management is responsible for maintaining effective internal control over financial reporting and for its assessment of the effectiveness of internal control over financial reporting, included in the accompanying (*title of management's report*). Our responsibility is to express an opinion on the company's internal control over financial reporting based on our audit.

(Scope paragraph)

We conducted our audit in accordance with the standards of the Public Company Accounting Oversight Board (United States). Those standards require that we plan and perform the audit to obtain reasonable assurance about whether effective internal control over financial reporting was maintained in all material respects. Our audit of internal control over financial reporting included obtaining an understanding of internal control over financial reporting, assessing the risk that a material weakness exists, and testing and evaluating the design and operating effectiveness of internal control based on the assessed risk. Our audit also included performing such other procedures as we considered necessary in the circumstances. We believe that our audit provides a reasonable basis for our opinion.

(Definition paragraph)

A company's internal control over financial reporting is a process designed to provide reasonable assurance regarding the reliability of financial reporting and the preparation of financial statements for external purposes in accordance with generally accepted accounting principles. A company's internal control over financial reporting includes those policies and procedures that (1) pertain to the maintenance of records that, in reasonable detail, accurately and fairly reflect the transactions and dispositions of the assets of the company; (2) provide reasonable assurance that transactions are recorded as necessary to permit preparation of financial statements in accordance with generally accepted accounting principles, and that receipts and expenditures of the company are being made only in accordance with authorizations of management and directors of the company; and (3) provide reasonable assurance regarding prevention or timely detection of unauthorized acquisition, use, or disposition of the company's assets that could have a material effect on the financial statements.

(Inherent limitations paragraph)

Because of its inherent limitations, internal control over financial reporting may not prevent or detect misstatements. Also, projections of any evaluation of effectiveness to future periods are subject to the risk that controls may become inadequate because of changes in conditions, or that the degree of compliance with the policies or procedures may deteriorate.

(Opinion paragraph)

In our opinion, ABC Company maintained, in all material respects, effective internal control over financial reporting as of December 31, 20X2, based on (*identify control criteria, e.g., "criteria established in Internal Control—Integrated Framework issued by the Committee of Sponsoring Organizations of the Treadway Commission (COSO)"*).

(Explanatory paragraph)

We have also audited, in accordance with the standards of the Public Company Accounting Oversight Board (United States), the (*identify financial statements*) of ABC Company and our report dated (*date of report, which should be the same as the date of the report on the effectiveness of internal control over financial reporting*) expressed (*include nature of opinion*).

(Signature)

(City and State or Country)

(Date)

Sample Combined Audit Report on Financial Statements and on the Effectiveness of Internal Control Over Financial Reporting
Report of Independent Registered Public Accounting Firm

To the shareholders and the board of directors of W Company

Opinions on the Financial Statements and Internal Control over Financial Reporting

We have audited the accompanying balance sheets of W Company (the "Company") as of December 31, 20X8 and 20X7, and the related statements of [_titles of the financial statements, e.g., income, comprehensive income, stockholders' equity, and cash flows_] for each of the years in the three-year period ended December 31, 20X8, and the related notes [_and schedules_](collectively referred to as the "financial statements"). We also have audited the Company's internal control over financial reporting as of December 31, 20X8, based on [_Identify control criteria, for example, "criteria established in Internal Control - Integrated Framework: (20XX) issued by the Committee of Sponsoring Organizations of the Treadway Commission (COSO)."_].

In our opinion, the financial statements referred to above present fairly, in all material respects, the financial position of the Company as of December 31, 20X8 and 20X7, and the results of its operations and its cash flows for each of the years in the three-year period ended December 31, 20X8 in conformity with accounting principles generally accepted in the United States of America. Also in our opinion, the Company maintained, in all material respects, effective internal control over financial reporting as of December 31, 20X8, based on [_Identify control criteria,_ _for example, "criteria established in Internal Control - Integrated Framework: (20XX) issued by COSO."_].

Basis for Opinion

The Company's management is responsible for these financial statements, for maintaining effective internal control over financial reporting, and for its assessment of the effectiveness of internal control over financial reporting, included in the accompanying [_title of management's report_]. Our responsibility is to express an opinion on the Company's financial statements and an opinion on the Company's internal control over financial reporting based on our audits. We are a public accounting firm registered with the Public Company Accounting Oversight Board (United States) ("PCAOB") and are required to be independent with respect to the Company in accordance with the U.S. federal securities laws and the applicable rules and regulations of the Securities and Exchange Commission and the PCAOB.

We conducted our audits in accordance with the standards of the PCAOB. Those standards require that we plan and perform the audits to obtain reasonable assurance about whether the financial statements are free of material misstatement, whether due to error or fraud, and whether effective internal control over financial reporting was maintained in all material respects.

Our audits of the financial statements included performing procedures to assess the risks of material misstatement of the financial statements, whether due to error or fraud, and performing procedures that respond to those risks. Such procedures included examining, on a test basis, evidence regarding the amounts and disclosures in the financial statements. Our audits also included evaluating the accounting principles used and significant estimates made by management, as well as evaluating the overall presentation of the financial statements. Our audit of internal control over financial reporting included obtaining an understanding of internal control over financial reporting, assessing the risk that a material weakness exists, and testing and evaluating the design and operating effectiveness of internal control based on the assessed risk. Our audits also included performing such other procedures as we considered necessary in the circumstances. We believe that our audits provide a reasonable basis for our opinions.

Definition and Limitations of Internal Control Over Financial Reporting

A company's internal control over financial reporting is a process designed to provide reasonable assurance regarding the reliability of financial reporting and the preparation of financial statements for external purposes in accordance with generally accepted accounting principles. A company's internal control over financial reporting includes those policies and procedures that (1) pertain to the maintenance of records that, in reasonable detail, accurately and fairly reflect the transactions and dispositions of the assets of the company; (2) provide reasonable assurance that transactions are recorded as necessary to permit preparation of financial statements in accordance with generally accepted accounting principles, and that receipts and expenditures of the company are being made only in accordance with authorizations of management and directors of the company; and (3) provide reasonable assurance regarding prevention or timely detection of unauthorized acquisition, use, or disposition of the company's assets that could have a material effect on the financial statements.

Because of its inherent limitations, internal control over financial reporting may not prevent or detect misstatements. Also, projections of any evaluation of effectiveness to future periods are subject to the risk that controls may become inadequate because of changes in conditions, or that the degree of compliance with the policies or procedures may deteriorate.

Critical Audit Matters [if applicable]

[Include critical audit matters]

[_Signature_]

We have served as the Company's auditor since [_year_].

[_City and State or Country_]

[_Date_]

PCAOB on Reporting Whether a Previously Reported Material Weakness Continues to Exist

After studying this lesson, you should be able to:

1. Know the PCAOB requirements, in general, when an auditor is engaged to report on whether a previously reported material weakness in internal control over financial reporting continues to exist under Auditing Standard No. 4.

2. Know management's specific responsibilities before an auditor can report on whether a previously reported material weakness in internal control over financial reporting continues to exist.

3. Understand the auditor's specific responsibilities when reporting on whether a previously reported material weakness in internal control over financial reporting continues to exist.

I. **"Reporting on Whether a Previously Reported Material Weakness Continues to Exist"**

II. **Applicability**—When engaged to report on whether a previously reported material weakness in internal control over financial reporting continues to exist as of a date specified by management. (The date specified by management must be a date after that of management's most recent annual assessment.) PCAOB standards do not require reporting on whether a previously reported material weakness continues to exist, so such an engagement is voluntary.

III. **The Auditor's Objective**—In an engagement to report on whether a previously reported material weakness continues to exist to express an opinion about the existence of a specifically identified material weakness as of a specified date (does not relate to the overall effectiveness of internal control over financial reporting); may report on more than one material weakness as part of the same engagement.

IV. **Conditions for Engagement Performance**—Cannot report on whether a previously reported material weakness continues to exist unless all of the following are met:

A. Management accepts responsibility for the effectiveness of internal control over financial reporting.

B. Management evaluates the effectiveness of the specific control(s) that it believes addresses the material weakness using the same control criteria that management used for its most recent annual assessment of internal control over financial reporting and management's stated control objective(s).

C. Management asserts that the specific control(s) identified is (are) effective in achieving the stated control objective.

D. Management supports its assertion with sufficient evidence, including documentation.

E. Management presents a written report that will accompany the auditor's report that contains all the elements required by the PCAOB:

1. Statement of management's responsibility for establishing and maintaining effective internal control over financial reporting;

2. Statement identifying the control criteria used by management to conduct the required annual assessment of internal control;

3. Identification of the material weakness that was identified as part of management's annual assessment (or by the auditor's report on it);

4. Identification of the control objective(s) addressed by the specified controls and a statement that the specified controls achieve the stated control objective(s) as of a specified date; *and*

5. Statement that the identified material weakness no longer exists as of the specified date because the specified controls address the material weakness.

V. Performing the Engagement

A. An individual material weakness may be associated with a single stated control objective (or more than one)—A *stated control objective* is the specific control objective identified by management that, if achieved, would result in the material weakness no longer existing.

B. Auditor uses materiality at the financial-statement level, rather than at the individual account-balance level, in evaluating whether a material weakness exists.

C. Obtaining an Understanding of Internal Control over Financial Reporting

  1. The extensiveness of the required understanding of internal control increases with the pervasiveness of the effects of the material weakness.

  2. Must perform a walkthrough for all major classes of transactions that are directly affected by controls specifically identified by management as addressing the material weakness—An auditor who has reported on internal control in accordance with PCAOB auditing standards for the most recent annual assessment is not required to perform a walkthrough for this engagement.

  3. Successor auditors may determine that they are unable to obtain a sufficient basis for reporting on whether a previously reported material weakness continues to exist without performing a complete audit of internal control over financial reporting in accordance with PCAOB auditing standards.

D. Testing and Evaluating Whether a Material Weakness Continues to Exist

  1. If management has not supported its assertion with sufficient evidence (a required condition) the auditor cannot complete this engagement.

  2. Auditor should evaluate the appropriateness of management's chosen date—for example, controls that operate daily and continuously can be as of almost any date of management's choosing; controls that operate over the company's period-end reporting process can usually only be tested in connection with a period-end.

  3. Auditor should obtain evidence about the effectiveness of all controls specifically identified in management's assertion (all controls that are necessary to achieve the stated control objective should be specifically identified and evaluated)—Determine whether the specified control operated as designed and whether the person performing the control possesses the authority and qualifications to perform the control effectively.

E. Using the Work of Others—The auditor may consider the work of others in deciding the nature, timing, or extent of the work that should be performed. (The auditor should perform any walkthroughs, however, because of the judgment involved.)

F. Obtain Written Representations from Management—About various matters (ranging from management's responsibility for establishing and maintaining internal control, management's evaluation of the effectiveness of the specified controls, describing any fraud issues, and stating whether there were material subsequent events, among other matters).

VI. Auditor's Report—In reporting on whether a previously reported material weakness continues to exist, the auditor may express an **opinion** (as to whether the material weakness continues to exist or does not) or a **disclaimer of opinion**;

A. See the sample below for a *continuing auditor* who has previously reported on the company's internal control over financial reporting in accordance with PCAOB auditing standards as of the company's most recent year-end.

B. Report Modifications—For any of the following conditions:

  1. Other material weaknesses that were reported previously by the company as part of the company's annual assessment of internal control are not addressed by the auditor's opinion.

2. A significant subsequent event has occurred since the date reported on.

3. Management's report contains additional information—express a disclaimer of opinion on the additional information.

Sample Auditor's Report for a Continuing Auditor Expressing an Opinion That a Previously Reported Material Weakness No Longer Exists

Report of Independent Registered Public Accounting Firm

We have previously audited and reported on management's annual assessment of XYZ Company's internal control over financial reporting as of December 31, 200X based on (identify control criteria, e.g., *"criteria established in Internal Control—Integrated Framework issued by the Committee of Sponsoring Organizations of the Treadway Commission (COSO)."*) Our report, dated (*date of report*), identified the following material weakness in the Company's internal control over financial reporting:

(Describe material weakness)

We have audited management's assertion, included in the accompanying (*title of management's report*), that the material weakness in internal control over financial reporting identified above no longer exists as of (*date of management's assertion*) because the following control(s) addresses the material weakness:

(Describe control(s))

Management has asserted that the control(s) identified above achieves the following stated control objective, which is consistent with the criteria established in (*identify control criteria used for management's annual assessment of internal control over financial reporting*): (*state control objective addressed*). Management also has asserted that it has tested the control(s) identified above and concluded that the control(s) was designed and operated effectively as of (*date of management's assertion*). XYZ Company's management is responsible for its assertion. Our responsibility is to express an opinion on whether the identified material weakness continues to exist as of (*date of management's assertion*) based on our auditing procedures.

Our engagement was conducted in accordance with the standards of the Public Company Accounting Oversight Board (United States). Those standards require that we plan and perform the engagement to obtain reasonable assurance about whether a previously reported material weakness continues to exist at the company. Our engagement included examining evidence supporting management's assertion and performing such other procedures as we considered necessary in the circumstances. We obtained an understanding of the company's internal control over financial reporting as part of our previous audit of management's annual assessment of XYZ Company's internal control over financial reporting as of December 31, 200X and updated that understanding as it specifically relates to changes in internal control over financial reporting associated with the material weakness described above. We believe that our auditing procedures provide a reasonable basis for our opinion.

In our opinion, the material weakness described above no longer exists as of (*date of management's assertion*).

We were not engaged to and did not conduct an audit of internal control over financial reporting as of (*date of management's assertion*), the objective of which would be the expression of an opinion on the effectiveness of internal control over financial reporting. Accordingly, we do not express such an opinion. This means that we have not applied auditing procedures sufficient to reach conclusions about the effectiveness of any controls of the company as of any date after December 31, 200X, other than the control(s) specifically identified in this report. Accordingly, we do not express an opinion that any other controls operated effectively after December 31, 200X.

Because of its inherent limitations, internal control over financial reporting may not prevent or detect misstatements. Also, projections of any evaluation of the effectiveness of specific controls or

---

internal control over financial reporting overall to future periods are subject to the risk that controls may become inadequate because of changes in conditions or that the degree of compliance with the policies or procedures may deteriorate.

(Signature)

(City and State/or Country)

(Date)

Auditing Employee Benefit Plans

After studying this lesson, you should be able to:

1. Identify the two types of employee benefit plans that are associated with the Employee Retirement Income Security Act of 1974 (known as ERISA).

2. Identify the basic types of welfare plans and pension plans under ERISA.

3. Know when employee benefit plans are generally required to be audited under ERISA.

4. Know the circumstances that might permit an ERISA section 103(a)(3)(C) audit (formerly known as a limited-scope audit) engagement for an employee benefit plan.

5. Know the structure of the auditor's report for an ERISA section 103(a)(3)(C) audit engagement of a pension plan.

Note

Employee benefit plans are a unique, technical subject matter for which extensive professional guidance is available, including the AICPA's Audit and Accounting Guide, Employee Benefit Plans, which exceeds 800 pages. The purpose of this lesson is to introduce the fundamental issues associated with auditing employee benefit plans.

The Employee Retirement Income Security Act of 1974 (ERISA) applies to most employee benefit plans. ERISA is comprised of four sections: Title I deals with the Department of Labor (DOL) responsibilities, including reporting and disclosure (and auditing) requirements; Title II specifies the tax law requirements; Title III identifies specific enforcement-related matters; and Title IV addresses multiemployer plan issues, including plan termination procedures. Additional resources are provided on the website of the Employee Benefits Security Administration (EBSA).

I. **Basic Issues Related to Employee Benefit Plans Under ERISA**

A. There are two fundamental types of employee benefit plans under ERISA:

1. **Welfare plans**—These provide benefits such as healthcare, disability, death, unemployment, job training, and vacation.

2. **Pension plans**—These provide benefits involving retirement income or deferral of income beyond an employee's period of employment.

B. **Eligibility Requirements**—The plan must specify the eligibility requirements.

1. ERISA specifies minimum eligibility requirements for pension plans. The minimum age to be eligible to enter the plan cannot be set above age 21, and the minimum employment to enter the plan is generally 12 months (2 years if the plan is fully vested); generally, an employee has to work at least 1000 hours for the year to count toward eligibility.

2. ERISA does not provide specific eligibility requirements for welfare plans.

C. **Nondiscrimination Requirements**—ERISA requirements promote the participation of a broad set of employees in an employee benefit plan; for example, the plan features dealing with contributions and vesting applicable to highly compensated employees usually must be the same for other participants.

D. **Vesting Requirements**—ERISA establishes specific minimum vesting standards for pension plans; pension plans may vest more quickly than these requirements, but they cannot vest less quickly. [Note: Benefits are "vested" when the employee has earned the rights to those benefits without any further performance requirements or conditions.]

E. **Funding Requirements**—"Qualified" pension plans (those having tax-exempt status) are subject to specific funding requirements; welfare plans are not required to be funded, although plan documents typically do address funding issues.

F. Exemptions from ERISA—ERISA provides certain specific exemptions from some or all of ERISA, but the auditor is not responsible for determining whether a plan is subject to ERISA requirements or whether the plan must be audited (although the auditor may, of course, assist in determining those matters); the plan sponsor's legal counsel should be involved in those determinations.

G. GAAP classifies employee benefit plans into either of two categories:

    1. Defined benefit plans—The actual benefits are specified in the plan design; the plan's obligations are based on the determination of an actuary.

    2. Defined contribution plans—The benefits are limited by the specified contributions to each participant's specific account.

    3. ERISA requires that pension plans be funded whether they are viewed as defined benefit or defined contribution plans.

II. Welfare Plans—Basic Terminology

A. Welfare plans may be classified as defined benefit or defined contribution plans.

    1. Defined benefit plans—These are common (e.g., a specific commitment to provide healthcare coverage) and usually do not create separate accounts for each participant.

    2. Defined contribution plans—Individual accounts are maintained separately for each participant, and benefits are limited to the balance in the individual's account; an example that has grown in popularity is medical flexible spending accounts.

B. Unfunded versus Funded Plans

    1. Unfunded plans—The benefits are either paid from the employer's assets or by insurance coverage (or a combination of those); ERISA exempts unfunded plans, which exempts most welfare plans. (The auditor is not responsible for determining whether the plan is "unfunded" or "funded; the plan sponsor's legal counsel should be involved in determining that.)

    2. Funded plans—If any portion of an ERISA benefit plan is deemed "funded," then all of the plan's activities are subject to the ERISA audit requirements; in this case, the plan assets are required to be held in trust.

III. Pension Plans—Basic Terminology

A. Defined Contribution Plans

    1. 401(k) plans—These permit employees to defer a portion of their income to the pension plan; taxes are deferred until a distribution is made at a future date.

        a. The employer may make a matching contribution, although employer contributions generally are not required.

        b. Roth 401(k) contributions—Subject to specific tax requirements, contributions are made with after-tax dollars so that neither the original contribution nor the investment earnings will be subject to taxes when distributed.

    2. 403(b) plans—Similar to 401(k) plans, these are associated with charitable organizations and public school entities; there are numerous technical requirements, including a "universal availability" requirement that nearly all employees are entitled to participate in the plan; also, plan assets may be held in a custodial account and need not be held in trust.

    3. Employee stock ownership plans—ESOPs are stock incentive plans primarily invested in the employer's securities; these plans are subject to many complex technical issues that require auditors to study the underlying plan document in detail.

B. Defined Benefit Plans

    1. Traditional plans—The benefits are based on the plan's benefit formula, and the accounting considerations are based on various actuarial concepts.

    2. Cash balance plans—In such plans, participants may choose to take lump-sum cash distributions or to take distributions as annuities.

IV. General Audit Considerations

A. ERISA Audit Requirements—ERISA requires an annual audit by an "independent qualified public accountant" of the financial statements of employee benefit plans (i.e., those that are not exempt from such a requirement).

    1. Pension plans—An audit normally is required for a pension plan covered by ERISA having at least 100 participants at the start of the plan year (considered a "large" plan); the number of "participants" is based on those eligible to participate regardless of the number actually participating.

    2. Welfare plans—An audit is normally required for a welfare plan covered by ERISA having the following characteristics: (a) it is a "large" plan having at least 100 participants at the start of the plan year (based on those who have actually elected to participate), and (b) the plan is "funded" (meaning that assets are held in trust or an account is established in the plan's name).

    3. Additional exemptions—There is a general exemption for pension plans of any number of participants when (1) the benefits are provided by an insurance contract for each participant, and (2) those insurance contracts are funded by premiums paid from the employer's general assets (perhaps paid in part by participants' contributions); there is a similar general exemption for welfare plans of any number of participants.

Note

Determining whether an audit is required for an employee benefit plan requires careful study of the underlying plan documents. The plan administrator may need to consult with an attorney knowledgeable about ERISA in making that determination.

B. DOL Form 5500—The DOL requires plan financial statements to be filed on Form 5500, *Annual Return/Report of Employee Benefit Plan*; the financial statements may be based on GAAP, the cash basis, or the modified cash basis of accounting; the DOL also requires the auditor to express an opinion on whether the financial statements and supplemental schedules comply with applicable DOL requirements.

C. Inquiries about the plan's tax status—The auditor should inquire of management (and obtain appropriate written representations) as to whether the plan complies with applicable laws and regulations affecting the plan's qualified tax status; the auditor should also read any correspondence with the IRS.

D. GAAS—Audits of employee benefit plans should be conducted according to generally accepted auditing standards; the audit takes into consideration relevant compliance issues, but the audit is not designed to ensure compliance with applicable laws (such compliance is the responsibility of the plan administrator, not the auditor).

V. GAAS is specified by SAS No. 136, *Forming an Opinion and Reporting on Financial Statements of Employee Benefit Plans Subject to ERISA*

A. This SAS addressed requirements associated with the following issues:

    1. Engagement acceptance issues—There are additional conditions that management must agree to, including maintaining a plan instrument and administering the plan and providing a substantially complete draft Form 5500 to the auditor.

    2. Risk assessment and linkage of planned audit procedures

      a. Should read the plan instrument and consider the risk of material misstatement

      b. Plan tax status—Should consider whether management has performed relevant compliance tests affecting the plan's tax status under the Internal Revenue Code

    c. Prohibited transactions—Any identified prohibited transactions should be appropriately reported in the ERISA-required supplemental schedules

  3. **Communication with those charged with governance** (specifically regarding reportable findings)

    a. Reportable findings—Involving one or more of the following: (1) noncompliance with applicable laws or regulations; (2) a significant finding that is relevant to those charged with governance; or (3) any identified significant deficiencies in internal control

    b. Communication of reportable finding—Should be timely communicated in writing to those charged with governance (include an explanation of the potential effects on the financial statements or the plan)

  4. **Responsibilities involving required supplemental schedules and the ERISA—related Form 5500**

    a. Should read the draft Form 5500 before dating the auditor's report to identify material inconsistencies with the audited ERISA plan financial statements

    b. If there are material inconsistencies—Determine whether the financial statements or the draft Form 5500 should be revised

    c. If there is material misstatement of fact in the Form 5500—Should discuss the matter with management; may suggest that management should consult with a qualified third party (such as legal counsel) for guidance

B. **ERISA section 103(a)(3)(C) audits** (formerly known as limited-scope audits)

  1. DOL regulations permit the plan management to elect to omit certain investment information from the audit when such investments are held and certified by a qualified institution (e.g., an insurance company, a bank, or a trust company that is subject to periodic state or federal examination)

  2. **Required certification**—The qualified financial institution holding these plan assets must furnish a certification that the investments and related investment activity are "complete and accurate; without an acceptable certification, an ERISA section 103(a)(3)(C) audit is not permitted (a mere confirmation is not an acceptable substitute for such certification).

  3. The plan administrator may then direct the auditor not to perform any audit procedures on the investment assets or activities that are the object of the qualified financial institution's certification; these investments typically represent the preponderance of the plan's assets.

  4. Auditor responsibilities regarding the certification—The auditor should (1) read the qualified financial institution's certification, (2) agree the certified information with that reported in the plan's financial statements, and (3) verify that the financial statement disclosures regarding the certified information are in accordance with GAAP requirements and in compliance with DOL requirements.

  5. Audit focus in an ERISA section 103(a)(3)(C) audit—The auditor should evaluate the noninvestment activity of the plan, including: (1) employee and employer contributions, (2) payments of benefits, (3) participant demographic and payroll data, (4) loans to participants, (5) the allocation of investment income to individual participants, (6) liabilities and plan obligations, and (7) administrative expenses.

  6. See the following AICPA sample audit report for a defined contribution plan when management has elected an ERISA section 103(a)(3)(C) audit:

Scope and Nature of the ERISA Section 103(a)(3)(C) Audit

Independent Auditor's Report

[Appropriate Addressee]

We have performed audits of the financial statements of ABC 401(k) Plan, an employee benefit plan subject to the Employee Retirement Income Security Act of 1974 (ERISA), as permitted by ERISA Section 103(a)(3)(C) (ERISA Section 103(a)(3)(C) audit). The financial statements comprise the statements of net assets available for benefits as of December 31, 20X2 and 20X1, and the related statement of changes in net assets available for benefits for the year ended December 31, 20X2, and the related notes to the financial statements.

Management, having determined it is permissible in the circumstances, has elected to have the audits of ABC 401 (k) Plan's financial statements performed in accordance with ERISA Section 103(a)(3)(C) pursuant to 29 CFR 2520.103-8 of the Department of Labor's Rules and Regulations for Reporting and Disclosure under ERISA. As permitted by ERISA Section 103(a)(3)(C), our audits need not extend to any statements or information related to assets held for investment of the plan (investment information) by a bank or similar institution or insurance carrier that is regulated, supervised, and subject to periodic examination by a state or federal agency, provided that the statements or information regarding assets so held are prepared and certified to by the bank or similar institution or insurance carrier in accordance with 29 CFR 2520.103-5 of the Department of Labor's Rules and Regulations for Reporting and Disclosure under ERISA (qualified institution).

Management has obtained certifications from a qualified institution as of December 31, 20X2 and 20X1, and for the year ended December 31, 20X2, stating that the certified investment information, as described in Note X to the financial statements, is complete and accurate.

Opinion

In our opinion, based on our audits and on the procedures performed as described in the Auditor's Responsibilities for the Audit of the Financial Statements section

- the amounts and disclosures in the accompanying financial statements, other than those agreed to or derived from the certified investment information, are presented fairly, in all material respects, in accordance with accounting principles generally accepted in the United States of America.

- the information in the accompanying financial statements related to assets held by and certified to by a qualified institution agrees to, or is derived from, in all material respects, the information prepared and certified by an institution that management determined meets the requirements of ERISA Section 103(a)(3)(C).

Basis for Opinion

We conducted our audits in accordance with auditing standards generally accepted in the United States of America (GAAS). Our responsibilities under those standards are further described in the Auditor's Responsibilities for the Audit of the Financial Statements section of our report. We are required to be independent of ABC 401(k) Plan and to meet our other ethical responsibilities, in accordance with the relevant ethical requirements relating to our audits. We believe that the audit evidence we have obtained is sufficient and appropriate to provide a basis for our ERISA Section 103(a)(3)(C) audit opinion.

Responsibilities of Management for the Financial Statements

Management is responsible for the preparation and fair presentation of the financial statements in accordance with accounting principles generally accepted in the United States of America, and for the design, implementation, and maintenance of internal control relevant to the preparation and fair presentation of financial statements that are free from material misstatement, whether due to fraud or error. Management's election of the ERISA Section 103(a)(3)(C) audit does not affect management's responsibility for the financial statements.

In preparing the financial statements, management is required to evaluate whether there are conditions or events, considered in the aggregate, that raise substantial doubt about ABC 401(k) Plan's ability to continue as a going concern for [insert the time period set by the applicable financial reporting framework].

Management is also responsible for maintaining a current plan instrument, including all plan amendments, administering the plan, and determining that the plan's transactions that are presented and disclosed in the financial statements are in conformity with the plan's provisions, including maintaining sufficient records with respect to each of the participants, to determine the benefits due or which may become due to such participants.

Auditor's Responsibilities for the Audit of the Financial Statements

Except as described in the Scope and Nature of the ERISA Section 103(a)(3)(C) Audit section of our report, our objectives are to obtain reasonable assurance about whether the financial statements as a whole are free from material misstatement, whether due to fraud or error, and to issue an auditor's report that includes our opinion. Reasonable assurance is a high level of assurance but is not absolute assurance and therefore is not a guarantee that an audit conducted in accordance with GAAS will always detect a material misstatement when it exists. The risk of not detecting a material misstatement resulting from fraud is higher than for one resulting from error, as fraud may involve collusion, forgery, intentional omissions, misrepresentations, or the override of internal control. Misstatements are considered material if, individually or in the aggregate, they could reasonably be expected to influence the economic decisions of users made on the basis of these financial statements.

In performing an audit in accordance with GAAS, we:

- Exercise professional judgment and maintain professional skepticism throughout the audit.

- Identify and assess the risks of material misstatement of the financial statements, whether due to fraud or error, and design and perform audit procedures responsive to those risks. Such procedures include examining, on a test basis, evidence regarding the amounts and disclosures in the financial statements.

- Obtain an understanding of internal control relevant to the audit in order to design audit procedures that are appropriate in the circumstances, but not for the purpose of expressing an opinion on the effectiveness of ABC 401(k) Plan's internal control. Accordingly, no such opinion is expressed.

- Evaluate the appropriateness of accounting policies used and the reasonableness of significant accounting estimates made by management, as well as evaluate the overall presentation of the financial statements.

- Conclude whether, in our judgment, there are conditions or events, considered in the aggregate, that raise substantial doubt about ABC 401(k) Plan's ability to continue as a going concern for a reasonable period of time.

Our audits did not extend to the certified investment information, except for obtaining and reading the certification, comparing the certified investment information with the related information presented and disclosed in the financial statements, and reading the disclosures relating to the certified investment information to assess whether they are in accordance with the presentation and disclosure requirements of accounting principles generally accepted in the United States of America.

Accordingly, the objective of an ERISA Section 103(a)(3)(C) audit is not to express an opinion about whether the financial statements as a whole are presented fairly, in all material respects, in accordance with accounting principles generally accepted in the United States of America.

We are required to communicate with those charged with governance regarding, among other matters, the planned scope and timing of the audit, significant audit findings, and certain internal control-related matters that we identified during the audit.

Other Matter—Supplemental Schedules Required by ERISA

The supplemental schedules of [identify title of supplemental schedules and periods covered] are presented for purposes of additional analysis and are not a required part of the financial statements but are supplementary information required by the Department of Labor's Rules and Regulations for Reporting and Disclosure under ERISA. Such information is the responsibility of management and was derived from and relates directly to the underlying accounting and other records used to prepare the financial statements. The information included in the supplemental schedules, other than that agreed to or derived from the certified investment information, has been subjected to the auditing procedures applied in the audits of the financial statements and certain additional procedures, including comparing and reconciling such information directly to the underlying accounting and other records used to prepare the financial statements or to the financial statements themselves, and other additional procedures in accordance with GAAS. For information included in the supplemental schedules that agreed to or is derived from the certified investment information, we compared such information to the related certified investment information.

In forming our opinion on the supplemental schedules, we evaluated whether the supplemental schedules, other than the information agreed to or derived from the certified investment information, including their form and content, are presented in conformity with the Department of Labor's Rules and Regulations for Reporting and Disclosure under ERISA.

In our opinion

- the form and content of the supplemental schedules, other than the information in the supplemental schedules that agreed to or is derived from the certified investment information, are presented, in all material respects, in conformity with the Department of Labor's Rules and Regulations for Reporting and Disclosure under ERISA.

- the information in the supplemental schedules related to assets held by and certified to by a qualified institution agrees to, or is derived from, in all material respects, the information prepared and certified by an institution that management determined meets the requirements of ERISA Section 103(a)(3)(C).

[Signature of the auditor's firm]

[City and state where the auditor's report is issued]

[Date of the auditor's report]

Introduction to Attestation Standards

> **After studying this lesson, you should be able to:**
>
> **1.** State the definition of an "attestation engagement" and the three different kinds of attestation engagements identified in the definition of "attestation engagement."
>
> **2.** Describe the non-authoritative principles associated with attestation engagements, consisting of (a) purpose and premise; (b) responsibilities; (c) performance; and (d) reporting.

Statements on Standards for Attestation Engagements (SSAEs) are issued by the AICPA's Auditing Standards Board (ASB) and are applicable to the preparation and issuance of attestation reports for nonissuers. In April 2016, the ASB replaced substantially all of the then-existing SSAEs with "clarified" SSAEs, similar to what the Auditing Standards Board previously did with the Statements on Auditing Standards and to what the Accounting and Review Services Committee did with the Statements on Standards for Accounting and Review Services. The main purpose of this project was to make the clarified SSAEs easier to read and understand and, therefore, to improve the application of these standards in practice; a further purpose was to more closely align U.S attestation-related professional standards with international standards.

Accordingly, the ASB adopted clarity drafting conventions, such as the following: (1) specified objectives for each of the clarified sections of the AT-C (i.e., the clarified SSAE sections); (2) included a section on definitions, as applicable, in each AT-C; (3) separated the professional "requirements" from the "application and other explanatory material" parts of each AT-C; and (4) adopted formatting techniques (e.g., using bullet lists) to improve the flow and readability of each AT-C.

The clarified SSAEs were issued as SSAE No. 18, *Attestation Standards: Clarification and Recodification*. It was comprised of the following primary sections:

- AT-C Preface, *Preface to the Attestation Standards*
- AT-C Section 105, *Concepts Common to All Attestation Engagements*
- AT-C Section 205, *Examination Engagements*
- AT-C Section 210, *Review Engagements*
- AT-C Section 215, *Agreed-Upon Procedures Engagements*
- AT-C Section 305, *Prospective Financial Information*
- AT-C Section 310, *Reporting on Pro Forma Financial Information*
- AT-C Section 315, *Compliance Attestation*
- AT-C Section 320, *Reporting on an Examination of Controls at a Service Organization...*
- AT-C Section 395, *Management's Discussion and Analysis*

The previously issued AT Section *701, Management's Discussion and Analysis*, was adopted as is without being issued in clarified format. The ASB concluded that practitioners rarely report on such MD&A presentations, so the existing guidance would be classified as AT-C Section 395 in unclarified form at until further notice.

Compliance with the SSAEs is enforceable under the AICPA Code of Professional Conduct, specifically the *Compliance With Standards* Rule (ET Sec. 1.310.001).

I. Definition

> **Definition**
>
> *Attestation Engagement*: "An examination, review, or agreed-upon procedures engagement performed under the attestation standards related to subject matter or an assertion that is the responsibility of another party."

II. Structure of the Attestation Standards

A. Section 105—This section addresses the concepts that are common to any attestation engagement.

B. Section 205, 210, and 215— These sections address the additional "level of service" requirements and guidance applicable to examination, review, and agreed-upon procedures engagements, respectively.

C. 300-Level Sections—These sections address the additional "subject-matter" requirements and guidance associated with certain specific topics.

III. Principles for Understanding Attestation Engagements (Not Authoritative)

A. Purpose and Premise

1. Purpose—"The purpose of an attestation engagement is to provide users of information, generally third parties, with an opinion, conclusion, or findings regarding the reliability of subject matter or an assertion about the subject matter, as measured against suitable and available criteria."

2. Premise—"An engagement in accordance with the attestation standards is conducted on the premise that the responsible party is responsible for:

a. The subject matter (and, if applicable, the preparation and presentation of the subject matter) in accordance with (or based on) the criteria;

b. Its assertion about the subject matter;

c. Measuring, evaluating, and, when applicable, presenting subject matter that is free from material misstatement, whether due to fraud or error; *and*

d. Providing the practitioner with:

i. Access to all information of which the responsible party is aware that is relevant to the measurement, evaluation, or disclosure of the subject matter;

ii. Access to additional information that the practitioner may request from the responsible party for the purpose of the engagement; *and*

iii. Unrestricted access to persons within the appropriate party(ies) from whom the practitioner determines it is necessary to obtain evidence."

B. Responsibilities—"Practitioners are responsible for complying with the relevant performance and reporting requirements established in the attestation standards."

C. Performance

1. Performance responsibilities—"In all services provided under the attestation standards, practitioners are responsible for

a. Having the appropriate competence and capabilities to perform the engagement,

b. Complying with relevant ethical requirements,

c. Maintaining professional skepticism, *and*

d. Exercising professional judgment throughout the planning and performance of the engagement."

2. **For an examination engagement**—"To express an opinion in an examination, the practitioner obtains reasonable assurance about whether the subject matter, or an assertion about the subject matter, is free from material misstatements, whether due to fraud or error. To obtain reasonable assurance, which is a high but not absolute level of assurance, the practitioner

    a. Plans the work and properly supervises other members of the engagement team.

    b. Identifies and assesses the risks of material misstatement, whether due to fraud or error, based on an understanding of the subject matters, its measurement or evaluation, the criteria, and other engagement circumstances.

    c. Obtains sufficient appropriate evidence about whether material misstatements exist by designing and implementing appropriate responses to the assessed risks. Examination procedures may involve inspection, observation, analysis, inquiry, reperformance, recalculation, or confirmation with outside parties."

3. **For a review engagement**—"To express a conclusion in a review, the practitioner obtains limited assurance about whether any material modification should be made to the subject matter in order for it to be in accordance with (or based on) the criteria or to an assertion about the subject matter in order for it to be fairly stated. In a review, the nature and extent of the procedures are substantially less than in an examination. To obtain limited assurance in a review, the practitioner

    a. Plans the work and properly supervises other members of the engagement team.

    b. Focuses procedures in those areas in which the practitioner believes increased risks of misstatements exist, whether due to fraud or error, based on the practitioner's understanding of the subject matter, its measurement or evaluation, the criteria, and other engagement circumstances.

    c. Obtains review evidence, through the application of inquiry and analytical procedures or other procedures as appropriate, to obtain limited assurance that no material modifications should be made to the subject matter in order for it to be in accordance with (or based on) the criteria."

4. **For an agreed-upon procedures engagement**—"To report on the application of agreed-upon procedures, the practitioner applies procedures determined by the specified parties who are the intended users of the practitioner's report and who are responsible for the sufficiency of the procedures for their purposes. As a result of the engagement, the practitioner reports on the results of the engagement but does not provide an opinion or conclusion on the subject matter or assertion. In an agreed-upon procedures engagement, the practitioner

    a. Plans the work and properly supervises other members of the engagement team.

    b. Applies the procedures agreed to by the specified parties and reports on their results."

D. **Reporting**—"Based on evidence obtained, the practitioner expresses an opinion in an examination, expresses a conclusion in a review, or reports findings in an agreed-upon procedures engagement."

Attestation Standards—Common Concepts

After studying this lesson, you should be able to:

1. Describe the guidance that is applicable to attest engagements, including Statements on Standards for Attestation Engagements (SSAEs), interpretive publications, and other attestation publications.

2. Identify the two types of professional requirements ("unconditional requirements" and "presumptively mandatory requirements") and the language associated with each.

3. Describe the preconditions that are applicable to attestation engagements.

I. General Comments

A. Written Assertion
A written assertion as to whether the subject matter is measured or evaluated according to suitable criteria is required when performing an examination or review engagement; a written assertion is not required for an agreed-upon procedures engagement under the attestation standards.

1. **When the engaging party is the responsible party and refuses to provide a written assertion for an examination or a review engagement**—The practitioner should withdraw from the engagement when that is permitted.

2. **When the engaging party is not the responsible party and the responsible party refuses to provide a written assertion for an examination or a review engagement—** That refusal should be disclosed in the practitioner's report, and the report's use should be restricted to the engaging party.

B. Definitions

> **Definitions**
>
> *Engaging Party*: "The party(ies) that engages the practitioner to perform the attestation engagement."
>
> *Responsible Party*: "The party(ies) responsible for the subject matter. If the nature of the subject matter is such that no such party exists, a party who has a reasonable basis for making a written assertion about the subject matter may be deemed to be the responsible party."

1. The practitioner's firm has a responsibility to establish and maintain a system of quality control over its attestation practice to provide reasonable assurance that: (a) personnel comply with professional standards and applicable legal and regulatory requirements; and (b) reports issued by the firm are appropriate in the circumstances.

2. Attestation standards apply to individual attestation engagements, whereas quality control standards apply to the firm's attestation practice as a whole.

II. Guidance Applicable to Attestation Engagements

A. Two Categories of Professional Requirements in the SSAEs

1. **Unconditional requirements**—Must be complied with in all relevant circumstances and are indicated by the word "must."

2. **Presumptively mandatory requirements**—Allow for rare exceptions and are indicated by the word "should." For any such exceptions, the practitioner should perform alternative procedures to meet the requirement's intent.

B. "Application and Other Explanatory Material" (Including Appendices of SSAEs)
These are not "requirements" and are presented separately within the SSAEs. Indicated by the words "may," "might," or "could," they may explain what a requirement means or provide examples of appropriate procedures.

C. The Role of "Interpretive" and "Other" Publications

1. **Interpretive publications**—The accountant should consider the guidance of applicable interpretive publications in performing the engagement. These are recommendations, not requirements, on the application of SSAEs in particular circumstances after Auditing Standards Board members have had the opportunity to comment on the proposed interpretations.

2. **Other attestation publications**—The accountant may evaluate the relevance and appropriateness of such guidance to the engagement, but other attestation publications have no authoritative status.

III. Preconditions for an Attestation Engagement

A. Three Fundamental Preconditions Applicable to Any Attestation Engagement

1. The practitioner must be independent.

2. The responsible party must take responsibility for the subject matter.

3. The engagement must have the following four characteristics:

   a. The subject matter is appropriate.

> **Note**
>
> Subject matter is "appropriate" if it is (a) capable of consistent measurement or evaluation, and (b) can be subject to procedures to obtain sufficient appropriate evidence to support the opinion, conclusion, or findings, as applicable.
>
> If the subject matter is not appropriate for an examination, it is not appropriate for a review.

   b. For an examination or a review engagement – The criteria to be used are suitable and available.

> **Note**
>
> Suitable criteria have these characteristics: (a) they are relevant to the subject matter; (b) they are free from bias; (c) they allow reasonably consistent measurements/evaluations; and (d) they do not omit relevant factors.
>
> Criteria established by a body designated by the AICPA are considered to be suitable.
>
> If criteria are "unsuitable" for an examination, they are also unsuitable for a review.
>
> When criteria are available only to specified parties, the use of the practitioner's report is required to be restricted to the specified parties.

   c. The practitioner expects to obtain the necessary evidence related to the opinion, conclusion or findings.

   d. The practitioner's opinion, conclusion, or findings is to be expressed in a written report.

B. If Any of These Preconditions Are Not Met—The practitioner should attempt to resolve the issue(s) with the engaging party. If the engagement has already been accepted, the practitioner should determine whether it is appropriate to continue with the engagement, and (if so) how to communicate the matter in the report.

IV. Other Considerations Common to Any Attestation Engagement

A. Acceptance and Continuance—Appropriate procedures related to acceptance and continuance of attestation engagements should be followed. The practitioner should not accept an attestation engagement unless he or she has reached an understanding with the engaging party as to the terms of the engagement.

B. Acceptance of a Change in the Terms of the Engagement—"Reasonable justification" is required to change the terms of an engagement to a lower level of service.

1. **If there is reasonable justification**—The practitioner's report should not reference the original engagement, any procedures that may have been performed, or scope limitations that caused the engagement to change.

2. A change in the nature of the engagement originally requested may not be considered reasonably justified if that change is motivated by an inability to obtain sufficient appropriate evidence regarding the subject matter.

C. Using the Work of Other Practitioner(s)

1. Obtain an understanding about the other practitioner's independence and competence.

2. Communicate with the other practitioner about the scope and timing of the other practitioner's work. Be involved with the work of the other practitioner when assuming responsibility for that work.

3. Evaluate the adequacy of other practitioner's work for purposes of the engagement.

4. Determine whether to reference the other practitioner in the report.

D. Engagement Documentation

1. **Documentation completion date**—The practitioner should assemble the final engagement file no later than 60 days following the report release date.

   a. **Deletions**—After the documentation completion date, the practitioner should not delete or discard any documentation prior to the end of the retention period.

   b. **Additions**—After the documentation completion date, additions may be made, but the practitioner must document the reasons for the additions as well as when and by whom the additions were made/reviewed.

2. **Retention**—The practitioner should adopt reasonable procedures to retain the documentation for a period sufficient to meet his or her needs and any legal/regulatory requirements.

3. **Confidentiality**—The practitioner should adopt reasonable procedures to protect the confidentiality of the documentation.

4. **Departures from presumptively mandatory requirements**—The practitioner should document the justification for such a departure and how alternative procedures met the intent of that requirement.

E. Engagement Quality Control Review

1. When such a review is required, the engagement partner should discuss with the quality control reviewer the significant findings; the engagement partner should not release the report until the engagement quality control review is completed.

2. The engagement quality control reviewer should evaluate the significant judgments and conclusions reached, including the following:

   a. Discussing significant findings with the engagement partner;

   b. Reading the written subject matter/assertion and proposed report;

   c. Reading selected documentation for significant judgments and conclusions reached; *and*

   d. Considering whether the proposed report is appropriate.

Note

The AICPA issued SSAE No. 20, *Amendments to the Description of the Concept of Materiality*, in 2019 to better align AICPA Professional Standards with the treatment of materiality by the U.S. courts, the PCAOB, the SEC, and the FASB. This SSAE, which is specific to examination and review engagements, is similar to the coverage in SAS No. 138 issued at the same time and having the same title.

SSAE No. 20 describes materiality as follows: "In general, misstatements, including omissions, are considered to be material if there is a substantial likelihood that, individually or in the aggregate, they would influence the judgment made by intended users based on the subject matter."

Examination Engagements

After studying this lesson, you should be able to:

1. Understand the practitioner's responsibility to obtain a written assertion for an examination engagement.

2. Understand the practitioner's responsibilities in performing an examination engagement, including obtaining written representations.

I. Definition

> **Definition**
>
> *Examination Engagement*: "An attestation engagement in which the practitioner obtains reasonable assurance by obtaining sufficient appropriate evidence about the measurement or evaluation of subject matter against criteria in order to be able to draw reasonable conclusions on which to base the practitioner's opinion about whether the subject matter is in accordance with (or based on) the criteria or the assertion is fairly stated, in all material respects."

> **Note**
>
> The guidance for examination engagements is provided in the Clarified SSAEs, specifically by AT-C 205, *Examination Engagements*. In addition, the practitioner is required to comply with AT-C 105 (*Concepts Common to All Attestation Engagements*) as well as any applicable subject-matter sections.
>
> Compliance with these attestation standards is enforceable under the AICPA's Code of Professional Conduct (specifically, the *Compliance With Standards* Rule).

II. Agreeing on the Terms of the Engagement

A. The practitioner and the engaging party should agree on the terms of the engagement, which should be documented in an engagement letter (or other suitable form of written agreement).

B. The terms of the engagement should include the following:

1. The objective and scope of the engagement;

2. The responsibilities of the practitioner;

3. The responsibilities of the responsible party and the engaging party, if those are different;

4. A statement that the engagement will be conducted according to AICPA attestation standards;

5. A statement about the inherent limitations of an examination;

6. A statement identifying the criteria for measurement or evaluation of the subject matter; *and*

7. Acknowledgment by the engaging party to provide the practitioner with a representation letter at the conclusion of the engagement.

C. Such an agreement should be obtained for each engagement, but, if the terms of the preceding engagement have not changed, the practitioner may simply remind the engaging party of the terms of the engagement (and document that communication).

III. Request a Written Assertion about the Subject Matter

  A. If the Engaging Party Is the Responsible Party and Refuses to Provide a Written Assertion—The practitioner should withdraw when that is permitted.

  B. If the Engaging Party Is Not the Responsible Party and the Responsible Party Refuses to Provide a Written Assertion—The practitioner need not withdraw but should disclose that refusal in the practitioner's report and restrict the use of the report to the engaging party.

  C. The responsible party is still responsible for the subject matter as a whole, and the practitioner should request a written assertion covering the entire relevant period(s), even when the responsible party was not present during some (or all) of the period covered by the practitioner's report.

IV. Planning and Performing the Engagement

  A. Engagement Planning–Related Matters

  1. The practitioner should establish an overall strategy that specifies the scope, timing, and direction of the engagement, including considering factors significant to the engagement team as well as the necessary resources.

  2. The practitioner should develop an engagement plan that specifies the nature, timing, and extent of procedures to be performed.

  3. The practitioner may need to revise the overall strategy and engagement plan due to unexpected events or changes in conditions.

  4. The practitioner should perform risk assessment procedures to identify the risks of material misstatement and to design appropriate procedures in response to that assessment; he or she should also obtain an understanding of internal control over the preparation of the subject matter.

  B. Engagement Performance–Related Matters

  1. Tests of control—The practitioner should perform tests of control about the operating effectiveness of relevant controls when (a) intending to rely on controls for purposes of designing other procedures; (b) procedures other than tests of control cannot provide sufficient appropriate evidence; or (c) the subject matter is internal control.

  2. Procedures other than tests of control—The practitioner should design and perform tests of details or analytical procedures, unless the subject matter is internal control.

  3. Analytical procedures performed in response to assessed risks—The practitioner should (a) determine the suitability of specific analytical procedures; (b) evaluate the reliability of the data from which an expectation is developed; (c) develop an expectation that is sufficiently precise to identify material misstatements; and (d) investigate significant differences from the expectation by inquiry or other procedures.

  4. Procedures regarding estimates—The practitioner should evaluate (a) whether the responsible party has appropriately applied the criteria to any estimates; and (b) whether the methods underlying estimates are appropriate and have been consistently applied (and that any changes in the estimates or methods used are appropriate).

  5. Fraud and noncompliance with laws and regulations—The practitioner should (a) consider the risk of material misstatement due to fraud or noncompliance with laws or regulations, (b) make inquiries of appropriate parties about such matters, and (c) evaluate whether there are any unusual relationships that might indicate risks of material misstatement due to fraud or noncompliance with laws or regulations.

  6. Communication responsibilities—The practitioner should communicate to the responsible party (and also to the engaging party, if different) (a) any known or suspected fraud, (b) any known or suspected noncompliance with laws or regulations, (c) uncorrected misstatements, and (d) identified internal control deficiencies.

7. **Using the work of a practitioner's specialist**

   a. When planning to use the work of a practitioner's specialist, the practitioner should (1) evaluate the specialist's competence and objectivity; (2) obtain an understanding of the specialist's expertise; (3) agree with the specialist regarding the scope of the work to be performed, the parties' roles, the need for communication, and the need to meet confidentiality requirements; and (4) evaluate the specialist's work for the practitioner's purposes.

   b. The practitioner's procedures when planning to use the work of a specialist will vary with the circumstances, including the risks of material misstatement and the practitioner's experience working with the specialist.

   c. An agreement between the practitioner and the practitioner's specialist often is obtained in the form of an engagement letter (but it is not technically required).

8. **Using the work of internal auditors**

   a. When planning to use the work of the internal audit function (either in obtaining evidence or in providing direct assistance), the practitioner should evaluate the **competence** and **objectivity** of the internal audit function;

   b. When planning to use the work of the internal audit function in obtaining evidence, the practitioner should also evaluate whether the work was subject to a **systematic and disciplined approach**.

   c. When planning to use the internal auditors to provide direct assistance, the practitioner should obtain written acknowledgment from the responsible party that the internal auditors will be allowed to follow the practitioner's directives without interference.

   d. The practitioner is responsible for all significant judgments and should appropriately supervise and review the work of the internal auditors.

9. **Considering subsequent events and subsequently discovered facts**

   a. The practitioner should inquire whether the responsible party (and the engaging party, if different) is aware of any subsequent events up to the date of the report that could have a significant effect; and if there are, the practitioner should perform appropriate procedures regarding those events.

   b. The practitioner has no responsibility to perform additional procedures after the report date; however, if there are subsequently discovered facts that may have caused revision of the report if known at the report date, the practitioner should respond appropriately to those facts.

V. **Written Representations**

   A. The practitioner should request written representations from the responsible party, including the responsible party's assertion about the subject matter.

   B. **When the Engaging Party Is Not the Responsible Party**—The practitioner should request additional written representations from the engaging party.

   C. **If the Responsible Party Refuses to Provide the Requested Written Representations**

      1. **When the engaging party is the responsible party**—The practitioner should discuss the matters with the appropriate party (parties) and take appropriate action if the matters are not resolved satisfactorily.

      2. **When the engaging party is not the responsible party**—The practitioner should

         a. Make inquiries of the responsible party and seek oral responses.

         b. **If satisfactory oral responses are obtained**—The practitioner should restrict the use of the report to the engaging party.

    c. If one or more of the requested representations are not provided (either in writing or orally) —A scope limitation exists, and the practitioner should determine the effect on the report.

  D. The representations should address the subject matter and periods covered by the practitioner's report.

  E. The written representations letter should have the same date as the practitioner's report.

VI. Documentation

  A. The documentation should permit an experienced practitioner without any connection to the engagement to understand the work performed and the basis for the primary decisions.

  B. The practitioner should prepare documentation sufficient to comply with AICPA Professional Standards and applicable legal and regulatory requirements, including these six matters:

    1. The identifying characteristics of the specific items tested;

    2. Who performed the work and the date the work was completed;

    3. The discussions with the responsible party (or others) about significant findings or issues, including the nature of the matters discussed (and when and with whom the discussions occurred);

    4. The actions taken when the engaging party is the responsible party and will not provide one or more of the requested written representations (or when representations provided are not seen as reliable);

    5. The oral responses provided when the engaging party is not the responsible party and the responsible party will not provide the requested written representations; *and*

    6. Who reviewed the work performed and the date of that review.

  C. The documentation normally addresses the following additional matters: (1) compliance with relevant ethical requirements, including applicable independence requirements; (2) conclusions about acceptance and continuance of client relationships and engagements; and (3) conclusions about any consultations that occurred during the engagement.

  D. If information has been obtained that is inconsistent with the practitioner's final conclusion about a significant matter, the practitioner should document how he or she dealt with the inconsistency.

Examination Reports

1. Recognize the elements that are required in a practitioner's unmodified examination report for an attestation engagement.

2. Identify the various types of modified reports that might be issued for an examination engagement and the circumstances that would result in each type of modification.

I. Focus of the Practitioner's Report

A. May either report on the responsible party's written assertion or report directly on the subject matter.

B. When reporting on the assertion, the assertion should accompany the practitioner's report (or the assertion may be clearly stated in the report).

II. Content of an Unmodified Examination Report

A. **A standardized format for the examination report is not required for all examination engagements**—The report is to include the identified basic elements but may be tailored to the circumstances of the engagement.

B. These 12 elements should be included in the unmodified report:

1. A title that includes the word "independent"

2. An appropriate addressee

3. Identification of the applicable subject matter or assertion, including the point in time or period of time involved

4. Identification of the criteria against which the subject matter was measured or evaluated

5. A statement that identifies (a) the responsible party and its responsibility, and (b) the practitioner's responsibility to express an opinion

6. A statement that (a) the examination was conducted in accordance with AICPA attestation standards, (b) those standards require the practitioner to plan and perform the engagement to obtain reasonable assurance (whether the subject matter is in accordance with the criteria in all material respects or whether the responsible party's assertion is fairly stated), and (c) the practitioner believes the evidence obtained is sufficient and appropriate to provide a reasonable basis for the opinion

7. A description of the nature of an examination engagement

8. A statement describing any significant inherent limitations associated with the engagement

9. An opinion about whether the subject matter is in accordance with (or based on) the criteria in all material respects or whether the responsible party's assertion is fairly stated in all material respects

10. The signature of the practitioner's firm (either manual or printed)

11. The city and state where the practitioner practices

12. The date of the report

C. AT-C Section 205 provides several examples of unmodified examination reports.

Example
Practitioner's Unmodified Examination Report on the Subject Matter

The following is an illustrative practitioner's report for an examination engagement in which the practitioner has examined the subject matter and is reporting directly on the subject matter.

Independent Accountant's Report

[*Appropriate Addressee*]

We have examined [*identify the subject matter; e.g., the accompanying schedule of investment returns of XYZ Company for the year ended December 31, 20XX*]. XYZ Company's management is responsible for [*identify the subject matter; e.g., presenting the schedule of investment returns*] in accordance with (or based on) [*identify the criteria; e.g., the ABC criteria set forth in Note 1*]. Our responsibility is to express an opinion on [*identify thesubject matter; e.g., the schedule of investment returns*] based on our examination.

Our examination was conducted in accordance with attestation standards established by the American Institute of Certified Public Accountants. Those standards require that we plan and perform the examination to obtain reasonable assurance about whether [*identify the subject matter; e.g., the schedule of investment returns*] is in accordance with (or based on) the criteria, in all material respects. An examination involves performing procedures to obtain evidence about [*identify the subject matter; e.g., the schedule of investment returns*]. The nature, timing, and extent of the procedures selected depend on our judgment, including an assessment of the risks of material misstatement of [*identify the subject matter; e.g., the schedule of investment returns*], whether due to fraud or error. We believe that the evidence we obtained is sufficient and appropriate to provide a reasonable basis for our opinion.

[*Include a description of significant inherent limitations, if any, associated with the measurement or evaluation of the subject matter against the criteria.*]

[*Additional paragraph(s) may be added to emphasize certain matters relating to the attestation engagement or the subject matter.*]

In our opinion, [*identify the subject matter; e.g., the schedule of investment returns of XYZ Company for the year ended December 31, 20XX or the schedule of investment returns referred to above*], is presented in accordance with (or based on) [*identify the criteria; e.g., the ABC criteria set forth in Note 1*], in all material respects.

[*Practitioner's signature*]

[*Practitioner's city and state*]

[*Date of practitioner's report*]

Example
Practitioner's Unmodified Examination Report on an Assertion

The following is an illustrative practitioner's report for an examination engagement in which the practitioner has examined the responsible party's assertion and is reporting on that assertion.

<u>Independent Accountant's Report</u>

[*Appropriate Addressee*]

We have examined management of XYZ Company's assertion that [*identify the assertion, including the subject matter and the criteria; e.g., the accompanying schedule of investment returns of XYZ Company for the year ended December 31, 20XX, is presented in accordance with [or based on] the ABC criteria set forth in Note 1*]. XYZ Company's management is responsible for its assertion. Our responsibility is to express an opinion on management's assertion based on our examination.

Our examination was conducted in accordance with attestation standards established by the American Institute of Certified Public Accountants. Those standards require that we plan and perform the examination to obtain reasonable assurance about whether management's assertion is fairly stated, in all material respects. An examination involves performing procedures to obtain evidence about management's assertion. The nature, timing, and extent of the procedures selected depend on our judgment, including an assessment of the risks of material misstatement of management's assertion, whether due to fraud or error. We believe that the evidence we obtained is sufficient and appropriate to provide a reasonable basis for our opinion.

[*Include a description of significant inherent limitations, if any, associated with the measurement or evaluation of the subject matter against the criteria.*]

[*Additional paragraph(s) may be added to emphasize certain matters relating to the attestation engagement or the subject matter.*]

In our opinion, management's assertion that [*identify the assertion, including the subject matter and the criteria; e.g., the accompanying schedule of investment returns of XYZ Company for the year ended December 31, 20XX, is presented in accordance with [or based on] the ABC criteria set forth in Note 1*] is fairly stated, in all material respects.

[*Practitioner's signature*]

[*Practitioner's city and state*]

[*Date of practitioner's report*]

III. **Modified Opinions**

A. **Modify the Opinion—**

1. When sufficient appropriate evidence has not been obtained in all material respects (regarding the scope); *or*

2. When the subject matter is not in accordance with the criteria in all material respects (regarding the presentation).

B. **When Modifying the Opinion**—Include a separate paragraph in the report that describes the reason(s) for the modification.

C. **Qualified Opinion**—Express a qualified opinion when the possible effect of the scope limitation "could be material, but not pervasive" or when the misstatement of the subject matter "is material, but not pervasive" to the subject matter.

D. **Adverse Opinion**—Express an adverse opinion when the misstatement of the subject matter is both "material and pervasive" to the subject matter.

E. **Disclaimer of Opinion**—Express a disclaimer of opinion when the possible effect of the scope limitation could be both "material and pervasive."

F. When Expressing Either a Qualified or an Adverse Opinion Due to Misstatement of the Subject Matter—Express the opinion directly on the *subject matter*, not on the assertion (even if the assertion acknowledges the misstatement).

G. Change the description of the practitioner's responsibility for modified opinions.

1. **When expressing a qualified or an adverse opinion**—Amend the description of the practitioner's responsibility to express the belief that the evidence obtained is sufficient and appropriate to provide a basis for the modified opinion.

2. **When expressing a disclaimer of opinion**—Amend the description of the practitioner's responsibility to say that the practitioner was engaged to examine the subject matter (or assertion).

IV. Other Examination Reporting Considerations

A. Restricted Use Paragraph—An alert to restrict the use of the report should be added in three circumstances:

1. When the criteria used to evaluate the subject matter are appropriate only for a limited number of parties;

2. When the criteria used to evaluate the subject matter are available only to specified parties; or

3. When the engaging party is not the responsible party and the responsible party does not provide the requested written representations but does provide appropriate oral responses —The practitioner's report should be restricted to the engaging party.

B. Reference to the Practitioner's Specialist

1. Should not refer to the work of the practitioner's specialist in a report having an unmodified opinion.

2. May refer to an external specialist when the opinion is modified and reference is relevant to understanding the modification.

C. Other Information

1. **If the practitioner's report is included in a document that contains the subject matter or assertion, along with other information**—Read the other information for material inconsistencies.

2. **If there is a material inconsistency (or if a material misstatement of fact exists in the other information)**—Discuss the matter with the responsible party and take appropriate action such as:

   a. Request that the appropriate party consult with a third party (such as legal counsel);

   b. Seek legal advice about possible actions;

   c. Communicate with third parties (such as a regulator);

   d. Describe the material inconsistency in the report; or

   e. Withdraw, when that is permissible].

3. "Other information" does not include information on the appropriate party's website.

D. If a Written Report Is Readily Available—The practitioner may also report orally or by using symbols (such as a web seal with a hyperlink to a written report).

Review Engagements

After studying this lesson, you should be able to:

1. Understand the practitioner's responsibility to obtain a written assertion for a review engagement.

2. Understand the practitioner's responsibilities in performing a review engagement, including obtaining written representations.

I. Definition

Definition

Review Engagement: "An attestation engagement in which the practitioner obtains limited assurance by obtaining sufficient appropriate review evidence about the measurement or evaluation of subject matter against criteria in order to express a conclusion about whether any material modification should be made to the subject matter in order for it to be in accordance with (or based on) the criteria or to the assertion in order for it to be fairly stated."

Note

The guidance for review engagements is provided in the Clarified SSAEs, specifically by AT-C 210, *Review Engagements*. In addition, the practitioner is required to comply with AT-C 105, *Concepts Common to All Attestation Engagements*, as well as any applicable subject-matter sections.

Compliance with these attestation standards is enforceable under the AICPA's Code of Professional Conduct (specifically, the *Compliance With Standards* rule).

AT-C 210 specifically prohibits review engagements involving (a) prospective financial information; (b) internal control; or (c) compliance with the requirements of specified laws, regulations, rules, contracts, or grants.

II. Agreeing on the Terms of the Engagement

A. The practitioner and the engaging party should agree on the terms of the engagement, which should be documented in an engagement letter (or other suitable form of written agreement).

B. These terms should include the following:

1. The objective and scope of the engagement;

2. The responsibilities of the practitioner;

3. The responsibilities of the responsible party and the engaging party, if those are different;

4. A statement that the engagement will be conducted according to AICPA attestation standards;

5. A statement that a review is substantially less in scope than an examination and that, accordingly, no opinion will be expressed;

6. A statement identifying the criteria for measurement or evaluation of the subject matter; *and*

7. Acknowledgment by the engaging party to provide the practitioner with a representation letter at the conclusion of the engagement.

C. Such an agreement should be obtained for each engagement, but, if the terms of the preceding engagement have not changed, the practitioner may simply remind the engaging party of the terms of the engagement (and document that communication).

III. **Request a Written Assertion about the Subject Matter**

A. **If the engaging party is the responsible party and refuses to provide a written assertion—**The practitioner should withdraw when that is permitted.

B. **If the engaging party is not the responsible party and the responsible party refuses to provide a written assertion—**The practitioner need not withdraw but should disclose that refusal in the practitioner's report and restrict the use of the report to the engaging party.

C. The responsible party is still responsible for the subject matter as a whole and should request a written assertion covering the entire relevant period(s), even when the responsible party was not present during some (or all) of the period covered by the practitioner's report.

IV. **Planning and Performing the Engagement**

A. The practitioner should obtain a sufficient understanding of the subject matter and circumstances of the engagement to design and perform procedures to achieve the objectives of the engagement.

B. **Procedures to Be Performed**

1. The practitioner should design and perform analytical procedures and make inquiries to obtain limited assurance.

2. Analytical procedures may not be applicable when the subject matter is qualitative instead of quantitative. In that case, the practitioner may need to perform other appropriate procedures.

3. The practitioner should increase the focus in the areas of the engagement that have increased risks of material misstatement.

C. **Analytical Procedures**

1. The practitioner should: (a) determine the suitability of specific analytical procedures (considering the subject matter and assessed risks of material misstatement); (b) evaluate the reliability of data from which the expectation is developed; and (c) develop an expectation that is sufficiently precise to identify material misstatements.

2. The practitioner should investigate significant differences from expectations by (a) inquiring of the responsible party and (b) performing any other procedures considered necessary.

D. **Inquiries and Other Review Procedures—**The practitioner should inquire of the responsible party about the following:

1. Whether the subject matter has been prepared according to (or based on) the criteria;

2. The practices used by the responsible party to measure and record the subject matter;

3. Questions arising in connection with the other review procedures; *and*

4. Communications from regulatory authorities or others, if any.

E. **Fraud, Laws, and Regulations—**The practitioner should make inquiries to determine whether the applicable parties have any knowledge of fraud (including suspected or alleged fraud) or noncompliance with laws or regulations affecting the subject matter.

F. **Incorrect, Incomplete, or Otherwise Unsatisfactory Information—**The practitioner should perform additional procedures to obtain limited assurance as to whether any material modifications should be made to the subject matter.

G. **Using the Work of a Practitioner's Specialist or Internal Auditors—**The practitioner should apply the same requirements stated in AT-C 205 (regarding examination engagements).

H. **Considering Subsequent Events and Subsequently Discovered Facts**

1. The practitioner should inquire whether the responsible party (and the engaging party, if different) is aware of any subsequent events up to the date of the report that could have a

significant effect; if there are, the practitioner should perform appropriate procedures applicable to those events.

2. There is no responsibility to perform additional procedures after the report date. If there are subsequently discovered facts that may have caused revision of the report if known at the report date, the practitioner should respond appropriately to those facts.

V. Written Representations

A. The practitioner should request written representations from the responsible party, including the responsible party's assertion about the subject matter.

B. **When the Engaging Party Is Not the Responsible Party**—The practitioner should request additional written representations from the engaging party.

C. **When the Responsible Party Refuses to Provide the Requested Written Representations**

1. **If the engaging party is the responsible party**—The practitioner should withdraw from the engagement (when withdrawal is permitted under applicable law or regulation).

2. **When the engaging party is not the responsible party**—The practitioner should

   a. Make inquiries of the responsible party and seek oral responses.

   b. **If satisfactory oral responses are obtained**—The practitioner should restrict the use of the report to the engaging party.

   c. **If one or more of the requested representations are not provided** (either in writing or orally) —A scope limitation exists, and the practitioner should withdraw from the engagement, if possible.

D. The representations should address the subject matter and periods covered by the practitioner's report.

E. The written representations letter should have the same date as the practitioner's report.

VI. Documentation

A. The documentation should permit an experienced practitioner without any connection to the engagement to understand the work performed and the basis for the primary decisions.

B. The practitioner should prepare documentation sufficient to comply with AICPA Professional Standards and applicable legal and regulatory requirements, including the following matters:

1. The identifying characteristics of the specific items tested;

2. Who performed the work and the date the work was completed;

3. The discussions with the responsible party (or others) about significant findings or issues, including the nature of the matters discussed (and when and with whom the discussions occurred);

4. The actions taken when the engaging party is the responsible party and will not provide one or more of the required written representations (or when representations provided are not seen as reliable);

5. The oral responses provided when the engaging party is not the responsible party and the responsible party will not provide the required written representations; *and*

6. Who reviewed the work performed and the date it was reviewed.

C. The documentation normally addresses the following additional matters:

1. Compliance with relevant ethical requirements, including applicable independence requirements;

2. Conclusions about acceptance and continuance of client relationships and engagements; *and*

3. Conclusions about any consultations that occurred during the engagement.

D. If Information Has Been Obtained that Is Inconsistent with the Practitioner's Final Conclusion about a Significant Matter—The practitioner should document how the practitioner dealt with the inconsistency.

Review Reports

I. Focus of the Practitioner's Report

A. May either report on the responsible party's written assertion or directly on the subject matter.

B. When reporting on the assertion, the assertion should accompany the practitioner's report (or the assertion may be clearly stated in the report).

II. Content of an Unmodified Review Report

A. A standardized format for the review report is not required for all review engagements. The report is to include the identified basic elements but may be tailored to the circumstances of the engagement.

B. The following elements should be included in the unmodified review report:

1. A title that includes the word "independent;

2. An appropriate addressee;

3. Identification of the applicable subject matter or assertion, including the point in time or period of time involved;

4. Identification of the criteria against which the subject matter was measured or evaluated;

5. Statement that identifies (a) the responsible party and its responsibility and (b) the practitioner's responsibility to express a conclusion;

6. Statement that (a) the review was conducted in accordance with AICPA attestation standards, (b) those standards require the practitioner to plan and perform the engagement to obtain limited assurance whether any material modifications should be made (either to the subject matter or to the responsible party's assertion), (c) a review is substantially less in scope than an examination so disclaim an opinion, and (d) the practitioner believes the review provides a reasonable basis for the conclusion;

7. Statement describing any significant inherent limitations associated with the engagement;

8. The conclusion about whether any material modifications should be made to the subject matter or to the responsible party's assertion;

9. The signature of the practitioner's firm (either manual or printed);

10. The city and state where the practitioner practices; *and*

11. The date of the report.

C. AT-C Section 210 provides several examples of review reports.

Example
Practitioner's Review Report on Subject Matter; Unmodified Conclusion

Note: The following is an illustrative practitioner's report for a review engagement in which the practitioner has reviewed the subject matter and is reporting directly on the subject matter.

Independent Accountant's Review Report

[*Appropriate Addressee*]

We have reviewed [*identify the subject matter; e.g., the accompanying schedule of investment returns of XYZ Company for the year ended December 31, 20XX*]. XYZ Company's management is responsible for [*identify thesubject matter; e.g., presenting the schedule of investment returns*] in accordance with (or based on) [*identify the criteria; e.g., the ABC criteria set forth in Note 1*]. Our responsibility is to express a conclusion on [*identify the subject matter; e.g., the schedule of investment returns*] based on our review.

Our review was conducted in accordance with attestation standards established by the American Institute of Certified Public Accountants. Those standards require that we plan and perform the review to obtain limited assurance about whether any material modifications should be made to [*identify the subject matter; e.g., the schedule of investment returns*] in order for it to be in accordance with (or based on) the criteria. A review is substantially less in scope than an examination, the objective of which is to obtain reasonable assurance about whether [*identify the subject matter; e.g., the schedule of investment returns*] is in accordance with (or based on) the criteria, in all material respects, in order to express an opinion. Accordingly, we do not express such an opinion. We believe that our review provides a reasonable basis for our conclusion.

[*Include a description of significant inherent limitations, if any, associated with the measurement or evaluation of the subject matter against the criteria.*]

[*Additional paragraph(s) may be added to emphasize certain matters relating to the attestation engagement or the subject matter.*]

Based on our review, we are not aware of any material modifications that should be made to [*identify the subject matter; e.g., the accompanying schedule of investment returns of XYZ Company for the year ended December 31, 20XX*], in order for it be in accordance with (or based on) [*identify the criteria; e.g., the ABC criteria set forth in Note 1*].

[*Practitioner's signature*]

[*Practitioner's city and state*]

[*Date of practitioner's report*]

Example

Practitioner's Review Report on Subject Matter; Qualified Conclusion

Note: The following is an illustrative practitioner's report for a review engagement that expresses a qualified conclusion because the review identified conditions that, result in a material, but not pervasive, misstatement of the subject matter, based on the criteria. The practitioner has reviewed the subject matter and is also reporting on the subject matter.

Independent Accountant's Review Report

[*Appropriate Addressee*]

We have reviewed [*identify the subject matter; e.g., the accompanying schedule of investment returns of XYZ Company for the year ended December 31, 20XX*]. XYZ Company's management is responsible for [*identify thesubject matter, for example, presenting the schedule of investment returns*] based on [*identify the criteria; e.g., the ABC criteria set forth in Note 1*]. Our responsibility is to express a conclusion on [*identify the subject matter; e.g., the schedule of investment returns*] based on our review.

Our review was conducted in accordance with attestation standards established by the American Institute of Certified Public Accountants. Those standards require that we plan and perform the review to obtain limited assurance about whether any material modifications should be made to [*identify the subject matter; e.g., the schedule of investment returns*] in order for it to be in accordance with (or based on) the criteria. A review is substantially less in scope than an examination, the objective of which is to obtain reasonable assurance about whether [*identify the subject matter; e.g., the schedule of investment returns*] is in accordance with (or based on) the criteria, in all material respects, in order to express an opinion. Accordingly, we do not express such an opinion. We believe that our review provides a reasonable basis for our conclusion.

[*Include a description of significant inherent limitations, if any, associated with the measurement or evaluation of the subject matter against the criteria.*]

[*Additional paragraph(s) may be added to emphasize certain matters relating to the attestation engagement or the subject matter.*]

Our review identified [*describe condition(s) that, individually or in the aggregate, resulted in a material misstatement, or deviation from, the criteria*].

Based on our review, except for the matter(s) described in the preceding paragraph, we are not aware of any material modifications that should be made to [*identify the subject matter; e.g., the accompanying schedule of investment returns of XYZ Company for the year ended December 31, 20XX*], in order for it to be in accordance with (or based on) [*identify the criteria; e.g., the ABC criteria set forth in Note 1*].

[*Practitioner's signature*]

[*Practitioner's city and state*]

[*Date of practitioner's report*]

III. Modified Conclusions

A. Misstatement of Subject Matter

1. The practitioner should consider whether qualification of the conclusion in the "standard practitioner's report" is an adequate way to disclose the misstatement of the subject matter. If that is not an adequate way to disclose the matter, then the practitioner should withdraw from the engagement.

2. The practitioner may express a qualified conclusion with the phrase "except for the effects of . . ." when the effects are material but not pervasive. In such a case, the practitioner should report directly on the subject matter, not on the assertion (even if the assertion acknowledges the misstatement).

3. If the effects of the misstatement are material and pervasive, the practitioner should withdraw from the engagement when that is permissible.

B. Scope Limitations—If sufficient appropriate review evidence is not obtained, a scope limitation exists, and the practitioner should withdraw when that is permissible.

IV. Other Review Reporting Considerations

A. Restricted-Use Paragraph—An alert to restrict the use of the report should be added in the following circumstances:

1. When the criteria used to evaluate the subject matter are appropriate only for a limited number of parties;

2. When the criteria used to evaluate the subject matter are available only to specified parties; or

3. When the engaging party is not the responsible party and the responsible party does not provide the requested written representations but does provide appropriate oral responses. In this case, the practitioner's report should be restricted to the engaging party.

B. Reference to the Practitioner's Specialist

1. The practitioner should not refer to the work of the practitioner's specialist in a report having an unmodified conclusion.

2. The practitioner may refer to an external specialist when the conclusion is modified and reference to the specialist is relevant to understanding the modification.

C. Other Information

1. **If the practitioner's report is included in a document that contains the subject matter or assertion, along with other information**—The practitioner should read the other information for material inconsistencies.

2. **If there is a material inconsistency** (or if a material misstatement of fact exists in the other information)—The practitioner should discuss the matter with the responsible party and take appropriate action [e.g., (a) request that the appropriate party consult with a third party (such as legal counsel); (b) seek legal advice about possible actions; (c) communicate with third parties (such as a regulator); (d) describe the material inconsistency in the report; or (e) withdraw, when that is permissible].

Agreed-Upon Procedures Engagements

I. Relevant AICPA Guidance

The relevant AICPA guidance in the clarified attestation standards is provided by AT 215, *Agreed-Upon Procedures Engagements* (SSAE No. 19, issued 2019).

    A. The practitioner is also required to comply with AT-C 105 (*Concepts Common to All Attestation Engagements*) as well as any relevant subject-matter sections.

    B. Objectives of the practitioner—To apply specific procedures to subject matter, to issue an appropriate report that describes the procedures performed and the findings, and to communicate further as required by applicable AT-C sections.

    C. Compliance with these attestation standards is enforceable under the AICPA's Code of Professional Conduct, specifically the *Compliance with Standards Rule*.

II. Definition

> **Definition**
>
> *Agreed-upon Procedures Engagement: "An attestation engagement in which a practitioner performs specific procedures on subject matter and reports the findings without providing an opinion or conclusion."*

> **Note to CPA Candidates Testing Prior to October 1, 2021:**
> The changes associated with SSAE No. 19, "Agreed-Upon Procedures Engagements," will not be tested until **October 1, 2021**. Before that date, the guidance in a prior SSAE applies. Most importantly, remember that through September 2021, the following requirements apply to agreed-upon procedures (AUP) engagements:
>
> 1. The practitioner is required to obtain a written assertion from the responsible party;
>
> 2. The distribution of AUP reports must be restricted to the specified parties; and
>
> 3. The specified parties must take responsibility for the adequacy of the procedures for their purposes.

III. Overview of Primary Differences—SSAE No. 19 versus Prior Attestation Standards

    A. No longer requires the practitioner to obtain an assertion from the responsible party

    B. No longer requires the practitioner to restrict the distribution of the report to so-called specified users; now allows for the possibility of a general-use report

    C. No longer requires the intended users of the report to take responsibility for the adequacy of the procedures; however, the engaging party must still do that

    D. Now permits procedures to be developed during the engagement (and allows the practitioner to assist in developing the procedures) as long as the engaging party acknowledges the appropriateness of the procedures prior to issuance of the report

IV. Agreeing on the Terms of the Engagement

A. The practitioner and engaging party should agree upon the terms of the engagement, which should be specified in an engagement letter (or other suitable written agreement) addressed to the engaging party.

B. The agreed-upon terms should include the following:

1. The nature of the engagement

2. Identification of the subject matter and the responsible party

3. The responsibilities of the practitioner

4. A statement that the engagement will be conducted according to AICPA attestation standards

5. A statement that the responsible party is responsible for the subject matter

6. A statement that the engaging party agrees to provide a written agreement and acknowledgment that the procedures performed are appropriate for the intended purpose of the engagement

7. A statement that the engaging party agrees to provide a representations letter (if the engaging party is not the responsible party, include a statement that written representations may be requested from the responsible party)

8. If known at the start of the engagement, identification of any other parties that will be requested to agree to the procedures and acknowledge that the procedures are appropriate for their purposes

9. Reference to the expected form and content of the AUP report, including any restrictions, if applicable

10. Identification of any disclaimers expected to be included in the report, if applicable

11. Identification of any assistance to be provided to the practitioner

12. Identification of any practitioner's external specialist to be used

13. Identification of specified thresholds for reporting exceptions, if applicable

V. Planning and Performing the Agreed-Upon Procedures Engagement

A. Procedures to be performed—The practitioner should not agree to perform procedures that are vague or otherwise open to varying interpretations.

1. Examples of unacceptable terms (due to vagueness) include the following: note, review, general review, limited review, evaluate, analyze, check, test, interpret, and verify.

2. Examples of acceptable terms include the following: inspect, confirm, compare, agree, trace, inquire, recalculate, observe, and mathematically check.

B. Using the work of a practitioner's external specialist

1. Any involvement of a practitioner's external specialist should be agreed to by the engaging party.

2. The practitioner's report should describe any assistance provided by the practitioner's external specialist.

C. Using the work of internal auditors—Only the engagement team (or other practitioners), not internal auditors, should perform the agreed-upon procedures referenced in the practitioner's report; internal auditors may prepare schedules and accumulate data for the practitioner's use.

D. Appropriateness of the procedures performed—Prior to the issuance of the AUP report, the practitioner should obtain from the engaging party a written agreement of the procedures and acknowledgment of the appropriateness of the procedures for the intended purpose of the engagement; if the engaging party refuses to provide that, the practitioner should withdraw from the engagement.

    E. Written representations—Should be requested from the engaging party

        1. These written representations should include the following:

            a. A statement that the responsible party is responsible for the subject matter

            b. If applicable, a statement that the engaging party has obtained from all necessary parties their agreement to the procedures and acknowledgment that the procedures are appropriate for the intended purposes

            c. A statement that the engaging party provided all relevant information and access, as applicable, as agreed to

            d. A statement that all known matters contradicting the subject matter and any communications from regulatory agencies or others relevant to the subject matter have been disclosed to the practitioner

            e. A statement that the engaging party is not aware of any material misstatements in the subject matter

            f. A statement that the engaging party has disclosed all known subsequent events that would be material to the subject matter

            g. Any additional representations deemed appropriate by the practitioner

        2. When the engaging party is not the responsible party—Should also consider requesting written representations from the responsible party

        3. The written representations should be dated the same as the date of the practitioner's report.

        4. If the requested written representations are not provided or are not reliable—Should discuss the matter with the appropriate parties and take appropriate action if the matters are not satisfactorily resolved (e.g., if the responsible party refuses to provide requested written representations, that refusal should be identified in the practitioner's report).

    F. Documentation—The practitioner should document the following:

        1. The agreement with the engaging party regarding the procedures to be performed and the appropriateness of those procedures

        2. The nature, timing, and extent of the procedures performed to comply with AICPA attestation standards and applicable legal and regulatory requirements, including:

            a. The identifying characteristics of specific items tested

            b. Who performed the work and the date the work was completed

            c. Matters related to situations when the appropriate party does not provide requested written representations or when those written representations do not appear to be reliable

            d. Who reviewed the work performed and the date and extent of that review

        3. The results of the procedures performed and the evidence obtained

VI. Agreed-Upon Procedures Reports

    A. A standardized format for the report is not required for all agreed-upon procedures engagements—The report should include the identified basic elements, but it may be tailored to the circumstances of the engagement.

    B. The practitioner's report should include the following elements:

        1. A title that includes the word "independent"

        2. An appropriate addressee

        3. Identification of the engaging party

4. Identification of the relevant subject matter

5. Identification of the responsible party when not the engaging party

6. A statement that the engaging party acknowledges that the procedures performed are appropriate for the intended purpose of the engagement

7. Identification of the intended purpose of the engagement

8. A statement that the practitioner's report may not be suitable for any other purpose

9. A statement that users are responsible for determining whether the procedures performed are appropriate for their purposes

10. A description of the procedures performed and the related findings

11. A description of any specified threshold established by the engaging party for reporting exceptions, if applicable

12. A statement that the engagement was conducted in accordance with AICPA attestation standards, that the practitioner was not engaged to conduct an examination or a review, that the practitioner does not express an opinion or conclusion, and that other matters might have been reported had the practitioner performed additional procedures

13. A statement regarding the practitioner's requirement to be independent of the responsible party and to meet other ethical requirements

14. A description of the assistance of a practitioner's external specialist, if applicable

15. A statement regarding any reservations concerning procedures or findings, if applicable (including any alert to restrict the use of the report to specified parties, when applicable)

16. A manual or printed signature of the practitioner's firm

17. The city and state of the practitioner's office

18. The date of the report (no earlier than when the procedures were performed and findings determined, including reviewing the attestation documentation and the preparation of the written presentation of the subject matter)

Example
Sample Report: Practitioner's Agreed-Upon Procedures Report Related to a Statement of Investment Performance Statistics

INDEPENDENT ACCOUNTANT'S REPORT

[Appropriate Addressee]

We have performed the procedures enumerated below on *[identify the subject matter, for example, the accompanying Statement of Investment Performance Statistics of XYZ Fund for the year ended December 31, 20X1]. [The responsible party, for example, XYZ Fund]* is responsible for *[the subject matter].*

[The engaging party, for example, XYZ Fund] has agreed to and acknowledged that the procedures performed are appropriate to meet the intended purpose of *[identify the intended purpose of the engagement, for example, assisting users in understanding the Statement of Investment Performance Statistics of XYZ Fund for the year ended December 31, 20X1].* This report may not be suitable for any other purpose. The procedures performed may not address all the items of interest to a user of this report and may not meet the needs of all users of this report and, as such, users are responsible for determining whether the procedures performed are appropriate for their purposes.

The procedures and the associated findings are as follows:

[Include paragraphs to describe the procedures performed detailing the nature and extent, and if applicable, the timing, of each procedure and to describe the findings from each procedure performed, including sufficient details on exceptions found.]

We were engaged by [*the engaging party, for example, XYZ Fund*] to perform this agreed-upon procedures engagement and conducted our engagement in accordance with attestation standards established by the AICPA. We were not engaged to and did not conduct an examination or review engagement, the objective of which would be the expression of an opinion or conclusion, respectively, on [*identify the subject matter, for example, the accompanying Statement of Investment Performance Statistics of XYZ Fund for the year ended December 31, 20X1*]. Accordingly, we do not express such an opinion or conclusion. Had we performed additional procedures, other matters might have come to our attention that would have been reported to you.

We are required to be independent of XYZ Fund and to meet our other ethical responsibilities, in accordance with the relevant ethical requirements related to our agreed-upon procedures engagement.

[*Additional paragraphs may be added to describe other matters.*]

[*Signature of the practitioner's firm*]

[*City and state where the practitioner's report is issued*]

[*Date of the practitioner's report*]

Prospective Financial Information

I. Definitions

Definitions

Financial Forecast: "Prospective financial statements that present, to the best of the responsible party's knowledge and belief, an entity's expected financial position, results of operations, and cash flows. A financial forecast is based on the responsible party's assumptions reflecting conditions it expects to exist and the course of action it expects to take."

Financial Projection: "Prospective financial statements that present, to the best of the responsible party's knowledge and belief, given one or more hypothetical assumptions, an entity's expected financial position, results of operations, and cash flows. A financial projection is sometimes prepared to present one or more hypothetical courses of actions for evaluation, as in response to a question such as 'What would happen if ...?' A financial projection is based on the responsible party's assumptions reflecting conditions it expects would exist and the course of action it expects would be taken, given one or more hypothetical assumptions."

Partial Presentation: "A presentation of prospective financial information that excludes one or more of the applicable items required for prospective financial statements as described in chapter 8 of the [AICPA Guide]."

Applicability: AT-C 305, *Prospective Financial Information*, applies to **examination** or **agreed-upon procedures** engagements involving prospective financial information, specifically to such reports issued on or after May 1, 2017.

II. Examination Engagements on Prospective Financial Information

A. **Preconditions**—The practitioner should not accept an engagement to examine a

1. Forecast or projection unless the responsible party has agreed to disclose the significant assumptions;

2. Projection unless the responsible party has agreed to identify which of the assumptions are hypothetical and to comment on the limitations of the projection's usefulness; *or*

3. Partial presentation that does not comment on the limitations of the presentation's usefulness.

B. **Requesting a Written Assertion**—The practitioner should request a written assertion from the responsible party; if that party refuses, the practitioner should withdraw when that is permitted by applicable law or regulation.

C. **Planning**—The practitioner should establish an overall engagement strategy that guides the development of the engagement plan to determine the scope and timing of the work and should obtain an appropriate level of knowledge about the entity's industry (and accounting principles used) and the key factors underlying the prospective financial information.

D. Examination Procedures

1. The practitioner should perform the procedures considered necessary to report on whether the assumptions underlying the forecast (or projection) are suitably supported and provide a reasonable basis for the forecast (or projection).

2. The practitioner should evaluate the support for significant assumptions individually and in the aggregate. They are viewed as suitably supported if each significant assumption is supported by the "preponderance" of the information.

3. **For a forecast**—The practitioner should evaluate whether there is a reasonably objective basis for the forecast and whether sufficiently objective assumptions can be developed for each key factor identified.

4. **For a projection**—The practitioner should evaluate whether the hypothetical assumptions are consistent with the purpose of the projection; the practitioner need not obtain support for the hypothetical assumptions, however.

5. **Evaluating the preparation and presentation of a forecast or projection**—The practitioner should obtain reasonable assurance that

    a. The presentation reflects the identified assumptions;

    b. Any computations made are mathematically accurate;

    c. Assumptions are internally consistent;

    d. Accounting principles used are appropriate;

    e. Information is presented according to the AICPA Guide; *and*

    f. Assumptions have been adequately disclosed.

E. Written Representations in an Examination Engagement

1. **For a forecast**—In addition to the representations required by AT-C 205 (regarding examination engagements), the practitioner should request the following from the responsible party:

    a. The forecast presents the expected financial statements and reflects expected conditions;

    b. The underlying assumptions are reasonable and suitably supported; *and*

    c. If the forecast is expressed as a range, the range was not selected in a misleading manner.

2. For a projection—In addition to the representations required by AT-C 205, the practitioner should request representations from the responsible party that:

    a. Identify the hypothetical assumptions (and identify any of those that are considered to be "improbable");

    b. Describe the limitations of the usefulness of the presentation;

    c. The projection presents expected financial information based on present circumstances, expected conditions, and the occurrence of the hypothetical events;

    d. The assumptions (other than the hypothetical assumptions) are reasonable and suitably supported; *and*

    e. If the projection is expressed as a range, the range was not selected in a misleading manner.

3. **Regarding the requirement in AT-C 205 that the subject matter is presented in accordance with "the criteria"** —Specifically, the practitioner should reference the AICPA Guide.

4. The practitioner should request the required written representations from the responsible party (even if the engaging party is not the responsible party). There is no alternative to obtaining the requested representations, so the responsible party's refusal to furnish the representations is a scope limitation that may preclude an unmodified opinion and warrant withdrawal.

F. Content of a Report on an Examination of a Forecast

1. A title that includes the word "independent;

2. An appropriate addressee;

3. Identification of the prospective financial information involved;

4. Identification of the criteria as the AICPA Guide;

5. A statement that identifies the responsible party and its responsibility and that identifies the practitioner's responsibility;

6. A statement that identifies that the examination was performed in accordance with attestation standards established by the AICPA, that describes the role of those standards, and that expresses the belief that the evidence obtained provides a reasonable basis for the opinion;

7. A statement that describes the nature of the examination engagement;

8. An opinion whether the presentation is in accordance with the AICPA Guide, and whether the underlying assumptions are suitably supported and provide a reasonable basis for the forecast or projection;

9. A statement that the prospective results may not be achieved and identifying any other significant inherent limitations;

10. A statement that there is no responsibility to update the report for events occurring after the date of the report;

11. The signature of the practitioner's firm;

12. The city and state of the practitioner; *and*

13. The date of the report.

14. **When the prospective information is presented as a range**—The practitioner should include a separate paragraph stating that the responsible party has chosen to present the expected results (of one or more assumptions) as a range.

G. Additional Elements for a Report on an Examination of a Projection

1. Identification of the hypothetical assumptions;

2. Description of the purpose for which the projection was prepared; *and*

3. An alert to restrict the use of the report to the specified parties. Modified opinions should be expressed for the following circumstances:

   a. **If the prospective financial information departs in a material way from AICPA presentation guidelines**—The practitioner should express a *qualified or adverse* opinion.

   b. **If the prospective financial information fails to disclose any "significant assumptions" or if one or more of the significant assumptions are not suitably supported or do not provide a reasonable basis for the forecast or projection**—The practitioner should express an *adverse* opinion.

   c. **If unable to obtain sufficient appropriate evidence as a basis for the opinion**—The practitioner should express a *disclaimer of opinion*.

Note

Any type of prospective financial statements (either a forecast or a projection) would be appropriate for limited use; however, only a forecast is appropriate for general use.

A forecast has to be based on a realistic premise that is supportable; however, the premise for a projection need not be supportable, although the hypothetical assumptions should be consistent with the presentation's purpose. In evaluating assumptions other than hypothetical assumptions, the practitioner can conclude that they are suitably supported if each significant assumption is supported by the "preponderance" of information.

H. Partial Presentations

1. The practitioner should consider whether key factors affecting elements, accounts, or items that are related to those in the partial presentation have been taken into consideration and whether all significant assumptions have been disclosed.

2. Partial presentations usually are appropriate only for limited use. The practitioner should include a description of any limitations on the usefulness of the presentation.

I. AT-C 305 provides examples of unmodified examination reports on a forecast and on a projection that do not contain a range.

Example

Practitioner's Examination Report on a Financial Forecast

Independent Accountant's Report

[*Appropriate Addressee*]

We have examined the accompanying forecast of XYZ Company, which comprises [*identify the statements; e.g., the forecasted balance sheet as of December 31, 20XX, and the related forecasted statements of income, stockholders' equity, and cash flows for the year then ending*], based on the guidelines for the presentation of a forecast established by the American Institute of Certified Public Accountants. XYZ Company's management is responsible for preparing and presenting the forecast in accordance with the guidelines for the presentation of a forecast established by the American Institute of Certified Public Accountants. Our responsibility is to express an opinion on the forecast based on our examination.

Our examination was conducted in accordance with attestation standards established by the American Institute of Certified Public Accountants. Those standards require that we plan and perform the examination to obtain reasonable assurance about whether the forecast is presented in accordance with the guidelines for the presentation of a forecast established by the American Institute of Certified Public Accountants, in all material respects. An examination involves performing procedures to obtain evidence about the forecast. The nature, timing, and extent of the procedures selected depend on our judgment, including an assessment of the risks of material misstatement of the forecast, whether due to fraud or error. We believe that the evidence we obtained is sufficient and appropriate to provide a reasonable basis for our opinion.

In our opinion, the accompanying forecast is presented, in all material respects, in accordance with the guidelines for the presentation of a forecast established by the American Institute of Certified Public Accountants, and the underlying assumptions are suitably supported and provide a reasonable basis for management's forecast.

There will usually be differences between the forecasted and actual results because events and circumstances frequently do not occur as expected, and those differences may be material. We have no responsibility to update this report for events and circumstances occurring after the date of this report.

[*Practitioner's signature*]

[*Practitioner's city and state*]

[*Date of practitioner's report*]

Example

Practitioner's Examination Report on a Financial Projection

Independent Accountant's Report

[*Appropriate Addressee*]

We have examined the accompanying projection of XYZ Company, which comprises [*identify the statements; e.g., the projected balance sheet as of December 31, 20XX, and the related projected statements of income, stockholders' equity, and cash flows for the year then ending*] based on the guidelines for the presentation of a projection established by the American Institute of Certified Public Accountants. XYZ Company's management is responsible for preparing and presenting the projection based on [*identify the hypothetical assumption; e.g., the granting of the requested loan as described in the summary of significant assumptions*] in accordance with the guidelines for the presentation of a projection established by the American Institute of Certified Public Accountants. The projection was prepared for [*describe the special purpose, for example, the purpose of negotiating a loan to expand XYZ Company's plant*]. Our responsibility is to express an opinion on the projection based on our examination.

Our examination was conducted in accordance with attestation standards established by the American Institute of Certified Public Accountants. Those standards require that we plan and perform the examination to obtain reasonable assurance about whether the projection is presented in accordance with the guidelines for the presentation of a projection established by the American Institute of Certified Public Accountants, in all material respects. An examination involves performing procedures to obtain evidence about the projection. The nature, timing, and extent of the procedures selected depend on our judgment, including an assessment of the risks of material misstatement of the projection, whether due to fraud or error. We believe that the evidence we obtained is sufficient and appropriate to provide a reasonable basis for our opinion.

In our opinion, [*describe the hypothetical assumption(s); e.g., assuming the granting of the requested loan for the purpose of expanding XYZ Company's plant as described in the summary of significant assumptions*] the projection referred to above is presented, in all material respects, in accordance with the guidelines for the presentation of a projection established by the American Institute of Certified Public Accountants, and the underlying assumptions are suitably supported and provide a reasonable basis for management's projection given the hypothetical assumption(s).

Even if [*identify the hypothetical assumption; e.g., the loan is granted and the plant is expanded*], there will usually be differences between the projected and actual results because events and circumstances frequently do not occur as expected, and those differences may be material. We have no responsibility to update this report for events and circumstances occurring after the date of this report.

The accompanying projection and this report are intended solely for the information and use of [*identify specified parties, for example, XYZ Company and DEF National Bank*] and are not intended to be and should not be used by anyone other than these specified parties.

[*Practitioner's signature*]

[*Practitioner's city and state*]

[*Date of practitioner's report*]

Example

Practitioner's Agreed-Upon Procedures Report Related to a Forecast

Independent Accountant's Agreed-Upon Procedures Report

[*Appropriate Addressee*]

We have performed the procedures enumerated below, which were agreed to by [*identify the specified parties; e.g., the boards of directors of XYZ Corporation and ABC Company*], on [*identify the statements; e.g., the forecasted balance sheet as of December 31, 20XX, and the related forecasted statements of income, stockholders' equity, and cash flows of DEF Company, a subsidiary of ABC Company, for the year then ending*]. DEF Company's management is responsible for preparing and presenting the forecast in accordance with the guidelines for the presentation of a forecast established by the American Institute of Certified Public Accountants. The sufficiency of these procedures is solely the responsibility of those parties specified in this report. Consequently, we make no representation regarding the sufficiency of the procedures enumerated below either for the purpose for which this report has been requested or for any other purpose.

[*Include paragraphs to enumerate procedures and findings.*]

This agreed-upon procedures engagement was conducted in accordance with attestation standards established by the American Institute of Certified Public Accountants. We were not engaged to and did not conduct an examination or review, the objective of which would be the expression of an opinion or conclusion, respectively, about whether the forecast is presented in accordance with the guidelines for the presentation of a forecast established by the American Institute of Certified Public Accountants or whether the underlying assumptions are suitably supported or provide a reasonable basis for management's forecast. Accordingly, we do not express such an opinion or conclusion. Had we performed additional procedures, other matters might have come to our attention that would have been reported to you.

There will usually be differences between the forecasted and actual results because events and circumstances frequently do not occur as expected, and those differences may be material. We have no responsibility to update this report for events and circumstances occurring after the date of this report.

This report is intended solely for the information and use of [*identify the specified parties; e.g., the boards of directors of ABC Company and XYZ Corporation*] and is not intended to be, and should not be, used by anyone other than these specified parties.

[*Practitioner's signature*]

[*Practitioner's city and state*]

[*Date of practitioner's report*]

III. Agreed-Upon Procedures Engagements on Prospective Financial Information

    a. **Preconditions for an Agreed-Upon Procedures Engagement**—The practitioner should not perform such an engagement on a forecast or projection unless the prospective financial information includes a summary of significant assumptions.

    b. **Content of the Practitioner's Agreed-Upon Procedures Report**

        1. A title that includes the word "independent";

        2. An appropriate addressee;

        3. Identification of the prospective financial information and the nature of the engagement;

        4. Identification of the specified parties;

        5. A statement that the procedures performed were agreed to by the specified parties;

        6. A statement that identifies the responsible party and its responsibility for presenting the forecast or projection in accordance with AICPA guidelines;

        7. A statement that the specified parties are responsible for the sufficiency of the procedures performed and that the practitioner makes no representation regarding the sufficiency of the procedures;

        8. A list of the procedures performed (or reference to those procedures) and related findings. (The practitioner should not express a conclusion);

        9. Description of any agreed-upon materiality limits, as applicable;

        10. A statement that (a) the engagement was conducted in accordance with AICPA attestation standards; (b) did not conduct an examination or a review; (c) does not express such an opinion or conclusion; and (d) had additional procedures been performed, other matters might have been identified that would have been reported;

        11. Description of any assistance provided by a practitioner's external specialist, as applicable;

        12. A statement that the prospective results may not be achieved and identifying any other significant inherent limitations;

        13. A statement that there is no responsibility to update the report for events occurring after the date of the report;

        14. Any reservations concerning procedures or findings, as applicable;

        15. An alert restricting the use of the report to the specified parties;

        16. The signature of the practitioner's firm;

        17. The city and state of the practitioner; *and*

        18. The date of the report.

    c. AT-C 305 provides an example of an agreed-upon procedures report on a forecast.

Pro Forma Financial Information

After studying this lesson, you should be able to:

1. State what is meant by the term "pro forma" financial information.

2. Identify the two kinds of engagements associated with pro forma financial information under the clarified attestation standards.

3. Recognize the elements that are required in a practitioner's examination or review report on pro forma financial information.

I. Definitions

Definitions

Criteria for the Preparation of Pro Forma Financial Information: "The basis disclosed in the pro forma financial information that management used to develop the pro forma financial information, including the assumptions underlying the pro forma financial information."

Pro Forma Financial Information: "A presentation that shows what the significant effects on historical financial information might have been had a consummated or proposed transaction (or event) occurred at an earlier date."

Applicability: AT-C 310, *Reporting on Pro Forma Financial Information*, applies to **examination** or **review** engagements involving pro forma financial information.

It does not apply to agreed-upon procedures engagements involving pro forma financial information or when parties request a comfort letter on pro forma financial information in connection with a stock offering.

For example, pro forma financial information may be used to show the effects of (a) business combinations; (b) changes in capitalization; (c) dispositions of significant business segments; (d) changes in the form of business organizations; or (e) proposed sales of securities.

II. Examination or Review Engagements on Pro Forma Financial Information

A. Preconditions (in addition to those identified in other relevant AT-C sections)

1. The document containing the pro forma financial information must also include the historical financial statements (or the historical financial statements must be readily available);

2. For an examination, the historical financial statements must have been audited; for a review, the historical financial statements must have been either audited or reviewed—they cannot express a higher level of assurance on the pro forma information than on the historical financial statements;

3. The audit report or the review report, as applicable, must be included in the document containing the pro forma financial information (or it must be readily available); *and*

4. The practitioner should obtain an appropriate level of knowledge of the entity's accounting and financial reporting practices to perform the necessary procedures to report on the pro forma financial information.

B. Requesting a Written Assertion—The practitioner should request a written assertion from management; if management refuses, the practitioner should withdraw from the engagement (when that is permitted by law or regulation).

C. Assessing the Suitability of the Criteria—The criteria used by management are considered "suitable" when the criteria address the following matters:

1. That the financial information is extracted from the applicable historical financial statements;

2. That the pro forma adjustments are directly attributable to the transaction (event), are factually supportable, and consistent with the entity's applicable financial reporting framework and its accounting policies; *and*

3. That the pro forma financial information is appropriately presented, including adequate disclosures for users' understanding.

D. Examination and Review Procedures—The practitioner should apply the following procedures to the assumptions and pro forma adjustments for either an examination or a review engagement:

1. Obtain an understanding of the underlying transaction (event);

2. Obtain an understanding of the accounting and financial reporting practices of the entity (entities); if another practitioner performed the audit/review of the historical financial statements, the practitioner still should obtain this understanding;

3. Discuss with management their assumptions about the effects of the transaction/event;

4. Obtain sufficient evidence regarding the adjustments;

5. Evaluate whether pro forma adjustments are included for all significant effects;

6. Evaluate whether management's underlying assumptions are presented in a clear, comprehensive manner;

7. Evaluate whether the pro forma adjustments are consistent with each other and with the data used to make them;

8. Evaluate whether the computations of the adjustments are mathematically accurate and whether the pro forma column properly applies those adjustments to the historical financial statements; *and*

9. Read the pro forma financial information and evaluate whether (a) the transaction/event, the underlying assumptions, and the pro forma adjustments (and any significant uncertainties) have been adequately described; and (b) the source of the historical financial information involved has been properly identified.

E. Written Representation in an Examination and a Review Engagement

1. The practitioner should request the following written representations (in addition to those identified in other relevant AT-C sections):

    a. That management is responsible for the underlying assumptions used;

    b. That the assumptions are factually supportable (meaning that they are supported by the "preponderance" of the information);

    c. That the assumptions (a) provide a reasonable basis for presenting the significant effects, (b) the related adjustments properly reflect those assumptions, and (c) the pro forma amounts properly reflect those adjustments to the historical financial statements;

    d. That the pro forma adjustments are consistent with the entity's applicable financial reporting framework; *and*

    e. That the pro forma financial information is properly presented with proper disclosure of the significant effects directly attributable to the transaction/event involved.

2. Management's refusal to provide the requested written representations is a scope limitation sufficient to cause the practitioner to withdraw from the examination or review engagement. There is no alternative for obtaining the requested written representations from management for an engagement to examine or review pro forma financial information.

III. Content of the Practitioner's Report

A. Examination Report

1. A title that includes the word "independent;"

2. An appropriate addressee;

3. Reference to the pro forma adjustments included;

4. Reference to management's description of the transaction (or event);

5. Description of the pro forma financial information being reported on;

6. Identification of the criteria used to evaluate the pro forma financial information;

7. Reference to the financial statements from which the historical financial information is derived (refer to any modification of the auditor's report);

8. Statement that the pro forma adjustments are based on management's assumptions;

9. A statement to identify management's responsibility and to identify the practitioner's responsibility to express an opinion;

10. A statement that the examination was conducted in accordance with attestation standards established by the AICPA and other statements describing the examination engagement;

11. A statement describing the objectives and limitations of pro forma financial information;

12. An opinion whether management's assumptions provide a reasonable basis for presenting the significant effects and whether the pro forma adjustments give appropriate effect to those assumptions and the pro forma amounts reflect the proper adjustments to the historical financial statement amounts;

13. The signature of the practitioner's firm;

14. The city and state where the practitioner practices; *and*

15. The date of the report.

B. Review Report

1. A title that includes the word "independent;

2. An appropriate addressee;

3. Reference to the pro forma adjustments included;

4. Reference to management's description of the transaction (or event);

5. A description of the pro forma financial information being reported on;

6. Identification of the criteria used to evaluate the pro forma financial information;

7. Reference to the financial statements from which the historical financial information is derived (the practitioner should state whether the financial statements were audited or reviewed and identify any modification of such report);

8. A statement that the pro forma adjustments are based on management's assumptions;

9. A statement to identify management's responsibility and to identify the practitioner's responsibility to express a conclusion;

10. A statement that the review was conducted in accordance with attestation standards established by the AICPA and other statements describing the review engagement;

11. A statement describing the objectives and limitations of pro forma financial information;

12. A conclusion whether the practitioner is aware of any material modifications that should be made to: (a) management's assumptions for them to provide a reasonable basis for presenting the significant effects, (b) the pro forma adjustments for them to give appropriate effect to those assumptions, and (c) the pro forma amounts for them to reflect the proper adjustments to the historical financial statement amounts;

13. The signature of the practitioner's firm;

14. The city and state where the practitioner practices; *and*

15. The date of the report.

AT-C 310 provides examples of an unmodified examination report and an unmodified review report on pro forma financial information.

Example

Practitioner's Examination Report on Pro Forma Financial Information: Unmodified Opinion

Independent Accountant's Report

[*Appropriate Addressee*]

We have examined the pro forma adjustments giving effect to the underlying transaction (or event) described in Note 1 and the application of those adjustments to the historical amounts in the accompanying pro forma condensed balance sheet of X Company as of December 31, 20X1, and the related pro forma condensed statement of income for the year then ended (pro forma financial information), based on the criteria in Note 1. The historical condensed financial statements are derived from the historical financial statements of X Company, which were audited by us, and of Y Company, which were audited by other accountants, appearing elsewhere herein [*or "and are readily available"*]. The pro forma adjustments are based on management's assumptions described in Note 1. X Company's management is responsible for the pro forma financial information. Our responsibility is to express an opinion on the pro forma financial information based on our examination.

Our examination was conducted in accordance with attestation standards established by the American Institute of Certified Public Accountants. Those standards require that we plan and perform the examination to obtain reasonable assurance about whether, based on the criteria in Note 1, management's assumptions provide a reasonable basis for presenting the significant effects directly attributable to the underlying transaction (or event), and, in all material respects, the related pro forma adjustments give appropriate effect to those assumptions, and the pro forma amounts reflect the proper application of those adjustments to the historical financial statement amounts. An examination involves performing procedures to obtain evidence about management's assumptions, the related pro forma adjustments, and the pro forma amounts in the pro forma condensed balance sheet of X Company as of December 31, 20X1, and the related pro forma condensed statement of income for the year then ended. The nature, timing, and extent of the procedures selected depend on our judgment, including an assessment of the risks of material misstatement of the pro forma financial information, whether due to fraud or error. We believe that the evidence we obtained is sufficient and appropriate to provide a reasonable basis for our opinion.

The objective of this pro forma financial information is to show what the significant effects on the historical financial information might have been had the underlying transaction (or event) occurred at an earlier date. However, the pro forma condensed financial statements are not necessarily indicative of the results of operations or related effects on financial position that would have been attained had the above-mentioned transaction (or event) actually occurred at such earlier date.

In our opinion, based on the criteria in Note 1, management's assumptions provide a reasonable basis for presenting the significant effects directly attributable to the above-mentioned transaction (or event) described in Note 1, and, in all material respects, the related pro forma adjustments give appropriate effect to those assumptions, and the pro forma amounts reflect the proper application of those adjustments to the historical financial statement amounts in the pro forma condensed balance sheet of X Company as of December 31, 20X1, and the related pro forma condensed statement of income for the year then ended.

[*Practitioner's signature*]

[*Practitioner's city and state*]

[*Date of practitioner's report*]

Example

Practitioner's Review Report on Pro Forma Financial Information: Unmodified Conclusion

Independent Accountant's Report

[*Appropriate Addressee*]

We have reviewed the pro forma adjustments giving effect to the transaction (or event) described in Note 1 and the application of those adjustments to the historical amounts in the accompanying pro forma condensed balance sheet of X Company as of March 31, 20X2, and the related pro forma condensed statement of income for the three months then ended (pro forma financial information), based on the criteria in Note 1. These historical condensed financial statements are derived from the historical unaudited financial statements of X Company, which were reviewed by us, and of Y Company, which were reviewed by other accountants, appearing elsewhere herein [*or "and are readily available"*]. The pro forma adjustments are based on management's assumptions as described in Note 1. X Company's management is responsible for the pro forma financial information. Our responsibility is to express a conclusion based on our review.

Our review was conducted in accordance with attestation standards established by the American Institute of Certified Public Accountants. Those standards require that we plan and perform our review to obtain limited assurance about whether, based on the criteria in Note 1, any material modifications should be made to management's assumptions in order for them to provide a reasonable basis for presenting the significant effects directly attributable to the underlying transaction (or event); the related pro forma adjustments, in order for them to give appropriate effect to those assumptions; or the pro forma amounts, in order for them to reflect the proper application of those adjustments to the historical financial statement amounts. A review is substantially less in scope than an examination, the objective of which is to obtain reasonable assurance about whether, based on the criteria, management's assumptions provide a reasonable basis for presenting the significant effects directly attributable to the underlying transaction (or event), and, in all material respects, the related pro forma adjustments give appropriate effect to those assumptions, and the pro forma amounts reflect the proper application of those adjustments to the historical financial statement amounts, in order to express an opinion. Accordingly, we do not express such an opinion. We believe that our review provides a reasonable basis for our conclusion.

The objective of this pro forma financial information is to show what the significant effects on the historical financial information might have been had the underlying transaction (or event) occurred at an earlier date. However, the pro forma condensed financial statements are not necessarily indicative of the results of operations or related effects on financial position that would have been attained had the above-mentioned transaction (or event) actually occurred at such earlier date.

Based on our review, we are not aware of any material modifications that should be made to management's assumptions in order for them to provide a reasonable basis for presenting the significant effects directly attributable to the above-mentioned transaction (or event) described in Note 1, the related pro forma adjustments in order for them to give appropriate effect to those assumptions, or the pro forma amounts, in order for them to reflect the proper application of those adjustments to the historical financial statement amounts in the pro forma condensed balance sheet of X Company as of March 31, 20X2, and the related pro forma condensed statement of income for the three months then ended, based on the criteria in Note 1.

[*Practitioner's signature*]

[*Practitioner's city and state*]

[*Date of practitioner's report*]

Compliance Attestation

I. Definitions

Definitions

Compliance with Specified Requirements: "An entity's compliance with specified laws, regulations, rules, contracts, or grants."

Material Noncompliance: "A failure to follow compliance requirements or a violation of prohibitions included in the specified requirements that results in noncompliance that is quantitatively or qualitatively material, either individually or when aggregated with other noncompliance."

Applicability: AT-C 315, *Compliance Attestation*, applies to **examination** or **agreed-upon procedures** reports dated on or after May 1, 2017, related to compliance with specified requirements (or agreed-upon procedures related to internal control over compliance).

The practitioner may be engaged to report directly on the subject matter (compliance), on management's assertion about compliance, or on internal control over compliance.

II. Examination Engagements

A. Preconditions (in addition to those identified in other relevant AT-C sections)

1. Management accepts responsibility for compliance with specified requirements and the entity's internal control over compliance; *and*

2. Management evaluates the entity's compliance with specified requirements.

B. Practitioner Should Request a Written Assertion from Management—If management refuses, the practitioner should withdraw from the engagement when that is permissible.

C. Examination Procedures

1. The practitioner should obtain an understanding of the specified requirements, including:

   a. Consideration of laws, regulations, rules, contracts, and grants relevant to the specified requirements;

   b. Consideration of knowledge obtained through prior engagements and regulatory reports; *and*

   c. Discussion with appropriate personnel within the entity.

2. **When the entity involved has operations in several components**—The practitioner should determine the nature, timing, and extent of testing at the individual components.

3. **Internal control over compliance**—The practitioner should obtain an understanding of internal control over compliance and assess the risks of material noncompliance; should consider the kinds of potential noncompliance and design appropriate tests of compliance.

4. **Compliance with regulatory requirements**—The practitioner should review reports and communications involving the regulatory agencies; may make inquiries of the regulatory agencies (e.g., about any examinations in progress).

D. **Written Representations in an Examination Engagement**

1. The practitioner should request written representations from management (in addition to those required by AT-C 205) that:

   a. Management takes responsibility for internal control over compliance;

   b. Management has performed an evaluation of the entity's compliance with specified requirements; *and*

   c. Management has provided its interpretation of any compliance requirements that are subject to different interpretations.

2. Management's refusal to furnish the required written representations is a scope limitation sufficient to preclude an unmodified opinion and may warrant withdrawal when that is permitted; there is no alternative to obtaining the required written representations (as discussed in AT-C 205).

E. **Content of the Practitioner's Examination Report**

1. A title that includes the word "independent;

2. An appropriate addressee;

3. Identification of the compliance matters being reported on (or the assertion involved);

4. Identification of the specified requirements; should also identify the criteria, if those criteria are not included in the compliance requirement;

5. Statement identifying management's responsibility for compliance and the practitioner's responsibility to express an opinion;

6. Statement that the examination was conducted in accordance with attestation standards established by the AICPA and other statements describing the examination engagement;

7. Statement describing the nature of an examination engagement;

8. Statement that describes any significant inherent limitations;

9. Statement that the examination does not provide a legal determination;

10. An opinion whether the entity complied with the specified requirements, in all material respects, or whether management's assertion is fairly stated;

11. The signature of the practitioner's firm;

12. The city and state where the practitioner practices; *and*

13. The date of the report.

F. AT-C 315 provides example of an unmodified examination report on compliance, which is presented below near the end of these materials.

III. **Agreed-Upon Procedures Engagements**

A. **Preconditions** (in addition to those identified in other relevant AT-C sections)

1. Management accepts responsibility for compliance with specified requirements and the entity's internal control over compliance; *and*

2. Management evaluates the entity's compliance with specified requirements.

B. **Written Representations in an Agreed-Upon Procedures Engagement**—The practitioner should request written representations from management (in addition to those required by AT-C 215) that:

1. Management takes responsibility for internal control over compliance;

2. Management has performed an evaluation of the entity's compliance with specified requirements or internal control over compliance;

3. Management has provided its interpretation of any compliance requirements that are subject to different interpretations; *and*

4. Management has disclosed any known noncompliance occurring subsequent to the period covered by the practitioner's report.

C. **Content of the Practitioner's Agreed-Upon Procedures Report**

1. A title that includes the word "independent";

2. An appropriate addressee;

3. Identification of the specified requirements being reported on;

4. Statement identifying management's responsibility for compliance with the specified requirements;

5. Identification of the specified parties;

6. Statement that the specified parties are responsible for the sufficiency of the procedures performed;

7. A list of the procedures performed (or reference to them) and the findings;

8. A description of any agreed-upon materiality limits, if applicable;

9. Statement that the agreed-upon procedures engagement was conducted in accordance with attestation standards established by the AICPA and other statements pointing out that it was not an examination or a review and include a disclaimer of opinion or any other conclusion;

10. A description of the assistance provided by a practitioner's external specialist, if applicable;

11. Any reservations about the procedures or findings, if applicable;

12. An alert that restricts the use of the report to specified users;

13. The signature of the practitioner's firm;

14. The city and state where the practitioner practices; *and*

15. The date of the report.

D. AT-C 315 provides examples of an unmodified examination report on compliance and an agreed-upon procedures report on compliance, which follow.

Example

Practitioner's Examination Report on Compliance; Unmodified Opinion

The following is an illustrative practitioner's examination report for an engagement in which the practitioner is reporting on subject matter (an entity's compliance with specified requirements during a period of time).

Independent Accountant's Report

[*Appropriate addressee*]

We have examined XYZ Company's compliance with [*identify the specified requirements, for example, the requirements listed in Attachment 1*] during the period January 1, 20X1, to December 31, 20X1. Management of XYZ Company is responsible for XYZ Company's compliance with the specified requirements. Our responsibility is to express an opinion on XYZ Company's compliance with the specified requirements based on our examination.

Our examination was conducted in accordance with attestation standards established by the American Institute of Certified Public Accountants. Those standards require that we plan and perform the examination to obtain reasonable assurance about whether XYZ Company complied, in all material respects, with the specified requirements referenced above. An examination involves performing procedures to obtain evidence about whether XYZ Company complied with the specified requirements. The nature, timing, and extent of the procedures selected depend on our judgment, including an assessment of the risks of material noncompliance, whether due to fraud or error. We believe that the evidence we obtained is sufficient and appropriate to provide a reasonable basis for our opinion.

Our examination does not provide a legal determination on XYZ Company's compliance with specified requirements.

In our opinion, XYZ Company complied, in all material respects, with [*identify the specified requirements; e.g., the requirements listed in Attachment 1*] during the period January 1, 20X1, to December 31, 20X1.

[*Practitioner's signature*]

[*Practitioner's city and state*]

[*Date of practitioner's report*]

Example

Practitioner's Agreed-Upon Procedures Report Related to Compliance

The following is an illustrative practitioner's agreed-upon procedures report related to an entity's compliance with specified requirements in which the procedures and findings are enumerated rather than referenced.

Independent Accountant's Report on Applying Agreed-Upon Procedures

[Appropriate Addressee]

We have performed the procedures enumerated below, which were agreed to by [identify the specified parties; e.g., the management and board of directors of XYZ Company], related to XYZ Company's compliance with [identify the specified requirements; e.g., the requirements listed in Attachment 1] during the period January 1, 20X1, to December 31, 20X1]. XYZ Company's management is responsible for its compliance with those requirements. The sufficiency of these procedures is solely the responsibility of those parties specified in this report. Consequently, we make no representations regarding the sufficiency of the procedures enumerated below either for the purpose for which this report has been requested or for any other purpose.

[Include paragraphs to enumerate procedures and findings.]

This agreed-upon procedures engagement was conducted in accordance with attestation standards established by the American Institute of Certified Public Accountants. We were not engaged to and did not conduct an examination or review, the objective of which would be the expression of an opinion or conclusion, respectively, on compliance with specified requirements. Accordingly, we do not express such an opinion or conclusion. Had we performed additional procedures, other matters might have come to our attention that would have been reported to you.

This report is intended solely for the information and use of [identify the specified parties; e.g., the management and board of directors of XYZ Company] and is not intended to be, and should not be, used by anyone other than the specified parties.

[Practitioner's signature]

[Practitioner's city and state]

[Date of practitioner's report]

Management's Discussion and Analysis (MD&A)

When the Auditing Standards Board issued the clarified attestation standards, the ASB decided to retain the "old" guidance with respect to attestation engagements involving MD&A presentations. Rather than issue "clarified" guidance applicable to MD&A presentations, the ASB simply designated the existing guidance as AT-C Section 395. The justification was provided in a note that follows:

"The Auditing Standards Board (ASB) has not clarified AT section 701 because practitioners rarely perform attest engagements to report on management's discussion and analysis prepared pursuant to the rules and regulations adopted by the U.S. Securities and Exchange Commission. Therefore, the ASB decided that it would retain AT section 701 in its current unclarified format as section 395 until further notice."

I. Applicability

A. When attesting to MD&A that has been prepared according to the requirements of the SEC and that MD&A is presented in annual reports or in other documents.

B. Can even apply to a nonpublic entity that provides a written assertion that the SEC requirements were used as criteria for the presentation of the MD&A.

C. **Precondition to accept an MD&A engagement**—Must have audited the annual financials for the latest period applicable to the MD&A presentation; any other financials involved must have been audited (or at least reviewed if interim/quarterly financials) by the practitioner or a predecessor auditor.

II. Examination of MD&A—Results in Positive Assurance

A. **Purpose**—To express an opinion on whether:

1. **Required elements**—The presentation includes the elements required by the SEC:

   a. Discussion of **financial condition** (liquidity and capital resources);

   b. Discussion of **changes in financial condition;**

   c. Discussion of **results of operations.**

2. **Historical amounts**—The historical financial amounts are accurately derived from the financials.

3. **Basis for conclusions**—The underlying information, assumptions, etc., provide a reasonable basis for the disclosures within the MD&A.

B. **Four Assertions Implicitly Embodied in the MD&A Presentation**

1. **Occurrence**—Whether reported events actually occurred during the period.

2. **Consistency with the financials**—Whether historical amounts have been accurately derived from the financials.

3. **Completeness of the explanation**—Whether the description of matters comprising the MD&A presentation is complete.

4. Presentation and disclosure—Whether information in the MD&A is properly classified, described, and disclosed.

C. Primary Dimensions of an Examination of MD&A

1. Planning the examination (similar to an audit engagement)—Develop an overall strategy that limits "attestation risk" to an acceptably low level.

   a. Inherent risk—Varies with the assertion involved.

   b. Control risk (same as previously discussed).

   c. Detection risk (same as previously discussed).

2. Consideration of internal control applicable to MD&A (similar to an audit)—Pertains to assessment of control risk, documenting the understanding, and communication of significant deficiencies.

3. Obtain sufficient evidence—Varies with the circumstances but includes reading the MD&A for consistency with the financials, examining related documents, reading minutes, reading communications from the SEC, and obtaining written representations from management, among other things.

4. Consideration of subsequent events (SEC expects MD&A to reflect events at or near the filing date)—Read minutes and available interim financials; make inquiries of management and obtain appropriate representations in writing.

D. Reporting on MD&A—Financial statements with the auditor's report should accompany the document containing the MD&A (or be incorporated by reference to documents filed with the SEC).

1. Title—"Independent Accountant's Report."

2. Unmodified examination report—Four paragraphs:

   a. Introductory paragraph (four sentences).

     i. Identify MD&A presentation;

     ii. Identify management's responsibility;

     iii. Identify accountant's responsibility; *and*

     iv. Refer to related audit report.

   b. Scope paragraph—Three sentences:

     i. Refer to attestation standards established by AICPA;

     ii. Describe scope of examination; *and*

     iii. Say that examination provides reasonable basis for opinion.

   c. Explanatory paragraph—Three sentences:

     i. Comment on the need for estimates and assumptions;

     ii. Comment on the role of future expectations; *and*

     iii. State that actual results may differ.

   d. Opinion paragraph—One long sentence. Indicate whether (1) the presentation includes elements required by SEC; (2) the historical amounts are accurately derived; and (3) the underlying information and assumptions provide a reasonable basis for the MD&A.

3. Dating report—As of completion of the examination procedures.

4. Modifications of the examination report

   a. Reservations as to presentation—Results in a *qualified* or *adverse* opinion.

   b. Reservations as to scope—Results in a *qualified* opinion or a *disclaimer* of opinion.

c. Division of responsibility—May refer to another practitioner's report on MD&A for a specific component as a partial basis for one's own report.

d. Emphasis of a matter—Presented as a separate paragraph (e.g., information included beyond the SEC's requirements).

Sample Examination Report on (Annual) MD&A when Reporting Directly on the Subject Matter, Not on Management's Assertion

Independent Accountant's Report
(Introductory paragraph)

We have examined ABC Company's Management's Discussion and Analysis taken as a whole, included (incorporated by reference) in the Company's (insert description of registration statement or document). Management is responsible for the preparation of the Company's Management's Discussion and Analysis pursuant to the rules and regulations adopted by the Securities and Exchange Commission. Our responsibility is to express an opinion on the presentation based on our examination. We have audited, in accordance with auditing standards generally accepted in the United States of America, the financial statements of ABC Company as of December 31, 20X3 and 20X2, and for each of the years in the three-year period ended December 31, 20X3, and in our report dated [Month and day], 20X4, we expressed an unqualified opinion on those financial statements.

(Scope paragraph)

Our examination of Management's Discussion and Analysis was conducted in accordance with attestation standards established by the American Institute of Certified Public Accountants and, accordingly, included examining, on a test basis, evidence supporting the historical amounts and disclosures in the presentation. An examination also includes assessing the significant determinations made by management as to the relevancy of information to be included and the estimates and assumptions that affect reported information. We believe that our examination provides a reasonable basis for our opinion.

(Explanatory paragraph)

The preparation of Management's Discussion and Analysis requires management to interpret the criteria, make determinations as to the relevancy of information to be included, and make estimates and assumptions that affect reported information. Management's Discussion and Analysis includes information regarding the estimated future impact of transactions and events that have occurred or are expected to occur, expected sources of liquidity and capital resources, operating trends, commitments, and uncertainties. Actual results in the future may differ materially from management's present assessment of this information because events and circumstances frequently do not occur as expected.

(Opinion paragraph)

In our opinion, the Company's presentation of Management's Discussion and Analysis includes, in all material respects, the required elements of the rules and regulations adopted by the Securities and Exchange Commission; the historical financial amounts included therein have been accurately derived, in all material respects, from the Company's financial statements; and the underlying information, determinations, estimates, and assumptions of the Company provide a reasonable basis for the disclosures contained therein.

(Signature)

(Practitioner's city and state)

(Date)

III. Review of MD&A—Results in Negative Assurance

A. Purpose—To report whether the practitioner has any reason to believe that:

1. The presentation does *not* include the elements required by the SEC;

2. The historical financial amounts are *not* accurately derived from the financials; *and*

3. The underlying information, assumptions, etc., do *not* provide a reasonable basis for the disclosures within the MD&A.

B. Primary Dimensions of a Review of MD&A

1. Obtain an understanding of the SEC requirements regarding MD&A.

2. **Plan the engagement**—Develop an overall strategy;

3. Consider relevant portions of internal control affecting MD&A presentation;

4. Apply *analytical procedures* and make *inquiries* of management (usually do not have to obtain corroboration);

5. Consider subsequent events; *and*

6. Obtain written representations from management.

C. Unmodified Review Report—Usually consists of five paragraphs (if including a restricted-use paragraph at the end of the report); the accountant may review the entity's annual MD&A presentation or an interim MD&A presentation.

1. **Title**—"Independent Accountant's Report"

2. **Introductory paragraph**—Three sentences. Delete the sentence on accountant's responsibility and

   a. Identify MD&A presentation;

   b. Identify management's responsibility; *and*

   c. Refer to related audit report.

3. **Scope paragraph**—Four sentences. Add a disclaimer:

   a. Refer to attestation standards established by the AICPA;

   b. Describe a review engagement;

   c. Say that scope is less than that of an examination; *and*

   d. Disclaim an opinion.

4. **Explanatory paragraph**—Three sentences. Same as for an examination report:

   a. Comment on the need for estimates and assumptions;

   b. Comment on the role of future expectations; *and*

   c. State that actual results may differ.

5. **Conclusions paragraph**—One long sentence. Negative assurance as to whether presentation does not include elements required by SEC, historical amounts are not accurately derived, and underlying information and assumptions do not provide a reasonable basis for the MD&A.

6. **Restricted-use paragraph**—One sentence. Restrict the distribution when the MD&A presentation and the practitioner's report are not intended to be filed with the SEC under the 1933 and 1934 Securities Acts.

7. **Dating report**—As of completion of the review procedures.

8. **Changes to the usual review report**—Reservations as to presentation resulting in a qualified review report; reference to other practitioners; or emphasis of a matter.

Assurance Services

Definition

Assurance Services: Independent professional services that improve the quality or context of information for decision makers. (Quality includes the *reliability* and *relevance* of information and *context* refers to how the decision maker uses the information.)

I. **Relationship of Assurance to Auditing and Attestation**—Auditing and attestation both involve enhancing the *reliability* of information (auditing specifically focuses on historical financial statement subject matter, whereas attestation is not limited to financial statements subject matter); assurance is broader than attestation, since assurance may address the relevance of information in addition to the *reliability* of information.

II. **AICPA Assurance Services**

A. **Trust Services**—The AICPA and Canadian Institute of Chartered Accountants developed SysTrust (to provide assurance on systems generating information and representations generally) and WebTrust (to provide assurance specifically related to e-commerce activities).

1. Five principles and criteria associated with Trust Services (these are organized in four broad areas: policies, communications, procedures, and monitoring):

a. **Security**—The system is protected from unauthorized access.

b. **Availability**—The system is available for operation and use as committed or agreed.

c. **Processing integrity**—System processing is complete, accurate, timely, and authorized.

d. **Confidentiality**—Information designated as confidential is protected as committed or agreed.

e. **Privacy**—Personal information is collected, used, retained, and disclosed in conformity with the commitments in the entity's privacy notice and with criteria set forth in generally accepted privacy principles issued by the AICPA/CICA.

2. **WebTrust**—To earn the WebTrust seal (which provides assurance to participants about transaction integrity and information security in e-commerce transactions with an entity's Web site), the entity must comply with all five of the principles above and engage a CPA-licensed professional to provide WebTrust-related services; the seal displays a digital certificate and can be displayed until the designated expiration date (the WebTrust seal is managed by a third-party *seal manager*).

3. **SysTrust**—To earn the CPA's unqualified opinion for a SysTrust engagement, an entity's system would also have to meet the above Trust Services principles; the SysTrust engagement would evaluate management's written assertions about the effectiveness of controls over the entity's system relative to applicable attestation standards.

B. **PrimePlus (formerly known as ElderCare) Services**—PrimePlus has a connotation primarily involving financial/lifestyle planning issues, whereas ElderCare has a connotation primarily involving healthcare (the AICPA says it will continue to support both brands).

Definition

PrimePlus/ElderCare Services: "A unique and customizable package of professional services—both financial and nonfinancial—intended to help older adults maintain, for as long as possible, their desired lifestyle and financial independence."

---

1. Financial services include the following: receiving, disposing, and accounting for client receipts; making bill payments and handling banking services; submitting claims to insurance companies; estate planning; providing tax planning and tax return preparation; evaluating investments and trust activity; managing portfolios; protecting elderly from predators; etc.

2. Nonfinancial services include the following: coordinating support and healthcare services; communicating family expectations to care providers; managing real estate and other assets; establishing performance monitoring systems; managing real estate and other assets; coordinating services involving healthcare, legal, and other professionals; etc.

3. Markets for PrimePlus/ElderCare services—There are three primary markets: (a) older clients themselves; (b) children of older adults; and (c) other professionals who deal with those older adults (such as lawyers and healthcare professionals).

C. The AICPA has established a senior committee known as the **Assurance Services Executive Committee** (ASEC) to oversee the ongoing development of assurance services.

1. ASEC's role—To identify trends and assurance opportunities; to develop assurance guidance (including applicable criteria); to communicate those opportunities and guidance to AICPA members; and to create alliance with industry, government, or others to facilitate those assurance opportunities.

2. ASEC has appointed several task forces to focus on developing assurance opportunities: (a) XBRL Assurance Task Force (regarding the development of guidance on the assurance of XBRL-related documents); (b) Trust/Data Integrity Task Force (regarding the development of principles/criteria for assurance on the security, availability, process integrity of systems and the confidentiality and privacy of information); and (c) Risk Assurance Task Force (regarding enterprise risk management issues).

Index

A

Account balances:
four assertions for, 216–217, 221
opening balances–initial audits, 298–301
tests of ending balances, 164

Accounting, auditing vs., 78–79

Accounting estimates, 127, 188–191

Accounting policies and practice, critical, 127

Accounting principles:
for members in business, 55
for members in public practice, 12

Accounting records, 167

Accounts payable, 156, 235–236

Accounts receivable, 221–222

Accuracy, valuation and allocation assertion:
for account balances, 216–217, 222
for accounts receivable, 222
for current liabilities, 235
for fixed assets, 233
for inventory, 224
for investments, 229–231
for long-term liabilities, 237
for stockholders' equity, 238

Activity ratios (turnover; efficiency ratios), 165

Actuarial services, 46

ADAs (audit data analytics), 107–110

ADR (alternative dispute resolution), 25

Adverse opinion:
audit reports of, 288–290
on ICFR, 384–387

Advertising, by members in public practice, 17

Advisory services for investments, 51

Advocacy, by members in public practice, 11

Affiliates, of members in public practice, 23–24

Agreed-upon procedures (AUP) engagement,
430–434
agreeing on terms for, 430–431
on compliance attestation, 447–451
planning and performing, 431–432
on prospective financial information, 441
related to financial forecast, 440

Agreed-upon procedures (AUP) report, 432–434

AICPA, *see* American Institute of Certified Public
Accountants

Alert to restrict the use of audit report, 312–313

Alternative audit procedures, 187

Alternative audit reports, 261

Alternative dispute resolution (ADR), 25

**American Institute of Certified Public Accountants
(AICPA):**
assessing control risk under standards of, 135–138
Clarified Standards, 79
clarity and convergence project, 79, 80
Code of Professional Conduct, 2. *See also* Code of
Professional Conduct
independent auditor's report, 367
Statements on Auditing Standards, 380–388
Statements on Standards for Accounting and Review
Services, 87

Statements on Standards for Attestation Engagements,
87
use of term GAAS and guidance associated with it, 82

Analytical procedures, 105–106
documenting, 182
planning, 105–106
and risk of material fraud, 112
substantive, 163–166

Annual reports, other information in, 302–304

Applicable financial reporting framework, defined, 78

Application of requirements of framework reports,
326–327

Applied criteria, 317

Appraisal services, 46

Arm's-length transactions, 201

ASB (Auditing Standards Board), 407

Asserted claims, 195

Assertions:
for account balances, 216–217, 221
accuracy, valuation and allocation, 216–217, 222, 224,
229–235, 237, 238
classification and presentation, 239–240
completeness, 216, 222, 225, 231–236, 238, 239
cutoff, 239
for examinations, 415
existence/occurrence, 216, 221, 223–224, 231, 233, 234,
238, 239
in obtaining audit evidence, 168–173
for review engagement, 423
rights and obligations, 216, 222, 225, 231, 234, 236–238

Assurances, in comfort letters, 346–347

Assurance levels, 87–88

Assurance services, 456–457

Attestation standards, 407–413

Attest engagements, 87, 408–409

Attributes sampling, 241, 243–244

Audits:
initial, 94–95
level of assurance with, 88
planning, *see* Planning activities
preconditions for, 94
that are changed to review engagements, 378–379

Audit and professional engagement period, 57–58

Audit committees, 45, 127–129
administration of engagement by, 62
communications with, 206

Audit data analytics (ADAs), 107–110

Audit documentation, 180–185
ownership and custody of, 180
purposes of, 180
revisions to, 181

Audit engagement team, 58

Audit evidence, 163–240
accounting estimates, 188–191
accounts receivable, 221–222
"assertions" in obtaining, 168–173
audit documentation, 180–185
audit procedures, 171–173
cash, 218–220